JOURNAL FOR THE STUDY OF THE OLD TESTAMENT
SUPPLEMENT SERIES
248

Sheffield Academic Press

A Search for the Origins of Judaism

From Joshua to the Mishnah

Etienne Nodet

translated by Ed Crowley

Journal for the Study of the Old Testament
Supplement Series 248

Originally published as
*Essai sur les origines du judaisme: de
Josue aux Pharisiens*
© 1992 Les Editions du Cerf, Paris

Copyright © 1997 Sheffield Academic Press

Published by
Sheffield Academic Press Ltd
Mansion House
19 Kingfield Road
Sheffield S11 9AS
England

Typeset by Sheffield Academic Press
and
Printed on acid-free paper in Great Britain
by Bookcraft Ltd
Midsomer Norton, Bath

British Library Cataloguing in Publication Data

A catalogue record for this book is available
from the British Library

ISBN 1-85075-445-4

CONTENTS

The present enquiry developed on the margins of a French translation and commentary on the *Jewish Antiquities* of Flavius Josephus. The enquiry was initiated as a result of two surprises and one particular question in regard to the history of Judaea and Judaism.

It is striking how poorly informed we are on the history of Israel for most of the period which extends from the destruction of Jerusalem (587 BCE) with the deportation of the inhabitants to Babylon by Nebuchadnezzar down to the installation of the Hasmonaeans about 150 BCE. However, this period of more than four centuries encompasses the Exile, the Return, the rebuilding of the Temple, the beginnings of Judaism and the putting into writing of a great part of the Hebrew Bible; the contrast with what we know of the four following centuries is surprising.

We are well informed, however, about the great empires that ruled that part of the world during this period, thanks to the Greek historians and the discoveries of archaeologists. How is it then that the cultural history of Palestine for the Persian and Hellenistic periods has not managed to extricate itself from a dense fog, or that the elements for a synthesis amount to no more than a few isolated points that constantly give the impression of being shaky or arbitrary? Josephus is no better informed than we are and we often have the feeling that he is deliberately drawing out a meagre documentation in order to fill up centuries that are especially empty. Since by Graeco-Roman cultural standards the only thing that counted was that which was ancient, Josephus's explicit concern, after the destruction of Jerusalem in 70 CE, is to show the antiquity of his nation, especially using the Bible to begin with (*Jewish Antiquities*), then by putting it up against the external testimony of historians (*Against Apion*). He even tries to give precise chronologies, going so far as to suggest that Moses was the most ancient of all lawgivers. His non-biblical sources are for the most part lost, but, given his purpose, we may credit him with not having left out any important document, at least voluntarily. The balance sheet on his investigation, however, is disturbing. With regard to the history of Israel and Judah, the sources cited from before the second century BCE do not agree with the Bible, and later sources, when they do agree, are really dependent on it. Frequently the suspicion arises that he is aware of the weakness of his proofs, taken individually, and tries to substitute a heavy barrage for accuracy of aim. Several centuries later, in his *Preparation for the Gospel*, Eusebius of Caesarea undertook a comparable project for similar reasons, but his results are no more conclusive. This is the first surprise.

The second surprise relates to the status of the Bible in Judaism. The Samaritans, the Sadducees, Philo, Josephus or even the Epistle to the Hebrews assign a central place to the Bible, especially to the Pentateuch, as a source of law, history and meaning. On the contrary, the rabbinic tradition, in its oldest layers, shows no sign of a biblical foundation, but only of secondary offshoots from the Bible; it can therefore in no way pass for a 'religion of the Old Testament'. Oral tradition predominates, similar to the ancestral customs characteristic of the Pharisees according to Josephus, and these are anything but a jurisprudence drawn from the Bible. It was only at the beginning of the second century CE that an innovative school developed around Rabbi Aqiba which postulated and wanted to demonstrate the profound unity of what was written and what was oral. It would be interesting, however, to know why this problem, by nature an old one, had abruptly become so urgent. A little later, the Mishnah, a compilation of oral traditions of diverse origins, quite often situated itself downstream from what was written, while at the same time remaining very independent of it; but what results is an edited synthesis designed for study, and not a Pharisaic handbook in the strict sense.

To go back earlier, sources from before the destruction of Jerusalem in 70 CE are very fragmentary and the excavations in the Judaean desert provide no significant clarification. In a more distant past, the books of Ezra and Nehemiah show the emergence of a new relationship with the law of Moses, but writing seems to have a preponderant role, although this was something new and in opposition to more ancient customs. The question remains then: what happened so that a group appealing to Moses had traditions so autonomous and so lasting? There is no direct answer, nor any decisive evidence in regard to the events as to what could have brought about such a major change. It must then be supposed that it was a question of a structural phenomenon, to be situated in the rather confused sociology of the various currents of ancient Judaism. Although he calls himself a Pharisee, Josephus gives no satisfactory explanation for this, since he is too preoccupied with showing the continuity of his people from the time of Abraham.

On the fringe of these extensive areas of obscurity, the particular question raised looks very much restricted. At the time of the persecutions under Antiochus Epiphanes, in 167 BCE, Mattathias fled to the hills and, to prevent the massacre of his defenceless comrades, decided without invoking any precedent that armed defence on the Sabbath would be authorized from then on. How is it that such an elementary security problem only came up at such a late date? What was the relative importance of the Sabbath and of war prior to that time? Moreover, this issue may be raised in regard to a neighbouring people and their history, owing to the fact that the Samaritans of Shechem, in spite of being well known for their observance, claimed at that time that they had only recently received the Sabbath from the Jews, but that they were ready to abandon it in order to avoid harassment.

The approach followed in this study starts off by drawing up an inventory of certain classical difficulties in regard to the whole so-called Second Temple period, extended to cover the period down to the appearance of rabbinic Judaism. The questions raised ultimately focus on the Maccabaean crisis, as well as on the authority and vicissitudes of the sacred collection of books and on the origin of the oral traditions. A reorganization is then proposed under the form of a comprehensive line of argument built on a series of studies on limited themes, which are developed starting from the two subjects just singled out: the Sabbath and the Samaritans. The general method is set forth in the conclusion of Chapter 1.

The documentation used, besides the Bible, is that gathered together by Schürer,[1] but very special attention is paid to the rabbinic sources. They are very fragmented, and always deal with apparently secondary questions, which are more juridical than historical. So they are generally insufficiently utilized, although they contain all kinds of ancient materials, especially useful for portraying institutions, though they poorly inform us on any specific event.

The overall result obtained is quite different from Josephus's synthesis,

---

1. E. Schürer, *The History of the Jewish People in the Age of Jesus Christ* (trans. and ed. G. Vermes *et al.*; 3 vols.; Edinburgh: T. & T. Clark, 1973–87).

which still largely predominates in modern historiography. A certain number of reference points between 200 BCE and 200 CE are proposed. Although I do not provide any really new information, I hope to show that the simplest way to take into account various anomalies and many scattered bits of information is to presuppose, schematically, the following: that the Samaritans of Gerizim were the most direct heirs of the ancient Israelites and their cult; that the material in the Hexateuch should generally be attributed to them, with the conspicuous exception of the weekly Sabbath; that Judaism, dispersed throughout the whole Seleucid Transeuphrates, was an import from Babylon and was made up of ancestral traditions and memories of the Kingdom of Judah; that the union in Judaea between these two, that is to say, between two quite restricted groups, took place a little before 200 BCE, and was followed by an intense literary activity; that at this time Judaism was given legal status at Jerusalem by Antiochus III the Great, but this produced an unstable balance, because of the presence of an ancient cult to which it was not accustomed, and as a result there next arose different parties, including the Hasidaeans or Essenes, and finally the Maccabaean crisis; that on this occasion an Aaronite (maybe Zadokite) dynasty, originating from Samaria, ended up installed in Jerusalem, and its later supporters were the Sadducees; that the Pharisees were Babylonian in origin and were installed in Jerusalem, where they accepted the sacred Scriptures connected to the Temple, but in the same way that Nehemiah had, that is, without renouncing their customs; that the rabbinic tradition, firmly rooted in Galilee (from Hillel to the Mishnah), just as the beginnings of Christianity were, crossed paths several times with the Babylonian traditions and with the very diverse contributions of the Pharisees of Judaea (and those scattered throughout the whole Empire), which had a more biblical touch.

There were therefore two sources, as symbolized in the subtitle of this work: Joshua was the one who locally established in writing a statute and a law at the Shechem assembly, while the Mishnah was the ultimate metamorphosis of the traditions brought from Babylon and mixed in with Judaean influences.

The propositions formulated have the character of an interpretative model. Therefore, they can appear improbable. But this work is the opposite of a synthesis; it only aspires to open a debate. This English edition reshapes the French original to a considerable degree; in addition to numerous corrections and clarifications, it offers a clearer analysis of the Maccabaean crisis (Chapter 6, §4–5), as well as new developments on the Sadducees (Chapter 6, §6) and on Jewish Galilee (Chapter 7, §5). In this way the coherence of the whole work is strengthened.

Jerusalem, November 1993

Note

In addition to the footnotes, some technical explanations appear in the main text in a smaller type size. The general reader may skip over these passages and still follow the main flow of the argument.

ABBREVIATIONS

AASOR	Annual of the American Schools of Oriental Research
AB	Anchor Bible
AGJU	Arbeiten zur Geschichte des antiken Judentums und des Urchristentums
AGSU	Arbeiten zur Geschichte des Spätjudentums und Urchristentums
ALGHJ	Arbeiten zur Literatur und Geschichte des hellenistischen Judentums
AnBib	Analecta biblica
ANET	J.B. Pritchard (ed.), *Ancient Near Eastern Texts*
AOAT	Alter Orient und Altes Testament
ASTI	*Annual of the Swedish Theological Institute*
ATD	Das Alte Testament Deutsch
ATR	*Anglican Theological Review*
BA	*Biblical Archaeologist*
BASOR	*Bulletin of the American Schools of Oriental Research*
BJPES	*Bulletin of the Jewish Palestine Exploration Society*
BJS	Brown Judaic Studies
BZAW	Beihefte zur *ZAW*
CAT	Commentaire de l'Ancien Testament
CBQ	*Catholic Biblical Quarterly*
CBQMS	*Catholic Biblical Quarterly*, Monograph Series
DBAT	*Dielheimer Blätter zum Alten Testament*
DBSup	*Dictionnaire de la Bible, Supplément*
DJD	Discoveries in the Judaean Desert
EBib	Etudes bibliques
EncJud	*Encyclopaedia Judaica*
FRLANT	Forschungen zur Religion und Literatur des Alten und Neuen Testaments
HAT	Handbuch zum Alten Testament
HSM	Harvard Semitic Monographs
HTR	*Harvard Theological Review*
HUCA	*Hebrew Union College Annual*
IDBSup	*IDB*, Supplementary Volume
IEJ	*Israel Exploration Journal*
JAOS	*Journal of the American Oriental Society*
JBL	*Journal of Biblical Literature*
JJS	*Journal of Jewish Studies*
JNES	*Journal of Near Eastern Studies*

JQR	*Jewish Quarterly Review*
JSJ	*Journal for the Study of Judaism in the Persian, Hellenistic and Roman Period*
JSOT	*Journal for the Study of the Old Testament*
JSP	*Journal for the Study of the Pseudepigrapha*
JSS	*Journal of Semitic Studies*
JTS	*Journal of Theological Studies*
LCL	Loeb Classical Library
MGWJ	*Monatsschrift für Geschichte und Wissenschaft des Judentums*
NovTSup	*Novum Testamentum* Supplements
NTS	*New Testament Studies*
OBO	Orbis biblicus et orientalis
OTL	Old Testament Library
OTP	*Old Testament Pseudepigrapha*
OTS	*Oudtestamentische Studiën*
PAAJR	*Proceedings of the American Academy of Jewish Research*
PEQ	*Palestine Exploration Quarterly*
PG	J. Migne (ed.), *Patrologia graeca*
PGM	K. Preisendanz (ed.), *Papyri graecae magicae*
PL	J. Migne (ed.), *Patrologia latina*
RB	*Revue biblique*
REg	*Revue d'égyptologie*
REJ	*Revue des études juives*
RevQ	*Revue de Qumran*
RHR	*Revue de l'histoire des religions*
SANT	Studien zum Alten und Neuen Testament
SB	Sources bibliques
SBLSCS	SBL Septuagint and Cognate Studies
SBT	Studies in Biblical Theology
SC	Sources chrétiennes
SJLA	Studies in Judaism in Late Antiquity
SNTSMS	Society for New Testament Studies Monograph Series
SPAW	Sitzungsberichte der preussischen Akademie der Wissenschaften
SPB	Studia postbiblica
TT	*Teologisk Tidsskrift*
TU	Texte und Untersuchungen
UUÅ	Uppsala universitetsårsskrift
VT	*Vetus Testamentum*
VTSup	*Vetus Testamentum*, Supplements
WBC	Word Biblical Commentary
WMANT	Wissenschaftliche Monographien zum Alten und Neuen Testament
WTJ	*Westminster Theological Journal*
ZAW	*Zeitschrift für die alttestamentliche Wissenschaft*
ZDMG	*Zeitschrift der deutschen morgenländischen Gesellschaft*
ZDPV	*Zeitschrift des deutschen Palästina-Vereins*
ZNW	*Zeitschrift für die neutestamentliche Wissenschaft*

Chapter 1

FROM CYRUS TO THE MISHNAH: SOME PROBLEMS

Although this preliminary chapter intends to review this long period, it will do so from a limited point of view: it will not deal with history as such nor with institutions for their own sake, but merely with the main problems bound up with the history of the central institutions of Judaism as they are presented or understood in the most recent publications. The principal sources we will study and discuss are Ezra–Nehemiah and Josephus, but we will not exclude occasional references to other ancient historians. The method generally used consists of an examination of the relationships between the various classical problems, while noting the principal points of controversy as they come up; then various ways of resolving differences will be outlined. We follow in this first phase the chronological order of the periods as they are usually presented; it seemed useful besides to provide an outline of the principal dynasties up to the Roman period (Table 1 below).

1. *Cyrus and Darius*

In 539 BCE, Cyrus, the Achaemenid king of Persia,[1] conquered Babylon, which had been holding among others the captives from Judaea. Having dominion in this way over the whole Near East, Cyrus established a new imperial policy, based on respect for the culture of local populations, backing it up with a flexible, efficient and centralized administration. From this approach he gained a reputation as an enlightened liberator, as

---

1. For the general presentation of the Persian period, I mainly follow G. Widengren, 'The Persian Period', in J.H. Hayes and J.M. Miller, *Israelite and Judaean History* (London: SCM Press, 1977), and W.D. Davies and L. Finkelstein (eds.), *The Cambridge History of Judaism*. I. *Introduction: The Persian Period*; II. *The Hellenistic Age* (2 vols.; Cambridge: Cambridge University Press, 1984–89), I, chs. 4 and 7.

A Search for the Origins of Judaism

is borne out by Greek historians as well as the Bible (Isa. 45.3-4, where Cyrus is called 'Anointed of YHWH'). The evidence from inscriptions of that time is indeed quite precise: he reinstated the gods who dwelt in the vassal regions and rebuilt for them their temples; he allowed deportees to return to their traditional homelands.

Neo-Babylonians

Nebuchadnezzar II	604–562
Evil-Merodach	561–556
Labashimarduk	556–555
Nabonidus	555–539

Achaemenids

Cyrus (Babylon 539)	559–529
Cambyses	529–522
Darius I	521–486
Xerxes	485–465
Artaxerxes I Longimanus	465–425
Darius II	425–405
Artaxerxes II Mnemon	405–359
Artaxerxes III Ochus	359–339
Darius III Codommanus	339–331

Macedonians

Alexander (Issus 333)	336–323
(The Wars of the Diadochi	323–301)

Seleucids

Seleucus I Nicator	301–281
Antiochus I Soter	281–261
Antiochus II Theos	261–246
Seleucus II Callincos	246–225
Seleucus III Soter	225–223
Antiochus III the Great	223–187
Seleucus IV Philopator	187–175

Lagides

Ptolemy I Soter	301–282
Ptolemy II	
Philadelphus	282–246
Ptolemy III Euergetes	246–222
Ptolemy IV Philopator	222–205
Ptolemy V Epiphanes	204–180

Judaea

(Hasmonay-Asamonnias)
(Simon)
(John)

Seleucids		Judaea		Lagides	
Antiochus IV Epiphanes	175–164	Jason	175–171	Ptolemy VI Philometor	180–145
		Menelaus	171–163		
		(Mattathias	167–166)		
Antiochus V Eupator	163–162	(Judas Maccabeus	166–160)		
Demetrius I Soter	162–150	Alcimus	162–159		
Alexander Balas	152–145	Jonathan (160)	152–144	Ptolemy VII	145–144
Demetrius II Nicator	145–140	Simon	144–134		
Antiochus VI Epiphanes	175–164			Ptolemy VIII Euergetes II	(170)–116
Diodorus Tryphon	142–137				
Antiochus VII Sidetes	137–129	John Hyrcanus	135–104		
Demetrius II Nicator	129–125				
		Alexander Jannaeus	103–76		
		Alexandra	76–67		

Table 1. *Babylonian, Persian, Hellenistic and Judaean Dynasties*

In the context of the above-mentioned inscriptions, the proclamation of Cyrus which opens the book of Ezra seems plausible:

> The first year of Cyrus, king of Persia, to fulfil the word of YHWH spoken by Jeremiah, YHWH stirred up the spirit of Cyrus, king of Persia, who issued a proclamation—and even had it publicly displayed throughout his kingdom: 'Cyrus, king of Persia, says this: YHWH, the God of heaven, has given me all the kingdoms of the earth and has appointed me to build the temple at Jerusalem in Judah. Any among you who form part of this people, may their God be with them, and let them go up!'

Objections have been raised however in regard to the authenticity of this text, since the same book relates further on that Darius, one of the successors of Cyrus, discovered a copy of the same decree later on in the archives of Ecbatana, on the occasion of a dispute in Jerusalem, instigated by groups opposed to the construction of the temple. But this other version contained in Ezra 6.3-5 is in Aramaic and differs considerably from the first one; besides, it contains a number of literary difficulties. In a famous study, Roland de Vaux deals with the problem by way of general history:[2] he shows, through a study of the imperial policy of Cyrus and Darius I, that it would be hard to believe that there had not been a decree about restoring the Jerusalem temple.[3] The problem about the authenticity of the biblical versions of this document is then shifted and in fact reduced to a more limited question: since the official decree really existed, the only thing that need be done is to verify whether its text is well preserved. The demonstration then turns to the archive scroll recovered by Darius. The objections to its authenticity can be countered—whether they be external difficulties from the fact that it is included in a long section in Aramaic (4.6–6.18) which is hard to see as a homogeneous source, or internal difficulties in the composition itself. Finally, the author concedes that the two forms of the decree are too different to be traced back to the same text, but he contends that it is not necessary to choose between the two, which would amount to rejecting the version of Ezra 1, since the diplomatic and literary forms of the version in Ezra 6.3-5 agree sufficiently with the style of Archaemenid documents. It would be quite enough to admit that there were two decrees: the first more general one with the offer of the return (Ezra 1), the second regulating the construction of the Temple.

---

2. R. de Vaux, 'Les décrets de Cyrus et de Darius sur la reconstruction du Temple', *RB* 46 (1937), pp. 29-57.

3. He relies in particular on the famous Cyrus Cylinder; cf. *ANET*, pp. 315-16.

This division into two decrees is nevertheless a desperate solution; fundamentally it explains very poorly the radical difference between documents which came from the same administration and in which, besides, the first one certainly shows traces of reshaping by the biblical editor (v. 3: 'YHWH, the God of Israel', etc.); this finally discredits it irreparably. Elias Bickerman in the meantime has provided the final component of the answer, by concentrating specifically on making sense of the difference in style and language. By examining the formulas used in each of the two texts, he shows[4] that there are two documents which are independent, from the literary point of view, although they refer to the same decree. The scroll from the archives of Ecbatana was a memorandum (דכרונה, ὑπόμνημα, Ezra 6.2), namely, an internal administrative document, whereas the first version in Ezra 1.2-4 appears to be a notice proclaimed and displayed throughout the whole Empire, quite obviously in the local languages; this did not, however, preclude further retouchings. The difference between the two versions need not then be a priori unsettling and it is really a matter of just one decree. This whole theory has the advantage of clarity, but it perhaps starts off by overestimating the extent of Cyrus's policy, which did not really systematically repatriate the previously displaced populations.[5] By any hypothesis, only a small Jewish minority returned from exile.

We are told that Cyrus, having enacted this decree, handed over the Temple vessels, which had been seized by Nebuchadnezzar, to Sheshbazzar, prince of Judah (1.8; cf. 5.14-15). The latter laid the foundations of the Temple (5.16). If we may rely on the demand addressed to Darius for confirmation of the decree, it was still Sheshbazzar who, some years later, was directing the unfinished construction. However, when the governor of Transeuphrates, author of the demand, had come to enquire about the legality of the construction, it was then under the direction of

4. E.J. Bickerman, 'The Edict of Cyrus in Esdras 1', in *Studies in Jewish and Christian History* (Leiden: Brill, 1976), I, pp. 72-108.

5. A. Kuhrt, 'The Cyrus Cylinder and Achaemenid Imperial Policy', *JSOT* 25 (Sheffield: JSOT Press, 1983), pp. 83-97, observes that too much may have been demanded of the text of this cylinder, since Cyrus restricts himself to restoring in Babylon the cult of Marduk, while returning the neighbouring gods (but not the populations associated with them), according to a formula of a very ancient Mesopotamian type; we cannot directly infer from this then the order to re-establish the temple and community of Jerusalem, and we must in that case propose reasons that are more local, such as the consolidation of the Egyptian frontier (or even a policy like that of the Seleucid Antiochus III; cf. Chapter 6, §2).

Zerubbabel and Jeshua, aided by the prophets Zechariah and Haggai (Ezra 5.1-2). Sheshbazzar and Zerubbabel are separate individuals, and the consequent redactional effect gives a continuity from one to the other. What is more, the setting up of the altar (3.2) by Jeshua and Zerubbabel, even before the building of the Temple, is really the pursuit of the same work. As a consequence, the interruptions in the work mentioned in the time of Cyrus, Xerxes and then Artaxerxes (Ezra 4), before the confirmation by Darius, formally contradict this suggestion of continuity.

To recover the events then, it is absolutely necessary to correct the presentation of the text. So, taking the persons Jeshua and Zerubbabel as a reference point, it is necessary to connect the inauguration of the altar with Darius. And in order, besides, to take seriously the continuity in the construction, it is necessary to put everything before the incidents in the time of Xerxes and Artaxerxes. The usual correction since the time of Josephus (*Ant.* 11.31) involves this rearrangement, and understanding Darius not as Darius II (425–405 BCE, after Artaxerxes I), but as Darius I, who succeeded Cyrus in 521, after the brief reign of Cambyses, son of Cyrus who had died in 529.[6] Since according to Ezra 6.15 the dedication of the sanctuary took place 'the sixth year of the reign of King Darius', we obtain 515 as the date of that inauguration.

According to this correction, and taking into consideration that the roster of the repatriates of Ezra 2 combines distinct lists, so as to create an impression of a mass return after a period of complete abandonment (cf. 2 Chron. 36.17-21), a first group would have left quickly, led by Sheshbazzar, the prince of Judah, named governor by Cyrus. Sheshbazzar was perhaps a son of Jehoiachin, who was deported in 598 and died in 561 (1 Chron. 3.18 LXX), in which case Cyrus would be following the Persian custom of picking the heads of royal houses to govern the provinces[7] (cf. Herodotus 3.15). Eventually, other caravans would have followed, one of them bringing Jeshua, a descendant of Zadok, and Zerubbabel, grandson of Jehoiachin and perhaps a nephew of Sheshbazzar. The latter, whom some identify with the anonymous Jewish governor of Ezra 2.63, would have died in the intervening period, and Zerubbabel, of Davidic descent, would have naturally succeeded him, but he appears strangely absent from the inaugural Passover.[8]

---

6. Cf. Widengren, 'Persian Period', p. 322, and Bibliography.

7. The Davidic lineage of Sheshbazzar (distinct from Zerubbabel) which presupposes in fact an identification of שׁשׁבצר with שׁנאצר is considered impossible by P.R. Berger, 'Zu den Namen שׁשׁבצר und שׁנאצר', *ZAW* 83 (1971), pp. 98-100, but his discussion does not directly affect the discussion here.

8. There is no information on the end of his mandate, but it is usually admitted

The various phases of the reconstruction of the Temple could be linked with the successive migrations: beginning of the work under Cyrus, with Sheshbazzar, interruption by the 'enemies of Judah and Benjamin' (4.1), a resumption under Darius I, an investigation by the governor, the royal confirmation and completion of the sanctuary, and finally the dedication for the Passover of 515. Even then, several texts cause difficulties, especially in regard to the continuity of the work after Sheshbazzar (5.16), and the resumption of worship with Zerubbabel and Jeshua *before* the foundations laid by Sheshbazzar (3.2-6). One long-standing solution to remove this last inconsistency is to suppose that Sheshbazzar is merely the Persian name of Zerubbabel. But, even then, their actions cannot really be superimposed one on the other, especially if we take into account other evidence: 1 Esdras 3–4 (selection of Zerubbabel by Darius), as well as Haggai 1 and Zechariah 1–8 clearly imply the restarting of work under Darius; the accentuated continuity then becomes very uncertain. Finally, if as a last resort it is conjectured that the narrativies involving Cyrus and Darius are more or less overlapping doublets describing the same events, then the distinction established between the edict of Cyrus and its confirmation by Darius is inevitably compromised, with one of the two accounts (in fact, the first one) coming under suspicion of being merely a very free doublet of the other. The personages then seem to elude a clear grasp.

As for the work on the sanctuary, what had happened between the decree of Cyrus and the inauguration of 515 BCE, 24 years later? It could be supposed that local obstructions delayed the work or that the precarious situation of the community of repatriates (cf. Hag. 1.10-11) left few resources for carrying out a large-scale project. But the exact consistency of the activities remains blurred: how is it possible to reconcile the renewal of worship on a rebuilt altar before the laying of the foundations of the Temple (Ezra 3.3-6) with the mention of the beginning of the work on the Temple right after the arrival of the first convoy of repatriates (Ezra 5.16)?

Lexicographical solutions have been suggested: in Ezra 3.6 the Hebrew root יסד would not mean 'foundation' but rather 'restoration', and hence ultimately 'completion of the work';[9] while in 5.16 אשיא would designate in Aramaic not 'foundations', but more generally 'preliminary excavations'[10] (cf. 4.12). These proposals to separate the Hebrew word from the Aramaic word only take the edge off the problem

that because of a royal-messianic claim (cf. Zech. 6.13) he would have been removed by Darius. This hypothesis is still arbitrary, or at best unverifiable; cf. J.D. Purvis, 'Exile and Return', in H. Shanks (ed.), *Ancient Israel* (Washington, DC: Biblical Archaeological Society, 1988), p. 167.

9.   A. Gelston, 'The Foundations of the Second Temple', *VT* 16 (1966), pp. 232-35.

10.   Cf. C.G. Tuland, '"*Ussaya*" and "*Ussarna*": A Clarification of Terms, Date and Text', *JNES* 17 (1958), pp. 269-75.

without really resolving it, since both the Targum and Esdras B of the LXX show that they were considered equivalent terms, no matter what their precise technical meanings might be. Besides, the foundation work appeared to be still ongoing under Artaxerxes, therefore long after Darius I, even though it is not known precisely whether it refers to the restoration of the city (4.12) or the Temple (4.24).

The real problem, however, lies elsewhere: if the restored altar was ready for use, that is to say, if it was good enough for the carrying out of sacrifices 'as it is written in the law of Moses', there is room to wonder exactly what further role was played by the 'temple' (היכל), or more precisely its 'foundation'. To reply, by referring to the descriptions of the sanctuary of Moses or of Solomon's buildings, that it was a matter of the covered place where the Ark (Holy of Holies) was to be kept, resolves nothing, since according to 3.2-5 all the requirements of the cult could have been carried out on this altar.

In this regard, it has been suggested, based on the reference to an important 'keystone' (את האבן הראשה, LXX: τὸν λίθον τῆς κληρονομίας) in Zech. 4.7, that it could have indicated a symbolic foundation stone, taken from an ancient building and meant to show the continuity of worship.[11] The 'foundation' in this sense had an exalted meaning, as can be seen in the curse of Joshua on anyone who rebuilt Jericho ('He will lay its foundation [ייסדנה] on his eldest son', Josh. 6.26), and the meaning of the passage we are discussing would then be that worship according to the law of Moses would have been resumed with the altar alone *before* the establishment of a continuity with the Temple of the age of the monarchy. This distinction is interesting, if compared with the epic of Judas Maccabeus, who succeeded in purifying and dedicating the altar, and not the Temple (1 Macc. 4.52-59). In the period under consideration, under Cyrus and Darius I, it involved the re-establishment of the ancient cult, well before the development of Judaism under Ezra and Nehemiah: this is precisely what is indicated in the return of the cultic vessels carried off by Nebuchadnezzar.

As a matter of fact, there is little information from either archaeology or texts about what happened to the Temple in the period between the fall of Jerusalem and Cyrus: according to 2 Kgs 25.13-21, it was dismantled and looted, perhaps even destroyed. It has been suggested[12] that in

---

11. Cf. D.L. Petersen, 'Zerubbabel and Jerusalem Temple Reconstruction', *CBQ* 36 (1974), pp. 366-72, utilizing R.S. Ellis, *Foundation Deposits in Ancient Mesopotamia* (Yale Near Eastern Research, 2; New Haven: Yale University Press, 1968), which especially shows that the essential element of the 'foundation deposit' is an inauguration ritual, at the beginning or the end of the construction; this deposit could leave or not leave a material trace detectable by archaeology.

12. E. Janssen, *Juda in der Exilszeit: Ein Beitrag zur Frage der Entstehung des*

the course of the fifty years during which we have no precise information on Jerusalem, except that King Jehoiachin was freed and remained
in Babylon, there were attempts at restoration, which were considered to
have been illegitimate by the new immigrants and this caused a delay in
the re-establishment of a bond of continuity. Yet, this hypothesis of internal conflicts within the Judaean community, or more exactly between
those who had not been exiled and the returnees from exile gives rise to
ambiguity about the authority and the precise mission of Sheshbazzar
and Zerubbabel, and casts doubt on who really were the intended
recipients of the edict of Cyrus. In fact, if the edict was authentic, Judaea
should be considered to have been administratively homogeneous, and
local opponents ('enemies of Judah and Benjamin', 4.1; 'people of the
country', 4.4) must have been non-Judaeans. Since the opposition in one
instance (under Artaxerxes, 4.10) was attributed to Samaritan colonists,
and since the Samaritans constituted the only organized nation that
would be jealous of Jerusalem (2 Kgs 17), all the attempts to obstruct
the restoration of the Temple are usually blamed on them.[13] This is what
Josephus had already done (*Ant.* 11.19, under Cyrus), obviously for the
same reasons.

If the customary meaning, 'foundation', is retained, it is still possible to work out
some reconstruction of the events, or two such reconstructions. The first method
would consider Ezra 3 a full account of the restoration of the Temple, under the
direction of Zerubbabel and Jeshua. Everything culminated in an inauguration feast
(vv. 10-13), whose natural conclusion is reported in 6.19-22, when the Passover was
celebrated. The narrative is stretched out by the intrusion of the obstruction in the
time of Cyrus (4.1-5) and by the long passage in Aramaic (4.6–6.18). The reconstruction would have taken place then between a seventh month (feast of Booths) and
a first month (feast of Passover), probably in the first years of the activities of
Zerubbabel and Jeshua. But on the one hand such a presentation is more stylized
than historical; and on the other it can be noted that it is closely related to the activity
of Sheshbazzar, and that any allusion to Darius disappears, which gives an impression of everything happening quickly. Furthermore, there is an implicit assumption
that the intrusion of the fragments (4.1-5; 4.6–6.18) which separate the narrative into
two parts would be purely accidental. In that case, it may be asked whether it is
legitimate to formulate a literary hypothesis for reasons of historical consistency.

Another method, which avoids this reef, makes use of the Aramaic section (5.1–
6.18), which was omitted in the above reconstruction. The intense enthusiasm expressed for Zerubbabel and Jeshua by the prophets Haggai and Zechariah is decisive,
notwithstanding the affirmation of a continuity with the deputation of Sheshbazzar

---

Judentums (Göttingen: Vandenhoeck & Ruprecht, 1956), pp. 7, 102-103.
    13. Up to Purvis, 'Exile and Return', p. 168.

(5.16). Despite the various obstacles, which explain the long delay between the decree of Cyrus and the Passover of 515, everything was completed in the sixth year of Darius (6.15). The return of the cult vessels guaranteed the link with the ancient sanctuary. In this form, the account draws nearer to the details provided by Haggai 1 and Zechariah 1–8. Furthermore, the lustre it brings to the surrounding narrative then takes on an unquestionable significance. Unfortunately, the dividing up of the narrative highlighted in this way gives the impression of a doublet; besides, since it brings back to a great extent the dividing up of the decree between Cyrus and Darius, there is once again the difficulty mentioned above.

As a matter of fact, all the attempts to give a historical interpretation fail to provide a result clearer than the text as it stands, since there always remains an unusable residue. Not only are the details objectively few in number and incomplete, but they always seem to be overburdened with an excess of contradictory information, which weakens them by enveloping them in a fog of imprecision. And this fuzziness is so systematic that we get the impression that no new element provided by archaeology or epigraphy can clarify the totality of facts, since it would destroy a very precarious literary equilibrium. This observation raises a question about method: can a text so resistant to reconstruction—just like the Temple—be seriously considered, as is supposed by most critics, a *sloppy* text, a problematic outcome of a fortuitous accumulation of incoherent documents?

2. Nehemiah and Ezra

The immediate outcome of the events just discussed is lost now, and there certainly is a chronological gap. However, Ezra 7.1 provides a quick linking of events, since 'after these events' there immediately follows the story of Ezra, which covers Ezra 7–10, and this is continued in Nehemiah 8, where Ezra solemnly reads the Law (1 Esdras joins these two passages together), and perhaps in Nehemiah 9–10. The book of Nehemiah is presented as the 'Memoirs of Nehemiah' (a title borrowed from 2 Macc. 2.13), in the first person, supplemented by other material, especially about Ezra. The consequence of this is that they become contemporaries: Ezra was authorized to establish the Law in Jerusalem; Nehemiah rebuilt the city; and both carried out religious reforms. Nevertheless, the chronological details provided separate them a little: the dates given in the report of Ezra fell within the seventh year of an Artaxerxes (Ezra 7.7-8 and 10.9), while Nehemiah lived in Judaea from the twentieth to the thirty-second year of an Artaxerxes and returned later under this same king (Neh. 1.1 and 13.6). As a matter of fact, the only passage not editorially overloaded where Ezra and Nehemiah are mentioned together is Neh. 12.26; it is a redactional summary joining Ezra and Nehemiah together with the dynasty of high priests.

In addition, a third episode 'in the time of Artxerxes' is recounted: it involved a forced interruption of the work in Jerusalem, on the initiative of the 'people of Transeuphrates' (Ezra 4.7-24). As there were three Artaxerxes, it is necessary first of all to connect these events to precise reigns. For Nehemiah, Artaxerxes III is ruled out, since he reigned only 22 years (358–336), but there is room for doubt between Artaxerxes I (465–424) and Artaxerxes II (404–358). Here, an external element provides some help: a letter included in the Elephantine papyri, and dated 408–407, mentions Yohanan, high priest of Jerusalem, as well as Dalaiah and Shelemiah, sons of Sanballat, governor of Samaria.[14] But Johanan was the grandson of the high priest Eliashib (Neh. 12.10), a contemporary of Nehemiah, and Sanballat was his adversary (2.10; etc.). Nehemiah came, therefore, in the twentieth year of Artaxerxes I, or 445. It is natural then to connect Ezra, as well as the Samaritan opposition, to the same reign, prior to Nehemiah.

This first general interpretation,[15] grouping these occurrences together in the same reign, respects to a great extent the order of the texts and gives a plausible meaning, since the administrative and social work of Nehemiah presupposed the religious reform of Ezra and logically relied on it. Such a synthesis, however, runs into numerous difficulties. If Nehemiah came after Ezra, how could he have contrasted the justice of his government with the injustices of his predecessors (Neh. 5.15)? Why did Ezra have no worries about reconstruction, if the city was still in ruins and a community nonexistent, to judge from the appeal of the Samaritans to Artaxerxes (Ezra 4.12-16)? Finally, rebuilt or not, the city was very much depopulated when Nehemiah arrived, and we cannot see Ezra preaching in the desert.

This is why for a century there has existed an inverse hypothesis according to which Ezra would have come after Nehemiah.[16] He would

---

14.   A.E. Cowley, *Aramaic Papyri of the Fifth Century BC* (Oxford: Clarendon Press, 1923), pp. 108-122 nn. 30-31.

15.   So R. de Vaux, 'Israël', *DBSup* 4 (1949), cols. 764-65.

16.   Since A. Van Hoonacker, 'Néhémie et Esdras, une nouvelle hypothèse sur la chronologie et la restauration juive', *Le Muséon* 9 (1890), pp. 151-84, 315-17, 389-401. Cf. the overall review and general acceptance of this hypothesis in Widengren,

then have been connected with Artaxerxes II, and his mission in the seventh year would therefore be in 398. A confirmatory detail is provided by the Elephantine papyri: they are prior to 400, and contain many legal texts; none of these, however, is based on the authority of the law of Moses, and it must be concluded that the Mosaic laws were promulgated by Ezra only later on. Even then, obscurities remain. First of all, given that according to Ezra 3.2 the sacrifices in the time of Darius, consequently much earlier, would have been re-established according to the law of Moses, the argument based on Elephantine not only proves nothing, but again creates a grave difficulty, since one has to wonder who these Jews could have been who seem to be ignorant of the authority of the Law. Besides, the two missions of Nehemiah are very different in nature: if he rebuilt the city in the first one, which would seem natural before the work of Ezra, in the second he promoted religious reform according to the Law, something Ezra had only sketched out. It is tempting then to put Ezra between the two journeys of Nehemiah, but that returns to the starting point above, which is exactly what the book of Nehemiah does, by tending to make them contemporaries. Yet, based on elements identifiable before any modifications are introduced, they were not contemporaries and, what is more, they were totally unaware of each other.

Let us consider them separately then, before trying to propose a relationship between the two of them. They seem in fact to be open to being treated independently: the biblical tradition (Sir. 40.13; 2 Macc. 2.13) magnified Nehemiah, as if he had been the real restorer[17] of post-exilic Judaism, and forgot Ezra, while in the rabbinic tradition on the contrary Ezra was elevated and even identified with the prophet Malachi.[18] As for Ezra, he was a priest, but his genealogy is peculiar: he was claimed to be an immediate descendant of the high priest Seriah, taken captive to Babylon by Nebuchadnezzar (2 Kgs 25.18; cf. 1 Chron. 6.14), which would have put him long before Cyrus. Yet he was sent by Artaxerxes

'The Persian Period', pp. 504-505, with a refutation in particular of F.M. Cross, 'A Reconstruction of the Judean Restoration', *JBL* 94 (1975), pp. 4-18. Cross, by restoring the dynasties of the high priests making use of the finds from Wadi Daliyeh and various conjectures, wishes to restore Ezra before Nehemiah (cf. an additional critique in Davies and Finkelstein, *History of Judaism*, I, p. 138 n. 2).

17. Cf. U. Kellerman, *Nehemia: Quellen, Überlieferung und Geschichte* (BZAW, 102; Berlin: Töpelmann, 1967).

18. Targum on Mal. 1.1 and *b. Meg.* 15a.

to restore the practice of the Law and strengthen the organization and financing of the Temple in Jerusalem. This official mission, conveyed in a royal firman in Aramaic which should be considered authentic, presupposed a Jewish population in Judaea. Interestingly, however, it issued a general invitation to travel to Jerusalem addressed to all the people of Israel and drew attention to a royal offering 'to the God of Israel who dwells in Jerusalem'. In addition, Ezra was entrusted with the appointment of scribes and judges throughout all the land west of the Euphrates, to ensure that instruction and justice flourished. These instructions, which confuse to a slight extent Judah and Israel, are hard to reconcile with the resistance of the Samaritans, and in particular with the stoppage of the reconstruction ordered by Artaxerxes (Ezra 4.21), under the pretext that the kings of Jerusalem had ruthlessly ruled over all Transeuphrates.

It is still not clear if it referred to the same Artaxerxes. One fact and one imperial political objective are open to speculation. The fact would be that the Judaeans, and more broadly the Israelites, constituted a minority scattered throughout the whole satrapy, possibly eventually presenting a danger. The political objective then would be to reorganize these people in legal and religious matters, so that the whole area on the frontier with Egypt would be at peace, especially by strengthening Jerusalem as a centre. In the eyes of the Persians, then, this was the group best structured and able to be a faithful vassal if granted sufficient autonomy. Yet, in contrast with this important project, the recorded activity of Ezra was strictly Judaean and took on the appearance of a liturgical pilgrimage like the Exodus: there were concerns about the Levites, care exercised for the Temple offerings, the doing of penance, the breaking up of marriages with foreigners, and the proclamation of the Law in Jerusalem. No matter what the historical reality had been, the resultant narrative was essentially theological.[19]

The reading of the Law by Ezra was integrated into a celebration of the feast of Booths[20] 'as it had not been done since the days of Joshua, the son of Nun' (Neh. 8.17). This formula is reminiscent of the Passover of Josiah, 'as it had not been celebrated since the time of the Judges' (2 Kgs 23.22; 2 Chron. 35.18a: 'since the days of the prophet Samuel').

---

19. Cf. K. Koch, 'Esdras and the Origins of Judaism', *JSS* 19 (1974), pp. 173-97.

20. Deut. 31.9-13 prescribes a reading of the Law (or 'of that Law') on the feast of Tabernacles, but only 'at the end of every seven years, at the time fixed for the year of remission'.

The comparison is expressly made by 1 Esdras, which begins with the reform of Josiah. Just as Ezra was connected to the high priesthood from the end of the monarchy, so his reform completed what could not be carried out before the catastrophe. Continuity is assured in this way, but it may be asked what were the real historical facts on which it is based, since the whole restoration by Zerubbabel is made to disappear, even though it too had involved a feast of Booths at the inauguration of the altar, and a Passover at the inauguration of the whole sanctuary, not to mention the very deliberate allusions, as has been shown, to the preservation of the continuity with the ancient Temple.

The passage which follows the Ezra feast of Booths (Neh. 9) is not directly connected to it. It amounts to another reading of the Law, without Ezra,[21] inserted into an atonement ceremony, where the emphasis is placed on the 'separation of those of Israelite stock from those of foreign origin'. It culminates in a long historical psalm whose essential theme is the possession of the land, whereas the present slavery means great distress (9.36). The following piece (Neh. 10) is a solemn renewal of the Covenant and its stipulations. It fits into the context, but is signed by Nehemiah and his companions. It can be argued that the list of signatories, inserted in an odd place, intrudes into the proceedings, in which case an actual connection of the piece with Ezra would be possible;[22] but it must be admitted that the stipulations of the Covenant generally correspond better with the reform of Nehemiah[23] on the occasion of his second mission (Neh. 13) than with the activity of Ezra himself (Ezra 9–10), since it had just been inaugurated. As should have been anticipated, the two opposing ways of understanding the renewal of the Covenant remain in fact equal in merit, since it could have equally well preceded or followed the reform. In one case, it is naturally connected with Ezra; in the other, with Nehemiah.

To sum up, the mission of Ezra becomes problematic because of literary features which detach it from any precise historical setting; it blends together a continuity with the preceding period and an affirmation of a reforming newness, but without a clear link with the work of Sheshbazzar and Zerubbabel.

The Memoirs of Nehemiah cover two missions, one of twelve years beginning in the twentieth year of Artaxerxes, the other of undetermined duration.[24] The first mission (Neh. 1–7) focused its attention on

21. In 9.5 the psalm is introduced in the LXX (Esd. B 19.6) by the words 'And Ezra said', but this is an addition (which is not exactly at the beginning of the poem) making clear most likely the intention of the compiler.

22. The opinion of Peter Ackroyd in Davies and Finkelstein, *History of Judaism*, I, pp. 145-46.

23. See de Vaux, 'Israël', col. 764.

24. The phrase for permission to leave, in Neh. 13.6 ולקץ ימים, is usually rendered

the reconstruction and repopulation of Jerusalem, despite the repeated obstructions from neighbouring peoples, represented especially by Sanballat the Horonite, Geshem the Arab and Tobiah the Ammonite. A passage on internal social difficulties that Nehemiah had to smooth over is slipped in too (Neh. 5); it gives the impression that the main objective of his task as governor was to manage skillfully a mostly rural province, by restoring a strong administration. Yet, in this context it is not clear how the problem of volunteers building fortifications and the repopulation of Jerusalem would fit in, since these activities were perceived by neighbouring peoples as steps toward independence, in contravention of the fidelity expected of a governor formally appointed by the Persian authorities (Neh. 2.6-8).

What is more, one of the main steps in pacification realized by Nehemiah was the remission of debts; abuses had created tensions among members of the community. That matter was regulated in the name of the fear of God (5.9), but it is strange that Nehemiah should not have appealed to the law of the year of remission (or Sabbatical Year), referred to in the renewed Covenant (10.32), all the more so since it was institutionally and literarily connected to the Sabbath, which Nehemiah defended so energetically later on (13.15-22). In the final presentation of the book, the difficulty is toned down, since Ezra proclaims the Law between the two missions of Nehemiah, but it was shown above that Ezra and Nehemiah must be historically dissociated. To sum up, the two missions of Nehemiah are difficult to combine, and it is to be feared that the Memoirs are nothing more than a defence of a dissident undertaking in relation to the Persian authority. His justification would then have been based on the appearance of a religious restoration, from which stems Ezra's putting of the Law into effect and the insistence on a reform.

The beginning of the Memoirs reports bad news from Jerusalem reaching Susa, where Nehemiah happened to be: the situation of 'the remnant rescued from captivity' was disastrous and the city was in a deplorable state. In spite of the lists of the returnees 'from the beginning' which at that time he drew up for the repopulation of Jerusalem and which merely repeated the list in Ezra 2, Nehemiah was not linked to a return from exile, unlike Ezra (Ezra 7.28), but was appointed to attend to the Judaeans already in the country. This presentation not only omits Ezra, which is defensible if Ezra came later, but it also highhandedly ignores the convoys of Sheshbazzar and Zerubbabel and therefore their restoration efforts. Already then at this

---

'at the end of a certain time'; here perhaps it has the more precise meaning of 'at the end of a year', cf. S. Talmon, 'Ezra and Nehemiah', in G.A. Buttrick (ed.), *IDBSup*, p. 320.

stage there was an amplification of Nehemiah's role. As for the neglected condition of the city and its walls, it may, for lack of a better explanation, be connected with the stoppage of work 'by force of arms' in the time of Artaxerxes, as described in Ezra 4.8-23. The correspondence is not that close and there is no guarantee that it would be the same Artaxerxes, but the literary amplification pointed out skips over these uncertainties and sets its sights on the state of Judaea after Nebuchadnezzar. For Nehemiah ultimately appears as a prudent religious leader as well: he foils external and internal opposition (cf. Neh. 6.17-19) by combining action and prayer (4.8; 6.10). The meticulous reconstruction, with all the help coming from Judaea (Neh. 3), is implicitly attributed to him, even though it seems to have been directed by the high priest Eliashib, whether or not the latter was the same person as the Eliashib of the second mission and an accomplice of Tobiah and an adversary of Nehemiah (13.4-5). Nehemiah is furthermore presented, always implicitly, as the originator of the reorganization of the Temple in the short summary of Neh. 12.44-47, which paints a picture of an ideal epoch, in the context of lists of notable families and their functions (Neh. 11–12) which extends beyond the epoch of Nehemiah himself. More generally, however, the second mission of Nehemiah, which is not clearly dated and is vastly different from the first one (outside of a tenuous reference to the high priest Eliashib), is entirely centred on a religious reform parallel to that of Ezra (even beginning with a reading of the Law, 13.1). Perhaps this was artificially attributed to Nehemiah, in order to enhance his stature.

If there was such an enhancement of Nehemiah's role, there rises again the question raised earlier about the legitimacy in the eyes of the Persian authorities of Nehemiah's work in Jerusalem. According to the Memoirs, he had at his disposal documents accrediting him to provincial authorities, so that the local opponents had no legal title to cause him difficulties. Nevertheless, they denounced the enterprise as illegal. They seem to emerge as a more and more compact block and to act in a repetitive manner, but it is a good idea to examine them closely, since the first list refers only to Sanballat and Tobiah. Tobiah, the Ammonite slave (עבד), is certainly to be understood as a governor, 'servant' of the Great King, just as later on the Tobiads were to be the allies of the Seleucids, and he had good support in Judaea (6.17-19). As for Sanballat the Horonite, he is seen later on intervening before the court of Samaria (3.34), but, although he would certainly be a high dignitary (13.28), he had no official title, whereas external documents refer to several Sanballats, all of whom were governors of Samaria; they probably were natives of Mesopotamia and in any case were appointed by the Persians. There is definitely room then to wonder whether Nehemiah's undertaking, supported more by his God than by the secular Persian authority, would have been in the beginning really legitimate, and whether he had indeed been appointed governor (Neh. 5.14) quickly, as many historians would have it.[25]

25. Such as de Vaux, 'Israël', col. 768; E. Stern, 'Palestine in the Persian Period', in Davies and Finkelstein, *History of Judaism*, I, p. 74; P.R. Ackroyd, 'The Jews in Palestine in the Persian Period', in Davies and Finkelstein, *History of the Jews*, I, p. 148.

In regard to the Samaritan opposition to the restoration of the city in the time of Artaxerxes, which ended up as a stoppage by force of arms (Ezra 4.7-24), some place it under Artaxerxes I, therefore just before Nehemiah became governor, even if it underscores the changeability of this sovereign;[26] others observe that the composition of the complaint and the royal response exaggerated considerably the danger in the rebuilding of Jerusalem, by bringing up the 'powerful kings who had reigned in Jerusalem and lorded it over all Transeuphrates' (4.20), and conclude that there must have been numerous attempts at restoration and that this episode must refer to one such attempt, with no definable link to Ezra or Nehemiah.[27] The research of Ephraim Stern on the Persian period, based on archaeology, shows that in Palestine there were two culturally distinct regions: one comprised Judaea, the countries of Ammon and Moab and to a lesser degree Samaria; the other, Galilee and the coastal plain. Persian influence is hardly noticeable in material culture, but is much clearer in administrative matters, which can be seen from the seals and coins;[28] at the end of the fifth century there is evidence of decentralization. These conclusions are consistent with what we know from texts about Persian imperial policy. They can provide a context for the struggle for the control of Jerusalem, but they do not help decide which side had the legitimate claim. Nehemiah's Persian mandate was therefore problematic for the first mission; it was likewise for the second, since he clearly acted on his own authority.

As in the case of Cyrus and Darius, the balance sheet from the investigation of Ezra and Nehemiah is disappointing. Taken separately, they are unaware of one another, and each one could pass for the real founder of Judaism, although there would still be serious chronological and political uncertainties. What is more, as soon as we try to fit them

26. Cf. de Vaux, "Israël", who places the incident between Ezra and Nehemiah, and who should then suppose that the returnees with Ezra had begun to restore the walls, which is not mentioned at all. A. Lemaire, *Histoire du peuple hébreu* (Coll. 'Que sais-je?', n. 1898; Paris: Presses Universitaires de France, 1981), p. 72, puts Ezra after Nehemiah, as most authors do, but maintains that after Artaxerxes I stopped the work, Nehemiah succeeded in having himself appointed governor 'to straighten out the situation'.

27. Cf. Ackroyd, 'The Jews in Palestine', p. 148; it is strange that, in the same volume, Stern, 'Palestine', p. 74, totally ignores this episode.

28. E. Stern, *Material Culture of the Bible in the Persian Period 538–322 BC* (Warminster: Aris & Phillips, 1982), pp. 239-45.

together, it can only be done in a fairly rough synthesis, quite close to that produced by combining the actual books of Ezra and Nehemiah, since all the individual events, whether political or religious, appear systematically confused as a result of doublets or, as above, by 'contradictory overdetermination'. The same question of how to deal with this comes up, with still more urgency: is there something deliberate in the persistent haziness which surrounds the events, slight enough not to rule out a general view, but at the same time dense enough to prevent any precise scrutiny? What then had to be concealed, or rendered unverifiable?

3. *Alexander, Jerusalem and the Samaritans*

After the work of Ezra and Nehemiah, the Bible provides no further information with any semblance of being historical, or at least no narrative, until the Maccabaean crisis.[29] Josephus works hard to fill in the end of the Persian period: he draws out to the maximum the story of Esther, which he places under an Artaxerxes, after having put Ezra and Nehemiah under Xerxes, and he adds, right at the end of the period, some trifling ups and downs of the court, which are in fact connected to the more important event of Alexander's arrival in Jerusalem (*Ant.* 11.317-39). One possible conclusion is that, following the work of Ezra and Nehemiah, Judaea, 'recognized as a sacred territory having its own law, continued to enjoy a certain autonomy'.[30] But it is difficult to conclude that there was no trouble, under the pretext that none is reported. In fact, archaeology throws limited light on the period,[31] but it does provide evidence of several destructions, apparently linked to the tensions between the Persians and Egypt, although their correlation with events known to historians is not always clear. What is more, there was considerable Greek influence in Judaea, as can be seen from Attic pottery and silver coins that imitated Attic drachmas. Even though Judaea was a small region that we might think was turned in on itself, it does not follow in that case that the country would remain sheltered from all upheavals. On the contrary, even if the links to world history remain obscure, we note all through the books of Ezra and Nehemiah the seeds

29. From this, according to *Apion* 1.39, comes the lesser authority of the later historian-prophets, since their testimony is not continuous.

30. Cf. de Vaux, 'Israël', col. 769.

31. Cf. Stern, *Material Culture*, pp. 254-56.

of crises, both internal and external, which had little chance of being spontaneously extinguished.

Internally, the Judaean exclusiveness of the founders, constantly being brought up, leads to the thought that there was not unanimity on the doctrine of absolute separation: while Nehemiah was absent, the high priest Eliashib associated with Tobias the Ammonite (Neh. 13.5), and then one of his grandsons married a daughter of Sanballat the Samaritan (13.28-29). Josephus (*Ant.* 11.302-303) confirms that many priests from Jerusalem were in the same situation. Opposition existed then between an assimilationist party and a separatist party, as was the case later on in the time of the Maccabees or under Herod. This is the sweeping view proposed by Morton Smith.[32]

Externally, with regard to the Samaritans here met again, the repeated conflicts referred to above in the preceding periods reappear later on in the Hellenistic period, with all the expected intensity. If the synthesis of G. Widengren is accepted,[33] it must be assumed that the tension had not diminished, since the schism seemed in fact of long standing. According to Samaritan sources, which are fairly late, it went back to the time of Eli and the temple at Shiloh, and it was Solomon who crystallized it by building the temple in Jerusalem.[34] According to Judaean historiography, the separation took place after the fall of Samaria, when the new Assyrian colonists partially adoped the Yahwist cult, which led to a syncretized religion (2 Kgs 17). Josephus systematized this point of view by making the Samaritans the permanent opponents of those who had returned from exile beginning in the time of Cyrus, and he described them as

32. Cf. M. Smith, *Palestinian Parties and Politics That Shaped the Old Testament* (Lectures on the History of Religion, NS, 9; New York: Columbia University Press, 1971), pp. 148-92, who thinks that Josephus had no precise knowledge of the Samaritans before the time of Antiochus Epiphanes and projects into the past conflicts of a later time.

33. Widengren, 'Persian Period', p. 511, who bases himself on E. Meyer, *Die Entstehung des Judentums* (Halle: Niemeyer, 1896); H.H. Rowley, *Men of God: Studies in Old Testament History and Prophecy* (London: Nelson, 1963), pp. 246-76; and G. Widengren, 'Israelite–Jewish Religion', in C.J. Bleeker and G. Widengren (eds.), *Historia Religionum* (Leiden: Brill, 1969), pp. 225-317.

34. J. Macdonald, *The Samaritan Chronicle No. II (or: Sepher ha-Yamim) From Joshua to Nebuchadnezzar* (BZAW, 107; Berlin: Töpelmann, 1969); cf. R.J. Coggins, *Samaritans and Jews: The Origins of Samaritanism Reconsidered* (Oxford: Basil Blackwell, 1975).

fickle: with their mixed origins, they called themselves Jews or Mesopotamians according to the demands of the moment. It still seems unnecessary, Widengren continues, to connect the split to a unique and definitive event, but to see it rather as a progressive distancing, a gradual development away from Judaism by small jolts, hardened finally into an insurmountable opposition in regard to the legitimate priesthood and the true sanctuary: Jerusalem versus Gerizim. It is possible that the establishment of Judaea into a relatively autonomous province, as the mission of Nehemiah prescribed, would have embittered an antagonism that had been at first political and then religious, just like the ancient conflict between Israel and Judah after Solomon. The exclusivism of the Jews in Judaea, set up by Ezra and Nehemiah—the foundation of Judaism—left Samaria in an antecedent religious condition: the Samaritan religion would have been a more traditional and conservative, perhaps more popular religion. As a matter of fact, later Samaritan tradition vilified Ezra, but not Nehemiah.

These are the main lines of the nuanced synthesis of Widengren, who incorporates numerous earlier studies. He concludes that the date of the construction of the Gerizim temple 'probably falls outside the Persian period, since the Persians obviously favoured the temple of Jerusalem over Samaritan cult-places'. This is precisely what is said by Josephus, who connects this temple at Gerizim with the arrival of Alexander (*Ant.* 11.306-47). In fact, an echo of such conclusions can be provided by the finds in the caves of Wadi Daliyeh, north of Jericho, especially the coins and texts, which show that the Samaritan refugees went there to escape a general disaster, right at the end of the Persian era.[35] One major difficulty still remains: on the one hand, before Nehemiah, the Samaritan religion was more conservative and traditional than Judaism, but later in the time of Alexander, the building of the Samaritan sanctuary of Gerizim would be the result of a dissidence that was Jewish in origin (see *Ant.* 11.309-12), while the Judaism of Jerusalem remained more conservative.

---

35. The material is supposed to be dated before 332 BCE, but it is really difficult to determine whether the refugees had fled Persian persecutions or Alexander's conquest, or even the repression of a revolt which occurred shortly after (reported by Curtius). Cf. below, and both Stern, *Material Culture*, p. 255, and F.M. Cross, 'Papyri of the Fourth Century BC from Dâliyeh: A Preliminary Report on their Discovery and Significance', *New Directions in Biblical Archaeology* (Garden City, NY: Doubleday, 1971), pp. 5-69.

It is appropriate, here, to reconsider the circumstances of Alexander's arrival, and therefore return to Josephus's account, which is comprised of two parts, one Samaritan, the other Judaean (*Ant.* 11.313-20). It is first related that after the victory of Issus (333 BCE) Alexander began the siege of Tyre. On learning of this, Sanballat, though governor of Samaria owing obedience to Persia, hurried to proclaim his allegiance to Alexander, while asking his permission to construct a temple at Shechem, so as 'to split up the power of the Jews', which had to be something of interest to the conqueror. Sanballat returned, built his temple, installed as priest Manasseh, brother of the high priest in Jerusalem, and then died. Nevertheless, Alexander, after a siege of seven months at Tyre and two at Gaza, came to Jerusalem, and bowed down before the high priest, to the surprise of everyone, since the Jews, in contrast to Sanballat, had remained faithful to the Persians; but Alexander had had a vision and was in this way assured of giving to God true worship. This was then confirmed for him by a reading of the prophecies of Daniel. After this edifying episode, Alexander granted privileges to the Jews, which he then refused to give to the Samaritans, who had come to Jerusalem on hearing the news of his arrival there; he did this on the pretext that they were not Jews. This second part happened at most nine months after the first, and probably much later than that, since it presupposed that Sanballat had passed away and that a delay in the construction of the temple at Gerizim had to be taken into account. It is astonishing then that the Samaritans seemed to be unknown to Alexander, and that there was no more echo of Sanballat, nor of his deeds, in particular the installation of the *Jewish* high priest at Gerizim.

Commentators have not failed to challenge the historical accuracy of this account: it combines, in the well-known setting of Alexander's conquest of Phoenicia and Egypt, elements of the Judaeo-Samaritan polemic, with each of the two sides claiming that its temple had received the support of Alexander, with the whole thing being revised to the advantage of the Jews.[36] The other sources for these events are legendary (Pseudo-Callesthenes, rabbinical traditions) or very much passing references, as can be seen from the following examples. Arrian 2.25.4 says that Palestine submitted to Alexander at the time of his Egyptian campaign. Curtius Rufus 4.5 states that it was while Alexander was in Egypt that Samaria revolted against Andromachus, prefect of Coele-Syria, and that on his return Alexander dealt severely

---

36. Cf. F.-M. Abel, 'Alexandre le Grand en Syrie et en Palestine', *RB* 43 (1934), pp. 528-45; *RB* 44 (1935), pp. 42-61, and the discussion of Ralph Marcus, in Josephus, *Jewish Antiquities Books IX–XI* (trans. H. St.J. Thackeray *et al.*; LCL; London: W. Heinemann, 1937), Appendix C, pp. 521-32.

with them. Pliny, *Historia Naturalis* 12.25.17, in dependence on Theophrastus, connects the development and the reputation of the 'balm of Jericho' to the passage of Alexander through the country. Byzantine sources, beginning with Eusebius, attribute to the Macedonian the foundation of Hellenistic cities, in particular Samaria. All this ultimately amounts to nothing more than unverifiable rumours—that is to say, reinterpretations of real facts, perhaps from much later times, but difficult to situate, and it should be remembered that Alexander was already a legendary figure before his death and was quickly divinized afterwards.[37] Yet, even if he did not come to Jerusalem, as is probable, Josephus wishes to emphasize the importance of the Jews and their Temple, and by contrast the secondary character of the Samaritans and their temple.

Josephus appears then to confirm the synthesis presented by Widengren. This synthesis is, however, less clear than first seems, and two difficulties are to be noted. On the one hand, it is based on a supposedly clear vision of the restoration of the Temple and of the institution of Judaism in the preceding period, with Ezra and Nehemiah, but it has been shown that their relation to the sanctuary and to the work of Zerubbabel is problematic. On the other hand, it implies incoherent views of the Samaritans: were they traditionalists who offered resistance to the emergence of Judaism, or were they a secondary and degenerate branch of the same religion? If they were late-comers, it is hard to see the meaning of the story of their origin in 2 Kings 17 and of their opposition to the restoration of Jerusalem, since Judaean historiography would only have benefited from declaring them late-comers. If they were really ancient, the account of the arrival of Alexander, reduced to its bare outline, no longer had any direct meaning, or would have rather had as its principal function to conceal their antiquity, by belittling their temple in comparison to the one in Jerusalem. The 'fickleness' of which Josephus regularly accused them was perhaps then the transformation into a polemical argument of a historical reality, namely, that the Samaritans would have had several 'parties', or even a hybrid origin; this polemic would have arisen from a combination of ancient Israelite tradition (from the Persian period or earlier) with late Jewish influences (from the Hellenistic period).

Before taking up again the examination of the sources in this direction, it is not irrelevant to observe that one can say the same thing of Judaism: no matter the epoch in which the reforms of Ezra and Nehemiah are placed, they run up against internal resistance, as seen

37. Cf. C. Saulnier, *Histoire d'Israël. III. De la conquête d'Alexandre à la destruction du Temple (331 AC–135 AD)* (Paris: Cerf, 1985).

above, and it is necessary to presuppose several parties. More importantly still, at the time when the newcomers brought something new, the texts emphasized the continuity of the cultic installations, the Davidic ancestry of Zerubbabel, the priestly character of Ezra, and so on. It would be risky to characterize this renewal as 'syncretism', but it is reasonable to see here, from the morphological point of view, a hybridization. There are reasons to suppose that it is not the same as that of the Samaritans, but at the same time there is always hope that they clarify one another.

One detail indeed gives rise to an extreme mistrust about the homogeneity of Judaism: Josephus, almost omnipresent behind the principal points of modern historiography, from Cyrus and Cambyses to Alexander, does his best to erase every important difference among Israelites, Hebrews and Jews/Judaeans, and he never stops laying stress on the continuity of Judaism with the royal epoch and with Moses. It is essential to determine why he tones down the rifts, and especially how he does it, since he did not have at his disposal any details significantly different from ours for the period under consideration, and since, as a good courtier, he knew how to present facts in a convincing way (cf. *Ant.* 14.1-3). The account of the coming of Alexander follows precisely this technique: it is clearly legendary, but is meant to leave the reader with at least a trace of the reality of the primacy of the Jerusalem Temple. There is then a mystification to expose and this very reality must be questioned if it is based only on legendary deeds.

But it must be emphasized here that there is much at stake: the origins of Judaism, distinct from the reconstruction of the sanctuary under the patronage of Cyrus and Darius, fit in very poorly in the Persian period, but seem certainly earlier than the arrival of Alexander, since he was impressed with the Temple and with the worship there, and since he bestowed on the Jews privileges which he refused to the Samaritans. If this episode fades away as fictional, however, there is no longer anything which would appear to guarantee so ancient a date for these origins.

4. *From Alexander to Antiochus IV Epiphanes*

After the death of Alexander in 323, the situation in the region was rather confused, because of rivalries among the claimants: the satrap of Egypt, Ptolemy, wished to control Phoenicia and occupied Coele-Syria including Palestine three times, but twice had to fall back immediately. In

301, following the battle of Ipsus, the empire of Alexander was gradually split up into four kingdoms, including the Lagides in Egypt and the Seleucids in Transeuphrates. But Coele-Syria, which had been part of the latter since the time of the Persians, was at that time occupied by the Ptolemy Lagos, and was not handed back. This disequilibrium was the cause of numerous wars between the Lagides and the Seleucids, but this region in fact remained under Egyptian domination for a century.

Josephus (*Ant.* 12.4-10) reports, following Agatharchides of Cnidus, a historian of the second century BCE, that in one of Ptolemy's incursions Jerusalem was captured by surprise on a Sabbath, and many Jews and Samaritans were deported to Egypt. This historian ridiculed the disastrous consequences of Jewish superstitions; but the episode is in fact either very polemical or very edifying, according to the meaning given to it, since it presupposed in Jerusalem a beautiful unanimity, which is historically improbable. Josephus describes this event more completely elsewhere (*Apion* 1.184-212), by having it preceded by another episode, drawn this time from Hecateus of Abdera and dated to the 117th Olympiad, according to which, on the occasion of another conquest of Syria by Ptolemy, many of the inhabitants, on being made aware of his benevolence, spontaneously followed him to Egypt; among them was a 'high priest' (ἀρχιερεύς) Hezekiah, who produced well-documented propaganda in favour of emigration for his compatriots.

These two episodes, in regard to campaigns by a Ptolemy, are naturally connected to the period 323–301, before the stabilization of the Lagide dynasty and its domination over Palestine. Yet, they are so dissimilar that it is difficult really to attribute them to the same Ptolemy. In *Against Apion*, Josephus is not worried about this aspect, since his only purpose is to gather together the testimonies of historians. In the *Jewish Antiquities*, on the contrary, he composes a somewhat involved paragraph, beginning with the prisoners captured owing to the observance of the Sabbath, and ending with the voluntary migrations on account of Ptolemy's benevolence. He does not quote Hecateus, but he bridges the gap by indicating that Ptolemy understood, from their response to the messengers of Alexander after the defeat of Darius (cf. *Ant.* 11.318), that the people of Jerusalem were the most faithful and the most reliable in keeping a sworn allegiance; consequently, he assigned a large number of them to his garrisons and gave them the same freedom of the city in Alexandria as the Macedonians. To come up with this explanation, Josephus actually makes use of his own writings on Alexander (cf. 11.318), along with an organizing of some facts from the *Letter of Aristeas*, which he knows and paraphrases in what follows. As a matter of fact, the decision of Ptolemy II Philadelphius to have the Law translated was accompanied by the emancipation of Jewish slaves (12.45-50) 'brought by the Persians', after which some of them were given responsibilities in the army.

The facts are therefore quite confused, and Josephus really tries to merge the two accounts into one single campaign, as if he had concluded that it was a matter of two versions of the same events.[38] In any case, the origin of these Jewish prisoners is not clear, just like the policies of the Ptolemies. The emigration of the priest Hezekiah to Egypt is reminiscent of the exodus of Onias, who went to build his temple in Egypt at the time of the Maccabaean crisis. Finally, the capture of the Jews on the Sabbath is reminiscent of another episode connected with the same crisis[39] (2 Macc. 5.23-26). All this raises some doubts about the solidity of the documentation of the historians mentioned, but what is clearly seen is the advantage that Josephus could draw from testimony from the time of Alexander on the religious observance of the Jews in a fortified Jerusalem, that is to say, leading the existence reorganized by Nehemiah.

During the century of Lagide domination, Palestine was given certain privileges, certainly intended to strengthen their loyalty, since the Seleucids several times tried in vain to reconquer the area. Ancient cities received the constitution and privileges of Greek cities, often with a new name: Ptolemais (Akko), Scythopolis (Beth-Shan), Philadelphia (Rabbat Ammon), and so on. About the Jews themselves, there is little information. To describe this period, Josephus fills his pages with secondary or doubtful details, a method he readily uses (cf. the example of the book of Esther above). He stretches out at length the *Letter of Aristeas*, then alludes to the privileges granted to the Jews of Antioch and Ionia, which are probably nothing more than the literary prologues to statutes granted long after by the Romans, and do not in any way provide

38. The difficulty did not ecape the notice of the author of *Ep. Arist.* either; he was acquainted with the work of Hecateus of Abdera (§31), but did not follow him, at least according to what Josephus reports. According to *Ep. Arist.* (§13), Ptolemy I brought captives from Syria, and Ptolemy II Philadephus alone deserves credit for introducing liberal measures, but this conclusion leads to certain historical difficulties; cf. A. Pelletier, *La lettre d'Aristée à Philocrate* (SC, 89; Paris, Cerf, 1962), pp. 66-67, 105 n. 1. According to Loeb, it is not impossible that what Josephus says on the captives taken to Egypt comes from *Ep. Arist.* As a matter of fact, he explicitly uses this text later on (*Ant.* 12.11-12), following it to attribute to Ptolemy II the emancipation of the Jerusalem captives brought by his father; this stands in contradiction to the liberalism of his father, which he had just mentioned. The opinion of Reinach, according to which Josephus produced his own synthesis in the section being studied (or used someone else's synthesis) without using *Ep. Arist.* seems very plausible: when he repeats this later on to produce a paraphrase, he does not guard against the contradiction.

39. Cf. P. Schäfer, 'The Hellenistic and Maccabaean Period', in Hayes and Miller, *Israelite and Judaean History*, p. 570, who points to coins from this period (found at Tel Gamma, near Gaza) which mention a 'governor Hezekiah'; cf. the discussion of M. Stern, *Greek and Latin Authors on Jews and Judaism* (3 vols.; Jerusalem: Magnes, 1974–84), I, p. 40.

information on the rule of the Ptolemies.[40]

From the time of the Seleucid king, Antiochus III (223–187), the information becomes more controllable. Antiochus, like his predecessors, attempted to reconquer Coele-Syria, but was defeated at Raphia in 217 and had to retreat. He tried again in 201 and, after an initial reverse, defeated the Lagide army at Banyas the following year. Coele-Syria then gradually became Seleucid. Antiochus practised an imperial policy worthy of Cyrus,[41] and in particular granted a charter to Judaea and Jerusalem[42] (12.138), allowing the Jews to live according to their ancestral laws, partially exempting them from taxes, helping in the restoration and upkeep of the Temple, and through taxation privileges encouraging more people to settle in the city.

Outside of this charter, the only information in regard to Judaea for this period (*Ant.* 12.160-222)—and once again it is of minor importance and hard to date—is the story of Joseph, son of Tobias, who obtained the contract for the tributes of Coele-Syria, apparently in the service of Ptolemy III (246–222).[43] The Tobiads had in addition the surveillance of the frontiers of the desert in Ammanitis, and practically constituted a dynasty ruling over Judaea. In regard to this dynasty, several facts should be noted: the papyrus of Zenon,[44] dated 259–258, shows the importance of the Judaean family of the Tobiads, but, notwithstanding various administrative and judicial fragments pertaining to a number of places in Judaea and Idumaea, they contain no identifiable allusion to Judaism (law of Moses, monotheism, etc.). On the other hand, Josephus reports (12.168) that when Joseph, nephew of the high priest Onias and son of Tobias and living in Jerusalem, left for Egypt to obtain from Ptolemy the lease for taxes in Judaea, he needed money and borrowed it from 'his friends in Samaria'. This alliance of Tobiads and Samaritans is exactly like the primitive form of opposition to Nehemiah's work of restoration in Jerusalem (Neh. 2.10; etc.); the context here is about some connivance with Ptolemaic Egypt. In a

40. According to Josephus himself (*Ant.* 14.186-87), all the privileges granted to the Jews before the Romans, whether they were given by the Persians or by the Macedonians (Seleucids or Lagides), were to be considered doubtful, since they were only recorded among the Jews and 'among certain other barbarian peoples' (cf. also Chapter 2, §5).

41. Confirmed by a Greek stele found near Hefzibah, close to Bet-Shean; cf. Y.H. Landau, 'A Greek Inscription Found near Hefzibah', *IEJ* 16 (1966), pp. 54-70.

42. E.J. Bickerman, 'La charte séleucide de Jérusalem', in *Studies in Jewish and Christian History* (AGJU, 9; 3 vols.; Leiden: Brill, 1974–86), II, pp. 4-35.

43. The chronology of Josephus is questionable; cf. V.A. Tcherikover, *Hellenistic Civilization and the Jews* (Philadelphia: Jewish Publication Society of America, 1959), pp. 158-59, and below, Chapter 6, §3.

44. Gathered together in V.A. Tcherikover and A. Fuks, *Corpus papyrorum iudaicarum* (Cambridge, MA: Harvard University Press, 1957).

complementary way, the Seleucid charter for Judaea, as referred to above, super-imposes itself easily upon the work of Nehemiah, who afterwards supplants, at the time of his second mission, a Tobiah associated with nobles of Judaea (Neh. 6.17-19) and even with a high priest, Eliashib (13.4-9). This closeness is suggestive, but evidently it proves nothing, except the mobility in time of certain narrative models conveyed by tradition. The same could be said of the relationship between the statute granted by Alexander to Judaea and the charter of Antiochus III.

The successor of Antiochus III, Seleucus IV Philopator (187–175), at first followed the policies of his father, but financial difficulties led him to covet the treasures of the Jerusalem Temple. According to 2 Macc. 3.1-40, which opens the account with a marvellous presentation of this incident, Seleucus, who had contacts in Jerusalem, instructed Heliodorus, his administrator, to confiscate these funds, but the latter was prevented from doing so by the high priest, Onias III; the ostensible religious reason given for this refusal was probably hiding a pro-Lagide tendency through ties with Hyrcanus the Tobiad. The tension increased and, apparently to contain the risk of civil war, Onias tried to make a personal appeal to Seleucus, but the latter was meanwhile assassinated by the same Heliodorus. It was Antiochus, brother of Seleucus, however, who then became king. He had been a hostage at Rome, after the defeat of his father Antiochus III at Magnesia (189 BCE). The latter, emboldened by a matrimonial alliance with Egypt, had attempted despite the Romans to re-establish Alexander's empire, but finally had to withdraw to Syria and Mesopotamia (treaty of Apamea, 188).

With the coming to power of Antiochus IV Epiphanes (175–164), the documentation becomes more abundant, but the difficulties become more complex, since the sources contradict one another. The Greek historians considered this sovereign enlightened and tolerant, only fighting obscurantism. In Jewish tradition, he is an insane persecutor, who personifies evil and arrogance (cf. Dan. 7.25). As the stake in the conflict was acknowledged to be of crucial importance by later traditions, many commentators have tried to reconstruct the events and especially to interpret the revolt of Mattathias and Judas.

The facts are presented in contradictory ways in the sources: according to 1 Macc. 1.12-15, Antiochus granted the Hellenizing Jewish party (the 'renegades') the right to have pagan institutions, and then, in returning from a campaign in Egypt, looted the Temple. 'Two years later', Jerusalem was conquered by Judas the Mysarch, then completely transformed with the practice of the Law being forbidden by the king. This resulted in the persecution of those who rebelled and led to the holy war of Mattathias and his sons. According to 2 Macc. 4.7-20, after Antiochus had come to power, Jason the brother of Onias III, paid a high price for the office of high priest, while promising to Hellenize Jerusalem. He received Antiochus there on his way to a first campaign in Egypt, but 'at the end of three years' a certain Menelaus obtained the priesthood for an even higher price, and Jason had to flee. The latter, thinking that Antiochus had died in a second Egyptian campaign, wanted to reconquer Jerusalem. Informed of the civil war, Antiochus arrived, looted the Temple, persecuted the Jews and established pagan cults. Judas Maccabeus then fled to the hills.

According to *War* 1.31-33, it was really a quarrel in Jerusalem between Onias and the Tobiads; the latter were expelled but took refuge with Antiochus, who invaded Judaea, took Jerusalem, looted the Temple and prohibited the practice of Judaism, while Onias, who had taken refuge in Egypt, built a temple there. These accounts are hard to harmonize, but one of their common traits is that neither shows clearly what interest a sovereign could have had in carrying on a religious persecution, once order had been re-established and the Temple plundered.

For Bickerman,[45] the crisis was first and foremost a civil war with religious origins, for which the Seleucid authority had no terms of reference, except the fear of alliances with the Lagides. It was the Hellenized Jews who, wishing to be accepted by the neighbouring peoples, instigated decrees persecuting those who wanted to be strictly faithful to the Torah. Subsequently, the pro-Hasmonaean redaction of 1 Maccabees attempted to play down the internal tensions in Judaism and reinterpreted the revolt as a response to the persecutions of Antiochus Epiphanes. This thesis of internal tensions has been adopted and developed by others, especially Hengel, who goes so far as to say that the real authors of the decrees are Menelaus and the Tobiads.[46] This explanation matches the views of Josephus, for whom the Maccabaean crisis began as a conflict among the Jewish upper classes. Later on he stigmatized the internal dissensions for being responsible for the ruin of Jerusalem and the Temple. It is nevertheless true that if Josephus, especially in *The Jewish War*, tends to throw into relief the dissensions in the heart of Judaism, this is done to give an explanation for the final ruin of Jerusalem that does not reflect on the Romans.

45. E.J. Bickermann, *Der Gott der Makkabäer: Untersuchung über Sinn und Ursprung der makkabäischen Erhebung* (Berlin: Schocken Books, 1937; ET: *The God of the Maccabees: Studies on the Meaning and Origin of the Maccabaean Revolt* (SJLA, 32; Leiden: Brill, 1979).

46. M. Hengel, *Judaism and Hellenism* (trans. J. Bowden; 2 vols.; Philadelphia: Fortress Press, 1974), I, p. 289. This opinion, which is close as well to the thesis of Smith, *Palestinian Parties* (above, n. 32), has produced sarcastic reactions from Stern, 'Review of M. Hengel's "Judentum und Hellenismus"', *Kiryat Sefer* 46 (1970), pp. 94-99.

Tcherikover[47] is especially attentive to the social conflicts: Hellenization was the programme of rich families, and the drama increased when
in the name of that aristocracy Jason, the brother of Onias III, usurped
the high priesthood and tried to obtain permission from Antiochus for
Jerusalem to become a Greek *polis*, another Antioch (2 Macc. 4.7-9).
The persecution of Antiochus would then be the repression of a revolt of
humbler people, mounted by the Hasidaeans against this project of Hellenization. The 'Abomination of Desolation' in the Temple would have
been nothing more that the worship brought in by the Seleucid soldiers
come to restore order.

More recently, Bringmann[48] concentrates on the policy of the king,
Antiochus, who wanted to make his kingdom a second Rome; this would
call for effective authority and sufficient resources. He observes that the
choice of a person like the high priest directly depends on what he
agrees to pay. Looting the Temple and a clumsy attempt to strip it of its
Jewishness, at least economically, and all this with the complicity of the
pro-Seleucid aristocracy, provoked the revolt. Subsequently, the sources
reinterpreted all this as purely religious persecutions.

In his lengthy commentaries, Goldstein[49] presupposes sufficient homogeneity in the core of Judaism at this time that a major conflict would
not have developed on its own, and tries to understand in another way
the reasons for the persecution by Antiochus. There is no other example
of such a policy in Greek history, but a comparison with the suppression
of the Bacchanalia by the Romans, a short time before (186 BCE), suggests that Antiochus was trying to imitate the civil and religious policies
of Rome.

According to Bickermann, the crisis was first and foremost Jewish;
according to Tcherikover it was due to the initiatives of Antiochus; and
the other opinions are distributed between these two poles. In an attempt
to reconcile all the opinions, Bunge[50] expands the investigation and

47. Tcherikover, *Hellenistic Civilisation*, pp. 189-90.
48. F. Bringmann, *Hellenistische Reform und Religionsverfolgung in Judäa:
Eine Untersuchung zur jüdisch-hellenistischen Geschichte (175–163 v. Chr.)*
(Göttingen: Vandenhoeck & Ruprecht, 1983).
49. J.A. Goldstein, *I Maccabees: A New Translation with Introduction and
Commentary* (AB, 41; Garden City, NY: Doubleday, 1976); *II Maccabees: A New
Translation with Introduction and Commentary* (AB, 41A; Garden City, NY:
Doubleday, 1983); .
50. J.G. Bunge, *Untersuchungen zum zweiten Makkabäerbuch* (unpublished

thinks that the incidents in Jerusalem were connected to the campaign of Antiochus in Egypt. The 'Abomination of Desolation' would originally have been a celebration of the victory of Antiochus, the 25 Kislev 167, a celebration asked for or even imposed by a royal emissary. Some offered resistance to this, but the 'Hellenists' would have reacted by institutionalizing this cult, with a bitter crisis and the royal repression resulting. By putting the eruption of internal opposition in this way, between two Seleucid interventions, the first an incidental one and the second more siginificant, the two opposing points of view become complementary; nevertheless, the facts remain complicated.

Finally, in a recent introductory study, Harrington[51] is impressed by the variety of literary works that the crisis generated: obviously Daniel and 1–2 Maccabees, but also Judith, the *Testament of Moses*, the *Habbakuk Pesher* from Qumran, not to mention other works to which the name of the Maccabees was attributed. A great variety of interpretations are therefore possible. As for the facts, the crisis was the effect of a will for political and religious independence. Its outcome, once the risks of dissolution were overcome, was the definitive establishment within Judaism of the centrality of the Torah and the Temple.

This last statement is certainly true, though vague, and has the merit of trying to discover the stakes involved by looking at the consequences of the events instead of their causes, since the facts and the exact circumstances are not directly accessible.

In this connection, some contradictory statements should be noted. 1 Maccabees, which makes no mention of any high priest at the time when the persecutions of Antiochus began, is the book of the foundation of the Hasmonaean dynasty (using the terminology of Josephus): the priest Mattathias revolts, his son Judas reconquers the Temple, then his brothers Jonathan and Simon become high priests, *strategoi* and ethnarchs, continue the fighting, and establish relations with Rome and Sparta. The book concludes when, at the death of Simon, his son John Hyrcanus succeeds him, that is to say, when the dynasty has been established.

In 2 Maccabees, on the contrary, the book opens with a detrimental excess of high priests, while the Temple is the setting for marvels.[52] The book ends before the death

diss.; Bonn, 1971), cited in P. Schäfer, 'Hellenistic and Maccabaean Periods', p. 562).

51. D.J. Harrington, *The Maccabaean Revolt: Anatomy of a Biblical Revolution* (Old Testament Studies, 1; Wilmington, DE: Michael Glazier, 1988).

52. Cf. R. Doran, *Temple Propaganda: The Purpose and Character of 2 Maccabees* (CBQMS, 12; Washington: Catholic Biblical Association, 1981), p. 84,

of Judas, with the institution of the commemoration of the victory over Nicanor, a Seleucid general (corresponding to 1 Macc. 7.48). This victory was in fact the repulse of a last attempt by the fallen high priest Alcimus to be restored to office. It has been agreed for a long time that it is not enough, in order to explain why 2 Maccabees is shorter, to say that it was written earlier, before the conclusion of the events reported in 1 Maccabees: it gives much more information at the beginning, although it presents itself as an *abridgement* of an earlier work (2.23). The perspectives of the two books are not the same. Besides, if the books are also etiological accounts of the feast of Dedication, it is strange that 1 Macc. 4.59 calls it 'the inauguration of the altar' (ἐγκαινισμός), while for 2 Macc. 10.6 'they celebrate eight festive days with rejoicing in the manner of the feast of Booths [σκηνωμάτων τρόπον], remembering how not long before (they had celebrated) the feast of Booths in the mountains'.[53] It was shown above that there was precisely such ambiguity about the feast of Booths, which could have celebrated the inauguration of the altar (Zerubbabel) or the reception of the Law with the building of shelters (Ezra, outside the Temple). It should be noted finally that Josephus calls the Dedication, 'Feast of Lights', but he admits that he does not know why; in fact, this title is not explained at all by the story in 1 Maccabees which he follows (*Ant.* 12.325), since it presupposes another foundation account. The very nature of the commemoration is therefore doubtful.

Towards 200 BCE, the charter of Antiochus III does not seem to have provoked divisions, since tradition unanimously celebrates the virtues of the high priest of that epoch, Simon the Just. Nevertheless, a generation later, in the time of the crisis, there were several parties, whose backgrounds have been lost. After the crisis, the redactional complexities and the varieties of opinions referred to in passing suggest that there were several tendencies or movements in the heart of Judaism, each one of which reinterpeted the facts through displacements, expansions or consolidations. It is advisable then to consult Josephus once again as he relates the continuation of the history of the Hasmonaeans.

who notes that the pleading for the Temple is tragic, since its means of functioning are missing.

53. M.D. Herr, 'Hanukkah', *EncJud* 7 (1971), cols. 1280-86, conjectures that it is just a compensation for the feast of Booths, become possible at that time in a manner analogous to the substitute Passover described in Num. 9.10-13. This interpretation does not explain, however, either the term 'Dedication' (mentioned in the summary of 2 Macc. 2.19, but ignored in the account in 2 Macc. 10.6), nor the intrinsic relationship between this new commemoration and one aspect of the feast of Booths (inauguration of the altar).

5. *Pharisees and Sadducees*

From the Maccabees to Herod the Great, Josephus's documentation is very extensive. Yet, since he is especially interested in political history, the indications that he gives on the various opinions and tendencies, or even on the specifically religious conflicts, are brief. Outside of a few accounts in which he defines on several occasions the three principal schools, namely, the Pharisees, the Sadducees and the Essenes, and even adds a 'fourth philosophy', the particulars on the real life story of these groups and their evolution are rare, but still significant.

In *The Jewish War*, the Pharisees come on the scene when Alexandra gives a share in her government to this 'Jewish sect which is accounted to be the most pious of all' (1.110); under Herod, they are powerful adversaries (1.571); under Agrippa II, after 66 CE, they form part of those who protest against the claim of the Zealots to put a stop to sacrifices by foreigners (2.411). In the *Jewish Antiquities*, they appear in the narrative on the occasion of a sequence of episodes which go from John Hyrcanus to Alexandra (13.288-92, expanding on *War* 1.110); later on, when Herod has subdued Judaea, he counts up his supporters, and among them are the Pharisees Shemaiah and Abtalion (*Ant.* 15.3, 370; the teachers of Hillel and Shammai, according to *m. Ab.* 1.12); yet, on another occasion, Herod deals severely with the Pharisees (*Ant.* 17.41-45, expanding on *War* 1.571).

The allusions to the Sadducees are briefer still: outside of the banquet of Hyrcanus and the summary notices, which will be examined later, the only person whom Josephus calls a Sadducee is Ananus the Younger, who around 62 CE had James, brother of Jesus, put to death for having broken the Law (*Ant.* 20.199-200). As for the Essenes, they are expressly said to be later (*War* 2.162), and need not occupy us here, at least not immediately.

In *War* 1.67-69 Josephus recounts briefly that John Hyrcanus, having assumed power, provoked jealousy because of his prosperity; he, nevertheless, lived happily for thirty-three years, but his sons were faced with revolts. When he repeats this passage later on (*Ant.* 13.288-98), Josephus inserts an account which he had not mentioned in the summary[54] and which brings the Pharisees and the Sadducees into the picture. It is stated there that Hyrcanus disliked the Pharisees, even though he had been their disciple and much loved by them. In fact, during a banquet, when one of them asserted that Hyrcanus's mother had been a prisoner

---

54. The 'summaries' of each book of *Ant.* are sketches certainly drafted prior to the work itself and drawn from the primary source, in this case, *The Jewish War*; cf. E. Nodet *et al.*, *Flavius Josèphe: Les antiquités juives*, I–III (Paris: Cerf, 2nd edn, 1992), p. viii.

in the time of Antiochus Epiphanes, which would mean a legal incapacity for the high priesthood, he felt insulted by them all and went over to the side of the Sadducees. He therefore tried to abrogate the non-biblical Pharisaic traditions, which led to the people's hatred of him and his sons, since the Pharisees had great influence over the people, and had introduced among them the customs of the Ancients.

This short account has a Talmudic parallel, connected to Alexander Janneus and not Hyrcanus. Its insertion in the context of Hyrcanus in the *Jewish Antiquities* is awkward, but fits much better under the reign of Janneus, who massacred a number of Jews during a banquet (13.380), and who, at the moment of death asked his wife Alexandra, who was going to succeed him, to reconcile herself with the Pharisees, whom he had outraged.[55]

Josephus has, therefore, displaced this account, with the specific consequence that Simon, brother and successor of Jonathan, would have really given his son John a Pharisaic education. The Hasmonaeans, at the time when the dynasty was well established, had then, according to Josephus, a starting point that is clearly Pharisaic. Later, on the contrary, while Alexandra was really under their influence (but Josephus holds her in contempt, 13.432), Janneus dealt severely with them, as did Herod later on. On the occasion of narratives on the latter, Josephus cannot refrain from expressing what he spontaneously thought of the Pharisees, in terms worth noting:

> *There was a sect* [or: a party] of the Jews who prided themselves on very strictly observing the law of their fathers and affected a great zeal for the divinity [...], people capable of standing up to kings, far-sighted and openly daring to fight them and injure them.

This passage takes no account of all that is said of the Pharisees in Book 13, where there are two references (§173 and 298) to the account in *War* 2.119-66. Consequently, it is an earlier composition,[56] done at a

---

55. The version attributed to Alexander Janneus is given in *b. Qid.* 66a, but another *baraita* says that Hyrcanus, after a life of fidelity, became a Sadducee; there is, therefore, a multiform tradition, but E. Main, 'Les Sadducéens vus par Flavius Josèphe', *RB* 97 (1990), pp. 190-202, shows convincingly, in going over the modern arguments, that Janneus is to be preferred.

56. It could be maintained, with D.J. Schwartz, 'Josephus and Nicolaus on the Pharisees', *JSJ* 14 (1983), pp. 157-71, that Josephus is here following his source passively ('without reflection', Reinach concludes too); in this case his source is Nicolaus of Damascus, who was certainly not pro-Pharisee, and Josephus (or an

time when Josephus had no interest in having the influence of the Pharisees on the people reach back to the time of Hyrcanus. There was, therefore, a turning point in Josephus's apologetic, at some time after the *The Jewish War* and in between on the one hand the composition of the summaries for the *Jewish Antiquities*, which were unaware of any kind of allusion to the 'parties' in Book 13, and on the other the final redaction of Book 13: he had become pro-Pharisaic, and did his utmost to show that this was really the position of the first Hasmonaeans. The general arrangement of 1 Maccabees shows a similar tendency, but the important thing here is to note that this result is achieved at the price of some literary contortions which have left their mark.

The accounts describing the parties provide an insight into the ideas of Josephus. The first appears in *War* 2.119-66; after having named in order the Pharisees, the Sadducees and the Essenes, the rest of the account is devoted almost entirely to the Essenes (§119-61), as if they had pride of place with the author.

In the *Jewish Antiquities*, this list is found in two places: first in 13.171-73, which refers to the previous list in *The Jewish War* and indeed generally follows it in regard to the Pharisees and the Sadducees, but slips between them a single-sentence summary on the Essenes. The reason for this account in this place, in connection with the youth of John Hyrcanus, is to give to understand that the Pharisees and the Sadducees were already clearly defined and that they ran schools. This could not be put before Mattathias and Judas, since that would have necessitated situating these tendencies in relation to the Hellenistic parties of that time, and, as will be shown later on (Chapter 6, §3), Josephus could not allow such a comparison. Between Judas and Simon, father of John Hyrcanus, Josephus seems to have profited from the unique quiet interval in an otherwise feverish account, when Jonathan renews ancient alliances with Rome and Sparta.

The second account (18.11-22) is in the place corresponding to that of *The Jewish War*, after the revolt of Judas the Galilean. Josephus refers to this account from *The Jewish War* and has it in front of him, but this new presentation has two peculiarities, useful for our purposes: on the one hand, the Sadducees have become very dignified scholars, but are inactive and practically obedient to the Pharisees; on the other hand, the followers of Judas the Galilean (say, the Zealots), close to the Pharisees in doctrines, are raised to the rank of 'fourth party', even though Josephus cannot refrain

---

assistant) passively transcribed the opinion of the latter. Yet in other places and especially in the parallel developments of *War* and *Antiquities* in general (and in particular here the corresponding passage, *War* 1.571) we see that Josephus constantly adapts his sources and, therefore, unless there is formal proof to the contrary, he must be held responsible for the result. Here, then, it is more simple to admit that when he composed this passage, he subscribed to the opinion expressed, but that later on, when he had changed his outlook, he failed to retouch it, not having an index of references at his disposal.

from recalling that their movement is 'madness', since he holds it responsible for the war and the final ruin. In all this recomposition, the Pharisees dominate, as if in spite of Josephus, and it is astonishing that he declares elsewhere, but belatedly (*Life* §10), that he freely chose this party from his youth.

This portrayal of Judaism made up of four parties, in which Josephus has no real leaning towards either the Zealots or the Pharisees, was probably forced on him by circumstances—that is to say, perhaps by the primacy of the Pharisees in the Diaspora, and/or by a composite assembly descended from the Sanhedrin from before the fall of Jerusalem—since the four parties ended up by representing for Josephus the totality of Judaism.

The overwhelming influence of the Pharisees among the people since the time of Hyrcanus or even earlier, as proclaimed by the *Jewish Antiquities*, should not be taken literally. Moreover, the appearance of three parties in the time of Jonathan is unintelligible in the context of the epic of Judas, which is recounted by Josephus according to 1 Maccabees. If Mattathias had united the observant Jews in a federation, and if Judas his son had eliminated the Hellenizers, it is hard to see how a difference could have developed between Pharisees and Sadducees, at least as important and not just marginal groups, even while admitting that the Essenes were later, something that is in no way demonstrated. This tidying up having been carried out, there still remains Alexandra, with whom the Pharisees governed, according to *War* 1.110-12 where Josephus is in no way preoccupied with glorifying them. There remains as well that rumour according to which a great Hasmonaean king, either Hyrcanus or Janneus, moved over from the Pharisaic party (or the 'Wise') to the Sadducean party (arrogant advocates of the non-written Law), in circumstances that are obscure: the dynasty has changed parties and has become evil.

Through all these developments, there can be discerned in the background one fact and one opinion of Josephus. The fact is the rise to power of the Pharisees, as a popular movement in Judaea and abroad at the end of the second century BCE, to the point of becoming politically important.[57] The opinion is reflected in a commentary with a Pharisaic

---

57. This fact remains obscure, but archaeology can provide some clarification: according to an oral communication of Gérald Finkielsztejn, Rhodian jar-handle stamps are no longer found in Jerusalem (while they are found elsewhere in Judaea), from about the 145–140 BCE level (hence, under Jonathan or at the beginning of Simon); this allows us to conclude that the importing of oil, or more probably wine, had stopped. This change must be connected with new religious requirements (cf. the gymnasium, 1 Macc. 1.14), and fits in with the efforts of Jonathan to reinforce the

leaning, connected with the account in 1 Maccabees, and can be formulated in this way: the Hasmonaeans have become Sadducees, therefore bad, whereas in the beginning, namely with Judas, they were Pharisees and therefore good. The implicit conclusion suggested by Josephus is that the high priest to be desired should be a Pharisee, which is very debatable,[58] and that the Sadducees have no status.

Nevertheless, in considering the exploits of the leading Hasmonaeans, from Simon to Janneus, no major difference is apparent among them, relative to the point under consideration: all are high priests, all are ethnarchs or kings, all are likewise preoccupied with politics and court intrigues. No episode provides a satisfactory context for a lasting and irreversible 'change of party', a context where one could discern major religious and national matters at stake. After an examination of the whole period, one question comes up: what was the real relationship between Judas and the Hasmonaeans? A quick investigation above showed that 2 Maccabees completely isolated Judas from the whole dynasty, but it cannot be determined at this stage whether it was a matter of some mischance in the primitive narrative or an anti-Hasmonaean rewriting. In reality, even 1 Maccabees, which shows signs of reworkings, makes Judas stand out: this important conqueror who restored the Torah to the Temple, son of a priest and brother of future high priests, did not himself become a high priest. It could be objected that since the high priesthood was a concession of the Seleucid authority, that period would have been an inauspicious time for it. Later on, Jonathan obtained the high priesthood on the occasion of a civil war between Demetrius I and Alexander Balas (1 Macc. 10.17-20), by allying himself with one of the parties; next,

city and isolate the citadel (1 Macc. 10.11 and 12.36), along with a change of the composition of the population. There is therefore an observant group, cf. Chapters 6, §4 and 8, §7.

58. The view that the Pharisees had ended up taking control of worship in the Temple, or that they would even have had that control very early in the Hasmonaean period is based on *Ant.* 18.15: 'They have so much prestige among the people that in everything involving divine matters, the prayers [εὐχῶν] and 'sacred things' [ἱερῶν] are regulated according to their practical interpetations [ποιήσεως ἐξηγήσει τῇ ἐκείνων]'; Main, 'Les Sadducéens', pp. 187-88 is interested in the complete absence of a bond between the Pharisees and the Temple, according to Josephus, and shows very clearly, against most modern commentators, that the 'sacred things' in which the Pharisees intervene are not the sacrifices, but the practices of daily life (purity, food, etc.), which to a great extent took precisely the place of specifically cultic practices.

Simon received it under analogous circumstances. Nevertheless, even if they were really brothers of Judas, they were ready to compromise for the high priesthood, which jars with the absolute intransigence of Judas, as though for the latter obtaining this dignity would not have been one of his objectives, since it necessitated an intolerable submission to the Seleucid power. It is worth noting that Judas is not mentioned among the predecessors of Simon in the document binding the whole assembly (1 Macc. 14.27-49). But in that case, what does it mean for Judas 'to bring back the Torah to the Temple', without requiring a guarantee of its application immediately by a high priest and appropriate institutions?

The propaganda of 1 Maccabees is meant to show that the Hasmonaean dynasty has a Jewish legitimacy above any suspicion. There is something to hide then, and Josephus felt that the demonstration was not flawless. Perhaps possessing other sources, but especially armed with his rhetoric, he made various revisions, of which one at least is significant for the point in question: as he clearly saw that it was illogical that Judas had not become high priest, he patched up the error (*Ant.* 12.414), but not without introducing an incongruity, since he states that 'the people gave the high priesthood to Judas'. This cannot be a real historical piece of information, for such a nomination could only be made by the Seleucid authority, or at least with its approval, since the office had important fiscal aspects.

As for the homogeneity that Josephus claims for the Hasmonaean dynasty after Judas, it remains unconfirmed. In fact, Alexander Janneus had had difficulties in inspiring respect for his legitimacy to be high priest, because of a suspicion about his mother (*Ant.* 13.372), and Josephus asserts that previously Alexander's father, John Hyrcanus, had seen his legitimacy questioned by the Pharisees for the same reason, on the occasion of the banquet referred to above (13.280). If this episode is reconnected to Janneus, all the doubts are concentrated on the latter, which suggests a certain discontinuity between him and Hyrcanus. As a matter of fact, 1 Maccabees is only aware of a dynasty up to Hyrcanus, son of Simon; what is more, the succession to Janneus, which began with the brief reign of Aristobulus, is obscure. In these circumstances, the ultimate complicity of Janneus with the Sadducees, after the failure of the alliance with the Pharisees, followed by a persecution, makes room for a conjecture about a forceful political emergence of these parties at this time, on the occasion of a dynastic crisis; this does not however imply in any way a sudden outburst of movements at that time. In fact, these 'parties' are founded not on shades of political sensitivity, but on a profound religious difference, since some were acquainted with the Bible alone, while others remained faithful to ancestral customs. As for the crisis itself, the fact that Josephus blurs in order to emphasize a dynastic homogeneity is not necessarily ostentation or negligence, since it recalls a similar effort to impose homogeneity at work in 1 Maccabees. There is room then to ask whether the presentation by Josephus is not responding to apologetic motives.

It will have to be enough for now to conclude these observations by formulating two problems. To begin with, according to the accounts of Josephus, the Sadducees are to be defined only in a negative way, in comparison with the Pharisees, as if they were in a defensive position, or culturally subordinate; the two are then in a certain sense inseparable. But the enquiry must be broadened, since the research on the origins of the separation between the Pharisees and the Sadducees has led to questions about the real relationship that existed between Judas Maccabeus and his brothers, and on the nature of their relationship to the Temple. It is natural then to draw from the difference between 1 Maccabees and 2 Maccabees a working hypothesis, already glimpsed from another angle by Niese;[59] according to this hypothesis Judas and his epic would be clearly intrusive in the history of the origins of the Hasmonaeans, that is to say, the history of the descendants of the priest Mattathias. In other words, it is a question of inquiring into whether the difference between Judas and Mattathias can be superimposed on the divergence which separates the Pharisees and the Sadducees; the name Sadducees necessarily brings to mind the high priest Zadok, in the time of Solomon (1 Kgs 2.35), that is to say, the ancestor of every legitimate high priest according to Ezek. 40.46 (the LXX has: Σαδδουκ). We could glimpse then a strong correlation between these 'parties' and the circumstances prior to the Maccabaean crisis, in which there would be represented a well-defined body called the Hasidaeans (1 Macc. 2.42; etc.), who must certainly be identified with the Essenes.[60] Certain further questions call for

59. B. Niese, *Kritik der beiden Makkabäerbücher: Nebst Beitragen zur Geschichte der Makkabäischen Erhebung* (Berlin: Weidman, 1900), pp. 61-62.

60. Cf. E. Puech, *La croyance des Esséniens en la résurrection des morts: Immortalité, résurrection, vie éternelle* (EBib NS, 21; Paris: Gabalda, 1993), pp. 21-26, who shows that the Greek term transcribes an Aramaic plural חסיא ('Εσσαîοι) or חסין ('Εσσηνοί), an exact equivalent of the Hebrew חסידים from which comes 'Ασιδαîοι (perhaps by way of an Aramaicizing form חסידיא).

examination, especially the exact meaning of the Dedication, or the feast of the arrival at the Temple, and the content of the sacred library gathered together by Nehemiah and by Judas (2 Macc. 2.13).

The second problem involves, beyond the crisis, the posterities of the Sadducees and the Pharisees after the destruction of Jerusalem. According to the usual historiography,[61] resistance to foreign domination was a driving force at the heart of Judaism, from the time of the Maccabaean crisis, right up to the time when it reached a violent climax against the Romans; but apart from Josephus, the sources are nearly silent on the events surrounding the ruin of the Temple. In any case, the Pharisees were the ones who best resisted the crisis, and they gradually reorganized themselves, thanks to the academy at Jabneh-Jamnia in Judaea. National life passed from the Temple to the synagogue (public prayer replaced the cult; the teachers took the place of priests), and much of the cultic ritual was transferred to domestic life (the Passover). The descendants of the Babylonian Hillel were reinstated in the patriarchate, but the propensities of the Zealots again gave rise to many upheavals, up to the crushing of Bar Kochba's revolt in 135 CE. After the death of Hadrian, a restoration began to take place in Galilee. In these circumstances, rabbinic Judaism took shape; the Pharisees had as their successors the *Tannaim*, teachers who determined precisely the authority of oral tradition, by connecting it to Moses; it was they who edited the Mishnah, a little after 200 CE.

This outline contains one major difficulty however, because this form of Judaism has some very new aspects, in substance as well as in form, and fits in very poorly with the statements of Josephus, which are centred on Jerusalem: how is it possible to comprehend exactly how the *Tannaim* are faithful to the oral traditions and simultaneously innovators in a time of crisis, or after several crises? The question is analogous to the one raised above about the Samaritans of Gerizim, who were viewed at the same time as both conservative and open to deviation. Commentators vacillate between two extreme attitudes. They either consider that rabbinic Judaism is an entirely new creation developed as a reaction to disasters and to the rise of Christianity;[62] or on the contrary they admit

61. Cf. S.J.D. Cohen, *From the Maccabees to the Mishnah* (Library of Early Christianity, 7; Philadelphia: Westminster Press, 1987); L.H. Schiffman, *From Text to Tradition: A History of Second Temple and Rabbinic Judaism* (New York: Ktav, 1991).

62. According to A. Paul, *Leçons paradoxales sur les juifs et les chrétiens*

that after the Maccabaean crisis, Judaism, buffeted by the surrounding world, remained unstable, divided by various tendencies and tensions, until it reached maturity and equilibrium under the rabbinic form,[63] the only one that could last. As for the first view, it could be objected that it fails to recognize the nature of an oral tradition, which by definition cannot arise from a crisis; in regard to the second, the objection to it would be that it is too deterministic, since Samaritans and Christians availed themselves of other responses to the same challenge of Hellenization, and especially persistently claimed besides to be the true Israel. It could be assumed that the Tannaitic tradition is connected through the Pharisees with Judas Maccabeus, but in fact it ignores Judas, while it has a thorough knowledge of the *hassidim*, who are related to the Hasidaeans.[64] The question must be re-examined, all the more so since rabbinic sources are to be used to supplement Josephus. It is certainly not inappropriate to give these sources some status.

6. *Rabbinic Tradition and Galilee*

Morphologically, rabbinic literature, which begins with the Mishnah, has every appearance of being an innovation, in style, language and content. It is not interested in history as such, and mentions events only in connection with juridical or homiletical developments. In every case, the particulars that can be gleaned from it on persons and events are not very numerous. Among them, few are earlier than the war of Bar Kochba (destruction of Jerusalem), and still fewer are prior to the destruction of the Temple in 70 CE. Besides, the Mishnah is a kind of 'oral literature', supposed to be transmitted[65] from master to disciple,

(Paris: Desclée, 1992); Schürer and Vermes end their study at the Bar Kochba war, and so ignore the most creative part of the period of the Tannaim; but they still use the rabbinic literature (E. Schürer, *The History of the Jewish People in the Age of Jesus Christ* (trans. and ed. G. Vermes *et al.*; Edinburgh: T. & T. Clark, 1973–87).

63. According to E. Will and C. Orrieux, *Ioudaïsmos, Hellènismos: Essai sur le judaïsme judéen à l'époque hellénistique* (Nancy: Presses Universitaires de Nancy, 1986).

64. J. Kampen, *The Hasideans and the Origin of Pharisaism: A Study in 1 and 2 Maccabees* (SBLSCS, 24; Atlanta: Scholars Press, 1988).

65. On prohibiting the writing of *halakha*, cf. *b. Tem.* 14b (*b. Giṭ.* 60b) with the formula כותבי הלכות כשורפי תורה. Rashi is the first to assert (on *b. Šab.* 13b) that the Mishnah had not been written. The prohibition does not apply, however, to the *Haggadah*, nor to the pre-Tannaitic writings (*Meg. Taʿan., Sefer Yuḥasin*). It seems

and not to be handed over to any reader. This is characteristic of a closed group. In other respects, even if the Bible is not missing, this literature is in no way a biblical exegesis,[66] since it proceeds from another source. At the turn of the first century CE, Ishmael and Aqiba, the leading figures of this tradition at that time, were innovators in striving to show, by the use of certain hermeneutical laws, that oral tradition and the Bible form one Torah alone, and not two; that is to say, that the oral tradition, which alone is normative, can be considered to be proceeding from what is written. This is summarized in a rabbinic axiom: 'The words of the scribes are more important than those of the [written] Torah' (*y. Sanh.* 11.6). It is strange however that this systematic reappropriation of what is written only happened so late.

These features show a remarkable contrast with the work of Philo of Alexandria, for whom the Law, which he strives to explain according to the Decalogue, is derived in its entirety from the Bible, in fact essentially from the Pentateuch. Besides, he had the explicit desire to publish it and make it understood by everyone, since this Law, or *nomos*, is the law of the world, whose unity is that of a *logos*; that is why it begins with Creation. It involves a Stoic view, connected to the utopia of an ideal city. For Philo this has two consequences: on the one hand, the one who observes the Law, and this one alone, is a true inhabitant of the world, or *cosmopolitès*;[67] on the other hand, the written laws, as a system of positive law, come second, though not secondarily. It was in this way, he

that writing was in fact tolerated, but only for private usage (correspondence, memoranda; cf. *b. Ket.* 49b, *y. Git.* 5, 3, etc.); H. Albeck, *Introduction to the Mishnah* (Tel Aviv: Devis, 1959), pp. 11-12. In regard to the sixth-century Talmudic inscription in the Rehob mosaic, S. Lieberman, 'The Halakhic Inscription from the Beth-Shean Valley', *Tarbiz* 45 (1975), pp. 54-63, observes that it is the oldest example known of the 'publication' (פרסום) of *halakha*, namely, of an exposition of any kind. According to 2 Esd. 14.42-47, Moses would have foreseen, besides a written Law for everyone, books reserved for the wise alone; shortly after the destruction of the Temple, then, there developed some sort of theory of esoteric knowledge, to explain the Mosaic authority of the oral tradition.

66. On the contrary, the *Mid. Halakha*, which connects to the Bible the precepts of the Mishnah (and the associated compilations) is secondary in comparison to the Mishnah itself; cf. J.N. Epstein and E.Z. Melamed, *Introductions to the Tannaitic Literature* (Jerusalem: Magnes, 1957), pp. 537-38 (on Ishmael and Aqiba).

67. According to *Abr.* §§5, 16, 46, 261, 276; *Migr. Abr.* §130; *Vit. Mos.* 1.28, 158, 162; *Spec. Leg.* 4.149-50, the Law is destined to be the definitive legislation for all the cities.

explains in a preamble to the treatise on the Decalogue, that the patriarchs before the time of Moses are incarnations of the Law; consequently, they express by their being, a non-written law (νόμους ἀγράφους αἱ ἱεραὶ βίβλοι δηλοῦσιν): the genuine sage is the one who gives direction without relying on any written text,[68] that is to say, without any external precept, and this can only be the result of a divine pedagogy or a divine election. Moses is at one and the same time king, priest and prophet, or again 'a living law and gifted with speech' (λογικός). There is consequently inspiration, *habitus*, and not dictation of an oracle. In other words the 'non-written law', universal and in conformity with nature, is not for Philo an external traditional datum, but the result of a harmony with the created world. Of course, this in no way excludes the existence of a system of laws, or even of an oral tradition completing the written law,[69] but Philo was not very concerned with this. In *Spec. Leg* 4.150, Philo declares that whoever obeys written laws should not be congratulated, since this is done under constraint and out of fear of chastisement; but observance of non-written laws deserves praise, since it proceeds from virtue. Although he sets a major value on the non-written laws too, this idea is the opposite of oral tradition in the rabbinic sense,[70] which is not only positive, and consequently not natural (in the sense of nature as experienced), but also in some way private and not public. The ultimate goal of the Torah and its precepts is the acceptance of the 'yoke of the Kingdom of Heaven' and the 'yoke of the commandments', which frees from the yoke of nature (*Shema Israel*; cf. *m. Ber.* 2.2).[71]

This contrast stresses the existence of a non-biblical source of the oral

---

68. As Plato wanted: *Politics* §§202-203. According to *Vit. Mos.* 1.162 and 2.4, the legal being of the king is νόμος ἔμψυχος; cf. A. Myre, 'Les caractéristiques de la loi mosaïque selon Philon d'Alexandrie', *Science et Esprit* 27 (1975), pp. 35-69. According to *Spec. Leg.* 4.149, whoever observes the non-written law is worthy of praise, for 'the virtue that is shown is freely willed'; cf. I. Heinemann, 'Die Lehre vom ungeschriebenen Gesetz in jüdischen Schrifttum', *HUCA* 4 (1927), p. 155.

69. As is assumed by *Vit. Mos.* 1.4, *Spec. Leg.* 1.8, among others.

70. S. Sandmel, *Philo's Place in Judaism: A Study of Conceptions of Abraham in Jewish Literature* (New York: Ktav, 1971), pp. 24-31, summarizes the many earlier discussions on the possible links between Philo and the rabbinic traditions, and concludes that the numerous points of contact observed can neither prove direct dependence nor above all conceal the profound differences in point of view.

71. Cf. E.E. Urbach, *The Sages: Their Concepts and Beliefs* (Jerusalem: Magnes, 1973), p. 291 nn. 22-24.

tradition. Again the testimony of Josephus in regard to the Pharisees is relevant. Nevertheless, Josephus, who calls himself a Pharisee and in any case wishes to be accepted as such, is not afraid to present Judaism under the form of a biblical paraphrase, while in numerous places he gives instructions that do not have a biblical origin and are found in the rabbinic tradition.[72] Taken as a whole, then, the Pharisees are connected to two sources which are not reducible one to the other; this evidently can allow for varying tendencies that are more or less biblical. This is illustrated well, each in its own way, by the New Testament and the rabbinic tradition. There remains, nevertheless, the matter of deciding how the coming together of the two could have taken place. The book of Nehemiah as it stands serves as a model and an example of how this happens: the proclamation of the law of Moses to the people (Neh. 8) happened within a group of returnees who already had their own cohesiveness. As a matter of fact, the community commitment which follows does not agree with what we read in the Law; indeed, the subsequent expulsion of foreigners (Neh. 13) is contrary to the verse of Deuteronomy specifically cited, although in a shortened form; the Bible is in some way assimilated and used as a guarantee for another tradition. The trail splits then into two persons and two places: the person of Nehemiah, especially in that second mission, arrives from Babylon with his precepts and is unaware of Ezra, while the Law is proclaimed at Jerusalem by Ezra, who is unaware of Nehemiah. The (peaceful) fusion is only brought about by the book itself, and, what is more, as indicated above, this fusion evidently needs to be assigned a date.

In other respects, even if both of them are Pharisaic in spirit, Josephus and the rabbinic tradition strangely ignore one another. Josephus knows of Jamnia-Jabneh, but totally ignores the fact that there was an academy there at the time of the destruction. On the subject of salvaging institutions, the only thing he mentions is a more or less forced migration of priests from Jerusalem to Gophna, in Judaea (*War* 6.114). The prologue of *Pirke Abot* mentions, as ancestors responsible for the transmission of the tradition, Shemaiah and Abtalion, then Hillel and Shammai, with a certain discontinuity between the two pairs, but all in the time of

---

72. Cf. *Ant.* 4.197-98. By perhaps confusing things a little, Eusebius, *Demonstratio evangelica* 6.18.36 (291b), says that Josephus knew the ἔξωθεν Ἰουδαϊκαὶ δευτερώσεις, where this term is an equivalent of מִשְׁנָה ('mishnah', in the sense of 'second part', or 'dividing into two parts'), as is attested also by Epiphanius, *Panarion* 33.9 and Jerome, *In Isaiam* 3.8.

Herod. Josephus knew the first two, at least late in life (*Ant.* 14.172; 15.3), but not the second two. Now, Hillel was a Babylonian, and his elevation to head of the school, on the occasion of some crisis, happened in the Babylonian colony of Bathyra (Golan), founded by the same Herod.[73] This marginal situation implies that the rabbinic tradition, although wanting to be heir to the memories of Jerusalem and the Temple, had its origin in fact far from the ruling circles of Jerusalem. This would explain perfectly why Josephus ignores them altogether, or even would not want to know about them. In a similar way, Josephus only discovered Christianity in Rome, when he could not deny it a certain social importance.[74]

This reference to Hillel at Bathyra draws attention to neighbouring Galilee, which was far from Judaea and separated from it besides by a hostile Samaria. As a matter of fact, while Galilee on the whole plays no role in the Bible, three historical phases make it necessary to take it seriously: first of all, shortly after the time of Herod, Jesus recruited disciples there in a rural setting with strong religious traditions; then, at the time of the war of 66 CE, Josephus disparages the Galileans, but cannot hide their strong religious motivations; finally, toward the end of the second century CE, the Mishnah originated there, again in rural surroundings, and there are grounds for wondering whether this was a natural cradle for it, or the random result of a forced migration after the prohibition of Judaism in Judaea in 135 CE; it must be added that this Mishnah was immediately adopted (or imposed) in Babylonia. In short, it is a matter of evaluating the origins of this Jewish Galilee, so remote from Jerusalem that it could be considered more cosmopolitan ('Galilee of the nations'); the preceding observations suggest, nevertheless, that it would not be a stranger to the flow of Babylonian immigrants, even in very late periods.

7. *Conclusion: Outline of a Method*

The preceding analyses are all incomplete and the overall result obtained gives an impression of uniform confusion, in which no fixed point is secure. Some considerations on method are in order here, before gathering together some conclusions in order to pursue the further stages of

73. By combining *Ant.* 17.23-24 and *y. Pes.* 6.1; cf. Chapter 7, §4, below.

74. Cf. E. Nodet, 'Jésus et Jean Baptiste selon Josèphe', *RB* 92 (1985), pp. 321-48.

the search: the points encountered are to a great extent interdependent, since they deal with historical moments succeeding one another in time, but, for each of them, any clarification suggested fails to impose itself for lack of factual evidence. Yet, since they are problems arising in periods that are clearly distinct, two approaches are possible: the first is the one that has been put in perspective in this chapter. It consists of an attempt to settle in the best way possible each case individually and locally, beginning in a more self-contained way, and elaborating for each of them a probable solution starting from what has been established in the preceding cases. Suppose, for example, that we find a solution that is 70 per cent probable, which is more than respectable, for the elucidation of events under Cyrus and Darius. If we then rely on this result to interpret Ezra–Nehemiah with the same internal probability of 70 per cent, the two taken together will, however, have only a 49 per cent chance of being true, and will then in reality be improbable. If we continue and build the solution of a third problem on the solutions to the two preceding problems, we end up, under the same conditions, at 34 per cent, and so on. The progression of this positivistic method of establishing facts becomes very quickly disastrous, all the more so since the brief review of problems and authoritative opinions proposed above shows that the threshold of 70 per cent is most often highly inacessible.

The second approach, which will be adopted in what follows, is based on the fact that none of the literature studied is dated as annals would be. What is more, there is always the suspicion that it has undergone modifications, since it came out of a culture which tried to express its unity even in dissimilar contexts. Our procedure then will be to start from explicit cultural questions or interests, and we will construct, through successive approximations, models for the interpretation or the restoration of facts. The criterion for the validity of such models is not their historical exactitude, since this is inaccessible almost by definition, but their capacity to coordinate a maximum number of fragments scattered through historical discourses. These fragments come from the methodical analysis of the sources. In more classical terms, it will be a matter of putting into effect converging arguments.

With these preliminaries established, it is evident from the overview done in this chapter, intended to identify the uncertainties about the origin of Judaism, that the epic of Judas Maccabeus constitutes a pivotal point. Before him, any historical traces, however certain, are difficult to understand clearly; and it should be noted that they are grouped around isolated moments, all flawed by great uncertainties: the decree of Cyrus-Darius, the activity of Ezra–Nehemiah, the arrival of Alexander and the charter of Antiochus III. After Judas, the information is more abundant, and matters have obviously changed, even though a precise causal connection cannot be determined.

The delineation of changes implies institutions which eventually are transformed, and there is one of these which all through these events appears to be of decisive importance: the Sabbath, to which is connected the Sabbatical Year (the sabbath of the land; cf. Lev. 25.2-7). It is an essential element of what Nehemiah wanted to promote, in connection with the enclosure of the City. Additionally, it is something at stake in grave situations: when Alexander granted Judaea the exemption from the tax of the Sabbatical Year, the Samaritans saw themselves refused the same privilege, since they were Hebrews but not Jews (*Ant.* 11.344). No matter what the truth of the account of Alexander's visit to the Temple in Jerusalem, the statement about an institutional split among the 'Hebrews' (a term equivalent to 'Israelites' in Josephus) is of primary importance, all the more so since it arises again at the time of the persecutions of Antiochus IV. When the Samaritans learned the fate met by the Jews, Josephus relates (*Ant.* 12.259) that they wrote to Antiochus that their ancestors had adopted the Jewish custom of celebrating the Sabbath out of superstition, but that he should not compare them with the Jews; they won their case. Once again, the observation (or not) of the Sabbath was decisive.

In the same context, when the Jews get killed in the desert on the Sabbath day without defending themselves, Mattathias and his friends decide to allow armed defence on the Sabbath (1 Macc. 2.41). This decision is noteworthy since it appears to be entirely new, and does not appeal to any precedent. This would be understandable, if it were with Mattathias that Judaism began to be involved in political-military activity. But what were they up to in the time of the kings of Judah and Israel? Another curious question comes up in the same way, very much later. In the time of Herod the Great, before Hillel the Elder had been promoted to the rank of patriarch, he first faced a strange question: that year the Passover (14th Nisan) fell on the Sabbath, and nobody knew which of the two events took precedence over the other. This is a little like a priest in the present Christian calendar not knowing what to do should Christmas (December 25th) fall on a Sunday, and wondering whether it should be postponed to the next Monday. In the Jewish lunar calendar, the concurrence takes place on average one year in seven; and since the rituals were popular, we can scarcely understand how the problem raised could have been new at such a late date, and how it could be puzzling for a congregation entitled to choose a patriarch.

Leaving for now history in the strict sense, we begin by considering the ups and downs of the Sabbath, especially in relation to war in the late documentation. Then the evolution of the biblical institution will be examined, to throw into relief the work of Nehemiah. Subsequently, to simplify matters, I use 'city of Nehemiah' or 'model of Nehemiah' to designate a community structure defined by a limited and protected space, where the Torah—and especially the Sabbath—could be observed without any hindrance.

As for the Samaritans, who seem to have an ambiguous relationship with the Sabbath, it has been shown that they appear at each important moment in the development of ancient Judaism, and that Josephus in particular systematizes their opposition, from Cyrus to the Maccabees. If the two camps are at this point inseparable, a re-evaluation of these peculiar Hebrews should shed some light on their neighbours to the south.

Lastly, the Temple in Jerusalem is difficult to fit in: artificially magnified in the story of Alexander, it is astonishingly marginal for Nehemiah as well as for the Pharisees, which does not, however, prevent strong claims being made about it. In this regard, the precise result of the activity of Judas Maccabeus, although commemorated as the Dedication of the altar, is in reality uncertain, since the surprise attack, 25th Kislev 164 BCE, did not have immediate institutional consequences. Of course, it is evidently not the building which is at issue, but the real functioning of Jewish religious institutions. It is necessary then to re-evaluate this crisis and its consequences, in their context, which will provide some clarification of the famous parties of Josephus. At this point, the rabbinic tradition, duly situated, will provide instructive supplementary information. Since the conclusions reached differ considerably on the whole from the historical fresco painted by Ezra–Nehemiah, I shall sketch finally a literary analysis of these books, in order to control the coherence of everything. These various aspects will be dealt with one after the other in the following chapters.

Chapter 2

THE SABBATH AND WAR

Other than the text quoted at the end of the previous chapter (1 Macc. 2.41), in which Mattathias allowed armed defence on the Sabbath, one cannot find in all the rest of the Bible any allusion to whether or not the Sabbath and war were compatible. Undoubtedly, the problem is present, since on the one hand, at the time of the intervention of Mattathias, the carrying and use of arms on the Sabbath was prohibited, even for legitimate defence, but on the other hand, the long wars of Joshua and David necessarily presuppose that the Sabbath would not have interrupted combat and given an easy advantage to an adversary.[1] Leaving aside for the moment the ancient periods to concentrate on the Hellenistic epoch, it can be noted first of all that the initiative of Mattathias and his followers is marked by a certain boldness, since, according to 1 Macc. 2.42, it created a movement, which began from limited circles without any particular authority, and banded together little by little various resistance groups, in particular the Hasidaeans. Like all initiatives by minority groups, this one too was marked by controversy, at least implicitly,[2] since 2 Maccabees not only ignores Mattathias and his decision, but also specifies that in Judas's war the Sabbath was respected (2 Macc. 8.26-27); 2 Maccabees even takes care to emphasize that if Judas was attacked by surprise, he would not defend himself, on account of the holiness of this day (15.1-5, blasphemies of Nicanor). The campaigns of Judas took place after those of Mattathias, and therefore the book appears to reject Mattathias's decision, and in any case ignores it.

---

1.   This assumption is made by M.D. Herr, 'The Problem of War on the Sabbath in the Second Temple and the Talmudic Period', *Tarbiz* 30 (1961), pp. 242-56; 341-56, from whom I borrow many elements in the development that follows, but in a presentation which leads to opposite conclusions.
2.   It is made explicit later on in rabbinic sources; cf. below, §4.

Josephus, who reports the episode making use of 1 Maccabees,[3] introduces some modifications which have the effect of leading his readers to believe that there was a process by which the Jews in general had adopted this novelty (*Ant.* 12.275-78). The refugees join Mattathias, make him their chief, and it is only then that Mattathias, whose zeal is above any suspicion, convinced them to fight even on the Sabbath, so that they would not all perish. The priest Mattathias is in this way given the part of a master entitled to teach (ἐδίδασκε[4]), whose sole task is to instruct new followers. Consequently, Josephus tones down the novelty of the decision and its marginal origin, but does not hide the fact that its general adoption is definitely due to Mattathias, endowed with the proper authority. He even underlines this point by enlarging the horizon, saying that fighting on the Sabbath is so necessary that it is maintained 'to the present day', but he avoids qualifying this 'fact' (τὸ καὶ σαββάτοις μάχεσθαι) as a law or a venerable custom.[5] He does not specify, however, that it was a matter of defence alone. It is possible that such a broadening would involve an element of self-justification, since Josephus himself had waged war. Josephus is prudent on sensitive topics. Yet, when as in this case he appears to restrict himself to reporting, while refraining from prescribing laws, he is not afraid, as in *Apion* 1.212, to show the greatness of those who put the observance of the Law, and in particular of the Sabbath, above defending their lives and even above the destiny of the nation. Furthermore, there are good reasons to think that the question was debated in Judaism by those with different leanings after the destruction of the Temple (cf. Chapter 1, §5 and below, §3).

3.   The exact form of the Maccabaean account that Josephus had before him is difficult to determine. In the immediate context, some details show a certain independence of Josephus in relation to 1 Maccabees: the king's officer who had come to Modin to impose apostasy and was killed by Mattathias (1 Macc. 2.25) becomes in *Ant.* 12.270 Appeles, *strategos* of the king. At the time of the challenge to the guerillas on the Sabbath, 1 Macc. 2.38 speaks merely of an attack, but *Ant.* 12.274 says that they were burnt in the caves, like 2 Macc. 6.11. For a survey of the discussions on this point, cf. L.H. Feldman, *Josephus and Modern Scholarship (1937–1980)* (Berlin: de Gruyter, 1984), pp. 219-26.

4.   An imperfect as in the Loeb edition and in most manuscripts, instead of the aorist, found in P only and adopted by Niese; this choice will be justified elsewhere.

5.   Whereas in 12.273 he states clearly that the *law* of warfare (πολέμου νόμος), which has little likelihood of being a recent innovation, is clearly in conflict with the custom of Sabbath rest (ἀργεῖν γὰρ ἡμῖν ἐν αὐτῇ νόμιμόν ἐστίν). It is no longer question of a 'tradition of the ancients', of the Pharisaic kind; cf. Chapter 7, §3.

It can already be seen that the debate that began with Mattathias revolves around defence on the Sabbath and does not take into account at all the more serious matter of offensive wars in more ancient times, such as those of Joshua or of David, as already mentioned. This is an additional reason not to project later debates back into remote times, since this would amount to making vanish the point to be established, namely, that the Sabbath institution had always been the same.[6]

1. *The Sabbath and the City*

In the *Jewish Antiquities*, Mattathias's insurrection is surrounded by other narratives on the theme of respect for the Sabbath. In particular, I referred above (Chapter 1, §4) to the taking of Jerusalem by Ptolemy, at the end of the fourth century BCE, making use of a ruse that allowed him to lay siege to it during the Sabbath rest. Some of its details help to clarify matters (*Ant.* 12.4):

> He came into the city on the Sabbath, as if he would offer sacrifice, without the Jews offering the least opposition [ἀμυνομένων], since they did not suspect any hostile act; unsuspicious and because of the day, they were passive and unconcerned [ἐν ἀργίᾳ καὶ ῥαθυμίᾳ]; he made himself master of the city without any difficulty and ruled it harshly.

This wording is worth noting, since it implies that if the people of Jerusalem had had any suspicions about him, they would have defended themselves. In other words, the teaching of Mattathias does not appear to be truly new, and we may ask then why Josephus does not connect it more explicitly to an authentic custom.

This difficulty is cleared up if we keep in mind Josephus's source,

---

6. Herr, 'Problem of War', p. 247 follows others in finding a continuity by proposing that Mattathias's decision is not precisely formulated, that it must imply in addition the possibility of offensive warfare, and finally that there was no difference between the Pharisees and the Sadducees on this point. This final assertion seems arbitrary, since it neglects the essential problem of the relationship with Scripture for the religious meaning of a decision of this importance (cf. *Ant.* 13.293-94), but it is interesting, since it flows almost mechanically from Josephus's presentation. According to him, the distinction between Pharisees and Sadducees is put prematurely, in the time of Simon, or even Judas, but is later than the time when Mattathias and Judas were active together. I indicated in Chapter 1, §5 that there is room to doubt Josephus's coherence and objectivity, and this is seen clearly here: with the dates he provides, it is impossible to assign a definite date for a Sadducean *religious* opinion.

Agatharchides of Cnidus, since he gives a longer citation from him in *Apion* 1.209-212. It gives precise details on ceasing all work on the Sabbath, and the defeat is clearly attributed to the deliberate refusal to take up arms.[7] The effect of surprise is therefore not present, and Josephus's account is seen to be contradicted on this point. He seems to have projected forward a customary situation to a period later than the decision of Mattathias, but this could be due to simple inadvertence, or even to using a secondary source already reformulated, since he did not try to make it a precedent. It can be assumed besides that if he had at his disposal a written source fitting in more directly with his aims, he would not have failed to cite it, as he readily does elsewhere.

In order to delimit still more the implication of Josephus's editing, I note first another modification which he introduces into the same source: he attributes to Ptolemy the intention of offering a sacrifice in the Temple, and this trite motif of royal devotion[8] is a way to trick the people. Now, Agatharchides does not mention this at all; but what is more he shows the Jews, in a very well fortified Jerusalem (ὀχυρωτάτην πασῶν), occupied in prayer all day long with arms extended in *their* temples. This plural suggests places of prayer, and not the Temple, and the absence of an allusion to any sacrifice tends to confirm that sacrifice is not involved: the comparison with the city of Nehemiah, well

---

7.   J. Klausner, *The History of the Second Temple* (2 vols.; Jerusalem: Massada, 1952), II, p. 111 notes the contradiction between the account of Josephus and the remarks cited from Agatharchides, which are focused on a critique of superstitions, and especially of martyrdom. Herr, 'Problem of War', p. 242 n. 5 holds on the contrary that if Josephus had seen such a contradiction, he would not have failed to point it out; this argument from silence fails to recognize the way in which Josephus generally uses his sources. Reinach (ed.), *Contre Apion*, p. xxxv, gives excellent examples of the way in which Josephus would have people believe that Manetho or Berossus backs up his statements, when the citations provided demonstrate nothing of the sort. In *Antiquities of the Jews*, the same thing happens over and over again. For example, in *Ant.* 9.283-84, after having recounted the conquest of Israel by Shalmaneser, he describes how the king of Assyria invaded Syria and Phoenicia, and quotes a compiler of the archives of Tyre, who referred to this particular event. However, the text produced does not mention the name of the king, and makes no allusion to the biblical episode. Strictly speaking, the citation proves absolutely nothing. In regard to the point raised here, there is no contradiction, but slight intentional modifications.

8.   Cf. for Alexander, *Ant.* 11.336; for Pompey, *Ant.* 14.72. Later on, however, Josephus reports that foreigners abstained from sacrificing, out of respect for the law of Moses (*Ant.* 3.319).

protected and centred on daily life, is once again suggestive.

Other details are provided by another account of a victory over Jerusalem by the use of trickery, which is worth referencing too, even though it involves a Seleucid and not a Lagide aggression, and, what is more, is a century later, at the time of the persecutions of Antiochus Epiphanes. According to 2 Macc. 5.23b-24, Antiochus,[9] having plundered the Temple, and 'holding towards the Jews a deep-seated hostility', sent the mysarch Apollonius with orders to massacre the men and sell the women and children. His success there came through a deception, by organizing a parade of his fully armed soldiers outside the city on the Sabbath. With no apprehension, the people came out, and Apollonius could then enter with the armed soldiers and kill a multitude that had no defence. This text reflects a very clear socio-political situation: these people knew how to defend themselves, but if they did not take up arms on the Sabbath, it was because they were protected by the walls, whose entrances were properly closed. The deception consisted of the request to the Jews, asking them not to close the gates; this would work if they thought themselves protected by a sympathetic army, because of the spectacle of fully armed soldiers parading outside the walls. By comparing this with the Ptolemy incident, it can be seen that the account by Agatharchides is incomplete, and ultimately tendentious: if the city is so well fortified, it is incomprehensible how it could have been captured after a siege of one day, except by a deception allowing an army to enter. The slight alterations of Josephus have the effect, in particular, of filling in this gap: Ptolemy entered in order to offer a sacrifice; this could be done with a retinue and bedecked dignitaries, a spectacle very much like a parade of fully armed soldiers. The impression which Josephus gives is that they would have defended themselves if they had been on the alert, therefore that they could have defended themselves with arms on the Sabbath. This impression comes then quite simply from the fact that he omits mention of walls and gates: defending themselves by closing the gates on the Sabbath is an obvious necessity, completely independent of the decision of Mattathias, a decision obviously made outside the city, at the time of a flight into the wilderness (1 Macc. 2.29-30). We

---

9. An indication of a redactional seam after the preceding episode is provided by an awkwardness (or a deception) in style. It seems that it was the high priest Menelaus, lording it over his compatriots (v. 23a), who organized the massacre. This makes v. 23 a strange verse, which led to corrections by copyists; cf. Goldstein, *II Maccabees*, p. 262.

must conclude then that the accounts, even if their variations confer on them a legendary touch, witness to a precise reality, of which a basic element is the close connection between the walls and the strict observance of the Sabbath. Here again we see the work of Nehemiah, who restored the walls and their gates, and, more generally, the theme of Jerusalem as a Holy City, namely separated, with or without the Temple, possibly reduced to a quarter.

It is remarkable that these accounts refer neither to Temple nor priesthood, and the retouching by Josephus, who reintroduces them by the expedient of the royal sacrifice, brings this detail into relief. According to the context of the story of Apollonius, first (2 Macc. 5.21-23) Antiochus, having pillaged the Temple, returned to Antioch, leaving representatives: one at Jerusalem, 'Philip, by birth a Phrygian, in character more barbarous than the one who appointed him; one on Mount Gerizim, Andronicus; and besides these, Menelaus who lorded it over his compatriots worse than the others did'. Menelaus was a high priest who had bought his office from the Seleucids, and he really acted as governor of the country from his sanctuaries.[10] After this account, the story is told (2 Macc. 6.1-11) of how Antiochus sent Geron, an Athenian, to abolish the ancestral law of the Jews and to pollute the temples in Jerusalem and Gerizim, dedicating one to Olympian Zeus, and the other to Zeus, Patron of Strangers. Between these two passages, which have a similar origin and could pass for doublets, or as an introduction followed by a further development, the expedition of Apollonius does not really fit: not only does it ignore the Temple, but especially it does not fit in with the project of administrative domination and fiscal exploitation. The oddity is lessened by the fact that Antiochus is presented as insane with arrogance and incapable of a judicious policy: 'He thought, in his arrogance, because his mind was elated, that he could sail on the land and walk on the sea' (2 Macc. 5:21). It can be admitted that this pleasant description would help to heighten what was really the unstable character of this prince, but it does not entirely hide the difficulty in the narrative. In particular, the similar account in 1 Maccabees, describing the pillaging of the city by the mysarch of Judah, who rebuilt the City of David and installed a foreign population, seems more plausible: the elimination of Jews, according to 2 Maccabees, would make more sense in fact, if it was for settling foreign colonists, but this is not stated.[11]

10. We may note in passing that 'our nation' takes in Judaea and Samaria; cf. Chapter 6, §4.

11. This version of the story, oddly unknown to 2 Maccabees, offers strange details which imply that it evolved from an anti-Jewish version; cf. Chapter 6, §3. The suggestion by Goldstein, *II Maccabees*, p. 263, of joining the two accounts in order to restore the Common Source (cf. *II Maccabees*, pp. 38-39) is certainly too mechanical, since it assumes that these accounts are clearly documentary (objective). This gives rise to artificial questions: for example, why (according to 1 Maccabees)

More importantly still, this insertion of an account of a massacre is the occasion for bringing into the picture Judas Maccabeus, the ardent resistance fighter who then retired to the wilderness (1 Macc. 5.24), although he will appear in an active role only later (8.1), after lengthy periods of persecution. In other words, in a context pointing out foreign domination over the Temple, there finally occurs the addition of a sort of medallion, picturing the persecution of the city, in connection with the Sabbath, together with the rebellious Judas who will save the city later. It could not be said more clearly than in this way, that he is presented as a defender of Nehemiah's work. Nevertheless, the final redaction weakens this effect to a great extent, but it is premature to determine whether this was done deliberately or not.

As for determining the origin of the accounts of massacres resulting from deceptions, and whether it is necessary to see here a Lagide initiative with Agatharchides or a Seleucid one with 2 Maccabees, or even whether there were several similar occurrences, the matter is hard to settle. If we rule out as improbable the hypothesis that the inhabitants of Jerusalem had several times shown the same naiveté when faced with the same deception, there still remain two possibilities: either the small differences among the accounts were stabilized, so that quite different events would have been transmitted in a same heroic narrative mould; or, on the contrary, these differences are to be attributed to the ups and downs of oral transmission, so that diverse accounts would have dealt with the same disaster, which could even be quite late, since Agatharchides, the principal witness, is later than Antiochus Epiphanes.[12]

2. *Jerusalem or Babylon?*

In an entirely different context, after the death of Caligula (January 41 CE), which cut short the unfortunate incident of the statue of the Emperor in the Temple, Josephus recounts the strange story of the two brothers, Asineus and Anileus in Babylon (*Ant.* 18.310-79), having referred to it in the opening summary as a catastrophe. This long excursus, which forms the last episode in Book 18, does not seem to have been motivated by the need to divert the attention of the reader in order to conceal the serious gaps in the main narrative, since the following book returns to take up the end of Caligula's reign as well as his misdeeds. But, before inquiring into the reasons for this story and the place that

---

after such a disaster on a Sabbath (a detail provided by 2 Maccabees) did Mattathias not arrive at his decision earlier?

12. Cf. Stern, *Greek and Latin Authors*, I, p. 104.

Josephus assigns it, here is an overview of his account, since he is its only witness.

Asineus and Anileus were natives of Neerda (Nehahardea[13]) which was one of two fortified Jewish towns in Babylon, with Nisibis being the other; at Neerda and Nisibis the legal collections for Jerusalem were gathered together. The two brothers, after the death of their father, learned the trade of linen weaving, but after being beaten by their employer, they fled to the hills, where some unemployed workers and other disaffected people joined them; they carved out an estate by holding up the country for ransom. The Parthians' power was weak, but they eventually reacted, and the brothers found themselves threatened on the Sabbath by the forces of the satrap of Babylon. The rebels took it for granted that it was impossible to defend themselves on the Sabbath day, even in open country (διὰ τὸ κατείργεσθαι προαγορεύσει τῶν πατρίων εἰς τὸ ἀργεῖν). Anileus decided to act otherwise, however, and preferred to die, if necessary, to take vengeance for having to break the law (παρανομεῖν). He triumphed and the power of the two brothers was confirmed. The king of the Parthians, Artabane, preferring to use their power rather than fight it, entrusted them at this time with maintaining order in Babylon. The prosperity of the two brothers lasted until Anileus married by force the wife of a neighbouring Parthian chief after having had him killed. This woman introduced foreign cults,[14] and a grave crisis among the Jewish entourage of the two brothers followed. On this occasion, Asineus, who wanted his brother to get rid of his Parthian wife, was poisoned by her. Left in full control, Anileus plundered the son-in-law of the king, Mithridate, who set out in pursuit of him, but Anileus defeated him through a deception, by violating the Sabbath once more. Mithridate, captured and then released, set out again on a campaign and in collusion with the Babylonians ended up defeating Anileus. With Anileus dead, the Babylonians gave free rein to their hatred of the Jews, fostered by the endless discord provoked by the

---

13. A centre, in the time of the Talmud, of the exilarch and a famous academy, directed in the third century CE by Samuel, who received the Mishnah there.

14. 'Having been led away captive, she concealed the images of the ancestral divinities of her husband as well as her own, since it is the custom of the people of that region to have in their home their cult objects and to carry them along when they travel to a foreign land' (18.344). This comment brings to mind Rachel and the teraphim of Laban (Gen. 31.19); cf. M. Greenberg, 'Another Look at Rachel's Theft of the Teraphim', *JBL* 81 (1962), pp. 239-48.

incompatibility of their respective laws, and they attacked them. The Jews, unable to do battle, took refuge at Seleucia, but there, after a few years, the Greeks and Syrians succeeded in conspiring against them and carried out a great massacre. The survivors withdrew to Ctesiphon, then to the fortified towns of Neerda and Nisipis.

This account forms a kind of loop and returns to the two cities which were its starting point. It teems with the usual interesting details, but contains some improbabilities with a legendary look and ultimately presents very little precise information: the infrequent proper names mentioned, such as Artabane and Mithridate, are Parthian chronological references as vague as a Ptolemy or Cleopatra would be in Egypt.[15] Through this historical vagueness, the account is really very edifying, since it shows the inexorable consequences both of not observing the Sabbath and of imprudent unions with foreign women, who bring their cult with fatal consequences. Whether the story has a real foundation or not, it is written in the form of a tale, stigmatizing impiety and explaining the origin of the strong establishments of Neerda and Nisibis. For our purposes here, some observations will suffice: first of all, the two points of the Law thrown into relief—the observance of the Sabbath and abstention from marriage with foreigners—are precisely the same two aspects with which Nehemiah, at the time of his second voyage back from the King of Babylon, thrashed the Jewish society of Jerusalem[16] (Neh. 13.15-29). In the same spirit there is the emphasis at the two extremities of the narrative on the importance of the fortified places of Nisibis and Neerda, with their good natural defence; in such places, there cannot be a surprise attack on the Sabbath. It is clear that the controversy between Asineus and his companions about the defensive war on the Sabbath is the same as that happening around Mattathias. Finally, it is remarkable that Josephus seems to be inconsistent, since here the war

15. If this is real history, various details allow this attempt at 'Jewish autonomy' to be situated around 20–35 CE, under Tiberius. Cf., following others, Jacob Neusner, *A History of the Jews in Babylonia*. I. *The Parthian Period* (SPB, 9; Leiden: Brill, 1965), pp. 51-55. Josephus's narrative neglects completely, however, the Jewish institutions in place in the two cities, which inevitably should be taken into account in this autonomy, since at least a fiscal administration was found there. Besides, the matter is complicated by the coming to power at this time of the Jewish king of Adiabene, Izates I (about 30 CE; cf. *Ant.* 20.34-35).

16. Josephus could not have made such a connection, for he recounts the story of Nehemiah according to 1 Esdras (*Ant.* 11.159-83), which lacked the second voyage (cf. Chapter 7, §7).

on the Sabbath, even a defensive war, is an impious infraction, which
definitely leads to persecutions, and there is no redactional effect tending
to weaken this diagnosis.

The lack of logic could be attributed to a collaborator, but this would
be a desperate solution and certainly an illusory one, since such a long
passage necessarily means that Josephus is responsible for it, all the more
so since it is already mentioned in the earlier summary. At most, the
context in which the episode is placed suggests that the tradition corresponding to it was contemporaneous, at least in Babylon.

On the occasion of other narratives, Josephus has more difficulty
making up his mind, but these deal with Jerusalem, and not Babylon.
This is how it was when, at the time of Pompey's invasion, the Romans
took advantage of the Sabbaths to prepare for the assault on Jerusalem,
by building up an embankment and by preparing their engines, while
guarding themselves carefully against any direct attack: 'Although the
law allows one to defend oneself when the enemy joins battle and begins
an assault, it forbids it outside of these cases, whatever the enemy does'
(*Ant.* 14.63). This measure, already described briefly in *War* 1.146,[17]
seems consistent with the teaching of Mattathias, and yet its argument,
to avoid destruction when the threat was beyond all doubt, could have
allowed the right to defence to be extended to include the right to
preventative action. It implicitly follows from this, as Josephus has
already given to understand, that according to him Mattathias had only
made a plea for an older tradition. The parallel passage, *War* 1.146, had
already presented the same prohibition, while insisting in a proportionate
way on the bravery of the Romans, who endured extreme hardships,
and on the admiration of the Romans for the Jews' fidelity to their Law.
Were it not for the Sabbath rest, Pompey would not have been able to
triumph. A military defeat is in this way turned into a victory of another
kind, freely chosen.

Josephus had been himself confronted with this problem, during the
campaign in Galilee. He had to face up to a threat of an insurrection at
Tiberias, on the eve of the Sabbath (*Life* 159-61): 'I had dismissed my
soldiers from Tarichea to their homes; since the next day was a Sabbath,
I did not want the Taricheans to be subjected to any annoyance
[ἐνοχλεῖσθαι] from the presence of the military.' It was not just a

---

17. And mentioned by Strabo, *Geography* 16.2, who speaks of 'days of fasting'
and not Sabbaths, since people thought that the Jews fasted on the Sabbath; cf.
Suetonius, *Augustus* §76.

matter of protecting the Sabbath of civilians, Josephus continues, since 'I was reluctant to recall my forces, because, even if they were called back, they would not have been able to carry arms the next day, since our laws prohibit it [κωλυόντων ἡμᾶς τῶν νόμων]'. The context shows clearly that it involved a preventative action, not acceptable on the Sabbath, and not immediate defence, but Josephus does not bring up this nuance.

In *War* 2.632-37, the factual account is slightly different: the scene was again on the eve of the Sabbath, but the soldiers from Tarichea had gone foraging, and the only effect indicated from the approach of the Sabbath is that Josephus is prevented from acting for one more day, even though the forces of King Agrippa II are a threat. The elements common to the two versions suffice for our purposes here: according to Josephus, the Sabbath prevented him from taking up arms, but apparently it does not have the same inhibiting effect on Agrippa and his troops. Josephus's submission to the Law is in this way discretely emphasized, in contrast to the pro-Roman Jewish camp which is ready to compromise; but it is to be feared that this presentation, on the whole legendary, is tendentious.[18] In a similar way he accuses

18. S.J.D. Cohen, *Josephus in Galilee and Rome: His Vita and Development as a Historian* (Leiden: Brill, 1979), p. 146, points out several examples of parallel passages in *War* and *Life*, where the latter lays great stress on showing Josephus to be observant. Here, however, the difference between the two accounts in regard to the Sabbath is apparently not that great, as Cohen recognizes, p. 94 n. 33. Another point needs to be stressed: the account in *Life* seems more plausible than the *War* account. Judge for yourself: according to *War*, many things happened the same day. A Roman detachment turns up at Tiberias, whose important citizens had officially banished Josephus, since they thought that the arrival of Agrippa and his troops was imminent. The news reaches Josephus at Tarichea, just when he is dispersing his soldiers; he completes this, then assembles two hundred and thirty small craft scattered on the lake. Next he pretends to threaten Tiberias with this squadron which was not armed. Approaching the city, he harangues the rebels, then demands their submission with ten of the principal men being a guarantee; having placed these on board a ship, he asks for fifty more and puts them on board, and little by little lures the six hundred members of the Tiberias Council and two thousand other distinguished citizens toward the empty boats, and this whole convoy is sent at full speed toward the prisons of Tarichea, while Josephus stays behind and punishes the instigator of the revolt, who oddly only appears at this point in the story and is denounced by the townspeople *after* the capture of all the distinguished residents— and 'such was the means by which [Josephus], with empty ships and seven guards, enslaved an entire population and brought back Tiberias under his authority'. All this took place on a Friday without any profanation of the Sabbath; but a few days later the city again defected. In *Life*, the performance is less extreme: it is Josephus himself who sees the Roman detachment around Tiberias. His troops being at rest for the

his adversary John of Gischala of having deceived Titus at the siege of Gischala by making him think that he was properly observing the Sabbath (*War* 4.99).

As for the exact content of the precept observed here, two interpretations are possible: the Law brings to a halt all military activity on the Sabbath, with or without allowance being made for direct legitimate defence through a counterattack. The episode at Tiberias makes no allusion to such an exception being possible. Alternatively, it may be admitted if need be that the teaching of Mattathias or the custom in the time of Pompey are not formally contrary to this, but the crucial situation is poorly deliniated.

These redactional fluctuations, in which whatever is significant is evaded, leave room for the suspicion that Josephus, perhaps for rhetorical concerns, avoids taking a position that was too clear-cut in a controversy over the limits of legitimate defense. This is the case in *War* 2.517, when, on the occasion of the feast of Booths, with all the people in Jerusalem, the threat of war at the gates led to an interruption of the feast and a rush to arms 'without even taking into account the weekly rest, since it was really a Sabbath, which they observed so scrupulously'.[19] It amounted to a pre-emptive strike toward Gabaon, therefore outside the walls, and not a strictly legitimate defence. In the same way, in the great exhortation of Agrippa in 66 to divert the people of Jerusalem from going to war against the Romans, he brings up the deprivation of divine help, since the war will oblige them to break the ancestral law of rest on the Sabbath (*War* 2.393): it involves once again some initiative, whether it be clearly preventative or not.

Sabbath the next day, he asks each of the important citizens of Tarichea to lend him a boat with a pilot; through trickery he then obtains from Tiberias, with only the same seven guards, the ten notable prisoners, and little by little 'the whole Council', as well as many well-known citizens. The guilty one is then denounced and punished. The account is a little less heavy, the numbers are skirted round, and the new defection brought up at the end is transferred back to before the episode. There is no good reason to suppose that this second account is more authentic than the first; it is just reorganized to tone down the implausibilities, without obliterating them, and to enhance the Sabbath precept. As for the reason for the extravagance of the first account, which only develops the synthetic account quoted on the reconquest of Tiberias and combines it with the episode of the punishment of a guilty party, this would require a more extensive study.

19. Perhaps that day was actually the Sabbath which of necessity is included in the eight days of the Feast, but in that case the redaction is at best clumsy, since 'the Sabbath day' may simply indicate the first or last day of the feast, either the fifteenth or twenty-second day of the seventh month (Tishri) which are clearly defined as Sabbaths (Lev. 23.39, שבתון; the LXX has ἀνάπαυσις, which weakens the comparison). It is possible then that in the original text of *War* it was a question of the 'Sabbatical rest', since the feast is a Sabbath, and that the translation, merging it with the Saturday, had to add an explanatory gloss 'because it was really a Sabbath' (ἦν γὰρ δὲ τὸ [...] σάββατον).

Nevertheless, it can be shown that Josephus's imprecisions are merely redactional, since they still permit a glimpse of very clear principles. In fact, by reintroducing the purpose of the walls, which Josephus persists in implying, the various incidents fall into line: the gates of Tiberias were closed during the Sabbath. Likewise, as long as the earthworks of the Romans built to besiege Jerusalem were not yet high enough, the walls fulfill their protective role. In the same way, the massacre of the Romans by Eleazar on the Sabbath was a disgrace and would draw down divine anger, since the siege of Jerusalem by Metilius had just been lifted, and there was no longer a need of defence (*War* 2.455-56). The problem only came up then when there were no longer any fortifications left, or if they had been neutralized or if the fighting took place in open country. It was then that legitimate defence became imperative, and this is what is clearly discernible in two cases: when it involved the defence of Judaea (Mattathias) or of Jerusalem (Pompey), it was allowed, but when it involved a defence of any conquest in Babylon (Anileus), it was not. As for Galilee, it did not exactly possess the Judaean norms, or at least those that seemed natural to Josephus: in fact, the taking of Asochis[20] (Shihin) by Ptolemy on a Sabbath, under Alexander Janneus (*Ant.* 13.337), and the observance witnessed to by Josephus himself imply that the protection of territory made sense, but that armed defence was not allowed on the Sabbath. The Jews of Galilee displayed customs of a Babylonian type (cf. Chapter 7, §6), for which Josephus showed respect.

We may surmise then that in the background there were varying war situations depending on the locality, but Josephus has obviously avoided making the situations clear, and in the *Jewish Antiquities*, where he has taken on a Pharisaic profile without any political pretensions against the Romans, it is not by accident that the last literary reference to the problem is the story of Anileus and Asineus, and their defeat is linked to the profanation of the Sabbath by the taking up of arms. The reference having again become Babylonian, there are no longer any walls or a Jewish state; consequently, the two brothers have become examples *in no way* worthy of imitation. This Pharisaic view fitted in with the custom in force in Babylon or Galilee, and was borne out by Judas

---

20. The taking of Asochis is already mentioned in *War* 1.86, but without any allusion to the Sabbath. We cannot tell whether this detail is historical, but what matters here, is Josephus's concern, in this case and in his own activity, to attest to a consistent observance of the Sabbath, probably of a Pharisaic tendency. In this, he bears witness more to principles than to their actual application.

Maccabeus, but it did not fit in with the custom of the governing circles of Jerusalem, heirs at least apparent of Mattathias.

3. *Rabbinic Sources: Holy War*

Josephus had therefore blurred the specific problem of war on the Sabbath and, through it, that of the meaning of war, but without managing to obscure the importance of the 'model of Nehemiah'. For lack of more direct data,[21] I now try to clarify the question using rabbinic sources, since it became a matter for study in relation to the remembrance of ancient events. It is nevertheless necessary, in order to locate the problem of war on the Sabbath, to clarify first of all the status of war in general,[22] since, viewed from the religious angle, it should be connected with the Promised Land. Furthermore, this survey is going to provide useful insights on the epic of Judas Maccabeus.

At the moment when Judaea was being reconquered and the battle of Emmaus was beginning, 1 Macc. 3.50-60 relates that Judas prepared his troops by following fairly closely the procedures provided for in Deut. 20.1-9, a passage that might be qualified as a ritual for holy war. The Mishnah (*Sot.* 8.1), contrary to its custom of keeping a certain distance from the biblical text, offers a literal commentary on this passage:

> The Messiah of war [משוח מלחמה 'anointed of war'], at the moment of speaking to the people, it is in sacred language [בלשון הקדש] that he speaks, for it is said [שנאמר]: 'And when you will be [in the plural] [LXX "you will be" (in the singular)] ready for combat, the priest shall come forward'—it is the Messiah of war—'and he shall speak to the people'—in sacred language—'He shall say to them: Listen, Israel, you are today about to fight against your enemies'—and not against your brothers—'[...] may your heart not be faint, [...] for it is YHWH your God who marches with you to fight for you against your enemies, in order to save you'—this is the camp of the Ark.

21. R. de Vaux, *Ancient Israel* (New York: McGraw–Hill, 1961), pp. 258-67 assembles the biblical information on holy war. The *Rule of War* of Qumran (1QM) describes the eschatological war of the 'Sons of Light', with clear references to the Pentateuch; cf. M. Delcor, 'Qumrân: Livre de la Guerre', *DBSup*, 9 (1983), cols. 919-31; J. Duhaime, 'The War Scroll from Qumran and the Greco-Roman Tactical Treatises', *RQ* 13 (1988), pp. 133-51.

22. Here I take up again some details already developed in Nodet, 'La Dédicace, les Maccabées et le Messie', *RB* 93 (1986), pp. 321-75, but without referring to its conclusions, since the main points proposed there in regard to 1–2 Maccabees are very inaccurate.

This *pesher* presents some interesting features. First of all, it takes the form of an interlinear commentary, in which the explanations are inserted in the text, and this combination follows a brief introduction, with the transition being provided by the connective 'for it is said'. Such a formula is normally supposed to justify some assertion about a verse, but here it produces a defective sequence: it is not the passage cited from Deuteronomy which speaks of 'sacred language' or 'Messiah of war', but the commentaries which are inserted into it.[23] In other words, the authority cited, and therefore existing before the redaction of the Mishnah, is the totality formed by the text and its *pesher*. Moreover, the explanatory glosses clearly innovate in comparison to the text of Deuteronomy: in addition to the two phrases cited, which are not biblical, there is no mention in this text of the 'camp of the ark', and it is not formally forbidden for brothers to become enemies.

I begin with this last point, which has to do with civil war. After 'and not against your brothers', the Mishnah added a gloss, omitted above: 'Judah against Simeon or Simeon against Benjamin, for if you fall into their hands, they will be lenient with you, as it is said [2 Chron. 28.15, commenting on the Syro-Ephraimite war]: "The men [of Israel] […] took charge of the prisoners [from Judah] with the booty; they clothed those of them who were naked […] and took them back to their people." It is against your enemies that you will go, and if you fall into their hands they will not be lenient with you.'

If I understand this gloss correctly, it is trying to say that there is no reason to fear domination or conquest by compatriots, and therefore there is no need to conduct a defensive war against them. In other words, only a defensive war is being considered. There is no question here of a war of conquest like that of Joshua or a venture at territorial expansion, but it may be asked whether a war of liberation or of reconquest, like that of Judas Maccabeus in time of persecution, or even like that which Agrippa wanted to avoid, are comparable to a defensive war. Finally, it may be noted that the reinterpretation of the Syro-Ephraimite war (between Israel and Judah) is not pointless: biblical Judah and Benjamin correspond more or less with the Judaea of

---

23. The Talmud (*b. Soṭ.* 42a) saw clearly that the passage from Deuteronomy, when stripped of its *pesher*, proves nothing, and tries to complete it with another argument: in Exod. 19.19, it is said that Moses *spoke* and God answered through the 'voice', therefore in sacred language. Here the priest *speaks*, therefore, because of word similarity, in sacred language. The proof is a weak one, and we observe elsewhere (*Tosafot* הכי; cf. *y. Soṭ.* 8.1, p. 22b) that in the *Shema Israel* it is stated: '[…] and you *will speak* through them', and the same analogy could apply, since it is by the same words (*Shema Israel*) that the priest addresses the people. However, according to the list cited in *m. Soṭ.* 7.1, the *Shema* can be said in any language. The failure of the reasoning underlines the absence of a strictly biblical proof.

the repatriates (Ezra 1.5; etc.), and Simeon is the tribe barely visible in the midst of Judah (and approximately corresponding to Idumaea of later times). The problem of civil war is therefore closely linked to minority groups in Judaea (cf. Chapter 6, §4).

The leniency of compatriots is certainly more a wish than an actual fact: the text cited from 2 Chronicles follows a reference to the intervention of prophets, who, after a ferocious war between Judah and Israel, compelled the victors to be generous to the defeated. Indeed, civil war seemed a permanent threat: the Maccabaean crisis is to begin with internal, and a leitmotif of Josephus is that the great defeats suffered by the Jews were first and foremost caused by their internal divisions. One particular case is interesting in a different way: from the Hasmonaean period, Josephus refers to the civil war between Hyrcanus and Aristobulus (*Ant.*14.25-28; cf. *War* 1.127) and reports how the latter, besieged in Jerusalem, was defeated by his rival, thanks to the aid given by the Romans. The episode is reported in a different way in a *baraita* (*b. Soṭ.* 49b): the defender of the Temple was defeated by an elder who knew Greek wisdom; in this way worship was interrupted and the Law abolished. The victory of Hellenism over the Temple evidently recalled the crisis under Antiochus Epiphanes, but it recalled too Hyrcanus (or Janneus) going over to the side of the Sadducees, and the abolition of the Law (cf. Chapter 1, §5). The civil war had religious implications, but it was connected too with the acceptance or non-acceptance of foreign domination.

As for defensive war itself, it calls for the examination of other texts, which can be approached by way of a difficulty relative to Deut. 20.1-8: the procedure begins with a short speech by the priest to the people, imploring them not to be afraid. Then the officers or scribes (שׁוֹטרים, γραμματεῖς) intervene, asking those who have a new house, a new vineyard or a young wife to return to their homes. Lastly, they intervene a second time to dismiss those who are afraid. It can be maintained that it is somewhat illogical to encourage the fearful and then get rid of them. The Mishnah is silent about this difficulty, but a Tannaitic parallel (*baraita*, cited *b. Soṭ.* 42a-b), suggests a response, by distinguishing several phases:

> [The priest] speaks to them twice, first at the frontier [בספר[24]], then at the moment of battle, with the scribes serving as translators or a megaphone. The first time he says to them: 'Listen to the words of the military leaders [מערכי מלחמה] and return home'; before the battle he says to them: 'May your heart not weaken'.

24. This text has several parallels, with numerous variants; one of these has בספי, that is 'in sight of the battlefield' (or 'towards the scouts', בצופים), and not 'in a fixed place'; cf. S. Lieberman, *Tosefta kifshuṭah: A Comprehensive Commentary on the Tosefta* (8 vols.; New York: Jewish Theological Seminary of America, 1955–73), VIII, p. 687.

The obvious meaning of this text seems to be that it is a war of expansion, in which the army is going to be involved beyond the frontier, but there is nothing preventing it being interpreted as a crossing of the frontier in the opposite direction for a conquest or reconquest coming from the exterior. There was a tradition which interpreted in this same way Phinehas, son of Eleazar, son of Aaron, as an 'anointed of war' (*t. Soṭ.* 7.17, on Num. 31.6).[25]

An immediate problem which comes up however is that of the 'frontier', whether it was for coming in or going out. It could be the limit of Joshua's conquests, in which case a war of expansion beyond these borders is hardly realistic, at least in a religious perspective (Promised Land). It could be a somewhat reduced Judaea as well, such as that of Nehemiah or of Judas Maccabeus, which in width went from Emmaus (Amwas) to Jericho, and in length from Beth-zur to Bethel (Beitin) in which case the expansion would only be a reconquest.

For all wars are not alike, as Josephus implies. The Mishnah envisages several cases (*m. Soṭ.* 8.7):

> It is an optional [רשות] war about which there is question [in Deuteronomy, with the selection by the scribes], but for the prescribed [מצוה] war all should go out; R. Yehuda [bar Ilai] says: 'It is a prescribed war that is spoken about [in Deuteronomy], and it is for an obligatory [חובה] war that all go out.'

The three kinds of war named here seem difficult to define, since the Tosefta considers the Yehuda controversy to be purely verbal (*t. Soṭ.* 7.23): it merely plays on words, and therefore there would only be two categories. But even then the debate is not closed: for some, one is mandatory, limited to wars of conquest (Joshua, but also the campaigns against Amalek, Exod. 17.9 and Deut. 25.19), and the other is more contingent, to be decided by a Sanhedrin of seventy-one members (*m. Sanh.* 1.5); according to others, these two categories were, in the one case, the defensive war, which is mandatory without delay, and, in the other, the war of aggression, which is not mandatory (*t. Soṭ.* 8.7). The traditional commentators[26] considered that this last case was that of expansion beyond the borders. According to this system, however, one case remained undecided, that of a war of reconquest: there were no longer any clear criteria available to judge whether it was analogous to the wars of Joshua and therefore equally necessary, or whether it should be controlled by the Sanhedrin. This case, from the speech of Agrippa before the destruction of

25. A parallel (*S. 'Ol. R.* 18a) prudently introduces this view by 'Some say [יש אומרים]'; it is a debated opinion then, and we will see that it is opposed to that of Yehuda.

26. Maimonides, *Hilkot Melakhim* 7.2; cf. Lieberman, *Tosefta kifshuṭah*, VIII, p. 696.

Jerusalem up until the Tannaitic period, was the most grave, since it underlay several Jewish revolts against foreign domination, right up to the ultimate attempt at reconquest by Bar Kochba. The epic of Judas Maccabeus, as recounted in 1 Maccabees, formed at the same time the model and the literary background for these revolts. But the rabbinical sources discredited Bar Kochba's venture to such a degree that it is hard to explain how Aqiba, the undisputed master of the Mishnah, could have been in favour of him (*baraita* cited *y. Ta'an.* 4.7, p. 68d). It is not exaggerating to assume sharp controversies.[27] Although that may be so, the intervention of the Tosefta, reducing the cases from three to two for reasons said to be purely semantic, was really a major initiative, since it lessened the problem: the war of reconquest disappeared, and was not a precept.

The war of reconquest is poorly handled in the Mishnah, but a controversy over it is already evident in the differences in the presentation of Judas's war between 1 Maccabees and 2 Maccabees. According to 1 Macc. 2.1, the priest Mattathias fled from Jerusalem to settle in Modin, outside of Judaea, and as such this was the starting point, at least the literary one, of a route of reconquest toward Jerusalem. The decisive element, after Judas took command, was the capture of Emmaus, at the edge of the mountainous area of Judaea. Before the battle, the ritual that Judas followed conformed to Deuteronomy 20, as made clear by the *baraita* above calling for two interventions by the priest: after having organized the army (like Jethro, Exod. 18.21-22), he dismissed 'at the frontier' those who had another obligation to fulfill, then just before the battle he delivered a warlike discourse. Before that, the Torah had been solemnly read; then there was a collection of priestly offerings, a public prayer, and the sounding of trumpets (1 Macc. 3.46-54). It is therefore a prescribed (מצוה) war, carried out in conformity with the Law.

---

27. The following section of the *baraita* cited shows a violent dispute, at the time of the siege of Betar, between the Sages and Bar Kochba, and the town is captured when the latter end up assassinating the pious Eliezer of Modin, which reminds us of the martyrdom of Eliezer in 2 Macc. 6.18-31, killed by the Seleucids (or their Judaean representatives). In a slightly different context, the Haggada for Passover (ritual of the Passover meal) includes, after the account of the Exodus, an invitation to debate freely about the coming out from Egypt, and it is reported that four Sages, come to celebrate at the home of Aqiba at Bene-Beraq, continued the debate all night in a cave, far from their families. The historical context is the revolt of Bar Kochba, and it is hard to think that current events would have been absent from the debate, especially since Gamaliel, president of the Sanhedrin and known for his relations with the Romans, is notable by his absence; cf. M.M. Kasher, *Hagadah Shelemah: The Complete Passover Hagadah* (Jerusalem: Tora Shelema Institute, 1967), lines 70-76.

On the contrary, the parallel redaction in 2 Macc. 8.12-20, which contains comparable elements, avoids any appearance of conformity to any ritual emanating from the Law: there was no selection of combatants, Judas was merely a military leader and not a priest, and it was a defensive war, decided on in an atmosphere of panic. The reading of the 'Sacred Book' is mentioned, but in the context of an appeal to Providence, and the victory is finally obtained thanks to providential help, which could not constitute a precedent. This inevitable war is not the fulfillment of a particular precept and we encounter in it the two cases given by Yehuda, but not those of his opponents: the account in 2 Maccabees corresponds to his obligatory or inevitable (חובה) war, while for 1 Maccabees it is, as has been shown, a prescribed war. The two accounts therefore apply to the same war entirely different legal statutes. In this respect, it is striking that according to 2 Macc. 8.26-28, it would be precisely this inevitable war which breaks off just before the Sabbath: it was not then a formal precept which could invalidate other precepts.

As for Judas himself, it is important to determine whether he was a priest or not, since, according to Deut. 20.2, it is *the* priest (הכהן) who arouses the whole country, but his exact position in the hierarchy is not specified. It is not at all impossible that it is the high priest in person. On the other hand, it has been shown that there was a doubt about the priestly position of Judas, a doubt that Josephus tried to remove. But the Mishnah, commenting on this chapter on holy war, replaces the priest by an original person, the 'anointed of war', and it is not known at this stage whether it refers to an anointing *for* war, therefore before, or of an anointing *by* the war, namely, a consecration after the event.

Another passage of the Mishnah provides some important pieces of information (*m. Mak.* 2.6), attributing them to the same Yehuda bar Ilai as above: the death of the 'anointed of war' had the same effect as that of the high priest as far as the freeing of those guilty of involuntary murder went. This is a reference to cities of refuge, a Mosaic institution and a Levitical statute. In these cities, anyone who involuntarily killed someone had to take refuge to escape the 'avenger of blood', and he stayed there 'until the death of the high priest whom he has anointed [אשר משח אותו, LXX ὃν ἔχρισαν] with holy oil' (Num. 35.25). This final clause of the verse is a curious gloss, in which you hardly know who did the anointing: 'he' in the MT; 'someone' in the LXX. The question then is to know whether the 'anointed of war' had this role when he had a high priest over him, who anointed him (or named him) *for* the war, as in the example mentioned above where Phineas coexisted with Aaron his grandfather, then with Eleazar his father, or when he was alone. Examination of the context of the Mishnah cited proves that the death of the 'anointed of war' had the desired effect only in the absence of the high priest, but that at the same time there must be a high priest. That seems contradictory, but the inevitable conclusion was still, for Yehuda, that the 'anointed of war' filled the role of high priest, at least to a certain extent. We must then imagine circumstances in which the nomination of the high priest was impossible, but there was the possibility of the promotion of an 'anointed of war', who took his place, though the ritual anointing would be important. These circumstances are remarkably close to those of Judas Maccabeus who would then be 'anointed *by* the war' or, as Josephus says, elected high priest by acclamation of the people after the reconquest of the Temple.

What the two ways of understanding the 'anointed of war'[28] have in common is that they make him unreal, at least according to the Mishnah's way of seeing things. In one case there would have to have been a high priest over him; in the other, there was needed a triumphant *recital* about a war, interpreted as a holy war. But the Mishnah was unaware of any procedure for nominating a high priest and did not seem to care particularly about accounts of holy war. That amounts to saying that holy war was nothing more than a subject for study.[29] As for the book of 1 Maccabees, while it was no longer in the sacred library, its suppression had left some traces behind, coupled with censures. The sayings of Yehuda, disciple of Aqiba and therefore later

28. A *baraita* (*b. Soṭ.* 42a), commenting on Deuteronomy 20, ignores the idea of 'the anointed of war', and simply says that the priest who speaks to the people should be appointed (ממונה), but it does not specify by whom (probably not by a foreign authority); he is not then high priest himself. With the same point of view, another *baraita* (*b. Hor.* 13a) points out that only the high priest can receive the anointing. These two texts are therefore opposed to the idea of the direct anointing of 'the anointed of war'. From another angle, 'the anointed of war', according to *t. Hor.* 2.10, has a rank between the high priest and his substitute (סגן, who replaces him in case of an unexpected blemish; cf. *m. Yom.* 3.9); he is still not quite a high priest, however, since he is not bound to the perpetual offering of wheat flour (*y. Hor.* 3.3, p. 47c-d; cf. Lev. 6.13).

29. This lack of realism is equally striking in other syntheses drawn from 1 Maccabees and Greek sources, for example, Maimonides, *Hilkot Melakhim*, 7.1: 'The prescribed war and the optional war follow the same procedures: a priest is picked to speak to the people, and he is anointed with oil; it is he who is called Anointed of War'; it is not stated who consecrates him, and the oil of anointing of Aaron and Eleazar had disappeared since the First Temple.

than the defeat of Bar Kochba, can only be explained through this book, but they have subsequently undergone some tampering, cutting them off from their source, which had become proscribed.[30] On the other hand, it should be pointed out that even if this book was originally a piece of Hasmonaean propaganda, this fact no longer has any importance here: already in the case of Josephus it had become, after the ruin of the Temple, a source on the fringe of the sacred library, freed from the conditions of its formation, namely, presenting a sort of model of the holy war.

One final detail of the Mishnaic commentary on holy war accentuates again its lack of realism: the divine accompaniment in battle (Deut. 20.4: 'YHWH your God goes with you to fight for you') was represented by the Ark, or, more exactly, the Israelite army was effectively sustained, since 'it is the camp of the Ark'. The Tosefta (*t. Sot.* 7.17-19) filled out this declaration by furnishing information drawn from the accounts of the wandering in the desert: the Ark contained the divine name (and all its titles), with the tablets of the Law (Num. 31.6: 'Moses sent [...] the sacred vessels'); according to another opinion, there were two arks, one in the camp, one in front (Num. 10.33: 'and the ark of the covenant of God marched three days in front'), and so on.[31] The scene was thus transported back to the times of Moses and Joshua. The Mishnah did not go this far, but it called for an ark, the sole guarantee that God would be at the side of the combatants. The criteria applied also for civil war, in which there could only be one 'camp of the Ark', in the same way as for the reconquest. For want of the ark, and such was the case during the period of the Second Temple,[32] there was no legitimacy to war being of divine inspiration, and it was recognized that even the campaign of Judas Maccabeus could only be validated after the event: he was really consecrated *by* the war.

It must be admitted then that this 'anointed of war', in the person of Judas, was a literary and not a historical entity. On the one hand,

30. Cf. *m. Sanh.* 11.1: 'All Israel has a part in the Kingdom that is to come, except [...] those who read the outside [חיצונים] books'; this refers to the apocryphal books, rejected to the outside, among which 1 Maccabees certainly figures prominently, since Origen (cited by Eusebius, *Historia Ecclesiastica* 6.25.2), besides the 22 books of the canon, draws attention to one unique book 'on the exterior', that of the Maccabees, to which he gives a Hebrew title; it is still close to the official corpus. Cf. S.Z. Leiman, *The Canonization of Hebrew Scripture* (Transactions of the Connecticut Academy of Arts, 47; Hamden: Archon Books, 1976), p. 159 n. 229, discussed in *RB* 92 (1985), pp. 589-96. Cf. Chapter 6, §1.

31. Various texts indicate, with several variants, that these arks contain the pieces of the first tablets of the law, the second tablets, the Torah scroll or the vestments of the high priest; cf. Lieberman, *Tosefta kifshutah*, VIII, p. 686.

32. In this regard, it is striking that on certain coins of the Jewish state established by Bar Kochba there is represented a sanctuary (*temenos*), with the silhouette of the ark clearly visible (with cherubim); cf. L. Mildenberg, *The Coinage of the Bar Kokhba War* (Typos, 6; Frankfurt am Main: Sauerländer, 1984), Large Silver Series, nn. 1-104.

according to 1 Macc. 2.66, Mattathias before dying named Judas general of his armies, and this could not be considered an anointing, which in any case had disappeared with the First Temple, nor could it mean that Judas would have in some way at this moment been made a substitute for the high priest for legal effects. All this became true only after a consecration by the victory. But, on the other hand, Judas presided at the starting up of the holy war in such forms as if he had the priestly qualifications or the requisite anointing. There was then, on the level of the unfolding of events, a contradiction. In other words, the presentation of a holy war according to Deuteronomy 20 was a literary reconstruction arising from the success of the campaign, which then became *after the event* a cultic success, for which Judas had not been expressly qualified at the beginning. The result, according to this interpretation, was that the strange designation 'anointed of war', which in that case became simple and clear, was a reconstruction *ex post factum*, to qualify an atypical case due to the absence of any visible or acceptable high priest (at least in literary terms, in 1 Maccabees, since 2 Maccabees drew attention to high priests). One of the good points about this reconstruction is that the historical question of ascertaining whether Judas was really a priest becomes secondary, but the least we can say here is that the doubt expressed in regard to this is not cleared up.

4. *Rabbinic Sources: The Sabbath and War*

The book of Jubilees, which is entirely centred on the Sabbath, issues an absolute prohibition: whoever takes up arms on the Sabbath is punishable by death (50.12), as if it involved a profanation similar to other forbidden activities, for which the sanction was stoning (Num. 15.32). The context of Mattathias's decision according to 1 Maccabees leads one to surmise a prohibition just as strong, even if the penalty is not indicated there.

The controversy which emerges from the comparison of 1 Maccabees and 2 Maccabees is found clearly expressed in the Mishnah, which begins by prohibiting going out (לא יצא) on the Sabbath with arms, whether for defence or offence. Eliezer then objects that arms are ornaments (תכשיטים), but the sages retort that they are instead a disgrace, for it is written (Isa. 2.4): 'They broke their swords to make them into plowshares and their spears to make them into sickles. They will no longer lift a sword nation against nation, they will no longer learn to make war' (*m. Šab.* 6.4).

This passage, however, was not concerned with actual armed action, but only with the symbolic meaning of the simple fact of bearing arms outside one's home, since another text dealt specifically with questions of actual defence:

> If the nations (גוים) advance on the towns of Israel, the people should go out armed against them and because of them profane the Sabbath. In what circumstances? When they threaten the lives [...] If they advance on towns near the frontier (הסמוכות לספר), even if it is to collect straw, the people should go out armed (*t. 'Erub.* 3[4].5).

It is clearly a matter of national and territorial defence, against military activity or looting by armed bands.

The parallel recensions have some variations. The Babylonian Talmud took an opposite starting point (*b. 'Erub.* 45a), while appearing to give the same directions:

> If foreigners besiege the towns of Israel, the people do not go out against them armed, and do not profane the Sabbath because of them. What case is involved? When they come to steal; but if they come to kill, the people go out against them armed, and profane the Sabbath because of them...

The issue to be interpreted just limited a permission in the first case, and toned down a prohibition in the second. There were therefore originally two conflicting formulations of the licit reaction to the attack of foreigners, and just before this text there is cited a Babylonian formulation giving a blunt prohibition, without the usual casuistry: 'Yehuda relates that Rab says: "If foreigners attack the towns of Israel, the people should not go out against them armed nor profane the Sabbath".'

The analytical explanations which had the effect of reducing the two sayings one to the other according to a usual rabbinic method, should be considered secondary, even if the parallel in the Jerusalem Talmud[33] gives a synthesis which leaves no room for the distinction between a primitive text and its commentary.

The passages examined provide therefore a 'Judaean view', according to which armed defence on the Sabbath was licit, as opposed to a 'Babylonian' view,[34] in which it was not. So we meet again the elements

33. *y. 'Erub.* 4.3, p. 21d: 'If the nations come against the towns near the frontier even to take straw, even wood, the people should go out against them armed, and afterwards bring back the arms to their place; if it is against towns in the interior, they do not go out armed, unless there is a threat of death.'

34. The next section of the Talmud comments on the complete *baraita*, and not

extracted above from Josephus, according to which the decision of Mattathias was valid for Judaea, but not for Babylon, judging by the story of Anileus and Asineus.

It is interesting to observe besides that the 'Babylonian' doctrine was attributed to Rab, the authority who had brought the Mishnah from Galilee to Babylon, and had founded there the Academy of Sura, at the beginning of the third century CE. Now, all the versions cited have the status of *baraita*, consequently annexed Tannaitic traditions, while the Mishnah, the only official authoritative compilation, was silent on this question, or rather only knew the general case of danger of death, which took precedence over all other precepts. Every action likely to save lives ought to be undertaken (נפש חקום), and besides 'the one who returns after a life-saving operation can bring back with him his equipment' (*m. Roš Haš.* 4.5).

In that case the question arises whether the possibility of fortifications played a role, dispensing from the immediate use of arms on the Sabbath, as is evident from the testimony of Josephus. The Tosefta quoted above continued by pointing out a change in usage:

In the past they deposited the arms in premises near the rampart, but it happened one day when they went for them that they jostled one another in taking their arms, and they killed one another; it was decreed right away that each was to take his arms home.

For lack of a more precise context, the exact meaning of this text is obscure;[35] perhaps it was about a raid outside the town against an aggressor in the surrounding country, but the important thing is that it referred to a wall, and that a particular indication would have been given if it was not about Jerusalem.

Another case drew attention to the poorly defended town or village (*m. 'Erub* 3.5). A condition can be put on its 'extension of territory on the Sabbath' (ערובו): 'If foreigners (גוים) come from the east, my extension will be to the west [...].' It seems to involve the organization of the withdrawal in case of an attack, but another version of the same text (designated *b. 'Erub.* 36b as coming from Palestine), said on the contrary that the stated condition is to carry out the extension in the direction from which the foreigners come. A formal solution to the contradiction was then proposed: the two versions can both be valid at the same time according to whether the

the brief form of *Rab*. Thus Nehardea (Neerda of the story of Anileus, the site of the rival academy of Shemuel) is assimilated to the towns close to the frontier, and the development is illustrated by 1 Sam. 23.1-2, where David sets out to fight the Philistines who have attacked a threshing floor at Keila. The technical interest in this text is that it links up the question of the defence of territory on the Sabbath to the wars of David (cf. *Tosafot* א).

35. Cf. Lieberman, *Tosefta kifshuṭah*, III, p. 342.

foreigners in question are friends or enemies, without any allusion to an actual war situation, since it is a matter of keeping the Sabbath displacement within the law. Nevertheless, this Mishnah has a literary connection to the Tosefta quoted on 'the foreigners who come', where it definitely is a question of war, and the two forms transmitted (to flee the enemy or go to meet him) correspond well to the two opposing forms of the *baraita* singled out: permission or not to go out armed on the Sabbath. The controversy remains present, but there are no walls: it is therefore necessary to allow for a displacement, in one direction or the other.

All the actual cases examined involved defensive action, in the face of a move by an opponent, and the confrontation of two points of view came up regularly. For some, the permission to fight on the Sabbath was linked to the defence of territorial integrity and economic goods: it proceeded therefore from the consideration of a national political responsibility for the dimensions of a region too extensive practically to be surrounded by a wall. For others, on the contrary, the well-balanced prohibition is connected rather to the concept of the life of a minority, on the border, facing the covetousness of the powerful. In this connection, there was a remarkable blurring of the model of Nehemiah, centred on the city, whose walls allowed at the same time for political autonomy and a defence without arms on the Sabbath. In fact, for the masters of the Mishnah, the times had changed, and Jerusalem as a free city was far away: on the one hand, there remained a remembrance (idealized) of the Hasmonaean or Herodian state, whence the permissive tradition; on the other, the real situation of the Jews of Galilee, after the defeat of Bar Kochba in the second century CE and the *damning of his memory*, involved a largely rural existence without proper defence and completely submissive to the Roman power, whence the restrictive tradition.

As for offensive war, it seemed to be entirely proscribed on the Sabbath in the Hellenistic period, even in Judaea. It was clearly not included in the decision of Mattathias nor in the grounds for that decision, and there is no literary trace of it elsewhere, since even the assault on Gezer, in 2 Macc. 10.33 lasted only five days. The expansionism of John Hyrcanus or Herod was not a model to be followed.

Later on, an authorization attributed to Shammai the Elder developed: 'You must not mount an attack on a foreigner's town less than three days before the Sabbath.'[36] There is a commentary on this declaration (*baraita, y. Šab.* 1.8, p. 4a-b): 'What you

---

36. This text is handed down in several forms, with varying difficulties (in particular an indecisiveness about terminology on the *compulsory* or *prescribed* war; cf. above, §3); cf. Herr, 'Problem of War', pp. 249-52, and Lieberman, *Tosefta kifshutah*, III, pp. 342-43.

speak of is optional war, but in the case of compulsory war it is allowed even on the Sabbath, for we find that Jericho was besieged specifically on a Sabbath, and it is written (Deut. 20.20): "[...] until it falls", *therefore even on the Sabbath* war was permitted'. The parallels show that the biblical support is not found in what is connected to Shammai, but is the work of a Tannaitic teacher, Yashya. On the other hand, it is hard, if we retain the attribution to Shammai, to see the occasion of such a teaching in the time of Herod or Archelaus. This could be a taking into account by tradition—in the beginning not necessarily Pharisaic—of more ancient events, such as the wars of Alexander Janneus, by way of a rereading of history by the Pharisees, at a time when their influence was increasing.[37]

If this teaching is an innovation, even a decree, which the text does not claim, the only agitation which would have had a real posterity (and in a variety of forms) in this period was the movement of Judas the Galilean: in *War* 2.56, Judas, son of Ezechiah, from Sepphoris in Galilee, organizes a religious movement, but the uprising is put down by Varus, come in haste from neighbouring Syria (2.68). Later (2.117), after the reign of Archelaus, Judas the Galilean—this title supposed him known in Judaea—is presented as the instigator of a religiously inspired resistance movement and there is no indication of its repression. It would be a matter of a doublet,[38] presenting two opposing points of view on the same events. Here we have the origin of the Zealots, and later of the 'Fourth Philosophy', which Josephus finally declared close to the doctrine of the Pharisees, no doubt reluctantly. A connection of these events with Shammai is suggestive, but unverifiable, all the more so since it is not proved that the attribution to Shammai of the opinion referred to might not have occurred later on (cf. Chapter 7, §3).

Whatever its possible relationship with Janneus or the Zealots, the significant fact for our purpose is precisely the attribution to Shammai. Even if the subsequent *halakha* actually depended on this story, it was indicated to begin with that it was not from the majority school of Hillel, and besides it is not in the Mishnah, but in the collection of outside traditions (*baraita*). Moreover, whatever might have been the ups and downs of an armed Jewish force in Judaea after the ruin of the Temple, it should be noted that the teaching presented on offensive warfare, including the question of the Sabbath, is connected to the accounts of Joshua's campaigns, especially to the taking of Jericho, since that operation lasted seven consecutive days, and remains in the sphere of influence of the precept of holy war (Deut. 20). Whether it was a matter of practical urgency or not, the important thing to note is the effort to unify the oral tradition transmitted (Shammai) and the Bible, by means of a reflection on the inner coherence of the Bible itself, since the precepts in regard to the Sabbath do not agree spontaneously with the accounts of long wars.

37. Herr, 'Problem of War', p. 253, following G. Alon, *Jews, Judaism and the Classical World: Studies in Jewish History in the Times of the Second Temple and the Talmud* (Jerusalem: Magnes, 1977), pp. 18-47.

38. Cf. Schürer, 'Zu II Macc. 6,7', I, p. 48-52, and M. Hengel, *Die Zeloten: Untersuchungen zur jüdischen Freiheitsbewegung in der Zeit von Herodes I bis 70 n, Chr.* (AGSU, 1; Leiden: Brill, 1961), pp. 337.

A final point will clarify a little more the chronological problem of the changes undergone in the practice of the Sabbath between ancient times and the Maccabees: it is the matter of Jewish mercenaries in foreign armies, which is closely connected to the Sabbath. In the account of Alexander's visit to Jerusalem, he promised those who wanted to enlist in his army that they could follow their ancestral laws (τοῖς πατρίοις ἔθεσιν), and a great number accepted (*Ant.* 11.339). Later, in the *Letter of Aristeas*, which Josephus quotes (12.47), Ptolemy II, writing to Eleazar the high priest to request the translation of the Law, congratulates himself on having recruited for his army the best of the Jews living in his kingdom. Whatever the truth of these documents, they at least contain a rumour, difficult to date, pointing to the voluntary presence of Jews in Greek armies, and it is hard to see how the Sabbath, and the prohibition of carrying arms and marching (cf. *Ant.* 13.252), could be observed. Later on in fact, in the time of Hyrcanus II, a request to Dolabella, governor of Asia, to dispense the Jews from serving in the army, is officially approved (around 40 BCE) and the decree quoted by Josephus (14.226) expressly declares that such service is incompatible with the Sabbath, because of the carrying of arms and the travelling. Other decrees of the same period point in the same direction, and Roman historians confirm that the Jews were conscientious objectors.[39] The problem raised by these decrees is to determine whether they are not the trace of new privileges, following on a reform with a Pharisaic touch. Politically, Rome could have an interest in implementing such measures, as a way to keep the Jews disarmed, especially if they were under the influence of reformers arrived from the hostile Parthian kingdom.

The amount of information prior to the first century BCE is not great, but there is enough to draw attention to the disturbing case of the Greek armies, even if the difficult instance of the military colonies of the Samaritans in Egypt (*Ant.* 11.345 and 12.7) is disregarded. It is hard to believe that these armies were considered better than the Roman army for those observant of the Sabbath. Must it be concluded that in this

---

39. *Ant.* 14.228-232, 234, 236-40; 16.27-60 (a persecution of the Jews of Ionia stopped by Herod; it included enlistment in the army); 18.81-85 (expulsion of Jews from Rome after the Fulvia affair; some at that time preferred martyrdom to forced enlistment in the Roman army). Tacitus, *Annales* 2.85 (expulsion from Rome under Tiberius, in 19 CE) and Suetonius, *Tiberius* §36, testify—disapprovingly—to the same refusal to enlist; cf. discussion of the sources in Stern, *Greek and Latin Authors*, II, pp. 69-73.

more remote period the Jews did not observe it, or observed it less strictly than later on? The taking of Jerusalem during a Sabbath under Ptolemy Lagos, as recounted by Agatharchides of Cnide (cf. above, §1), and reported by Josephus *before* the *Letter of Aristeas*, tends to show the observance as ancient. There is a contradiction therefore, which could explain Josephus's uneasiness.

5. *Conclusions*

The investigation carried out in this chapter leads to useful results, which brings us back once again to the activities of Judas Maccabeus. Let us begin with the last point discussed.

1.   The contradiction between the history of Agatharchides and the ease with which the Jews fitted into the Egyptian army can easily be disposed of: *they were not the same Jews.* Even if the episode about the taking of Jerusalem is probably an anachronism, as has been suggested, the important difference is that in the latter case the Jews were complying with the 'model of Nehemiah', while in Egypt they ignored it. It certainly will not do to consider these latter as Jews of loose morals, since according to *Ant.* 11.339 they could enlist while retaining all their customs. For greater clarity, I call these from now on 'Judaeans'.

2.   The decision of Mattathias was in reality an innovation, but it was subject to dispute, as is evident in the contrast between 1 and 2 Maccabees. The prototype was always the city of Nehemiah, but it could only be one of its quarters, since the defence by means of the walls was valued more than the Temple. The crisis brought into conflict Jews and Judaeans, but in circumstances which are still to be investigated, there came a time when Judas the observant, therefore with him the Jews, reached the Temple.

3.   The resistance of the Jews of the Diaspora to enlistment, which came up in an acrimonious way at the end of the Hasmonaean period, should be brought into relationship with the growing power of the Pharisees at that same time or a little before, since they 'ended up imposing on the people their ways of doing things', perhaps through itinerant preachers (cf. Acts 15.21). The result of this was a reconciliation that needs to be examined of 'Jews', Pharisees and the Judas of 2 Maccabees.

4.   The rabbinic traditions, compiled from around 200 CE, were separated from these events by two major disruptions: the destruction of the Temple, which certainly contributed to magnifying its veneration, and

the definitive failure of Bar Kochba, that is to say of the 'fourth philosophy' of Josephus. Correlatively, the sources, where we rediscover at the same time traces of the controversy represented by 1 Maccabees and 2 Maccabees, were affected by two series of transformations: the first, perhaps following the book of 1 Maccabees, restored a certain lustre to the Hasmonaean dynasty, at least in its beginning (by contrast with Herod, who constituted a sort of foil). The second watered down a little bit the problem of the war of reconquest, by treating war in general as an object of study, and, from a more practical point of view, by grouping together all the occasions of breaking the Sabbath to deal with a threat under the unique rubric of 'danger of death'. These developments in the tradition were under the influence as well of two important factors: on the one hand, the special living conditions in Galilee in the second century, that is to say, after the expulsion of the Jews of Judaea; and on the other hand the necessity of seeing the whole Bible as homogeneous: it was necessary then to show that the Sabbath, as set out in the written Torah, had effectively regulated the whole of life—including war—from Moses to the Exile.

5.   This last remark in fact raises a problem: even a cursory reading of the biblical passages (from the Pentateuch to Nehemiah) expressly pertaining to the Sabbath gives an immediate impression, to repeat the distinction mentioned before, that the Jews observed it, but the Judaeans did not, with the Israelites and Samaritans being a special case still to be cleared up. The issue then is whether this is just one more manifestation of the periodic alternation between the observant and the worldly, as desired by many commentators, of whom M. Smith is the most extreme, or whether these Jews with Judas did not constitute the first emergence in a socially perceptible and contentious way of what had been until then only a small group, fervent but marginal, although perhaps ancient.

6.   To formulate a hypothesis on this last point, which brings up for discussion the redaction and promulgation of the Bible, it should be observed in the first place that 1 Maccabees and 2 Maccabees give some coverage to the sacred library: according to 2 Macc. 2.13-14, Nehemiah established a library, and Judas Maccabeus reconstituted it. According to 1 Macc. 12.9, Jonathan, the first Hasmonaean high priest, declared that he no longer really needed, as his predecessor Onias formerly did, a treaty of friendship with the Spartans, 'having for consolation [παράκλησιν] the holy books'. Josephus (*Ant.* 13.167) tones down the formula: 'Meanwhile we have no more need of this demonstration,

because of the conviction [διὰ τὸ [...] πεπιστεῦσθαι] stemming from our holy books.' This text and documents associated with it pose different historical problems on the relations between Judaea and Sparta or Greece,[40] but relevant here is the reference to new facts relative to authoritative writings, one of whose fundamental roles is to attest to the antiquity of a culture:[41] a new state of affairs for the Bible, or rather the sacred library, had become evident.

7. This new state of affairs should be compared with the 'model of Nehemiah' and with the debates over the exploits of Judas, in which the 'Jewish' observance of the weekly Sabbath played an essential role. The Hexateuch as a whole can with great difficulty be considered the work of Nehemiah–Judas, since on the one hand the narrative part superbly ignores Jerusalem and very largely gravitates around Shechem and Mount Gerizim and therefore applies more to the Samaritans then to Judaea, and on the other hand the Babylonian model of the Sabbath, close to that of Nehemiah, does not agree with the basic biblical ideas. Some of the accounts referred to above indicate besides that these same Samaritans, although attached to the Pentateuch, denied that they observed the Sabbath like the Jews, at least in the time of Antiochus IV, as if the Sabbath precept had no further force. In dispensing with the biblical narratives then, it is advisable to examine the legislative sections, especially those dealing with the Sabbath: Is it possible to picture a Pentateuch without the weekly Sabbath of the Creation?

40. Cf. A.R.C. Leaney, 'Greek Manuscripts from the Judaean Desert', in J.K. Eliott (ed.), *Studies in New Testament Language and Texts* (Festschrift G.D. Kilpatrick; NovTSup, 44; Leiden: Brill, 1976), pp. 283-300. The replacement of fraternal friendship with Sparta by the 'holy books' was an evaluation in terms of a pursuit of antiquity. Cf. Chapter 6, §7.

41. Cf. the summary of apologetic principles from the Hellenistic and Roman periods in A.J. Droge, *Homer or Moses?* (Hermeneutische Untersuchungen zur Theologie, 26; Tübingen: Mohr [Paul Siebeck], 1989), pp. 12-35. Cf. also E. Nodet, 'Flavius Josèphe: Création et histoire', *RB* 100 (1993), pp. 5-40.

Chapter 3

THE SABBATH IN THE BIBLE

Many biblical texts deal with the Sabbath, or at least mention it. A great majority of them are connected, directly or indirectly with the week and the weekly rest, and we must associate with these the Sabbatical Year, since it is described in similar terms. Some passages more or less clearly designate as Sabbath the feasts defined as full moon by the lunar calendar, that is, falling on the 14th or 15th of the month: the Passover of 14th Nisan (Lev. 23.10) and the feast of Booths 15th Tishri (23.39). Similarly, certain passages in the Prophets associate the Sabbath with the New Moon (חדשׁ, LXX νουμηνία), as a festival following the new moon (Isa. 1.13; 66.23; Hos. 2.11; Amos 8.5). There is a suspicion then that the same term covers different solemnities, more or less unified as a result of the work of redactors in favour of the dominant weekly Sabbath.

Two external details especially call for a thorough examination: on the one hand, in the preceding chapter it became evident that the weekly Sabbath, based on the rest of the seventh day, was well adapted to what has been called the city of Nehemiah, but fitted in poorly with the accounts of wars in ancient times; on the other hand, the famous calendar found in *Jubilees* divided the solar year (of 364 days) into four seasons of thirteen weeks, with each season always beginning on the fourth day of the week, namely, a Wednesday. This calendar therefore in principle fixed the first full moon of each quarter on a Wednesday, and in particular Passover and the Feast of Booths on a Wednesday, in the first and third quarter. But Wednesday, according to the Creation account, is precisely the day of the moon, which determines the time of feasts.[1] There was consequently some competition between a weekly system of the Sabbath and a lunar system which comes up again in the dual motive for the fourth commandment of the Decalogue: in Exod. 20.11,

---

1.   Cf. A. Jaubert, *La date de la Cène: Calendrier biblique et liturgie chrétienne* (EBib; Paris: Gabalda, 1957), pp. 23-36.

the remembrance of the Sabbath is clearly linked to the work of Creation in seven days, but in Deut. 5.15, the observance of the Sabbath, said to be weekly, seems nevertheless to be put in relationship with the remembrance of the coming out from Egypt, therefore with Passover or the Feast of Unleavened Bread, that is to say, with a full moon.

These questions have long been debated, but most often starting from considerations internal to the Bible. The traditional position tends to consider these lunar allusions as unproved, or at best as residues from earlier times. This position is really based, however, on the assertion that the weekly Sabbath is very ancient in Israel: it is in fact found in the Decalogue, the Elohist Covenant Code (Exod. 23.12), the Yahwist Code (Exod. 34.21) and the Priestly Code (Exod. 31.12-17). Its presence in such divergent traditions is a good argument to show that it was in existence prior to their separation,[2] even if it must be conceded that the texts presuppose a considerable evolution between the practice in the monarchical period and the new views that came up during the Exile because of the disappearance of the Temple. It is advisable therefore to begin by taking a bearing on this subject, before attempting to confirm the proposed hypothesis of a Pentateuch without a weekly Sabbath, in relation to the newness of Mattathias's decision and to the special characteristics of the Samaritans of Shechem.

1. *The Sabbath: Full Moon or Saturday?*

Before dealing with the Pentateuch for its own sake as well as for the problems in its legislation, let us consider the passing allusions to the Sabbath in the Prophets, both the Early Prophets and the Latter Prophets. The texts referred to above suggest a comparison with the full moon, and Isa. 1.13 expressly alludes to sacrifices. In the Elisha cycle, the husband of the woman from Shunem was astonished that she would want to go and see the prophet at Mount Carmel on a day that was neither a New Moon nor a Sabbath (2 Kgs 4.23-24). It is clear then that a trip to a sanctuary was usual only on these feasts. The sanctuary (of YHWH in Jerusalem) was again the setting in the capture of Athalia (2 Kgs 11) on a Sabbath when the guard coming on duty and the guard being relieved could be present together. In all these accounts, no allusion is made to the seventh day, but it was a matter of a sanctuary, in a

---

2.   A good example is the characteristic reasoning of de Vaux, *Ancient Israel*, pp. 479-80.

city or not, of consultation of a prophet and of a trip outside the home, all of which clash with the weekly Sabbath, for which it had been prescribed (Exod. 16.29): 'On the seventh day no one is to leave home.'

All the texts mentioned, no matter what the date of their final redaction, were connected to the history of the period of the monarchy, and the constitutive elements of this Sabbath, which could be called lunar, did not indicate any difference between Israel and Judah. Nevertheless, as the institution was only mentioned, but not defined, we cannot know whether the pieces of information gleaned here and there form a coherent whole, and it is natural, in order to clarify a general view obtained by simple addition, to search for parallels from the same period in the Near East.[3]

For a century the Sabbath has been compared to Babylonian *šabattum* or *šapattum*, which designated the 15th day of the lunar month, and in general this means the full moon; it was also the 'day to rest the heart' *(um nuḥ libbi)*. We have at our disposal very ancient records of this day and its name from the Old Babylonian period, but we do not know too much about what celebrations could have been attached to it. The special designation, whose origin is not otherwise made clear,[4] leads one however to think that there was really a minimum of ritual.[5]

---

3.   I am using here the documents assembled by A. Lemaire, 'Le sabbat à l'époque royale israélite', *RB* 80 (1973), pp. 161-85. For the extra-biblical sources, see H. and J. Lewy, 'The Origin of the Week and the Oldest West Asiatic Calendar', HUCA 17 (1943), pp. 1-152.

4.   An attempt has been made to see in it a distortion of a feminine dual *šab'antum* ('two times seven'), but the purely numerical sense is without doubt secondary, and 'seven' exists under the form *šibitum*; the comparison with the verb *šabatu*, 'to conclude' (synonym of *gamaru*) gives a better meaning (completion of growth), but the derivation is not typical. See M. Jastrow, *Hebrew and Babylonian Traditions* (London: Fisher-Unwin, 1914), pp. 134-37, who proposes שבתון, 'celebration of the Sabbath', as the most exact equivalent of *šabattum*. Lemaire 'Le sabbat', pp. 173-78, prefers the Aramaic usage, attested as early as the Elephantine papyri, of connecting *šabbat* and *šabattum* to the binary root *šbb*, 'to grow, increase', which fits in with the full moon.

5.   Cf. B. Landsberger, *Der kultische Kalender der Babylonier und Assyrer* (Leipziger Semitische Studien, 6; Leipzig: Hinrichs, 1915), pp. 131-36. At Ugarit too, we find traces of a cult of the new moon (*ym ḥdt*) and of the full moon (*ym mlat*), on the fifteenth day; cf. P. Xella, *I testi rituali di Ugarit, I* (Studi Semitici, 54; Rome: Consiglio Nazionale di Ricerca, 1981), pp. 42, 49, 55. Other names for the full moon come up in diverse but converging occurrences: *ksa* in Ugaritic (Xella, *Testi rituali*, p. 216); *bks'm* (= בכסאם, in the plural) in a Phoenician inscription from

Furthermore, a Mesopotamian astrological tradition, not attested earlier than the seventh century BCE, drew attention to some 'dangerous days', the 7th, 14th, 19th, 21st, 28th days of the month, in which the 19th was merely the 49th of the preceding month. The septennial rhythm is clear, and apparently was connected with the four phases of the moon, but in no way was it associated with the name *shabattum*. The comparison of this computation with the weekly Sabbath has of course been made, but the problem is to insert the evolution of the dominant meaning of 'Sabbath', from the full moon to seventh day, into the history of the Israelite religion. In fact, scholars have pointed to an upheaval in regard to the calendar, for which they have attempted to settle on a date between 622, date of the publication of Deuteronomy (under Josiah), which still used the ancient Canaanite system in which the months had names, and 587, date of the fall of Jerusalem, in which the months were named by ordinal numbers and in which the beginning of the year passed from September to April. If we accept these dates as secure, the most cogent hypothesis would settle on a date for the change about 604, following the battle of Carchemish, which marks the beginning of Babylonian supremacy over Syria-Palestine.[6] Another component of this change at that time would have been the development of the weekly system, used to begin with perhaps for the period of seven weeks leading up to the Feast of Weeks, then generalized to the detriment of the feast of the new moon; and the priestly redaction, which insisted on the seventh day to the extent of making it go back to Creation, is only properly understood if there was something new there, which provided a context for the energetic measures which Nehemiah took to enforce the Sabbath rest.

This general view, which in its main points is the presentation of André Lemaire,[7] has the advantage of accentuating the appearance of a new institution, but some obscurities remain: in the first place, certain

Cyprus: cf. H. Donner and W. Röllig, *Kanaanäische und aramäische Inschriften* (3 vols.; Wiesbaden: Otto Harassowitz, 1966–69), n. 43; כסא in the Bible, in Prov. 7.20 and Ps. 81.4, texts difficult to date.

6. Cf. Lemaire, 'Le sabbat', p. 175, making use of E. Auerbach, in particular 'Der Wechsel des Jahres-Anfang in Juda im Lichte der neugefundenen babylonischen Chronik', *VT* 9 (1959), pp. 113-21.

7. See also A. Lemaire, 'Le Décalogue: Essai d'histoire de la rédaction', in A. Caquot and M. Delcor (eds.), *Mélanges bibliques et Orientaux en l'honneur de H. Cazelles* (AOAT, 212; Neukirchen–Vluyn: Neukirchener Verlag, 1981), pp. 259-85.

texts imply that not only the change in calendar was pre-exilic, but also the origin of the regulation on the seventh day.[8] It follows from this then that Nehemiah's reform, especially in the light of what has been said in ch. 1, where we saw in particular that he was not inspired by any precedent, is not very intelligible at such a late period, since it is hard to see to what 'law of Moses' his adversaries or his predecessors could be referring. This question necessitates a re-examination of the texts, but it is advisable, as a preliminary step, to attempt to consider for itself the term 'Sabbath' and its preservation despite a change of meaning. There are three difficulties: (1) the passage from a rhythm bound to the new moon to a purely weekly system, independent of the moon, implies a rupture; (2) the preservation of the same name for a different institution indicates a relationship, not attested in the Mesopotamian sources; (3) finally, the eventual connection between the Sabbath and a 'dangerous day' is at least questionable, since it does not seem to be clearly evident in the biblical texts.

Let us begin with this last point which is really the easiest: the principle of absolute rest on the Sabbath, of which God gave an example in the Creation narrative, was extended in the Decalogue to servants and domestic animals. The context of the reference is rural, but it can be asked whether it is realistic. Other details suggest more clearly some restrictions in the face of certain dangers: not to leave one's place (Exod. 16.29, as at the approach to Sinai, 19.12-13), not to light or rekindle a fire (Exod. 35.3), nor cook anything. And there must be added to this an extreme case, complete abstention from work on the Day of Atonement, which was also a 'Sabbath of complete rest', שבת שבתון (Lev. 23.32), and on that day it was prescribed that they mortify themselves (וְעִנִּיתֶם אֶת נַפְשֹׁתֵיכֶם).

It could be argued that these precepts were variations on the general prohibition of work, but the case of fire,[9] at least, tempts one to look for more. Various passages make allusions to respect for fire or to its threat: for example, in Num. 15.32-36, the case of someone who gathered wood on the Sabbath, very likely to light a fire, was

---

8. Cf. J. Briend, 'Sabbat', *DBSup* 10 (1985), cols. 1132-70, particularly cols. 1139-40.

9. The prohibition of fire especially interferes with the work of blacksmiths, and so some have sought a Qenite origin (Arabia, Midian) for the Sabbath, but useful documentation is very inadequate, and above all the explanation is too materialistic; cf. de Vaux, *Ancient Israel*, pp. 478-79 and N. Negretti, *Il settimo giorno* (AnBib, 55; Rome: Pontifical Biblical Institute, 1973), p. 71 and authors cited in n. 113.

something new, and Moses had to consult God. It was therefore not contrary to the Sabbath rest, since apparently the precept not to work was not involved. The importance of fire became obvious in the Dwelling in the desert and in the Temple, since two of Aaron's sons, having presented a 'strange' or 'profane' fire (זרה אשׁ), were devoured (Lev. 10.1-3) and later the second festal letter of 2 Maccabees (1.10–2.18) took care to show the continuity of sacred fire from the time of Moses at least up to the Exile. The study in the preceding chapter has shown too the danger from war, and the importance of enclosure walls for the observance of the Sabbath: they protect private life, 'at home'. These scattered notations are witnesses to rumblings, vague at this stage of the analysis, but enough not to cut off all possible links between the Sabbath and the 'dangerous days', on which it was necessary to ward off some menace by not participating in something.

We can add besides a significant outside witness. At the time of the persecutions of Antiochus IV, the Samaritans wrote to him and explained, to make it very clear they were not Jews, that they were ready to give up the practice of the Sabbath, which was a recent importation for them. It was their ancestors who 'after droughts devastated the country, obeying an old superstition, adopted the custom of celebrating the day which the Jews call the Sabbath' (*Ant.* 12.259; cf. Chapter 4, §6). The allusion to superstition implies that it definitely referred to warding off a danger.

As for the permanence of the name for different institutions, first the question should be expanded, by observing that in the Bible the term 'Sabbath' can have related meanings, in addition to the obvious meanings of 'day of the new moon' and of 'consecrated seventh day'. In accordance with the first case, it also designated, as we saw, feasts falling in the middle of the month (Passover, Booths), and in accordance with the second, it can designate the week.

This last meaning is especially important in several respects. In fact, a text defining the feast of Pentecost calls for counting 'seven whole Sabbaths [שבתות, LXX ἑβδομάδας]'; it consequently involves the week. What is more, reckoning begins 'from the day after the Sabbath [ממחרת השבת], the day of the presentation of the first fruits' (Lev. 23.15). This last phrase involves a famous ambiguity (*m. Ḥag.* 2.4; *m. Men.* 10.3): according to the dominant rabbinic tradition, the Sabbath in question was the first day of the Feast of Unleavened Bread, which lasted seven days, but according to the Boethusians and the Sadducees (or other sectarian groups), it was the Saturday which of necessity fell in this period of seven days. The Samaritans and the Caraites still follow this practice, which makes Pentecost a Sunday, and the whole present-day Christian tradition does the same. A more unusual meaning however was attested, according to which the Sabbath designated the whole week of the feast; this is what was prescribed by the book of *Jubilees*, for which Pentecost should fall on the Sunday, the 15th of the third month (15.1). A calculation backwards of seven whole weeks (from Sunday to Saturday) led to Saturday, the 25th of the first month, which would be an aberration, unless one considers that for the verse the first Saturday was not the one after Passover (Saturday within the octave), but the one after the octave of Passover.[10] The 'day after the Sabbath' was deferred then in this way after the octave of Passover, and the *entire* seven weeks should be strict Sabbaths, from Sunday to Saturday. In the passage this meaning is the only one which unifies the whole verse, since then the word Sabbath refers both times to 'week', and it is not unreasonable to consider it primitive. This calendar model is found in the priestly additions of the Hexateuch,[11] but also among the Qumran sectarians,[12] and even, and this is a very significant fact, in a curious Western variant of Lk. 6.1, where a Sabbath is referred to as δευτερόπρωτον ('second first'), which only makes sense if it is at one and the same time the second Saturday after Passover and the first for the computation of Pentecost.[13]

In this way a two-fold result is obtained: not only is the Sabbath in the sense of 'week' sound,[14] but above all, in regard to Passover, it can designate the whole festive week. Now, it is worth noting that the great feasts of the middle of the month (Passover, Booths) are not limited to one day only, but form an octave (7 + 1). What follows from this is a joining together of two meanings for 'Sabbath': the full moon *and* the week, that is to say, the date of the feast *and* its duration. Whatever the history and meaning of these festivities, there is enough to conclude here that there exists the possibility of passing from the date to the duration, and vice versa, through a relationship expressed by the same word, and

10. Jaubert, *Date de la Cène*, p. 24.

11. Jaubert, *Date de la Cène*, p. 33.

12. D. Barthélemy, 'Notes en marge de publications récentes sur les manuscrits de Qumrân', *RB* 59 (1952), pp. 199-203.

13. Cf J.-P. Audet, 'Jésus et le "calendrier sacerdotal ancien": Autour d'une variante de Luc 6,1', *Sciences Ecclésiastiques* 10 (1958), pp. 361-83, in which the author explains the meaning of the variant well, but sees it as merely an ancient gloss, underestimating as a result the importance of the Western text; also M.-E. Boismard and A. Lamouille, *Le texte occidental des Actes, reconstruction et réhabilitation* (Synthèse, 17; Paris: Etudes et Recherches sur les Civilisations, 1984).

14. It is also the usual New Testament expression, for example: μιᾷ τῶν σαββάτων, 'the first day of the week' (Mt. 28.1; Mk 16.2; Lk. 24.1; Jn 20.1; Acts 20.7; 1 Cor. 16.2), or πρώτη (σαββάτου), Mk 16.9.

this all the more so since the full moon falls on the 14th or 15th day of the month, since a month lasts about 29.5 days. The full moon appears then at the end of two weeks (in French, 'quinze jours' has the meaning of 'vierzehn Tage' in German).

A final point still remains to be discussed, the passage from lunar to weekly computation. The four quarters of the moon have an immediately understood meaning that is universally recognized. The interval between quarters is about 7.38 days, which the 'evil days' rounded off to a week of seven days. At the end of the month, the discrepancy was then about 1.5 days on average. The decisive factor was therefore the overstepping of the monthly limit at the time of the following new moon, since there were only two possibilities: either to resume the calculation of the 'evil days' beginning with the new moon, or else to continue the rhythm of the week by ignoring the discrepancy, which stretched and then cut the link with the moon. The series of 'evil days' pointed out above included the 19th of the lunar month, namely, the 49th of the preceding month, which provided a clear sign of the breaking of the monthly limit through the rhythm of the week. The system was composite, but contained a beginning of an emancipation from obedience to the moon. Likewise, the feast of Pentecost was constructed as well on a 49th day; it ignored not one but two new moons, those of the second and third months.[15] Curiously, the feast has no name in Lev. 23.15-18, and the derivative term, '50th day', becomes a proper name, indicating a dependent definition. The name 'feast of Weeks' (חג שבועות, LXX ἑορτὴν ἑβδομάδων), from Deut. 16.10, reveals something else: it really is a question of the feast of the 'number 7' squared.

The context, however, is not completely clear, since according to Deut. 16.9 the reckoning begins 'from the time the sickle is first put to the standing grain'. This is not necessarily identical to 'the day after the Sabbath' of Leviticus 23, and the *Temple Scroll*[16] interprets this text as a cycle of successive 'periods of 50 days', beginning with the first fruits of the harvest of barley, then that of wheat, then of grapes, and so on. Obviously there is something at stake here, the victory of this number (7 or 49), associated with the success of the harvest. The adversary was

15. Cf. Lewy and Lewy, 'Origin of the Week', *HUCA* 17(1943), pp. 1-152; S.H. Horn and L.H. Wood, 'The Fifth-Century Jewish Calendar at Elephantine', *JNES* 13 (1954), pp. 1-20.

16. Y. Yadin, *The Temple Scroll* (3 vols.; Jerusalem: Magnes, 1977–83), I, pp. 99-122.

definitely the moon, since to follow the rhythm of the phases of the moon implied a sort of cult of the moon. We meet this conflict in all the biblical vestiges of Astarte or Asherah, and in the week of Creation as well, which limits as much as possible any regulation by the moon. We meet it finally in the calendar of *Jubilees*, in which the third month is a 'sabbatical': it begins on a Sunday, not a lunar day, and culminates in the feast of Weeks, in a prolongation of a Saturday. As for the reasons for resisting the lunar cult, beyond the numerical complications, they are simple: the moon ruled the rhythm of human fecundity, and the issue was whether it was recognized or not as a goddess of fertility.

It is significant that in the rabbinic tradition, as in Acts 2.1-4 and already in *Jub.* 17.21, Pentecost would also have been the feast of the gift of the Torah to Moses at Sinai, since it was it which determined the primacy of the weekly Sabbath, and which more generally determined a new state of law and other affairs. Exod. 19.1 indicates merely that the Israelites arrived at Sinai in the third month, which makes this interpretation at least possible. *Jubilees* connects the revelation to Moses with Exod. 24.16: 'The glory of YHWH settled on Mt Sinai, and the cloud covered it for six days; on the seventh day, YHWH called to Moses out of the cloud.' This week is seen as a metaphor of the week of Creation: the revealed knowledge of the story of beginnings culminated in the Sabbath, which Moses had to prescribe for the Israelites (*Jub.* 2.26) and which then closes the book (50.6-10).

The transition from the lunar system to the weekly system was consequently remarkably unstable, due to the importance of the moon. The Sabbath could fluctuate between a date (full moon) and a period (a quarter of a lunar month), but there was a struggle to free it from its relationship to the moon, a struggle whose outcome was marked by an annual feast. The transition repeated itself each year from Passover to Pentecost.

Jewish customs that are still in existence show that this interval, called the period of the *Omer*, from the name of the sheaf of the first fruits, has been the ritualization of an uncertainty: it is prescribed that there should be a daily count, without interruption, of the number of days and weeks. Certain attitudes of mourning, therefore of abstention, are maintained throughout the whole period; in particular, marriage is forbidden during these seven weeks, with the exception of the 33rd day after the Passover (ל״ג בעומר, *Lag ba'Omer*), that is to say, the 49th day of the year (since 1st Nisan), which could be understood as a sort of veiled message about the victory of 7. The stake in this ritual is full of meaning: marriage is a prescribed way into fecundity; therefore, it should not be put under the sign of the moon, or Astarte; so it is necessary to await the ritualized victory of the Sabbath, or at least a precursory sign. The tradition, furthermore, attributes a strong conjugal symbolism to the Sabbath. It is remarkable that these customs should be well known in the rabbinic tradition, but still be poorly explained (cf. *b. Yeb.* 62b). They came then from previous usages whose origin was lost, but which must be connected to Hillel the Babylonian (cf. Chapter 7, §3). On the other hand, Pentecost had also in the rabbinic tradition the name עצרת, 'closure' (*Targ. Onq.* on Num. 28.26), a name already attested by Josephus (*Ant.* 3.252), that is to say, the same name as the eighth day of the feast of Booths (Num. 29.35). Pentecost would then be the close of Passover, after the successful outcome of the ritual system of weeks.

All the indications accumulated in the preceding considerations are quite varied. They only show, under the heading of perhaps diffuse Mesopotamian influences, that it is not pointless to admit that the same term Sabbath could have designated two institutions that were notably different, but whose common element was the duration of a quarter of a lunar period, or about seven days. A certain tension between the two was never completely overcome, seeing that it had become ritual. It remains to discern whether the bold innovation of the weekly Sabbath could have been a (pre-exilic) Israelite institution, or something peculiarly Jewish (Nehemiah). To do that the biblical texts should be examined, and in particular the Decalogue.

2. *The Sabbath and the Decalogue*

The principal argument in favour of the antiquity of the weekly Sabbath, and therefore against the attribution of any significance to the fragments still visible in the Bible of a Sabbath associated with the new moon, is its presence in the Decalogue. It may be possible to brush aside the difficulty by showing that the Decalogue is a late creation,[17] or at least that the fourth commandment is a late insertion. Such solutions are certainly too drastic, since the history of the redaction is not that simple. As a matter of fact, it has been stressed that there are several 'Decalogues' or collections of laws grouped into collections of ten.[18] Specifically, the holiness code of Leviticus 19 contains two of them, with each

---

17. Cf. among others J. Meinhold, 'Die Entstehung des Sabbats', *ZAW* 29 (1909), p. 92.

18. Cf. E. Auerbach, 'Das Zehngebot-Allgemeine Gesetzes-form in der Bibel', *VT* 16 (1966), pp. 255-76.

one containing a commandment concerning the Sabbath: both of them have את שבתותי תשמרו, 'You must keep my Sabbaths' (vv. 3 and 30), with the second adding ומקדשי תיראו, 'And you must reverence my sanctuary'.[19] Not only is there no allusion to the rest or to the seventh day, but the allusion to a temple brings up the sacrifices and the displacements in the texts noted above, where the Sabbath was associated with the feast of the new moon. It could be claimed that the feast of the new moon is missing here precisely in order to support the Sabbath as full moon. One could respond, however, that the issue was the feasts of the full moon (Passover and Booths, in the first and seventh months), which lasted exactly an octave: they would be Sabbaths par excellence, as we have seen, much more important than simple new moons, celebrations of just one day.

Even if it is objected that the collection of precepts in Leviticus 19 is secondary, and merely a dislocation of the elements providing the foundation of the two versions of the Decalogue itself (Exod. 20 and Deut. 5),[20] the observations just made open up the possibilities of a Sabbath commandment which would not necessarily have been weekly, even though it could be adapted to a new situation, and even include Pentecost. They allow besides for the principal feast days (Passover and Booths) to be placed in the condensed compilations of laws. The absence of these feasts in the two principal forms of the Decalogue has intrigued commentators.[21] We now turn to these two forms of the Decalogue.

These two forms are noticeably different, their clauses vary a great deal in extent and it is an effort to recover from them the precise number of ten precepts, even though this number is clearly indicated in Deut. 4.13 and 10.4 ('the ten words which he inscribed on the two stone tablets'). We may consider by way of example a classical approach to rediscovering a primitive form of the Decalogue. As many others had done, H. Cazelles[22] examined the structure of similar codes from Mesopotamia or from Egypt, made up of a variable number of brief apodeictic

19. The LXX translates this as καὶ ἀπὸ τῶν ἁγίων μου φοβηθήσεσθε, 'You shall fear my sanctuaries', that is to say, it reads קדשׁי in the plural with a preposition 'of my sanctuaries, of my holy things'; cf. Ezek. 22.8: 'You have despised my sanctuaries [קדשׁי, LXX τὰ ἅγιά μου], and profaned my Sabbaths'; the singular in the MT of Lev. 19.30 is probably a *tiqqun*.

20. H. Cazelles, 'Les origines du Décalogue', in *W.F. Albright Volume, Eretz-Israel* 9 (1969), pp. 14-19.

21. H.G. Reventlow, *Gebot und Predigt im Dekalog* (Gütersloh: Gerd Mohn, 1962), p. 46.

22. Cazelles, 'Origines', p. 16.

formulas. He proposes a reconstruction of ten primitive prohibitions in the biblical Decalogue, of which the fifth, in regard to the Sabbath, would become לא תעשה כל מלאכה בו, 'You shall do no work on it', where בו, 'on it', expanded by the versions[23] (cf. Table 2 below, line 7), had to develop into 'the seventh day', from the beginning of the verse (cf. line 5). The commandment restored in this way is, nevertheless, not very intelligible; the frequency and the meaning of this seventh day are unclear, since there is not even a mention of the word 'Sabbath', even though this commandment follows after clear cultic prohibitions ('You shall not take the name of YHWH in vain') and precedes no less clear moral prohibitions ('You shall not kill', etc.). Besides, if this is nevertheless the core of the commandment, before its redactional expansion and its influence on other passages, it is hard to account for the forms examined above from Leviticus 19. If they are derivative forms, it is strange that they do not mention what is essential, namely, the rest on the seventh day, and if they are primitive, then the proposed restoration, also primitive according to the hypothesis, finds itself refuted. By way of a general observation on method, it can be added that it has not been established that the number of commandments as ten is primitive,[24] since it is just because of the preciseness of this number, which in addition fits in badly with the Decalogue itself,[25] that the biblical indications differ from the parallels provided by the neighbouring ancient cultures.

The explanation proposed above by way of example is merely a variation on a long exegetical tradition seeking a primitive shape of the Decalogue, through an analysis of the two versions, starting from formal considerations, either by extracting a 'common denominator', or by restoring the texts in the framework of some form established in advance. In the case of the fourth commandment in particular, these two approaches necessarily develop all or part of the common portion, represented

---

23. Sam., LXX, Vet. Lat. The *Nash Papyrus* has לוא תעשה בה כל מלאכה, where בה is masculine; cf. F.C. Burkitt, 'The Hebrew Papyrus of the Ten Commandments', *JQR* 15 (1903), pp. 392-408.

24. Cf. M. Lestienne, 'Les "dix paroles" et le Décalogue', *RB* 79 (1972), pp. 491-93; W. Johnstone, 'The Decalogue and the Redaction of the Sinai Pericope in Exodus', *ZAW* 100 (1988), pp. 361-65.

25. The division of the Decalogue into ten commandments is traditionally delicate, since it has thirteen sections (cf. *Bible d'Alexandrie*, 2.59). The first two, in the first person, stand out from the others; this is why the rabbinic tradition (*b. Mak.* 24a) explained that they were delivered by God directly. Josephus joined them together and modified the first one, basing himself on the *Shema Israel* (Deut. 6.4) which suggests a joint usage, as can be seen in the *Nash Papyrus*. See also S.A. Cook, 'A Pre-Massoretic Biblical Papyrus', *Proceedings of the Society of Biblical Archaeology* 25 (1903), pp. 34-56, to be supplemented by Burkitt, 'Hebrew Papyrus', pp. 392-408. Josephus made the prohibition of all animal representation the second commandment, gathering together into just one the two following paragraphs; as for the last two commandments, Josephus united them into a tenth commandment. Philo, *Dec.* §§51-53 proceeded in almost the same manner.

especially by lines 3-10 (Table 2 below), and tend to underestimate the significance of the differences, which are considerable.

Franz-Lothar Hossfeld has drawn up an important overview of studies done on the Decalogue over more than a century. Here is a brief extract on what concerns the Sabbath.[26] A majority of authors consider the first sentence (line 1) to be the source of the whole development of the two forms of the commandment; they hesitate, however, about choosing between שמור, 'take care' and זכור, 'remember', or differ about the point of knowing whether even this primitive short form (analogous to that of Lev. 19) is or is not an insertion (post-exilic) into a Mosaic Decalogue already formed beforehand. Others expand the enquiry to parallel non-Priestly texts prescribing a stoppage of work on the seventh day, that is to say, they search for the 'kernel' of the precept, which is not necessarily the same as its origin: two such texts are Exod. 23.12, coming right after the abstention from working of the land in the seventh year, and Exod. 34.21, which specifies 'even at ploughing time and harvest' and precedes an allusion to the feast of Weeks. The guiding idea in that case is that these last two texts, being primitive and not containing the term 'Sabbath' (but using the verb שבת, 'to keep a feast, to abstain from work'), would be more or less independently at the origin of the two elaborations of the Decalogue.

Table 2. *The Sabbath Commandment in the Decalogue*

	Deut. 5.12-15		Exod. 20.8-11	
1	שָׁמוֹר את יום השבת לקדשו	12	זָכוֹר את יום השבת לקדשו	8
2	כאשר צוך יהוה אלהיך			
3	ששת ימים תעבד	13	ששת ימים תעבד	9
4	ועשית כל מלאכתך		ועשית כל מלאכתך	
5	ויום השביעי	14	ויום השביעי	10
6	שבת ליהוה אלהיך		שבת ליהוה אלהיך	
7	לא תעשה כל מלאכה אתה		לא תעשה כל מלאכה אתה	
8	ובנך ובתך וְעַבְדְךָ ואמתך		ובנך ובתך עַבְדְךָ ואמתך	
9	וְשׁוֹרְךָ וַחֲמֹרְךָ וְכָל בְּהֶמְתֶּךָ		וּבְהֶמְתֶּךָ	
10	וגרך אשר בשעריך		וגרך אשר בשעריך	
11			כי ששת ימים עשה יהוה	11
12			את השמים ואת הארץ	
13			את הים ואת כל אשר בם	

26. Cf. F.-L. Hossfeld, *Der Dekalog: Seine späten Fassungen, die Originale Komposition und seine Vorstufen* (OBO, 45; Freiburg: Vandenhoeck & Ruprecht, 1982), pp. 35f.

14   וינח ביום השביעי

15   למען ינוח עבדך ואמתך כמוך
16   15   וזכרת כי עבד היית
17   בארץ מצרים
18   ויצאך יהוה אלהיך משם
19   ביד חזקה ובזרע נטויה
20   על כן צוך יהוה אלהיך לעשות   על כן ברב יהוה
21   את יום השבת   את יום השבת ויקדשהו

Here are the conclusions of Hossfeld himself, who successfully follows this latter route, which J. Briend[27] adopts as well, since these conclusions will be of use as the basis for fuller observations:

1. In Deuteronomy 5, following on the opening which is considered in n. 5 below, the four propositions of vv. 13-14a (lines 3-10) take up again the abstention from work on the seventh day, by developing the prohibition in two contrasting parts ('You shall labour [...], you shall do no work') of Exod. 23.12 and 34.21. At the centre of the commandment, a nominal clause (lines 5-6) solemnly identifies the seventh day with the Sabbath. The list of beneficiaries of the Sabbath (lines 8-10) and the sentence which concludes the list (line 15) are already found in Exod. 23.12.

2. The comment in v. 15 is constructed according to a pattern of reminding of God's benefits ('Remember that you were slaves [...] and YHWH brought you out [...]') with a conclusion ('That is why [...]') returning to the observance of the Sabbath. This pattern (וזכרת כי עבד היית [...] על כן) is met again in Deut. 15.15 and 24.18.22, as well as for Pentecost, with the feast to be kept by everyone (Deut. 16.11-12); but in this last text, in a revealing way, the redactional systematization (על כן) is missing; this provides a parallel in theme and vocabulary with the conclusion of Deut. 5.14 (line 15).

3. The version of Exodus 20 follows the same outline, but the corresponding commentary (v. 11) is a reminder of Creation and returns to the opposition between six days of activities and a day of rest, and it can be shown that it closely depends on Genesis 1, in adding here the 'rest', just as in Exod. 31.17b ('but on the seventh day he rested and was refreshed').

4. We find the Deuteronomic expression 'YHWH your God' four times in Deuteronomy 5, but just once in Exodus 20, in fact, in a parallel passage (line 6). It can be concluded from this that Exod. 20.9-10 is derived from Deut. 5.13-14. Besides, the comment (Exod. 20.11), which twice contains YHWH without any apposition, is clearly secondary in relation to the precept and has a distorted conclusion (lines 20-21) which does not exactly refer back to the prescribed law (contrary to the normal usage of the expression 'that is why'); it follows from this that the version of Exodus 20 depends on Deuteronomy 5, and not vice versa.

5. As for the opening (line 1), there is no difficulty in considering שמור in Deut. 5.12 as primitive, especially when associated with עשה of the conclusion (line 20),

---

27. Briend, 'Sabbat', cols. 1149-51.

since this is the usual form in Deuteronomy to introduce a precept (and is found again in Lev. 19), while זכר (Exod. 20.8) is used in the same sense in later Priestly texts. In a general way, furthermore, the slight differences between the two versions (indicated by words underlined in varying ways in Table 2, lines 1-11) do not form an obstacle to the sense of dependence indicated, although Exodus 20 has some shortening of the text. Finally, Deuteronomy 5 introduces the peculiarity (lines 2 and 20) of twice referring back to an earlier promulgation of the law, and the examination of the formulas used in other analogous cases (in particular for the commandment on parents, where Deut. 5.16 has a reference back, but Exod. 20.12 does not) shows that there is actually a reference back to the model used, Exod 23:12. It is clear then that a similar reference back has no purpose in Exodus 20, since the Decalogue appears there as a preface to the whole legislation, and *a fortiori* no purpose before the Code of the Covenant of Exod. 34.10-28.

Hossfeld's presentation explains the many difficulties of the double text, and concentrates attention on Deuteronomy 5, but it implicitly permits the assumption that the important commandment about the Sabbath, although it takes up a third of the Decalogue, is a creation formed from Exod. 23.12 and 34.21 and placed in Deuteronomy 5, then transferred with revisions to Exodus 20. It would appear then that such a large section is in no way connected with one item of a pre-existing list. This is not the place to take up again for its own sake the question of a primitive list of 'ten words', but two observations must be made: on the one hand, the first proposition formulating the precept (Deut. 5.12) is remarkably close, in vocabulary, to Lev. 19.30 already quoted ('You shall keep my Sabbaths and revere my sanctuary'); on the other hand, the motivation for the precept, explained by the coming out of Egypt, is in general considered a simple, more or less fortuitous appendix, but the literary sequence is faulty. As a matter of fact, this appendix is not strictly speaking explanatory (like the כי of Exod. 20.11) and can give the impression of being a purely homiletical development,[28] therefore an arbitrary comment. In regard to this point, it is certainly not enough to say that the link between the Exodus and Sabbath is 'a little artificial',[29] since the qualification 'a little' presupposes exactly such a relationship. It is precisely this which must now be determined.

This 'comment' is very close, in meaning and vocabulary, to other

---

28. Cf. J. Loza, *Las palabras de Yahve: Estudio del decálogo* (Biblioteca Mexicana, 4; Mexico: Universidad Pontificia, 1989), p. 228.

29. Cf. F. Michaeli *Le livre de l'Exode* (CAT, 2; Neuchâtel: Delachaux & Niestlé, 1974), p. 182.

Deuteronomic passages, beginning with the first commandment: Deut. 5.6 ('I am YHWH, your God, who brought you out of Egypt, from the house of slavery'); Deut. 26.6-8 ('My father was a wandering Aramean, [...] and YHWH brought us out of Egypt with a strong hand and an outstretched arm'); Deut. 6.21 ('We were slaves of Pharaoh, in Egypt, and YHWH made us come out with a strong hand, [...] but he made us come out from there'), among others. This last text is interesting, since it is the response of a father to his son, who had asked him what then are 'these instructions, these laws and these customs which YHWH our God has prescribed for us?' This brief dialogue is very much like others, situated in proximity to various phases of the coming out of Egypt. One of them merits special attention: in Exod. 13.8, on the occasion of the setting up of the precept about seven days of unleavened bread, it is prescribed for the subsequent celebration: 'This day, you shall speak in this way to your son: "It is because of what YHWH has done for me at the time of my coming out of Egypt".' In other words, it recalls the Passover, and if we keep in mind that this is a Sabbath, it is no longer possible to see the contested link as artificial. By removing vv. 13-14 from Deuteronomy 5 (lines 3-14 of Table 2), which gives the development about the rest on the weekly Sabbath, there results a commandment to observe the paschal Sabbath analogous to that on Pentecost (Deut. 16.11-12), and the formula 'as YHWH your God has commanded you' can be understood still better, since the reference is then to the very first commandment, given at the very moment of the exodus from Egypt, before the (intrusive) weekly Sabbath of Exodus 16 and before the body of legislation connected to Sinai. In other words, we can continue to admit, if necessary, that the development on the weekly Sabbath in the Decalogue is derived from Exod. 23.12 and 34.21, but it must be maintained that this reworking transforms a pre-existent commandment, where the Sabbath had another meaning.

For the sake of completeness, it must be admitted that if the observance of the 'Sabbath day' can be connected to Passover, it fits in rather poorly with the week of unleavened bread, after what has been proposed above concerning the Sabbath of the full moon as a date and a period of time; but all that has to be done is to remove in vv. 12 and 15 the word יום, 'day of' (or eventually to put it in the plural ימי). There then remains: 'Keep the Sabbath to sanctify it' (or 'the days of the Sabbath') and we meet a formula very close to Lev. 19.3 and 30.[30] The

---

30. In Lev. 19.3, the commandment on respect for parents is placed before the

word 'day' would have been added twice then to confirm the transformation of the Sabbath into a weekly rest of one day, which defines
precisely the nominal clause of Deut. 5.14: 'And the seventh day is a
Sabbath for YHWH your God.'

It follows from this that there remains a trace, in the Decalogue, of a
feast of the exodus from Egypt, which resolves a difficulty already mentioned. As for knowing whether there really existed a primitive collection, a proto-Decalogue, including a lunar Sabbath, and whether its commemoration could have been monthly or annual, these questions do not
fall within the horizons of the present study. It is sufficient for our
purposes to have shown that the weekly Sabbath can be detached from
the Decalogue in its present state and allow for the appearance of
another institution which it had veiled, since it is actually the Decalogue,
or more exactly the recension of Deut. 5.12-15, which redefines the
Sabbath as a rest on the seventh day of the week. The more homogeneous version of Exodus 20 has effaced the ancient residues turned
into parasites.

Other texts follow the same pattern of redefinition of the Sabbath as a seventh day.
Exod. 31.13-17 first (v. 13) develops the observance of the Sabbath ('You shall
observe my Sabbaths, since it is a sign between me and you'), then specifies (14a)
that whoever profanes it will be put to death. Finally a second development (14b-17)
identifies the Sabbath with the seventh day, with an allusion to the week of creation,
and insists on the abstention from all 'work' under pain of death (ונכרתה). It is
agreed that the two last parts, where the language is more evolved, are successive
additions to the first part,[31] which, unaware of the seventh day, is very close to the
formulas of the law of holiness (Lev. 19). Whatever the exact meaning of these last
parts, the third part, which alone refers to the seventh day in order to redefine it as
Sabbath, or 'day of the Sabbath', is easily detached.

The weekly framework ('six days [...], but the seventh day [...]') is repeated
again in the formulas of Exod. 35.1-3 and Lev. 23.3, where the day of rest is identified with the 'sabbatical Sabbath' (שבת שבתון), which can be translated as 'Sabbath
of complete rest', or 'Sabbath of solemn rest'. The first text forms an independent
paragraph, easily separable, and the second, placed at the head of a ritual for feasts of
the year, is an insertion too, framed by a repetition (vv. 2b and 4: 'These are my
solemn festivals'). A final insertion, Num. 28.9-10, which defines the sacrifices

---

Sabbath, the inverse of the Decalogue, which limits an overly direct comparison; cf.
Briend, 'Sabbat', col 1144.

31. Cf. M. Noth, *Exodus: A Commentary* (OTL, 2; Philadelphia: Westminster
Press, 1962), pp. 240-45; R. de Vaux, *Ancient Israel* (New York: McGraw–Hill,
1961), p. 394; J. Briend, 'Sabbat', *DBSup* 10 (1985), cols. 1145 and 1158.

prescribed for the 'day of the Sabbath', is placed at the head of a calendar of feasts, just before the feast of the new moon.

There remains finally a foundation narrative for the rest of the seventh day, identified with the Sabbath: it is the episode of the manna and quails (Exod. 16). Its redaction is complex and there are reasons for thinking that it was originally independent of the general framework of the book of Exodus and was a basic Priestly narrative,[32] but the question remains open for discussion. In any case, certain literary characteristics ('sabbatical Sabbath', vv. 23; 'during six days [...], but the seventh day, it is the Sabbath') connect its sabbatical elaboration to analogous prescriptive texts.

All the texts considered up to here are in literary terms connected to the final redaction of the fourth commandment, identifying the Sabbath with the seventh day of rest. All the references to the seventh day are easily removed, without any distortion of the literary setting, and their suppression enhances the traces of another Sabbath, linked to the full moon, to the Passover (with the development on the feast of unleavened bread; cf. Lev. 23.4-8) and to the sanctuary, not without some competition between the lunar rhythm and the weekly rhythm. All this literary activity is thought to be Priestly, but the situation is certainly more complex, since no role is given to the Temple, and the law of holiness (Lev. 19) refers to the Sabbath of the first kind only, with no mention of the seventh day.

3. Seventh Day, Seventh Year

It must be agreed that the preceding conclusions just displace the problem: the reinterpretation of the Sabbath in the setting of another institution assumes in fact that this latter pre-existed the literary modifications. As a matter of fact, the method adopted for analyzing the Sabbath commandment has expressly appealed to other passages, which refer to the seventh day, but not the Sabbath. These texts, Exod. 23.12 and 34.21, must be examined now, and with them the model of prime importance, the first Creation narrative.

On the occasion of the Covenant concluded at Sinai in connection with the second tablets of the Law, a legislative unit (Exod. 34.10-26), resembling a sort of calendar, is introduced; sometimes it is referred to as a cultic Decalogue because of v. 28 ('the words of the Covenant, the

---

32. E. Ruprecht, 'Stellung und Bedeutung der Erzählung vom Mannawunder (Ex 16) im Aufbau der Priesterschrift', *ZAW* 86 (1974), pp. 269-307.

Ten Words').[33] Between the redemption of the first-born (vv. 19-20) and a brief mention of the feast of Weeks and the feast of Ingathering (v. 22), relating to first fruits, the precept of weekly rest appears (v. 21): 'For six days you shall work (תעבד), but the seventh day you shall cease work (תשבת, LXX καταπαύσεις); even at ploughing time and harvest you shall cease work.' The first clause gives the shortest of all the formulations on the seventh day. The expression 'during six days you shall work', in which it is a matter first and foremost of working the earth,[34] is found again in the synthesis of the Decalogue (line 3 of Table 2). It is then developed into 'and you shall do all your work' (line 4), which could be understood of all sorts of activities, and it is this last turn of phrase alone which is found in the wording described above for Sabbath rest.

Notwithstanding the lexical relationship, the verb שבת does not mean 'observe the Sabbath', but 'stop',[35] and it is replaced elsewhere by the noun 'šabbat', which is itself made more specific by religious terms, 'holy' and 'for YHWH' (cf. Exod. 23.16 שבתון שבת קדש ליהוה). This evolution makes the complete absence of a motivation for the precept about ceasing work stand out. The arrangement of the immediate context of Exodus 34 can provide some clarifications: vv. 18-26 as a whole forms a sort of religious calendar, which assumes the installation in Canaan and gives rules for various aspects of the sacrifices. It can stand by itself as pre-existing the composition of the charter of the Covenant[36] (vv. 10-28). Now, in this 'calendar' the precept which immediately precedes the ceasing of work on the seventh day, namely the redemption of the first-born (vv. 19-20), seems incongruous in the calendar, except perhaps for the final sentence, which refers to the pilgrim feasts ('No one shall come into my presence with empty hands'). This impression is reinforced by the fact that in Exod. 23.15, this same sentence closes the feast of Unleavened Bread.

33. But such a term is improper; cf. H. Kosmala, 'The So-Called Ritual Decalogue', *ASTI* 1 (1962), pp. 31-61.

34. F.-E. Wilms, *Das Jahwistische Bundesbuch in Exodus 34* (Munich, 1973), p. 165.

35. Cf. G. Robinson, 'The Idea of Rest in the Old Testament and the Search of the Basic Character of Sabbath', *ZAW* 92 (1980), pp. 32-42. The LXX sometimes renders the verb שבת by σαββατίζειν (Exod. 16.30; Lev. 23.32; 26.35-36; 2 Chron. 36.21; cf. also 2 Macc. 6.6), but always in contexts where the word σάββατα expressly appears. Along with the usual vocalization of the imperfect ישׁבת, with a *holem* in the last syllable, there is one occurrence of תשׁבת, with a *pathah* in the last syllable, in one of the cases cited (Lev. 26.35), and it is possible that in this stative form it is derived from 'sabbat'; cf. G. Bettenzoli, 'Lessemi ebraici de radice "ŠBT"', *Henoch* 4 (1982), pp. 129-62.

36. De Vaux, *Ancient Israel*, p. 448.

In Exodus 34, the same precept of Unleavened Bread in identical terms precedes the one on the first-born, but with this same concluding sentence placed after the precept on the first-born. The passage on the first-born is therefore, from a literary point of view, inside the one on Unleavened Bread, and the juxtaposition recalls Exodus 13. If it is omitted, we get an interesting contact between this feast, whose relationship to the exodus from Egypt is clearly expressed (in which 'during seven days you will eat unleavened bread'), and the ceasing of work the seventh day, which, without any other explanations or reasons, forms with it then a natural complement indicating that the week of commemoration culminates in a day of rest, or an actual feast. We rediscover in this way the day of rest conclusion of Lev. 23.8 or Deut. 16.8. It would be a matter then of a particular week, and no longer a permanent weekly rhythm.

In short, the feast of Unleavened Bread comes at the head of the calendar, a sign of its importance. It commemorates the leaving of Egypt and we rediscover in this way the emphasis placed on the festive week, divided into two phases. It is this period which has been compared elsewhere to the Sabbath of the full moon. However, the absence of the term Sabbath itself would tend to weaken this explanation. But it must be noted that the date indicated for the feast, usually understood (34.18) 'at the appointed time, in the month of Abib' (למועד חדש האביב) through implicit identification with the 15th of the first month, on the day after the Passover, can be interpreted more simply 'at the pilgrim feast of the new moon of Abib', therefore at the beginning of the month; taken literally in this way, it is then not a lunar Sabbath.

This last hypothesis can be supported with other details. The precept to stop work on the seventh day is completed by a very concise, rather sibylline specification (34.21): 'At ploughing time and harvest you shall cease work' (בחריש ובקציר תשבת). The precept could be understood to be limited to these two times, but the preceding observations are opposed to this. On the contrary it could be generalized, by considering that the cycle of ploughing/harvest is perpetual and covers the whole year, without further specification[37] (as in Gen. 45.6 or 1 Sam. 8.12), and this would be a way of extending the weekly model of Unleavened Bread to the entire year. But this interpretation is implicitly governed by the model of the weekly Sabbath, and especially agrees poorly with the generally precise style of calendars. Another possibility,[38] more in keeping with ritual style, consists of seeing agrarian feasts in the Ploughing and Harvest. This Harvest could be compared to the feast of Weeks, which is mentioned just after (v. 22) and corresponds to the first fruits of wheat, whereas the feast of Ploughing would be situated in the autumn. No matter what their identification, these two feasts, joined to Unleavened Bread, form a triad which agrees very well with the precept on pilgrimages, which follows (v. 23): 'Three times a year, the whole male population will present themselves before the Lord YHWH, God of Israel.' There is a consistency then to what the precept of ceasing

37. J. Halbe, *Des Privilegrecht Jahwes Ex 34,10-26* (FRLANT, 114; Göttingen: Vandenhoeck & Ruprecht, 1975), p. 188.

38. H. Cazelles, 'Ex XXXIV: 21 Traite-t-il du sabbat?', *CBQ* 23 (1961), pp. 223-26, and also Briend, 'Sabbat', col. 1139, who refers to a Phoenician inscription mentioning a sacrifice for these two feasts.

work conveys, first in regard to Unleavened Bread, then finally in regard to these three feasts.

The literary history of this calendar of Exodus 34 is certainly complex, but it suffices for us to show here that the seventh day rest is fundamentally a stranger to the Sabbath under all its forms, even if the final redaction lends itself easily to a reinterpretation in the framework of the weekly Sabbath.

The commandment to rest on the seventh day comes up again, with the same terminology but without the details about the feasts, in another quite different legislative passage (Exod. 23.12): 'For six days you may do your work [תעשׂה מעשׂיך], but stop on the seventh day, so that your ox and your donkey may rest, and the son of your servant and the stranger [והגר] may refresh themselves.' This precept appears just after another similar one on the year of remission (vv. 10-11) and before a sort of paranetic conclusion (v. 13: 'You shall be attentive [תשׁמרו, *niphal*, LXX φυλάξασθε] to every word of mine and you shall not invoke the names of other gods'), which has the effect of separating it from a slightly gentler version of the liturgical calendar considered above in Exod. 34.18-26. In comparison with the formulation of Exod. 34.21, the absence of an allusion to any feast is noticeable, and there is a difference in vocabulary[39] ('You shall do your work'), as well as a list of subordinate living beings (human and animal), which presupposes another social context. The reference is no longer to the one who lives directly from his work, even living a settled life (cf. Gen. 2.5 'There was no one to till [לעבד] the soil'), but, in a more diversified social organization, to one who manages a business in which others work for him (cf. 1 Sam. 25.2, on Nabal: 'A man of Maon had a business (ומעשׂהו) at Carmel'). It has been possible to show that these compositional effects link the commandment under this form to another collection of laws, Exod. 22.20–23.9, from a time when they were giving their attention to the situation of the stranger in the community.[40] To sum up, the precept in Exodus 23 is intentionally detached from the context of feasts with which it was still associated in Exodus 34, although already in a diminished form there too.

---

39. It has been noted that this difference in vocabulary comes up again in Exod. 23.16, where first fruits and harvests of 34.22 become 'the first fruits of your works' and 'the harvest of your works', suggesting an expansion in meaning; cf. W. Richter, *Recht und Ethos: Versuch einer Ortung des weisheitlichen Mahnsprüches* (SANT, 15; Munich: Kösel, 1966), p. 94.

40. Halbe, *Privilegrecht*, p. 420.

This displacement, combined with a proximity to the year of remission, whose septenary rhythm would seem to be perpetual, imposed on the seventh day rest the sense of a permanent weekly rest, but independently of all identification with the Sabbath.[41] A problem of coherence comes up then, for if the weekly rest is defined apart from the Sabbath, we are forced to deduce from it that the redefinition of the Sabbath such as is seen in the Decalogue does not have the effect of generalizing the rhythm of the week, but of obliterating the importance of the lunar Sabbath, by transferring its holiness to the weekly Sabbath. Before concluding this point, it is necessary to examine the year of remission, understood usually as 'a year of letting the land lie fallow', since according to the observations just made, it is this septennial rhythm which seemed to govern the generalization of the weekly rest; there is therefore a presumption that it pre-existed it.

Under the general name of Sabbatical Year[42] there are gathered together institutions in reality distinct, at least originally, but later joined together.[43] In the passage just studied, it seems to be a matter of letting the land lie fallow the seventh year for the benefit of the poor (Exod. 23.10-11): 'For six years you may sow the land [...], but in the seventh year [והשביעית] you shall let it lie fallow [תשמטנה, LXX ἄφεσιν ποιήσεις]; you shall leave it alone [ונטשתה, LXX καὶ ἀνήσεις αὐτήν] [...], so that the poor of your people may eat.' It is not stated when the counting of years began and especially whether it was applicable to the whole country or whether it was connected to the date of a particular purchase or to a private practice. This last possibility would be the most logical, since in this way products of the earth would be permanently left for the poor. In literary terms, it is close moreover to the rights of 'Hebrew' slaves, which is not connected to a general calendar either

41. And it is difficult to admit, with A. Lemaire, 'Décalogue', p. 272, that the precept of rest on the seventh day, as in Exod. 34 and Exod. 23, would only be a by-product of the priestly redaction imposing the weekly Sabbath.

42. De Vaux, *Ancient Israel*, pp. 173-75 puts together the different texts on the seventh year (remission, Sabbath) in order to compose a unique ancient institution with multiple effects. The Mishnah joins together the year of remission and the year of the land being fallow/giving up the harvest under the same title of *Seventh Year* (שביעית), but makes no allusion to the notion of a Sabbatical Year itself.

43. Cf. S.A. Kaufman, 'A Reconstruction of the Social Welfare Systems of Ancient Israel', in W.B. Barrich and J.R. Spencer (eds.), *In the Shelter of Elyon: Essays on Ancient Palestinian Life and Literature in Honor of G.W. Ahlström* (JSOTSup, 31; Sheffield: Sheffield Academic Press, 1984), pp. 277-86.

(Exod. 21.2): 'During six years he shall work [יעבד; LXX adds σοι], but the seventh [ובשביעית; LXX adds ἔτει, "year"] he shall go free, without paying anything.' Yet, when letting the land lie fallow in the seventh year is put parallel with the seventh day rest, it tends, by an effect of reciprocal meaning, to impose the same universal permanence on both of them.

It is this permanence which is found very clearly in Lev. 25.2-7:

> When you enter the land I am giving you, the land shall observe a Sabbath for YHWH; six years you shall sow [...], but the seventh year the earth will have a Sabbath of complete rest, a Sabbath for YHWH [...]. You may eat what the land yields during its Sabbath—you, your male and female servants [...].

Nevertheless, the institution is only apparently the same; it is not a matter of abandoning the products of the field to the poor that year, but of the proprietor and his household living from the previous harvests. The model used and the vocabulary employed are exactly those found in all the Priestly texts prescribing Sabbath rest for YHWH. This is the same literary level and we observe in v. 18 supplementary affirmations meant to convince that there is no reason to fear scarcity. This law was put into practice, and it is interesting that an exact trace of it is found at the time of the Maccabaean crisis, when the Sabbath was a major concern: at a given moment, the Jews lacked provisions, 'for it was a Sabbatical Year for the land' (1 Macc. 6.49-54).

These details, by taking into account any differences and avoiding unwarranted harmonizations, allow for a better understanding of the law on the so-called year 'of letting the land lie fallow'. It could be, as the LXX understood it, a year of remission (the meaning of which will be examined later on) and in that case it was prescribed that during it the harvest was left for the poor, but the earth was not left fallow in the strict sense; this is more consistent with the fear of real scarcity expressed on the occasion of the real Sabbatical Year. So this year of remission was a kind of solidarity tax of one seventh of the general income, without any centralized administration. There is really a septennial rhythm, but it has no link here with the seventh day rest. This being so, the proposed comparison with the rights of the Hebrew slave becomes more pertinent: there are no grounds for thinking that this law enacted a general measure applicable on a fixed date for the whole country. In any case, this detour confirms what has already been said: putting the two precepts of Exodus 23 parallel created a new meaning which in no way pertained to them originally. There was no weekly rest.

The year of remission (שְׁמִטָּה; LXX ἄφεσις) in the strict sense is defined quite differently in Deut. 15.1-18: in the seventh year there took place the return of personal effects that had been kept for the payment of a debt (vv. 1-6) and there also took place the liberation of the Hebrew slave (vv. 12-18, repeating Exod. 21.2-6). These two passages imply that the calculation of time began anew in each case, especially v. 2 ('he shall not exploit his neighbour or his brother, when this one shall have appealed to YHWH for remission') and v. 12 ('he shall serve you six years; the seventh year [...]'). However, there is inserted between the two commandments (vv. 7-11) a parenetic development, which repeats the vocabulary of the first one, on the fear of lending when the seventh year approached, which presupposed a general remission carried out on a fixed date. Comparison with the preceding text displays the same two phases: the remission linked first of all to each individual case, later transformed into a remission on fixed dates.

The practical problem of the remission of debts leads us to Nehemiah. Between the two intrigues of the adversaries opposed to the reconstruction of the ramparts, there is presented in Nehemiah 5 a sort of report on the whole of the first mission. In particular, in order to face up to a deep-rooted situation of excessive debts between 'the common people and their fellow Jews', Nehemiah imposed a general remission of debts, personal and material. There is no allusion to a pre-existing law,[44] and the terms used (in 5.10, נַעֲזֹב נָא, LXX ἐγκαταλίπωμεν, 'let us cancel'; in 5.11, הָשִׁיבוּ, LXX, ἐπιστρέψατε, 'give back, return') ignore the technical term 'remission'. It is the same in Neh. 10.32, at the time of the formal promise made by the community, always in the context of the first mission, when the observance of the Sabbath is recalled in very pragmatic terms and is followed by a commitment: 'and we will forego [נִטֹּשׁ; LXX ἀνήσομεν] the seventh year[45] and all debts [וּמַשָּׁא כָל יָד; LXX ἀπαίτησιν πάσης χειρός].' This formula is worth comparing with Exodus 23, since the two principal ideas again occur, but in a more sober form, without allusions to the poor, and in a slightly less technical way: the gathering and leaving of the harvest. The issue is not a matter of a Sabbatical Year in the sense of Leviticus 25, and it is not clearly

---

44. As N.P. Lemche observes in 'The Manumission of Slaves—the Fallow Year—the Sabbatical Year—the Yobel Year', *VT* 26 (1976), pp. 38-59.

45. Most translations add 'of the soil', so as to recover the sabbatical fallow, but it is definitely question here of the *harvest*, which in no way implies a fallow.

stated that the so-called remission is something general and on a fixed date. What is more, the redaction of Exodus 23 is a development of Neh. 23.10-11 and not vice versa.

The conclusion is obvious: the text of Nehemiah is aware of the Sabbath day and remission, but without the connection, still timid but suggestive, built by Exodus 23; it should be dated earlier then, and *a fortiori* before the elaborations of the Decalogue and the subsequent multiplication of references to the 'Sabbath day of YHWH'.[46] The pre-scription of Deut. 31.10-11 to read the Law 'every seventh year, the year of remission, during the feast of Booths', is clearly derivative, but, in referring back in this way to Neh. 8.14, it opens up the perspectives that will be examined in Chapter 8, §2.

4. *Closing Remarks*

Many other texts deal with the seventh day and the Sabbath. It is enough here to show briefly that they do not affect our topic in any way. The first account of creation (Gen. 1.1–2.4a) certainly has a complex history: we find there ten commands ('And God said [...]'), expressing the setting up of all the objects of the cosmos as well as the living beings, with everything organized into six days and a seventh day; this latter, after the total completion of the work, is a stop (וישבת) and not a momentary rest. The first week is unique, and liturgically like a procession:[47] it is first of all the prototype of the feast, before being that of ordinary time.[48] The hymn of Nehemiah (9.5-37) celebrates the creation in the same terms as Genesis 1, but as a unique work without a succession of days, and the 'holy Sabbath' only appears at the time of the revelation at Sinai (v. 14), therefore specifically after the episode of the manna. In other words, the first account of creation can be

46. This point has an effect on the establishment of the relative antiquity of the Holiness Code (H) of Leviticus 17–26 in comparison to the rest of the Priestly Document P; cf. the discussion of I. Knohl, 'The Sabbath and the Festivals in the Priestly Code and in the Laws of the Holiness School', *Shnaton* 7–8 (1983–84), pp. 109-46.

47. Cf. P. Beauchamp, *Création et séparation: Etude exégétique du premier chapitre de la Genèse* (Bibliothèque de Sciences Religieuses; Paris: Aubier-Montaigne, 1969), pp. 57-65.

48. This fact clearly stands out in contrast with the presentation of Josephus (*Ant.* 1.33) and *Jub.* 2.1-5; since the seventh day is for them the prototype of the human weekly Sabbath, they are obliged to say that God *rested*.

considered to be entirely independent of the promotion of the weekly Sabbath, even if Exod. 20.11 uses it expressly for this end, and it is useless for our purposes to enquire into what can remain when an attempt is made to remove from it the seven-day framework.

The case of Ezekiel and Isaiah is just as interesting. Ezekiel contains passages on the profanation of the Sabbaths (20.12-24; 28.8-26; 23.38), with allusions to the sanctuary, which are connected to Lev. 19.3.30 ('You shall keep my Sabbaths').[49] In 45.17–46.7, it is a question of the Sabbath ritual in the Temple, in relation to the new moon, the Passover and Unleavened Bread. All this seems earlier than the weekly Sabbath, but there is a sentence which could make one think the opposite: in 46.1, after 'six working days' (שֵׁשֶׁת יְמֵי הַמַּעֲשֶׂה), when the gate of the interior court must remain closed, comes a 'Sabbath day' on which it should be open, just as on the day of the new moon. It should be noted right off that the context of the Temple and the idea of a gate open on the Sabbath are quite distant from Sabbatical rest, and more generally from the model of Nehemiah with closed gates. So the questionable words 'six working days' can either be considered to be a gloss, since these words are otherwise missing from the rest of the passage, which continues to deal with Sabbaths and new moons;[50] or, in the context indicated just above (45.23) of 'seven days of the feast of Unleavened Bread', they can be interpreted in the light of 'the rest of the seventh day' of Exod. 34.21, which, as has been shown, applied primitively to the seven days of Unleavened Bread. In short, Ezekiel knew only the lunar Sabbath.[51]

---

49. The comparison is made by W. Eichrodt, 'Der Sabbat bei Hezekiel: Ein Beitrag zur Nachgeschichte des Prophetentextes', in H. Gross and F. Mussner (eds.), *Festschrift H. Junker* (Trier: Paulinus Verlag, 1961), pp. 65-74, but he deduces from it that Ezekiel 20 is interpolated, since Lev. 19 is very late; this last point, however, is not proved, at least for the Sabbath.

50. This is the opinion of Lemaire, 'Sabbat', p. 183; cf. J. Hermann, *Ezechiel* (Sellin Kommentar zum Alten Testament, 11; Leipzig: Hinrichs, 1924), p. 291.

51. Lemaire, 'Sabbat', deduces from this that Ezekiel 'proposes a return to the traditional ritual as it was already attested at Ugarit for the feast of the full moon', and one may surmise that the implicit argument would be: 'beyond the novelties imported with the Babylonian calendar, after the battle of Carchemish in 604 [cf. p. 179], among which was the Sabbath rest.' Would it not be more simple—and more coherent with the vicissitudes of the Sabbath rest—to say that Ezekiel very naturally proposes a return to what he was acquainted with, even if that must affect the date of the arrival of the Babylonian calendar in Judaea.

As for Isaiah, the invectives from the very beginning (1.13) against the sacrifices of the new moon and Sabbaths were mentioned in the prologue of this chapter. Other allusions to the Sabbath, toward the end of the book, remain again and again unacquainted with the notion of the seventh day: in 66.23, mention is made, in the conclusion, of new moons and Sabbaths, twinned and favourably evaluated, which forms an *inclusio* with the beginning of the book; in 56.2-6, it is a matter of 'observing the Sabbaths' without profaning them. This is language analogous to that of Ezekiel 20 and Leviticus 19, with allusions besides to the welcoming of the 'sons of foreigners', the eunuchs and all peoples, which is certainly not part of Nehemiah's reform. Finally, at the end of an exhortation to care for the poor and oppressed (58.1-12, similar to Jer. 7.1-15; Hos. 6.4-6; Amos 5.21-24), is found an invitation to observe the Sabbath: 'If you refrain from trampling the Sabbath and doing business on the holy day, if you call the Sabbath "Delight" and the holy day of YHWH "Honourable" [LXX: "delightful, holy for your God"] [...].' There is no allusion to the week and the phrase "Sabbath day" is missing. It appears then that, although it has a Priestly look, this passage presents a notion of the Sabbath similar to that of Amos 8.5, which speaks out against those who want to do away with new moon and Sabbath (i.e., the full moon) to carry on more business,[52] but there is no objection to seeing there a gloss joining together exhortation and cult, stemming from phrases in the Decalogue, perhaps by way of the language of the year of remission in favour of the poor. Outside of a slight doubt in regard to this last occurrence, it can be seen that the book of Isaiah did not know of the weekly Sabbath either.

The strict delimitation of the weekly Sabbath refers back from every direction to Nehemiah. We saw that the precept of remission of debts was an undertaking of his first mission, and the observance of the Sabbath day a pivotal point of his second mission (13.15-22), for which we find a development in Jer. 17.19-27,[53] which insists on the closing of the gates and stopping of traffic on the Sabbath. The two precepts are placed side by side without being joined together in the promises made by the community (Neh. 10.32), a passage which appears in the first mission (closely related to Ezra), but is connected in literary terms to the second (cf. Chapter 1, §2), which is not precisely dated.

André Lemaire's conclusion was that 'the idea of the Sabbath, a rest

---

52. This is the opinion of Lemaire, 'Sabbat', p. 184.
53. Cf. Lemaire, 'Sabbat', p. 182 and the references in nn. 104-105.

every seventh day, is only put in place after the return from exile, with the Priestly compilation and its implementation by Nehemiah and Ezra'. It will suffice to clarify this opinion by pushing to the limit the logic of Nehemiah's renewal: it is arbitrary to place earlier than him what he did not utilize, whether this be the year of remission or the Sabbath, all the more so since no literary evidence really calls for it. The 'Priestly redaction', which has been shown to be complex, must be placed after him, at least in the case of anything which pertains to 'the holy day of the Sabbath for YHWH', but certainly before the redaction of 1 Maccabees. All the corresponding passages are easily detached from the Pentateuch, while leaving behind very clear traces of festive weeks and a lunar Sabbath, especially for the feasts of Unleavened Bread and Booths, and more generally a whole legislative corpus which we can assume to have been in force. The Sabbath in the ancient way is especially well documented in the Prophets, including Trito-Isaiah, which is considered to be expressing the preoccupations of the first returnees from exile.[54]

This is not the place to assess the consequences of these affirmations. Here it will be enough to emphasize that the dating of Nehemiah (two missions and Memoirs) must play an essential role. In this regard, it is important to point out that the extra-biblical institutions mentioned, in particular those found in Mesopotamia (calendar, *šabattum*, evil days), have only been useful for bringing something to light, and not as dateable artifacts, by suggesting structures of interpretation which are then set free from their model: from Abraham to Antiochus IV and beyond, the movements along the Fertile Crescent or in Transeuphrates have been sufficiently numerous and varied so that no migration could be ascertained and dated, without a special study. It is significant in this regard that the Semitic proper name, *Šabbetai*, which derives from 'šabbat' would be of Babylonian, and not Hebrew, origin: the most ancient attestations arise from non-Judaean documents discovered at Elephantine (from about 400 BCE), and it is really improbable that the bearers of this name would be proselytes.[55]

Before reconsidering Nehemiah and the problems that his memoirs raise, it is necessary to remain for a little while longer on the periphery,

---

54. Cf. J.L. McKenzie, *Second Isaiah* (AB, 20; Garden City, NY: Doubleday, 1968), pp. xv-xxiii; P.R. Ackroyd, *Israel under Babylon and Persia* (The New Clarendon Bible Old Testament, 4; Oxford: Clarendon Press, 1970), pp. 233-36.

55. Cf. B. Porten, 'The Diaspora. D—The Jews in Egypt', in Davies and Finkelstein (eds.), *History of Judaism*, I, pp. 372-400, with references on pp. 387-88.

while considering the case of the Samaritans, whose relationship to the Sabbath is problematic, and by analyzing the ins and outs of the Maccabaean crisis, so as to establish landmarks for the historical framework.

Chapter 4

THE SAMARITANS AND SHECHEM

Summed up briefly, the problem of the Samaritans, their origin and relation to Judaism, can be expressed through the contradiction already outlined (cf. Chapter 1, §3): on the one hand, in the time of Ezra and Nehemiah and probably earlier they constituted the prototype of the conservative opposition to the return from exile—perhaps with the complicity of certain Judaeans—and more generally the symbol of the resistance to that innovation constituted by Judaism; on the other, in various passages and especially in the account of the coming of Alexander as told by Josephus, they appeared instead as a degenerate branch of Judaism, gathered around the late and undistinguished temple of Gerizim. Just like Josephus, who called them unstable, present-day researchers struggle to explain how they could have been in ancient times conservative and then later on laxists, and strive, in order to have the contraries coexisting, to rediscover various evolutions, even tendencies and parties. It is advisable to begin with a statement about how things stand, before resuming the analysis of the main texts concerning the Samaritans, in the light of the hypotheses and results of the preceding chapters.

1. The Elusive Samaritans

The most recent comprehensive view is provided by James D. Purvis,[1] who describes the contribution of recent discoveries, in particular the discoveries in the Judaean Desert. He begins with a series of questions about the origin of the Samaritans. What was the essential characteristic of the group when they attained a distinct and autonomous stage? What

---

1. J.D. Purvis, 'The Samaritans and Judaism', in R.A. Kraft and G.W.E. Nickelsburg (eds.), *Early Judaism and its Modern Interpreters* (Philadelphia: Fortress Press, 1986), pp. 81-98, supplemented by J.D. Purvis, 'The Samaritans', in Davies and Finkelstein (eds.), *History of Judaism*, II, pp. 591-613.

were the stress lines which established and maintained a permanent chasm between the Samaritans of Shechem and the Jews of Jerusalem? When was the rupture produced? What was its ideological or theological motif, in relation to the sacred tradition of Israel and the Pentateuch?

Since the historical documents are few in number and have little in common, the response to these questions depends on the order of importance attributed to the sources by the various authors. According to a first group of texts, the Samaritans themselves claimed to be descendants of the tribe of Joseph and of a levitical clergy established at Shechem and on Gerizim since Joshua's conquest. They considered themselves to be the only ones faithful to the Mosaic Torah, while Judaism was a heresy arising from the schism of Eli when he built a sanctuary at Shiloh; that error was confirmed by the establishment of the cult centre at Jerusalem (by Solomon), then by Ezra's falsification of texts. In other words, the Samaritans would be the genuine descendants of the ancient Israelites. This is the way they present themselves, through a few, poorly preserved texts but some historians admit that they are partly correct.[2]

A second series of documents contains the Judaean views represented by some of Josephus's accounts and by the rabbinic tradition, which are all based on the one biblical passage that deals with the Samaritans (שומרונים), 2 Kgs 17.24-41. It is recounted there that they were originally colonists come from Mesopotamia to replace the deported Northern tribes, but that they eventually adopted the local cult of YHWH. Josephus knew that they called themselves descendants of Joseph, but he declared that this was just opportunism and that they still carried out the pagan rites of their ancestors (*Ant.* 9.290-91). The rabbinic tradition expressed doubts as to the validity of their conversion, since it had taken place under the threat of lions, but it still considered them Israelites in many ways and scrupulously faithful (*b. Qid.* 76a; cf. Chapter 6, §8). The assertion that the Samaritans had a pagan origin can throw some light on their ancestors, but these views have especially been utilized to determine in what circumstances they had emerged before the Exile as a kind of Israelite sect.

The third ancient interpretation was peculiar to Josephus, who highlighted a post-exilic schism, without too much coherence with his

---

2. So M. Gaster, *The Samaritans: Their History, Doctrine and Literature* (London: British Academy, 1925), and J. Macdonald, *The Theology of the Samaritans* (London: SCM Press, 1964), pp. 11-27.

interpretation of 2 Kings 17. He explained (*Ant.* 11.302-325) that in the time of Alexander a brother of the high priest Jaddua, having married the daughter of Sanballat, governor of Samaria, was expelled from Judaea and that the temple of Gerizim was built for his benefit. Later on, some Jews who were not very observant (especially in regard to the Sabbath and mixed marriages) took refuge too in Samaria (§§346-48). This presentation is accepted by the majority of modern commentators, in spite of some serious difficulties. The account about Alexander is suspect, Sanballat remains difficult to identify, the story of the rejection of the brother of the high priest, referred to in Neh. 13.28, was in no way the origin of a major schism, and Josephus himself seemed illogical, since he had previously described the pre-exilic schism, without implying that it would have been a kind of etiological narrative projecting back in time later events.

These three models remain in competition, but recent discoveries have provided useful additional information. In the first place, the biblical fragments discovered in the Judaean desert have helped clarify paleographic questions and real or orthographic variants, and the outcome of this is that the Samaritan Pentateuch cannot be earlier than the second century BCE.[3] Moreover, the excavations of Shechem (Tel Balatah) and of the temple of er-Ras on Mount Gerizim have shown that there was a revival there in the Hellenistic period.[4] In particular, it has been established that these developments were well before the schismatic Pentateuch. Finally, the documents found in the caves of Wadi Daliyeh have made it possible to distinguish, as a result of evidence of papponymy, between Sanballat, the adversary of Nehemiah, and a Sanballat who would be a contemporary of Alexander.[5] The statements of Josephus with regard to the temple on Gerizim, Purvis continues, turn out in this way to be to a great extent confirmed, and we have at our disposal additional information that makes it possible to provide a global outline.

1. Shechem was rebuilt by rebel nobles from Samaria, after their expulsion because of their revolt against the Macedonians, a fact known

---

3. Cf. F.M. Cross, 'Aspects of Samaritan and Jewish History in Late Persian and Hellenistic Times', *HTR* 59 (1966), pp. 201-111; H.G. Kippenberg, *Garizim und Synagogue: Traditionsgeschichtliche Untersuchungen zur Samaritanischen Religion der aramäischen Periode* (Berlin: de Gruyter, 1971), pp. 92-97.

4. G.E. Wright, *Shechem: The Biography of a Biblical City* (New York: McGraw–Hill, 1965).

5. Cross, 'Papyri', pp. 45-69.

from classical sources. Ever since their settlement in Samaria by the Assyrians, they had had a long tradition of independence in relation to Jerusalem, and already a deep-rooted hostility, as was shown by their repeated opposition to the returnees from exile in the Persian period (cf. Ezra–Nehemiah). Conversely, they were looked down on by at least some of the Judaeans because of their hybrid ethnic and religious origins. The Samaritans who rebuilt Shechem were nevertheless attached to the Hebrew God, even if their ancestors had worshipped other gods.

2.　While restoring Shechem, the Samaritans had erected a sanctuary to YHWH on nearby Gerizim, making in this way a deliberate gesture of attaching themselves to the ancient Israelite tradition, as a way of gaining favour with the local population, a little like Jeroboam I creating a sanctuary at Bethel to stabilize the secession of the North (1 Kgs 12.26-29). These practices fit in with what we observe in other places in the ancient eastern Mediterranean world, where, in reaction to the foundation of a Greek colony, we see the local population forming a union around an ancestral sanctuary.[6]

3.　Contrary to what Josephus implied, it is not clear that the priesthood of Gerizim would have been a branch of the Zadokites of Jerusalem, since the Samaritan genealogies ignore Jerusalem and David. Yet, since the Jewish and Samaritan traditions are tendentious, the choice between the two theses is difficult: the dominant opinion however is to accept the independence of the Samaritan priesthood, taking into account that Sanballat could have without any difficulty found an Aaronite family endowed with the desired pedigree.[7] Others stick to the Zadokite dissidents of Josephus,[8] or combine the two possibilities, by suggesting that after the service of a number of dissident high priests a proper Samaritan dynasty was installed.[9]

4.　The building of the temple on Gerizim was therefore an independent activity, and not right away a schism with regard to

6.　E.J. Bickerman, *From Ezra to the Last of the Maccabees: The Historical Foundations of Post-Biblical Judaism* (New York: Schocken Books, 1962), pp. 43-49.

7.　Kippenberg, *Garizim und Synagogue*, pp. 60-68; Coggins, *Samaritans and Jews*, pp. 142-44.

8.　Cf. J. Bowman, *The Samaritan Problem: Studies in the Relationships of Samaritanism, Judaism and Early Christianity* (Pittsburg: Pickwick Press, 1975), pp. 33-46.

9.　Cf. J.D. Purvis, *The Samaritan Pentateuch and the Origin of the Samaritan Sect* (HSM, 20; Cambridge, MA: Harvard University Press, 1968), pp. 116-17.

Jerusalem, although certainly a counterbalance—another place for an allegiance within Judaism as a whole, but without pretensions about claiming unique legitimacy.

5.   It was only later that relations deteriorated, to the point of ending up as a real schism in the second century because of political tensions arising from the rivalries between Seleucids and Lagides over control of Palestine; then because of a difference in attitude at the time of the Hellenization crisis, with the Jews reproaching the Samaritans for their submission to Antiochus IV; and because meanwhile the respective diasporas found themselves in conflict too (*Ant.* 13.74-79). These difficulties came to a head with the expansionism of John Hyrcanus, all the way up to the destruction of Gerizim in 128 BCE and of Shechem in 107, events which we know from Josephus (*Ant.* 13.254-81).

6.   At a time difficult to determine, but at the latest in the second century, the Samaritans edited a Pentateuch, with some emendations[10] which tended to establish their exclusive legitimacy. It is this claim, confirmed by the rejection of 'Judaean' literature (Prophets, Writings) and not the mere fact of the temple at Gerizim, which rendered the chasm between Jews and Samaritans impassable.

7.   Finally, if we consider Judaism in a very broad sense as the totality of groups claiming legitimately to represent the Israelite tradition, then the Samaritans can be considered a Jewish sect, and this in certain aspects is what the rabbinic tradition did. Moreover, the traces of divergencies within the sources show that the Samaritans did not form a single block. Evidence of this would especially be the Dosithean movement, identifiable from the second century and with an anti-sacerdotal tendency, which reminds us of what the Pharisees were like in relation to the Sadducees.[11]

This overview, which depends on a large number of works, still continuously gives an impression of uneasiness, of assertions immediately retracted. Typically, there is a hesitation to set precise goals for present research, as if the clarification of obscure points could only ruin the edifice. Here are some examples of this fragility. Why have confidence in Samaritan sources when they claim that the Gerizim priesthood is from old Levitical stock and does not come from Jerusalem, and at the

10.   Cf. J.D. Purvis, 'Samaritan Pentateuch', *IDBSup*, pp. 772-75.

11.   Bowman, *The Samaritan Problem*, pp. 37-56; Kippenberg, *Garizim und Synagogue*, pp. 128-71; S.J. Isser, *The Dositheans: A Samaritan Sect in Late Antiquity* (SJLA, 17; Leiden, Brill, 1976).

same time challenge them when they declare that the Samaritan tradition is from old Israelite stock? How is it possible to understand at one and the same time a deeply rooted antipathy between Jews and Samaritans, with an ethnic-religious foundation and dating back to the monarchical period, and the *non-schismatic* erection of the temple of Gerizim? The late dating of the Samaritan Pentateuch obviously causes a problem, but is it reasonable to compare it with a Jewish (or Judaean) Pentateuch supposed in that case to have been fixed for centuries? As for the 'totality of Judaism' as a depository of Israelite tradition, the least that we could say is that it is a poorly defined notion, given the uncertainties, noted in Chapter 1, about the social context of the reforms of Nehemiah as well as of the Maccabaean crisis. It could even be said that the possibility of doubling Sanballat by papponymy, far from usefully resolving the tension between Nehemiah and Josephus, tends to paralyze the contradictory data[12] and to reduce the urgency for historico-literary criticism of one as well as of the other, namely, of the texts which present these facts.

Of course, whether we accept him or reject him, Josephus constitutes the principal source, and his evidence must be re-evaluated. That is the object of this next section.

2. *Josephus and the Samaritans*

The most recent and most instructive study on this subject, is that of Rita Egger,[13] who systematically and meticulously examines the vocabulary used by Josephus in the *Jewish Antiquities*. He speaks in fact more or less vaguely of Cuthaeens (Χουθαῖοι, כותאים, כותים of the Targum and the rabbinic tradition), of Samaritans (Σαμαρεῖται, Σαμαρεῖς), to say nothing of the allusions to the faithful of Gerizim, to the Shechemites, even to the Sidonians at Shechem, and we experience some trouble in discerning in each case whether the reference is to citizens of the city of Samaria (later Sebaste), of inhabitants of the region

---

12. L.L. Grabbe, 'Josephus and the Reconstruction of the Judean Restoration', *JBL* 106 (1987), pp. 231-46; D.R. Schwartz, 'On some Papyri and Josephus' Sources and Chronology for the Persian Period', *JSJ* 21 (1990), pp. 175-99, shows that the papyri from W. Daliyeh do not confirm the statements of Josephus, but explain how he could have been mistaken.

13. R. Egger, *Josephus Flavius und die Samaritaner: Eine terminologische Untersuchung zur Identitätsklärung der Samaritaner* (Novum Testamentum et Orbis Antiquus, 4; Freiburg: Vandenhoeck & Ruprecht, 1986).

of Samaria, of members of the Samaritan religion, indeed even of groups of diverse origins more or less attached to one of these three entities.

She studies in particular the occurrences of four principal terms or groups of terms, while giving in each case an assessment:

1. Σαμαρεῖς: this term, identified in places with Χουθαῖοι (10.184; 11.114, 117, 303), can designate either the inhabitants of the region or of the city of Samaria, or the Samaritans themselves. The unequivocal designation of Samaritans can only be applied after the construction of the temple of Gerizim, in the time of Alexander. The indications given by Josephus suggest that these Samaritans are of Jewish (or at least Judaean) origin and that their activities formed part of the history of Judaea. Furthermore, the frequent use of Σαμαρεῖται and Σαμαρεῖς alternately in the same passages does not seem to be derived from a clear differentiation: in this case the two terms should be considered equivalent.

2. Σαμαρεῖαι: this name, used less frequently, does not appear before the Assyrian conquest of 721. We find it especially in the Persian period; then it tends to be replaced by Σαμαρεῖς to designate the Samaritans.

3. Σικιμῖται, οἱ ἐν Σικίμοις Σιδώνιοι: this would refer to Judaean dissidents from before the Maccabaean crisis, confused by Josephus with ancient Phoenician colonists (of Sidon). The complete schism between Jews and Samaritans only took place in the time of the Hasmonaeans.

4. Χουθαῖοι: the point is to identify the development of this term, which appears in the list of Babylonian immigrants of 2 Kings 17: on the testimony of *War* 1.63, and of the Samaritan Targum on Gen. 10.19, we conclude that it can be identified with Sidonian, and that it was probably used in Samaria.

The very careful work of R. Egger in fact only leads to the reproduction of the historiography of Josephus: the Samaritans, as a religious community, a little before but especially after the construction of the temple of Gerizim, constituted according to Josephus, in the time of Alexander, an illegitimate branch of Judaism. Before that decisive moment, nothing had clearly emerged on the origin and nature of the inhabitants of Samaria, despite the permanence of Samaritan opposition to the Jews from the time of Cyrus, and the confusion surrounding this double origin (local and Judaean) was expressed by Josephus, using a reproachful tone, in terms of fickleness.

The pivot of this reconstruction, and also of Josephus's presentation, is precisely the account of Alexander's arrival, with the erection of the temple of Gerizim for the dissident Judaeans. In fact, if we define the Samaritan religious community in function of the Gerizim temple, it is not astonishing that we cannot recover definite traces of it beforehand, either in the Persian period, or *a fortiori* at the time of the Assyrian conquest. Now, the examination of the account in question has shown that Josephus's statements are less clear than they seem at first sight. Archaeology probably confirms, as was said above, some of the details concerning Shechem and Gerizim, but the dating of the finds is less clear than first seemed, and above all the confirmation could not be automatically extended to the picture that Josephus gave of Jerusalem and Judaea.

Before trying to explain the failure of the investigation just mentioned to break free from Josephus's ideas, we should consider another point: the Samaritan hostility in the Persian period is expressed in numerous ways in *Ant.* 11. What were Josephus's sources? Egger rightly points out that one particular incident (11.114-19) does not correspond to any passage in Ezra–Nehemiah, but that he repeats to some extent an attack previously reported (§§97-99), in which the Samaritans (Σαμαρεῖται) brought about the rediscovery by Darius of the document in which Cyrus had prescribed the reconstruction of the Temple at the expense of the treasury, together with the upkeep of the cult through local tributes. Here, the Samaritan hostility provoked a complaint by the Jews to Darius, who responded with a letter to the notables of Samaria, reminding them of the order to provide for the sacrifices from the tribute of that region. In the end, Josephus had no other documents on the Jews than the biblical books and known apocrypha, but he went far beyond his sources, by systematizing under the guise of Samaritan opposition various cases of local resistance since the time of Cyrus (11.19-22). The origin of this Samaritan opposition was the refusal by the Jews to see this obstinate people participate in the construction of the Temple (§85), which would have given them some rights there. Josephus depended here on Ezra 4.1-6, but he suggested to a greater extent that the Samaritans, though venerating God (σεβόμεθα, instead of MT וּלָהֶם‎, LXX ἐπιθύομεν, which implied a cultic installation), did not have their own temple. The passage under consideration mixes together the terms Σαμαρεῖς and Σαμαρεῖται, and accentuates the obvious continuity, on the occasion of which the equivalent name Χουθαῖοι is recalled (11.88). Eggar concludes however that no indication exists of a link between these Samaritans, who recalled their Persian origin, and the community of Gerizim; they were therefore inhabitants of Samaria, but not Samaritans in the religious sense of the term.

This last conclusion is interesting, because it is at the same time arbitrary and rigid: arbitrary, since it does not take into account the *religious* (and political) jealousy expressed; rigid, since it is in reality forced to reaffirm a Samaritan discontinuity which is in fact necessitated by the premises, while Josephus was much less logical.

It is logic that has forced Egger to dismantle more than Josephus did any clear meaning, national or religious, for the Samaritan entity. Under the same name, with a geographical origin, are found, more or less arbitrarily, various groups and religions, subdivided into as many sects as is necessary according to circumstances of time and place. The Cuthaeans, being enemies of the Jews, could not be Samaritans in the strict sense, but descendents of the ancient colonists; the Sidonians of Shechem, ready to apostatize, could not be true Samaritans either, but must have been Phoenicians, and so on, and Josephus was mistaken if he implied the contrary.

All these results come up against numerous objections in regard to details, of which many will be dealt with in what follows. At the outset there is however one central option, which consists of following the governing idea of Josephus, for whom the only true Samaritans (monotheists) came from a Jewish dissidence. In other words, the Jews had priority, since they alone had a meaningful antiquity and continuity. Now, this governing idea is precisely what was produced by the story of Alexander's conquest. I stated briefly that it was legendary (cf. Chapter 1, §3), but it is now necessary to conclude that this legend conformed to an *urgent* objective, and therefore to re-examine the texts from this perspective.

3. *Alexander and Gerizim*

The account of Alexander's visit to Jerusalem was placed by Josephus in the framework of the high priestly genealogies of the Persian period. After having presented brief episodes from the time of the two Artaxerxes, he came to the reign of the high priest Jaddua (*Ant.* 11.302), under the last Darius. That is how the narrative in view begins. It is made up of two main units, as will be shown: 1. a story in which the central figure is Sanballat, governor of Samaria, who succeeded, with Alexander's blessing, in erecting the temple of Garizim for some dissident Jews (§§303-25a); 2. the account of Alexander's visit to Jerusalem (§§325b-45a), in which Alexander completely ignored Sanballat and Gerizim. These two stories had independent origins, but they were merged by Josephus into a single composition.

That redaction added some facts from general history on the journey of Alexander: a note summarizing the beginning of the conquests before the battle of Issus (§§304-305), then an allusion to this battle and its consequences for the Phoenician coast (§§313-20). In this last passage there are added a first note laying out Sanballat's projects (§315) and a second showing the fidelity of the Jerusalem high priest to his sworn word (§§317-18).[14] To this redaction should be connected

14. I follow, in a different direction, the excellent analysis of A. Büchler, 'La

too the final piece of information (§345, prepared for in §342) according to which Alexander took along to Egypt the soldiers of Sanballat, since Josephus strongly emphasized the contrast between Sanballat who relied on his soldiers, and Jaddua who trusted in God. On the other hand, he stated a little farther on that the Samaritan colonists (in Upper Egypt) would have been in fact descendents of prisoners taken by Ptolemy I in a later conquest of Samaria (cf. below).

The link between the two main units is the death of Sanballat, at the end of a narrative which culminates in the erection of the Gerizim temple and the installation as high priest of his son-in-law Manasseh, a dissident brother of Jaddua, the high priest of Jerusalem. It is remarkable that throughout this whole affair, the only allusion to the Samaritans is the fact that Sanballat, sent by Darius, was like them of the Cuthaean race (§303): the enterprise took place then in Samaria, but on the margin of the Samaritans properly. The conclusion, after Sanballat had obtained from Alexander, who was besieging Tyre, authorization to build a temple, arouses some suspicions (§§324-28): 'As fast as he could, Sanballat built his temple and installed Manasseh as priest [...]. After the siege of Tyre had lasted seven months and that of Gaza two months, Sanballat died.' The disappearance of Sanballat was indispensable for the sequel of the narrative, which recounted the coming of Alexander to Jerusalem and his complete ignorance about what had been taking place in Samaria. The interval is extremely short, and it could be suggested that Josephus would have extended it for the sake of credibility, if he was not bound by the necessity of making specific sources compatible. There is besides an inconsistency, since the conquest of Tyre and then the beginning of the siege of Gaza had already been reported (§§320-22); there is then a doublet. Furthermore, it was at this moment that 'Sanballat, judging the occasion to be favourable [νομίσας δὲ καιρὸν ἐπιτήδειον ἔχειν], came to Alexander, whom he found beginning the siege of Tyre'. It appears then that the introduction of the story of Sanballat into the setting of historical events about the advance of Alexander is a little artificial.

Sanballat's goal no longer seems clear, since it is given in two forms. At the time of his appointment (§303), he had a precise political design:

> Knowing that Jerusalem was a flourishing city, whose kings had given a lot of trouble to the Assyrians and the inhabitants of Coele-Syria, he lost no time in marrying his daughter Nikaso to Manasseh, a brother of the

high priest, in the hope that this union would be a guarantee that the whole
Jewish people ['Ιουδαίου ἔθνους] would be well-disposed towards him.

It was a matter of unification then, and there was nothing about a
temple. Moreover, the argument about the misdeeds of ancient kings
recalls the petition, addressed to Artaxerxes by the officials of Samaria
and Transeuphrates, to stop the restoration of the city and the walls
of Jerusalem by the returnees from exile (Ezra 4.11-16). That opposition has been compared to the resistance to the work of Nehemiah
(Chapter 1, §2), at least in the first mission. Later on, Sanballat formulated another goal, by developing in a meeting with Alexander (§322)
(having already thought of it in the time of Darius [§§311-13]) a scheme
to divide the Jews by creating a dissident sanctuary as a means of
gathering together all those who had contracted marriages with
foreigners, by giving them certain advantages. The goal was divide in
order to rule, and we find again in this another form of the opposition to
the work of Nehemiah (cf. second mission, Neh. 13.23-30).

These two opposing policies were based on the same elements: on the
one hand, the power of the Jews should be controlled or used, and on
the other, the external marriage of the brother of the high priest served
as a lever to attain this. The transition between these two moments of
the narrative was assured by the appearance of a religious factor: the
Elders ('Ιεροσολυμιτῶν πρεσβύτεροι), followed by the people and
finally the high priest Jaddua himself, judged the marriage of Manasseh
to be contrary to the Law and intolerable, because it was a bad example.
To be more precise, the new factor which appeared was what Josephus
called here 'the Elders', who were obviously opposed to the milieu of
high priests and their spontaneous religious customs, since they had
permitted such a marriage to take place. Once again, there is an echo of
Nehemiah in his second mission (which Josephus did not know about):
'One of the sons of Jehoiada, son of the high priest Eliashib, was the
son-in-law of Sanballat the Horonite. I chased him away from me.' The
comparison should however be made cautiously, since, according to
Josephus, it involved the great-grandson of Eliashib and not a grandson,
and besides the role of Nehemiah is taken by 'the Elders'. Finally, there
is no proof that it would be the same Sanballat, since it is now clear that
there were several.

No matter what the historical details, the important thing is the similarity of a form of religious intervention (the Elders and Nehemiah)
controlling the priesthood, which was susceptible to collusion with the

royal authority. We see it clearly through a significant detail in the narrative of Josephus (§310): when Manasseh, after being summoned to choose between high-priestly dignity in Jerusalem and the daughter of Sanballat, came to see Sanballat to tell him that he preferred the high priesthood, Sanballat told him that he would obtain it, as well as the succession to him as governor, if he just kept his daughter. The next phrase mentions the project of a temple on Gerizim as already approved by Darius, but this is just a clumsy harmonization with what follows (§315), and it must be understood that Sanballat was in fact promising him, to start with, the high priesthood in Jerusalem.[15] The account of Manasseh's expulsion was therefore, fundamentally, rather anti-high-priestly: not only was authority returned to the Elders, but the high priesthood was in the hands of the Persians. In the narrative about Alexander at Jerusalem, that dependency is transformed into heroism, since the high priest Jaddua, rejecting allegiance to the new master out of loyalty to the Persians, made a profession of independence.

To sum up, the story of Sanballat, which seemed to originate in a rather uncertain Persian policy, regains its coherence if we consider it from a Jewish point of view, since it brings together all the elements attached to Nehemiah: Sanballat had thought that by the marriage of his daughter he would secure control of Jerusalem, but the result of his intrigues was that he only succeeded in gaining control of the dissident faction of Gerizim, which was very modest for a satrap. The independence of Jerusalem asserted itself, thanks to the Law, and if an account of the foundation of Gerizim and its temple is given, that does not necessarily imply that it would have been Samaritan in origin:[16] in fact, in its present form it is not in the least in praise of the Samaritans, since they went even so far as to buy their faithful (§312). Seen from this angle, the specific role of Alexander in the account is no different from that which Darius could have played. On this subject, in regard to the

---

15. This is the opinion of Reinach, who thinks it is even necessary to change the end of §311, where Manasseh thought of receiving from Darius the office of high priest, 'for Sanballat was then already very old'; to avoid implying that Sanballat was a high priest, he corrects it with the name of the high priest of Jerusalem: 'for Jaddua was then [...]'. Loeb, less sensitive to the literary effects of harmonization, thought that Sanballat promised Manasseh the high priesthood 'of the Samaritans, of course, cf. §324'.

16. As Büchler would like ('La relation', and others after him), but he is aware that the insistence on the fact that the first high priest of Gerizim was a brother of the one in Jerusalem was strange on the part of a Samaritan (p. 21).

dating of the episode, it must be observed that Sanballat is made out to be a satrap of Samaria, a small district of Coele-Syria, and not of Transeuphrates, a great province. Now, the division of the Persian heritage into small units was no earlier than the Seleucids.[17] Josephus's source was therefore later than Alexander, or at the very least was revised in the Hellenistic period. Furthermore, new excavations on Mount Gerizim (*Luza*), still incomplete, show an important Hellenistic building in the vicinity of the sanctuary on the summit, whose beginnings could go back to early in the period.[18] As for the account of Pseudo-Hecateus (quoted by Josephus, *Apion* 2.43), according to which Alexander gave Samaria to Judaea, free of tribute, it is nothing more than an attempt to overlay the Hasmonaean conquests of the second century with the authority of Alexander.[19]

4. *Alexander at Jerusalem*

The second unit is the story of Jaddua receiving Alexander at Jerusalem. It begins after the death of Sanballat, but is introduced by an exchange of letters at the time of the siege of Tyre (§§317-20). That exchange breaks the thread of the narrative about Sanballat: in fact, the 'favourable occasion' for Sanballat is the beginning of the siege of Tyre, referred to in §317a, and §321 connects to it very naturally. In other words, even if the connection of Sanballat to Alexander is artificial, it is prior to the joining of the two units, and it must be admitted that the reason for this connection is still not cleared up. On the other hand, the story of Jaddua is also centred on Alexander, without any link to Sanballat, and we uncover in this way in literary terms the narrative necessity for the death of Sanballat at this juncture between the two narratives.

The relations between Alexander and Jaddua offer some interesting features. To begin with, as far as probability is concerned, there are two kinds of difficulties: on the one hand, geography would have required that Alexander come by Jerusalem between Tyre and Gaza, and not after the conquest of Gaza, all the more so since the reception of the

---

17. E.J. Bickerman, *Institutions des Séleucides* (Bibliothèque Archéologique et Historique, 26; Paris: Geuthner, 1938), p. 200.

18. Cf. Y. Magen, 'A Fortified Town of the Hellenistic Period on Mount Gerizim', *Qadmoniot* 19 (1986), pp. 91-101, and *Qadmoniot* 24 (1991), pp. 70-96.

19. Cf. Stern, *Greek and Latin Authors*, I, p. 44.

king by the high priest took place on Mount Scopus, that is to say, on the northern approach to Jerusalem, which would be the right route from Antpatris and Jaffa by way of the valley of Aijalon and Beth-horon, whereas the Gaza[20] entrance would have had to be by the south, as we can see in the account of Philip and the Ethiopian (Acts 8.26). The insertion of Jerusalem in the passage of Alexander is therefore a little forced, at least as far as terrain is concerned. On the other hand, the general historicity of the events has inspired doubts for a long time, since the narrative is to a great degree marvellous: while the plan for a puni-tive expedition, when Jaddua refused to profess allegiance, is plausible, the reversal by Alexander on meeting the high priest, thanks to a pre-monitory vision, is difficult to accept as a bare fact, all the more so since the coming out in a grand procession[21] was certainly a royal reception, and since the episode is rounded out (11.337) with the reading of Daniel, where Alexander noted that he was in the process of fulfilling a prophecy (cf. Dan. 8.16-19, already interpreted in this way in *Ant.* 10.273). This last motif, whose probability is likewise very weak, was utilized else-where by Josephus: in *Ant.* 11.5, Cyrus also read in Isaiah the prophe-cies concerning himself, and marvelled at being able to realize them.

The narrative is therefore legendary, since the marvellous element is at its centre, and cannot be omitted without destroying the coherence of the whole narrative. Since they are in this way largely detached from historical contingencies, the elements of the narrative are therefore almost entirely determined by the redactional goals, eventually in

20. The place of the meeting is called *Saphin* (*Ant.* 11.329: Σαφῖν, Σαφᾶν according to the manuscripts, which Josephus translated by 'observation post'). Since the time of Schürer, it has been identified with the corresponding Aramaic word (צפין) from the Hebrew צופים, 'observers', indicated by *m. Pes.* 3.8 as the northern boundary of Jerusalem. In *War* 2.528, the word is translated in Greek Σκοπός, from which comes Scopus. According to *Meg. Ta'an* (repeated in *b. Yom.* 69a) on the 'day of Gerizim' (21st Kislev), the meeting took place at Antipatris, the name given by Herod to Kefar Saba (Καφαρσαβᾶ in *Ant.* 13.390 and 16.142, there-fore כפר סבא), and it has been suggested for a long time that *saba* and *sapha/saphin* could have accidentally been exchanged. The facts are probably more complex, since on the one hand the point where they met could have been displaced on the route for reasons of geographical probability (between Tyre and Gaza by land, Alexander had to pass by Antipatris), and on the other hand כפר סבא is, according to *y. Dem.* 2.1, a Samaritan location (cf. 1 Macc. 11.34 on the 'Samaritan' districts transferred to Judaea), which gives another complexion to the story.

21. Bickerman, 'Charte séleucide', p. 49.

successive and contradictory stages. In particular, the problem of war, or of the participation of Jews in foreign armies (cf. Chapter 2, §§1-2), provides some useful distinctions. In the prologue (§§317-20), Alexander wrote to Jaddua demanding for himself military assistance and the tribute previously contributed to Darius. Jaddua's response referred only to his loyalty to Darius and not at all to the fact that the Torah, especially the observance of the Sabbath, could make service in a foreign army difficult. In doing that, the high priest showed himself to be leader of the Judaeans, and not of the Jews, following the distinction defined in Chapter 2, §5. When Alexander assembled the 'Jews', however, to find out what they were demanding, the high priest became their mouthpiece, and they obtained from Alexander exemption from tribute every seventh year (§338), which corresponds obviously to the Sabbatical Year on a fixed date. I have shown (Chapter 3, §3) that the Sabbatical rest and the Sabbatical Year are connected. It is remarkable, furthermore, that in obtaining the exemption the high priest himself did not take the initiative, and that he was just a mouthpiece of the people. In the same way, we see that the request addressed to Alexander that the Jews of Babylon and Media be allowed to follow their ancestral customs (πατρίοις ἔθεσιν) was formulated by the people, and not by the high priest. It follows from this that the narrative is not homogeneous: there is a 'Judaean' part, with the high priest and the temple, without any allusion to the Sabbath, and a 'Jewish' part, alongside the high priest, with the ancestral traditions and the Sabbatical Year. The combining of the two parts was achieved through a compromise sentence (§339), effusively explaining that a great number joined the army of Alexander in return for the promise of being able to observe the Law, which was certainly not very realistic for those who were Jews in the strict sense, as the decrees and privileges in the time of Caesar fully showed (cf. Chapter 6, §6).

This second unit had therefore, independently of its connection with the unit about Sanballat, at least a double purpose: the most obvious was to show that Alexander himself bore witness to the eminent dignity of the Temple and its priesthood. The other, less obvious, but no less important, was to indicate clearly as self-evident, that the priesthood of the Temple and the Judaism of Nehemiah went hand in hand. This second purpose had already been present in the version peculiar to Josephus of a massacre of the inhabitants of Jerusalem on a Sabbath by means of a deception (cf. Chapter 2, §1), in which he deliberately introduced a sacrifice in the Temple. In this unit, it has been shown that the theme of the king's reading of the prophecy seemed to be peculiar to Josephus. There is therefore a strong presumption that he would have been the one who would have carried out these important modifications to introduce his own views.

There is one last element of Alexander's visit left to consider. Once they had seen the favours granted the Jews, the Samaritans made a move to obtain the same.[22] But listen to Josephus, since the details are important (§340): 'The Samaritans, whose capital was at that time at Shechem, situated near Mount Gerizim and inhabited by dissidents [ὑπὸ τῶν ἀποστατῶν] from the Jewish people, saw that Alexander had so lavishly treated the Jews, and decided to pass themselves off as Jews.' This sentence immediately raises some issues: the Samaritans were therefore something different from the dissident Jews, but these latter were living in their new capital of Shechem. There is in some way a hybridization. Next, Josephus commented[23] on the changeability of the Samaritans:

> When they see the Jews faced with adversity, they deny being from the same race as the Jews, in that case acknowledging the truth; but when they see them favoured by fortune, they immediately boast about kinship with them and declare that they are close relatives, tracing their origins back to the sons of Joseph, Ephraim and Manasseh.

It is remarkable that this assessment did not consider the simplest point in the context, that is to say, kinship by dissidence: the Samaritans were therefore quite distinct from the movement promoted by Sanballat, in the first literary unit. In fact, at the time of the meeting with Alexander, he refused them the exemption from the tax of the seventh year, because, though saying they were Hebrews, they could not say that they were Jews. Again, the narrative raises speculation: wishing to pass as Jews, they did not succeed. In reality, their response is in accord with the commentary of Josephus. Their eventual kinship would have come from the fact that, being descendents of Joseph, they were Israelites, but that

22. In *Apion* 2.43, Josephus, quoting Hecateus of Abdera, declared that Alexander added the district of Samaria (Σαμαρεῖτιν χώραν) to the territory of the Jews without tribute. It is a matter, with a customary anachronism, of the three districts granted by Demetrius II (1 Macc. 11.34); cf. below, Chapter 6, §4.

23. Already begun in *Ant.* 9.291, in regard to their beginnings under the Assyrians.

was not enough for them to be Jews, in the meaning of the Sabbatical Year.

A certain working outline emerges from these muddled features: on the one hand, the fickleness of the Samaritans, which will be examined later on for its own sake, had no practical effect with regard to the Jews, whose identity was warranted by their keeping the weekly Sabbath, as stated before. It actually belonged then to their challenging the Judaeans. On the other hand, the dissident minority at Shechem played no further role in the narrative. Finally, the clumsiness of the Samaritans, who did not know how to claim to be Jews, is to be attributed to Josephus, who, as we have seen, constantly tried to consider Jews and Judaeans as identical.

It follows from all these observations that neither the Judaeans nor the Samaritans were acquainted with the Sabbath (cf. below, §5) or the Sabbatical Year. In this regard a rabbinic tradition provides strange testimony: according to *y. Šeb.* 6.3, p. 36c some Cuthaeans were exempt from the Sabbatical Year since the time of Joshua, son of Nun.[24] Since Joshua was the one who had assured the introduction of the law of Moses in the Promised Land, this could have meant that there were places where this Law imposed neither Sabbath nor Sabbatical Year, which draws closer to the issue of a Pentateuch without a Sabbath (cf. Chapter 3, §2). On the contrary, Jews and dissidents at Shechem knew of these institutions, if only by transgression (§346). In other words, the privileges of some and the envy of others presupposed these institutions, and it may be concluded that there must have been a mixed population, as much in Judaea as in Samaria: Jews and Judaeans on the one hand, dissident Jews and Samaritans on the other. It is therefore logical that the Samaritan petition to Alexander would have been later than the building of the dissident temple, and we then catch a glimpse of the principle of Josephus's chronological organization. On the one hand, it was worth his while to overlay with the authority of Alexander not only the splendour of the Jerusalem temple, but also a debate on the Sabbatical Year which is certainly from a later time, as shown below; on the other hand and especially, it was in no way to his advantage to move back in time the building of the Gerizim temple, and that is why he put Sanballat just before, under the same Alexander.

---

24. Cf. G. Alon, 'The Origin of the Samaritans in Halachic Tradition', *Tarbiz* 18 (1947), pp. 146-56; in regard to Joshua, cf. Chapter 8, §4.

In a parallel rabbinic tradition (*Meg. Ta'an.*, 21st Kislev, 'Day of Gerizim', scholion), it is recounted that the Cuthaeans (כותיים) asked for the Jerusalem temple from Alexander, telling him to give them five *kur* of land on Mount Moriah; provided with an authorization they arrived, but the inhabitants of Jerusalem chased them away, and informed Simon the Just. The latter came with great pomp before Alexander at Antipatris (אנטיפטרס); he was denounced as a rebel, but to the surprise of everybody Alexander bowed down before Simon and admitted having been deceived by the Cuthaeans. The Judaeans (יהודאין) then left to plough up Mount Gerizim, that is to say, to do to the Cuthaeans what they had thought of doing to the Temple.

This narrative combines elements from several epochs: Alexander the Great dominates, but Jaddua is replaced by Simon II the Just (about 200, under Antiochus III; cf. Chapter 7, §2); then the construction of the Gerizim temple is replaced by its destruction under John Hyrcanus (about 107; cf. *War* 1.65 and *Ant.* 13.281); and finally the meeting on Scopus is placed at Antipatris, Herodian name for Kefar Saba (*Ant.* 13.390 and 16.142-43). From a literary point of view, we see immediately that Simon, who did not chase the Cuthaeans and did not go to Gerizim, is useless in the account of the struggle between the Judaeans and Cuthaeans: he is added, and with him the error of Alexander and their meeting at Antipatris. This motif of the condemnation of Jerusalem by Alexander, followed by the dazzling and unexpected recognition of the truth about its cult is the same as in the Josephus account, but it is used here solely to affirm the absolute supremacy of the Jerusalem cult since the time of Alexander, without any allusion to any statutory or fiscal advantage (Sabbatical Year), which is more consistent. In fact, this legend makes no distinction between Cuthaeans (or Samaritans, of Mesopotamian origin) and dissident Jews, since it in no way envisages the latter. Under these conditions, there is no obstacle to moving the existence of Gerizim back to very distant times. Furthermore, this legend is only concerned with the fight between the two temples, without any specifically Jewish focus, except perhaps through the presence of Simon the Just, instead of John Hyrcanus or Jaddua. Now, it is worth noting that Simon the Just would be the only high priest retained in the list of transmitters in *m. Ab.* 1.1 (cf. Chapter 7, §2), which certainly expressed the views of the Pharisees. In a word, even if the composition had a final Pharisaic touch, through the choice of Simon, it did not start off that way, and it appears again in a symmetrical Samaritan form, preserved in an abridged version: 'At that time Alexander, king of Macedonia, appeared: it was he who bowed down before the high priest, Hezekiah, who had come out to meet him with the leaders of the Samaritans.'[25]

To summarize: the account of Alexander's coming is fictional, and is an answer to the central problem of Josephus's apologetics. If we take a

---

25. E.N. Adler, 'Une nouvelle chronique samaritaine', *REJ* 45 (1902), p. 73, where Alexander is written אסכנדר, through the influence of Arabic ('*al*' is omitted because it was taken to be the article, and there is metathesis of '*x*' to '*sk*').

view opposed to Josephus's, we obtain contrasting assertions: 1. the magnificence of Jerusalem cannot pride itself on the authority of Alexander; 2. the antiquity of the Samaritans, or Hebrews without a weekly Sabbath, should be affirmed in comparison with the Jews; 3. since the chronological elements are still confused, the time of Alexander no longer constitutes the *terminus ante quem* for the reforms of Ezra–Nehemiah; 4. the matter of the Jewish emigrants in Samaria, or more exactly at Shechem and on Gerizim, with traces of debates on the purity of the priesthood and on the observance of the Sabbath, expresses a further interaction, in which the influences relative to the Sabbath and to cult have emerged.

5. *Antiochus IV and the 'Sidonians'*

The dissidents at Shechem, who were not identical with the Samaritans, according to Josephus had the name 'Sidonians',[26] and this name is strange, since it brings to mind a Phoenician origin: Tyre was the 'chief city of the Sidonians', according to coins from the time of Antiochus IV. However, those called Phoenicians by the Greeks called themselves Canaanites: Josh. 13.4 speaks of 'the land of the Canaanites which belonged to the Sidonians', and historians who spoke Greek, with Genesis in mind, said that Abraham left Ur of the Chaldeans to come to Phoenicia.[27] In *Ant.* 1.138-40, Josephus listed, in dependence on Gen. 10.15-19, the clans descended from Canaan, among whom were Sidonios, founder of Sidon, and Samaraios (as in LXX, as opposed to צמרי of the MT) which definitely suggests Samaria, but the posterity of Canaan was destined to be destroyed by the Hebrews (ancient name of the Judaeans). Josephus did not establish any link with the primitive genealogies, of which he had obviously lost sight when he spoke of the Samaritans: their Mesopotamian origin was certainly an allusion to 2 Kgs 17.24-41. On the other hand, we know that Phoenicia had been a Macedonian colony since Alexander the Great. The same was true for

26. *Ant.* 11.344 has: τῶν δ' εἰπόντων Ἑβραῖοι μὲν εἶναι, χρηματίζειν δ' οἱ ἐν Σικίμοις Σιδώνιοι, translated by Loeb as '[...] they were Hebrews but were called the Sidonians of Shechem', and by Reinach: '[...] that they were Hebrews, but that the inhabitants of Shechem were called Sidonians'; this second translation reflects better the chiastic structure of the text, and avoids identifying the Samaritans as a whole with the Sidonians of Shechem.

27. Eupolemos, come down to us through Alexander Polyhistor, who was quoted by Eusebius, *Praeparatio Evangelica* 9.17.8.

the city and the region of Samaria, as the result of a conquest in circumstances that are unclear. If the term Sidonian really referred to Phoenicia, it could then have referred either to Canaanite origins or to influence from Hellenized Phoenicia. This fits the Samaritans very poorly, whether it be in their own mouth or in that of their detractors, that is to say, whether they are taken to be Assyrian colonists, or descendants of Joseph or Jewish dissidents, with or without a temple on Gerizim.

The term 'Sidonians' comes up again specifically in a major text from the time of Antiochus Epiphanes, in 166 BCE. Josephus describes, to a large extent following 1 Macc. 1.16-54, how Antiochus, returning from Egypt, plundered the Jerusalem temple, then installed pagan worship there, by constructing the abomination of desolation. At this point, the nearly parallel account in 2 Macc. 6.2 indicates that the king sent Geron an Athenian, 'to defile the temple in Jerusalem and to dedicate it to Olympian Zeus, as well as the one at Gerizim, [by dedicating it] to Zeus-the-Friend-of-Strangers [Διὸς Ξενίου], as the people who lived in that place felt it to be [ἐτύγχανον²⁸]'. Josephus deviates at this point from 1 Maccabees, by giving the impression of considerably developing the information from 2 Maccabees. He cites a petition of the Samaritans asking Antiochus to spare them the fate met by the Jews. This document had been under suspicion of being a forgery, until Bickerman clearly established its authenticity.²⁹ I propose to show here on the one hand

28. Since Niese, *Kritik*, p. 106, a correction is often made to ἐνετύγχανον, from which comes 'as the people who lived in that place requested [...]'; cf. J. Starcky and F.-M. Abel, *Les livres des Maccabées* (La Sainte Bible; Paris: Cerf, 1961), p. 256. This is in fact a harmonization with Josephus, but it is unnecessary, since there is no direct dependence here between him and 2 Maccabees, which is in no way unfavourable to the Samaritans (cf. Chapter 6, §2, and the 'good Samaritan', who was hospitable too). The discrepancy in regard to the name of the temple is not insurmountable: the direct meaning of *Xenios* in the context is surely 'hospitaller', as commentators hold (cf. Goldstein, *II Maccabees*, p. 274), but it may conceal another meaning, perhaps more primitive, of 'foreigner, imported', close to *Hellenios* of Josephus, which also denotes a foreign origin: an expressly imported name is superimposed on the local god. As for knowing which of the two terms is original, the presumption is in favour of *Hellenios* (contrary to the opinion of Goldstein, *II Maccabees*), since the document cited by Josephus seems very authentic, which is something that cannot be said of 2 Maccabees.

29. E.J. Bickerman, 'Un document relatif à la persécution d'Antiochus IV Epiphane', *RHR* 115 (1937), pp. 188-223 (republished in *Studies in Jewish and Christian History* [Leiden: Brill, 1980], II, pp. 105-135). With occasional

that his conclusions should be followed in their entirety, since any suspicions about falsification which remain are to be attributed to Josephus's revisions, and on the other hand that this document provides useful insights into relations between Jerusalem and Gerizim, as well as the reasons for the revisions by Josephus. The significance of this text in the Maccabaean crisis itself will be evaluated in Chapter 7.

Josephus then reports (*Ant.* 12.257-64) that the Samaritans, seeing the grave reverses suffered by the Jews—or Judaeans—wanted to give up being accepted as their kinsfolk and to abandon any claim that the Gerizim temple was the temple of God Almighty (μεγίστου θεοῦ). They said that they were colonists belonging to the Medes and Persians, which Josephus confirms in a parenthesis (καὶ γὰρ εἰσιν τούτων ἄποικοι). Then, after these comments, he continues, giving his source:

> A. 'This is why [οὖν] they sent a delegation to Antiochus with a letter drawn up in this way: "To King Antiochus Theos Epiphanes, memorandum of the Sidonians of Shechem [ὑπόμνημα παρὰ τῶν ἐν Σικίμοις Σιδωνίων]: after droughts had desolated the country, our ancestors, obedient to a certain ancient religious scruple [ἀρχαίᾳ τινὶ δεισιδαιμονίᾳ], adopted the custom [ἔθος ἐποίησαν] of observing [σέβειν] the day that the Jews call 'sabbath' [λεγομένην τῶν σαββάτων ἡμέραν]. They had also erected on the mountain called Gerizim an unnamed temple, and they offered there appropriate sacrifices [καθηκούσας θυσίας]. These days, as you have treated the Jews as they deserved for their wickedness, the royal officers, thinking that as a result of our kinship with them we must do[30] the same things, charge us with the same offences, whereas we are Sidonians by origin [ὄντων ἡμῶν τὸ ἀνέκαθεν Σιδωνίων], as is evident from [our[31]] public archives. We

reservations, the critics have basically followed his conclusions; cf. Egger, *Josephus Flavius*, pp. 286-91.

30. The text (οἰόμενοι κατὰ συγγένειαν ἡμᾶς ταὐτὰ ποιεῖν) is translated in this way by Reinach: 'thinking that it is a result of our kinship with them that we follow[...]'. This translation suggests that the motive for the charge by the royal officers was the kinship, and not the actual fact of the practices, whereas the memorandum admitted them. That brings out the difficulty of Antiochus's response, who established that the Samaritans had *done* none of those things for which the Jews were blamed. Loeb has 'in the belief that we follow the same practices as they through kinship with them', which is more neutral and does not dismiss the simple presumption of practices. Likewise Egger, *Josephus Flavius*, p. 261, renders 'glaubend, aufgrund unserer Verwandtschaft handelten wir auf dieselbe Weise wie jene'.

31. This is the way Loeb and Reinach reconstruct it, but not Bickerman. It could

therefore petition you, as our benefactor and saviour, to order Apollonius, the governor of the district, and Nikanor, the royal agent, not to harass us by bringing against us the same charges brought against the Jews, since to us they are aliens by race as well as customs, and we ask that the unnamed temple be given the name of Zeus Hellenios. In this way we will no longer be harassed, and being able from now on to attend in complete security to our work, we shall increase your revenues."'

To this petition of the Samaritans the king replied:

B. 'King Antiochus to Nikanor. The Sidonians of Shechem [οἱ ἐν Σικίμοις Σιδώνιοι] have submitted the enclosed memorandum. Since their messengers have confirmed before us and our friends sitting in council [συμβουλευομένοις ἡμῖν μετὰ τῶν φίλων] that they have done none of those things of which the Jews are accused, but that they want to live according to the customs of the Greeks, we consider them clear of all charges, and order that their temple, as they have requested, be known as that of Zeus Hellenios.'

The final point is then mentioned:

C. 'The king also wrote that[32] to Apollonius, the district governor, in the 46th year,[33] the 18th day of the month of Hekatombaion of Hyrcanus.'[34]

This correspondence presents several difficulties, in content and in form. Josephus in his account refers in fact to three documents: (A) an

be an appeal to the archives of the addressee, therefore an *ad hominem* argument; in fact, the royal response entirely ignores any verification of the matter. In an analogous way, Justin Martyr addressed the emperor by making an allusion to the *Acta Quirini* and to the *Acta Pilati*, that is really to say, since such notarized documents had never been published, by appealing to the public archives, whose existence the emperor could not deny, but which he was perhaps not in a position to consult; cf. P. Prigent, *Justin et l'Ancien Testament* (EBib; Paris: Gabalda, 1964), p. 282.

32. Reading ταῦτα, namely, a copy of the *two* documents indicated (as in Loeb), and not ταὐτά, 'the same things', suggesting that the letter to Apollonius did not contain the two documents (as in Reinach).

33. The text is restored to read '146th year' (Seleucid), 167–66 BCE (2 Macc. 1.9 has a similar omission).

34. Or 'Hyrkanios'; the first name of the month is Attic, and not Macedonian (which would be *Loos*, for July–August) and the second is unknown, but it could come from a corruption of Kronios, which, according to Plutarch, *Theseus* 12, is the ancient name of Hekatombaion; cf. Loeb, *ad loc.* This word, with the form of an adjective in the genitive, could also come from a faulty copying of an archival mark on the document, indicating that it belonged to a 'Hyrcanian collection' (John Hyrcanus, rather than Hyrcanus II).

undated Samaritan petition asking King Antiochus to intervene with Apollonius and Nicanor; (B) an undated response from the king to Nicanor, the second in the indicated precedence, where it is described as a document attached to the preceding petition; (C) an identical response to Apollonius, with the date and the title of the addressee both indicated, but without the contents specified. The most natural and the most probable conclusion is to consider, with Bickerman, that Josephus did not have access to two distinct archival sources, with different origins, but to just one, which gave the query appended to the response. (A) was therefore known to Josephus as an annex of (B). Furthermore, (C) should come before (B), according to the precedence expressed in the petition. The first inversion is easily explained as necessitated by a presentation in chronological order. The second seems odder, but it can be explained by the mechanism of coordinated responses: the chancelry had addressed the royal instructions to Nicanor, as well as a copy to his senior in rank Apollonius. This copy should have contained a dispatch note duly addressed and dated, the actual copy of the instructions without formularies of state etiquette and, in order that the instructions be intelligible, a copy of the 'attached document', without formularies as well, namely, the petition. In other words, Josephus had access to the archives of Apollonius, or at least to the letter that he had received, in which (C) would have introduced (B) and its appended document (A), and he re-established the chronological order in which (C) evidently came last.

The forms are therefore very plausible, despite an appearance of being complicated, or rather owing to it, and the title given to the king, 'Antiochus Theos Epiphanes', could only have been written in this way between 169 and 166, as the evidence from coins indicates. The content of these texts is nevertheless difficult. In fact, there seems to be a contradiction between the petition and the response: the latter implied that the Samaritans wanted to change their customs, and particularly had done none of those things which the Jews were accused of doing. On the contrary, the petition not only did not deny that they were following customs that were originally Jewish (Sabbath and an unnamed temple), even if for reasons that were superstitious in origin, but it was entirely centred on the ethnic question of absence of kinship. Bickerman resolves the difficulty by considering that the contentious point is not the observance of such or such a custom in itself, but the fact that the *ethnos* of the Jews, juridically dependent on Jerusalem, no longer had the right to follow the law of Moses, since the edict of 167 (1 Macc. 1.44), by which Antiochus Epiphanes, by imposing Greek customs, had annulled a customary state of things which had been confirmed moreover in 200 by the charter of Antiochus III (*Ant.* 12.138-44).

This explanation is accurate in regard to form, in that it accounts for the coherence of the document, and preserves the Samaritans' fidelity to the law, despite their foreign origin, since the rededication of the sanctuary to Zeus involved no change in cult, and constituted only a minor concession.[35] In regard to the content, the petition itself and the context of Samaritan history lead to some obscurities persisting: 1. the petitioners said that they were different from the Jews by race and *by customs* (ἔθος); the observance of the Law would therefore not have been the same at Jerusalem and at Shechem; 2. the promise to procure better revenues for the king implied that the charge (the 'wickedness of the Jews') had a fiscal effect; 3. the royal officials had not really established that there were infractions, but had presumed them inevitable owing to the incriminating kinship. The combination of these three aspects suggests some difference in observance, not as yet determined, but with fiscal consequences, and therefore liable to provoke civil prosecution. Now, the account of the visit of the Samaritans to Alexander, after the concession of privileges to Judaea, provides a model case: the exemption from taxes in the Sabbatical Year, granted to the Jews but refused to the Samaritans.

In the petition, the allusion to ancient droughts was connected to the adoption of the 'Sabbath day', but a special care of the ground such as periodically letting it lie fallow would fit in better with a rural problem.[36] So had Josephus made a very slight alteration in his document, by putting in the singular what was originally in the plural, 'the days of the sabbaths',[37] which could be a semitism to designate both the weekly rest and the Sabbatical Year? The meaning of the request then was that they

35. Bickerman, 'Document relatif', p. 215. It is a matter of a simple request for an administrative registration, as is the custom of the Greeks, but without any explicit consequences in local practice.

36. According to Philo of Byblos (in Eusebius, *Praeparatio evangelica,* 1.10.7), it was as a result of droughts that the Phoenicians began to worship the 'Lord of Heaven, or "Zeus" in Greek' (בעל שמים). It could be a matter of something commonplace, but such is also the origin of the 'Abomination of Desolation', whose installation in the sanctuary at Jerusalem was the cause of the revolt; cf. Chapter 6, §1.

37. An assumption already made by A. Schalit, 'Die Denkschrift der Samaritaner an König Antochos Epiphanes', *ASTI* 8 (1972), pp. 131-83.

were not demanding exemption from taxes, as they had done in the time of Alexander. In the same spirit, the new name for the sanctuary must have had a fiscal effect, by inserting it into a system of royal supervision, since the order from Antiochus was not concerned with the local designation, but only with the official name. In this way the response established, on two essential and connected points, that the Samaritans should live well as befitted subjects of the Greek empire, and should pay the normal taxes. In this way, they could 'observe the customs [ἔθεσι χρώμενοι] of the Greeks', while remaining faithful to the Law.

As for the matter of foreign ancestry, it is more delicate to assess. Josephus, who seemed to forget what he had said about dissident Jews in the time of Sanballat and Alexander, insisted on the Mesopotamian extraction in his introductory paraphrase, but the royal letter made no mention of it, and restricted itself to asserting that the accusations against the Jews did not concern the Samaritans. In reality, it was not a matter of race, but of *ethnos*, that is to say, of a population seen as a juridical and cultural unit.[38] Here there were evidently two such units, gravitating around two cities endowed with sanctuaries, Jerusalem and Shechem. In this way, in spite of the tendentious interpretations of Josephus, it is clear that the documents studied make no allusion to the existence or not of a strictly ethnic kinship, in the modern sense of the term, between Samaritans and Jews: in particular, the eventual migration of dissident Jews, if they were integrated into the local cult, should have been considered from the legal point of view a change in *ethnos*.

The Samaritans, however, expressly called themselves Sidonians. It has been shown that this term, which could have been a metaphor for Phoenicians, indeed even Canaanites, was inappropriate, and Josephus, under the influence of his own report on the narrative of 2 Kings 17 about their origins, interpreted it as 'Mesopotamians'. It must be admitted however that he respected his source, since he did not maintain the interpretation which he had previously given, and since he could have easily made the whole difficulty disappear by replacing 'Sidonians' with 'Cuthaeans' or any other term agreeing more explicitly with 2 Kings 17. Furthermore, it is noteworthy that the style of the petition was not without its studied ambiguities, since it certainly was a matter of delicate negotiations: the Samaritans wanted to give an impression of submission, but, as Bickerman has clearly seen, 'correctly understood, the petition of the year 166 in no way expressed a disavowal by the Samaritans of their

38. Bickerman, *Institutions*, p. 164.

paternal religion'. In other words, they declared that the observance of the weekly Sabbath and/or the Sabbatical Year was a casual Jewish influence. This hybridization, moreover, could very well have been connected with the migrations of Jews, as Josephus had suggested with regard to the building on Gerizim and in connection with those who took refuge there later on (*Ant.* 11.346), and as is suggested too by the introduction into the Pentateuch of the weekly Sabbath.

Finally, it is not stated that they would be 'from Sidon' or 'from Phoenicia', but merely 'Sidonians'. It is not said then that they would be Phoenicians (or Canaanites) who had adopted Jewish customs, but in a rapid reading we are induced—especially in Josephus's context—to come to this conclusion, which the response of Antiochus did not do. The term 'Sidonians' was part of a systematic double meaning.

6. *Sidonians of Shechem*

It was Josephus who referred to these Sidonians of Shechem as Samaritans, without any allusion to any kind of internal subdivision of these latter into parties or tendencies. But his presentation, as we have just seen, distorted the meaning of the petition. Now, if we return to what is known of the Seleucid administration, it is a good idea not to lose sight of the fact that the seat of the governor of Samaria (and perhaps of all of Palestine), in this case Apollonius, was the city of Samaria. The people of Shechem did not intermix with the subjects of the province as a whole. On the occasion of the visit of Alexander (*Ant.* 11.340), two entirely distinct groups are clearly apparent: the Samaritans in general, and the 'dissident Jews' connected with the Gerizim temple. Even if Josephus's presentation is tendentious, since he always tried to denigrate the Samaritans (cf. Chapter 5), there is a certain duality, represented by the two cities of Samaria and Shechem. In other words, the petition just studied did not concern all the Samaritans, but only a group revolving around Shechem and the unnamed temple. In these conditions, the interpretation of 'Sidonians' as 'Phoenicians' or 'Canaanites', conceivable for the population of Samaria as a whole (especially if compared with the biblical allusions to 'dwellers in the land' [יושב הארץ]), can no longer be suitable for the sub-group observing the law of Moses, whether we would have them derived from Jerusalem or from the sons of Jacob.

Outside of the passages which clearly refer to the inhabitants of Sidon, we note in Josephus, beyond the two passages already considered, only one other example in which Sidonians could have been connected with all or part of the Samaritans. In *Ant.* 13.329, to encourage Ptolemy Lathyrus to come from Cyprus to help the coastal towns who were being threatened by Alexander Janneus (a little before 100), the inhabitants of Ptolemais indicated to him that he would have as probable allies the people of Gaza, as well as Zoilus, and added that there would be joining these 'the Sidonians and many others' (ἔτι γε μὴν Σιδωνίους καὶ πολλοὺς ἄλλους). The context does not formally rule out their being inhabitants of Sidon, or even Phoenicians. It was indicated shortly before (§324), however, that the only coastal towns still resisting were Ptolemais and Gaza, as well as Straton's Tower (the future Caesarea Maritima) and Dora, ruled by the local governor Zoilus just mentioned. In the immediate narrative setting, Sidon was therefore not on the list, as simple geography could lead us to expect. Here then the 'Sidonians' were a separate social category, whose territorial attachment remained imprecise. The general situation at that moment was rather confused, due to internal disputes in Syria as well as in Egypt, and in a more distant context (*Ant.* 13.276-79), it is reported that, after the destruction of Shechem and the temple of Gerizim, the Samaritans, besieged by John Hyrcanus, had appealed to Antiochus IX Cyzicenus to deliver them, and he got help from the same Ptolemy Lathyrus, at that time ruler of Egypt before being driven out by his mother Cleopatra III, who was favourable to the Jews (§285). There is no formal political contradiction in seeing the Samaritans or more exactly the Shechemites in the mention of the 'Sidonians', but perhaps this is stretching the text.

The 'Sidonians of Shechem' were Shechemites who had retained a trace of another attachment, of having been made satellites of some kind, either with respect to Samaria, or with respect to Jerusalem. Since the origin of the term 'Sidonians' in this case was not territorial, and since its use is only well attested by Josephus, it is on the whole advisable to seek its source in Josephus's own culture rather than in the Hellenistic world. Since older testimony is lacking, rabbinic literature provides some useful information.

Gen. 25.27 ('And Esau became a skillful hunter [צַיִד יֹדֵעַ], a man of the open country [שָׂדֶה אִישׁ]') was usually understood[39] as expressing the double-dealing of Esau, as opposed to Jacob's integrity (תָּם אִישׁ). The ancient midrash *Gen. R.* developed a play on words on שָׂדֶה/צַיִד[40]: צָד בְּבַיִת צָד בְּשָׂדֶה צַידְנִי סַדְנִי, where צַידְנִי,

---

39. Rashi, *ad loc.*, giving the literal sense. Yet Jacob in this episode is more cunning than his brother, but Esau is traditionally reinterpreted, in the light of all the texts concerning him—in particular, the third oracle of Balaam, Num. 24.18—as a symbol of the Byzantine Empire; cf. recently, among others, J. Neusner, *Comparative Midrash: The Plan and Program of Genesis and Leviticus Rabbah* (BJS, 111; Atlanta: Scholars Press, 1986).

40. *Gen. R.* 63.9, p. 693; the variants in the mss. and the parallel passages given

'devoted to hunting', became 'deceitful, two-faced' (from צד). Technically speaking, this midrash, transmitted by a third-century master, is interesting, since the same idea would have been easier to extract from other passages on Esau: in fact, it contradicts the immediate context here, and to arrive at it the author had to mobilize subsidiary semantic resources. The possibility cannot be excluded, however, that one of the goals was precisely to accentuate these. Whatever it might have been, there was a play on צידני (slightly different from צידוני[41]), by using the skill of a hunter (or 'Sidonian') as a coded symbol for duplicity.

In the Mishnah, we meet a singular example of 'Sidonian' (*m. Kel.* 4.3; cf. *t. Kel. B. Qam.* 3.11). In the setting of debates on the spreading of impurity, a question came up about containers with bottoms that were not flat, and therefore useless unless supported, since they could not stand by themselves. Owing to the fact that in principle only a free-standing and directly usable utensil was susceptible of impurity, the problem then was to define the juridical situation of such containers which could not be used by themselves. The Mishnah examined different cases, in particular the שולי קורפיות ושולי קוסים צידוניים and concluded, in conformity with its idea of intentionality as expressed in the treatise *Makshirin*, that they were real utensils, since they were conceived as such and given an appropriate name. It was in fact given two names: the first, קורפיות, is commonly interpreted as being derived from Greek κορυφαῖος 'tapering',[42] and designated in an understatement a vase with a pointed bottom; the second was explained by the traditional commentators as being a different object, a Sidonian vase, otherwise unknown. Such a commentary was hardly an explanation, but rather a simple paraphrase, to camouflage their ignorance. It was based on the hypothesis that the *waw* which joined the two expressions was an addition, and therefore organized a list of different articles. Yet, the fact that a Greek name is followed by a Hebrew name gives rise to a doubt, and leads us to attribute to this *waw* an explanatory value, or, which comes to the same thing, to see here a phonetic corruption of או, 'or'. Such an occurrence is not rare in the Mishnah,[43] and fits well here: the Greek term is explained as referring to a 'lateral' vase, namely one which lies on its side and not on its base. The explanatory gloss, now a doublet, generated the 'vases of Sidon', impossible to explain. The meaning thus extricated for צידוני, 'Sidonian' simply came from צד, 'side', and an eventual connotation of duplicity or trickery constituted a secondary development.

---

in the footnotes show that the two adjectives are really derived respectively from ציד and שדה, through some unknown factors, but in a way that constitutes phonetically one unique derivative from the root צדד.

41. The spellings צידון/ציידן and צדוני/צדני alternate in the sources; cf. *Arukh* 6.25, צדד[5].

42. *Arukh* 7.210, כרף. The use of a technical Greek term implies the adoption of a utensil of foreign origin, but with a use that was well defined and had become very common.

43. Cf. J.N. Epstein, *Mavo lenusah hamishna* (Jerusalem: Magnes, 1964), pp. 1070-90.

With regard to the Sidonians of Shechem, the term, whether in Hebrew or in Aramaic, indicated therefore that they were 'laterals'; the question left to answer is who named them in this way and in relationship to what: Samaria, Shechem or Jerusalem. It seems probable that such a designation would have come from others (just like that of the Pharisees, 'separatists'). Yet, according to the petition to Antiochus, they themselves used this word (cf. the Pharisees, who would end up by referring to themselves with this term invented by others), perhaps cleverly taking advantage of a possible double meaning. But as they were trying to obtain a favour and only displayed very modest pretensions, it is not difficult to admit that they would have used a term coined by others. For lack of other information, the simplest way is to follow Josephus and admit that the term came from Jerusalem, and consisted of a sort of hypocoristic to refer to the community attached to the Gerizim temple. Accepting the testimony of Josephus on this point does not involve, however, taking him literally, when he spoke of Jewish dissidents: the story about Sanballat was tendentious, but it certainly had as a substratum a kinship to clarify between Jews and Shechemites.

A final detail on the Sidonians can be presented: at the beginning of this century, the excavation of the tombs at Marisa provided all kinds of information on the life of a Hellenized city in the Lagide period.[44] In particular, a funerary inscription was dedicated to the head of a colony of 'Sidonians of Marisa' (τῶν ἐν Μαρίσηι Σιδωνίων), who had been in command for thirty-three years in the second century.[45] The most direct interpretation, according to which the colony in question would have originated from Sidon, would make impossible any useful comparison with the Shechemites.[46] Yet, it is recounted in *Ant.* 13.275 that, at the time when John Hyrcanus, emancipated from the Seleucids, besieged Samaria (later Sebaste), he was 'full of resentment against the Samaritans, because of all the harm they had done, at the instigation of the kings of Syria, to the people of Marisa, colonists stemming from the Jews and allied with them'. Like Idumaea as a whole, Marisa was colonized and Judaized by Hyrcanus (§257), but some commentators wonder how Samaria could have moved against Marisa, in the middle of Idumaea.[47] Seen

44. Schürer, *History*, II, with bibliography, p. 4 n. 8.

45. Cf. F.-M. Abel, 'Tombeaux récemment découverts à Marissa', *RB* 35 (1925), p. 275.

46. As opposed to the opinion of M. Delcor, 'Vom Sichem der Hellenistischen Epoche zum Sychar des Neuen Testaments', *ZDPV* 78 (1962), pp. 34-48, who assumes that the Shechemites would be from Sidon, just like the Sidonians of Marisa. For the latter, that possibility cannot be ruled out; cf. Egger, *Josephus Flavius*, p. 268.

47. Reinach, followed by Loeb, suggests correcting 'Marisa' to 'Samaria' (the

from the Jewish side, we can meanwhile certainly admit that the expansionism of Hyrcanus would have come up against Samaritan, or 'Sidonian', opposition, coming from communities dispersed throughout the territory, without it being necessary to suppose an *ad hoc* expedition sent from Samaria (or from Shechem). The disputes between Jews and Samaritans in Egypt (*Ant.* 12.10, and especially 13.74-79, under Ptolemy VI Philometor, a contemporary of the Maccabaean crisis) on the respective merits of their temples would have provided a plausible context, since these were purely local crises.

7. Conclusions

The community at Shechem, focused on its temple, was therefore clearly distinct from the city of Samaria. The confusion could have occurred after the ruin of Samaria, following Alexander's conquest, when the capital was transferred to a rebuilt Shechem, which did not imply that the whole province had automatically become identified with the cult at Gerizim.

The contradiction expressed in the introduction of the chapter remains, but it divides up into different aspects. Ethnically, there is a trace of a foreign origin of the Samaritans: if the portrayal of the community of Gerizim as Phoenicians or Canaanites from Sidon appears unsatisfactory, there remains Josephus's insistence, following 2 Kings 17, on showing the Mesopotamian (Cuthaean) origin of the Samaritans, as well as of Sanballat. To simplify matters, we can attach this origin to the city of Samaria. As for an Israelite kinship, Josephus reported that according to their own statements, the Samaritans were descended from Ephraim and Manasseh, but he himself declared that they were dissident Jews, and in particular he insisted on the Judaean origin of the Gerizim priesthood. Even if we concentrate the debate on Shechem, setting Samaria aside, the two opinions are incompatible.

Now, this is a major issue. In fact, on the one hand the petition of the Shechemites to Antiochus IV referred to the Sabbath and the unnamed temple as two significant axes of their cult. On the other hand, in studying the different forms of the account of the taking of Jerusalem by

region), assuming that after the conquest of Shechem, the Shechemites had put up resistance in their region. He relies on the fact that in 1 Macc. 5.66, Μάρισαν alternates in the manuscripts with Σαμάρειαν, because of the similarity in the writing of the uncials; but in *Ant.* we can only see the adjective Μαρισηνούς, which is somewhat longer than Σαμαρεῖς; Moreover in 1 Maccabees, 'Samaria' is a correction to give an easier reading (Abel).

surprise on the Sabbath, it is seen that Josephus surreptitiously, but artificially, introduced an incident of a sacrifice in the Temple, foreign to the structure of the narrative. The 'model of Nehemiah', with the walls and the Sabbath, was in fact to a considerable extent independent of the Temple, but Josephus tried to bring them together. Alexander, attracted by the Temple and its high priest, had granted an exemption from the taxes of the Sabbatical Year, at the request of the Jews (and not of the high priest, who is only a spokesperson).

These minor manipulations suggest that the Gerizim system had more intrinsic coherence, especially priestly coherence, than that of Jerusalem, which was something Josephus could certainly not admit, and therefore definitely had to hide: that could have been at the root of his unfavourable view of the Samaritans, of which he made no secret.[48] In these circumstances the two units forming the account of the coming of Alexander, although in literary terms discordant, were utilized in a coherent manner: at Jerusalem the temple dominated, while there would have been room to distinguish between Jews and Judaeans. At Gerizim, the priesthood was derivative and illegitimate, and was made up of refugees who observed the Sabbath poorly (11.346). Whatever the interval in time between them might have been,[49] these last two assertions are completely opposed to the declarations in the letter of the Shechemites. Who therefore was right?

Legends never occur by chance, and the rumours of Jewish dissidents at Gerizim must have been based on something. The matter of a degenerate priesthood does not entirely fit in, since the priestly lines in Jerusalem were imprecise, as will be shown (Chapter 6, §6), but a movement of institutions such as the Sabbath seems better, since it is based on clearer indications: the Samaritans of Shechem admitted to having adopted it. Furthermore, the Pentateuch, considered as a whole, goes better with Shechem than Jerusalem, as much from the narration (Abraham, Jacob, Ebal and Gerizim) as from the legislation (cult, importance of priests), and we saw in Chapter 3 that it was simple enough to imagine a stage of the Pentateuch without a weekly Sabbath, which especially brings up the question of the origin of *non-biblical* Jewish

48. Coggins, *Samaritans and Jews*, pp. 10, 16, 94, 99.

49. It can be ignored, since it is a matter of legends in which redactional activity by Josephus is certain, and especially because the visit of Alexander and the petition of the Samaritans are the only two cases in which Josephus uses the expression 'Sidonians of Shechem': the two pieces therefore belong to the same debate.

institutions (cf. Chapter 7). The Samaritan petition to Antiochus IV gives a chronological reference point then. At the time of the Maccabaean crisis, the cult at Gerizim had already received this new feature (and spoke of it as something recent), while the high priest in Jerusalem did not yet have sacred writings at his disposal, or at least did not yet have sufficient authority (cf. Chapter 6, §5).

The resulting hypothesis therefore is that the quasi-definitive formation of the Pentateuch must be situated somewhere towards the end of the third century in connection with Shechem (Gerizim), probably from a preceding briefer stage. The conclusions of F.M. Cross, according to which the formation of the Samaritan Pentateuch cannot have been earlier than the second century, must be qualified: in fact, if he does not reach a decision on the earlier stages, it is because of a lack of evidence from that earlier time. As for the paleographic argument, that the Samaritan alphabet is derived from Hebrew script of the second century, as is well attested, this is not a difficulty, since we only need admit that the definitive disappearance of the Gerizim temple, at the end of that same century, strongly contributed to reinforcing the role of their written Torah and to stabilizing its script. We see an analogous mechanism in Judaism, two centuries later.

The revisions in Josephus are imperfect, since they almost inescapably provoke doubts about his statements, but we do glimpse the enormity of what he had to hide. In particular, his tendency to homogenize the culture and the cult of Judaea, which turned up once again in this chapter, inspires a comparison with the propaganda characteristic of 1 Maccabees, which fits Judas, an intransigent man, into a Hasmonaean priestly dynasty which was perhaps founded on completely different principles. To make some progress, and in particular to fill out the hypothesis just formulated by finding a context for it, it is necessary to delay again the examination of the Maccabaean crisis, and study first other testimony on the origin of the Samaritans and their ancient history.

Chapter 5

ABOUT THE ORIGIN OF THE SAMARITANS

Direct Samaritan traditions only became known in modern times, and are in general very confused. For a long time the textual transmission had never come under the control of scribal schools,[1] and the revisions were so continuous that there are even events after the 1789 Revolution in some of the sacred chronicles. Other facts, however, induce careful consideration of what the Samaritans say about themselves. The narratives of the Hexateuch, which ignore the Judaea of Bethlehem and Jerusalem, leaves a major place for Shechem, from the time of the altar built by Abraham (Gen. 12.7) up to the great assembly of Joshua (Josh. 24), while treating in passing a solemn installation at Ebal and at Gerizim (Deut 11.29-30; Josh. 8.30-33). In the genealogy of the patriarchs, Judah is a son of Israel, and consequently the Northern Kingdom has precedence. So the most official canonical tradition preserves very clear indications relative to the precedence of the North over the South. The previous chapter showed that Josephus's demonstrations relative to the priority of the Jews and the Jerusalem Temple over the Shechem Samaritans were very suspect, and we have to find out whether we can bring together all these elements, in particular whether the opposition Israel–Judah supports an identifiable relationship with the twosome Samaritans–Jews. Such is the object of this chapter, in which there is an examination of the biblical texts and the Samaritan documentation, without losing sight of the reinterpretations of Josephus.

1. Assyrian Colonists in Samaria

In dependence on 2 Kgs 17.24-41, Josephus recounts that, at the time of the deportation by Shalmaneser V, Cuthaeans (Χουθαῖοι) were brought

---

1.   With the exception of certain techniques that made colophons unchangeable, at least for the Pentateuch; cf. Gaster, *The Samaritans*, pp. 108-10, in regard to copies of the Abisha scroll.

from Persia to Samaria (εἰς τὴν Σαμάρειαν) (*Ant.* 9.288-92).[2] But they brought their own cult, and as a result neglected the cult of God Most High (μέγιστον θεόν). They were then attacked by a pestilence, but obtained from the king of Assyria the repatriation of Israelite priests. And Josephus concluded: 'They strove to worship (God) with great zeal [...] Even today, the same rituals continue in use among these people, called Cuthaeans in the language of the Hebrews and Samaritans in that of the Greeks.' Whether 'Samaria' referred here to the city or the region (earlier, in 9.279, he states that the Cuthaeans were established as colonists at Samaria and in the land of the Israelites), it is clear that the derivative racial name had a lasting Israelite religious meaning, which seems difficult to restrict to the citizens of the city of Samaria alone. Besides, that state of affairs apparently lasted until the days of Josephus himself. At best it could be argued against this duration that the form 'even today' is just a clumsy transcription of the conclusion of the biblical account (17.34, 41: עד היום הזה: 'to this day'). Such lack of certitude on the part of Josephus was perhaps not innocent, as we have just seen. In any case, the connection of the Samaritan ritual to the ancient Israelite religion is in keeping with the account of the visit of the inhabitants of Shechem to Alexander at Jerusalem, in which the Samaritans, although Hebrews, could not call themselves Jews.

Josephus had begun by expressing in a different way the message that he wished to give concerning the origin of the Samaritans. He stated that the ten tribes of the North had been deported and replaced by the Cuthaeans (*Ant.* 9.278; 10.183), which did not stop him from reporting

---

2.   Josephus stated elsewhere (*Ant.* 9.288) that the newcomers were made up of five peoples, whom he did not name. The MT of 2 Kgs 17.24 in fact gives five names that are parallel: מבבל ומכותה ומעוא ומחמת וספרוים, whereas the LXX handles them differently: (καὶ ἤγαγεν...) ἐκ Βαβυλῶνος τὸν ἐκ Χουνθα καὶ ἀπὸ Αια καὶ ἀπὸ Αιμαθ καὶ Σεπφαρουαιν; for the LXX therefore, Χουνθα formed part of Babylon and constituted the principal source of the migration, while the contribution of the other three places was marginal. Josephus seemed to have the same understanding then as the LXX, by giving greater importance to the Cuthaean name and by situating *khoutha* in Persia (9.288), through an anachronism. Both of them seem to have proceeded from a text מבבל מכותה, without a connecting *waw*, and there were then only *four* peoples, all in Babylon, the first being the Cuthaeans, which is also attested by the rabbinic tradition. On the contrary, when Josephus mentioned *five* peoples (cf. Jn 4.18), he presupposed the *waw* (MT); he combined a reading like the MT with a tradition (witnessed to by the LXX) which gave a privileged place to the Cuthaeans.

(9.69), in dependence on 2 Chron. 34.6-7, that Josiah had visited and reformed those Israelites who had escaped the captivity. There seems to be a contradiction here, but this double account allowed him to play once again with the double origin of the Samaritans: they were Assyrian colonists or more or less Judaized Israelites, that is to say, outsiders or subordinates, which leaves intact the primacy of Judaea. As for the ten tribes who according to Josephus emigrated *from Judaea* (*Ant.* 9.280), their number did not come from a direct detailed count, which he would probably have had trouble explaining (Reuben, Gad, Simeon, Levi?), but from the fact that the kingdom remaining in the South comprised the two tribes of Judah and Benjamin alone (cf. 1 Kgs 12.21, although according to 2 Kgs 17.18 there remained only the tribe of Judah).

The context of 2 Kgs 17.24-41 seems ambiguous. According to 17.1-4, Hoshea, son of Elah, became king of Israel in Samaria in the twelfth year of Ahaz, king of Judah, and reigned there for nine years. Shalmaneser, king of Assyria, made Hoshea his vassal and imposed on him a tribute, but Hoshea tried to get out of this by seeking support in Egypt (סוא, Sais[3]), and Shalmaneser had him put in chains. According to 15.30, however, this Hoshea was a contemporary of Jotham, father of Ahaz, and close to the deportations of Tiglath-pileser. Against this uncertain background, it is next recounted (17.5-6) that the king of Assyria invaded the country and came to Samaria and laid siege to it for three years, at the end of which he deported the Israelites 'to Halah and on the Habor, a river of Gozan, and in the cities of the Medes'. This second account, in which the Assyrian king is not named, seems unaware of the preceding report, but is connected to it by the redactional indication that Samaria fell in the ninth year of Hoshea, therefore at the end of his reign.[4] Attributing all these activities to the same 'king of Assyria',

3.   Literally: 'He sent messengers to So [LXX Σηγωρ], king of Egypt' (Lucianic recension: 'to Adrammelech [cf. 17.31], the Ethiopian living in Egypt'); the identification of 'So' with 'Sais' (or 'the Saite') was proposed by W.F. Albright, 'The Elimination of the King "So"', *BASOR* 171 (1963), p. 66 (completing a note of H. Goedicke, 'The End of "So, King of Egypt"', *BASOR* 171 [1965], pp. 64-66) and accepted ever since. The form of the LXX (which renders in this way צוער, 'Zoar' from Gen. 19.22) is closer rather to צוען, 'Tanis'.

4.   According to the literary analysis of E. Würthwein, *Die Bücher der Könige* (*1 Kön. 17–2 Kön. 25*) (ATD, 11/2; Göttingen: Vandenhoeck & Ruprecht, 1984), p. 394, it would be a matter of two parallel reports, one (vv. 1-4) centred on Hoshea, the other (vv. 5-6) on Samaria, with the imprisonment of one corresponding to the siege of the other. For M. Cogan and H. Tadmor, *II Kings* (AB, 11; Garden City,

however, is contradicted by external documents: while it is indeed to Shalmaneser V, successor of Tiglath-pileser III, that the Babylonian Chronicle attributes the ruin of Samaria after a siege in 722–721, he died the same year, after a reign of five years, and it was Sargon II who deported in 721 or 720 a part of the population, '27,280 persons with their chariots and their gods', at the time of one or several subsequent campaigns,[5] and settled in Samaria rebels from afar captured in the deserts.

The accounts in 2 Kgs 17.1-6 have, therefore, from an Assyrian perspective, an identifiable historical foundation, but they are unsure about the reigns and exaggerate to a great extent in speaking of the deportation of all the Israelites. This exaggeration was motivated by a long reflection (17.7-23) on the complete ruin of Israel because of its sin, and the section on 'the origin of the Samaritans' comes next (17.24-41). This section contains two principal parts, combined at the end by a verse that gives a synthesis.

1. Verses 24-33 deal with the colonists settled by the Assyrians, their imported cults and their adoption of Israelite cult, thanks to a priest (LXX: 'priests') deported from Samaria who was repatriated to Bethel. The king of Assyria is not named. The new colonists were taken from five places with well-known cults (Babylon, Cutha, Avva, Hamath and Sepharvayim), which they retained along with their adherence to Yahwism. These colonists had not come voluntarily, but, in accordance with the regular custom of the Mesopotamian empires, they were themselves deported on the occasion of other Assyrian conquests, and the extra-biblical sources prove that they could not have come at the same time: some of the operations are prior to Sargon II (Hamat), while others are later (Babylon, in 689, by Sennacherib). According to Ezra 4.2, the 'enemies of Judah and Benjamin' stated that they had come under Esarhaddon (681–668). It was a question then of an imaginary synthesis of numerous migrations, and even the theme of devouring lions, which Josephus transformed into a pestilence, to make it more plausible, should be attributed to a literary motif of punishment for disloyalty.[6]

NY: Doubleday, 1988), pp. 195, 216, more sensitive to historical reconstructions, the two accounts stand in isolation, since, according to their interpretation of the Assyrian chronicles, the siege of Samaria began at the end of Hoshea's reign.

5. Cf. *ANET*, pp. 284-86; Cogan and Tadmor, *II Kings*, pp. 336-37.

6. Also 1 Kgs 13.24 and 20.36, and M. Weinfeld, *Deuteronomy and the Deuteronomic School* (Oxford: Clarendon Press, 1972), p. 123.

2. Verses 34-40, which follow after the reflections on the ruin (vv. 23 and 34: 'until this day'), speak, without any specification of time and place, of the unfaithfulness of the Israelites to the Covenant concluded by YHWH with Jacob, their father, with those who had come up from the land of Egypt. There is no mention then of colonists come from the East. Some authors consider,[7] because of the literary relationship of this passage with the long excursus on the causes of the exile (17.7-23), that it was a declaration depriving the exiles from Israel of the right to return, since they were persisting in their infidelity in the land of the Medes and Persians. Most think, however, that the diagnosis concerned the Israelites who had not been exiled. In fact, on the one hand the deportation had touched only a small number, and on the other hand, later on, the centralization of cult by Josiah was extended to the high places of Bethel and Samaria, built in connection with Jeroboam's secession (2 Kgs 23.15-20), and definitely the unfaithful Israelites were the ones affected. According to 2 Chron. 30.1-14 Hezekiah made an attempt to con-voke all Israel, 'from Dan to Beersheba', to celebrate the Passover in Jerusalem, but did not succeed in rallying much more than Judah. This account is probably not really historical, but it is testimony, at least in the time of the Chronicler, about the persistence of dissident Israelites in the North.

This presentation on the origin of the Samaritans calls for several observations, since its two parts are not homogeneous: there are in the first place foreigners who fear (יְרֵאִים) YHWH, then Israelites who do not fear (אֵינָם יְרֵאִים) YHWH. As a matter of fact, the first part is in itself complex: vv. 25-28 describes the urgent introduction of the cult of YHWH at Bethel, but v. 29 causes a break, by recalling the imported cults: 'And each nation began to make [וַיִּהְיוּ עֹשִׂים] its own gods and put [וַיַּנִּיחוּ] them in the temples of the high places that the Samaritans had made.' This proposition is the natural continuation of v. 24, giving the arrival of the aforesaid nations in the cities of Samaria, and the result of the present order is to make the threat of the lions a consequence of the absence of the cult of YHWH, and not of the importation of other cults as Josephus gave to understand in the passage quoted (9.288). In this way, the subsequent syncretism no longer brings about the same threat. This narrative effect, which does not necessarily imply successive redac-tional phases, culminates in v. 32, in which after the description of

---

7. M. Cogan, 'Israel in Exile—The View of a Josianian Historian', *JBL* 97 (1978), pp. 40-44.

foreign cults, it is explained, in the same style as the break in v. 29: 'And they began to fear [ויהיו יראים] YHWH and they appointed out of their own number priests[8] for the high places.'

A few consequences follow from these observations: first of all, the same name Samaria, which had designated the royal city at the time of the deportation, has a changed meaning and presupposes here a whole region, with cities and high places; next, in this group there is a very clear distinction between Bethel, heir of the traditions of the North, to which there had returned a priest of YHWH, and the high places with priests of the foreign cults, a distinction which came up again at the time of the reform of Josiah (2 Kgs 23.15, 19, 'altar of Bethel' and 'temples of the high places of the cities of Samaria'); finally, the Samaritans, according to this text (v. 29), are those who, before being deported, had built the temples of the high places, where the new cults are now found. To use precise terminology, according to this account, the name 'Samaritans' for these new occupants can no longer have the same meaning, and the name Cuthaean is more appropriate. The other part of the passage, however, makes an allusion to the persistence of unfaithful Israelites, guilty in particular of having built the high places (17.9-12): the same Samaritans, in the ancient sense, still survive 'to this day'. The confusion exists therefore at several levels.

Verse 34 contains moreover an unusual feature. According to the MT, its two hemistichs seem to be incompatible: they persist in their ancient laws, which could be said of the foreign colonists, and at the same time they do not follow their own laws (?) nor the precepts of God, which are only applicable to the ancient unfaithful Israelites.

עד היום הזה	ἕως τῆς ἡμέρας ταύτης
הם עשׂים	αὐτοὶ ἐποιοῦν
כמשׁפטים הראשׁנים	κατὰ τὸ κρίμα αὐτῶν.[9]

---

8. ויעשׂו להם מקצותם כהני במות; the LXX doubles the verse with two adjoining forms put end to end: the first version puts, in place of these words, καὶ κατῴκισαν τὰ βδελύγματα αὐτῶν ἐν τοῖς οἴκοις τῶν ὑψηλῶν 'and they installed their loathsome things in the temples of the high places', that is to say, with forms graphically very close, וישׂימו להם שׁקציהם בתי הבמות. The second version follows the MT, while omitting the word מקצותם (translated μέρος or ἐκ μέρους in 1 Kgs 12.31 and 13.33), which makes clear that there is no question of a levitical priest; this suggests that it is because of trouble with this problematic word that the doublet developed.

9.   The Lucianic recension, which otherwise follows the MT against the LXX, has for this line: κατὰ τὸ κρίμα αὐτῶν τὸ ἀπ' ἀρχῆς οἱ πρῶτοι, or כמשׁפטם הראשׁון הראשׁונים, with a doublet.

אֵינָם יְרֵאִים אֶת יְהוָה	αὐτοὶ φοβοῦνται
וְאֵינָם עֹשִׂים	καὶ αὐτοὶ ποιοῦσιν
כְּחֻקֹּתָם וּכְמִשְׁפָּטָם	κατὰ τὰ δικαιώματα αὐτῶν
וְכַמִּצְוָה [...]	[...] καὶ κατὰ τὴν ἐντολήν,
אֲשֶׁר צִוָּה יְהוָה [...]	ἣν ἐνετείλατο κύριος [...]

According to the LXX, on the contrary, they observed 'to this day' the command-ments given to the sons of Jacob as well as their own laws, that is to say, they followed an enduring hybridization. Without coming to any conclusion here on the relative precedence of these two versions,[10] we can see that the MT is longer (the underlined words), and can be understood in a Pharisaic perspective, with a reproach for not having followed the oral tradition, which was later than the ancient laws (cf. Chapter 7, §3). Verse 40, which according to the MT had just said after the discourse that they persisted in their infidelity, was included by the LXX in the precepts: 'And you shall not conform to their rituals, as they practice them [καὶ οὐκ ἀκούσεσθε ἐπὶ τῷ κρίματι αὐτῶν, ὃ αὐτοὶ ποιοῦσιν].' The modifications in vv. 34 and 40 were therefore coordinated, and it is worth noting that Josephus, who also pro-nounced on the faithfulness of the Samaritans, would be very close to the LXX, and would go so far as to omit v. 41, which summed up their syncretism in a sort of general conclusion. According to Josephus, the Samaritans were faithful, and their only flaw, which he periodically referred to, was to be of foreign origin. As for the LXX, we may understand either that the colonists had become faithful Israelites, like those who had come out of Egypt, or that there had remained, on the fringe of the colonists with the hybrid cult, ancient faithful Israelites.

The confusion seems inseparable from the history of the Samaritans: genuine Israelites more or less faithful, or colonists more or less cross-bred with Yahwism. Only the category of those who had been protected by Sanballat according to Josephus, namely 'dissident Judaeans', seems to be missing, but it may be rediscovered in the schism that had arisen among the heirs of Solomon (1 Kgs 12.20-24), in something close to an anachronism. From a chronological point of view, the whole pasage is certainly a synthesis from long after the events.

Geography however is going to provide some reference points: the cities of Samaria and Shechem were distinct, and it was to one of them, and not to Bethel, that we could expect to see the exiled priest return. Bethel comes up at several points, not as a city, but as a sanctuary, as its name suggests. It had been the altar of the golden calf, condemned after Jeroboam's secession (1 Kgs 13); it had been before that the sanctuary founded by Jacob (Gen. 28.19).

10.　　The determination of the relative antecedence of the MT and the LXX is dif-ficult here, as is also the exact nature of Josephus's biblical evidence (he puts vv. 29-32 before 25, follows the LXX in vv. 34 and 40, and omits v. 41).

2. *Aaron and Bethel*

Bethel was a sanctuary, which presupposes a priesthood. In every epoch, the high priestly dynasties in Jerusalem had the greatest trouble to connect themselves to Aaron. On the contrary, the Samaritan priesthood came to have a great importance, so much so that Josephus did not succeed in entirely discrediting it.

It is advisable then to take note first of what the texts say about the priestly connections of Israel. According to 1 Kgs 15.7, Abijam, son and successor of Rehoboam in Judah, made war on Jeroboam, king of Israel. The parallel in 2 Chron. 13.4-12 deals with the conflict in a much later context.[11] It modifies the profile of the belligerents and introduces before the battle a discourse by the king of Judah to all Israel, developing the legitimacy of the kingship of the sons of David and that of the priesthood of the sons of Aaron: 'Have you not driven out the priests of YHWH, the sons of Aaron [...], to make priests of your own "like the people of foreign countries" [כעמי הארצות, LXX ἐκ τοῦ λαοῦ τῆς γῆς[12]]: anyone who comes with a bull and seven rams to get himself consecrated, can become priest of what is no god at all'. On the other hand, the discourse is spoken to all Israel on Mount Zemaraim (צמרים in the dual) in the mountains of Ephraim.[13] The LXX has Σομορων, very close to שומרון, 'Samaria'. We have already noted (Chapter 4, §6) the same divergence between MT and LXX for Zemerites, son of Canaan, in Gen. 10.18. The discourse as a whole is fictional ('the midrash of the prophet Iddo', v. 22) and it is suggestive to see there an allusion to the Samaritans (with the dual form discretely referring to Gerizim and Ebal), but the question is to know which ones. In particular, it has not been proved that the deviancy blamed on the Aaronide priesthood is real, as I have shown that on this point Josephus, who made similar allegations relating to a later time, had a very tendentious presentation: the whole discourse could just be

11.   M. Delcor, 'Hinweise auf das samaritanische Schisma im Alten Testament', *ZAW* 74 (1962), pp. 281-91.

12.   This is the translation of *Traduction Œcuménique de la Bible* (Paris: Cerf, 1988); the JB translates: 'as the people of the region do', that is to say, the Canaanites. Now, the ritual referred to recalls Exod. 29.1-30, and therefore it should be a question of Israelites, as 1 Kgs 12.31 says. So M. Delcor, 'Samaritanische Schisma', p. 284 prefers the LXX (in fact, B, where כל which follows is translated πάσης, and therefore modifies γῆς) as less discordant. Rashi understands 'who are like the local people', in fact coming from the people; this gives a better literal sense, quite close to the LXX.

13.   Josh. 18.22 MT draws attention to a town with this name in Benjamin, along with Bethel. Since these two names are missing in the LXX (B), this could be an alteration corresponding to the conclusion on the war of Abija(m), in 2 Chron. 13.19, where Bethel and her outlying villages were taken by Jeroboam.

propaganda for Judaean usage, in the setting of a takeover of the Aaronide priesthood in Jerusalem.

Despite the discussions, which will be touched on later, there was certainly, at some stage in the tradition, a solid priestly bond between Bethel and Aaron. It has been noted for a long time that there was a literary relationship between the role of Aaron at the time of the episode of the golden calf (Exod. 32) and the narrative about the erection by Jeroboam of the golden calf at Bethel (and at Dan), where it was presented as an innovation[14] (1Kgs 12.28-33). Even if we admit that Jeroboam had begun again a ritual for which Aaron would have been the precursor, this could not have been originally any more reprehensible than the bronze serpent at Jerusalem,[15] or the divine throne formed by the Cherubim.[16]

Eleazar, the eldest son of Aaron, was buried according to Josh. 24.33 at Gibeah, the town of his son Phinehas, in the mountains of Ephraim, and at the time of the incident of the Levite from Ephraim, it was the same Phinehas who ministered before the altar at Bethel (Judg. 20.28). On the other hand, the link between Aaron and the Zadokites, who formed the traditional priesthood of Jerusalem, is only found in biblical texts that are very 'Judaean':[17] Ezra–Nehemiah, Chronicles (cf. the discourse of Abijah) and the Priestly source P.

At the time of Jacob's dream, moreover, use was made of the ancient name of Bethel, Luz (Gen. 28.19; 35.6; 48.3), which denotes 'almond' (cf. Gen. 30.37). Now, according to Num. 17.23, the branch of Aaron was an almond too, and the *menorah* which he was to guard (Lev. 24.4) must also resemble an almond[18] (Exod. 25.33-40). In fact, it was made in one piece and called to mind a tree, like a bell of a capital. There

14.   R.H. Kennet, 'The Origin of the Aaronite Priesthood', *JTS* 6 (1905), pp. 161-86.

15.   M. Aberbach and L. Smolar, 'Aaron, Jeroboam, and the Golden Calf', *JBL* 86 (1967), pp. 129-40, who find thirteen similarities between Jeroboam and Aaron; H. Motzki, 'Ein Beitrag zum Problem des Stierkultes in der Religionsgeschichte Israels', *VT* 25 (1975), pp. 470-85.

16.   H. Danthine, 'L'imagerie des trônes vides et des trônes porteurs de symboles dans le Proche-Orient ancien', in *Mélanges syriens offerts à René Dussaud* (Bibliothèque Archéologique et Historique 30; 2 vols.; Paris: Geuthner, 1939), II, pp. 857-66.

17.   E. Auerbach, 'Die Herkunft der Sadokiden', *ZAW* 49 (1931), pp. 327-28; H.H. Rowley, 'Zadok and the Nehustan', *JBL* 58 (1939), pp. 113-41.

18.   L. Yarden, *The Tree of Light: A Study of the Menorah* (Uppsala: Scriv Service, 1972), p. 41.

would have been therefore, at Bethel, the souvenir of a sacred tree.[19]

The examination of different texts gives reason to think finally that the bronze serpent in the Jerusalem temple (Num. 21.4-9), identified with the rod of Moses (Exod. 4.2-5) and done away with by Hezekiah, was then replaced, at least in the texts and not without some confusion, by the branch of Aaron, the badge of the priesthood of Bethel. Jeremiah, at the time of his vocation, said that he saw an almond branch.[20] It is worth noting finally that this *menorah* with seven branches of the Priestly texts, which has a Mesopotamian origin,[21] would have been entirely different from the 'lamp of God' of Shiloh (1 Sam. 3.3), from that of David at Jerusalem (1 Kgs 11.36) and from those of the temple of Solomon (1 Kgs 7.49).

The importance of the Zadokite priesthood seems very clear at Jerusalem, but it was not of levitical origin, its attachment to Aaron is historically doubtful, and it is in no way proved that the high priests of the monarchical period would have been of Zadokite ancestry:[22] it was therefore principally providing a literary backing for the post-exilic high priests.[23] On the other hand, if the Levites before Deuteronomy had only been what was left of a category of 'resident foreigners' (גרים), they became at that time, and they alone, capable of being chosen for the exercise of priesthood at the unique sanctuary; in Deut. 17.8-13, they are called levitical priests, and in Deut. 18.6, just Levites. Nevertheless, following on the reform of Josiah, the high priests had to be Zadokites, at least progressively (Ezek. 40.45-46), and later on this priesthood was connected to Aaron, presented as a Levite. Such are the main lines of the accepted synthesis,[24] but it poses more problems than it resolves, since it is entirely focused on Jerusalem, which produces the risk that a Judaean bias will be underestimated. But especially, by putting Deuteronomy, the reform of Josiah (2 Kgs 22–23) and Ezekiel's vision of the

---

19.   Mentioned in regard to the dream of Jacob in *Jub.* 27.20: 'He took one of the stones from the place and put it under *that* tree' (Ethiopic version; *that* is missing in the Latin and the Hebrew fragment from Qumran; cf. D. Barthélemy and J.-T. Milik, *Qumran Cave I* [DJD, 1; Oxford: Clarendon Press, 1955], p. 83).

20.   L. Yarden, 'Aaron, Bethel and the Menorah', *JJS* 26 (1975), pp. 39-47, with bibliography.

21.   G. Widengren, 'The King and the Tree of Life in Ancient Near Eastern Religion', *UUÅ* 4 (1951), pp. 64-67.

22.   J.R. Bartlett, 'Zadok and His Successors at Jerusalem', *JTS*, NS, 19 (1968), pp. 1-18.

23.   A. Cody, *A History of Old Testament Priesthood* (AnBib, 35; Rome: Pontifical Biblical Institute, 1969), pp. 92-96.

24.   Cody, *Old Testament Priesthood*, p. 150.

temple in a chronological series, we do not obtain a coherent historical view of the evolution of the priesthood, or more exactly we are induced to merge literary elaborations unifying the dynasties with historical episodes that are certainly more incompatible. What is more, even if we should see in this way the necessity of a connection between Zadok and the Levites, the introduction of Aaron into the dynasty seems strange, if he must be connected with the North and if he is supplanted by the Levites. Finally, this is a good place to observe that Ebal and Gerizim are the only cult places mentioned in Deuteronomy, which never specified which was 'the place YHWH has chosen'.[25] It is therefore not established, in fact the very opposite is true, that Judaea would have been the first addressee of this book.[26]

It is time to consider the texts. Ezekiel's future temple was situated on a high mountain (40.2, with 'like a city built to the south'[27]), and must be served by the priests,[28] sons of Zadok, since the Levites 'had gone astray' (44.10-14). The high mountain suggests the surroundings of Shechem, which is a central place for the ten tribes. The insistence on all Israel as well as the absence of any allusion in this passage to the name of Jerusalem, other than through a reference to Judaea (48.7-8), indicates a reunion perspective, which is made explicit in Ezek. 37.16-17.[29]

25.   Or 'will choose': MT has יבחר, the Samaritan Pentateuch has בחר. Cf. R. de Vaux, 'Le lieu que Yahwé a choisi pour y établir son nom', in F. Maass (ed.), *Das ferne und nahe Wort* (Festschrift L. Rost; BZAW, 105; Berlin: Töpelmann, 1967), pp. 219-28. The vagueness about the 'place' in Deuteronomy (but not in the Deuteronomistic History) will be discussed later.

26.   N. Na'aman, 'Shechem and Jerusalem in the Exilic and Restoration Period', *Zion* 8/1 (1993), pp. 7-32, shows that Deuteronomy 11 and 27, on Ebal and Gerizim (completed by Josh. 8 and 24), are late Deuteronomic additions, after the Exile and prior to the restoration by Cyrus and Darius; they would have been intended to promote the sanctuary at Shechem after the destruction of Jerusalem. The analysis of the literary elements, completed by an extensive bibliography, is excellent, and the conclusion just referred to, debatable since it is dependent on an unverified historiography, can easily be transposed. The sanctuary at Shechem existed before the establishment of a properly biblical cult at Jerusalem, which only appeared with Jonathan; cf. Chapter 6, §7).

27.   MT מנגב, LXX ἀπέναντι 'on the opposite side', from מנגד.

28.   Zadok and his sons, priests since the time of David and Solomon (2 Sam. 15.24; 1 Kgs 2.35), are not Levites; cf. Ezek. 48.11. The mention of 'sons of Levi' in Ezek. 40.46 is a (poorly placed) addition.

29.   Z. Weisman 'Reflexions on Lawgiving at Sinai and its Interpretations', *Shnaton* 5-6 (1978, published 1982), pp. 55-68, suggests that the two versions of the

Furthermore, there is no reference to the law of Moses.[30] According to Exodus, on the contrary, in the aforesaid law, and with various nuances, the story of the golden calf promotes, in opposition to Aaron, the Levites along with the Ark as heirs of Moses and guardians of the Law. Likewise, Deut. 33.1-7, with the wish 'to bring back Judah', does not declare a reform in Judah alone, but a bringing together of all Israel. We get in this way two models in conflict (relative to 'all Israel', therefore centred in the North), which leads us to compare the priests of Zadok and Aaron, but in contrasting perspectives, in which the Law constitutes a decisive element. According to Ezekiel, the Levites were pushed aside for the benefit of Zadok and his temple, which constituted (or represented) the Law. On the contrary, in the confrontation with Aaron, the Levites were made guardians of the law of Moses. There was therefore an opposition between two laws, with the Levites in the middle, that of the (future) Temple and that of Moses. The redefinition of Zadok as a descendant of Aaron clarified the conflict, and of course, if all became Levites, that is if everything was reoriented on a continual history of Jerusalem, the conflict vanished, but it left wounds behind.

In fact, the account of the golden calf (Exod. 32) clearly places in opposition Aaron, who made the idol and built the altar, and the Levites, who fought against the idolaters and supported Moses. The report of the episode of Deut. 10.6-8 calls to mind the anger of God against Aaron,[31] and throws into relief the choice of the Levites for the cult, despite the

Covenant in Exodus 23 and 34, represented by the double giving of the tablets, corresponds to two parallel recensions, one in Judaea (J) and the other in the North (E). He also suggests that the fight against the golden calf, which records them, represents the struggle against the division brought about by Jeroboam erecting the temple at Bethel, so that the reunion of the pieces of wood by Ezekiel would correspond to the same idea. These views are useful in so far as they focus attention on the difficulties: 1. According to Exodus, the golden calf, which characterized the schism, was incompatible with the tablets of the written Law, and it is hard to see that this would have been the 'recension of Jeroboam'; 2. Ezekiel, who ignored the law of Moses, criticized Jerusalem and sought rather to bring dissident Judaea into the bosom of Israel.

30.   The Law exists, but it is a matter of the 'law of the Temple' (תורת בית יהוה), Ezek. 43.11-12; 44.5, 24.

31.   Exod. 32.10 in the Samaritan Pentateuch as well as in 4QExª, inserts the anger of God against Aaron (nine words analogous to Deut. 9.20a, with התאנף; cf. 9.8 and 2 Kgs 17.18); cf. M. Baillet, 'Le texte samaritain de l'Exode dans les manuscrits de Qumrân', in A. Caquot and M. Philonenko (eds.), *Hommages à André Dupont-Sommer* (Paris: A. Maisonneuve, 1971), pp. 363-81.

reminder about the installation of Eleazar when Aaron died (cf. Num. 20.22-29). It is hard to dispute that in the episode of the golden calf Aaron would have had a priestly function,[32] and that there was a censure of the cult as it existed at Bethel (and Dan), on the occasion of which Aaron had abandoned the people, 'exposing them to the derision of their adversaries' (Exod. 32.25b). It is not Bethel itself that is criticized, but the cult that took place there. Nevertheless, the version in Exodus accuses the people (v. 31, 'This people has committed a grave sin'), and tends to exonerate Aaron.[33] In short, the worship of the idol is prohibited and the Levites are promoted, but there is a debate over the position of Aaron.

Such is what we find in the present text, but we may wonder about its origin, since in the end it is not stated clearly in any way that Aaron would have been the ancestor of the priests of Bethel.[34] In Exodus 32, the passage on the Levites (vv. 25-29) seems secondary ('the next day' of v. 30 follows either v. 24, or v. 20). From a narrative perspective, the context of the episode of the golden calf is Exod. 24.12-15, in which Moses, invited to come up the mountain, delegated to Aaron and Hur the task of replacing him. Aaron and Hur were the ones who aided Moses in the battle against the Amalekites (Exod. 17.8-14), and on that occasion, Moses received the order to write about the events in *the* book, and to speak them in the ears of Joshua (v. 14). The latter was therefore instituted heir, and we find him at the side of Moses in the golden calf incident (32.17), but he was absent from the parallel account in Deuteronomy 9. According to current literary and redactional criticism, the primitive account of Exodus 32 draws attention to Aaron.[35] According to some,[36] a primitive reference to Aaron (vv. 1-7) gives the golden calf a positive etiological dimension at first, but it is afterwards integrated into a polemical compilation. For others,[37] the

32.   A.H.J. Gunneweg, *Leviten und Priester* (FRLANT, 89; Göttingen: Vandenhoeck & Ruprecht, 1965), pp. 88-95.

33.   The account as a whole frees Aaron of any responsibility, while vv. 25b and 35b accentuate it; this leads us to suppose two redactional phases, but commentators do not agree in determining the account's primitive tendency; cf. Cody, *Old Testament Priesthood*, p. 149 (see n. 9).

34.   Since H. Oort, 'Die Aaroniden', *TT* 18 (1884), pp. 289-335; cf. Cody, *Old Testament Priesthood*, p. 147.

35.   O. Eissfeldt, *Hexateuch-Synopse* (Leipzig: Hinrichs, 1922), pp. 50-52, who after some discussion assigns it to E; H. Valentin, *Aaron* (OBO, 18; Göttingen: Vandenhoeck & Ruprecht, 1978), p. 266.

36.   W. Beyerlin, *Herkunft und Geschichte der ältesten Sinaitraditionen* (Tübingen: Mohr [Paul Siebeck], 1961), pp. 146-53.

37.   Cf. the studies of O. Eissfeldt, *Kleine Schriften* (6 vols.; Tübingen: Mohr [Paul Siebeck], 1962–79), IV, pp. 12-31 and pp. 209-214 (L source), followed by others; also de Vaux, *Ancient Israel*, pp. 398-401.

primitive element was an account of infidelity and punishment concerning Joshua, and the whole story of the golden calf, with or without Aaron, was superimposed. As a matter of fact, if literary criticism only reaches very uncertain results, as far as sources go, it is due to the preoccupation with recovering a real history of the Sinai Covenant and the priesthood sufficiently similiar to the apparent history of the final redactions.

If we remove this concern from the picture, we obtain, by using the observations made by the various commentators, simpler ideas, based on more obvious facts. By following the obvious features of the context, we note that neither Hur nor Joshua play significant roles in the account of the golden calf. What is more, the role of Aaron (and the Levites), which seems a major one, is found in two passages which are easily disconnected from the context (not counting a final gloss in v. 35b: 'the one that Aaron made'): vv. 1b-6, he made the calf, and vv. 21-25, he explained to Moses what had happened.[38] What is left over is a more homogeneous narrative, in which the people (eventually abandoned by Aaron, v. 25) made the calf and became corrupted; then Moses, having come down to restore order, went back up to beg for the mercy of God. The history of the redaction can extend into much more minute details, and the evaluation of the connection of the golden calf incident with the context depends then on the significance given to vv. 17-18, which introduce Joshua.

Therefore, if the episode of the Levites was also added at some later stage, it is in any case closely coordinated with Aaron. In other words, Aaron was connected at a later stage to the golden calf group, to whom the Levites were opposed. The golden calf itself was a retrojection into the Sinai narratives from the narratives about Bethel. The bond between Aaron and Bethel is therefore affirmed, but in an indirect way. The result of this is that the joining of Aaron to Bethel, no matter what its precise historical origin,[39] was not a bare fact, but a thesis, in which we can see an effort to exonerate him. In fact, if the calf incident, which indicated a rural cult, was something negative, it had a positive legacy too, which introduces the Levites, and which is expressed by the staff, the *menorah*, the almond, and is connected to the first name of Bethel.

3. *Shechem and Bethel*

The present context of the episode of the golden calf is that of infidelity to the Law given verbally at Sinai-Horeb, before the appearance of its

38.   J. Loza, 'La tradición antigua de Exodo XXXII y su prehistoria', in press; *idem*, 'Exode XXXII et la rédaction JE', *VT* 23 (1973), pp. 31-55.

39.   Cody, *Old Testament Priesthood*, p. 160, who considers that the Levitical cities of the Kohathites (Josh. 21.9-42), to which the Aaronides were connected, were in greater Judah and Benjamin.

written form (the tablets with the Ark, then the memorial stones of Deut. 27.3 and Josh. 8.32). Unlike Aaron, the Levites were expressly connected to the conservation of the written form of the law of Moses. Now, the question of the legacy of Moses, and in particular the enactment of the Law after his death leads to an examination of the account of the assembly of the Israelites at Shechem with Joshua (Josh. 24), in which the people and important members of the community, but not the Levites and priests, took part. In Joshua's discourse, Moses and Aaron are only brought in at the moment of the departure from Egypt and have no connection with the Law (Josh. 24.5),[40] but at the end of the account, when statutes and ordinances are laid down for the people, it is all put in writing in the book of the law of God (vv. 25-26). Joshua was therefore a founder (he offered them a choice) and legislator (he wrote). He was thus in competition with Moses and the Levites. In the passage that immediately follows, Joshua, 'servant of YHWH' (a title of Moses, Exod. 14.31, for whom Joshua is the substitute), dies, as well as the priest Eleazar, son of Aaron. The competition lies then between two presentations of Joshua as guardian of the Law: one in which he dominates, but without a successor, and in which Moses and Aaron have only a very vague (and perhaps secondary) role as initiators, and the other in which successions and roles are set, since Joshua succeeded Moses as servant of God (cf. Josh. 1.2), and Eleazar succeeded Aaron as priest.

The account of the assembly at Shechem is regarded, according to source criticism, as a late insertion, or more exactly as the deuteronomistic revision (pre- or post-exilic) of ancient material, connected to the Elohist source.[41] They would find there the trace of an entry into the Covenant of Northern tribes, who would perhaps be of Eastern origin, but in any case distinct from those connected to the traditions of the exodus and Sinai, and the whole thing would have been reworked in connection with a subsequent renewal of the Covenant, according to some (the reform of

---

40.   According to the MT; the LXX omits any mention of Moses and Aaron. In Mic. 6.4, Moses and Aaron appear with Miriam.
41.   Since M. Noth, *Das Buch Josua* (HAT, 1/7; Tübingen: Mohr [Paul Siebeck], 1953), pp. 135-38, which was based on the thesis of the amphictyony; cf. de Vaux, *Ancient Israel*, pp. 667-69, who presents various opinions on reconstructing the historical facts. J. Van Seters, 'Joshua 24 and the Problem of Tradition', in W.B. Barrick and J.R. Spencer (eds.), *In the Shelter of Elyon: Essays on Ancient Palestinian Life and Literature in Honor of G.W. Ahlström* (JSOTSup, 31; Sheffield: JSOT Press, 1984), pp. 139-58, maintains that it is a late composition, related to the work of the Yahwist, and intended for the exiles.

Josiah),[42] or of a return from exile, according to others. Yet, if the extent of the revision is as great as is claimed, the importance of Shechem is peculiar, for Josiah as for the return from exile. In particular the complete absence of any allusion to Moses as a legislator stands in contrast with the ritual of installation at Ebal-Gerizim of Josh. 8.30-35, which expressly refers to the law of Moses and to the Levites: this presupposes at least a parallel tradition (doublet), which made an assembly at Shechem an occasion for a continuation of Moses, perhaps to form in the final redaction a sort of prologue to the other assembly where Moses is not involved.

Shechem was connected then to the legislation of Joshua, with or without Moses in the background, but Bethel was connected to patriarchal legislation.[43] In fact, in the narrative on 'the origin of the Samaritans' of 2 Kings 17, which speaks of Bethel, there is a reference to the coming out of Egypt as well as to 'statutes, ordinances, law and commandments which YHWH had laid down for the sons of Jacob, who had been given the name Israel' (v. 34), with no allusion to Moses, nor even to any written document, since it had become necessary to send a priest for the colonists. It was a matter again of legislation for Israel which could be called 'pre-Mosaic', despite the Deuteronomistic redaction, and which was connected to the remembrance of the miraculous deliverance, but here without the opposition between Joshua who had established the people, and Jacob who had exiled them.[44] Finally, even if it is observed that Bethel was above all a sanctuary, while Shechem was first of all a city, it must be emphasized that in Genesis, Jacob is evidently connected to the two, or more exactly, we observe a superimposition of traditions on Jacob (heir of Abraham), linked to Shechem, with others on Israel, linked to Bethel,[45] and the double name is found in 2 Kings 17. So there is a trace of a difference, then of an identification.

Where was Bethel then? Gen. 28.11-22 is very vague, and Josephus, at this point, takes care in his paraphrase to provide no precise information (cf. *Ant.* 1.279). By way of a preliminary remark, it should be noted that in the Bible the twin peaks of Ebal and Gerizim are not clearly connected with Shechem, but are 'opposite Gilgal, near the oak of Moreh', according to Deut. 11.30. In the same way, the expedition of

42. R.G. Bowling and G.E. Wright, *Joshua* (AB, 6; Garden City, NY: Doubleday, 1982), pp. 533-36.
43. L. Perlitt, *Bundestheologie im Alten Testament* (WMANT, 36; Neukirchen–Vluyn: Neukirchener Verlag, 1969), pp. 239-84.
44. A.G. Auld, *Joshua, Moses and the Land: Tetrateuch–Pentateuch–Hexateuch in a Generation since 1938* (Edinburgh: T. & T. Clark, 1980).
45. De Vaux, *Ancient Israel*, p. 172.

Joshua 8 took place when Joshua was still in the camp at Gilgal, which raises in passing the problem of the relation of Gilgal to Jericho. The tradition well established by Josephus and the Samaritans having these mountains flanking Shechem will be examined below. But to return to Jeroboam's golden calves: 1 Kgs 12.28-30 relates that there were two, one at Dan and the other at Bethel, but the continuation of the narrative is exclusively centred on Bethel; it speaks of house (LXX: 'houses') of high places, institution of non-Levitical priests and feasts, condemnation by the man of God come from Judah. Furthermore, just before that it was stated that Jeroboam 'built Shechem in the mountain country of Ephraim and lived there' (v. 25). The only geographical detail which suggests a noticeable separation of Shechem from Bethel is the mention of Dan, which leads one to suppose that each of the two calves was at an extremity of the territory of the kingdom of Israel, parallel to the expression 'from Dan to Beersheba'. Apart from the fact that it is perhaps not too wise to create a place for worship in an outlying area in the conditions indicated,[46] the important thing here is to note that the introduction of Dan is in literary terms artificial,[47] and therefore Bethel and Shechem are 'close'.

The symmetry thus intended between Dan and Bethel suggests, in the light of the preceding observations, that we should consider anew the cults connected to Moses and to Aaron. In fact the Danites, at the time of their migration towards Laish, took as priest Jonathan, son of Gershom, son of Moses,[48] as well as his sons after him (Judg. 18.30), and everything needed for the cult: 'carved image, ephod, *teraphim*, the idol of cast metal.' The account is a composite one, but it has connections with Judah, since before his name is mentioned, the priest is referred to as a Levite from Bethlehem,[49] and since the Danites, while on the move, encamped at Kiriath-

46.   W. Ross, 'Is Beitin the Bethel of Jeroboam?', *PEQ* 73 (1941), pp. 22-27, who observes besides that the Bethel of Jeroboam should according to Amos 7.10-14 contain the palaces of the king and the high priest.

47.   But later the passage became an established source; cf. 2 Kgs 10.29, in regard to the permanence of the golden calves in the time of Jehu.

48.   MT has מֹשֶׁה (fully pronounced); LXX (AB) reads 'Manasseh' (cf. the wicked king of Judah in 2 Kgs 21.1-18); but some textual witnesses (including the Lucianic recension) ignore the *tiqqun* and read 'Moses'.

49.   At the beginning of the narrative (Judg. 17.7), he is a Levite from Bethlehem in Judah, of the clan (מִשְׁפָּחָה, LXX συγγενεία) of Judah, living as a *ger* there (גָּר שָׁם, which gives a 'good' etymology for Gershom, גֵּרְשֹׁם), and he tries to find a place to live elsewhere. On the meaning of this 'Levite', see de Vaux, *Ancient Israel*, p. 362; Gunneweg, *Leviten und Priester*, pp. 16-33, considers that it is not yet a question of a tribe, and that the appearance at the end of the account of the name of

Yearim. There is also a link with the highlands of Ephraim, since it was there that Micah resided, whose priest and utensils they stole. In other words, the cult of Dan, connected to Moses, had some morphological relationship with Aaron's calf. At the time of the revelation at the burning bush, a question was posed for Moses: 'Is there not Aaron your brother the Levite?' The relationship discussed is not extraneous to an eventual conflict, which brings into the picture the episode of the golden calf, and which suggests besides the theft of cult by the Danites. On the other hand, the story of the Danites closes with the indication that the dynasty of priests continued to function there until the exile, and that the carved image remained there even as long as the house of God was at Shiloh (vv. 30-31). We can admit that this last detail would be included for general consistency with the history of David and Solomon, but it is easy to see that the intrusion of the golden calf of Jeroboam is artificial. It was a matter of the literary coordination of the cults at Bethel and Dan, which had by themselves nothing reprehensible in those times, that is to say in reality, the reconciliation of Moses and Aaron, the two protagonists in the departure from Egypt (Josh. 24.5). All this, again, is well before any written Mosaic law, and shows how Moses could have become the young brother of Aaron, in a collection gravitating around Shechem and/or Bethel.

To connect Bethel to Shechem appears, however, to do violence to common sense and to the most solid evidence of the texts and of archaeology. In fact, the traditions and the facts appear to be unanimous in situating Bethel-Luz at Beitin, a small village north of Jerusalem. Yet, it can be shown that it is in reality a consensus with relatively little foundation.

The arguments are as follows:[50] 1. from a linguistic point of view the correspondence of Bethel or Beitil and Arabic Beitin is not a difficulty,[51] since in the same way Yizr'el became locally Zer'in,[52] and in these two cases, among many others, the words have no meaning in local Arabic, and have therefore resisted the attraction of the usual terms; 2. the excavations at Beitin have shown that it is the only site in the region which would have had an important occupation in the Middle and Late

---

the Levite, with a genealogy, comes from a revision (גר שם) which is at best a play on words with the name of his father.

50.   A.F. Rainey, 'Bethel is still Beitin', *WTJ* 34 (1970–71), pp. 175-88.

51.   Ever since the identification, by Edward Robinson and Eli Smith (E. Robinson and E. Smith, *Biblical Researches in Palestine* [3 vols.; Boston: Crocker & Brewster, 1841], III, pp. 161-68), which was accepted by the local Orthodox priests.

52.   It is in fact merely an alternation (or confusion in pronunciation) of נ/ל, occurring also in the ancient pronunciation of Hebrew. Josephus puts Ῥουβῆλος for ראובן (*Ant.* 1.304; found also in Syriac); in the same way, *t. Meg.* 1.3 affects the meaning through the confusion מסתכנין / מסתכלין.

Bronze periods, ending with a destruction level around 1250,[53] which fits in with the fact that Bethel had an ancient name (Luz) and appears in the history of the patriarchs and the conquest; 3. the biblical geography fits too: Judg. 21.19 speaks of Shiloh on the east of the route going from Bethel to Shechem, which must have a north–south axis, distinct from the route of Beth Horon (1 Sam. 13.18), from the route in the Desert (Josh. 8.15) and from the route of the Arabah (2 Sam. 4.7), which have lateral axes; 4. moreover, Bethel was in the lot of Benjamin (Josh. 18.22), but was occupied by Ephraimites (1 Chron. 7.28), since it was the 'house of Joseph' which went up there after the death of Joshua (Judg. 1.22), and all this fits in well with a position near the frontier between Benjamin and Ephraim, in the time of the tribes as well as in the period of the two monarchies; 5. finally Eusebius indicated that Bethel was still in his time a small village east of the route, in the vicinity of the twelfth milestone from Aelia (Jerusalem) on the way to Neapolis (Nablus).[54]

These arguments however prove very little: the local onomastic component factor is solid, but it cannot claim to do more than to have preserved on the site what Eusebius had indicated. The presence of a church commemorating Jacob's dream is mentioned by Jerome,[55] and can correspond without too much difficulty to one or other of the ruins of Byzantine churches found in the vicinity of Beitin. But Josephus, as has been said, was unaware of the location of Bethel, and the testimony of Eusebius was later lost, apparently with the disappearance of the village, since in modern times they resumed the search for its location all the way even to the vicinity of Shechem.[56] We know on the other hand that in the Byzantine period the holy places were multiplied as stages for Christian pilgrims, often without any other tradition than a simple biblical likelihood. In the case of Bethel, the text cited, Judg. 21.19, joined to the memory of the ascent of the Israelites from Gilgal (near Jericho) towards Ai and Bethel is quite clear: 'at Shiloh, which is north of Bethel, on the east side of the route [למסלה] that goes up from Bethel to Shechem, and to the south of

53.   J.L. Kelso, *et al.*, *The Excavations at Bethel (1934–1960)* (AASOR, 39; Cambridge, MA: American Schools of Oriental Research, 1968); the remains of the Hellenistic and Roman periods were also recovered. Important Byzantine ruins, consisting of two churches, have been recognized in the vicinity (Burj Beitin) by C.R. Conder and H.H. Kitchener, *The Survey of Western Palestine* (4 vols.; London: Palestine Exploration Fund, 1881–83), pp. 295-96 , 305-307, and have since been excavated.

54.   Eusebius, *Onomastikon*, p. 4, 1.28-30 ('Αγγαί, from העי, Ai), p. 40, 1.20-22 and p. 120, 1.9. This location is met again on the Madeba Map, which groups together Bethel, Rimmon and *Ephraea* (= Ophra), but it is not an independent source.

55.   Eusebius, *Onomastikon* (additions from the Latin tradition), p. 5, 1.29-31 ('Αγγαί); Ai itself was unknown to Eusebius as well as Jerome.

56.   C.R. Conder, *Tent Work in Palestine* (2 vols.; London: Bentley, 1879), II, pp. 106-107, who looked for 'heretical Bethel'; he suggested, following V. Guérin, a connection with Luza, a name retained for the ruins on the summit of Gerizim (according to Gen. 28.19, Luz is the ancient name of Bethel, and the Samaritan Pentateuch has לוזה). There will be more on this, below.

Lebonah.' The precision of this verse is really a very strong argument against any ancient local tradition, since it dispenses with searching elsewhere for the origin of the holy place. We are brought back to a simple question of biblical geography, that is to say, essentially to a literary problem. As for archaeology, it in no way bears out the preference accorded to Beitin, but the very opposite: the site stopped being occupied from the beginning of the Iron Age. Now, accepting the usual dates for biblical history, the archaeological finds can furnish a setting for the Abraham and Jacob narratives, which are connected to the Middle Bronze Age. Possibly a setting is provided too for the conquest by Joshua (although it would be Jericho and Ai which were destroyed, and not Bethel), which is dated at the transition between the Late Bronze Age and Iron I, but such a date is no longer acceptable either for the period of the Judges (the attack by the house of Joseph, who are really the ancestors of the Samaritans: Judg. 1.22, etc.) in Iron I, or for the time of Samuel (1 Sam. 7.16, etc.), or for the period of the monarchy (the passages cited above on the temple of Jeroboam; Elijah and Elisha: 2 Kgs 2.2, etc.), all dated to Iron II. It must be admitted therefore either that the site is elsewhere or that it was displaced at one time, either as to place *and* as to texts, or only in the texts, by way of a literary effect.[57] In this sense, archaeology is in no way opposed to the hypotheses proposed above, in regard to redactional effects bringing near or distancing Bethel from Shechem, according to circumstances to be defined. In this regard, it must be pointed out that the apparently so precise verse of Judg. 21.19 sounds strange in the LXX: 'at Shiloh, which is north of Bethel, toward the rising of the sun, *on* the highway [B; A reads: "*in* the route", supposing במסלה and not למסלה of MT] going up from Bethel to Shechem'; if this text is treated seriously, it must be recognized as obscure, and therefore some revisions should be presupposed.

As for the location of Ebal and Gerizim, Eusebius, followed by Jerome,[58] maintained that their localization around Shechem was a Samaritan falsification, since these mountains are near Gilgal according to Deut. 11.30 (and Josh. 8.30-35), and since according to Josh. 4.19 Gilgal is near Jericho; he added a tradition putting them around Jericho, but he did not know exactly where to situate them. The *Madaba Map* agrees with this testimony, but without more precise details. Josephus on the contrary links up with the 'Samaritan falsification', which a rabbinic tradition followed as well (*m. Soṭ.* 7.5); this tradition considered that the arrival of the Israelites at Ebal and Gerizim 'in Samaria, close to Shechem', took place right after the crossing of the Jordan, because of Deut. 27.4: 'The day you cross the Jordan, [...] you shall set up [...].' This view, which favours Deut. 11.30 ('These mountains are opposite Gilgal, near the oak of Moreh'; cf. Gen. 12.6, which puts

<hr>

57. D. Livingstone, 'Location of Biblical Bethel and Ai Reconsidered', *WTJ* 34 (1970–71), pp. 20-44, proposes el-Bireh, while noting the circular reasoning in the identification of Bethel with Beitin, and basing himself on topographical considerations, linked to the difficulties in locating Ai (there could also be here a play on words between עי, 'Ai', and עיבל, 'Ebal').

58. Eusebius, *Onomastikon*, pp. 64-65.

together the oak of Moreh and Shechem[59]), tends therefore to separate Gilgal from Jericho and to bring it nearer the ford of Adam (situated 'at a great distance', Josh. 3.16), if it must be left near the Jordan. Such a situation is incompatible with Josh. 4.19, for which Gilgal is 'on the eastern border of Jericho'. Eusebius made the opposite choice, preferring the reports of Joshua to the Pentateuch. A certain polemic on his part however is possible, since he knew Josephus's works, and what is more, in the story of the reign of Abimelech, son of Gideon-Jerubbaal, the discourse of Jotham to the leaders of Shechem (Judg. 9.7; LXX: 'people') is explicitly spoken from the summit of Gerizim, which leaves no doubt as to the locality. For our purpose, it suffices to note that in this account a temple of El-Berit ('Bethel-Berit') is mentioned in the vicinity of Shechem (9.46), which may or may not be the same Bethel.

In short, Bethel, which could have designated any temple to the god El, has in literary terms a double existence, at a point on the frontier of Benjamin, which corresponds to the Benjaminite accounts of the conquest of Joshua[60] and of the reconstitution of Benjamin (Judg. 21.19; the Ark was at Bethel, 20.27), and at another point in the mountains of Ephraim, which approximately corresponds to Shechem, or at least to an associated sanctuary. To this doubling there corresponds another, that of Gilgal, which can in itself designate any structure of dressed stones (cf. Josh. 22.10); it is situated either in the region of Jericho, because of the same Benjaminite accounts, or at another point closer to Ebal and Gerizim, which must be connected with Shechem. In this regard, from now on an important similarity between Josephus and the Samaritan book of Joshua must be kept in mind (cf. below, §7), for they both separate Gilgal from Jericho. A third doubling is superimposed on the previous ones and clarifies them: Eusebius distinguished Luz, an ancient name for Bethel (Gen. 28.19) from a substitute Luz 'in the land of the Hittites' (Judg. 1.26). He situated this latter 'near Shechem, nine miles from Neapolis',[61] and the ruins at the summit of Gerizim still have the name Luza, but that may be due to the subsequent influence of the Samaritans. Incidentally, the Samaritans' naming of their sanctuary as 'Mount Gerizim-Bethel' can be acknowledged to have an honourable

---

59.   Cf. Deut. 11.30 Samaritan Pentateuch, which, after 'near the oak of Moreh', adds שכם מול, 'opposite Shechem'. According to 2 Kgs 2.1 (Elijah and Elisha), Bethel is between Gilgal and Jericho, and *Onomastikon*, p. 67 (Jerome's translation) points to *aliam Galgalam*, which we meet again in the village of Jiljiliyeh, 7 miles north of Beitin, that is to say, in the mountains of Ephraim.

60.   De Vaux, *Ancient Israel*, pp. 606-10.

61.   Eusebius, *Onomastikon*, p. 120, l.11; Jerome has only 3 miles.

antiquity[62] despite the precariousness of their documentation. Nevertheless, while Bethel is near Shechem in the narratives of 1–2 Kings, it must
be recognized that in the Patriarchal narratives, the efforts to superim-
pose one on the other presuppose them to be distinct: there was a
pilgrimage which went from Shechem to Bethel[63] (Gen. 35.2-4), which
could give the impression that the distancing of Bethel in relation to
Shechem is a secondary phenomenon.

In conclusion, the criteria followed, consisting on the one hand of not
taking for granted the existence before Joshua of the 'law of Moses' (the
historical summaries of the coming out of Egypt systematically ignored
Sinai anyway) and on the other hand of following in the texts the
appearance of written laws, provide some contrasting results:

1. There was a trace of a (written) law at Shechem and/or Bethel,
    binding Jacob and/or Israel, without any connection with Moses.
2. Always in the North (Joshua), there was a split between Moses
    as legislator and Joshua as legislator, with a strong presumption
    that the first had replaced the second, who then became his
    heir.
3. The golden calf (Bethel or Sinai) was the adversary of the law
    of Moses, which was closely united to the Levites.
4. This golden calf, to which Aaron was connected with a certain
    priestly role, was certainly no more bizarre in the ancient stages
    of the cult than the carved image at Dan or the bronze serpent
    at Jerusalem.
5. This same Aaron was the undisputed high priest of the P
    (Priestly) documents, and it is tempting to bring him together
    with the non-Mosaic, in fact pre-Mosaic, law of Joshua, which
    would open the way to understanding why, at the time of the
    synthesis (of P and Deuteronomy), he was left a priest while at
    the same time becoming the elder brother of Moses.

---

62.   Eusebius, *Praeparatio evangelica* 9.17.13, quotes a passage from
Eupolemius which could be translated 'Mountain of the Most High'. A fragment of
a papyrus in Hebrew script from the first century CE was found at Masada in which
the place name הרגריזים is written as a single word; cf. the discussions of
R. Pummer, 'ΑΡΓΑΡΙΖΙΜ: A Criterion for Samaritan Provenance', *JSJ* 18 (1987),
pp. 18-25; and of H. Eshel, 'The Prayer of Joseph: A Papyrus from Masada and the
Samaritan Temple on ΑΡΓΑΡΙΖΙΜ', *Zion* 56 (1991), pp. 125-36.

63.   A. Alt, 'Die Wallfahrt von Sichem nach Bethel', in *Kleine Schriften zur
Geschichte des Volkes Israel* (3 vols.; Munich: Beck, 1953–59), I, pp. 79-88.

6. What results from these considerations is an important plan for
    literary analysis: in particular, the P collection certainly has had
    a long and complex history, as we have glimpsed in regard to
    the Sabbath in Leviticus, since, even in the limited perspective
    considered here, it included traces of a non-Mosaic cult (Aaron
    and the almond), and went as far as genealogical syntheses
    making Aaron and Moses brother Levites.

Before dealing with any questions about dates, it should be established
that the authoritative document with the title 'law of Moses' had appeared at a certain point in a literary and cultic history that was already
formed and centred in the North (Shechem or Bethel). The book of
Joshua, in its final redaction, obviously had among its tasks to assimilate
that occurence, without moving away from the North (Shechem). As for
the document itself, to be brief I call it the Pentateuch, it certainly had
distant sources, written or not, and it must be recalled that the narrative
about the patriarchs revolves to a great extent around Shechem, with
contacts, through appropriate journeys around the country, with Hebron
and the Negev as well as with Egypt and Mesopotamia.[64] By contrast,
Judaean historiography (Judges–Kings), which ignored the patriarchs to
a great extent and knew the law of Moses very poorly, constituted
something completely distinct. The highlighting of the Hexateuch just
proposed, as well as of Shechem and Bethel, leads back inevitably to the
Samaritans and their writings.

4. *Samaritan Pentateuch*

Before its rediscovery at the beginning of modern times and its publication in the *Polyglots* of Paris (1645) and of London (1657), the memory of the Samaritan Pentateuch (hereafter, SP) was only preserved by a
few Jewish and Christian traditions.

First of all, the Bible. Rabbinic tradition (*b. Sanh.* 21b) had maintained
a precise remembrance that the law had first been given to Israel in
Hebrew letters (כתב עברי). In the time of Ezra it was given anew, and
Israel chose Aramaic writing ('Assyrian', כתב אשורי; cf. *m. Meg.* 2.2),
leaving the Hebrew writing to the native population (הדיוטות, ἰδιῶται).

---

64.   I thus agree, from another angle, with the direction opened up by J. van
Seters, *Abraham in History and Tradition* (New Haven: Yale University Press,
1975), who advocates controlling literary criticism through the analysis of forms and
structures, and not the other way round.

And who are these 'natives'? The Cuthaeans, said R. Hisda, and their writing the 'Neapolitan'[65] (from Nablus). It is worth noting that this tradition was known by Christians at least since Origen.[66] I shall consider later on how to interpret these natives, who are none other than the 'people of the land' (עם הארץ; cf, Chapter 7, §4). What is to be observed here is that, according to this text, the Samaritans were the possessors of the ancient account of the Law, before Ezra, and therefore that they were extraneous to the return from exile, as a result of which the term Israel had been transferred to the returnees.

The continuation of the tradition just mentioned gave to this ancient writing the name *da'aṣ* (דעץ)[67], an Aramaic term which can refer to the engraving by a style on a hard support. In a parallel passage, a midrash proves that the form of the letters was known (*y. Meg.* 1.11): 'If we maintain that the Torah was given in *da'aṣ*, the letter *'ayin* was a miracle. In fact, the legend would have it that the letters were carved into the Tablets (since they were written "on both sides"), and the central part of *'ayin* (a closed oval or triangle, in the Hebrew-Samaritan alphabet) would have to fall out.'[68] Another text (*Tanhuma*, Vayesheb 2) calls this ancient writing *notaricum* (נוטריקון); that is to say, the writing of a notary or a stenographer. This could designate either profane usages,[69] as Hasmonaean coins show, or a special script

65.   J.A. Montgomery, *The Samaritans, the Earliest Jewish Sect* (Bohlen Lectures, 1906; Philadelphia: J.C. Winston, 1907; repr.; New York: Ktav, 1968), p. 282. The text has ליבונאה, which some tried to connect to Lebanon or to Lebona in Ephraim (cf. Judg. 21.19), but since J. Halévy, *Mélanges de critique et d'histoire relatifs aux peoples sémitiques* (Paris: A. Maisonneuve, 1883), p. 435 n. 15, a probable restoration would be ניבולאה (from Νεαπόλις, Shechem-Nablus), because of the phonetic confusion נ/ל, already suggested above in regard to Beitin.

66.   For references, cf. Montgomery, *The Samaritans*, p. 281 n. 25.

67.   The MSS most often have רעץ, but according to the testimony of Epiphanias, *De duodecim gemmis*, §63 (*PG* 43, 356), the five books of Moses were given to him at Sinai in *deession* writing which Ezra rejected, but which the Samaritans still used; cf. G. Hoffmann, 'Lexicalisches', ZAW 1 (1881), p. 334.

68.   The cited text continues: 'If the Torah had been given in Assyrian characters, the letter *samech* would be a miracle'; in this alphabet, the *samech* is a closed oval too.

69.   A passage of the Mishnah states precisely the boundary between the sacred and the profane: if a book of the Hebrew Scriptures is written in Hebrew letters, it does not soil (מטמא) the hands (*m. Yad.* 4.5), that is, it does not oblige the one who touched it to perform ablutions in water; only the 'Assyrian' alphabet was fitting for official sacred usage.

used for the tetragrammaton, as Origen and Jerome mentioned,[70] and as has been confirmed by the texts from Qumran.

As for the text itself, the Greek Christian tradition, since Origen, has preserved the trace of lessons from a *Samaritikon*,[71] but it has long been wondered whether this referred to the Samaritan Pentateuch properly so called or to a Greek translation more or less parallel to the LXX.

Since the publication of SP in the *Polyglots*, it has been realized that it had, besides obvious late alterations, curious contacts with the LXX against the MT, which could be used to weaken the authority of the latter. A new component was thus brought into the debates stemming from the Reformation in regard to the Deuterocanonicals, that is to say, on the authority respectively of the LXX and the MT. In an age when the religious wars were very far from being at an end, and when in the bosom of Catholicism the debates over the Latin Vulgate were very lively, the discussion fairly quickly moved out of the strictly humanist domain. At the beginning of the nineteenth century, Gesenius thought that he could demonstrate,[72] by classifying and analysing the variant readings of the SP, that it was a late counterfeit edition, without any value for textual criticism. As for the similarities with the LXX, which presented an obstacle to the thesis of arbitrary falsification, he tried to explain them merely by declaring that one as well as the other came from Hebrew manuscripts separate from the official tradition of the MT. In a major study, Geiger later on observed[73] that the type of text on which Gesenius based himself was not the best, and that the Samaritan text should not be considered as a late derivative of the MT, but as a witness to an ancient tradition, later on rejected with the establishment of the Jewish text. The comprehensive definition of the exact relationships among SP, MT and LXX remained uncertain, however, and the work began again. Even the relationship between the New Testament and SP was noticed and this set off new enthusiasm.[74] Once again, there were

70.   Origen, *In Psalmos* II, §2, *PG* 12.1104; Jerome, *Epistula* 25, *PL* 28.594; cf. G. Mercati, *Psalteri Hexapli reliquiae*, I (Rome: Vatican Library, 1958), p. 172.

71.   F. Field, *Origenis hexaplorum quae supersunt, sive veterum interpretum graecorum in iotum vetus testamentum fragmenta* (2 vols.; Oxford: Clarendon Press, 1875), I, p. lxxxii, has noted 43 definite references, and four probable ones.

72.   W. Gesenius, *De Pentateuchi Samaritani origine, indole et auctoritate commentatio philologico-critica* (Halle: Renger, 1815).

73.   A. Geiger, *Urschrift und Übersetzungen der Bibel in ihrer Abhängigkeit von der innern Entwicklung des Judentums* (Breslau: Heinauer, 1857), pp. 97-100.

74.   H. Hammer, *Traktat von Samaritanermessias: Studien zur Frage der*

facts of different kinds to explain: on the one side slight contacts without theological significance between the SP and the Old Testament as cited or referred to by the New Testament (discourse of Stephen in Acts 7, Heb. 9, Rev. 7); on the other, important scenes, such as the episode of the Samaritan woman, in which the phrase 'For salvation comes from the Jews' (Jn 4.22) is an addition,[75] or the mission of Philip in Samaria (Acts 8.4-25), for whom the connection with Jerusalem was secondary.[76]

In regard to specifically textual matters, Paul Kahle developed a new argument, by deducing[77] from these relationships that the Greek translation of SP was already in circulation at the time of the redaction of the New Testament, a conclusion corroborated by the discovery a short time before of Greek fragments of SP:[78] the *Samaritikon* in Origen's Hexapla was therefore really a translation.[79] As a consequence, SP, even with errors, should certainly be presumed to reflect an ancient tradition distinct from the MT. Therefore, Kahle, starting from the observation of many texts that seemed to be easier readings, formulated the hypothesis that there was a *popular* version established on the fringe of the received text, at a time long enough before that the fidelity of the transmission would not yet have the rigidity that eventually developed, and would allow for such variants. Such antiquity could explain the contacts

Existenz Jesu (Bonn: Carl Georg, 1913), went so far as to maintain, while only considering for the New Testament Franz Delitzsch's translation into biblical Hebrew, that Christianity was a Samaritan sect, which is certainly biased.

75.   M-E. Boismard and A. Lamouille, *L'évangile de Jean* (Synopse des quatre Evangiles, 3; Paris, Cerf, 1977), pp. 139-40.

76.   M-E. Boismard and A. Lamouille, *Les actes des deux Apôtres* (EBib NS, 13; 3 vols.; Paris: Gabalda, 1990), II, p. 176.

77.   P. Kahle, 'Untersuchungen zur Geschichte des Pentateuchtextes', in *Opera minora* (Leiden: Brill, 1956), pp. 3-37.

78.   P. Glaue and A. Rahlfs, 'Fragmente einer griechischen Übersetzung des Samaritanischen Pentateuchs', in *Mitteilungen des Septuaginta-Unternehmens* (Berlin: Weidermann, 1914), II, pp. 71-72; republished by E. Tov, 'Pap. Giessen 13, 19, 22, 26: A Revision of the LXX?', *RB* 78 (1971), pp. 355-83.

79.   In reality, these facts prove only the age of SP, and Origen could have used the original Hebrew, since he knew the phrase τὸ τῶν Σαμαρειτῶν Ἑβραικόν. The idea of supposing for him a Samaritan Greek version came from Epiphanius, *De mensuris et ponderibus*, §15, who claimed that Symmachus, a former Samaritan, had made his translation (Jewish) to counter that of the Samaritans; cf. references in Montgomery, *The Samaritans*, p. 285 nn. 31-33. I give another interpretation of this account later on.

observed between SP and the *Book of Jubilees* in regard to the chronologies of Genesis 5.[80] This same book of *Jubilees* had interesting points in common with the LXX against the MT as well, and this fact casts a new light on the significance of the some nineteen hundred contacts between the LXX and SP against the MT, all the more so since most of them do not really affect the meaning (for example, concomitant presence or absence of the linking *waw*), and are therefore significant for textual criticism. Kahle repeats one of Geiger's conclusions,[81] according to which SP, once its Samaritanisms and Aramaisms are removed, represents a very ancient recension, from which the LXX was derived. Now, we possess on this point the *Letter of Aristeas*, which among other things gives an account of the origins of this tradition.

This *Letter* is certainly not to be considered exact in regard to its details. In particular, Kahle continues, the interest shown by the Egyptian ruler Ptolemy II and the intervention of the Greek Aristeas are both imaginary: the *Letter of Aristeas* is certainly Jewish, and gives a justification for a translation made for the needs of the Diaspora communities, perhaps in particular for the liturgy.[82] This translation, as a cultural phenomenon, should be compared to those by Aquila-Onkelos and Theodotian-Jonathan,[83] which were based on the received texts (MT), or at least were revised on the basis of it. Kahle then observes that the multiplicity of Greek versions could have created some problems, and develops a theory of successive revisions, which however did not prevent the survival of faulty copies, that is to say, copies that were more ancient: it would be necessary then to recover the ancestor of SP, since

---

80.   A. Dillmann, 'Beiträgen aus dem Buche der Jubiläen zur Kritik des Pentateuch-textes', *Sitzungsberichte der deutschen Akademie der Wissenschaften zu Berlin* 11 (1883), pp. 320-40.

81.   A. Geiger, *Nachgelassene Schriften* (Leipzig: Kauffman, 1876), IV, pp. 54-67, 121-32.

82.   *m. Meg.* 2.1 indicates, at least for the Esther scroll, that it was not right to *read* a translation (*targum*), no matter what the language: the original had to be read, and the translation made as they went along. According to *y. Meg.* 2.1, it is the same for the Torah. For lack of any other precise indication, we cannot know whether these testimonies applied to the Judaism of Alexandria as well. The *Letter* limited itself to emphasizing the *legislative* importance of the Torah, which could square with an exclusively scholarly or juridical usage of the Greek version.

83.   It is a matter of two pairs of translations (Greek and Aramaic) each put under two forms of the same name; cf. Geiger, *Urschrift*, pp. 48f.; and D. Barthélemy, *Les devanciers d'Aquila* (VTSup, 10; Leiden: Brill, 1963), pp. 148-57.

the evidence of the various Greek versions was weakened. In particular, the *Letter of Aristeas* had as its function, among other things, to authenticate the revision (at least partial) according to the MT of an ancient translation made from a text of a SP type.

These remarks can be enlarged upon. In fact, the *Letter of Aristeas* displays a number of clues indicating textual and graphical uncertainties in regard to the text of the Pentateuch: 1. a difficult passage (§30) gives the impression that Demetrius, the librarian at Alexandria, had complained about having only an inexact text,[84] written in Hebrew characters (and not Chaldean), but that there were people at Alexandria capable of making an authoritative judgment; 2. the sending of a mission to Jerusalem was due to a desire to obtain a text 'which had the agreement of the majority', and therefore very likely in Chaldean writing;[85]

---

84. The letter distinguished clearly (§11 and 15) between the transcriptions (in Greek letters, μεταγράφειν) and the translations (διερμενεύειν) of foreign works; Demetrius declared that the books of the Jews 'were defective' (ἀπολείπει), since they were read in Hebrew characters and pronunciation, and were written down rather negligently and inexactly (ἀμελέστερον δέ, καὶ οὐχ ὡς ὑπάρχει σεσήμανται), 'according to competent people'. The meaning of σεσήμανται is disputed: 'were translated' (allusion to pre-existing translations); 'were vocalized' (Diels; cf. the translation of Paul Wendland, *ad. loc.*). E.J. Bickerman, 'Some Notes on the Transmission of the Septuagint', in *Studies in Jewish and Christian History* (Leiden: Brill, 1976), I, pp. 137-66, followed by others (cf. G. Zuntz, 'Aristeas Studies II: Aristeas on the Transmission of the Torah', *JSS* 4 [1959], pp. 109-126; Pelletier, *Lettre d'Aristée*, pp. 118 n. 3), plausibly supposes that it was a matter of Hebrew manuscripts (p. 143 n. 27), and understands 'were copied' (*notare*). Josephus prudently paraphrased with the same verb (σεσημάνθαι). The sentence remains difficult, since it indicates that these books 'were deficient', but also 'were on hand, although of poor quality'. The term could have referred to a library marking (*notare*, 'to annotate'), indicating a questionable work impossible to include in the official catalogue, in contrast with the desire of the librarian Demetrius, who wanted to establish a text 'of quality' (θῶμεν εὐσήμως, §32); cf. H. St J. Thackeray, 'The Letter of Aristeas', *JQR* 15 (1903), pp. 337-91. In any case, the meaning of the sentence is that there existed at Alexandria one or several copies in Hebrew (language and alphabet) that were considered defective, according to criteria that were not precise, and that it was necessary to import a new text from Jerusalem.

85. Or 'Assyrian', as the rabbinic sources called it. At Qumran were collected fragments of the Pentateuch written in palaeo-Hebrew, which clearly indicates that in the second century the scripts were still mixed. See K.A. Mathews, 'The Background of Paleo-Hebrew at Qumran', in C.L. Meyers and M. O'Connor, *The Word Shall Go Forth: Essays in Honor of D.N. Freedman* (ASOR spec. vol. ser., 1; Philadelphia: American Schools of Oriental Research, 1984), pp. 549-68, who gives

3. at the time of the promulgation of the translation, a solemn impreca-
tion was uttered against 'whoever alters the letter of the text'[86] (§311);
4. there is an allusion to earlier translations, with legends showing their
dangers (§314); 5. Philo had contacts with SP against the LXX which
shows that the ancient 'Samaritan' translation continued to exist (even
at Alexandria) on the fringe of the LXX, at least with a residual right,
which confirms that the latter was definitely the result of a revision;[87] 6.
subsequently, the Hexapla show that in the time of Origen at least three
recensions of the LXX were current, which proves that the unification
proclaimed by the *Letter of Aristeas* had not really succeeded.

On the fringe of the problem of the translation and its legitimacy, the
question of a revision presupposes not only several textual traditions, but
also conflicts about authority, and the *Letter of Aristeas* shows the trace
of the increasing (and decisive) weight of Jerusalem.

5. *More on the* Letter of Aristeas

The history of the translation related by the *Letter of Aristeas* is mentioned by two other sources. Aristobulus, a Hebrew philosopher and
counsellor of Ptolemy VI Philometor (181–146) wrote to the king that
since Plato various fragments had been translated into Greek (and pla-
giarized), and concluded: 'The complete translation of the whole Law
was done under the king by the name of Philadelphus, your ancestor,
when Demetrius had taken the matter in hand.'[88] It is a question neither
of Jerusalem, nor of Judaea, nor of a revision, but there remains, beyond
the platitudes of Jewish apologetics about the 'theft by the Greeks', a
sort of rumour about earlier translations. Moreover, it is not stated that
Aristobulus would have been a Jew (at least in Nehemiah's sense);
2 Macc. 1.10 states that he was descended 'from the family of anointed

---

as well a list of texts in Aramaic script with a divine name in palaeo-Hebrew.

86. For some (Wendland, *ad loc.*), the curse is just the echo of Deut. 4.2 or 13.1,
which is found again in Rev. 22.18-19. In fact, it could have been just the custom of
the times, but it is not found elsewhere.

87.   P. Katz, *Philo's Bible: The Aberrant Text of Bible Quotations in Some
Philonic Writings* (Cambridge: Cambridge University Press, 1950).

88.   Quoted by Eusebius, *Preparatio evangelica*. E.J. Bickerman, 'The
Septuagint as a Translation', in *Studies in Jewish and Christian History*, I, pp. 167-
200, defends its authenticity (p. 168 n. 2): this would be the Aristobulus 'of the
family of anointed priests' of the second festal letter (2 Macc. 1.10).

priests',[89] which does not imply any more than that. Finally, it should be noted that Clement of Alexandria was the first to quote him (*Stromates* 1.148.1), and it is disturbing, as far as the letter's authenticity goes, that it should have escaped the notice of Josephus as well as Alexander Polyhistor.[90]

Philo, for his part, mentioned (*Vit. Mos.* 2.25-44) that an annual feast on the island of Pharos commemorated the initiative of Ptolemy Philadelphus, who had obtained from the 'high priest and king of the Jews (for this was the same person)' competent translators. These individuals, working independently, 'prophesied' and produced identical results. The titles used here clearly pointed to the Hasmonaeans, and the 'Chaldean language' by which Philo described the original was an ambiguous designation,[91] at least when it referred to an alphabet: this could have been an allusion to Hebrew writing, since Moses the Hebrew was also presented as a Chaldean (*Vit. Mos.* 1.5), but also to Aramaic writing, since 'Chaldeans knowing Greek [...] finding themselves before the two versions at the same time [...], look at them admiringly [...] as one and the same work'. Philo seemed to avoid mentioning textual conflicts; in any case he did not have in mind an eventual revision of the LXX, but was anxious to stress its inspiration. What is more, even if he knew of the existence of the tripartite division of the Bible (*Vit. Cont.* §25), he was really only interested in the Pentateuch, like Aristobulus, and certainly is not a reliable witness as to the consistency of the Hebrew canon as a whole. Finally, Philo, in his biblical citations or allusions, had more contact with SP than with the LXX and/or the MT, so we must conclude that he is a witness only to a text of a proto-Samaritan type, more or less authenticated as Jewish by the story of Ptolemy.

In this regard, the testimony of Epiphanius stands out: he declared (*De mensuris et ponderibus* 15) that Symmachus, a former Samaritan converted to Judaism, did

89.   The reference, put in apposition with Aristobulus, who had already been described as the tutor of King Ptolemy, is a well-attested formula in Lev. 4.5, 16; 6.15; 21.10, 12, but not elsewhere. We have to surmise an addition either to give a Jewish dignity to Aristobulus, or to make him a priest acceptable to Judas and the Jews, the addressees of the letter; but it is not self-evident that such a priest would have come from Jerusalem.

90.   N. Walter, *Der Thoraausleger Aristobulos* (TU, 86; Berlin: Akademie Verlag, 1964), pp. 52-55, who brings up, following Bickerman, the usual objections to the authenticity of Aristobulus. It remains in doubt.

91.   Philo used 'Chaldean' for 'Hebrew', especially in the late works, but not for 'Israelite' or 'Jew'; on the other hand, he was unaware of the term 'Samaritan'.

his translation to counter that of the Samaritans.[92] This 'Samaritan translation' is nothing else but a form of the LXX (perhaps close to that of Philo), certainly less contaminated by the MT (or any pre-Masoretic text) than the recensions known today, which have all, to varying degrees, undergone revisions based on the MT. Similarly, there is a rabbinic tradition (*y. Meg.* 1.11) which relates that the proselyte Aquila translated the Torah before Eleazar and Jehoshua, and that he praised them.[93] There were two Pharisaic doctors from the end of the first century, renowned for their conservatism: according to the preceding considerations, it was not for them a question of promoting Greek, but of opposing a non-conforming tradition,[94] improperly spread in their view throughout the Hellenophone Diaspora. As a consequence, as opposed to the opinion of Kahle, caught up in his hypothesis of very ancient and constantly revised written targums, it is not necessary to look farther than the LXX, under one or another form, for traces of a Greek SP in New Testament times. In contrast, it must be concluded that the *Samaritikon* of Origen is not another Greek translation, but really a Hebrew text, although it does not exactly coincide with the present editions of SP, but rather with an Aramaic version.[95] As a corollary, we may note that the context of a general revision, considered urgent by Origen, appears still more clearly.

We now return to the *Letter of Aristeas* itself, since it includes some strange arrangements, relative to the setting up of the translation. In the first place, the high priest Eleazar of Jerusalem, to whom the king Ptolemy addressed his request, cannot be found in the known

92.	Epiphanius is not always coherent. Elsewhere in the same work (*De mens. et pond.*, III, PG 43, 242), he recounts the story of the translation by the seventy-two, with an interesting detail: after the seventy-two independent translations, they checked them and found that they were in agreement, that is to say, that in comparison with the original they added or dropped simultaneously the same words. This testimony agrees with the rabbinic tradition (*b. Meg.* 9a; cf. below), which also shows the unanimity of the translators for a *different* text.

93.	By citing Ps. 45.3: 'You are the most beautiful [יפיפית] of the sons of men', with a play on words on Japhet (יפת), ancestor of the Greeks. The term used for 'praise', וקילסו אותו, comes precisely from κάλος: they declared him to be 'well (and good)'; cf. S. Lieberman, *Greek in Jewish Palestine* (New York: Jewish Theological Seminary of America, 1942), pp. 17-19 (as opposed to Jastrow, who remains bound by the existence of the root קלס in the Bible, even though it has the opposite meaning of 'derision'). According to *y. Qid.* 1.2, Aquila did his translation before Aqiba (orally, in accordance with *m. Meg.* 2.1), and Jerome, *In Isaiam* 8.14, reports that Aquila was a disciple of Aqiba. According to Epiphanius, *De mens. et pond.* §14, Aquila would be a relative of the Emperor Hadrian, and his translation should be dated 128–129.

94.	Barthélemy, *Devanciers d'Aquila*, pp. 2-6, concentrates on the exegetical controversies in pre-Mishnaic Judaism, presumably Pharisaic.

95.	Field, *Origenis*, I, pp. lxxxii, 329-30.

genealogies,[96] and the conclusions of Chapter 4 leave a persistent doubt as to the quality of the relations between the Jews and the high priests of Jerusalem during the whole Hellenistic period. Furthermore, to find in Jerusalem six scholars from each of the twelve tribes to form a collection of translators was certainly a gamble in the period under consideration, not to mention earlier times. The list of those selected (§§47-56; Josephus omits it), is therefore fictional, but it contains two revealing details: on the one hand, the tribes are given in order by their number, without their name, which certainly resolved a difficulty of precedence; on the other hand, the lists corresponding to the first three tribes begins respectively with Joseph, Judah and Nehemiah, which makes the reader think, in order, of Samaria (house of Joseph), of Judaea, and of the founder of the sacred library (2 Macc. 2.13). The allusion cannot be forced too much, but it is certain that it is an arrangement wishing to show the unanimity of 'all Israel'. As for the number seventy-two, or twelve times six, it is frequently simplified to 'seventy' since Irenaus (seventy Elders[97]). The reference was certainly to a complete *gerousia*, that is to say, a group endowed with the desired credentials, therefore a tribunal (sanhedrin) which judged the text with authority,[98] and there is an allusion in the *Letter of Aristeas* to competent people. It was the admittance of the twelve tribes to equality that prompted a revision from seventy to seventy-two, and this is combined with the fiction about the interest brought to the enterprise by the Gentiles, which removed the need for a reference to a Hebrew tribunal, and replaced it with the competence of pagan authorities. Under the fiction of the *Letter of Aristeas*, there is a trace of an arbitration by a *gerousia*, let us say

96. Despite the assertion of Josephus, *Ant.* 12.157; cf. A. Büchler, *Die Tobiaden und die Oniaden* (Vienna: Holder, 1899), p. 41.

97. Quoted by Eusebius, *Historia Ecclesiastica* 5.8.11; cf, the texts collected by Pelletier, *Lettre d'Aristée*, pp. 81-84.

98. Gaster, *The Samaritans*, p. 119. The Samaritan tradition, as well as some colophons of SP manuscripts, indicate that the text is based on the authority of seventy Elders. The memory of the seventy Elders instituted by Moses is venerated among the Samaritans, since they received some of his spirit from him as the unique prophet (Num. 11.16-17); cf. J. MacDonald (ed.), *Memar Marqa* (BZAW, 84; 2 vols.; Berlin: Töpelmann, 1962), 4.1. The opinion advanced by A. Paul, *Le Judaïsme ancien et la Bible* (Paris: Desclée, 1987), p. 79, that the *Letter of Aristeas* shows that with the LXX 'the Jews had become Greeks', underestimates the variety and influence of groups and tendencies that survived in Judaea, Samaria and Galilee, at least up to the destruction of 66–73.

between Samaritans and Jews, in regard to which text was good.

It remains difficult however to determine clearly what exact form of text the *Letter* was supposed to present: on the one hand, it could very well have introduced the translation of Aquila, so close to the proto-Masoretic text, and on the other it could just as well be a fabrication authenticating a text still very close to SP. The testimony of Josephus, who would hardly be suspected of being favourable to the Samaritans, is therefore opportune. In his paraphrase of the Pentateuch, he used a text distinct from the MT and very closely related to the LXX, or more exactly to its Hebrew substratum, since it can be shown that he had not seen the LXX, at least under the form in which we know it.[99] A confirmation of the usual interpretation, according to which the *Letter* should be associated with something close to the present LXX, follows from this, along with one other piece of information: the Hebrew text according to which it was revised or redone was very close to that attested by Josephus, which indicates by contrast that the MT proceeds from another milieu.

The rabbinic traditions relative to the Greek translation of the Pentateuch provide some further glimpses. On Exod. 12.40 ('The sojourn of the Israelites in Egypt had lasted [...]'), the *Mekhilta*[100] gave a long variant ('the Israelites in *the land of Canaan* and in the *land* of Egypt and in the *land* of Goshen'), and indicated that such was one of the lessons 'that they wrote to the king, Ptolemy'. It is difficult not to see there an at least remote allusion to the history reported in the *Letter*. Nevertheless, taken literally, this passage recalled not the Greek translation, but a different Hebrew text,[101] sent in view of a translation or

99.   That is mainly, for the Pentateuch, ms. B (Vaticanus). Cf. Nodet *et al.* (eds.), *Flavius Josèphe*, p. xxvii (discussion) and note on the translation of *Ant.* 1.5 (references); see also Feldman, *Josephus and Modern Scholarship*, pp. 130-34.

100.   H.S. Horovitz and I.A. Rabin, *Mechilta d'Rabbi Ismael* (Frankfurt am Main: Kauffman, 1930; repr. Jerusalem: Magnes, 1970), pp. 50-51, with parallels in notes.

101.   The commentators have been partial to considering the modifications made by the translators (cf. V. Aptowitzer, 'Die rabbinischen Berichte über die Entstehung der Septuaginta', *Haqedem* 2 (1909), pp. 11-27, 102-122), or the readings proper to the Greek accepted by the revisers; cf. E. Tov, 'The Rabbinic Traditions Concerning the "Alterations" Inserted into the Greek Pentateuch and their Relation to the Original Text of the LXX', *JSJ* 15 (1984), pp. 66-89. E.J. Bickerman, *The Jews in the Greek Age* (London: Basil Blackwell, 1988), p. 106, suggests, starting from a slight difference between *Ep. Arist.* (§310-11) and its paraphrase by Josephus

even only of an arbitration. In fact SP has: 'in the land of Canaan and in the land of Egypt', just like the LXX, but in the inverse order; even Josephus (*Ant.* 2.318) presupposes a similar lesson. The *Mekhilta* continues by giving a list of thirteen differences, or more exactly a list of ten, followed by another list of three, of which the last one concerns the cited verse. The first of these lessons consists of rewriting Gen. 1.1 ('God created in the beginning [...]'), by reversing the order of the words, in such a way that it could not be believed that it was 'In the beginning' (or the entity בראשית) that created God, along with the heavens and the earth;[102] grammatically, the ambiguity is conceivable in Hebrew, but not in Greek, because of the declensions. This case confirms that it definitely was a question of variants of the Hebrew, and throws into relief the remarks of Philo indicating the details of translation that bilingual readers could notice.

An analogous list of variants appears in *b. Meg.* 9a-b, but it is preceded by a brief miraculous account, according to which Ptolemy summoned seventy-two Elders without telling them why, then separated them by putting them in seventy-two houses. He then asked each of them separately to 'write' the Torah, and each came up with the same result, that is to say, with the *same* variants, the list of which is given next: such is clearly the miracle. This passage recalls more and more the *Letter of Aristeus*, especially because of the strange number seventy-two. This short narrative is on the other hand a *baraita*, that is to say a Tannaitic tradition which is of the same antiquity and with the same authority as the list of variants, which are inserted in the later discussions. It is striking that it should not be clearly a question either of a translation or of Greek: the Talmudic context alone leads us to see what resulted from it, namely, a Greek translation, since this *baraita* is connected to an opinion of the Mishnah according to which the translation of the Torah into Greek had been authorized, but curiously it is explained that this was 'because of what King Ptolemy had done'. The discussion creates an optical illusion, tending to give the impression that for the translation ordered by Ptolemy permission had been given beforehand by the Sages (Pharisees)

(*Ant.* 12.108-109), that the lists of differences between Greek and Hebrew texts were destined for bilingual Jews who desired to correct their own scrolls personally. See also A.I. Baumgarten, 'The Rabbinical Accounts of the Translation of the Torah into Greek' (a paper to be published).

102. Rashi, *ad loc.*, also feels the need to remove the ambiguity.

These remarks show that it is more than improbable that the translation or the revision authenticated by the *Letter of Aristeus* had had the consent of the Pharisees. The explanation quoted ('they permitted the translation into Greek because of Ptolemy') can then be understood differently: because of Ptolemy and his initiative, ending up in their eyes in a non-conforming text, whether in Hebrew or in Greek, the Pharisaic Sages had to permit, or even promote, a translation of the MT meant to do battle against the ravages of the diverse texts in circulation, derived to a lesser or greater degree from SP. In this way, we meet again very naturally the interpretation proposed in the Talmudic passage quoted above celebrating the work of Aquila, as well as the meaning of the remarks of Epiphanius on Symmachus.

6. *Conclusion: Chronologies and Hypotheses*

The preceding considerations lead up to a consideration of the MT and its immediate derivatives as contrasted with a rather vast textual group, confirmed in varying degrees by SP, the LXX and Josephus. What is more, it is the MT which forms an anomaly in comparison with the others, and not vice versa. More than a century ago, Paul de Lagarde formulated a clear-cut analogous conclusion:[103] according to him, all the mediaeval Hebrew manuscripts of the MT came down from a single copy, a product of a specific recension in the time of Aqiba (c. 100 CE). The consequence of this is that the MT obscures its textual pre-history or, which comes to the same thing, that there is not strictly speaking any textual criticism of the MT. Another result, according to him, is that the LXX then becomes the principal witness to that pre-history. These views have been challenged, especially by Kahle,[104] who distrusted the LXX and its revisions and developed a theory according to which SP was a popular version, distinct from the MT, which was a scholarly edition more and more normative for the translations; the MT and SP, however, coexisted in the period of the Second Temple. In any case, it is admitted that if SP really represented an ancient form of the text, this was a result of a separation from the principal branch, which was Jewish, and this

---

103. P. de Lagarde, *Anmerkungen zur griechischen Übersetzung der Proverbien* (Leipzig: Hinrichs, 1863).

104. P. Kahle, *The Cairo Geniza* (Schweich Lectures, 1941; London: Milford, 1947), pp. 132-79.

separation went back to the first quarrels with the Samaritans (fifth century).

By way of a conclusion, I intend to show that the Qumran discoveries allow for a combination of the two theses, and consequently that there is no need to choose between SP and the LXX. The result of this will be some inferences relative to the Samaritan schism.

The finds in the desert of Judaea have provided new facts of foremost importance:[105] the most obvious discovery is that the Samaritan script is a quite late development of the Hebrew alphabet,[106] as it was in the Hasmonaean period, and the orthography of the corresponding manuscripts matches the epigraphy of that period. In other words, the separation of the texts should scarcely go back further than the Maccabaean crisis. As for the texts themselves, if we limit ourselves to the Pentateuch, fragments of SP type (Palestinian), of LXX type (Egyptian), as well as various mixed types have been discovered.[107] The conclusions of Cross[108] are first of all that there is not the least reason to suppose that the proto-Samaritan text, namely, a text stripped of obvious 'Samaritanisms' like the commandment relative to Gerizim, is a late sectarian recension; it is an intermediary between the Egyptian recension, still evident in the LXX, and the proto-Masoretic text.[109] He

---

105.   F.M. Cross, *The Ancient Library of Qumran and Modern Biblical Studies* (Garden City, NY: Doubleday, 1958), pp. 127-29.

106.   F.M. Cross, 'The Development of the Jewish Scripts', in G.E. Wright (ed.), *The Bible and the Ancient Near East: Essays in Honor of W.F. Albright* (New York: McGraw–Hill, 1965); R.S. Hanson, 'Jewish Palaeography and its Bearing on Text Critical Studies', in F.M. Cross, *et al.* (eds.), *Magnalia Dei, The Mighty Acts of God: Essays in Memory of G.E. Wright* (Garden City, NY: Doubleday, 1976), pp. 561-76.

107.   Baillet, 'Texte samaritain', pp. 363-81; E. Tov, 'Hebrew Biblical Manuscripts from the Judaean Desert: Their Contribution to Textual Criticism', *JJS* 39/1 (1988), pp. 5-37; cf. n. 96, where he questions Baillet's proposal, that from the contacts noted with the SP it could be concluded that it was a matter of specifically Samaritan texts; the argument put forward to refute the thesis is that it was a question of a sect, but it amounts in fact to a begging of the question.

108.   Cross, *Ancient Library*, p. 144.

109.   This tripartite division is probably insufficient, since there are types of texts which (at least according to the statistical methods of sorting out the variants) are connected to none of these three; cf. E. Tov, 'A Modern Textual Outlook Based on the Qumran Scrolls', *HUCA* 52 (1982), pp. 11-27.

proceeds by assuming[110] that the Egyptian text was separated from the proto-Masoretic text as early as the fifth century, and that the proto-Samaritan diverged shortly after, but he acknowledges that the origin of the proto-Masoretic text remains obscure. Even if the latter developed in official circles at the same time as other less accurate ones, there is still a need to explain the adoption of the Aramaic alphabet. This development could have taken place outside of Palestine, namely in Babylon,[111] and the repatriation of the text would thus have taken place subsequently, at the latest in the Maccabaean period. At first sight this conclusion would seem to be close to the hypothesis of Kahle,[112] but in fact it opposes it energetically,[113] preferring the term regional textual traditions, brought together in Palestine in the Hasmonaean period, well before the selection of one from among them by the editors of the MT.

This debate on official texts or local texts in reality hides a more serious problem, namely, the extreme difficulty in proposing a simple comprehensive view which would maintain unequivocally that the Samaritans were a sect derived from Judaism, and therefore that the Jewish Pentateuch is clearly prior to the Samaritan, although it has been demonstrated that the Samaritan texts have not borrowed substantially from the Jews.[114]

The priority of Judaism is precisely what Josephus claims: he declares, in connection with the arrival of Alexander, that the erection of the Gerizim temple was due to a Jewish dissidence. I have shown the difficulties in this presentation, connected in particular with the impossibility of clearly dating the emergence of Judaism a very long time before the Maccabaean crisis, let alone such a late appearance of the MT (for which we meet again the de Lagarde thesis).[115] These difficulties become

110. Following W.F. Albright, 'New Light on Early Recensions of the Hebrew Bible', *BASOR* 140 (1955), pp. 27-33.

111. Cf. also P.W. Skehan, 'The Biblical Scrolls from Qumrân and the Text of the Old Testament', *BA* 28 (1965), pp. 87-100.

112. Brought up to date by M. Greenberg, 'The Stabilization of the Text of the Hebrew Bible in the Light of the Biblical Materials from Qumran', *JAOS* 76 (1956), pp. 157-67.

113. F.M. Cross, 'The History of the Biblical Text in the Light of Discoveries in the Judean Desert', *HTR* 57 (1964), pp. 281-99.

114. Macdonald, *The Samaritan Chronicle No. II*, Preface.

115. Cf. the situation as presented by E. Ulrich, 'Horizons of Old Testament Textual Research at the Thirtieth Anniversary of Qumran Cave 4', *CBQ* 46 (1984), pp. 613-36, especially 622-24.

insurmountable with the new late dating of SP, which requires the separation of the dissidence of Gerizim from the 'sectarian' edition of the Pentateuch, and the reconstruction of events no longer conforms to any intelligible model.

It is therefore necessary to propose an inverse hypothesis, making use of the results from the preceding chapters:

1. The first appearance of the Pentateuch as an authoritative compilation able to be called 'law of Moses' is to be situated in Samaria (at Shechem, in connection with Gerizim and its priesthood), a generation or two before the date that Samaritan palaeography calls for, that is to say, c. 250–200 BCE[116] (cf. Chapter 4, §7).

2. A lay movement of Jews stemming from Babylon imported its alphabet and the weekly Sabbath (non-biblical) into Judaea, and there resulted from this, perhaps as a result of dissidence, a contamination of the Samaritans, from which there followed an important redactional activity, and eventually a common Pentateuch, which then spread into the Diaspora, especially into Egypt, and branched out little by little through the various movements.

3. These Samaritans of Gerizim and of the Pentateuch must be distinguished as a limited subgroup in the territory and population of Samaria as a whole, which was a more or less clearly defined blending of Canaanites, Israelites and Cuthaeans (or Assyrian colonists).

4. The Jewish movement, for reasons that are still obscure, had some sectarian aspects, but considered itself the heir of all Israel, and in Jerusalem collided with another tradition that was cultic, prophetic and perhaps royal. This forms the distant prehistory of the Maccabaean crisis.

5. Cross's conclusion, relative to the appearance in Palestine in the second century of all the textual types found at Qumran, should be retained, since it is a fact. All that is needed is to complete it by suggesting that the Pentateuch had previously had not a *textual* history (regional recensions, errors), but a

---

116. By different routes, mainly historical, G. Garbini, *History and Ideology in Ancient Israel* (London: SCM Press, 1988), pp. 146-51, arrives at a similar date for the Pentateuch, considered as a whole.

literary prehistory (sources, glosses, redactions), with it being understood that the two are sometimes difficult to distinguish in practice.

These hypotheses resolve many of the difficulties listed up to here, but they give rise to others, relative to the history of Israel and the editing of the whole Bible: schematically, why was this movement of repatriated Jews anxious to identify itself with Israel, whether under an inclusive form (Chronicler type) or an exclusive one (Ezra–Nehemiah type)?

Some preliminary remarks can be proposed immediately: first, the indications in 2 Macc. 2.13-15, attributing to Nehemiah the foundation of a library and to Judas Maccabeus its reconstitution, come into focus. From Judges to Kings, the history is reinterpreted in a way systematically favourable to Judaea. It occasionally mentions sources, such as the 'royal annals of Judah and Israel' ([...] דברי הימים) or the 'Book of the Just' (ספר הישר).[117] In particular, the account of the origin of the Samaritans (2 Kgs 17), which has been proved to be unhistorical,[118] could very well be a mere denial, in which the Jews would have accused the Samaritans of being what the Jews themselves were: intruders blending local traditions with Babylonian importations. Then, the astonishing mission of Ezra, to appoint scribes and judges all over Transeuphrates, 'that is for all those who know the law of your God' (Ezra 7.25-26) can come to have a precise meaning, since he arrived in Jerusalem as if in a liturgical procession: the Law had to be established in various places, in particular in Samaria, but it culminated *finally* at Jerusalem. The invention of Artaxerxes's firman, detected above (Chapter 1, §2), expressed therefore something factual, while consigning it to a distant past. Finally, the morphologically sectarian character of the Judaism of Nehemiah–Ezra has been pointed out for a long time,[119] with its particularly weak political claim, at least up to the Maccabaean crisis.

---

117.   The expression תורת משה, well attested in Joshua, Daniel, Chronicles–Ezra–Nehemiah, is not found in Judges–Samuel–Kings except in 1 Kgs 2.3 and 2 Kgs 14.6 and 23.25, passages inspired respectively by Deut. 8.6; 24.16; and 6.5.

118.   Cf. H.H. Rowley, 'The Samaritan *Schism* in Legend and History', in B.W. Anderson and W. Harrelson (eds.), *Israel's Prophetic Heritage* (Festschrift J. Muilenburg; New York: Harper, 1962), pp. 208-22.

119.   M. Weber, *Ancient Judaism* (Glencoe: Free Press, 1952), pp. 385-404, taken up again and developed by S. Talmon, 'The Emergence of Jewish Sectarianism in the Early Second Temple Period', in *King, Cult and Calendar in Ancient Israel* (Jerusalem: Magnes, 1986), pp. 165-201.

In regard to the 'sacred libraries' and sects, an observation on method is called for here: it is certainly anachronistic to project back into the Hasmonaean period the current difference between the Jewish Bible and the Samaritan Bible. We must suppose a very creative phase, in the second century, probably even before and certainly after that, in which all kinds of texts were produced or edited, in Palestine, in varied and more or less competing groups; the series of such assorted finds from the Judaean desert is proof of this. In this connection, there is no reason for making too clear-cut a distinction between the canonical literature and the so-called apocryphal literature or the pseudopigrapha: the discovery at Qumran of a fragment of Job in Hebrew characters, therefore theoretically connectable to the Samaritan literature, is interesting in this regard; conversely, the recent excavations on Gerizim collected inscriptions in Hebrew and Aramaic characters.[120] A few examples in the meantime will help us detect simple, but instructive, criteria to distinguish between libraries.

1. The literature focused on Jerusalem and Judaea (from Samuel to Nehemiah) had little chance of being retained in the North and, indeed, was not.

2. An 'apocryphal' book like Judith, the original of which was in Hebrew but which cited the Pentateuch according to the LXX (or SP), and was centred on Bethulia in Samaria (calling Bethel to mind), could not as such be in an official Jewish library, even though Jerusalem and its cult would also have been mentioned.[121]

3. The book of *Jubilees*, preserved in the Ethiopian canon and in fragments from Qumran, had contacts with SP and is centred too on Bethel, to which Jacob went up from Shechem to build an altar (31.3). Levi became high priest there (32.1), and they even had to bring the second tithe there (32.10), the one foreseen in Deut. 14.22 to be consumed 'in the place which YHWH has chosen as a dwelling for his name'. Once again, such a text is not very Jewish,[122] but the kinship of its calendar,[123] touched on in Chapter 3, §1, with the one underlying the Hexateuch, with that of the Qumran

120.   Cf. Y. Magen, 'Mount Garizim—A Temple City', *Qadmoniot* 23 (1991), pp. 70-90.

121.   But it was utilized by the midrash, which transferred Judith's brave deed to Jerusalem in the time of the Seleucid persecution, and, in this form, it was connected to the Dedication (cf. Chapter 8, §7).

122.   As for affirming with J. Schwartz, 'The "Temple of Jacob" and the Cult in Bethel during the Second Temple Period', in *Proceedings of the Ninth World Congress of Jewish Studies 1985* (6 vols.; Jerusalem: World Union of Jewish Studies, 1986), I, pp. 7-12, that Bethel, in *Jubilees*, is only a substitute for Jerusalem at the time when Jerusalem had become inaccessible under Judas Maccabeus, this is a gratuitous statement, which underestimates the connection established with Jacob: it refers to Israel, and not to Judah. On the matter of dates, since this is under discussion, it would seem more natural to interpret the dissuasion by the angel about building a temple at Bethel (32.16-20) in a context later than the ruin of the temple of Gerizim, in spite of J.A. Goldstein, 'The Dating of the Book of Jubilees', *PAAJR* 50 (1983), pp. 64-65.

123.   Jaubert, *Date de la Cène*, p. 33.

sect[124] and with that of the Samaritans[125] is of foremost importance.

4. The presence in the 'Greek Bible' of all these texts (it was a Greek version of *Jubilees* that was later translated into Ethiopian), combined with 'pan-Israelite' views about unanimity of the *Letter of Aristeas* and Philo, tends to show that at Alexandria they tried to minimize the petty factional quarrels between the various groups from Judaea and Samaria, even if it meant relying in that case on the authority of a foreign institution, the library of Alexandria. This had probably taken place before the end of the Hasmonaean period.

To sum up, two lines of research emerge: in the first place, if there is such a Samaritan precedence, what had happened in Judaea one or two generations before the Maccabaean crisis? We have turned up indications of a final redaction of the Pentateuch at this time, with Jewish influences of Babylonian origin, but great uncertainties too in regard to the priesthood of Jerusalem. The figure of Simon the Just, who was high priest in Jerusalem in this period, dominated in all the traditions,[126] the oldest having been provided by Ben Sira. The political and social setting of his emergence will be examined in Chapter 7.

As for the origin of the Samaritans, the title of this chapter could only be accepted if it had been a matter of a Jewish dissidence. What had it amounted to before the Jewish influence, of which the weekly Sabbath has been acknowledged as its major component? The examination of this question goes beyond the bounds of the present study, since Israelite history, ancient and less ancient, is without any doubt complex. There is

124. J. Bowman, *Samaritanische Probleme: Studien zum Verhältnis von Samaritanertum, Judentum und Urchristentum* (F. Delitzsch Vorlesungen, 1959; Stuttgart: Kohlhammer, 1967), p. 95. For the Samaritans, Pentecost was always a Sunday: they therefore counted the period of the *omer*, after Passover, as the Sadducees did.

125. Gaster, *The Samaritans*, p. 67; Jaubert, *Date de la Cène*, p. 73 n. 1; S. Powels, *Der Kalendar der Samaritaner* (Berlin: de Gruyter, 1977); Epiphanius, *De mens. et pond.*, §10, declares, in regard to debates about calendars, that the Essenes, whom he identifies with the Samaritans (or confuses with them), had persevered in the ancient way of doing things, without adding anything. The *Tolida*, a mediaeval text which gives the sequence of Samaritan high priests, draws up a complete enumeration of the jubilees from Adam up to Abraham and Moses, just as the book of *Jubilees* did, for which the death of Moses and the entry into the Promised Land were the centre of history.

126. Some attribute to him the final redaction of the Pentateuch; in regard to this, cf. B. Barc, 'Siméon le Juste, rédacteur de la Torah?', in M. Tardieu (ed.), *La formation des canons scripturaires* (Patrimoines, Religion du Livre; Paris: Cerf, 1993), pp. 123-54.

surely a local component, represented by the person of Joshua the legislator as well as by the traditions relative to Jacob–Israel. The cult of YHWH is certainly of local origin, Canaanite or Phoenician; the archaeological excavations have brought to light almost everywhere fertility figurines, which we can associate with the fact that the Bible never ceased to stigmatize every trace of the cult of Astarte, the lunar goddess of fertility.[127]

7. *Excursus 1: Samaritan* Chronicles

The literary examination of Bethel and of the literary narratives connected to the North has brought out the importance of the Hexateuch and the fundamental role of Joshua, but textual considerations in regard to the LXX and SP are especially associated with the Pentateuch. The Samaritans knew the book of Joshua (from now on, JosS), however, as well as other chronicles, but the condition in which the text has come to us is suspect, since they are all very recent manuscripts, with definite traces of continuous modifications and expansions, and it has always been suspected that the alterations are exclusively late.[128] Be that as it may, the important thing is to insist on the contrary on the presumption that, because of its content, the most likely possibility is that the book of Joshua came from the Samaritans to the Jews, and not vice versa.

In fact, at the time of the rediscovery in the West of the Samaritans in the sixteenth century, when Joseph Scaliger[129] wrote to the communities at Nablus and Cairo to buy manuscripts from them, one of the replies was favourable, with some reservations, but the second, dated 1598, was negative:[130] 'We are not allowed to sell you the book of Joshua or the

---

127. Cf. the synthesis of Garbini, *History and Ideology*, pp. 54-62

128. At the time of the publication of the Hebrew-Samaritan Joshua by M. Gaster, 'Das Buch Josua in hebräisch-samaritanischer Rezension', *ZDMG* 62 (1908), pp. 209-279 (text) and pp. 494-549 (discussion of the objections on the authenticity raised by A.S. Yahuda, 'Über die Unechtheit des samaritanischen Josuabuches', *SPAW* 39 [1908], pp. 887-913), the atmosphere was combative—cf. in the same volume of the *Zeitschrift* the reactions of Paul Kahle, pp. 550-51, and A.S. Yahuda, p. 754—there was however a misunderstanding as we will see later.

129. Cf. I. Ben-Zevi, 'The Samaritan Script in the Gaonic Literature', *BJPES* 7 (1939), pp. 30-33. Scaliger seems to have been informed about the Samaritans by his teacher, Guillaume Postel (1510–1563).

130. Quoted by M. Delcor, 'La correspondance des savants européens, en quête de manuscrits, avec les Samaritains du XVIe au XIXe siècles', in J.-P. Rothschild

Writing [מכתב, namely, the Pentateuch] when you are not Samaritans'. Thus these works were sacred, or at least venerated,[131] and that explains why the copies of JosS obtained by the searchers were generally not ancient manuscripts, but copies produced on demand, often very faulty. It was easy to find obvious inconsistencies in the text of JosS: the presence, in the list of cities, of Tiberias, Caesarea, Naim; the addition of verses from the Pentateuch; the influence of Arabic and Muslim invocations[132] (in 1.1: שלום יהוה עליו; cf. 'The peace of Allah be on him'; in 5.18: לית אלה אלה אלה אחד; cf. 'There is only one God, the Unique'). These alterations are real, and cannot be extraneous to the fact that the title is not the book of Joshua, but a 'Chronicle of events from the time of the entry of Joshua, son of Nun, into the land of Canaan up until this day'[133] in a continuous expansion, compiled and copied in an Arabophone environment.

Without going into a detailed analysis of the text, there are some

and G.D. Sixdenier (eds.), *Etudes samaritaines, Pentateuque et Targum, exégèse et philologie, chroniques* (Collection de la *REJ*, 6; Paris: Peeters, 1988), pp. 27-43. Scaliger had however obtained an Arabic translation as early as 1584, but it was only published later by T.W.I. Juynboll, *Chronicon samaritanum arabice conscriptum, cui titulus est Liber Josuae* (Leiden: Brill, 1848).

131. G. Postel, visiting the Samaritans at Nablus and Damascus in 1550, had described them as having 'nothing sacred outside of the Pentateuch'; cf. P. de Robert, 'La naissance des études samaritaines', in J.-P. Rothschild and G.D. Sixdenier (eds.), *Etudes*, pp. 15-26.

132. Yahuda, 'Über die Unechtheit', pp. 903-906, built up arguments to try to show that it was a Hebrew translation, influenced by the MT, of an Arabic composition dependent on the medieval chronicle of Abu'l-Fath. Yet, in concentrating on what is most obvious, he ended up with a not very realistic explanation, and especially neglected some facts hard to explain if the text is entirely fabricated; cf. below. He is actually defending the opinion of Juynboll, *Chronicon samaritanum arabice*, which placed its composition in Egypt in the thirteenth century, an opinion once again defended, on the basis of citations in Coptic works of this time, by G. Graf, 'Zum Alter des samaritanischen "Buches Josue"', *Biblica* 23 (1942), pp. 62-67. The convergent opinion of Arabic scholars for the dating of the version should be accepted, but it cannot demonstrate the absence of a Hebrew substratum, when there are other reasons which suggest that one should be postulated. Furthermore, there was a misunderstanding, since the JosS of Gaster, which is the only part relative to Joshua from Macdonald's *Chronicle II* (*Theology of the Samaritans* [London, 1964], pp. 44-46), is a chronicle of a different recension than that of Juynboll (*Chronicle IV* of Macdonald).

133. עד היום הזה; the Arabic manuscripts are generally *'ila yawmina haḏa*, literally 'up to this our day'.

indications that suggest that the ancient Samaritans always had a book of Joshua which was their own, before any Jewish or other influence.

1.   JosS, aside from easily recognizable and 'late' subsidiary expansions, is clearly shorter than the MT and the LXX, which hardly tallies with the thesis of a derivation from the MT, since the tendency toward expansion happens from all sides. This brevity is seen in examples, which apparently are not accidental, since they are in line with the analyses already done in §3 or proposed below: JosS reorganizes and abbreviates the whole apportioning of the tribes west of the Jordan (Josh. 14.6–21.45); the scene on Ebal and Gerizim (Josh. 8.30-35) is simplified, and neither the copy of the Law (תורה משנה), nor Moses is referred to; likewise, the account of the Shechem assembly is briefer, and in particular the discourse of Joshua omits the patriarchs[134] (24.2-5), the departure from Egypt and the conquest (24.6-13, replaced by Deut. 4.34); and the people omit the historical confession (24.17-21a). According to this redaction, the extreme oversimplicity of the conquest and the apportioning is again emphasized, and there are blunt recollections relative to Joshua as founder and legislator without any connection with the patriarchs or with Moses or his Law, in the double scene of Ebal-Gerizim and Shechem. There is more: the memory of the coming out from Egypt only appears in this passage from the injection of a verse of Deuteronomy, according to a procedure described below.

2.   Among the signs indicating the chanting of the MT, one of them, the *paseq*, formed by a vertical line between two words, is atypical, since it does not conform to the rigidity of the general system of conjunctive and disjunctive signs. M. Gaster has observed that when the MT has a *paseq*, the parallel in JosS, if it exists, offers a different text, often close to the LXX (A) for the minor variants;[135] he concludes from this that it is a pre-Masoretic sign[136] for textual control, presupposing a Jewish

---

134.   This peculiarity should be compared with a polemical remark of Benjamin of Tudel, criticized by Scaliger and according to which 'The Samaritans were missing the three letters ה, ח, and ע: ה of the name of Abraham, ח of the name of Isaac, ע of the name of Jacob. In their place they put an א [...]', quoted by de Robert, 'Naissance', p. 30. This is patently false, and besides Samaritan piety insisted more on the 'merits of the fathers' than the rabbinic tradition did.

135.   Gaster, *The Samaritans*, pp. 136-39.

136.   Which completes the study of James Kennedy, *The Note-Line in the Hebrew Scriptures, Commonly Called* paseq *or* pᵉsīq (Edinburgh: T. & T. Clark, 1903), pp. 19-21, who shows that this sign is ancient (and wrongly named by the Masoretes): 1. It is simple, and very obvious, almost cumbersome; 2. it always

collation on an ancestor of the present Samaritan text. Similarly, he has compared,[137] for the parallel passages, the divisions of the manuscripts of JosS into pericopes (*qiṣṣot*) and the massoretic divisions of Jos (*petuḥot* and *setumot* mixed up, as was verified for the Aleppo codex): the result is that, of thirty-seven divisions of JosS, thirty are met again exactly the same in the MT, four correspond imprecisely because of the difference of text, and only three do not correspond at all. These observations are only thrown so much into relief because there are other indications (below) which show that JosS *is not* derived from the MT.

3.   There are some significant contacts between JosS and Josephus's paraphrase: in Josh. 2.1 the spies, sent out, went first to the house of Rahab, but in JosS as in *Ant.* 5.5-15, they came first to give their report to Joshua. In Josh. 2.21, after their dismissal by Rahab, Josephus (*Ant.* 5.15) and JosS add again a report by the spies in front of Joshua and Eleazar. In Josh. 7.16, for the discovery and judgment of Achan, Josephus (*Ant.* 5.43) and JosS introduce Eleazar and the Elders into the procedure. Josephus (*Ant.* 5.48) and JosS omit the perpetual ruin of Ai and the execution of the king, as recounted in Josh. 8.28-29. In a striking way, Josephus (*Ant.* 5.20, 35) and JosS refer to Gilgal only in the vicinity of Ai, therefore far from Jericho (and near Shechem, because of Deut. 11.30), which is certainly a more 'Samaritan' notion, and they omit the circumcision at Gilgal of Josh. 5.2-9, after the crossing of the Jordan. One last contact worthy of note was the analogy of the passage on the apportionment of the conquered territory among the tribes (*Ant.* 5.80-87), very brief and arranged systematically in one as in the other

corresponds to a difficulty in the text, but, on the other hand, many difficulties are not indicated: they might be later; 3. it coincides often with the presence of a *qere*; 4. it is later than the introduction of the final letters in the Aramaic alphabet. On the contrary, I. Yeivin, *Introduction to the Tiberian Masorah* (trans. and ed. E.J. Revell; Masoretic Studies, 5; Missoula, MT: Scholars Press, 1980), pp. 216-18 (§§283-86), states that the *paseq*, while marking (as its name indicates) a slight pause after a word with a conjunctive accent, has a use which does not follow simple and clear rules; he deduces that its introduction was not contemporaneous with the general (and coherent) system of conjunctive and disjunctive accents. He therefore considers that this introduction is later, but he provides no arguments, and it can be objected: 1. that this supplementary sign was not necessary for the Masoretic system; 2. that it has an effect on the *bgdkpt* at the beginning of the following word, while it is hardly probable that the Masoretic pronunciation would have been modified after its establishment.

137.   Gaster, 'Das Buch Josua', p. 219.

from the south (Judah) to the north (Nephtali), with the only difference being that Josephus puts Dan at the end, probably because of its future migration to the north. This arrangement was not by chance, and can be characteristically attributed neither to the one nor the other, since it is encountered as well in the schematized view of Ezek. 47.15-21, with Reuben and Gad placed west of the Jordan, in the south. These few connections in content between Josephus and JosS should not obscure marked differences (for example, in regard to the curse on anyone who would rebuild Jericho in Josh. 6.26), but since it is really improbable that Josephus had sought Samaritan sources, or that the *Jewish Antiquities* would have had any influence on the present JosS, it must be concluded that one as well as the other, despite their reputation for inaccuracy, had drawn from a common source, less 'Benjaminite' than the MT and the LXX that we know: the text of Joshua was a flexible compilation, as is proved as well by various fragments from Qumran.

4. The present text of JosS is peppered with 24 citations of the Pentateuch, without specific Samaritan variants, of which 15 come from Deuteronomy. Such an occurrence is common in the texts from the desert of Judaea and is not rare in SP; we regularly meet the primacy of Deuteronomy, as the principal source of the inserted verses.

I can provide here two suggestive illustrations, drawn from Cave 4:[138] first 4Q158, a kind of chain formed by excerpts from Genesis and Exodus, contains (f. 6) a sequence formed from Deut. 5.27 + Exod. 20.19-22 MT + (addition) + Deut. 5.29 + (a corrupt phrase) + Deut. 18.18-22. If we omit the 'corrupt phrase', we obtain Exod. 20.19-21 SP exactly, but in square-letter Aramaic script of the time of Herod. It is part of the section which follows the Decalogue and consists of a passage in which God announces to Moses a prophet like himself. The other fragments of this batch have contacts in both content and form with SP, but are more free. The other example is provided by 4Q175, which is an anthology too (called *testimonia* by the editor) written in the square-lettered alphabet of the end of the second century BCE, but in it we find a sequence, Deut. 5.28-29 + Deut. 18.18-19, which is none other than Exod. 20.21b SP; then comes the third oracle of Balaam[139]

---

138. J.M. Allegro, with the collaboration of A.A. Anderson, *Qumran Cave 4, I (4Q158–4Q186)* (DJD, 5; Oxford: Clarendon Press, 1968), to be completed by the lengthy recension of J. Strugnell, 'Notes en marge du Volume V des "Discoveries in the Judaean Desert of Jordan"', *RevQ* 26 (1970), pp. 163-276.

139. Macdonald, *Theology of the Samaritans*, p. 160, in which 'the star that

(Num. 24.15-17) and the benediction of Moses on Levi (Deut. 33.8-11), two important texts for the Samaritans. In a conclusion appears an excerpt from the *Psalms of Joshua*, citing against Jerusalem a version of the curse of Josh. 6.26 without the mention of Jericho (cf. LXX), from which there would be grounds to think that they had some connection with a Samaritan tradition.[140]

These few facts show that the Samaritan biblical texts (SP and JosS) have preserved not only some variants, but some composition techniques well attested at Qumran, in which it is significant that the sorting of the fragments collected according to writing, Aramaic or Hebrew, is not consistent with the expected distinction between Samaritan and other writings. It is necessary then, we must repeat, to avoid the anachronism of projecting back into the Hasmonaean period, at least before the destruction of Gerizim and Shechem, clear-cut distinctions that are only clearly attested later.

The proposed renewal of interest in JosS should be extended to the whole Samaritan literary tradition, since its very conservative character allows a generalized presumption that it did not depend on Judaism, or at least that it was not subject to *learned* influence, more especially so since study was not a precept among the Samaritans. Now the Samaritan chronicles, following the book of Joshua, most often contain narratives up to the Exile which have extensive material in common with Judges, Samuel, Kings and Chronicles, but are joined to other elements, and a presentation of facts that is in general anti-monarchical, anti-Judaean and anti-prophetic. An observation made in regard to JosS applies again here: the narratives contain many expansions and glosses, but the biblical 'excerpts' represent a stringent selection, in which the motive is not straightforward blame, since certain passages very critical in regard to the North were kept, while others, more neutral, are omitted.[141] Beside various developments and alterations, these texts call for a careful examination, since they should contain elements to counterbalance the bias of Judaean historiography.

comes out of Jacob' can designate Moses, son of Jochebed, or the prophet to come, the restorer (*Taheb*); *II Chronicle* Judg. K:J* mentions a 'Book of Balaam'.

140. Cf. the discussion of Cross, *The Ancient Library*, p. 113; Baillet, 'Texte samaritain', p. 380; the Samaritan ritual contains an ancient Prayer of Joshua; cf. A.E. Cowley, *The Samaritan Liturgy* (2 vols.; Oxford: Clarendon Press, 1909), I, pp. 1-92.

141. Macdonald, *The Samaritan Chronicle No. II*, pp. 14-18.

To take one example, Judg. 12.13-15 gives a brief account about the judge Abdon, a very prolific individual, eventually buried at Pireathon, 'in the land of Ephraim, in the hill country of the Amalekites', which brings to mind episodes in the desert (Exod. 17.8-15). In place of this account, *II Chron.* Judg K:J*-R* (MacDonald's notation) puts in a narrative according to which strangers seduced the Israelites with Balaam's sorceries. This dissidence prospered (like the posterity of Abdon), and eventually took refuge in a place called Pireatha.[142] What is more, in *II Chron.* 1 Kings E:A*-M* there is a list of four tendencies or parties (פרקים) of the Israelites, in the time of Jeroboam: 1. the followers of Gerizim, descendants of the high priest Eleazar and of the house of Joseph; 2. the tribe of Judah with a large number of other people, faithful since David to Jebus-Jerusalem; 3. the inhabitants of Pireathon, following the strange gods of the nations, called 'Unreliables', or perhaps 'Slackers' (עזובים [sic]); 4. the rest of the tribes of Israel, called the 'Rebels' (סוררים), since they are obedient to Jeroboam, son of Nebat, who led them into adoring the golden calves, placed at Samaria and Dan.[143] This midrash, which does not directly consider the Samaritan diaspora, is suggestive: the development of the tribe of Judah is an allusion to the Hasmonaean conquests, or even to the conversions in the time of Herod. The fourth party is a doublet of the third, corresponding in literary terms to the time of Jeroboam, and perhaps in reality to the splendours of the Hellenistic city of Samaria. It is in any case a matter of idolatry, for one as well as for the other, and it is remarkable that each of them contains a major element of the story of Aaron in the desert: the golden calf, and the people who had 'lapsed' (פרוע, where we find the root of Pireathon), with the difficult gloss: 'since Aaron had let them lapse [...]' (Exod. 32.25). *II Chronicles* in this passage is not very favourable to Aaron, since the high priests are descendants of Eleazar and not of him; it derives perhaps from the erasing of the connection between Aaron and Pireathon. There is another element to the record: the coins of Samaria representing Gerizim, in the Hasmonaean period, show two sanctuaries side by side, one to Aphrodite and the other Samaritan. Idolatry prospered, or 'laxity' was not far away, which confirms that the Samaritans of Gerizim formed only a limited group, just like the community of Nehemiah or the companions of Mattathias.

In literary terms, the Samaritan *Chronicles* have the status of a midrash, like the biblical Chronicles: they cannot be used to establish the priority of the Samaritans over Judaism, without begging the question. This having been advanced through other criteria, which emphasized a major creative phase in the Seleucid period, the *Chronicles* then become usable to clarify matters.

142. The text has פרעתה ומקומות. There is a place called Far'ata, 7 miles southeast of Nablus.

143. The text mentions in passing that it was at Dan that treasures were hidden; we may compare the leather scroll 3Q15, which mentions the treasures hidden at Gerizim and at Jerusalem.

Chapter 6

THE MACCABAEAN CRISIS

The series of analyses developed in the preceding chapters, whether in regard to the emergence of the Sabbath and the 'model of Nehemiah', or the establishment of the sacred library and the questions connected with the Samaritans, or even the difficulties between Judaism and the Temple in connection with the ambiguities of Hellenization, all this tends to make the Maccabaean crisis a foundational moment, or at least a revelational moment, which is supposed to define its antecedents. We have also seen, however, that the exact circumstances of this crisis are difficult to piece together, since the accounts which relate them are tendentious and contradictory, and render almost unintelligible the policies of Antiochus IV as well as the relations between the rival high-priestly dynasties and the various groups claiming to go back to the spirit of the Covenant, not to mention the obscurities surrounding the origins of the feast of Dedication.

Besides the two books of Maccabees, the available documentation on this crisis comprises: the book of Daniel, which had prophesied the destruction of the Temple,[1] as Josephus indeed pointed out (*Ant.* 12.322);

---

1.   But not its restoration, from which it is usually concluded that it was composed before the death of Antiochus Epiphanes (164 BCE); cf. L.F. Hartman and A.A. di Lella, 'Daniel', in R.E. Brown, J.A. Fitzmeyer and R.E. Murphy (eds.), *The New Jerome Biblical Commentary* (London: Geoffrey Chapman, 1990), pp. 406-409 (with bibliography), even if it means that the events would have eluded the prophecies of a seer, as Goldstein, *I Maccabees*, p. 43, would wish. The argument is still weak for two reasons: 1. it is not demonstrated that the restoration by Judas had produced unanimity among the Jews, nor even that it would have been a major *historical* event (cf. below); 2. the prophetic genre, by nature, remains turned towards hope, and therefore leaves the future open, rather than closing it off with a limited event: for example, the conclusion of 2 Chronicles is a universalist proclamation, which ignores Ezra. Pseudo-Philo, in which the whole narrative prepares for the coming of David, finishes at the moment when he should appear, but one cannot

the two descriptions of events by Josephus (*War* 1.31-40 and *Ant.* 12.237-326), one very different from the other, with the second closely dependent on 1 Maccabees; certainly a significant part[2] of the Hellenistic Jewish literature and the texts from Qumran, but more by way of allusion than in factual accounts. On the other hand, the history of the rivalries between the Lagides of Egypt and the Seleucids of Syria, and in particular the reign of Antiochus IV Epiphanes, are sufficiently documented, apart from numerous inscriptions and coins, in the Greek historians (Polybius, Diodorus Siculus, Strabo, Porphyry, through the commentary of Jerome on Dan. 11), and in the Roman chroniclers[3] (Livy, Tacitus). The role of Rome, after the fall of Carthage, was already appreciable in the East, and its hegemony over the Greek world was definitively established during the period that extended from the Treaty of Apamea (188 BCE), in which Antiochus III had to accept the loss of part of his kingdom, to the destruction of Corinth by the Romans (146 BCE), after which Greece became practically a Roman province.

The purpose of this chapter is to re-examine the documents not from the angle of facts for their own sake, although it may be necessary to sort them out a little, but by trying as before to track the ups and downs of some major institutions. After a summary of the main historiographical difficulties, three principal domains will help in guiding the train of thought: 1. the sacred library founded by Nehemiah has already been mentioned, but the discussion must be completed on account of the strange correspondence with Sparta of the high priest Jonathan, the brother and successor of Judas Maccabeus; 2. the control of the city of Jerusalem is obviously a major stake throughout the crisis, and this fact must be connected to the 'model of Nehemiah', according to which the restoration of the city is an essential element for the observance of the Law; 3. in regard to the Temple, the nature of the Seleucid profanation is unclear, and the exact shape of the restoration commemorated by the

---

conclude that the narrative is incomplete. Likewise, the Acts of the Apostles, which is unaware of the destruction of Jerusalem, concludes with the arrival of Paul at Rome, but it cannot be concluded that it was composed before his death, nor even before the destruction.

2.   D.J. Harrington, *The Maccabaean Revolt*, pp. 109-123, in which he refers to the *Testament of Moses*, Judith, *Habakkuk Pesher*.

3.   For an excellent summary presentation of the viewpoints of these different sources on the crisis and the history of their interpretation, see Bickerman, *The God of the Maccabees*, pp. 9-31.

feast of Dedication is less clear than might seem, since the various accounts of its foundation are not very consistent.

1. *A Many-Sided Conflict*

The two principal accounts still available on the crisis, 1 Maccabees and 2 Maccabees, describe it in very different ways. For 1 Maccabees, it all began when Antiochus caused Hellenism to be introduced into Jerusalem, through the complicity of 'renegades'. There is no mention of any high priest at that time; then the resistance of Mattathias gained momentum, and his dynasty established itself, as stated before. For 2 Maccabees, it all began with the deposition of Onias, the best of the high priests, over a fiscal matter of minor importance, a 'conflict of nobles', according to *War* 1.31. Divisions and persecutions followed from this, and the resistance was launched by Judas Maccabeus alone, who was not a priest and had no known family connections, but scrupulously observed the Law, especially the Sabbath and purity. The book ends before his death, without any dynasty having been established, but with the restoration of a sublime temple, although without any priest in charge, and with the institution of a commemorative feast.

According to 1 Macc. 1.10-54, then, Antiochus Epiphanes became king in the year 137 of the Seleucid calendar (September 175 BCE) and 'in those days there arose in Israel a faction of renegades' who obtained from the king the authorization to follow pagan customs: they built a gymnasium in Jerusalem, disguised their circumcision and 'abandoned the holy covenant'. Antiochus then conducted a victorious campaign in Egypt, and on his return in 143 (169 BCE) advanced on Jerusalem with a strong force; he plundered the Temple and departed. Two years later, therefore in 145 (167 BCE), the king sent a sizeable detachment against Judaea and Jerusalem, which destroyed the city and constructed a citadel by building a wall around the city of David. The king next published a decree requiring that all should renounce their national customs, so that the kingdom would be made up of a single people. One specific result of this was a persecution at Jerusalem and in Judaea; the sanctuary was profaned, and finally, on 15th Kislev 145 (Dec. 7, 167), they built on the altar l of burnt offering the 'abomination of desolation' (a derisory distortion of *Baal Shamayim*, 'Lord of heaven').[4] The following section (1 Maccabees 2–4) recounts the resistance of the priest Mattathias, then of Judas Maccabeus, the reconquest and finally the restoration of the Jerusalem sanctuary. It was inaugurated with a solemn festival of eight days on the 25th Kislev 148 (Dec. 14, 164), or exactly three years

4.   The expression is traced to שקוץ שמם of Dan. 11.31; cf. F.-M. Abel, *Les livres des Maccabées* (EBib, 38; 2 vols.; Paris: Gabalda, 1949), pp. 28-29 (Excursus 1).

after the profanation (mentioned in 1 Macc. 1.59), and the annual commemoration of this dedication was then instituted. The wars of reconquest, under the leadership of Judas, continued. Meanwhile, Antiochus (6.1-13), who had been campaigning in Persia, after a defeat at Elymais,[5] was sadly returning to Babylon, when he learned of the liberation of Jerusalem. He became ill over this and died at Babylon, but not before recognizing that his dereliction was due to his sin against Jerusalem, namely, his completely irrational pillaging and exterminating.

Concentrating now on the origins of the crisis, this account is not coherent: 1. the party of Hellenizing 'renegades', which was present at the beginning, afterwards played no part, especially at the time of the destruction of the city; 2. the installation of settlers (1 Macc. 1.34) would appear to duplicate this party; 3. the Seleucid year 145 (167 BCE) seems to be very heavily loaded: restoration and colonizing of the City of David, persecutions, 'abomination of desolation'; 4. the setback of Antiochus before Elymais, followed by his sadness, sickness and death, is combined with his related setback at Jerusalem, followed by the same effects: there is a fusion of two motifs, and it is difficult to know whether his death should be situated before or after the dedication of the 25th Kislev. In fact, if we omit the strange episode of the installation of settlers in Jerusalem and the construction of the Akra (1.29-35), the first three inconsistencies disappear, and we arrive at a sequence of two simple narrative segments: a plundering on the return from Egypt, in the Seleucid year 143 (169 BCE), then a persecution aimed at Judaism, related to the emergence between 137 and 142 of the party of the 'renegades', and culminating in the new cult installed in 145 (167 BCE). Plundering and persecution are precisely the misdeeds that Antiochus acknowledged before dying. Even in this case, the lining up of the causes of the crisis remains confused, if we try to adopt a political point of view: the persecuted Jews are apparently anti-Seleucid, and the plundering fits in with the development of the pro-Seleucid party only if the latter is external to the Temple. This point is hard to establish, since no high-priestly dynasty is mentioned. In other words, according to this account we do not know who started things: the Hellenizing party, or the king with his plundering. For the reason indicated, this confusion is related in literary terms to the spiritual testament of Antiochus, in which he strangely accused himself by taking all responsibilty, whereas according to Hellenistic custom he had a perfect right to do what he did.[6] This tendentious account induces us to turn in the opposite direction, and to look for the causes of the crisis in the quarrel of two rival factions in Jerusalem, each calling the other 'renegades'. In any case, such developments certainly bring up in connection with this passage the problem of the evolution of the status of Jerusalem and its fiscal affairs in the Seleucid kingdom since the conquest of Antiochus III, seeing that each new king was entirely free to confirm or

5. On the ambiguity as to place, and the possible confusion with the death of Antiochus III, cf. F.-M. Abel, *Maccabées*, pp. 108-109.

6. The *Suda*, article βασιλεία: 'Neither nature nor law grants to men kingships, except to those who can command an army and carry out things sensibly [νουνεχῶς]: such was Philip and the heirs [διάδοχοι] of Alexander.'

redefine the statutes granted by his predecessors to the various parties in his kingdom.[7] This point will be examined below, §2.

Another account of the same facts is given by 2 Macc. 3.1–6.1, which is concentrated more decidedly in the preceding reign. Under Seleucus IV Philopator, who financed the operation of the Temple, Onias had proved to be the best high priest ever, but Simon the administrator of the Temple, following a fiscal dispute, out of jealousy went off to Apollonius governor of Coele-Syria to make known the enormous riches stored in the Temple: the king would therefore be able to enrich himself. The latter, informed of this, sent Heliodorus, who was miraculously struck down at the very moment he had gone to prepare an inventory of the Temple treasury, and who in the end repented and then offered a sacrifice. But Simon still had the ear of Apollonius, and denounced Onias as the one who had caused the attack on Heliodorus. The tension increased, and Onias, to re-establish public peace, resolved to appeal to the king. Seleucus IV having died, Antiochus IV Epiphanes had succeeded him, and Jason, brother of Onias, profited from this to usurp the high priesthood by buying the office. He paid besides a large sum for the right to establish Greek-type institutions. The cult became lax. Nevertheless, when Antiochus came to Jerusalem, he was received in triumph by Jason and the inhabitants. Three years later, Menelaus, brother of the administrator Simon, obtained the high priesthood from the king by paying even more money. Jason had to flee to the land of the Ammonites, and Onias, a refugee at Daphne[8] near Antioch, protested against the plundering of the Temple. Menelaus then arranged to have Onias assassinated by Andronicus, a deputy of the king. Antiochus was indignant over this and condemned Andronicus, but Menelaus managed by means of a bribe to escape punishment. Antiochus then embarked on an unfortunate campaign in Egypt and, following a rumour of his death, Jason tried to retake Jerusalem from Menelaus, but failed and once again took refuge in Ammonite territory, among the Nabataeans. Antiochus was furious at this and came in a hurry, carried out a massacre and plundered the Temple. Next he sent the mysarch Apollonius, who took Jerusalem by surprise on the Sabbath and carried out another massacre. Judas Maccabeus then took to the hills. Next, Geron an Athenian was sent to Jerusalem (and to Gerizim) to abolish the

7.   Cf. Bickerman, *Institutions des Séleucides*, pp. 11-13, in which he shows that the king was the living Law (νόμος ἔμψυχος), guaranteed by force alone, and pp. 136-37, in which he demonstrates that every charter granted to a city expired with the death of the king, and therefore had to be confirmed or modified by the successor, contingent on a tax for the 'crown'.

8.   About 5 miles from Antioch, Daphne was renowned for its temple of Apollo and Artemis, founded by Seleucus I, in which the right of asylum was recognized (Strabo, *Geography*, 16.2.6); this was certainly the place of refuge of Onias, apparently protecting himself more from Jason than from Antiochus IV, to judge from the context. 2 Macc. 4.33 has εἰς ἄσυλον τόπον, a technical term, as in 3.12 where it characterized the inviolability of the Jerusalem Temple; cf. 1 Macc. 10.43, where Demetrius I offered Jonathan refuge in the Jerusalem Temple. See also Bickerman's presentation, *Institutions*, pp. 148-49.

Law and replace the cult with a monthly feast to Dionysus. After the accounts of the martyrs (6.18–7.42), the story is told (8-9) of how Judas embarked on his campaign and defeated the Seleucid generals who had been especially sent. Learning of this, Antiochus, who had just returned from an unsuccessful expedition in Persia, went into a rage, but, struck with an incurable illness, he died admitting his misdeeds, not without having written a friendly letter to the Jews, in which he asked them, in consideration of the benfits they had received, to give a warm welcome to his successor. It was only then that the arrival of Judas in Jerusalem, the purification of the Temple and the institution of a commemorative feast were reported.

This account is very complex and well documented, but without the system of Seleucid dates found in 1 Maccabees. The profanation of the Temple is preceded by lengthy episodes on the rivalries of the high priests, associated more or less with the dissensions within the Seleucid power structure. All this is peculiar to 2 Maccabees, in which we find many inconsistencies, running through the ever-present important question of money: 1. It is not logical, when Seleucus had financed the Temple, that he would send Heliodorus to plunder it. 2. At the same time, it is not logically consistent that Onias, who had been fighting against Simon but dropped out of sight after the death of Seleucus, should reappear years later, exiled but fighting against Menelaus, brother of Simon. It is simpler to assume to begin with that the whole episode took place in the reign of Antiochus IV, but out of piety it would have been displaced to the preceding reign, as a way to focus on the virtue of Onias, who in this way would have had nothing to do with the manoeuvres of this wicked king. 3. The triumphant reception of Antiochus in Jerusalem by Jason and the people, after Hellenization, no longer makes any sense since Onias, who was respected by all, was still living. It must be assumed that his replacement had been accepted by the people, and therefore, to be able to magnify Onias as unique in an era of peace, a redactor had placed him under Seleucus. 4. After the abortive attack by Jason, it is hard to see what would have accounted for the extreme rage of Antiochus, who had concluded from it that Judaea was seceding. From this point in the narrative, Antiochus is presented as out of his mind, which completely obscures the divisions among the Jews. 5. As has already been noted (Chapter 2, §1), the massacre of the people of Jerusalem by Apollonius, brought about by the persistent fury of the king, and not by a desire for plunder or to install settlers, seems to be the work of a madman, especially in the light of what followed, in which Geron came to abolish the Law. 6. This last move concluded or repeated the Hellenization carried out by Jason: if it is a conclusion, the insane actions of Antiochus are not in their proper place, and if it is a repetition, it would imply that the opposing party had regained influence, but this is not stated. 7. The letter of Antiochus, presented as a sort of circular[9] which the king normally would send at the beginning of a campaign from which he might not return, is incompatible with the context of the defeat of the Seleucid generals, but it would fit very well during Jason's reign, that is at the time of one of the Egyptian episodes. This letter should be compared, in its general tone, to another one

---

9. The address (2 Macc. 9.19): Τοῖς χρηστοῖς Ἰουδαίοις τοῖς πολίταις is ponderous. Ἰουδαίοις is an addition; cf. Goldstein, *II Maccabees*, pp. 360-61.

(11.27-29; cf. below) addressed to the Jews, thanks to Menelaus, and once again presenting the king as a shrewd politician.

All these inconsistencies, many of which will be explained later, have the effect of putting the spotlight on the corrupt high priests and their henchmen, unstable accomplices of Antiochus, attached to money and equally to Hellenism, which by way of contrast preserved the memory of a bench-mark figure, Onias.

The version in the *Jewish Antiquities* of Josephus (12.237-47) follows 1 Maccabees, but develops its brief prologue (1.1-19) which goes from Alexander to the sack of Jerusalem by Antiochus returning from Egypt in 143 (169 BCE). This part, although better documented, is nevertheless independent of 2 Maccabees. There it records that Jesus (Hellenized to Jason) had been given the high priesthood on the death of his brother Onias, and not in place of him while he was still alive, since he was soon dismissed in favour of another brother, Onias, who was called Menelaus; the latter is therefore no longer the brother of the administrator Simon. There had been a rivalry between the brothers, and the people were divided between them. The Tobiads were on the side of Menelaus, but the latter, now with minority support, took refuge with Antiochus, asked for the abolition of the ancestral laws (πατρίους νόμους) and the adoption of a Greek constitution (πολιτείαν), which led to the construction of a gymnasium and the abandonment of circumcision. On returning from his first campaign in Egypt, Antiochus made his way into a divided Jerusalem with the help of his supporters and killed and plundered a number of his opponents.

This account presents some difficulties, both in itself and when compared to 2 Maccabees: 1. The identification of Menelaus as a brother of Onias and Jason, with Jason to boot called Onias too, is not convincing. It would amount to a revision by Josephus or his source to demonstrate dynastic homogeneity, and the information in 2 Maccabees is preferable.[10] 2. It is missing a link, showing the actual outcome of the Hellenization by Menelaus. According to 2 Maccabees, it was Jason who introduced it, which is more consistent, all the more so since he had changed his name, and later the rivalry between Jason and Menelaus would have been a squabble within the Hellenized camp. 3. As for the visit of Antiochus to Jerusalem, 2 Maccabees presents it as a triumphal entry with Jason, before his disgrace and the appearance of Menelaus, whereas 1 Maccabees turned it into a pillaging of the Temple. The persecution of Antiochus's opponents, indicated by Josephus, does not appear to have been able to affect the high priest Jason, since he held the Temple and nothing is said of it: it affected those who resisted Hellenization, and who constituted a threat.

It is at this point that the brief account in *The Jewish War* (1.31-34) provides a useful detail: at the time when Antiochus was disputing with the Lagides over Coele-Syria, the nobles in conflict in Jerusalem divided up into two camps; Onias (confused with Jason), whom we can suppose to have been properly appointed, expelled his adversaries, in particular the Tobiads (with Menelaus) who obtained the help of Antiochus. The latter took Jerusalem, putting Onias to flight; he took refuge

---

10.   A sentence in Josephus (12.239) lets it be understood besides that they were not really brothers: 'Jesus, the preceding high priest, revolted against Menelaus who had been named after him'; cf. Loeb, *ad loc.*, and Appendix G.

in Egypt, where he was able to recreate a city and a temple. By inserting this account into that of the *Jewish Antiquities* and 2 Maccabees, it is then necessary to understand that Jason, appointed first by the Seleucid government, had thought that he could draw closer to Egypt, due to the changing fortunes of Antiochus, but this was a mistake. The adversaries of Antiochus at Jerusalem, in assuming that this would be the right time to act, were then right off the pro-Lagide camp. Those opposed to Hellenization made up another category, identified later with the political adversaries of Antiochus: Josephus's version in the *Jewish Antiquities* was a first stage in this reinterpretation, that of 1 Maccabees (plundering of the Temple) was a second. That of 2 Maccabees is to be placed before the presentation of the conflict in terms of a rivalry between nobles, and steers clear of any connection of any high priest with Egypt: there is a total censorship in regard to the temple of Onias, and the temple of Jerusalem is the only one mentioned.

Many commentators, as a way of reconstructing the events, have attempted to add together the details from the two books;[11] the second presents itself as a digest of Jason of Cyrene, therefore a selection. This method leads however to some narrative contradictions, but especially it pays little attention to several important literary facts relative to Judas and his activity:[12]

1. In the solemn document of 18th Elul in the one hundred and seventy-second Seleucid year (Sept. 13, 140 BCE, 1 Macc. 14.28) in honour of Simon, there is mention only of Mattathias, a descendant of Joarib, and of the glorious deeds of Jonathan and Simon, his sons, who both became high priests, but there is mention neither of Judas Maccabeus nor his reconquest of the sanctuary. Likewise, in 1 Macc. 16.3, Simon, growing old, tells his sons to take his place and that of *his* brother: the singular indicates Jonathan, and Judas is again absent. At this stage, the reconquest had not yet taken on the importance it would later have. This fact fits in with the details of the first festal letter to the Jews of Egypt,[13] in which they are ordered to celebrate the feast of Dedication (called 'feast of Booths') the 25th Kislev; it is dated 124

11.   A very typical example would be Goldstein, *I Maccabees* and *II Maccabees*.

12.   For a different presentation, see Bickerman, *The God of the Maccabees*, p. 36.

13.   The first festal letter (2 Macc. 1.1-10) is dated 124 BCE, so under John Hyrcanus; it refers to a previous letter dated to 143, under Simon; cf. E.J. Bickerman, 'Ein jüdischer Festbrief vom Jahre 124 v. Chr.', in *Studies in Jewish and Christian History* (Leiden: Brill, 1980), II, pp. 136-58. The second letter is in homiletical style and hard to date, even though it gives the impression of being sent just before the Dedication itself (1.18).

(188 Seleucid) and recalls a previous letter along the same lines in 143 (169 Seleucid). The latter is most certainly a literary fiction, since it is actually the letter of 124 which endeavoured to institute the commemoration.

2. The 'renegade' party of 1 Maccabees, which procured Hellenization, parallels the activities of the high priest Jason of 2 Maccabees and his successors. Later, the decree abolishing the practices of Judaism culminating in the 'abomination of desolation' is parallel to the sending of Geron the Athenian who installed another cult. These two phases are separated by the plundering of the Temple by Antiochus as he returned from Egypt. They appear redundant, but in the first instance, the initiative came from the 'renegades' or from Jason; in the second, it was a decision of Antiochus: the double motivation is common to the two accounts. As for the plundering, it is a sober and clear enough account in 1 Maccabees, while for 2 Maccabees it is divided up between the aborted attempt of Heliodorus and the action of Antiochus, become crazed with *pride*; in fact, since the office of high priest had been sold to the highest bidder, the despoiling of the Temple could assume legal forms, without any anger being involved. In other words, the triumphal reception, according to 2 Macc. 4.21-22, of Antiochus returning from Egypt, given by Jason who had paid dearly for his office is quite parallel to 1 Macc. 1.21-23, which describes the plundering of Jerusalem and the Temple by Antiochus returning from Egypt, while introducing besides some details which are found in the plundering perpetrated by the same Antiochus on his return from a second Egyptian campaign (2 Macc. 5.15-16). There were therefore two points of view on the visit of Antiochus to Jerusalem: the one, Seleucid, which celebrated in him the guarantor of order, after the Hellenization (by Jason); the other, Jewish, which rejected him as the profaner of the Temple, or the persecutor, as Josephus called him. The second passage about Antiochus at Jerusalem (2 Macc. 5), situated more than three years after the first, is therefore a doublet and interprets it according to the second point of view. This is in no way a contradiction of the fact that Antiochus really carried out two campaigns in Egypt, separated however by one year only, and that in the second, in 168, he was forced by the Romans to leave Egypt[14]

14.   Cf. Titus Livius, *History* 45.11-12, following Polybius, *History* 29.27, who relates how the Roman senators had sent a legation led by Popilius Laenas to consolidate the rule of Ptolemy VI Philometor, threatened by Antiochus Epiphanes, since the latter wanted to counter Egyptian claims over Coele-Syria.

(cf. Dan. 11.30), which he did full of spite. The redactional effect deforms the historical source, which explains on the one hand why Antiochus would be presented as a demented person, since he no longer followed the logic of greed, and on the other hand why another account of a massacre (5.23-27) would be connected to that madness. It explains too the strange episode in which Jason attempted to retake the city from Menelaus, without any real success, except that Antiochus, disturbed by it, arrived. But his pillaging in the time of Menelaus (5.15) is only a continuation or a development of the indication about the power acquired by Menelaus in 4.50, in which he established himself 'as the chief enemy of his compatriots'. In this way, and taking into account the information provided by Josephus, the succession of 'renegades' appears more clearly, against the background of Antiochus's financial needs and Egyptian difficulties: there is a superimposition of a political problem and an issue of Hellenization, at first haphazard, then institutional.

3. The heroic reconquest by Judas 25th Kislev 164 BCE is itself strangely isolated, since on the one hand, according to the letter preserved in 2 Macc. 11.27-33, Antiochus had brought his persecution of the Jews to an end six months earlier, 15th Xanthicus of the one hundred and forty-eighth Seleucid year, and on the other hand the real restoration of the sanctuary, at least in the Hasmonaean sense, only took place 12 years later, with the arrival of Jonathan in 152, after the high priesthoods of Menelaus and then Alcimus (162–159), another representative of the opposing camp, followed by a phase of abandonment of cult. As far as dates are concerned, the death of Antiochus IV is dated in the one hundred and forty-ninth Seleucid year according to 1 Macc. 6.16, but a Babylonian tablet[15] has shown that news of it had reached Babylon in Kislev 148 (December 164), that is around the time of the Dedication, or rather a little before.[16] This concomitance is certainly

15.   A.J. Sachs and D.J. Wiseman, 'A Babylonian King List of the Hellenistic Period', *Iraq* 16 (1954), pp. 202-212 (British Museum Tablet 35 603).

16.   Goldstein, *I Maccabees*, p. 274, suggests that the Jewish *liturgical* year could have been a month or two in advance, due to the central Jewish authority not having been able to proclaim the intercalary months during the crisis, and therefore that the Kislev of the Dedication would be prior to the Kislev of Antiochus's death, the news of which however would have arrived at Jerusalem much later. This is unverifiable and even improbable, since the argument, based on the existence of an authority as presented by the rabbinic tradition, is an anachronism, if it is not confirmed by other sources; besides, if it is true that many ancient local calendars

behind the origin of the fusion, on the occasion of the sickness and death of Antiochus, of the setback at Elymais and of God's punishment for the sins committed against Jerusalem. In this way, Jewish teleology is respected.

A passage of *Meg. Ta'an.* (a list in Aramaic of feast days on which fasting and/or mourning is prohibited) brings a supplementary component to the debate: 'On the 28th Adar [Xanthicus] the good news reached the Judaeans [ליהודאי] that they should stop turning away [דלא יעדון] from the Torah. No mourning.' This refers to the end of a persecution of Jews in Judaea, which the accompanying *scholim* seems to situate long after the crisis under consideration: 'For the kings of wicked Edom had decreed a persecution [שמד] against Israel, by forbidding the circumcision of their sons, the keeping of the Sabbath, and by obliging the practice of idolatry [...];' liberation was finally due to the action of a certain Juda son of Shamoa who rallied the people. In Rabbinic literature, Edom was usually the Byzantine Empire, possibly the Roman Empire first, since the *Megila* cited was certainly composed before 150 CE. In this case Edom could be a corruption of Aram through an anachronism of a copyist (אדם for ארם). But Aram is Syria, and the three elements of the persecution and especially its interruption are difficult to situate under Roman domination, while they correspond particularly well to the measures taken by Antiochus IV, then revoked thanks to the activity of a man called Juda. Moreover, the date of the good news agrees completely with the letter cited by 2 Macc. 11.27-33, sent on 15th Xanthicus (Adar) 148 (164 BCE). Most commentators therefore see a parallel between the two documents.[17] Since it is clearly possible, in following 1 Maccabees, to date the death of Antiochus after the Dedication of 25th Kislev 148, there is no difficulty in imagining, at the price of certain clarifications in the calendar, that the new rights granted by the king would have been accepted by Juda and his people after their victory *and the Dedication*. If things were not that way, the necessary conclusion[18] is that this same Juda and his companions had conquered and obtained the desired concessions *before* 25th Kislev. The 'good news' only affected Jewish domestic life and said nothing about the Temple, and we meet up again with the presentation of 2 Macc. 8.33, in which the victory is celebrated at Jerusalem, with no date given and no connection with the Temple, before the death of Antiochus and independently of the insertion of the passage on the purification of the sanctuary on 25th Kislev.

---

remained in force during the Seleucid monarchy, it is striking that 1 Maccabees insists unequivocally on the official Seleucid era.

17.   H. Lichtenstein, 'Die Fastenrolle: Eine Untersuchung zur jüdisch-hellenistischen Geschichte', *HUCA* 8-9 (1931–32), pp. 257-351, with a discussion p. 279.

18.   Aside from reattributing the letter of 2 Macc. 11.27-33 to the young Antiochus V, so after Kislev 148, which is maintained by Goldstein, *II Maccabees*, pp. 418-19, at the cost of many complications in the calendar.

4. I now compare the parallel elements of the two accounts in 1 Maccabees and 2 Maccabees, beginning at the end, since this is the simplest. It is strange that Antiochus died after the Dedication according to 1 Maccabees, but before according to 2 Maccabees. The victory of Judas and his men, their arrival in Jerusalem and the victory celebrations are referred to briefly in 2 Macc. 8.31-33, thus before Antiochus had learned of them and then died because of them (9.4-10). The actual account of the Dedication and the institution of the commemoration is placed in what follows, but it concludes with the strange sentence: 'Such were the circumstances of [καὶ τὰ μὲν [...] οὕτως εἶχε] the death of Antiochus called Epiphanes' (10.9). This sentence in fact closes the preceding section, on Antiochus, and is separated from it by the account of the Dedication, which consequently forms an intrusion.[19] The location of this intrusion is more respectful perhaps of the real *historical* chronology, as has been noted, but if it is omitted, we meet up again with the *literary* chronology of 1 Maccabees,[20] necessary for the Jewish legend about Antiochus repenting and acknowledging his sin against God. A still more important fact is this: this intrusion creates a difference in meaning of primary importance, since if it is omitted, Judas, here just as at the time of his appearance in 5.27, no longer has any clear connection with the Temple, either in the account or in his genealogy, since he is not connected to the family of the priest Mattathias. This aspect will be

19. This is the conclusion of most commentators: for a contrary opinion, see Doran, *Temple Propaganda*, p. 61.

20. There is in fact a double chronological difficulty connected to the Dedication of 25th Kislev 148. First, in 2 Macc. 11.22-26 there appears among other letters dated in Xanthicus 148 (therefore four months later) an undated letter of Antiochus V recalling the death of Epiphanes his father, which had taken place in 149 according to 1 Maccabees; but it has been pointed out that this letter is later and is addressed to Judas, while the others refer to the Hellenized camp (cf. V. Tcherikover, 'The Documents of II Macc.', *Tarbiz* 1 [1930], pp. 39-43, elaborated upon by M.B. Dagut, 'II Maccabees and the Death of Antiochus IV Epiphanes', *JBL* 72 [1953], pp. 149-57). It is this error which would have induced the final redactor of 2 Maccabees to insert the Dedication after the death of Antiochus. Secondly, among the other letters, the third (11.27-32) supposes Menelaus still in charge, and so cannot be later than the victory of Judas. It has therefore been concluded that the official letters follow the official calendar (Macedonian), beginning in the autumn of 312 BCE (Dios, corresponding to Tishri), while the chronology of 1 Maccabees follows the Babylonian calendar, counted six months later (Nisan 311). In this way, the date of the Dedication is eight months after the letters, and not four months before; cf. Abel, *Maccabées*, p. 51. Schürer, *History*, I, p. 162, gives another explanation.

examined later. Therefore, in 2 Macc. 10.1-8, the account of the exploit is a literary intrusion, which is combined with the death of Antiochus IV and depends in reality on the festal letter of 1.18-29; furthermore, Judas had already celebrated his victories at Jerusalem in 8.31-33, but did not stay there, since his sights were set elsewhere.

5. With the actual political event disappearing (a point confirmed by Dan. 8.14, which suggests a restoration very much later), there remained however the memory of a symbolic event, promoted later on as a foundation exploit; in fact, on the twenty-fifth of each month there had been celebrated at the sanctuary in Jerusalem a sacrifice in honour of the king and 25th Kislev 164, which perhaps coincided with the winter solstice, was apparently the first occurence of the sacrifice *after* the death of Antiochus IV in Elam. A limited activity can be assumed then, content with a disruption of the royal cult on that day, but significant enough to be magnified later.[21]

Antiochus IV was not crazy, but he was a politician. There are in 2 Macc. 11.16-33 rather conciliatory letters in regard to the status of the Jews, which their context would tend to place under Antiochus V, the successor of Epiphanes, during the regency of Lysias, but which their date of Xanthicus 148 of the Seleucid year, or the beginning of 164 BCE, situates considerably before the Dedication and the death of Epiphanius. These documents present various problems.[22] In particular, they had been displaced by the author of 2 Maccabees, since they did not seem to agree with what he wanted to say about Antiochus IV, as they indicated that Judas, once he was victorious, negotiated 'in the interests of the people'. One of the letters announced to the 'gerousia' and to the people of Judaea that on the request of Menelaus all could return home and practise their laws. In reality, the king obviously ignored Judas and the rebels who had fled the persecution or who had gone underground: they were not the interlocutors, but it was on the contrary the high priest, who was not mentioned as such, who had

---

21.   The history of France, at least in the pedagogical presentation, offers interesting analogous examples: St Genevieve repulsing the Huns (but who were the barbarians?); the stopping of the Saracen invasion by Charles Martel ('Maccabee' has the probable meaning of 'hammer', 'marteau' in French, since it is derived from מקב); among others.

22.   Cf. Abel and Starcky, *Maccabées* (Paris, 1961), pp. 39-43; C. Habicht, 'Royal Documents in Maccabees II', *Harvard Studies in Classical Philology* 80 (1976), pp. 1-18, followed by Bickerman, *The God of the Maccabees*, p. 113.

sought the calming down. The clear result of this, since the fighting continued and Menelaus had previously been presented as the enemy of his fellow citizens, is that the struggle was carried on against what he represented, or at least that is the thesis that the account wanted to have accepted. The remarkable point is that there is no mention in this letter of the Temple, but of the re-establishment of the right to Jewish *private* practices. The stake in this struggle was not the Temple.

It must be concluded, once again, that there was a difference in points of view. According to the government, it was simply a question of a dissident party that had become more powerful than had been foreseen, which gave rise to the necessity to negotiate and provide a place for it. The rebels, on the contrary, saw themselves or were presented as the only Jews worthy of this name, in a struggle against the absolute evil represented by Menelaus and Antiochus, enemies of God. Moreover, the documents which show that the rebels too had political views have been transferred to another context, especially since according to the fourth letter the Romans had intervened in support of the requests of the dissidents (cf. 1 Macc. 8, the alliance of Judas and the Romans). This literary displacement is symmetrical with that of Onias: the genuine faithful could not be compromised with Antiochus. Finally, by tolerating a certain legal diversity among the 'Jews', Antiochus simply reverted back to what he wanted to do with the decree abolishing Judaism: the public order in 'the whole kingdom' that 'all were to become a single people' was to be understood as a policy of integration covering the whole kingdom, since the Jews were scattered throughout it, and he would have exploited their resources, or at least their cultic revenues. The control of this system was to be obtained by the Hellenization of the ruling circles of Jerusalem, since, once this was accepted and elevated to the level of law, whoever diverged from it was living outside the law.[23]

Judas Maccabeus was clearly dissociated from the institutional reconquest of the Temple and the establishment of an autonomous government in Judaea. We can note in passing that the usual term 'dynasty of the Maccabees', to designate the Hasmonaeans as a whole, exactly corresponds to the idea that 1 Maccabees wished to convey: namely, that Judas was its founder, whereas he was only its literary guarantor. As a matter of fact, his activity in defence of the persecuted Jews, which

---

23. Cf. Bickerman, *The God of the Maccabees*, pp. 30-32; the coins of the period make it possible to prove that Antiochus never had a systematic policy of forced Hellenization.

perhaps started at Jerusalem (2 Macc. 5.27), was in reality extended over a vast territory, comparable to the Judaea of Herod, which the rabbinic sources subsequently called the 'domain of those who came up from Babylon' (*y. Dem.* 2.1). The oral traditions came from Babylon, and Judas must be considered close to the later Pharisees. He had no priestly connections, so much so that Josephus, who had sensed the difficulty that a short-lived reconquest of the sanctuary portrayed, had him named high priest by acclamation of the people (*Ant.* 12.414), which is absurd in the context of unyielding Seleucid pressure, and, what is more, contrary to the facts. The document set out in 2 Macc. 11.27-33 shows that the high priest Menelaus remained in office after 25th Kislev 164, and the account in 1 Macc. 9.54-57 proves that his successor Alcimus died *after* Judas. Josephus himself forgot his own apologetic, and said in *Ant.* 20.237 that at the death of Alcimus the high priesthood remained vacant for seven years, up to the nomination of Jonathan.

In short, Judas Maccabeus must be detached from the dynasty of Mattathias: his presentation as a son of Mattathias and brother of Jonathan and Simon is therefore a literary artifice, due to motives which will become apparent later. In the same way, we see that the Maccabaean crisis itself, to judge from the results, had two aspects: a profanation of the Temple, a work of long duration, *and* a persecution of Judaism just about everywhere, brutal and short-lived. It was in response to this second aspect that Judas, whom we have seen waging war just about everywhere in defence of persecuted Jews, was really active.

2. *Jerusalem: Autonomous City or Centre of the Jews?*

The results of the crisis having been established, it is now a question of considering it against the background of its antecedents. If the policy of Antiochus IV was not insane, why was it nevertheless mistaken?

Behind the visionary language of Daniel, the various theocratic presentations of the books of Maccabees or the more rationalistic elements provided by Josephus, there are questions of statutes and law. The available documents especially concern the period of the crisis, but we can go back a generation earlier, when Antiochus the Great snatched Judaea from the control of the Egyptian Lagides.

Antiochus III, when he had definitively conquered Palestine, in 200 BCE, wrote to Ptolemy, son of Thraseas, governor and high priest of

Syria and Palestine,[24] a letter by which he granted Jerusalem an administrative charter that was religious and fiscal: the Jews could govern themselves according to ancestral laws and institutions (πατρίους νόμους); a royal contribution was set for the sacrifices, as well as assistance for reconstruction; a freeing of captives was decreed, and a fiscal incentive to repopulate Jerusalem. This document, mentioned by Josephus (*Ant.* 12.138-44), is authentic.[25] It was motivated by the reception given by the population of Jerusalem to Antiochus and his troops, and the assistance provided for the capture of the Egyptian garrison stationed in the citadel. As for the reconstruction and the repopulation, it is all explained by the fact that in 202 Antiochus had already captured the city from the Lagides, but the following year the latter had retaken it, then in 200 Antiochus recaptured it. Such upheavals certainly involved substantial destruction. On the other hand, the Jewish institutions indicated were evidently pre-existing, and the main question then is to know whether this charter created an entirely new juridical situation at Jerusalem, or merely confirmed arrangements previously in force.

Antiochus III, from the time of his accession to the throne in 223, had carried out an active policy of restoring the Seleucid Empire, not without a number of reverses and retreats. We know that for each city captured or recaptured he established rights and duties by decrees, and that most often it was a matter of restoring previous legislation, in many cases with certain fiscal advantages, at least momentary, to consolidate the loyalty of the newly conquered. These advantages are obvious in the document examined, but it is striking, seeing that the ancient legislation was admittedly pre-existent, that there is no indication that it was then in force: no high priest had been appointed, the Temple was unfinished, and the only source of power indicated before the war and the conquest was the Lagide garrison in the Citadel. What is more, the decree was addressed not to those involved, but to the governor of Syria, broadened at that time to include Palestine, that is to say, to the official in charge of taxes and public spending, who had a priestly rank. This arrangement was similar to the practices followed by the Persian chancelry, as the letters of Cyrus and Darius attest (Ezra 6.1-12).

24.   According to a Greek inscription found near Beth-shan, which shows that Palestine was at that time broadly controlled by this Ptolemy, a former Lagide general; see Landau, 'Greek Inscription', pp. 55-70, supplemented by L. and J. Robert, 'Bulletin épigraphique', *Revue des Etudes Grecques* 83 (1970), n. 627, pp. 469-73. According to Polybius, V.70.5, Scythopolis (Beth-shan) and Philoteria (K. Kerak, to the south of the Sea of Galilee) were handed over as early as 218 to Antiochus III.
25.   Cf. Bickerman, 'La Charte séleucide', pp. 44-85, who considers that Josephus had had access to an official copy addressed to Jerusalem, perhaps transcribed later on a stele (like the decree of Demetrius II; cf. 1 Macc. 11.37).

Now, in the Seleucid Empire, scattered throughout the territory there were free zones consisting of towns and peoples to whom the royal power for various reasons had granted certain liberties. They could have been Greek cities, Oriental sanctuaries, or local ethnic groups. These entities had in common the privilege of being under the immediate suzerainty of the king, and therefore of coming directly under the central administration, which did not prevent them from being able to organize among themselves, or to establish links with the outside, in particular with Rome.[26] What was Jerusalem's status in this regard?

In the various narratives of the Maccabees, there are several kinds of administrative relations between Jerusalem and the Seleucid government: in certain cases, the link is direct, and it is in this way that the high priest Onias tried to address the king directly at the time of the sinister affair of Simon and Heliodorus, which had disturbed the public peace (2 Macc. 4.1-6). Nevertheless, the fact that others, whether of a priestly family or not, could have been named high priests by the king, gives rise to some doubts about the real autonomy of Jerusalem, since we know that that function, seen from the central government, was first of all a responsibility of the regional governor. Besides, it was pointed out that the king 'defrayed from his own revenues, all the expenses for the sacrificial services' (3.2). We know that the other major sanctuaries, such as the temple mentioned at Daphne, had real estate revenues, or had the recognized right to collect certain taxes,[27] according to the circumstances. For Jerusalem, the administration of the Temple, according to the testimony just cited, depended entirely therefore on the government treasury, and the administrator Simon, whose quarrel with Onias set off the whole affair, is first of all a royal functionary (προστάτης τοῦ ἱεροῦ), although certainly recruited in Jerusalem. This administrator reported not to the king but more usually to Apollonius, governor of Syria-Phoenicia, who consulted the king on the matter, the result of which was the extraordinary mission of the highly-ranked Heliodorus.[28] All these factors permit a hybrid situation to come to light, in which there were two sources of effective power: the high priesthood, in so far as it is autonomous (since there was some control over the nominations), and the central administration with its regional representatives, a source of financing.

These facts clarify the impact of the charter of Antiochus III: it subsidized the autonomy of Jerusalem, which was linked to the cult, by offering, besides some interim help, a significant and regular contribution[29] to the Temple. These benefits were in kind and in cash, and the total indicated of 20,000 drachmas of silver needs further clarification: it represents 3.3 talents, or the annual salary of fifty to sixty day

26.	Bickerman, *Institutions*, pp. 141-42.

27.	M. Rostovtzeff, *Social and Economic History of the Hellenistic World* (Oxford: Clarendon Press, 1941); cf. his Index, for 'Temple', 'Temple Lands'.

28.	Cf. E.J. Bickerman, 'Héliodore au temple de Jérusalem', in *Studies in Jewish and Christian History*, II, pp. 159-91.

29.	The text does not specify the frequency, but the term used (σύνταξις) indicates a permanent contribution, barring explicit contrary stipulations; cf. 2 Macc. 9.16; 1 Esd. 6.28; and Bickerman, 'Charte séleucide', p. 53.

labourers converted to sacrificial offerings, the sum total of the annual production of a comparable number of families. It is a considerable sum for a private budget, but it would be income from a much smaller fund than the hundreds of talents paid by Jason or Menelaus to obtain new rights or to buy their offices.

Some of the details of the charter call for a widening of the investigation: in fact, on the fringe of the restoration of the city and the Temple, we note that the nation of the Jews did not coincide with the population of Jerusalem, nor even with that of Judaea. It is a matter of assembling in the city the dispersed (§139: συνοικίσαι τῶν διεσπαρμένων [...] συνελθόντων), and the ancestral laws are restored for 'all those who are members of the nation' (§142: πολιτευέσθωσαν πάντες οἱ ἐκ τοῦ ἔθνους), a formula reminiscent of the decree of Cyrus (Ezra 1.3). In other words, Antiochus proclaimed the unity of the *ethnos*, of the ancestral law, and of the Temple, with all these having to come to the fore in the 'city', which is not otherwise named. In this way we can understand why it did not refer to any *ethnarch* or high priest: what had perhaps existed previously was not taken into account as too local, and those who were to come afterwards were none other than those who emanated from ancestral institutions, under the control of the regional governor, as elsewhere in the kingdom. They must have originated particularly from among the 'gerousia' and the priests,[30] but we do not know the procedures for recruitment and promotion.

Josephus provides in addition two other documents, issued by the same king, which clarified his policy: a declaration relative to the status of the Jerusalem Temple (*Ant.* 12.145-46), and an ordinance showing that Antiochus held the Jewish *ethnos* worthy of confidence (*Ant.* 12.148-53). Let us examine these pieces.

The declaration protecting the Temple is authentic, despite some apparent improbabilities.[31] It is an official notice (πρόγραμμα) intended to be posted in a public place, which explains why the name of the city does not appear either. This notice, addressed to Jews as well as foreigners, consisted of various prohibitions in regard to access to the Temple, and in regard to the introduction of impure animals or their

---

30.   This was a kind of aristocracy (cf. *Ant.* 4.223 and 11/111), and not a democracy, the usual form of government in a Greek city; cf. Bickerman, *Institutions*, p. 165.

31.   For a discussion and conclusions, cf. E.J. Bickerman, 'Une proclamation séleucide relative au temple de Jérusalem', in *Studies in Jewish and Christian History*, II, pp. 86-104.

hides into the city. The offender was to be punished with a very large fine, to be paid to the priests. The text itself was neither signed nor dated, but its wording is Seleucid: in fact, it could neither be from the Hasmonaean period, during which the local authorities were free from Seleucid domination, nor from the Roman period, during which the corresponding crimes were punishable by death, as we can read from the inscription guarding the access to Herod's temple.[32]

Some observations can be made on the supervision by the central authority and correlatively on the fact that the notice is obviously intended for a mixed population. The religious policy for the city (and the sanctuary) did not emanate from local authorities, whereas the charter introduced or restored the traditional institutions of government. As for the mixed population, it must be kept in mind that Jerusalem could not be compared to Alexandria or Antioch: it was neither a port nor an important commercial or cultural centre. According to the *Letter of Aristeas* (§107), it was a city of moderate size surrounded by farmland. There would therefore be no reason to expect to find there a significant flow of foreigners in transit. The case of Zenon, still in the Lagide period, is characteristic: he had passed through Jerusalem and Jericho on minor business.[33] The 'foreigners' were, to a great extent, local population, which means that the Jews were not the only ones in the area: they formed a minority in the midst of the others. Strabo indicated that four *ethne* are mingled with the Syrians, the Coele-Syrians, and the Phoenicians, namely, Jews, Idumaeans, Gazaeans and Ashdodites.[34] In this respect, we see that the notice gave an absolute primacy to the ritual preferences of a particular *ethnos*, but offers foreigners the possibility of being incorporated into it.[35] In such a context, the provisions of the

32.   For bibliography and analysis, cf. E.J. Bickerman, 'The Warning Inscription of Herod's Temple', in *Studies in Jewish and Christian History*, II, pp. 210-24.

33.   Cf. C.C. Edgar, *Zenon Papyri* (Paris: Institut Français d'Archéologie Orientale, 1925–31), 1.59004; according to Hecateus, there were more neighbours (residents) than visitors (quoted in *Apion* 1.191).

34.   Literally 'Azotians' ('Αζωτίους); cf. Strabo, *Geography* C 749.

35.   The prohibition of access was meant for non-natives as well as for Jews 'except for those of them who had purified themselves [οἷς ἂν ἁγνισθεῖσιν]'; the possibility indicated by ἂν shows that the prohibition can be lifted for anyone. The foreign resident in the Bible—גר, translated by the LXX as προσήλυτος—and could become a fully fledged citizen (cf. Ruth). In the Greek world, on the contrary, an identical cult supported distinct ethnic groups, at least as far as citizenship was concerned; cf. W.S. Ferguson, 'The Attic *Orgeones*', *HTR* 37 (1944), p. 98.

charter, favouring in addition the return of exiles, had a clear meaning: the king desired, in a somewhat authoritarian way, to judaize or reju-daize Jerusalem, by assimilation as well as by repatriation.[36]

As for the prohibitions themselves, they were based on the 'ancestral law', which is the same well-worn formula.[37] Their details, however, do not agree with what the Bible says. According to Exod. 30.20, it was participation in sacrifice, and not access to the Temple that necessitated ritual purity. In the same way, Solomon in his prayer (1 Kgs 8.41-43, 2 Chron. 6.32) referred to the foreigner from a distant land who would come to pray in the Temple. The biblical prohibitions in regard to animals only concerned their carcass and their meat, whereas here the prohibition was extended to these same animals when alive, among which we note beasts of burden (donkey, horse, mule[38]) and wild animals (wild ass, panther, fox, hare). These small deviations in comparison with what is written, and the fact that the latter is ignored by the Seleucid documents could suggest that oral tradition, as jurisprudence derived from the decisions of the Ancients, was already very old.[39]

Although this may have been so, the most striking thing about the prohibitions was their extreme difference from the 'model of Nehemiah'.

36.   As John Hyrcanus did to the Idumaeans; on that occasion, as Josephus concluded (*Ant.* 13.258): 'they submitted to circumcision and to making their way of life conform to that of the Jews. From that time they have continued to be Jews [ὥστε εἶαι τὸ λοιπὸν Ἰουδαίους]'; cf. §318 (Ituraeans) and §397 (Pella). On the Rabbinic distinction between *ger toshab*, who remained pagan, and *ger ben berit*, actual converts, see G.F. Moore's synthesis on proselytism, *Judaism in the First Centuries of the Christian Era: The Age of Tannaim* (New York: Jewish Institute of Religion, 1970), I, pp. 327-29, and Schürer, *History*, III.1.170; more recently, M. Goodman, 'Proselytism in Rabbinic Judaism', *JJS* 40 (1982), pp. 174-85, introduced the political factor more clearly.

37.   Cf. Bickerman, *Institutions*, p. 135; subsequently, the Romans too confirmed 'ancestral laws'; the famous proclamation of Flamininus on liberty for Greece, in 196 BCE, re-established the Corinthians, Phocidians, and others in their 'ancestral laws' (Polybius, *History* 18.46).

38.   The absence of the camel (prohibited by the Bible) is worthy of note, since the Seleucid troops used them. The visions of the second part of Zechariah speak of a plague among the horses, mules, camels and donkeys of the enemies of Jerusalem (14.15), but also of the entry of the donkey of the Messiah (9.9) and the future consecration of horses (14.20).

39.   W. Bacher, *Die Agada der Tannaiten* (2 vols.; Strasbourg: Trübner, 1890), I, p. 76 n. 5; I.H. Weiss, *Dor dor udorshav* (2 vols.; Berlin: Platt & Minkus, 1871), I, p. 1.

The latter was concerned first and foremost with the observance of the Sabbath, on which all commerce became impossible, and with the purity of the *ethnos*, so that anything about union with foreigners was not even to be mentioned; at the same time its interest in the Temple, ritual purity and the priests was secondary, although not absent. We could hold that the Seleucid notice only helped to supplement the well-known requirements of the Law for the Jews; but this is still difficult to admit, since its prescriptions had obvious commercial effects, while there was no allusion to public holidays, particularly in regard to activities within the city, if we admit that the gates were at that time actually closed (cf. Neh. 13.19). In short, the Seleucid acts do not match Nehemiah's project,[40] which was, as we have seen, the foundation of the Jewish community itself (cf. Chapter 2). In theory a balance was possible, with certain precautions, but clashes must have been inevitable.

Antiochus III was not a philanthropist, but a prudent politician. He granted enormous fiscal advantages to the Temple and the people in his charter, but it was in return for a voluntary reorganization of the nation around its cult, with a strong point at Jerusalem. Josephus, always sensitive about the Temple, saw only benevolence in it, but Polybius, whom he quoted (*Ant.* 12.136-37) was more caustic when he described Antiochus's campaign: '...and shortly after there came over to him [προσεχώρησαν αὐτῷ] those Jews living around the sanctuary of Jerusalem, as it is called.' The Jews submitted to the power of the king, but all the subjects of the king were not in Judaea.

What goal was Antiochus pursuing? It was certainly necessary to consolidate the frontier with Egypt, in particular by securing for himself the loyalty of the local populations. Palestine had been Egyptian shortly before, and the Seleucid governor, Ptolemy, had been at that earlier time a high Egyptian official, who then changed sides. However, coastal cities like Ashdod and Gaza had a strategic importance far beyond that of Jerusalem: it was they who were on Alexander's route to Egypt, and they had not become in any way vassals of Jerusalem, since as ethnic

---

40. In this way, the controversy between Bickerman, 'Une proclamation', pp. 89-91, who states that the royal commands affected whoever was in Jerusalem, and I. Heinemann, *MGWJ* 82 (1939), p. 156, who thinks that it was intended for pagans only, becomes pointless. The king imposed on everyone respect for the ritual of the Temple, with the other precepts and their degree of obligation being within the competence of the Jewish *gerousia*.

groups they had remained very much distinct. The king's intentions must therefore be sought elsewhere.

Josephus quotes a document, close to the same period, although not dated, which provides some clarification. Troubles had broken out in Asia Minor (Lydia, Phrygia), and so Antiochus wrote to one of his loyal generals, Zeuxis, general governor of the Anatolian satrapies, asking him to install in those regions two thousand Jewish families from Babylon. Zeuxis was to furnish them with suitable conditions for rural settlement, allow them to follow their ancestral laws and exempt them from paying taxes for ten years. It was certainly a delicate matter, he admitted, but he maintained that they would be loyal guardians of Seleucid interests because of their piety towards their God (διὰ τὴν πρὸς τὸν θεὸν αὐτῶν[41] εὐσέβειαν). The letter is authentic,[42] and presupposes two facts significant for this study: on the one hand, the connection between fidelity to the king and piety is properly understood only in the setting of the charter, which placed the Jews in an obligatory situation; on the other hand the migration of two thousand colonists from Babylon with their families under advantageous conditions presupposes voluntary participation and not deportation, which implies that these migrants, although an appreciable number, really constituted a small part of the Jews of Babylon.

We know that unlike the Lagides, heirs of the Macedonian system of soldier-colonists, the Seleucids, in order to stabilize a region in which pacification was unstable, practised a civilian colonization, on plots of land that were to some extent confiscated.[43] An especially important question to settle, about which the documents are silent, is what was the protective system for these colonists, and in particular whether they

---

41.   Some manuscripts omit αὐτῶν, from which we get 'their piety toward God', with the meaning being that the Seleucides were pleased with monotheism, but they actually did not profess monolatry and honoured all the local cults; in particular, Antiochus III sacrificed to Athena and Apollos in Greece, while Chaldean astrology flourished in Babylon; cf. Bickerman, *Institutions*, pp. 250-51. The document itself must then have included the possessive, but Josephus, who sometimes made revisions, could have introduced such a monotheistic note, under the influence of Persian documents from Ezra–Nehemiah (temple of God, God of heaven).

42.   As is shown again by E.J. Bickerman, 'Une question d'authenticité: Les privilèges juifs', in *Studies in Jewish and Christian History*, II, p. 40; cf. the discussion of R. Marcus, *Josephus* (LCL, 7; London, 1943), pp. 764-66.

43.   Cf. Bickerman, *Institutions*, pp. 82-83. On the Jewish Babylonian colony established in Batanea (Bathyra) by Herod on a similar model, cf. Chapter 7, §4.

were subject to military service in the royal army. In the same region of Asia Minor, some available facts help in forming a hypothesis: we know of at least twelve rural communes of Macedonian colonists, set up by the Seleucids, whose population was distinct from Macedonians of the regular army. Moreover, a decree from Smyrna around 244 granted citizenship to a neighbouring population of colonists: these were civilians, living in villages defended by walls, and protected by detachments of soldiers. The absence of any military allusion in the texts relative to the Jews, whether a garrison at Jerusalem or a defence system in the colonies, warrants the presumption that they were exempt from all constraints of that kind, direct or indirect. We can even go further and conjecture with great probability that this was precisely the motivation for the king being interested in them. Since their religious devotion towards God was expressed especially through strict observance of the Sabbath, which implied the absolute impossibility of enlisting in a regular army for an attack, either friendly or hostile, this same religious devotion could only be a guarantee of political fidelity to the central authority.

The royal policy relative to this Jewish *ethnos* was in this way rational, and the effort to restore the coherence and strength of Jerusalem shows, by contrast, a hybrid situation in Judaism at that time: on the one hand a diaspora, strong on 'ancestral tradition', and on the other the sorry state of the Temple and Judaea.[44] Jerusalem was obviously not at that time a *polis*, but the reorganization of the *ethnos* around an urban sanctuary was certainly a first step towards granting a political autonomy that was advantageous for the king, one of its local elements being to promote citizenship, which could be interpreted, from a completely different point of view, in terms of proselytism. In the first phase of the process, under Antiochus III, one cannot speak specifically of autonomy,[45] as if it were the natural response to the unanimous desire of the population, but of a delegation of jurisdiction that was carefully limited and hedged in, with

44.   These observations contrast with those of Bickerman, *The God of the Maccabees*, pp. 34-36: since he does not make the comparison with the letter to Zeuxis, he assumes the charter to be of purely local interest; what is more, he infers from the military obligations of Jonathan and John Hyrcanus to the Seleucids (1 Macc. 10.36) that it was the same under Antiochus III, whereas there is nothing to indicate this.

45.   As would be claimed, along with others, by Tcherikover, *Hellenistic Civilisation and the Jews*, p. 84 (see n. 122); but it is then difficult to understand why the high priest would be named by the king, which is right at the root of the Maccabaean crisis.

all the guise of a benefit due to royal munificence.

We already begin to see how all the elements thus put in place were able to develop up to the eruption of the Maccabaean crisis. In fact, somewhere there had been a misunderstanding, since the Judaeans (Temple) and the Jews (of the diaspora) could not become one and the same. The subsequent secession of Onias, who left to found his temple in Egypt, indicated clearly that the Seleucid cultic reorganization was somewhat forced; this is also shown by the numerous presents of Ptolemy II to the Temple, as recounted in the *Letter of Aristeas* (§51-82) and 'in accordance with Scripture'. Relations with Egypt were not at all brought to an end.[46]

Still more importantly, while the problem of the 'return from exile' of the Jews, encouraged by the Great King, would appear in literary terms to be artificial in the setting of the restoration of the Temple in the Persian period (Ezra–Nehemiah), it becomes perfectly intelligible in the setting of the policy of the Seleucids,[47] and especially that of Antiochus III, another Great King (ὁ μέγας), since his influence extended from Egypt to the Bosphorus, and his cultural relations were with the West. These questions will be taken up later (Chapter 8, §3), but it is now necessary to go back over the immediate context of the Maccabaean crisis.

3. *Hellenization*

With Roman pressure increasing in the East, Antiochus III could not maintain his hold on Asia Minor, and was finally defeated by the army of Scipio Africanus at Magnesia in 189. According to the treaty of Apamea, which followed in 188, Antiochus among other things had to hand over to Rome hostages, among whom was his son, the future Antiochus IV, to ensure the maintenance of the Roman army in Asia Minor and also to pay an indemnity of 15,000 talents. Of that sum,

---

46. Polybius, *History* 5.86.10 indicates that the people mostly remained on the side of the Lagides, but this opinion could have been affected by a pro-Egyptian bias.

47. The hypothesis of Hengel, *Judaism and Hellenism*, p. 10 (following others; cf. his n. 34), according to which Antiochus would have acted like his Persian predecessors, or even like Alexander before him (cf. Tcherikover, *Hellenistic Civilisation*, pp. 49, 422), is not supported by any text, except perhaps by Ezra–Nehemiah, about which I have shown that there are some problems. More useful is the opposite hypothesis, namely, to suppose that the obvious institutional relationships between Persians and Seleucids permitted the projection back in time of episodes from the Hellenistic period; cf. below, Chapter 8.

3,000 had already been paid at the time of the ratification of Apamea. There remained therefore 12 instalments of 1,000 talents, and the principal part of the war debt had to be paid off by 176. Antiochus III was assassinated, however, as early as 187 in Elam, while attempting to plunder a sanctuary of Bel, which he had the right to do as long as private effects were not included.[48]

His son Seleucus IV was overburdened by the debts owed to Rome stemming from the defeat of his father and, at his death in 175, he still owed the equivalent of two instalments. What is astonishing, then, is the statement of 2 Macc. 3.3 that Seleucus financed from his own revenues (ἐκ τῶν ἰδίων προσόδων) the expenses connected with sacrifices. It could refer to a private budget of the king, if he in fact possessed private funds, separate from public finances and intended for his court. According to 1 Macc. 10.40, Demetrius I offered the Jerualem temple an annual allowance, 'chargeable out of the king's revenues [λόγων τοῦ βασιλέως] from appropriate places'. Nevertheless, this royal revenue was just a withdrawal from the revenues of the crown, whose property and resources formed a unique whole, managed by the administration of the kingdom. Under these conditions, to interpret the subsidy for the cult as coming from this private budget would suppose that in doing this there was some private interest, separate from the public good; this is not at all demonstrated in the case of Seleucus IV. What is more, the contributions provided for in the charter of Antiochus III came from the government, through the local authorities, and not from the king's private estate, since the piety that he invoked towards the Temple was strictly official, taking into account the personal character of the monarchy. Finally, the literary context is rather schematic (2 Macc. 3.2): 'It came about [συνέβαινε] that the kings themselves honoured the holy place and enhanced the glory of the Temple with magnificent presents.' These royal honours, which look perhaps extraordinary,[49] are allusions to important acts, under which can be grouped together the provisions of the charter of Antiochus III, and perhaps some Lagide favours as well, of which the *Letter of Aristeas* would be an echo. Moreover, the bestowal of this munificence is presented as a result of the piety of Onias, whose virtue would have been contagious: so it is a reinterpretation derived from the views on Providence of 2 Maccabees. The unfolding of this state of grace up to the time of Seleucus is therefore

48.   Cf. Bickerman, *Institutions*, p. 121.
49.   Cf. Goldstein, *II Maccabees*, p. 200.

something merely fictional, presenting an ideal economic and religious landscape in order to make the misdeeds to be recounted next stand out better.

This conclusion is confirmed by a contradiction in the account that follows (2 Macc. 4): it is not logical that Seleucus would on the one hand trust in the piety of Onias and then, on the strength of a denunciation by Simon, an official of modest social rank, believe the latter without any additional investigation and send Heliodorus to confiscate the wealth of the Temple. Relations between Seleucus and Onias were not then uncomplicated.

Nevertheless, it must be maintained that Seleucus, as suzerain authority, remained responsible for the proper functioning of the Temple, and that it was not at all in his interest to confiscate the part of its treasury which ensured its upkeep, for fear of alienating an *ethnos* that certainly included taxpayers in various parts of his kingdom: that is why Simon reported a surplus of deposits, which could eventually be confiscated, and not that ordinary part, which could not serve as a financial resource, and which therefore had to remain. Seleucus had need of money, and the rumour of an important deposit belonging to Hyrcanus the Tobiad, a general tax-farmer in Judaea for the Lagide account, was more than likely true, since this Hyrcanus, according to Josephus, was a second cousin of Onias (*Ant.* 12.160). He lived in Ammanitis (*Araq el-Emir*), on the border of the jurisdiction, if not of the territory that was specifically Seleucid, and was, according to Josephus, in bitter conflict with his brothers.

The problem of a connection with the Lagides, completely ignored by 2 Maccabees, calls for a brief examination here. In regard to this dynasty of the Tobiads, Josephus presents, in the setting of the reign of Antiochus III, a long fictionalized history (12.154-222), which presents a number of difficulties: 1. Antiochus III would have given Coele-Syria, Samaria, Judaea, Phoenicia to Ptolemy V Epiphanes, as a dowry for his daughter Cleopatra. The marriage had actually taken place in 194–93,[50] and it was afterwards that Joseph the Tobiad, 'governor' (προστάτης) of the Jews, would have obtained at Alexandria the farming of taxes of Coele-Syria for 22 years, as a result of the persistent refusal of the high priest Onias to pay taxes to Egypt. There is however nothing to suggest that Seleucus IV would not have still been reigning over the provinces, preserving the conquests of his father: the 'Sixth Syrian War' (170–168), referred to above, was launched from Egypt against his successor Antiochus IV in an attempt to recapture these provinces. 2. In the continuation of the narrative (§158), Josephus seems abruptly to set the fiscal problems of Coele-Syria under Ptolemy III Euergetes (246–222), but it was in the time of a high priest Onias, identified as a son of Simon the Just, about whom more below. Now Josephus had presented the latter as a brother of Eleazar, the high priest of the *Letter of Aristeas*, therefore a contemporary of Ptolemy II.[51] With Onias, a generation later,

50. Cf. Schürer, *History*, I, p. 140 n. 4.
51. This Eleazar is an intrusion in the high-priestly genealogy, but his position

it would therefore naturally be under Ptolemy III.

The account has ties both with Ptolemy V, with resulting historical difficulties, and with Ptolemy III (before the time of Antiochus III), in a more legendary setting. The simplest solution would be to say therefore that the episode of Joseph the Tobiad and his sons, which is a sort of tale, would really have taken place earlier,[52] under Ptolemy III, and that it was Josephus who put it under Ptolemy V. Nevertheless, the account, after extensively dealing with the feats of Joseph, then of his son Hyrcanus, abruptly ends: after having brilliantly returned from Egypt while foiling the plots of his brothers, Hyrcanus was suddenly afraid to enter Jerusalem and withdrew to Perea. This abrupt ending in reality occurs because of the necessity of combining the legend with a report that Josephus provided a little later on (§§228-36), in which Hyrcanus, during the high priesthood of Onias, brother of Jason, appeared less strong, and had excellent reasons for withdrawing, on account of an inevitable family quarrel. In other words, it must be concluded that the legend, placed by the storyteller (Josephus's source) at a time in the past that cannot be verified, then embellished and connected to the reign of Ptolemy III, was clearly based on real persons, Joseph and Hyrcanus. Josephus had a reason therefore for putting it where he did, but, as is so often the case with him, at the cost of revisions that are at the same time clumsy and inadequate, at the two extremities of the narrative.

The outcome of this examination is that, in literary terms, the matter of the dowry for Cleopatra is irrelevant to the legend, but is useful as a starting point. It is attached to the legend in an artificial manner, since there is no proportion between the 20 talents that Onias refused to remit and the enormous sum of 16,000 talents that Joseph paid to the king of Egypt and to his wife for the concession of tax-farming for the whole of Coele-Syria.

A legend, then, but one of significance: there was a rumour around about good relations between ruling circles of Jerusalem and of Alexandria, from the time of Antiochus III to the time of Antiochus IV, in a period when Coele-Syria was officially Seleucid. Such was furthermore the framework of the initial crisis according to the brief account in the *The Jewish War*, in which Onias, an ally of Ptolemy, began by expelling the 'sons of Tobiah', who took refuge close to Antiochus and persuaded him to invade Judaea. These Tobiads did not include Hyrcanus, who according to *Ant.* 12.236 committed suicide at the death of Ptolemy V Epiphanes, in 180. In the legend, the withdrawal of Hyrcanus to Ammanitis is a vestige of conflicts within ruling circles, in which there is no indication of any pro-Seleucid faction: kinship with the high priest certainly did not prevent clashes of interests. The situation thus made clear was very similar to that against which Nehemiah had struggled, when he expelled a Tobiah who had been in collusion in the Temple with a priest Eliashib (Neh. 13.4-9). This event will be commented on below. For the moment, it is a matter of confronting the above-mentioned rumour with Seleucid history, and in

---

shows how Josephus understood these accounts; cf. Reinach, *Œvres complètes*, on *Ant.* 12.157 (p. 82).

　　52.　　Cf. in agreement with others, Hengel, *Judaism and Hellenism*, pp. 56, 267-69; who places the legend at Alexandria between 150 and 100 BCE.

particular with the matter of the dowry of Cleopatra.

From 206 to 186, Upper Egypt had seceded[53] and in Lower Egypt the political situation had remained confused since the first victories over Antiochus III (Raphia, in 218). Ptolemy IV Philopator died before the age of 35, in 204, unpopular and decadent. In 197, Ptolemy V Epiphanes, who was not yet 14, was proclaimed of age and solemnly crowned, an indication of a certain stabilization of the court after years of intrigues. In 196, Antiochus III most likely tried to annex Egypt, all the more so since the news reached him of the death of the young Ptolemy. He was dissuaded from doing so, since the report was false, but especially because the Romans had just proclaimed at the Isthmian Games the freedom of the Greeks of Europe and of Asia: this was a warning to Antiochus, at first somewhat general, but expressly confirmed in 195 by a formal mission of a specially dispatched legate. It was in this context that Antiochus made peace with Egypt, then gave his daughter Cleopatra to Ptolemy: Lagide interests in this way became his own, but without annexation.

As for the famous dowry, it is suspect since there is no proof that Coele-Syria had ever been detached from Syria after the battle of Panias, in 200: Seleucus IV and then Antiochus IV never lost control of it at any time. This at least apparent political stability, however, did not rule out the possibility that the dowry might have consisted, at first, of specific revenues coming from this region. A first indication of this is provided by the deposits of Hyrcanus in the Temple (2 Macc. 3.11), coveted by Seleucus. A second indication is provided by the war of Antiochus IV with Egypt, in 170. The young Ptolemy was not of age, and the causes of that war are vague: it would definitely seem to have been a question of a claim to Coele-Syria,[54] perhaps to consolidate a de facto situation. In any case, Antiochus was not at all taken by surprise, and everything took place as if he was carrying out a programme for the reconquest of the whole region, both by force and by diplomacy.[55] At the time of the armistice with the opposing plenipotentiaries, near Alexandria, he challenged the thesis that Cleopatra had received Coele-Syria as a dowry (φερνῇ), and Polybius curiously adds that Antiochus 'convinced not only himself, but also his hearers' (28.20.10). It seems then that there really had been some such arrangement on the dowry,[56] even if it remained ineffective, at least politically, right up to the death of Cleopatra. Josephus's information is therefore not imaginary, and the tribute of 20

53. Cf. C. Préaux, 'Esquisse d'une histoire des révolutions égyptiennes sous les Lagides', *Chroniques d'Egypte* 11 (1936), pp. 531-36.

54. According to Diodorus 29.29, Ptolemy V had devised this plan, but he had been killed in 180, and there is no mention of a similar plan by Cleopatra, a sister of Antiochus IV and regent until her death, in 176.

55. Cf. O. Mørkholm, *Antiochus IV of Syria* (Classica et Mediaevalia, Diss. VIII; Copenhagen: Gyldendal, 1966), pp. 68-70.

56. Mentioned as well by Appian, *The Syrian Wars*, §5, who passes himself off as independent of Polybius; cf. E. Gabba, 'Sul libro siriaco di Appiano', *Atti dell' Accademia nazionale dei Lincei* 9 (1957), pp. 339-51.

talents, which the high priest Onias had to pay, seems like a plausible amount.[57]

This detour gives some perspective on the events reported by 2 Maccabees. Onias would have practised a policy which maintained an unstable equilibrium between Syria and Egypt, a remote consequence of the relative independence granted by the charter of Antiochus III. As for the failure of the mission of Heliodorus, sent by Seleucus to Jerusalem to confiscate the funds from the treasury, it is described in a marvellous way, but the important detail is the kindly reception by the high priest, followed by a friendly separation; parallel to this are the adverse rumours accusing Onias of having had Heliodorus attacked. In giving his account to Seleucus, Heliodorus himself declared (2 Macc. 3.38): 'If you have any enemy or any plotter against the government, send him there, and he will return to you well flogged, if he survives at all [...].' These words were prophetic, since Heliodorus was precisely the one who was going to assassinate the king in 175. A little before that, Antiochus, after 12 or 13 years of living as a hostage in Rome, was exchanged for Demetrius,[58] the still young eldest son of the reigning Seleucus IV. King Eumenes II of Pergamum then decided to recognize Antiochus and took the initiative in aiding him to obtain the throne of Syria by providing him an army. War was avoided, and Antiochus took power while making his nephew a joint ruler, which enabled him to push aside Heliodorus. An added significant detail should be noted: according to a decree discovered at Pergamum, the Athenians shortly after voted to honour Eumenes for having helped the Syrian Prince, declared a friend of the Athenian people.[59] In fact, the new king had been impressed by the Romans and was sincerely philhellenic. His later policies made him clash with Rome, to whom he still owed a part of his father's debt, but he always tried to regain prestige in the opinion of the Greek world, especially through numerous undertakings, often costly, in favour of Greek cities, particularly with public edifices. With the disappearance of Heliodorus, Onias of Jerusalem had certainly lost an ally.

The silence of 2 Maccabees about any connection between Judaea and the Lagides had as its goal to show the autonomy of the high priesthood of Jerusalem: Onias was not a client of Seleucus IV, and therefore had not been named by him. We thus rediscover the indication, from another angle, that Judaea was perhaps only nominally Seleucid. Furthermore, the legend of the Tobiads is very interesting because of the form of Judaism that it implicitly demonstrates: a perspective that is completely secular, with nationalist leanings, and one in which all means are good.

57.   Cf. E. Cuq, 'La condition juridique de la Coelé-Syrie au temps de Ptolémée V Epiphane', *Syria* 8 (1927), pp. 143-62.

58.   Apparently at the request of the Romans, since he was in no hurry to return to Antioch; cf. Mørkholm, *Antiochus IV*, p. 36.

59.   M. Holleaux, *Etudes d'épigraphie et d'histoire grecque* (6 vols.; Paris: A. Maisonneuve, 1938–57), II, pp. 127-47. This text indicates that there were statues of 'King Antiochus' on the Agora.

At his death, Joseph was venerated as 'an honest man, of good character, who had brought the Jewish people from poverty and a precarious situation and elevated them to a more brilliant destiny' (*Ant.* 12.224). References to the law are minimal—namely, the prohibition of marrying a foreigner, allusion to a custom of sacrifices connected with a birth. These are really very banal customs, and nothing is said about purity, diet or the Sabbath. We cannot speak however of a real or at least a complete Hellenization, since the reference to the Jewish *ethnos*, of which the Temple was the pivot, remained extremely strong. The cohesion was national and aristocratic, before being religious, which the Zenon papyrus had already shown, around 250. Tobias, ruler of Ammanitis, had no fear of making allusions to the gods[60] on commercial documents. The ease with which Joseph and Hyrcanus took on the role of courtier was in no way seen as decadent; neither should it be confused with the adoption of new institutions. The 'model of Nehemiah' was a long way off, and we must conclude, to return to the terminology defined above, that the high priests and the Tobiads are Judaeans,[61] and not Jews.

Where then at that moment were the Jews properly so called, those 'of Nehemiah' or the future martyrs of 2 Maccabees? The Maccabaean crisis would later on reveal their presence at Jerusalem and various places in Judaea and the neighbouring regions. The charter of Antiochus III, as we have seen, aimed at situating them as a well-defined *ethnos*, centred on the temple at Jerusalem. Nevertheless, they were hardly seen before the crisis, while fiscal problems had become paramount. In fact, the charter had foreseen, after a period of exemptions and aid, certain taxes being paid directly. There was no mention of a set tax, payable to the high priest or through a contract. Later, after the Maccabaean crisis, around 140, the high priest Jonathan requested the tax-farming concession from Demetrius II (1 Macc. 11.28), for a fixed sum of 300 talents (annually), and apparently obtained it. The question then is to know whether anything can be interpolated between this piece of evidence and the charter of Antiochus III.

60. Cf. the references in Hengel, *Judaism and Hellenism*, pp. 267-69.
61. J.A. Goldstein, 'The Tales of the Tobiads', in J. Neusner (ed.), *Christianity, Judaism and Other Greco-Roman Cults* (SJLA, 12/3; Leiden: Brill, 1975), pp. 85-123, reaches by different routes an analogous distinction into two groups, but he concludes that Josephus's source was Onias IV, who, in establishing the temple of Leontopolis, did away with the primacy of Jerusalem.

Since Bickerman's research,[62] it is generally believed that under the Seleucid regime, there had been a fixed annual tribute, which he estimated at around 300 talents under Antiochus IV, based on the request of Jonathan and the overbidding that preceded the crisis. This inference undervalues several facts, however, and through them the causes of the crisis: 1. First of all, there was no allusion to such a tribute in the charter, and especially there was no indication that the high priest (Onias) was to be named by the Seleucid government. 2. The conflict of Onias and Simon the administrator of the Temple, which involved fiscal matters, presupposed a direct control of taxation, in which the high priest was not in charge, rather than a fixed concession. Later, in fact, under Menelaus, there was a concession, of such a kind that the administrator could no longer circumvent the high priest, and had to present his dispute to the king *with him* (2 Macc. 4.27-29). 3. The Hyrcanus legend presupposed that the general farming of taxes was a new institution. 4. Jason's usurpation, with the accession of Antiochus IV, was nothing more than the acquisition of the farming of taxes, with the associated coercive powers: he had become general administrator, named by the Seleucid king. It was a priestly function, but he is only called 'high priest' in 2 Macc. 4.7 by analogy with the later Hasmonaeans, vassal kings-high priests. In the legend about the Tobiads, the title of 'governor [προστάτης] of the Jews' given to Joseph was characteristic, even if it was used too early in that case, since it was the same as that given to the administrator Simon.

Jason's motive was therefore, to a great extent, greed. If he at first offered a tribute of 360 talents, with a supplement of 80, it was because he expected to collect much more. That Antiochus would accept such an arrangement—which certainly offered a political advantage, keeping in mind Egyptian covetousness and the role of Onias— that fact alone was a major change in the status of Jerusalem and Judaea. According to 2 Macc. 4.7, Jason's nomination presupposed the deposing of Onias, while according to *Ant.* 12.237, Jason succeeded him. The account in 2 Maccabees is probably preferable: on the one hand, Josephus depended on a high priestly chronicle, a simple list giving the order of succession of the high priests, without biographical details,[63] and on the other hand, the ruin of Onias, a refugee in the pagan temple of Daphne, thus after the nomination of Jason, was embarrassing information for the compiler of 2 Maccabees and so he embellished the circumstances. In any case, there is no trace of any consultation of the *gerousia*; we do not know how the people accepted these things and it would be surprising if there was unanimity.

62.   Bickerman, *Institutions*, p. 107.
63.   Goldstein, *II Maccabees*, p. 223.

The subsequent stage, in which Jason purchased for 150 talents the right to establish a youth group and a gymnasium at Jerusalem was just a supplementary step in the same direction, which evidently fitted in with the philhellenic views of Antiochus IV: it was a matter of essential institutions for Greek cities[64] (education, physical and intellectual training), allowing in this way for a national and cosmopolitan openness, consequently as well for an increase in tax revenues and commerce which would certainly be greater than the proposed increase in tribute. The establishment of a list of Antiochenes in Jerusalem, also promised by Jason, was proof of this. The people frequenting the gymnasium were constituted into a juridical entity, *demos* (citizenry) or *politeuma* (bodies of citizens), within the *ethnos* and not alongside it, and a delegation afterwards went to the quadrennial games at Tyre, 'in the presence of the king'. The granting of such a status was not rare under the Seleucids, and especially under Antiochus IV, who granted it to 18 cities.[65] It did not yet amount, strictly speaking, to the complete establishment of Jerusalem as a Greek *polis*, even if there was a party of Antiochenes. The letters of Antiochus IV addressed later to the *gerousia* and to the *demos* of the Jews, and not to the 'Antiochenes' of Jerusalem, prove that the city was not renamed Antioch.[66] It was more an attempt to create in Jerusalem the conditions for a future formation of a *polis*, destined to assimilate little by little the various elements of the population, from which there would progressively be built up a list of Antiochenes, new citizens. This organizational model, which reappropriates the Temple, was parallel to the one set up by Antiochus III, but with a different orientation, and with the high priests its principal actors.

During all the fiscal manoeuvrering before the crisis, we find no reaction from the Jewish *gerousia*. This passivity suggests that the horrified comments of 2 Macc. 4.14-17, depicting the complete abandonment of the Temple, are not to be taken at face value: just as Onias was less unsullied than we are told, in the same way Hellenization, at this stage, was only a limited phenomenon. The nomination of Menelaus, who supplanted Jason and obtained from Antiochus IV the office of high priest, by offering an increase in the tribute of 300 talents (for a total of 890 talents), seems more significant. On this occasion, the fiscal pressure increased, and the delicate balance stemming from the charter of Antiochus was certainly disrupted, since its main component was the reestablishment of the Temple, whereas the statutory novelties were only concerned with the functioning of this Temple and the organizing of

64. Situated in Jerusalem near the Temple, as in other cities; cf. J. Delorme, *Gymnasium* (Bibliothèque de l'Ecole Française d'Athènes, 196; Paris: de Boccard, 1960), pp. 441-44.
65. Among them, Babylon; cf. Hengel, *Judaism and Hellenism*, p. 277.
66. Bickerman, *The God of the Maccabees*, pp. 38-42, 112 (*addenda*).

taxes. Seen from the side of the high priests, there was a struggle then between the pro-Seleucid faction, which seemed to dominate with these high priests, and the pro-Lagide faction, with Onias, in regard to which we do not clearly see how it could have fitted into a Seleucid charter. Jerusalem was indeed divided, but had it really become more so?

4. *Divisions in Jerusalem and Judaea*

We certainly have to support the thesis brilliantly defended by Bickerman, that the actual persecution of Antiochus Epiphanes was not the wanton fantasy of a mad king, but the result of the express request of the high priest–governor Menelaus, transformed into a royal decree. This process was explicit at the end of the persecution, during which the same high priest had always been in charge, when Antiochus wrote to the Jews: 'Menelaus has informed us that you wish to return home [...]' (2 Macc. 11.29). It was already implicit at the beginning: 'A generation of renegades came out of Israel and led many people astray, saying: "Let us go and make a covenant with the nations that surround us, for since we separated ourselves from them many disasters have come upon us".' (1 Macc. 1.11). The result of this was a decree by Antiochus IV, to which his son later expressly made an allusion: 'Having learned that the Jews do not approve of the adoption of Greek customs as desired by our father [...]' (2 Macc. 11.24). Nevertheless, the enactment of a new status for Jerusalem as a *polis* cannot be confused with the decreeing of a persecution.

In 168, during his second campaign in Egypt, Antiochus IV had won on the ground, but lost politically because of the Romans. According to 2 Macc. 5.5 the ousted high priest Jason, on the basis of a false rumour of the death of the king in Egypt, attempted to regain power and managed to lay siege to Menelaus in the citadel. Inevitably this attempt had appeared to be pro-Lagide, and was put down by the Seleucid troops,[67] with Jason ending up taking refuge in Egypt.

There is also an account of a Seleucid army taking the city through the use of deception and demolishing it in that same year, 168. According to 1 Macc. 1.29-37, the episode took place two years after the plundering of the Temple by Antiochus, on his return from Egypt, and

---

67. But not by Antiochus himself, as claimed by 2 Macc. 5.11-20: he had come and plundered the Temple after the first campaign in Egypt; cf. Bickerman, *The God of the Maccabees*, pp. 110-11.

no motive or pretext for it is provided. Having crushed Jerusalem, these troops rebuilt the City of David, fortified it, 'and it became for them a citadel' (εἰς ἄκραν), which sheltered as well 'a race of sinners'. These pieces of information imply that this City of David was rebuilt *beside* the razed Jerusalem, which raises some literary and topographical difficulties.[68] According to 2 Macc. 5.24-26, the episode took place on the heels of the pillaging by Antiochus (but we have seen that this happened earlier). The Syrian officer is named[69] and the deception is described more clearly, but the account does not conclude with the reconstruction of the City of David: this is omitted altogether and replaced with the report about Judas Maccabeus then taking to the hills. The massacre therefore had neither cause nor purpose, since it did not even end in a colonization. What is more, the citadel, in which Menelaus took refuge at the time of the Jason's attack, was clearly distinguished from the walls of the city (5.5). It had existed before these accounts as a refuge of the Seleucid garrison. It is necessary then to challenge the account of 1 Maccabees, according to which Jerusalem had been destroyed and replaced by another city, the Akra, from which there came the profanation of the Temple with a new cult and finally persecutions. In this way, in fact, the reader is necessarily induced into thinking that it was a matter of a Greek cult imposed by Antiochus. Furthermore, 2 Macc. 6.3-7 in a disordered way provides some suggestive indications in this regard: prostitution which was more or less sacred, feasts of Dionysus, monthly meals in honour of the birth of the king, and so on.

68.   The topography suggests the northern part of the hill bordering the Tyropean on the west (towards the present Jaffa Gate), but the subsequent history of the Hasmonaean city (the developments by John Hyrcanus) and the name of the city of David suggest rather the hill on the east of the Tyropean, that is to say to the north of the Temple, around the Antonia tower built by the Romans; see Goldstein's discussion, *I Maccabees*, pp. 214-19.

69.   Appolonius the 'Mysarch', who appears also in 1 Macc. 3.10, whereas in the parallel passage, 1 Macc. 1.29, he is not named, and his title there is ἄρχων φορολογίας, which supposes שׂר המיסים, a form which could be confused with שׂר המוסים, 'Commander of the Mysians'; cf. Abel, *Maccabées*, p. 15. Antiochus III had had mercenaries from Mysia, a satrapy situated near Phrygia (cf. *Ant.* 1.125, and *Targ. P* on Gen. 10.2, on the territories of the sons of Japheth), but we cannot rule out a legate with fiscal and military skills, since the name Apollonius was also the name of the one who represented Antiochus IV in Egypt (4.21). He would be a high-ranking person of the court, whose three sons were hostages in Rome with the young Demetrius.

The 'abomination of desolation' installed on the altar of holocausts, however, is just a new altar and not a new idol. The local god, who was no longer revered in the Temple itself, since it had been plundered, was now turned into something similar to Oriental Betyl deities,[70] and it is even stated that they 'built altars in the surrounding towns of Judah', which amounted to repetitions of the same arrangement (1 Macc. 1.54). According to the view of 1 Maccabees, the persecution flowed from the introduction of this cult and from the consumption of its sacrificial food. The god linked to the place was the same and remained without any kind of representation, but the cult had changed: it had become a *foreign cult*, and such was the name of a treatise of the Mishnah (*'Aboda Zara*), which especially dealt with the consumption of food sacrificed to idols. Those Jews who had become followers of this movement were renegades. In other words, these events had led to loss of control over the cult, and the resolution of that crisis was brought about through the recapture of Jerusalem by Judas Maccabeus, followed by the restoration of the *altar* and further battles.

The presentation in 2 Maccabees is completely different and more complex, since there are some episodes which overlap: Jerusalem and its walls coexisted with the citadel in the time of Menelaus and even of Jason, since the gymnasium was built close at hand (4.12). The defection of the priests provoked no reaction, and the same was true of Jason's triumphal reception of Antiochus in Jerusalem. On the other hand, the destruction of the city by Apollonius did not seem to affect the Temple or its surroundings. Finally, the victory of Judas over the Seleucid army was marked by a festive return to Jerusalem (8.31-39), but not to the Temple, if we omit the intrusive passage on the purification. The result of this then was that there were two entirely distinct crises. On the one hand, the partial erection of the citadel as a *polis*, under the high priests Jason or Menelaus, with as a consequence the introduction of a new cult, the flight of the pro-Lagide faction, the dedication of the Temple, or at least of the altar, to Olympian Zeus, and so on. On the other hand, there was a persecution in the city, in fact in another quarter, which was later destroyed for some reason that is not specified. The trickery of Apollonius was connected to the Sabbath, and the subsequent destruction of the walls (or at least the dismantling of the gates; cf. 8.33) made it impossible to observe it appropriately.

An important outcome of this, therefore, was that there were two

---

70.   Cf. Bickerman, *The God of the Maccabees*, p. 71.

clearly distinct entities in Jerusalem: the citadel controlling the Temple, let us say to be brief the city of the Judaeans, and the Jewish city, surrounded as well by ramparts, and conforming to the 'model of Nehemiah'. This situation may be compared to the multiplicity of internal walls in the city, as described later by Josephus.

The charter of Antiochus III evidently applied to the city as a whole, not without some tensions as we have said, since there was little chance that the high priestly authority over the Temple would have satisfied the Jewish city in every respect. Under these conditions, the 'renegades' could be of two types, Jews or Judaeans. The power struggles of the Seleucids and Lagides for the most part concerned the latter, while the resistance of the Jews was mostly local, with regard to the Judaean governing authorites, whoever they might have been. The destruction of the Jewish city brought about by the Seleucids should be considered an internal conflict, namely, the reaction of Judaeans in a religious and/or fiscal revolt, definitely in relation to the new status of the citadel. The actual persecution was just a development from this, under the form of reprisals, ultimately affecting only a few people.

The clearer presentation in 1 Maccabees is ultimately misleading, all the more so since it requires the conclusion that the Hasmonaeans were the restorers of the most orthodox Judaism, whereas I have shown (Chapter 1, §5) that that renders the emergence of the Pharisees and Sadducees unintelligible. The presentation of 2 Maccabees is therefore preferable: in spite of the revisions and reinterpretations according to its views on Providence, the account is better documented, and provides more useful data for reconstructing the complex situation in the city from the time of Seleucus IV. The flattering portrait of Onias corresponds to the embellished recollection of an ideal epoch, and it will be shown in the following chapter that it was not Onias, but Simon the Just, his father, the only one who had brought about the unstable synthesis of Jews and Judaeans (under Antiochus III).

5. *Mattathias and Judas*

The role and the history of Judas Maccabeus according to 2 Maccabees are perfectly clear: having escaped the destruction of Jerusalem, he organized the resistance (while scrupulously respecting the Law) and reconquered the Jewish quarter. Then, trying to rally the whole of Judaea and to defend the Jewish communities in the vicinity, he had to carry on an intermittent guerilla war against the Seleucid army, while remaining very much opposed to the high priest Alcimus, in charge under Demetrius I (around 160). The book ends with the defeat of Nicanor, without any allusion to the establishment of the Hasmonaean dynasty. The account in 1 Maccabees is less clear, because there are two successive outbursts of resistance, first with the priest Mattathias, then with his successor Judas.

Let us consider the chronology. The story of Mattathias (1 Macc. 2) is tenuously connected to the context. It begins with 'In those days', and ends with his death, dated in the 146th Seleucid year, so between April 20, 166 BCE and April 6, 165, whereas the 'abomination of desolation' had been installed December 6, 167. Then Judas renewed the struggle, and Antiochus IV, in need of money, left for Persia in the 147th Seleucid year (1 Macc. 3.37), having named Lysias as governor of all Trans-euphrates. The latter sent an army that was defeated at Emmaus by Judas. We do not know how this victory was politically exploited, but in the following year (4.28), the 148th Seleucid year, Lysias attempted to retake Judaea through Idumaea (Beth-Zur), and was again defeated. While he was gone again to seek reinforcements, Judas marched on Jerusalem, purified the Temple, and had a new altar inaugurated on 25th Kislev 148, around December 14,[71] 164, three lunar years after the profanation.

This delay of three years was thus occupied, to put it briefly, by a year of resistance by Mattathias, and two years by Judas (represented by the victories of Emmaus and Beth-Zur), but with an unequal tempo: compressed for Mattathias, who had a dazzling career, but more diffuse for Judas. After brilliant beginnings, the victory at Emmaus, probably during the summer of 165,[72] should have given access to Jerusalem where the Seleucid garrison was certainly inadequate, since he was able to conquer it the following year. The account ends, however, with a transitional sentence stating that 'a remarkable deliverance took place that day in Israel' (4.25). Likewise, the following year, the victory at Beth-Zur over Lysias opened the way to Jerusalem, at the beginning of

71.   Taking into consideration intercalary years; cf. Goldstein, *I Maccabees*, pp. 273-75.

72.   The *Meg. Ta'an.* reports, on 24th Ab, therefore in the summer, a 'return to the Law' (תבנא לדינא), and the scholion explains: 'In the time of the Greek kingdom, the laws of the Gentiles were in effect, and when the hand of the Hasmonean house was strongest, they annulled them...' Cf. Lichtenstein, *Fastenrolle*, p. 278. It could refer to a victory of Mattathias or of Judas, permitting a restoration of the Law.

the spring of 164, but the Dedication only took place at the end of the following autumn. What is more, two documents already considered above show that negotiations had begun after the battle of Emmaus: a letter of Lysias to the Jews (2 Macc. 11.16-21), dated the autumn of 165,[73] in which he acknowledged their demands, then the letter already quoted of Antiochus IV to the Jewish *gerousia* (vv. 27-33), dated 15th Xanthicus, in the spring of 164, and granting the freedoms requested by Menelaus. These datable pieces of information suggest that after each defeat the Seleucid government made a concession,[74] about which the account in 1 Maccabees is silent, since it tries to show a continuous battle culminating with the purification.

What results from this is that the entire chronology of Judas's campaigns in 1 Maccabees, which does not mention the documents just cited, had the effect of making the arrival of Judas in Jerusalem and the Dedication a unique and total victory over the Seleucids, which brought about the end of the persecution (but not of the war). In reality, the armistice with Antiochus IV was earlier by eight or nine months: peace was established in Judaea, but nothing was settled in Jerusalem.

Some have tried to lessen the difficulty by interpreting the Seleucid chronology differently, and by claiming that the computation of all the dates of 1–2 Maccabees began in the autumn of 312 BCE:[75] in that case, the Dedication would have to be advanced a year to December 165, that is some months before the armistice, and about a year before the death of Antiochus; the sequence of events is then better. The letters of Lysias and Antiochus IV, however, made no allusion to the Temple, nor

73. The name of the month is changed to διοσκορινθιου (Latin: *dioscordi*, *dioscor*), which must be restored, either following Josephus who understood *Dios* and transposed Marheshwan (the 24th is then the end of October or the beginning of November), or considering the Cretan month of Dioscoros for it, equivalent to Xanthicus or Nisan, or perhaps an intercalary month in the spring, just before Xanthicus; cf. Morkholm, *Antiochus IV*, p. 155 n. 61.

74. The consequence of this is that it is unnecessary to consider the Jewish victory at Beth-Zur fictitious, a kind of inverted doublet of the Jewish defeat at Beth-Zur by Antiochus V and the same Lysias (1 Macc. 6.28-50); cf. Goldstein, *I Maccabees*, p. 268.

75. Cf. K. Bringmann, *Hellenistische Reform und Religionsverfolgung in Judäa: Eine Untersuchung zur Jüdisch-hellenistischen Geschichte (175–163 v. Chr.)* (Abhandlungen der Akademie der Wissenschaftlichen zu Göttingen, 3/132; Göttingen: Vandenhoeck & Ruprecht, 1983), pp. 15-28; J.C. Vanderkam, 'Hanukkah: Its Timing and Significance according to 1 and 2 Maccabees', *JSP* 1 (1987), pp. 23-40; according to this computation, the indication of an interruption in the cult for just two years (2 Macc. 10.3) is easier to understand.

even to Jerusalem, while giving the impression of satisfying the demands of Judas. In fact, it was Menelaus, high priest and governor of the *polis* of the citadel, therefore necessarily in contact with the Temple, who had pleaded on behalf of the Jews and the *gerousia*, that is in favour of the demands of the *ethnos* living at Jerusalem and in Judaea, as if he himself was one of them: whether the Dedication had taken place before or after the armistice, Judaea was perhaps at peace, but the city was still divided.

We now return to the campaigns in Judaea. Mattathias was from Modein (al-Midiya), near Lod-Lydda, since it was the location of the family tomb (1 Macc. 2.70). He was a priest, a descendant of Joarib, and Josephus (12.265) even specifies that he was of the class (ἐξ ἐφημερίδος) of Joarib, that is the first of the twenty-four classes of the sons of Aaron drawn by lot according to 1 Chron. 24.7. The priestly lists from Qumran, however, leave some doubt about this primacy, and we can assume[76] a pro-Hasmonaean revision of 1 Chronicles. What is more, Josephus, who was familiar with the country, mentions only that Mattathias lived at Modein, but avoided saying that he was born there: he would have been there only as a refugee. He was apparently uncomfortable with the topography involved: the Judaea reconquered by Judas, which is very much like the Judaea of Nehemiah, had as its western border Emmaus, at the foot of the hilly zone, and for its southern frontier Beth-Zur. Modein, more to the west in the plain and not far from the sea (cf. 1 Macc. 13.29), was located in the three nomes of Aphairema-Ephraim, Lydda-Lod and Ramathaim-Rama,[77] severed from Samaria and officially annexed to Judaea by Demetrius II, about 145 BCE (1 Macc. 11.34). Mattathias is thus at best on the periphery, in relation to Judaea and Jerusalem,[78] and there is definitely room to question his genealogy, since serious consideration should be given to a possible Samaritan origin.

76.   Cf. Abel and Starcky, *Maccabées*, p. 94, n. *c*. The title 'Hasmonaean', introduced by Josephus (and preserved by the rabbinic tradition) is by right much less worthy of note than that of 'descendant of Joarib, of Zadok and of Aaron' (cf. 1 Chron. 24.3-7).

77.   Later, in the same way, the neighbouring town of Kfar-Saba (Antipatris) was taken to be a Samaritan locality, according to *y. Dem.* 2.1; cf. Chapter 4, §4.

78.   J. Sievers, *The Hasmonaeans and their Supporters: From Mattathias to the Death of John Hyrcanus I* (University of South Florida Studies in the History of Judaism, 6; Atlanta: Scholars Press, 1990), pp. 27-29, and the discussion of S. Schwartz, 'A Note on the Social Type and Political Ideology of the Hasmonean Family', *JBL* 112 (1993), pp. 305-309, but the latter tends to conclude that this remote origin explains the moderate religious zeal of the Hasmonaeans; cf. below, §6.

As for his resistance activity, it developed first at Modein itself (2.15-28), but he had to go underground in the hills, with his partisans. Other dissidents took refuge in caves in the desert (of Judah), but, refusing to defend themselves against attack on the Sabbath, they died in great numbers. It was then that Mattathias made his famous decision to permit counter-attacks on the Sabbath, and that the assembly (συναγωγή) of the Hasidaeans joined him. Subsequently nothing more in particular is recounted about the mighty deeds of Mattathias and his followers, other than that they attacked the renegades and circumcised 'all the children that they found in the territory of Israel'. These actions appear to have been more scattered over the area, especially in Samaria,[79] rather than directed against Jerusalem, with which ultimately Mattathias had very few connections. In any case, no retaliation by high priestly or Seleucid authorities is mentioned. It must be concluded that the dissidents were split up into various groups and that the forces united by Mattathias were more than modest, that is to say on the scale of the tiny region of Modein.

In this regard, the flight of Mattathias the observant believer at the time of the persecutions, was very similar to the withdrawal to the desert with some companions of Judas Maccabeus, another observant believer (2 Macc. 5.27), at the time of persecutions in Jerusalem. This latter text implies that Judas left Jerusalem, then that his return was a notable victory. What is more, his position as leader of the Hasidaeans (2 Macc. 14.6) provided a bond with Mattathias: he was his successor, perhaps by rallying to him (cf. 1 Macc. 2.42), but there is no proof that he went along with his decision relative to the Sabbath; in fact, the very opposite seems true.

Nevertheless, most of Judas's activities were outside Jerusalem, and the conclusion of 2 Macc. 15.37, declaring that beginning with the death of Nicanor 'the city remained in the possession of the Hebrews', certainly demonstrates what the intention of the abridger was, but corresponds poorly with the facts, since the citadel remained in the hands of the Syrians long after the death of Judas in 160.[80] In a similar way, in

79. J. Schwartz and J. Spanier, 'On Mattathias and the Desert of Samaria', *RB* 98 (1991), pp. 252-71.

80. According to 1 Macc. 13.51, it was Simon who took the citadel by force (141 BCE); in 136, Antiochus VII Sidetes claimed it again (1 Macc. 15.28) and, according to *Ant.* 13.246 (apparently in dependence on Posidonius), he besieged and captured Jerusalem in 134, but agreed to give it up definitively, in return for

1 Maccabees, Judas made just two very momentary incursions into Jerusalem, one which culminated in the Dedication, the other which failed when faced with the Syrians, but nearly all his guerillas were spread out over wide areas on both banks of the Jordan. The question of Jerusalem was therefore something exceptional: the reign of the high priest Menelaus extended beyond the actual crisis, since he died in 163 (2 Macc. 13.4). His successor Alcimus died perhaps as early as 159 (cf. 1 Macc. 9.54-57) and in any case at least two years before Alexander Balas named Jonathan high priest in 152 (1 Macc. 10.21). From the time of the Dedication by Judas Maccabeus, that is for 12 or 13 years, it is hard to see how the Temple could have functioned, were it not for un-friendly dynasties. According to 1 Macc. 6.18, those living in the citadel blocked access to the Temple in 163–162, and later Alcimus, about 159, tried 'to destroy the work of the prophets' (1 Macc. 9.54). The letter of Antiochus V to Lysias, in which he asked 'that the Temple be restored [ἀποκατασταθῆναι, restitui] to the Jews' (2 Macc. 11.25), can be no later than 162. If it is authentic, it had no appreciable effect on the Jews properly so called, since it did not mention anyone responsible for the cult who would be acceptable to Judas, and a fortiori recognized by the gerousia, and this situation lasted until the enthronement of Jonathan (in 152), but the subsequent developments are under suspicion of having been distorted by the propaganda of 1 Maccabees, which is their only witness. It must be admitted then that this restoration was not done for the Jews, the companions of Judas, but for traditional Judaean groups, represented by Alcimus. In other words, the distinction between Judaeans and Jews persisted, the latter remaining at a certain distance from the sanctuary.

What is the meaning then of the Dedication of the altar by Judas and his companions, since their activity in general was on the fringe of the Temple? According to 1 Macc. 4.36-51, when they arrived on Mount Zion they were faced with a painful spectacle of ruins, or perhaps of foreign cults, with sacred trees. The restoration of the site comprised two very distinct phases: on the one hand, the repairing of the Dwelling, its courts and its furnishings (candelabrum, altar of incense, table for offerings, curtains), and on the other hand the dismantling and then the reconstruction of the altar of burnt offerings, which had been profaned.

compensations, and to 'grant to the Jews their national constitution [πάτριον πολιτείαν]', which presupposes the official abolition of the polis; Bickerman, The God of the Maccabees, p. 60.

Consequently, the inauguration took place in two stages: in the Temple, or more exactly in the Dwelling, the resumption of worship (incense, lamps, bread of the Presence), without any indication of a date or a particular feast; then, on 25th Kislev, the solemn inauguration of the altar with holocausts according to the Law, in an atmosphere of great jubilation of all the people for eight days. There is a paradoxical difference in magnitude between the two events, since the one which was architecturally more significant, relating to the Dwelling, did not give rise to a particularly notable celebration. This pre-eminence of the altar over the sanctuary as a whole is very similar to that observed at the time of the resumption of the cult under Zerubbabel, when holocausts were restored on the altar 'while the foundations of the sanctuary of YHWH had not yet been laid' (Ezra 3.6). This comparison will be considered later.

The two acts, which the parallel account in 2 Macc. 10.3 confuses to some extent,[81] correspond in fact to two distinct distortions in the cult: the Hellenization by Jason, with gymnasium and *ephebeum* (youth centres), had as a first effect, according to 2 Macc. 4.12f., the abandonment of the Temple. Then, the decree of Antiochus IV resulted in the profanation of the altar of holocausts with the 'abomination of desolation', which, as we have seen, was a foreign cult of the same local god; as for the multiplication of similar altars in the towns of Judah (1 Macc. 1.34-64), there is no reason to believe that they were dedicated to new deities either. The revolt was not triggered by the Hellenization, one of whose consequences was the attribution of a name to the anonymous deity (Olympian Zeus; 2 Macc. 6.1-2), but by this decree of Antiochus IV, since it affected the cult at Jerusalem and *elsewhere*. It is remarkable that it was in the surrounding towns of Judah, and not in the vicinity of the Temple, that they destroyed the books of the Law or the copies of the covenant (1 Macc. 1.56-60), and that the resistance of Mattathias began at a point far from Jerusalem. Later, all the activities of Judas in Idumaea, in Galaad, in Galilee were meant to defend the Jewish communities (1 Macc. 5.2, etc.). The horizon of the resistance fighters was not Judaea, nor even Jerusalem, but Judaism, and we encounter again the conclusions of §1. In this way should be understood the concessions made by Antiochus V to the Jewish *ethnos*, in his letter to Lysias (2 Macc. 11.22-26): it was an edict of amnesty, and he invited the Jews, wherever they might have been from, even those living in Jerusalem, to return home,

---

81. Just as certain commentators do; Abel, *Maccabées*, pp. 416-17.

whether they might have been runaways or dissidents. He guaranteed them at least statutory protection.

It did not follow from this, however, that the Temple would have been secondary, and the account of the Dedication was intended to prove this. The charter of Antiochus III had granted it a 'Judaean' status, but not specifically a 'Jewish' one, since it had no explicit connection with the law of Moses. According to 1 Maccabees, those resisting had that Law and wanted to bring it back to the Temple. This was apparently a result of the persecution, but perhaps it was its cause as well.

An analysis of the terminology used in a dispute about interpretation shows the importance of the Temple as a symbol: where 1 Maccabees speaks of the Dedication (ἐγκαινισμός) of the altar, 2 Maccabees speaks of a purification of the Temple (νεώς, designating the actual building), and associates the name 'Booths' with the feast (10.6: σκηνωμάτων τρόπον, 'in the manner of the feast of Booths'; 1.9, 18: σκηνοπηγία τοῦ χασελευ μηνός, 'erection of a Booth *of* the month of Kislev'). A comparison has long been made with the temple of Solomon, whose dedication coincided with the feast of Booths[82] (1 Kgs 8.62, and more clearly 2 Chron. 7.5). We can recall too that the first holocausts on the altar of Zerubbabel were offered on the feast of Booths. The usual explanation, suggested by the text itself, according to which it was a matter of a substitution for the recent feast of Booths of Tishri, with the eight days, the branches and the palms, is not really satisfactory, since it merely takes note of a coincidence in the calendar.[83] Following this logic, had the purification taken place in the spring, we would have spoken of a substitute Passover. Now, the event concerns the Temple, and not the altar. The example of the temple of Solomon clearly shows that there was a significant connection, and not just an accidental one, between the feast of Booths and the inauguration of the Temple.

In fact, the term σκηνή, 'tent, hut', found frequently in the Bible, translates 245 times אהל, 'tent', and 93 times מֹשֶׁכָן, 'residence, dwelling'. The latter meaning fits particularly well the sanctuary in the strict sense, that is to say the edifice where the

---

82.   Vanderkam, 'Hanukkah', p. 33.

83.   In the opinion of Abel, *Maccabées*, p. 408; in regard to the *Skenopegia* of the month of Kislev, he thinks he is able to restore (p. 288) an original יֹמֵי חַג חֹדֶשׁ כִּסְלוֹ , in which חַג would have included 'feast of Booths', the feast par excellence (cf. 1 Kgs 8.2); but this explanation, possible in the case of the festal letter, no longer fits 2 Macc. 10.6. For Goldstein, *I Maccabees*, pp. 274-78, the year in Judaea was moved forward in comparison with the legal (Jewish) year by two intercalary months which had not been proclaimed the preceding years, so that the ninth month of one (Kislev) corresponded that year with the seventh month of the other (Tishri). This theory, which does not entirely take account of the texts, is hard to verify, and in particular is only concerned with explaining a coincidence of dates, devoid as such of any specific signification.

divinity resided. Two consequences follow from this: 1. the term 'tent' to designate the inauguration of the Temple is perfectly natural, particularly in the letter of 2 Macc. 1.9, and indicates that attention is directed to the (closed) Dwelling and not to the altar for sacrifices; 2. in comparison with the biblical 'feast of Booths', the problem is to be tackled in the inverse direction: what is its meaning, if it is not the commemoration of a dedication?

This feast of Booths accumulates various meanings, difficult to bring together in a single ritual: feast of the Ingathering (Exod. 23.16), the turning of the year (34.22), feast of pilgrimage to the chosen place, and also, according to Lev. 23.42-43, the precept to live in huts (סכות) made of boughs 'as at the time of the Exodus'. This is odd since the Israelites camped at that time in tents, and not in huts, which would be difficult to prepare in the desert. What is more, according to Deut. 31.10-11, this feast, calling the people together, was also the occasion of the reading of the Law. A passage already commented on provides an instructive example of these last arrangements: at the end of the proclamation of the Law by Ezra (Neh. 8.14-18), the people were sent to gather boughs to make huts: 'Each one on his roof, in their courtyards, in the precincts of the Temple of God, on the square of the Water Gate and the square of the Gate of Ephraim. The whole assembly [...] built huts in this way and lived in them.' It is then stated that the reading of the Law lasted during the seven days of the feast, the eighth day being a closing assembly. This cluttered compilation, with a complicated topography, is the result of the combination of the precept to make an announcement in all 'their' towns about the making of these huts to dwell in, and the proclamation of the Law by Ezra to all the people, assembled in Jerusalem before the Water Gate. There is therefore a merging, at least a literary one, of a commandment entirely independent of Jerusalem and the assembly just mentioned, with the Temple being of use particularly because of its precincts, without any allusion to the Dwelling. This very special 'feast of Booths' clearly had no connection with an inauguration of all or part of the sanctuary, and still it is added that the assembly was made up of 'those who had returned from captivity', and that 'the Israelites had never done such a thing since the days of Joshua, son of Nun'.

These 'new facts' are obviously very attractive for characterizing the relations of Judaism with Jerusalem and the Temple, against the background of an origin situated under Joshua. For the present discussion, they explain very simply the apparent obscurity of 2 Macc. 10.6, where the feast of 25th Kislev is celebrated 'in the manner of the feast of Booths', remembering how 'a short time before they had wandered in the mountains' as they celebrated the feast of Booths. The cumbersome nature of the explanation is the result of the double meaning possible for these 'booths' which can just as well be the huts used in their wandering as the Dwelling. The 'huts' of Leviticus 23 were not a souvenir of the desert, but of the wandering far from the Temple (a first substitution), and the inauguration on 25th Kislev was seen as a symbolic transfer from the wandering to the Temple (second substitution). These considerations raise some questions about Ezra–Nehemiah, which will be dealt with in Chapter 8, and others about the meaning of the 'huts' of Leviticus, which go beyond the horizon of the present study, all the more so since the play on meanings between 'hut' and 'dwelling' can occur *only in Greek*, and not in Hebrew.[84]

It has been pointed out that the passage on the purification of the Temple, 25th Kislev, of 2 Macc. 10.1-8 was in literary terms an intrusion. It must now be added that this passage has no other role than to try to explain, somewhat clumsily, the commemoration of the *skenopegia* or 'feast of Booths', or again 'feast of the Dwelling', prescribed in the letters appearing at the beginning of the book. These letters are addressed to the Jews of Egypt. Now, it was in Egypt that the traditional model of a sanctuary, taken up again in the Ptolemaic period, had as its essential element the dwelling of the god,[85] an edifice closed and inaccessible to the people, whereas the Semitic reference model, *bomos* or betyl, consisted of the stele and the altar, and stood in the open air, therefore accessible to everybody. The account of the dedication of the altar in 1 Maccabees corresponds to this latter model, all the more so since it was a matter, after the impious multiplication of altars during the persecution, of a return to the unity called for in Deuteronomy. As for the term 'dedication' (ἐγκαινισμός, חנוכה), it is inappropriate, since it assumes an official recognition by a competent authority: we have seen that such was not the case, either in the Seleucid documents, or on the part of the high priests really in office, or even from the side of the Jewish aristocracy.

What is left therefore of the real, or more exactly the factual, in the 'dedication' by Judas Maccabeus, the reports of which arrived several decades later in Egypt? First, according to Dan. 9.27, the persecution lasted three and a half years and in no way ended up with a restoration (cf. 11.31-39). Second, ignored by 2 Maccabees in its primitive form, as well as by the document summarizing the origin of the Hasmonaeans (1 Macc. 14.27-48), the heroic deed of Judas was at most a small-scale raid without any follow-up, similar to many others in the towns of Judah and elsewhere. Such a raid was launched successfully on a day of royal

---

84.   From σκηνή (and its derivatives), which is perhaps connected with the root שׁכן, 'to dwell'.

85.   It follows from this as well that the Jews of Egypt, who were considered faithful to the Jerusalem temple and not to the one at Leontopolis, were however supposed to understand it through what they knew; cf. Doran, *Temple Propaganda*, pp. 11-13. In the same spirit, it was definitely at Jerusalem and not elsewhere that, according to *Ep. Arist.* §§51-82, Ptolemy sent the cultic furnishings for the Dwelling 'in accordance with the Law'.

sacrifice (2 Macc. 6.7), which occurred on the twenty-fifth of each month,[86] whence the Dedication's great symbolic value, connected later to the winter solstice. It was perhaps quite quickly commemorated, at least in certain circles, since the Temple remained inaccessible, which could then explain its *literary* development into a complete restoration after the installation of the Hasmonaeans. We obtain in this way the 1 Maccabees account of a dynastic foundation. The visions of Daniel, which were unaware of the Dedication, developed according to a different point of view, more independent of the Temple (versus 2 Maccabees) and of the Hasmonaeans (versus 1 Maccabees), certainly more in accordance with dispersed Judaism, particularly in Mesopotamia, where the claims about the Temple were less strong (cf. Chapter 7, §4).

It is certainly exaggerating to conclude, as Bickerman does, that the achievement of Judas, as well as the providential relaxation of pressure, shortly after the siege of Jerusalem by Antiochus V and Lysias, assured the survival of Judaism and monotheism.[87] Judaism was indeed alive, but especially outside Jerusalem, and it was the crisis of the reconquest of the Temple, at the end of an unstable period of internal tensions, which gave it a social and political dimension unknown previously, while the high priestly circles obedient to the Seleucids lost ground.

Finally the chronologies are not above suspicion: for 1 Maccabees, the profanation of the altar lasted three years, made up of one year of struggles by Mattathias, then two years by Judas; for 2 Maccabees, the profanation lasted just two years, equivalent to the activity of Judas alone, which ignores Mattathias; for Daniel, the crisis lasted half a week, or three and a half years, which dissolves the importance of 25th Kislev; Josephus too, in *The Jewish War*, speaks of three and a half years, then briefly mentions the resistance put up by Mattathias and Judas, but ignores any commemoration. At the other extreme, rabbinic Judaism was acquainted with the Dedication of 25th Kislev, with a feast of Lights

86.   In regard to the monthly celebration of the anniversary, see Schürer, 'Zu II Macc 6,7', pp. 48-52. The attempt could have taken place in Kislev itself, as indicated; this is the opinion of Vanderkam, 'Hanukkah', p. 34. However, according to others the bunching together of dates under the form of an anniversary is artificial, just like the five events commemorated 9th Ab according to *m. Ta'an.* 4.6; cf. Doran, *Temple Propaganda*, p. 61 n. 41. It is difficult to settle if it really was in Kislev, difficult even to decide the year—165 or 164; these doubts are nevertheless of little importance, since the raid had been limited, and it was not with Judas that Lysias and Antiochus had dealt.

87.   Bickerman, *The God of the Maccabees*, p. 91.

(which Josephus mentions without understanding it), but ignored Mattathias[88] as well as Judas. All the traditions testify to the fact that there was a crisis linked to Seleucid pressure, but they have a remarkable flexibility. The account of 1 Maccabees accumulates the most elements, but they are unstable: Mattathias is ultimately only important as the ancestor of the high priests Jonathan and Simon; Judas was a memorable resistance fighter, but his brave feat of 25th Kislev is doubtful, with it being understood that something indeed had happened on a 25th Kislev (cf. Chapter 8, §7).

6. *Zadokites, Hasmonaeans and Sadducees*[89]

The dynasty which reigned in Judaea between the Maccabaean crisis and Herod the Great had the name Hasmonaeans in the sources, but its origin is obscure. Nevertheless, if we go by what 1 Macc. 2.1 and Josephus (*Life* §2) say, its founders were of the line of Joarib, the first of the 24 priestly classes, who were descended from Aaron and Eleazar, then from Zadok in the time of David, at least according to the suggestion of 1 Chron. 24.3, 7. They could then be referred to as Aaronites, or better still as Zadokites, a more prestigious title which would have precisely fitted the prescriptions of Ezek. 44.15. So why had they retained a less prestigious title? There is a problem of literary manipulations, and I intend to show that for apologetic reasons the dynasty had been presented as unified, but in reality certain disruptions had been concealed so that heterogeneous elements could be grouped together.

The book of 1 Maccabees concludes with the coming to power of John Hyrcanus (135 BCE), the grandson of Mattathias, but Josephus praises his accomplishments and declares that at the time of his death (104) he was at the same time king (to all intents and purposes), high priest and prophet (*Ant.* 13.299). Next, the account of the coming to power of Alexander Janneus (103–76) is odd. After the brief and strange reign of Aristobulus, his widow released his brothers from prison and placed on the throne one of them 'who *seemed* better fitted for it by reason of his age and moderate temperament' (13.320); but he

---

88.   In *b. Meg.* 11a there is mention (in a *baraita*: במתניתא תנא) of Mattathias as high priest, but he is distinguished from 'the Hasmonaean and his sons'; this is a kind of muddled rumour, and something not accepted as official.

89.   This section condenses E. Nodet, 'Mattathias, Samaritains et Asmonéens', *Transeuphratène* 7 (1994), pp. 94-106.

immediately killed another pretender, which indicated some instabilities. Then, according to *War* 1.88-91, the Jews rose in revolt against him during one of the feasts, and he crushed them with his mercenaries. The grounds for the uprising are not clear, but according to *Ant.* 13.372-73, it was a matter of the king officiating at the altar as high priest at the time of a feast of Booths, when he found himself accused of being an offspring of captives, and therefore legally unfit to exercise the office of high priest; this resulted, through various episodes, in massive and lasting repressions, without other specific reasons, fiscal or political, being given for this unrest. He seems to have been more or less systematically rejected as an intruder, without managing to establish a stable moral authority. The reproach is nevertheless strange, if Alexander is really the legitimate son of John Hyrcanus, whose legitimacy had not been questioned by anybody. In this connection Josephus referred to a significant tradition (13.322-23), according to which Hyrcanus hated this son, because it had been revealed to him that he would succeed him, instead of his elder sons whom he preferred, Antigonus and Aristobulus; besides Alexander had been brought up in Galilee. This account is legendary, but it does not disguise the fact that the future king was a stranger at the court of Hyrcanus, and was not the acknowledged heir.

A banquet scene, which Josephus (*Ant.* 13.289-98) wrongly connects to John Hyrcanus instead of Alexander Janneus,[90] provides some supplementary information: the king, who had invited his friends the Pharisees to a banquet, asked them if they had any criticism to make of him. Those present cried out in admiration, but one of them, named Eleazar, demanded that he give up the high priesthood, maintaining that he was descended from a captive. A Sadducean friend of the king, Jonathan, then asserted that Eleazar was only expressing the opinion of the Pharisees in general, and suggested, in order to prove their loyalty, that they be asked what punishment they thought Eleazar deserved for his insolence. Seeing that they did not call for his death, the king was annoyed and concluded that they were in collusion with him; he then went over to the Sadducean camp, abrogating on this occasion the oral traditions of the Pharisees.[91] The king's question to the Pharisees really implied not friendship but fear: he wanted to make sure of their support, since 'they have great influence with the people', as Josephus makes

90. Cf. Chapter 1, §5 and Main's discussion, 'Sadducéens', pp. 190-202.
91. According to *b. Qid.* 66a, these were later restored by Simon ben Shetach, brother of Queen Salome.

clear. The acts of violence that followed show either that the king was crazy, since he alienated the people over something so trivial, or that he already no longer had any influence over Pharisaic opinion. What is more, the suspicion of illegitimacy is not at all cleared up, and there arise again the difficulties already mentioned in regard to the king trying to make himself acceptable.

The account is still not very intelligible, since it has a distorted perspective in which there is no option other than Pharisaic or Sadducean; that is to say, the only option is one originating apparently in a mere squabble between schools in a court context. Yet, if the king mistrusted the Pharisees and they despised him, and if, however, he became a Sadducee only late in life and after a crisis, it was because 'Sadducean' was something other than the opposite of 'Pharisaic'. So this designation especially had a real politico-social content and besides provided a way to overlook the suspicion of illegitimacy, although there is still the problem of knowing how that would be possible.

At this point the antecedents of Mattathias and Simon have a role to play: since they were descendants of Joarib, they were Zadokites, at least according to 1 Chronicles. The term 'Sadducee' referred to Zadok as well, and there is a necessary connection between the two, since we do not know where to find another Zadok who could constitute a reference of the same weight. In fact, 'passing to the camp of the Sadducees', as the account above put it, could be understood to be nothing else but 'getting accepted as pro-Zadokite', that is, being accepted by a legitimist party, one with roots going back to Zadok. It could be questioned, nevertheless, how the Sadducees, in the politico-religious sense of supporters of the dynasty of Mattathias and Simon, had welcomed an outsider. The response is political: it was because of their common opposition to the Pharisees, who exerted an increasing influence over the people, in Judaea probably, but certainly more in Galilee and in the Diaspora, in the East as well as in the West. This is clearly seen on the occasion of the Roman decrees granted in favour of the Jews in the time of Hyrcanus II (*Ant.* 14.190-210; cf. Chapter 4, §4): exemptions from taxes in the Sabbatical Year, exemptions from military service, necessary for the observance of the Sabbath, permission for banquets and cultic gatherings. All these constituted new arrangements for communities which were not themselves necessarily new; the goal was to give official recognition to usages that were specifically Pharisaic, or more generally of Babylonian origin, at least partially. Besides, Pharisaic pressure was always present in

Jerusalem because of cultic taxes and pilgrimages; it is worth noting, too, that the reported revolt against Janneus broke out at the time of one of the three great pilgrimage feasts. In such circumstances, the suspension of oral traditions, which could have real effect only in Judaea, could not but satisfy the coalition of the king and the Sadducees. This important self-interest having been identified, one of its results among other things is that the origins of Janneus remained really dubious.

It could be objected in regard to the break introduced between Janneus and Hyrcanus that Josephus describes Mattathias and all his successors as Hasmonaeans (*War* 1.19, etc.). However, 1 Maccabees was unaware of this term, and only retained the much more important connection with Joarib. Why would Josephus have hidden a rupture in the dynasty, by making it lose a prestigious name? The reply is perhaps simply his personal vanity: he was himself descended from the Hasmonaeans through his mother,[92] and going back to Mattathias enhanced his

92. The antecedents that he gave (*Life* §§2-4) present some difficulties:

a. He began by saying that he belonged to the most illustrious of clans from the first of the 24 priestly classes. According to 1 Chron. 24.7, confirmed by other lists (cf. n. 11), it is the class of Joarib, which is also that of Mattathias (1 Macc. 2.1). Then he continued: 'I am even, through my mother, of royal stock, since the descendants of the Hasmonaean ['Ασαμωναίου], her ancestors, were for a long time high priests and kings of our people.' If we read him correctly, Josephus would therefore be a priest and descendant of Joarib through his father, while through his mother he would be of royal stock descended from the Hasmonaean. If the reigning Hasmonaeans really began with Mattathias, these two lines merge, but Josephus did not in any way suggest this here. On the contrary, he clearly let it be understood that the 'royal stock' had no connection with Joarib or even with a specifically priestly genealogy (Aaronide).

b. He then gave the genealogy of his father, but with some inconsistencies: his great-grandfather (or 'grandfather' in the broad sense, πρόπαππος) Simon the Stutterer was a contemporary of John Hyrcanus (135–104), but Matthias, the grandson of the latter, would have been born the first year of the same Hyrcanus (135) of a daughter of the high priest Jonathan, son of Mattathias (152–144); the two pieces of information are incompatible: this Matthias could not be at the same time grandson of Simon the Stutterer and of Jonathan. Then, this Matthias would have had a son Joseph in 70, then in 6 CE a grandson Matthias (the father of Josephus), or two generations in 141 years, which is improbable. There is then an artificial stretching out, the reason for which is obvious: the connection to Joarib through the high priest Jonathan. If this link is cut, we get four generations in the same 141 years, or some 35 years a generation, which becomes again plausible: when Josephus was born (in 38), his father was 32 years old. Schürer, *History*, I, p. 81, also considers that the list has been altered, through the negligence of the author or the error of a copyist, but

lineage. In this regard, Josephus's error, transferring the banquet scene to the reign of John Hyrcanus, no longer appears to be the result of simple negligence: while the reign of Alexander Janneus was plagued by civil wars, that of Hyrcanus ended up in an apotheosis, since he was said to be a prophet, king and high priest (*Ant.* 13.282 and 299; *t. Soṭ.* 13.5). Now, according to 1 Macc. 14.41, Simon was raised to the high priesthood and leadership in perpetuity, at least *until an accredited prophet should appear who would confirm him.* The prophet Hyrcanus had appeared, he had announced against his will the accession of Janneus, and the genealogical misgiving had been lifted; there is therefore an implicit confirmation. What is more, the Pharisees were discredited in the passage as seditious, which corresponds closely to the underlying thought of Josephus. Finally, all dynastic discontinuity between Hyrcanus and Janneus is eliminated. In this way, the reappearance in the time of Alexander Janneus of the same doubt as to his antecedents had infinitely less significance: it is nothing more than a well-known symptom of the permanent agitation of an ungovernable people. Another reason, connected to the pro-Pharisaic apologetic of Josephus, could also have dissuaded him from connecting the Sadducees to the descendants of Mattathias, although he still knew and used Chronicles. Josephus implied (*Ant.* 13.298) that Simon gave his son John Hyrcanus a Pharisaic education; in other words, the Hasmonaeans, which evidently included for him Judas Maccabeus (acclaimed as high priest), had from the beginning been close to the Pharisees.

In regard to the name 'Hasmonaean', the Rabbinic tradition was acquainted with the adjective *hashmonai*, which seemed to apply, as it

does not consider a deliberate modification of the sources. J. Jeremias, *Jerusalem in the Time of Jesus* (London: SCM Press, 1969), p. 214, assumes the accidental omission of two generations between the two Matthiases, but there then remains the difficulty of leaving Simon the Stutterer in the time of John Hyrcanus.

c. It follows from this that the connection of Josephus to Joarib, which there is no direct reason to question, since he was certainly a priest, did not come about through Mattathias and his sons, but apparently in more obscure ways (according to *Apion* 2.108, each priestly class was composed of more than five thousand men). This suffices to explain perfectly how in *Ant.* 12.265 he would have chosen another expedient to include Mattathias among his ancestors. He made him a fairly distant descendant of the Hasmonaean, which added more lustre to his own royal ancestry; but nothing is really precise or substantiated, since even in that case Mattathias and Josephus could go back to the same Hasmonaean through two independent branches.

did for Josephus, to the whole dynasty since Mattathias, since it is said in
m. Mid. 1.6 that 'the sons of the Hasmonaean hid the stones of the altar
that the Greek kings had profaned', an allusion to 1 Macc. 4.43-51.[93]
However, it must be stated that this tradition is not well documented,[94]
since it identified clearly neither Mattathias nor his sons Jonathan and
Simon,[95] but it still set up a clear distinction between John Hyrcanus,
whom it recognized and found fault with as a high priest (cf. *m. Ma'as.
Sheni* 5.15; *m. Soṭ.* 9.10), and Alexander Janneus, who is never referred
to as a high priest, but only as a king, and then condemned. There is still
therefore the trace of a discontinuity, and we cannot take literally the
assertion that this king was at first a Pharisee.

As for the origins of the term 'Hasmonaean', it has been pointed out
that there was a town in Judah called Heshmon (Josh. 15.27 MT; no
equivalent term in LXX), near the border of Edom and the Negev, therefore in the Idumaean area where there had been a forced conversion by
Hyrcanus; some have very naturally concluded from this that the term
hashmonai, which has the form of a derived adjective and not of a

---

93.   The tradition on this is mixed, since in v. 43 the priests removed the stones
of the defilement (τοῦ μιασμοῦ, therefore the 'abomination of desolation') to an
impure place, then in vv. 44-46 'they' deliberated over the profaned altar of holocausts, and finally decided to demolish it and put its stones away 'in a suitable place,
while awaiting the coming of a prophet who would give a ruling concerning them'.
We could understand that there were two different installations, with the abomination
being built *on* the altar; this was the view of *Ant.* 12.253, and then of Jerome, *In
Danielem* 12.7, who imagined it to be a statue of Zeus; see also Abel, *Maccabées*,
pp. 28-29. However, since Bickerman, *The God of the Maccabees*, pp. 38-40 and
especially pp. 53-56, it has been considered to have been the same installation,
rededicated to another cult; this moreover is supposed by the passage of the Mishnah
just quoted, since it was indeed the stones of the altar, and not a superstructure,
which had become the abomination. It should be noted finally that Judas himself was
absent from these purification activities.

94.   According to *b. Meg.* 11a, quoted above, the liberators in the time of the
Greeks were 'Simon the Just the Hasmonaean and his sons and Mattathias the high
priest'; the information is at least inexact, since according to this testimony, the
Hasmonaeans, who were looked on favourably, were connected to Simon the Just,
but this is natural since he is the only political person retained by the tradition of *m.
Ab.* 1; cf. Chapter 6, §2.

95.   The tradition knew of a Juda ben Shamoa in a scholion about the good
news of the end of the persecution of Antiochus (*Meg. Ta'an*, 28th Adar), but definitely identifying him with Judas Maccabeus remains doubtful; cf. Lichtenstein's
discussion, 'Fastenrolle', p. 279.

proper noun (חשמונאי), refers to an inhabitant or a native of this place, whereas there was no such parallel possible in Greek. This explanation of *hashmonai* was not necessarily flattering, especially if it depended on a belated manipulation of the text of Joshua, but in any hypothesis the term cannot indicate more than a modest origin, with no possible comparison with what the Aaronites or the 'sons of Zadok' could have evoked. It should be remembered that the rabbinic tradition too had retained a great mistrust in regard to the class of Joarib, that is of Jonathan and Simon, indeed even of Hyrcanus. This class was described as 'rejecting heaven' (cf. Chapter 7, §2); this could be because of what they had done or very likely because of their supporters, the Sadducees, who rejected the oral tradition (cf. *m. Sanh.* 10.1), as will become evident below. In any case, this reprobation, joined to the fact that the pieces of information preserved are very fragmentary, can also explain an extension of the term similar to what Josephus had done.

These few scattered observations suffice to underscore a discontinuity between John Hyrcanus, grandson of Mattathias, a descendant of Joarib, and the later kings, who alone can properly be termed Hasmonaeans. The latter were the enemies of the Pharisees, the heirs of Judas Maccabeus, and had become the more or less inevitable allies of the Sadducees with their Zadokite claims, who kept alive a certain bond with Mattathias and his sons. These rudiments allow for a return to the crisis itself: Judas having become isolated as we have indicated, there is still a need to consider the specifically cultic dimension of the crisis, and in particular its preliminary stages. In this regard, 1 Maccabees and 2 Maccabees offer a remarkable contrast on the build-up to the crisis. According to the first, the only local person whose stature was clearly established before the crisis was Mattathias who was in the group of future victors, and the high priestly dynasty then reigning was literally non-existent; according to the second, the principal character was the high priest Onias who, despite his striking personal merits, was irremediably in the group who would disappear, since relations with the Seleucid overlord created fatal instabilities, and his dynasty was in fact supplanted by rivals who were of much the same type (Menelaus, Alcimus the Aaronite). Besides, in conformity with the Pharisaic perspective of this book, it was the future victorious dynasty which was non-existent, since there is not the least allusion made to it. Combining these elements, it is clear that these two successive profiles of high priestly dynasties, of Mattathias and then of Onias, are not of the same kind. I will now attempt to characterize them.

7. *Sparta or Scripture? Onias or Mattathias?*

The life of the Jewish communities, in Jerusalem and elsewhere, had been unstable since the time of Antiochus III, despite the ideal picture which 2 Maccabees suggested with Onias. This picture culminated, not with established facts, but with a hope, with the dream of Judas, in which he saw Jeremiah and Onias, in a premonition of the victory of the 'Day of Nicanor', 13th Adar (2 Macc. 15.11-16). Other pieces of information make it possible to be more specific, but in circuitous ways. In the time of Demetrius II, at the beginning of the installation of the so-called Hasmonaean regime, there was a report that the high priest Jonathan confirmed and renewed friendly relations, in particular with Rome and Sparta. Rome, since the time of Antiochus III, had tried to contain Seleucid ambitions. Despite his victory, Antiochus IV was forced by legates, as I have shown, to withdraw from Egypt. Other legates, according to 2 Macc. 11.38, supported the requests of the Jews sent to Lysias, contributing apparently to the final concessions and the amnesty granted by the same Antiochus IV in 164. About 160, under Demetrius I, Judas sought the support of Rome, 'for they saw that the Greek empire was reducing Israel to slavery'. These few notations, which put in perspective the sending of a peace mission to Rome by Jonathan (between 145 and 143), form a coherent whole, but any examination of them brings up the problem of the consolidation of the Hasmonaean regime and does not directly shed light on the circumstances of the Maccabaean crisis. It is therefore outside the area of this study.

The object of relations with Sparta is much less clear, even if, politically, Sparta was indeed an ally of Rome, or at least a 'friend', since 205 (the peace of Phoinike, at the end of the first Macedonian War). After the war of Achaea, in 146, Rome reorganized Greece. Sparta remained independent and was even able to organize a confederation of the Lacedaemonians, but many other Greek confederations were in the same position, like Athens, and there is no clear reason to explain the special singling out of Sparta, all the more so since Josephus mentions (*Apion* 2.259-60) that the Spartans were in the habit of expelling foreigners, which would seem to exclude the presence of Jewish communities in the Peloponnese.

In any case, relations between Jews and Sparta were defined by a letter which Jonathan wrote to them (1 Macc. 12.6-18); in it he made reference to an older correspondence of the king of Sparta, Areus, with the high priest Onias. This second document is an appended letter (12.20-23), but it recalls a third, since it indicates 'that it has been discovered in a document concerning the Spartans and the Jews that they are brothers and of the race of Abraham'.

I begin with an examination of the letter of Areus. Josephus, who transmitted it (*Ant.* 12.226-27), after detaching it from Jonathan's letter, put it in what he thought was its chronological place, that is to say under Seleucus IV, since he identified Onias with the brother of Jason.

His version has a strange conclusion: 'Demoteles, the courier, is bringing these letters. The writing is square; the seal is an eagle holding tight a serpent.' In 1 Maccabees, the conclusion is briefer and the only part that corresponds would be the mention of Demoteles, without any editorial information: 'We have ordered therefore that you be given a message on this subject.' The explanations about the writing and the seal could be describing the famous rediscovered account (a third document), but then a copy would have been likewise appended, which is not the case. The conclusion describes the letter itself, and evidently cannot be part of it. It is nevertheless easy to see the reason for the error of Josephus, who included it there. In his source, that is to say in his version of 1 Maccabees, the letter of Areus, appended to the letter of Jonathan, had an editorial introduction. It was introduced by a sentence of the redactor (v. 19: 'Here is the copy of the letter that had been sent to Onias'), and it ended with a second redactional sentence on the writing and the seal, which no longer appears in the Greek version of 1 Maccabees.

As for the content of that letter, two observations cast a doubt on the authenticity of the document: 1. it is strange that the Spartans, by declaring their kinship with Abraham, could take pride in being Barbarians, and not Greeks;[96] 2. Sparta had only two kings named Areus (or Areios), one in 309–265, and the other dead at the age of eight in 255. Areus I was a contemporary of Onias I, in office about 300 (son of Yaddua; cf. *Ant.* 11.347), which could be suitable, at least in theory, since such a correspondence is difficult to situate in the setting of the struggle of the Diadochoi, or afterwards in the struggles for power around Areus.[97] Nevertheless, in Jonathan's letter, the allusion to Onias concerns the last one with that name, as Josephus clearly understood, Onias III, much later than Areus II. There is therefore a strong

---

96. Which did not stop Homer and Herodotus from acknowledging Egyptian and Phoenician ancestors, but this was exceptional; cf. E.J. Bickerman, 'Origines Gentium', *Classical Philology* 47 (1952), pp. 66-74 and below.

97. E. Will, *Histoire politique du monde hellénistique. I. D'Alexandre à Antiochus III* (Annales de l'Est, 30; Nancy: Publications de l'Université, 1979), p. 214.

presumption that the ancient letter of Areus would be a forgery, since it becomes undatable.[98]

Even if this letter was not from Areus, and is only a forgery intended to justify Jonathan's claim of friendship, one detail shows that it was not without significance. As a matter of fact, Jonathan's letter only tried to renew an ancient friendship. It says (v. 8) that Onias received the envoy of Areus with honour and 'accepted the letter in which a clear reference was made to alliance and friendship (περὶ συμμαχίας καὶ φιλίας)'. The 'letter of Areus' goes much further, by introducing without evident necessity a kinship with Abraham, based on a still earlier document (the third), and by declaring that the flocks (κτήνη) and the possessions of the Jews and the Spartans would be from then on held in common, which would appear to be highly unrealistic, taking into consideration the geographical distance between the Peloponnese and Judaea. Josephus had sensed the implausibility, and rendered it in a more general way: 'We shall consider what is yours as ours [...].' But, since it refers to Abraham, the peace between the flocks of the related owners forms an interesting antithesis to the disputes with Lot of Gen. 13.5-9, and to the complete separation between the posterity of Abraham and that of Lot (Deut. 23.4-6) after both had prospered in Egypt, which gives a certain consistency with the 'earlier account' rediscovered, possibly a fragment of an apocryphal Genesis.[99]

There would be the distinct echo then of a lost story of the origin of the Jews, or more exactly of the posterity of Abraham. But why Sparta? The legend of Cadmus (the Oriental), come from Phoenicia to Egypt to found Thebes, a legend already known to Homer (2.4.388), provides a theme: he sowed the teeth of a serpent, from which there came forth armed men, who were called 'Sowed', Σπαρτοί, a term very close to 'Sparta'.[100] It is therefore possible, in narrative terms, to establish a connection between Cadmus the Phoenician (or the Canaanite, in biblical terms) and Sparta. 'Sparta' could then represent the descendents of the Canaanites. Now, in the account in Genesis, at the time of the conflict between the shepherds of Abraham and those of Lot, it is recalled, without obvious necessity, that 'the Canaanites and the Perizzites were then dwelling in the land' (Gen. 13.7), which also provides a possible

98.   This is the opinion of Bickerman, 'Question d'authenticité', p. 40 n. 35, who observes that the chancellery of Jerusalem followed Greek customs. The name of the messenger, Demoteles, is not an indication of authenticity, since it was the name of a Spartan herald come to announce a victory (cf. Xenophon, *Hellenica* 7.1.32), and just as famous as the soldier from Marathon. Finally, the seal with the eagle and the serpent is more an Oriental than a Greek symbol (Abel, *Maccabées*, p. 224), which hardly authenticates a Spartan origin.

99.   M.S. Ginsburg, 'Sparta and Judaea', *Classical Philology* 29 (1934), pp. 117-22, assumes that the information had reached Areus through Hecataeus of Abdera; historical or not, the comparison is interesting, since the statements of Hecataeus (or of Pseudo-Hecataeus) about the Jews differ noticeably from the biblical accounts; cf. Stern, *Greek and Latin Authors*, pp. 20-23.

100.   Cf. Herodotus, *History* 5.57, and Feldman, *Josephus and Modern Scholarship*, pp. 218.

connection, but it could be asked whether 'Sparta' is thus entirely reduced to a play on words. In any case, this narrative material amply suffices to explain why the letter attributed to Areus[101] says more about this than the letter of Jonathan assumes: it would thus be the vestige of legendary developments in Judaea, among the scribes who compiled 1 Maccabees, in which a *literary* motif is transformed for political ends. It would be interesting in this respect if 'the square script' mentioned by Josephus could refer to the Aramaic alphabet, which appeared in the third century.

Jonathan's letter, whose authenticity is not seriously challenged, does however raise some questions. The context in which it is introduced indicates a renewal of friendship with Rome, Sparta and other places, and therefore gives the impression of very extensive diplomatic overtures, which arise again later, on the occasion of the Roman circular of 140, in the time of the high priest Simon (1 Macc. 15.15-24). There is cited however only a letter to the Spartans, in which it is specified (12.16) that it is these same envoys, Numenios and Antipater, who were given the responsibility, in a unique mission, to bring an oral message of friendship to Rome and the letter to Sparta. That letter is therefore the main document, indeed the only one, in connection with this whole diplomatic activity, and the same question arises, why precisely Sparta?

The content of the letter expresses a discontinuity in the relations with Sparta: Onias in his time received the message of Areus favourably. Then a notable period went by without explicit relations (about thirty years since the deposing of Onias III), and that silence was justified by a concern for discretion on the part of the Jews, since, though there had been hardships, the necessary help had come from Heaven. Finally Jonathan resumed the initiative, but, curiously, he declared it superfluous (12.9): 'We have no need of these, having for encouragement [παράκλησιν[102] ἔξοντες] the holy books in our possession.' If we read

---

101.   Many commentators are inclined to accept the authenticity of the document. See Goldstein, *I Maccabees*, pp. 447-49, who provides a well documented study of parallel examples, in the Hellenistic period, of treaties of fraternity (συμμαχίαι), with or without a genealogical substratum. According to the considerations developed here, this authenticity remains doubtful, but that does not detract in any way from the interest in the document, just the contrary.

102.   Not for the (divine) consolation of the one who is put to the test (cf. παρακαλέσοντα, 2 Macc. 11.32), as suggested by Abel, *Maccabées*, p. 222 (following A. Momigliano, *Prime linee di storia della tradizione maccabaica* [Rome: Foro Italiano, 1930], p. 168), but as encouragement for the struggle, as is implied by the context, therefore equivalent to אמץ (Deut. 3.28, etc.); cf. J.A. Goldstein, *I Maccabees*, p. 453.

closely, this means that such a 'consolation', available for Jonathan, was not for Onias, that is to say that he did not have the 'holy books' at his disposal. Josephus was disturbed by such an assertion,[103] and he put it back in the time of Onias, by making Jonathan say (13.167) that the letter of Areus explaining the relationship was well received, 'although we had no need of such evidence, since our own writings inform us of this [διὰ τὸ πεπιστεῦσθαι]'. Revised in this way, Jonathan's letter becomes absurd, since it implies that the account discovered by Areus says, 'like the holy books', that the Spartans are related to Abraham, which is obviously false. In the original, it was stated on the contrary that the importance of the kinship and/or the renewal of friendship *had become* secondary, since the holy books provided satisfaction in other ways.

Since it was so contrary to all he had tried to demonstrate, Josephus had refused to admit a fact which up to here has only been sensed, but whose major importance must now be emphasized: Onias, as high priest, did not possess the 'holy books', that is to say he did not have the Pentateuch, in which the genealogies were found; or at the very least, he sought other proofs of antiquity than these books, which were perhaps not really 'holy' for him. This fact, while identifying the Jews properly so-called with the group who were bearers of the Law, is going to make it possible to render an account of a whole bundle of minor difficulties left in suspense up to here.

In the first place, on the institutional level, it must be observed that Jonathan's letter is the only passage in 1 Maccabees in which there is any question of the Jewish *gerousia*, whose strange absence during the whole time of the crisis and of the nominations of the high priests we noted, whereas it is expressly mentioned in the charter of Antiochus III as forming part of traditional Jewish institutions. In other words, Jonathan included the *gerousia* in his reorganization, while previously it had been cut off from the Temple and the high priest, especially in the time of Onias. The *gerousia* was on the side of the persecuted Jews (cf. the letter of Antiochus IV, 2 Macc. 11.27). *Gerousia* and holy books were therefore in this way clearly associated. This does not in the least preclude the Temple from having had its own 'Judaean' traditions, but we thus find again that Jason's Hellenization did not directly affect Judaism, and in fact, at the time of the persecutions, there was no question of a destruction of the Law *in Jerusalem*.

103. In the summary (*Ant.* 12.5), he only speaks, in regard to Onias, of φιλία καὶ συμμαχία, omitting any real relationship.

In the second place, the perfection of Onias, which has already been under suspicion above, can now be appreciated in a more balanced way. He was a civil servant tolerated by the Seleucid government, he did not have 'holy books' at his disposal (which did not prevent him in any way from officiating as high priest), and there was always that rumour of Spartan kinship. Two facts can then clarify his real situation. First, at the time of his deposition, he took advantage of the right of asylum at Daphne (2 Macc. 4.33) (therefore of the protection of Apollo and Artemis), in a high place of Seleucid royal cult,[104] which could be considered an indication of Hellenization. On the other hand, his brother Jason, when he definitely had to retreat before Menelaus, took refuge in Egypt, then at Sparta, 'in the hope of finding refuge there in consideration of a common origin' (2 Macc. 5.9). The simplest hypothesis is therefore to admit that Jason and Onias were really Lacedaemonian in origin, or more exactly, since their Lagide connections are certain, that they were Egyptian descendants of Spartan colonists. Moreover, this does not conflict in any way with their having been named or recognized as high priests by the Seleucids: the governor-high priest of Coele-Syria to whom Antiochus III had addressed the Charter of Jerusalem was a former Egyptian general named Ptolemy. Likewise, according to 2 Macc. 6.1, Antiochus IV named an Athenian to rededicate to Zeus the sanctuaries of Jerusalem and Gerizim, and that function greatly resembled an appointment as high priest in the official Seleucid royal cult.

The Spartan qualifications of Jonathan then become intelligible: it was a matter of proclaiming a certain dynastic continuity, while taking into consideration some new facts. As for the legendary allusions in the letter of Areus, they were a secondary development which, owing to the 're-discovered account', gave expression to a good reason why Jerusalem could have tolerated an Egyptian high priest of Spartan origin, this good reason being the legendary kinship.[105] The Seleucid administration realized that the region was difficult and attracted by Egypt, and had to be handled tactfully, since the high priest had not been chosen (nor even proposed) by the *gerousia*, and realized too that the measures instituted by Antiochus III were meant to reunite radically different elements.

104. Bickerman, *Institutions*, p. 152.
105. Hecateus of Abdera (quoted by Diodorus, *Bibliotheca historica* 40.3.2) speaks of an expulsion of foreigners from Egypt on the occasion of a plague; some were expelled to Greece (Danaos and Dadmos), but most to Judaea; it is evidence of a tradition indicating a possible kinship, whether real or not.

It could be objected that these results relating to the origin of Onias and Jason contradict not only the statements of Josephus, which is not an insurmountable objection, but also the high priestly lists on which he based himself. But I have already shown that he himself had produced harmonizations in regard to Eleazar as presented in the Letter of Aristeas. What is more, his hesitancies are revealing (*Ant.* 12.237-38): he stated that Jesus (Joshua) changed his name to Jason, a related Greek form, whereas 2 Maccabees ignores, no doubt correctly, all Hebrew names. Then he artificially connected Menelaus to the high priestly dynasty, so as to retrieve a traditional assertion according to which Simon the Just would have had three sons as high priests. This last assertion however presents chronological problems, as will be seen in Chapter 7, §1. It is important to note here that this tradition goes back earlier than Josephus, and therefore that the high priestly lists which he utilized had already been touched up in order to obscure genealogies considered aberrant, and the least one could conclude from all this is that the reconstitution of a Zadokite dynasty before the crisis remains compromised. Besides, the very name Onias is not Hebrew, but Egyptian and similar to On, which the LXX (cf. Exod. 1.11, etc.) translates '(city of the) Sun'.[106] Its Hebrew equivalent is יוחנן, 'Johanan' (cf. Sir. 50.1), distinct from the transcription חוני of *m. Men.* 13.10. It was therefore natural for an Onias to have built (or restored) in Egypt, with royal authorization (cf. *Ant.* 13.62-80), a temple which had a certain connection with the sun, since the prophecy of Isa. 19.18 spoke of a 'city of the Sun'. This prophecy had announced the conversion of Egypt and the building of an altar to YHWH; it amounted to a reinterpretation.[107]

The Oniad dynasty having thus been set apart from any Zadokite or even Aaronite attachment, we can return to Jonathan, or rather to his father Mattathias. Despite an opening scene showing Mattathias fleeing Jerusalem and taking up arms on seeing the profanation of the cult in Judaea, his real show of resistance took place at Modein itself, the city of

---

106. Frequently found in the MT under the form און; significantly, there is a בית און near בית אל; cf. Josh. 7.3; 1 Sam. 13.5; and elsewhere. Joshua himself was buried in a place linked to the sun, *Timnat Heres* (Judg. 2.9: תמנת חרס), which Rashi understood as תמונת חרס: 'representation of the sun', which could seem a little more acceptable (Josh. 24.30 reads *Timnat Serah*, with a play on words סרח/חרס; cf. Jer. 49.7: נסרחה חכמתם).

107. In Isa. 19.18, the city is called עיר ההרס, 'city of destruction', according to the MT; this very slight modification is a *tiqqun*, since Sym. and the Qumran scroll have עיר החרס, 'city of the Sun', which makes sense. The rabbinic tradition knew of the two variants (*b. Men.* 110a: 'it is the city of the sun, destined to be destroyed'). In complete opposition to the MT, the LXX has πόλις ἀσεδέκ, 'city of Integrity', with a Hebrew word (underlining the fidelity of the translation, real or simulated) which allows for a comparison with Zadok. In Mesopotamia, the sun (*shamash*) is the god of justice. Cf. the data assembled in E. Nodet, 'La Dédicace, les Maccabées et le Messie', *RB* 93 (1986), pp. 350-54.

his ancestors, and in some of the surrounding deserts. At no time in his operations did he go near Jerusalem, but his epic is cut short at the end of a year, according to the chronology provided. He was a person of biblical bearing, compared to Phinehas (cf. Num. 25.7-13), and the poem with which he introduced his testament brings to mind a gallery of biblical portraits, from Abraham to Daniel (1 Macc. 2.51-64), with a useful anachronism in the case of the latter, and a perspective through-out that is reminiscent of the book of Chronicles. In contrast, in the praise of Judas there is no comparison to anybody (3.3-9). Moreover, Mattathias was a priest, and his resistance to apostasy was over a ques-tion that was strictly cultic, whereas Judas, if we prescind from the hero-ic deed of 25th Kislev, fought against actual physical persecutions.

A priest in the biblical references, Mattathias was therefore very differ-ent from Judas. Furthermore, he was from Modein, an outlying place not part of the Judaea reconquered by Judas, but rather in the Samaritan sphere of influence, and his activity was connected more with the 'desert of Samaria' (cf. §6 above). In addition, there was not yet a defin-itive divorce between Jews and Samaritans (2 Macc. 5.22-23), far from it in fact. Finally, if the Sadducees were really the later supporters of the heirs of Mattathias when the direct dynasty died out after John Hyrcanus, it must be observed that, although they were definitely settled in Jerusalem, they had a remarkable religious kinship with the Samaritans, namely over the primacy of Scripture and especially of the Pentateuch. A rabbinic tradition (*m. Mid.* 4.1) attributed the same status to a Samari-tan as to a Sadducee.[108] Faced with all these facts, the simplest thing is to assume that Mattathias was of Samaritan extraction. What follows from this is that the redactional uneasiness of 1 Maccabees over Mat-tathias, with his very brief chronology (he got old in a year) and his vague activities, is understood better: he was only brought into the pic-ture after the installation of the 'abomination of desolation' at Jerusalem, but there is no difficulty in taking him out of this setting, and having him begin his activity from the onset of the persecution of local cults (begin-ning in 175, with the coming of Antiochus IV, or even earlier, under

---

108. Cf. T.A. Caldwell, 'Dositheos Samaritanus', *Kairos* 4 (1962), pp. 105-107; J. Danielou, *Théologie du judéo-christianisme: Histoire des doctrines chrétiennes avant Nicée* (Tournai: Desclée, 1958), pp. 82-85, under the title 'La Gnose samaritano-chrétienne', gives some sources (in particular Justin, a native of Nablus, and Hegesippus, a convert from Judaism) that mention primitive Christian sects having relationships with Jewish or Israelite sects.

Seleucus). In other words, his activity would have been considerably earlier than that of the Jews of Judaea. It is understandable then how 1 Maccabees, whose perspective is strictly Judaean, had to erase this fact, or rather channel it.

With the institutional elements thus to some extent identified, and the symbolic 'raid' of Judas evaluated, we begin to catch sight of what kind of society existed. According to the proposed reconstruction, there would have been three groups in Jerusalem, involved in some way in the Maccabaean epic event, which was a foundation crisis: first, the high priests of varying origins, named or tolerated by the Seleucid government, and opportunists to a greater or lesser extent, for whom Onias constituted a prototype. Secondly, there were the more or less observant Jews repatriated from exile, scattered throughout the Seleucid empire but with a moderate number settled in Jerusalem. Their key figure, in the time of crisis, was Judas Maccabeus, along with the Hasidaeans and the Nehemiah of the second mission (Neh. 13). Finally, there were Israelite priests, without any specific break with their Samaritan origins, who took religious and then civil power in Judaea, whose prototypes were Jonathan and then Simon, sons of Mattathias. Each of these categories had complex internal relationships, with rivalries and ambitions: 2 Maccabees exposes struggles to obtain the priesthood; according to 1 Macc. 7.14, Alcimus was no less an Aaronite than Mattathias and his sons, and so on. The priesthood of Mattathias and the militant Judaism of Judas, who each represented only a part of the corresponding category, are combined in the book of 1 Maccabees for ulterior apologetic reasons, but, schematically, their heirs are really to be connected respectively with the Pharisees and Sadducees. The Jerusalem milieu was therefore complex, and certainly unstable, which explains the royal initiatives, attempting to take advantage of a 'conflict between nobles', as Josephus puts it, but gravely underestimating the Jewish capacity for resistance.

8. *Conclusion: Samaritans, Jews and Priests*

Various problems remain. To sort them out, I begin by gathering together some established points.

1. Judas Maccabeus must be separated from Mattathias and the Hasmonaeans, who are both ignored by 2 Maccabees. He was the champion of Jews living according to the 'model of Nehemiah', and he

organized just about everywhere the struggle against assimilation (cf. Chapter 8, §4). The account of the expedition to the Temple for the restoration of the altar (Dedication) was probably not extraneous to him to begin with, but in 1 Maccabees it was turned into a heroic deed of a founder, followed later by the festal letters placed at the beginning of 2 Maccabees. The account in 1 Maccabees had as its function, among other things, to show that the Hasmonaeans (in the usual sense) were heirs of the Judaism of Judas as well as of the high priesthood. At the beginning of Judas's campaigns, the build-up of the battle of Emmaus as holy war according to the written Law (Deut. 20), on the frontier of Judaea, was an artifice showing that it was he who was going to bring the Law back to the Temple at the end of a sacred reconquest.

2.　There would have been two clearly distinct crises: the first, a very long one, was a Hellenization of the Temple, certainly begun from the time of Onias, that is to say right after the succession to Simon the Just, in connection with the financial difficulties of the Seleucids; there was then no notable reaction from the *gerousia* or Jews in the strict sense. It culminated with the attempt to give Jerusalem the status of *polis*, which coincided with the inauguration of the new royal cult in the Temple, on 25th Kislev 167. The second, much briefer, was a persecution of these same Jews by Menelaus, under Antiochus IV, apparently because they had refused to comply with the new statute promulgated in the whole kingdom, which annulled to a great extent the charter of Antiochus III.

3.　These two crises had different outcomes, corresponding to the two commemorations in *Meg. Ta'an.*, 25th Kislev and 28th Adar: the second was settled initially by Antiochus IV himself, before his death, well before the dismantling of the 'abomination of desolation'. The king at the request of the same Menelaus revoked the measures forbidding the observance of the Law, which brought to an end the official persecutions but not the Jewish distrust of the high priests (Menelaus, Alcimus).

4.　The crisis in regard to cult had a slower outcome. We can assume that, under the date of 25th Kislev, there was a raid on the occasion of the royal sacrifice that took place on the twenty-fifth of each month, magnified later into a foundation event. It was a significant exploit, since that 25th Kislev seems to have corresponded at the same time to the winter solstice and to the date of the first royal sacrifice occurring after the death of Antiochus IV. In any case, Jonathan, son of Mattathias, had to wage war afterwards for a long time and obtained the high priesthood only in 152, or a dozen years later, taking advantage of the weakening of Seleucid power due to internal struggles. This does not imply the absence of high priests, except at the end, that is, well after the death of Judas. Menelaus remained in his position well after 25th Kislev 164, then Alcimus, recognized as an Aaronite by the Hasidaeans, succeeded him. It was only because the succession to the latter was obviously very controversial that Jonathan finally obtained the high priesthood. In other words, there would have been two distinct struggles, one for high priestly power, involving the family of Mattathias; the other for access to the sanctuary, that is, for the freedom of pilgrimages, consisting of the raid by Judas. The two were merged by 1 Maccabees, for which the arrival at the Temple was a political takeover, and for that reason there was a foundational feast called Dedication, commemorating a modest, but significant event. For 2 Maccabees, the only thing that mattered was free access to the sanctuary, whoever the high priest might have been, which was not the same kind of power; moreover, the commemoration was called feast of Booths, which indicated a pilgrimage.

5. The petition of the Samaritans renouncing the Sabbath and the account of a massacre of Jews through a deception on a Sabbath would lead one to suppose that the observance of the Sabbath, whose social and economic implications were very evident (interruption of commerce each week, a Sabbatical Year with no taxes), was one of the reasons for the insubordination of the Jews at the beginning of the second crisis, another being the distribution of forbidden foods, as is indicated by the accounts of the martyrs (2 Macc. 6.18–7.42). The difference between Judaea and Samaria in regard to the magnitude of the crisis was the result too of the fact that the Samaritans were a group only local in extent, whereas the Jews as an *ethnos* were extended throughout the *whole* kingdom of Antiochus IV. Judaea was highly symbolic, and the Jerusalem temple attracted financial resources, but only a minority of Jews was found there.

6. I called attention above (Chapter 1, §5) to the connections of the Hasidaeans, duly identified with the later Essenes, at the same time to Mattathias (1 Macc. 2.42), to Judas Maccabeus (their leader, according to 2 Macc. 14.6) and even to the high priest Alcimus, who represent three remarkably distinct camps. This eclecticism is interesting, particularly since Mattathias permitted armed defence on the Sabbath, but Judas did not, which constituted a major difference, as we have seen. One could try to resolve the contradiction by considering it a difference

in perspective between 1 Maccabees and 2 Maccabees, but it is more important to observe that according to 1 Macc. 7.12 these Hasidaeans were remarkably unacquainted with political intrigue and military matters. Now, a close analysis of 1 Macc. 2.29-41, in which Mattathias allowed defence on the Sabbath when he learned of the massacre of those who had taken refuge in the desert, shows that it was a matter of a passage independent of the account of the Hasidaeans rallying around Mattathias,[109] which follows. These Hasidaeans, who pre-existed the crisis, serve then as a *literary* guarantee for Mattathias and his decision, in the perspective of 1 Maccabees, but it is necessary to separate them from him in order to identify them. Active at Jerusalem and observant, they were close to the 'model of Nehemiah', which was explicitly Babylonian in origin and to which we can connect numerous waves of repatriates, up to Hillel the Elder and after. As for Judas, his connection with the 'model of Nehemiah' is explicit in 2 Macc. 5.27, since it was immediately after the massacre at Jerusalem on a Sabbath that he took to the hills with his companions, and, after observing ritual purity, he then organized the resistance. He was at that time regarded as leader of the Hasidaeans (2 Macc. 14.6), but later they separated from him. In this case again, this connection served as a literary guarantee, since Judas was completely ignored in the official documents cited (1 Macc. 14.27-49; 2 Macc. 11.16-21); this guarantee allowed for importance to be given to the mighty deed of 25th Kislev. The proposed comparison of Judas with the later Pharisees should therefore be qualified: it is the Hasidaeans who were their ancestors, with Judas representing only an armed section of them, a sort of prototype of a Zealot, venerated by 2 Maccabees.

7.   The difference between Judas and Mattathias has become clearer, under the veil of a common armed resistance. The latter has been recognized as an Aaronite, perhaps a Zadokite, with Samaritan connections. But what results from this is a problem relative to the Book of Chronicles, which described a cult installed in Jerusalem, in which the Davidic monarchy and the tribe of Levi (priests and Levites) held sway. Moreover, the interpretation of the line of Joarib and of Mattathias as Zadokites is based solely on the interpretation of the list in 1 Chron. 24.3-31. If it is omitted, it is still possible to compare the Sadducees with Mattathias and the Samaritans, but their name becomes again inexplicable.[110] The difficulty may seem artificial, since Chronicles is commonly

109.   Kampen, *The Hasidaeans*, pp. 209-22.
110.   Cf. M. Simon, 'Les Sadducéens', *DBSup* 10 (1985), cols. 1546-48.

dated to the Persian period or the beginning of the Hellenistic period, without any very definite relationship with the decree of Cyrus, or with the activities of Ezra and Nehemiah (cf. Chapter 8, §1). But Chronicles is to be dated after the 'Law of Moses', which they constantly mention. Jonathan's letter to the Spartans, in which he declared that he had the sacred scriptures at his disposal, which Onias did not have, or did not utilize, shows that the existence or at least the authority of the law of Moses (or of the 'holy books') among the circles directing the Temple could not have gone back a good while before the Maccabaean crisis. Moreover, certain observations of various sorts lead us to give Chronicles a special status and a late origin: a. the New Testament, which is certainly much closer to the Pharisees than the Sadducees, did not know about it.[111] b. The rabbinic tradition, largely Pharisaic in origin, implicitly debated its authority: thus, for example, *m. Sanh.* declared that the wicked king Manasseh would not have a share in the Kingdom of Heaven, even though it was objected (in vain) that according to 2 Chron. 33.13 he had repented.[112] c. On the contrary, the theology of this book, according to which people engendered their own misfortunes by their sins, or by their repentance determined their happiness, is very close to a governing idea of the Sadducees, for whom people were authors of their own destiny, with Providence being only a sort of mirror (*Ant.* 18.16 and parallels). d. The Chronicler endeavoured to show clearly that the Jerusalem temple was the original unique sanctuary of the North and the South together and, except perhaps for 2 Chronicles 13, was not hostile to the people of the North and drew attention favourably to their eventual attraction toward Jerusalem. e. His account begins with Saul and David, and consequently he watered down considerably the Mesopotamian origins of the patriarchs as well as the episodes in Egypt, in order to hold on to the local roots. f. The Chronicler concluded on an optimistic note, by issuing on behalf of Cyrus a general invitation 'to those who form part of all his people' to come to Jerusalem, a unique sanctuary protected by the master of the world at that time, as residents and

111. The references given by Nestlé–Aland (1 Chron. 16.35 cited by Acts 26.17 and 2 Chron. 20.7 cited by Jas 2.23) are concerned with passages which are not exclusively in Chronicles.

112. There are other examples of assertions of the Tannaim and Amoraim which formally contradict Chronicles: for example, in *b. Meg.* 3b-4a, R. Joshua ben Levi states that Joshua fortified Lud and Ono, and it is objected to him (in vain) that according to 1 Chron. 8.12 it was Elpaal who constructed them.

not as pilgrims, which presents a complete contrast with the ostracism of Ezra and Nehemiah. All these features added together induce us to ask whether the book of Chronicles might not have been the foundation document of the Sadducees, since furthermore it justified their name.

8.   The matter of Scripture reintroduces the Samaritans and their priesthood into the debate. The author of 2 Maccabees expressed no hostility towards the Samaritans of Gerizim: he included them (5.22-23) in 'our race', persecuted by Antiochus IV, and treated symmetrically the rededications to Zeus of the temples of Jerusalem and Gerizim. Later, at the time of Nikanor's campaign, Judas and his companions seemed to be safe 'in the neighbourhood of Samaria' (15.1). There comes up in passing an interesting question about the authority at that time of Deuteronomy, which insisted so much on the uniqueness of the 'place chosen' by God, but without ever naming it, outside of allusions to Ebal and Gerizim. In the same way, the text fragments collected around Qumran show the coexistence of palaeo-Hebrew-Samaritan and Aramaic-Jewish writings, and even the rabbinic tradition preserved a precise remembrance of the fidelity of the Samaritans, *at least to that which they observe* (cf. Chapter 7, §5). The legend about the Tobiads made allusions to Samaritan persecutions, but the ideology of the account, not very Jewish and centred on the Jerusalem court (Onias), was very much contrary to the ideology of a Nehemiah or of a Mattathias as well as to that of faithful Samaritans. The definitive religious split must have been much later, and the simplest solution is to look for it in the direction of the expansionism of John Hyrcanus, culminating in the ruin of Gerizim, in 107.

9.   Around 200, Antiochus III had attempted to orient the Jews, dispersed in the empire, towards Jerusalem. These Jews, always defined, to simplify matters, by the 'model of Nehemiah', kept alive the distant memory of a relationship with Judaea, perhaps understood in the sense of a very broad territory, more or less connected to the empires of a David, or even of a Solomon, since the fall of Samaria under Sargon was well before that of Jerusalem under Nebuchadnezzar. The corresponding Judaism had combined these memories with new developments in Babylon where the weekly Sabbath was a major institution. The Gerizim temple existed at this moment (end of the third century), connected to recollections of Israel (Jacob, then Joseph), to the accounts in the Pentateuch and to a priestly legislation, but without appreciable political importance. The reciprocal influence of the two groups must

have been prior to the charter of Antiochus III, which introduced a political separation.

Two problems are directly connected to the proposed analyses: the difficulties relative to the history and identification of the priesthood and the high priesthood, and the question of 'parties' or sects.

These two questions are intrinsically linked, since all the groups have as a reference a sanctuary, real or imaginary, with more or less pronounced analogies. Thus, for example, we have noted the institutional resemblances between the Qumran documents and the Samaritans, sometimes even through texts very remote in time.[113]

An essential element for the Samaritans was the absolute primacy of the priesthood,[114] in conformity with the Pentateuch, in complete contrast with pharisaic and then rabbinical Judaism, which was a lay democracy in which the dominant element was the teaching of tradition by the doctors of the Law. Among the Samaritans, all religious acts went through the priests, and in particular the seven feasts and the calendar. Contrary to what Josephus suggests, there are certainly no grounds for considering the Samaritan high priests as stemming from the Zadokite priests of Jerusalem, but quite the contrary; there were connections between Aaron and the cult in Samaria. Historically, in fact, the origins of the Zadokites are lost. Those origins surely did not involve the deposed dynasty from the time of the Maccabaean crisis, whose last representative, Onias IV, went into exile in Egypt, which more probably means that he returned to the land of his ancestors.

In literary terms, the Zadokites were the descendants of Zadok, high priest in the time of Solomon (1 Kgs 2.35), and himself a descendant of Aaron and Eleazar, according to the presentation in 1 Chron. 6.35-37. However, outside of this reconstruction, which could at best only give backing to Mattathias and his posterity, nothing clearly indicates that the high priestly dynasties of Judaea would have ever been Zadokites, since the priests repatriated with Ezra, to whom these dynasties were connected, were descendants of Phinehas and Ithamar, thus Aaronites but not Zadokites (cf. Ezra 8.2-14). There is a hint of a thesis in the texts: Zadok had been high priest at Jerusalem in the time of Solomon, but had no identifiable Aaronite connection, and it was the book of Chronicles which, while preserving this model, connected him to Aaron,

---

113. Cf. Baillet's short but excellent synthesis, 'Texte samaritain', pp. 363-66.

114. Coggins, *Samaritans and Jews*, p. 157; in agreement with Montgomery, *The Samaritans*, pp. 72, 187.

which made the dynasty of Joarib the first of 24 classes, and so the most worthy. There again, the Chronicler remarkably conforms with Sadducean ideology, which wanted to domicile and legitimize in Judaea elements come from the North; this provides one more argument for the thesis proposed above.

Of course, these interpretations are in conflict with the precepts of Deuteronomy, which gave greater importance to the Levites, and with the so-called reform of Josiah, which established a Deuteronomic cult at Jerusalem. Accordingly, it is very difficult to put an emergence of Deuteronomy before the Exile. Chronicles presents us with another attempt, more royal than high priestly, to domicile in Judaea biblical elements come from the North. Even after the destruction of their temple, the Samaritans still celebrated each year the Passover at Gerizim according to a strictly Deuteronomic rite (which does not necessitate a temple), very different from that prescribed by Chronicles, which Josephus and Philo attested having seen at Jerusalem.

The classical text on the priesthood of the sons of Zadok remains Ezek. 40.46: 'These are the sons of Zadok, those of the sons of Levi who approach YHWH to serve him' in a central sanctuary which resembles Gerizim more than Mount Zion. This definition tried to reconcile everything in eschatological views, but it could not conceal the fact that the allusion to Zadok was necessarily a reference to Jerusalem. In fact, in the Hasmonaean period, the sects of Damascus and Qumran recognized only the priesthood of the sons of Zadok, while at the same time limiting hereditary priestly power over their communities: this is how the *Damascus Document* 10.4-6 even grants the title 'Zadokite' to members who were not priests. The Teacher of Righteousness was a high priest and a son of Zadok, even if his identification is uncertain.[115] That in no way implies a direct relationship between the Essenes (Hasidaeans) and Sadducees. We can on the contrary even imagine a rivalry for the possession of the genuine Zadokite heritage, one extolling a future figure, without a precise genealogy, the other satisfied with a real dynasty, actually claimed to be Zadokite.

All these factors created a confused situation in the Hasmonaean period. The Hasidaeans were taken to be the ancestors of the Pharisees, but the fact that they could be compared to the Samaritans or the Essenes or the Sadducees indicates that the realities were more fluid

115. J. Murphy-O'Connor, 'The Judean Desert', in Kraft and Nickelsburg, *Early Judaism and its Modern Interpreters*, pp. 119-56, and discussion, p. 140.

than the strict classifications of Josephus would imply: for him, they were clear and simple, but he was a witness to a later state of affairs. In particular, his tendency to consider the Essenes as secondary in comparison with the antagonists, Pharisees–Sadducees, is perhaps just a political viewpoint, which did not take into account the real origins of the various tendencies.

This variety in Judaea however should not make us lose sight of the fact that Judaism was Babylonian in origin. In this regard, the exodus of Mattathias and the reconquest by Judas imply that the project of Antiochus III, establishing a centre for a widely scattered *ethnos*, had a moment of success, forming a synthesis between Jews and Judaeans distinct from that between Jews and Samaritans. That moment had existed: it was the period of Simon the Just, whose memory was relatively well preserved by rabbinic tradition, which had deep Babylonian ties. That is the next focus.

Chapter 7

SIMON THE JUST, HILLEL, THE MISHNAH

The rabbinic tradition is considered historically suspect. In any case, it was not very verbose about its own origins. It recognizes customs going back to Moses (הלכה למשה מסיני), which implied that it was not limited to post-biblical jurisprudence, but this fitted in poorly with the historical interpretation of the facts. However, Hillel the Elder, in the time of Herod the Great, was the pivotal figure: it was with him that controversies began to develop, and teaching was built up little by little on the margin of the Bible. Before him, only a few sporadic indications are to be found, always clearly distinct from the biblical text. The extreme importance given to 'oral' traditions, that is to say, non-scriptural ones, constituted an obvious point of comparison with the definition that Josephus gave of the Pharisees, so attached to the customs (νόμιμα) of the Ancients. The aim of this chapter is to consider the traditions in question from the time of the high priest Simon the Just up to their actual appearance in Galilee around 200 CE, in order to compare them with the information gathered up to this point.

Nevertheless, it is a real problem to define clearly the relations of the priesthood with those called the 'Jews', and then with the Pharisees and the rabbinic tradition. Furthermore, some scattered observations have shown that the establishment of high priestly dynasties in the Hellenistic period remained unsettled, since the Zadokite dynasty cannot be found before Mattathias. To establish a context for the appearance of Simon the Just before the Maccabaean crisis, it is advisable as a prologue to make clear what we know and do not know of the high priests of that time.

1. *Chronological Framework*

The relative uncertainties in regard to the high priests ends with the Maccabaean crisis, at least beginning with the elevation of Jonathan to the high priesthood. Before that, even limiting the enquiry to the Hellenistic period, the sources produce information bristling with difficulties.[1]

I present them following the order of reigns:

1. Neh. 12.10-11 gives a list of high priests going from Jeshua, a contemporary of Zerubbabel, to Jaddua, a contemporary of Alexander according to *Ant.* 11.302. According to Neh. 13.28, an uncle of Jaddua was the son-in-law of Sanballat the Horonite, but according to *Ant.* 11.306, this son-in-law would have been Manasseh, brother of Jaddua.

2. Onias I was a son of Jaddua, according to *Ant.* 11.347.[2] If we admit that Jaddua was really a contemporary of Alexander, then it is necessary to bring together this Onias with Areus, king of Sparta (309–265), as is mentioned in 1 Macc. 12.7-8. However, Josephus (12.225) put the episode of Spartan kinship under Onias III, not without probability, as shown in Chapter 7, §7.

3. Simon I the Just, son of Onias I and brother of Eleazar, the contemporary and correspondent of Ptolemy II Philadelphus (283-246), according to *Ant.* 12.43 and the *Letter of Aristeas.*

4. Manasseh, uncle of Simon I, who filled the interim period during the youth of Onias II (*Ant.* 12.157), under Ptolemy III Euergetes (246–221).

5. Onias II, son of Simon I, according to *Ant.* 12.158 a contemporary of Ptolemy III Euergetes, but according to the context of the story of the Tobiads (cf. §§223-24) supposedly a

---

1. It is strange that the recent synthesis of M. Hengel, 'The Political and Social History of Palestine from Alexander to Antiochus III (333–187 BCE)', in Davies and Finkelstein (eds.), *History of Judaism*, II, pp. 35-78, provides, despite its title, no assessment of the institutions of Jerusalem and Judaea nor any list of their principal officials.

2. According to Ps-Hecateus, quoted in *Apion* 1.187, there had been a high priest Hezekiah, a contemporary of Ptolemy I Lagos (301–283), who had left for Egypt with a colony of emigrants, but Josephus ignored him in his account. For a discussion of his identity, in connection with a fourth-century coin found at Beth-Zur and struck in the name of a governor יחזקיה, cf. Loeb, note on *Ant.* 12.9 and Stern, *Greek and Latin Authors*, I, pp. 40-41. It is worth noting incidentally that a Samaritan chronicle speaks of the meeting of Alexander and a Samaritan high priest Hezekiah; cf. C.H.R. Martin, 'Alexander and the High Priest', *Transactions of the Glasgow University Oriental Society* 23 (1969), pp. 102-114.

contemporary of Ptolemy IV Philopator (221–204) and Ptolemy V Epiphanes (204–180).

6. Simon II, a son of Onias II, about whom we know nothing, except that his son was Onias III. Sir. 50.1 mentions a 'Simon son of Onias', who reinforced Jerusalem and the Temple, which habitually leads to him being placed under Antiochus III, around 200, and being identified with Simon the Just.

7. Onias III, son of Simon II, a contemporary of Seleucus IV and Antiochus Epiphanes, around 175.

If we add to these high priests Jason and Menelaus, whom Josephus presented as brothers of Onias III, as well as the high priests who had reigned since the return from exile, as Josephus took them from Ezra–Nehemiah, beginning with Jeshua son of Jozadak, we obtain a total of 15 reigns, before Alcimus and the Hasmonaeans. This number agrees with the synthesis that Josephus provided in *Ant.* 20.231-34, in which he tried hard to show dynastic continuity since Aaron, in accordance with the principle which he repeated in *War* 6.114 and *Apion* 1.30.[3] Such a comprehensive result, for Jerusalem and Judaea, is extremely artificial, as was indicated in Chapter 5, §2. In limiting ourselves nevertheless to the pre-Maccabaean Hellenistic period, the following doubts must be noted:

1. In regard to the synchronism of Jaddua and the dissident Manasseh, son-in-law of Sanballat, there is an uncertainty of a generation between Josephus and Nehemiah. What is more, another Manasseh, son of the same Jaddua already in charge at the end of the Persian period, before 332, had succeeded his nephew Onias I after 246, almost a century after Alexander's conquest. It is possible that there was only one Manasseh, due to the uncertainty of a generation. In any case, such an extension of the time is not plausible.[4]

---

3.   And in conformity with the matrimonial principles established in Lev. 21.7, and repeated in *m. Sanh.* 4.2; cf. E.E. Urbach, 'Class-Status and Leadership in the World of the Palestinian Sages', in *Proceedings of the Israel Academy of Science and Humanity* 2 (1968), pp. 38-74.

4.   Büchler, *Die Oniaden*, p. 41, had already surmised that the introduction of Eleazar into the list by Josephus had confused matters: it would be necessary to understand that Manasseh was the brother of Simon I, and not his uncle. That is more logical, but then this Manasseh, uncle of an Onias, had still more chance of being identified with the dissident brother of Jaddua, father of Onias I.

2. Josephus had nothing to say about Onias II, who served only as an artificial prop for the story of the Tobiads, but we have given reasons for leaving the story, as Josephus spontaneously did, under Onias III, that is to say in fact under Seleucus IV. He had nothing to say either on Simon II, son of that Onias II. As a consequence, especially in the light of the preceding observation, there is a well-founded presumption that the repetitive sequence formed by Onias I, Simon I, Onias II and Simon II was artificially stretched out by papponymy, as a way to have the dynasty go back at least to the time of Alexander.

3. The connections, at least literary, of Onias III and Jason with Egypt and Sparta, discussed in Chapter 6, §5, prove the absence of a genealogical continuity between these high priests and their predecessors. The methods perceptible in the elevations to the high priesthood of Jason, Alcimus and Jonathan, by the Seleucid king, show, at least in 1 Maccabees, that dynastic continuity was not an absolute necessity. In the same way, Josephus did not conceal the fact that the high priestly family of Boethus was of Alexandrian origin (*Ant.* 15.320).

4. The final fact to be kept in mind is the complete absence of an allusion to any high priest in office at the time when Antiochus III granted his charter to Jerusalem. The Temple was badly in need of repair, and the suzerain king to a great extent took charge of its restoration and functioning.

It has long been agreed[5] that Simon the Just, well known in the rabbinic tradition, should be identified with Simon II, and not with Simon I as Josephus wanted, that is to say, he should be considered a contemporary of Antiochus III. In brief, the main arguments are the following:

1. The great deeds of Simon son of Onias, celebrated in Sir. 50.1-23, as already mentioned, especially his reinforcing of the Temple and the city, are to be placed around 200, under

---

5. Cf. G.F. Moore, 'Simeon the Righteous', in G.A. Kohut (ed.), *Jewish Studies in Memory of Israel Abrahams* (New York: Jewish Institute of Religion, 1927), pp. 348-64; G. Hölscher, *Die Hohenpriesterliste bei Josephus und die evangelische Chronologie* (Sitzungsberichte der Heidelberger Akademie der Wissenschaften, 30/3; Heidelberg: Winter, 1940); and the synthesis of R. Marcus, 'Appendix B: The Date of the High Priest Simon the Just (the Righteous)', Loeb, VII, pp. 732-36.

Antiochus III; that reputation justifies the attribution to him of the title 'Just', since there was no mention previous to that of any great person with this name.

2.   The rabbinic sources (*t. Soṭ.* 13.6 and parallels) indicate that it was 'Onias, son of Simon the Just', who left to found a temple in Egypt, which agrees with the version of *War* 1.31-33 and 7.420-36, according to which this enterprise was a consequence of the exodus to Egypt of Onias III.

3.   The prologue of *Pirke Abot*, which will be examined in more detail below, presents Simon the Just as the first of a series of seven generations of transmitters of the Torah, of which the last was represented by Hillel and Shammai, in the time of Herod the Great, and the third by Jose ben Joezer, a contemporary of the high priest Alcimus. A simple rule of three, attributing to each generation 25 to 30 years, again provides a date close to 200 for Simon the Just.

The preceding considerations make it possible however to go further, and simply identify Simon I with Simon II: it was Josephus or his source who, desiring to give some dynastic content to the third century, would have doubled an Onias and a Simon, which, when joined to a just as imaginary Eleazar, and perhaps to the strange Manasseh, provided three or four generations of high priests—that is to say, with the same average duration of generations, approximately the interval that separated Alexander from Antiochus III. A rabbinic legend already cited (*b. Yom.* 69a) relates that it was Simon the Just who, in his splendid priestly vestments, risked coming to meet Alexander in order to head off a Samaritan manoeuvre. It is natural, in making use of the critical period indicated, to replace Alexander by Antiochus III,[6] the only king come from the North who would have in some way given a favourable statutory arrangement. The account, which involved further elements as well, helps therefore to clarify matters, since it brings out the unforeseen return of the king, and the fact that previously the priesthood at Jerusalem was unknown to him. That 'surprise' contains indeed a historical echo, since it is corroborated by the absence of any allusion to the high priest in the Jerusalem charter, and by the fact that the name Onias

6.   Cf. S. Zeitlin, *Ner Ma'arabi*, 1925, pp. 137-41, quoted by Moore, 'Simeon the Righteous', p. 357 and Marcus, 'Appendix B', p. 734; Lichtenstein, 'Fastenrolle', p. 288, places the episode under John Hyrcanus, because of the destruction of the Gerizim temple.

for the father of Simon clearly indicates Egyptian connections (cf. Chapter 7, §7).

It is even possible that the 'temple of Onias', which Josephus had trouble in dating, since he linked it with Onias III (according to *War* 1.32) or with his son (according to *Ant.* 13.62-64), should in reality be connected to the father of Simon the Just. There is some evidence here and there suggesting this: 1. The episode of the completion of the sanctuary 'in conformity with the Law' under the careful and pious protection of Ptolemy and Cleopatra is legendary and poorly situated in time, but it does not disguise the fact that it concerned a pagan temple. 2. The duration of 343 years of this temple, coming to an end at the latest under Domitian (*War* 7.436), is interesting, since it presupposes, if we do not correct this number,[7] an inauguration under Ptolemy II Philadelphus, which would suit perfectly the period of the father of Simon. 3. The LXX of Exod. 1.11, by adding 'On, which is the city of the Sun'; to the store-cities that the Israelites had to construct in Egypt, introduced a polemic on the works done *prior to the gift of the law of Moses*, that is to say before the emergence of the Pentateuch.

Continuity in the high priestly dynasty before the Maccabaean crisis is therefore compromised. More exactly, the available lists split up into two blocks: on the one side a late series, with Onias, of Egyptian origin and culminating around 200 with Simon the Just, and on the other an older series, provided by Nehemiah and taken up by Josephus, from Jeshua to Jaddua. The latter in origin, or at least in allegiance, was Persian and then Seleucid. The synchronism of Jaddua with Alexander, proposed by Josephus, is obviously not very certain, and the examination of this point is deferred to the next chapter, in the setting of a revaluation of the details in Ezra–Nehemiah. Finally, the notion of a Zadokite line can be no more than an illusion, especially if it is necessary as well to connect it to Aaron: Josephus's synthesis is just not usable.

2. *The 'Great Assembly' and Simon the Just*

The rabbinic tradition put Simon the Just at the head of the chain of tradition of distinctive post-biblical teachers. The sequence is given in a

---

7. Commentators have observed that $343 = 7 \times 7 \times 7$ can have a symbolic meaning, in which the number 7 brings to mind the 'week of years' used by Dan. 9.22-27; according to Feldman, *Josephus*, p. 462, it suffices to subtract a hundred years to have a plausible duration.

famous text, the short prologue of the *Pirke Abot*:

(1) Moses received the Torah from Sinai. He handed it on to Joshua, then Joshua to the Elders, then the Elders to the Prophets. These handed it on to the 'Men of the Great Assembly'. They said three things: 'Be deliberate in judgment, raise up many disciples, build a fence around the Torah.'	משה קבל תורה מסיני. ומסרה ליהושע, ויהושע לזקנים, וזקנים לנביאים. ונביאים מסרוה לאנשי כנסה הגדולה. הם אמרו שלשה דברים: הוו מתונים בדין, העמידו תלמידים הרבה, עשׂו סייג לתורה.
(2) Simon the Just was one of the last of the 'Great Assembly'. He said 'The world depends on three things: on the Torah, on the cult and on charity'.	שמעון הצדיק היה משיירי כנסת הגדולה. הוא היה אומר: על שלושה דברים העולם עומד: על התורה, על העבודה ועל גמילות חסדים.
(3) Antigonus of Socho received from Simon the Just. He said [...]	אנטיגנוס איש סוכו קבל משמעון הצדיק. הוא היה אומר [...]

After this beginning, each generation is then represented by one or two teachers, inheriting from their predecessors up to Hillel and Shammai. Unlike the persons of the biblical period, from Moses to the prophets, there is attributed to each of them one or more maxims. At the juncture of the two series there appears a poorly defined entity, unknown to Josephus and called the 'Men of the Great Assembly'.

Before considering this important link in the chain, let us complete the examination of Simon the Just. There is no direct indication of his priestly rank. At most we can infer from his sayings that he was favourable to the Temple cult. Other rabbinical sources however knew of his high priestly function. They never stated that he was a high priest, but they mentioned activities characteristic of the high priest: he entered the Holy of Holies on the day of Atonement (*t. Soṭ.* 13.5-6), he sacrificed the red heifer (*m. Par.* 3.5[8]; cf. Num. 19.1-10), and so on.

Simon the Just was furthermore the only person in the prologue who had a priestly function and pronounced a maxim having to do with cult. The teachers of the tradition, the guardians of the Torah, were therefore all members of the laity with ordinary ancestry, and no pedigreed priest is mentioned, contrary to the constant declarations of the Bible, which in

---

8.   According to the majority opinion, which was reflected in the source used by Josephus when he dealt with the subject (cf. *Ant.* 4.81), the *first* two red heifers after Moses and Ezra were attributed to Simon the Just, which definitely suggests that the ritual only appeared in Judaism at that moment (whether in literary terms or historically).

various places designated the levitical priests as teachers of the Law.[9] These facts give rise to several observations on the supporters and successors of Simon. His succession in the list is not priestly: there is no trace of Onias or of the Hasmonaeans (in the broad sense, including the descendants of Mattathias), and this last feature fits in the Hebrew title of 1 Maccabees according to the rabbinic tradition, *Book of the Dynasty of God's Resisters*.[10] Such a title may indicate a violent opposition to the Hasmonaeans, and perhaps as well to the Zealot model represented by Judas Maccabeus (cf. Chapter 2, §4). On the other hand, many of the successors of Simon are referred to by their place of origin, just about anywhere in Judaea or elsewhere; one of them, Jose ben Johanan, was even from Jerusalem, and was therefore an exception. This diffuse sociology corresponded to what was glimpsed in 1–2 Maccabees, at the time of the Hellenization of the cult: it was especially outside Jerusalem that Judaism was persecuted, and the scrolls of the Law torn up; and as we saw the feast of Booths had some connection with wandering, represented by the scattered huts. It was at Modein that Mattathias took to the hills, and Judas was never really at Jerusalem.

Just as he did not have any posterity, Simon the Just had neither an identifiable genealogy nor a previous history in the *Pirke Abot*, whose words are carefully weighed. Furthermore, going back earlier in it than the 'Great Assembly', there is an absence of David and Solomon, and thus of the monarchy and the *first* Temple; then, there is the merging together into a single unit of all the prophets,[11] before and after the exile.

9. At least Lev. 10.8-11; Deut. 31.9-13; Ezek. 7.26; Hag. 2.11; 2 Chron. 15.3; Ezra 7.1-6. In regard to the authority established to deal with new cases, Deut. 17.9 introduces 'the levitical priests and the judge'; LXX (A) renders it as πρὸς τοὺς ἱερεῖς τοὺς Λευίτας καὶ πρὸς τὸν κριτήν, but (B) jumps from πρός to πρός, indicating only the judge, which is not necessarily an accidental omission.

10. Origen mentions the name σαρβηθσαρβανεελ (Eusebius, *Historia ecclesiastica* 6.25.2). Among the many interpretations that have been proposed (cf. J.A. Goldstein, *I Maccabees*, p. 21), the one most in conformity with the rabbinic tradition is to restore at the beginning σφαρ, from which we get ספר בית סרבני אל; *sarbaney*, 'objectors', is explained as 'resisters to God' (and not 'God's resisters') in *y. Ta'an.* 4.5; cf. Geiger, *Urschrift*, pp. 204-205 and D. Hoffman, 'Sarbane El', *MGWJ* 15 (1988), pp. 179-80. M. Avi-Yonah, 'The Caesarean Inscription of the 24 Priestly Courses', *Eretz Israel* 7 (1964), pp. 24-28, has shown that the addition of מרום מסרבי, 'rejecting heaven', to the name of Yehoyarib in the priestly lists collected in Palestine is very derogatory.

11. A scholion restores a missing link: 'Haggai, Zechariah and Malachi received [it] from the prophets and the "Men of the Great Assembly" received [it]

There is an absence too of the generation that returned from the exile, with Zerubbabel and Jeshua, and with them the foundation of what is conventionally called the second Temple. Read carefully, this literally means clearly that the Torah and the Prophets reached the genuine Temple, that is to say one that was valid in the rabbinic sense, only with Simon the Just. This inference would be somewhat far-fetched if it did not converge with the antecedents glimpsed of the Maccabaean crisis, and with the correspondence of Jonathan with Sparta (cf. Chapter 6, §7), which emphasized a new relationship between the high priest-ethnarch and the holy Books.

This should not come as a surprise: the rabbinic tradition did not set a high value on the Hasmonaeans or on Herod and gave absolute primacy to the teachers and to the Torah, as studied and practiced, and it must really be considered remarkable that a high priest would have found favour in their eyes. This occurred in an exceptional circumstance, which fitted in well with the situation created by the charter of Antiochus III: there would have been a scattered observant Jewish population, focused on Mesopotamia and the promotion of a Judaean cultic centre at Jerusalem, where Egyptian domination had been eliminated shortly before. The king endorsed the *gerousia* and the Temple, badly-matched entities, just as the Jews were with the Judaeans, and in circumstances of which we are unaware there happened to be a personality as high priest who was capable of momentarily blending all this together. This was Simon the Just. The idyllic and unstable vision which 2 Macc. 3.1-3 suggested in regard to the reign of Onias is suspect for that high priest, as I have shown, but it could have preserved a more or less embellished and simplified echo of the success of Simon the Just, heralded by Sirach 50. In a significant way, a legend (*t. Soṭ.* 13.6[12]) relates that he had had certain revelations in the Holy of Holies, and specifies that he had heard them *in Aramaic*, that is to say, in the language of Syria, as if it were not something obvious. That amounts to declaring that even if Simon had Egyptian origins, as a son of Onias, there was no problem about any attempt at Hellenizing the cult, whether it would be Seleucid or Lagide

---

from Haggai, Zechariah and Malachi [...]' (*ARN*, A-B, p. 1b).

12.   Developed in *Meg. Ta'an.* (22 Shebat). The revelation announced the end of an abomination in the Temple, which the context connects with the incident involving the statue of Caligula; this affair came to an end with his death in 41 CE, which cannot fit in with Simon the Just. This anomaly in the legend brings out the importance of the latter; cf. Lieberman, *Tosefta kifshuṭah*, VIII, pp. 739-40.

in origin. The *Letter of Aristeas* shows however that the reality was certainly somewhat different.

As for the 'Great Assembly', which appeared between the biblical period and Simon the Just, it is in no way clearly defined, and any idea that we can get in regard to it is at best partial and fragile, since it is very much dependent on other considerations. I will attempt to identify it by discussing the recent synthesis of Louis Finkelstein, which he presents after numerous publications on this subject.[13] According to him, there was a tribunal,[14] created by Ezra and Nehemiah to counterbalance the court (*gerousia*) dominated by the priests and the aristocracy. Although it possessed the Mosaic traditions, it did not have a monopoly on them, but its authority was supreme and corresponded to the authority foreseen in Deut. 17.8-13. Outside the rabbinic sources, the expression 'Great Assembly' is met just once, in 1 Macc. 14.28 (συναγωγὴ μεγάλη), in the decree installing Simon and the Hasmonaeans as high priests and ethnarchs. This document was issued by 'the Great Assembly of priests and people, princes of the nation and elders of the country'. It is clear that it was a major official act involving the entire nation.

Formally, it could be admitted in support of this thesis that, with Simon the Just being 'among the last' in the 'Great Assembly', and not 'the last', it would have lived on after him. Furthermore, in the Greek *polis* as at Rome,[15] the community of citizens was the ultimate source of all legitimacy, which agrees with the decree on Simon. However, it is difficult to conclude that the entity recalled here would be a permanent formal *tribunal*, supreme in juridical domains.

1. There is no trace of it in Josephus, even though he was spontaneously pro-Hasmonaean and would not have had reason to be silent about the 'Great Assembly' recalled in 1 Maccabees.

2. Symmetrically, the rabbinic tradition is anti-Hasmonaean, and it does not stand to reason that the same body would have been a supreme authority for the aforementioned tradition and at the same time at the origin of the suspect dynasty.

3. The term 'synagogue' regularly renders in the LXX the idea of

13.   L. Finkelstein, 'The Men of the Great Synagogue (circa 400–170 BCE)', in Davies and Finkelstein (eds), *History of Judaism*, II, pp. 229-44.

14.   This is the traditional Jewish opinion, which would see in it a sort of Sanhedrin; cf. Moore, *Judaism*, I, pp. 31-32.

15.   Cf. V.A. Tcherikover, 'Was Jerusalem a Greek Polis under the Procurators?', *Eretz Israel* 1 (1951), pp. 94-101.

people being assembled (קהל, עדה), and not a particular juridical institution.

4. A rabbinical saying (*ARN* A) declared that an assembly called
together in the name of heaven will survive (for example, the 'Men of
the Great Assembly),[16] and that an assembly called together for another
motive will not survive (for example, the generation of the Tower of
Babel). The comparison shows clearly that it concerned all the people,
and this persists throughout its traditions.

5. As for the creation of this authority by Nehemiah,[17] while it is
true that he had to struggle against the abuses of the priests and leaders
of the people (cf. Neh. 5.7; 13.11), it is in no way proved that the latter
would be the ancestors of the *gerousia* restored by Antiochus III, nor is
it indicated to any greater extent that he created a tribunal properly so-
called: according to Neh. 8.1, it was 'all the people gathered together as
one man' who heard the Law, and in the final written agreement were
found 'our leaders, our Levites, our priests [...] and the rest of the
people [...]' (10.1 and 29); likewise, it was in a very unaffected way that
y. Ber. 1.6, indicated that the assembly participating in that ceremony
was none other than the 'Men of the Great Assembly', and these were
still the ones who received the blessing of Neh. 9.5-37.[18]

6. Besides that, no rabbinic legend selected any of the individual
companions of Ezra and Nehemiah as members of the 'Great Assembly', or reported edifying facts in regard to them.

What appears therefore is not a specialized tribunal, but all the people
(redefined as separate from 'the people of the land'; cf. below), as a
source of legitimacy in important matters. Its juridical authority, that is
to say, its Mosaic filiation, cannot be contested. To the 'Great Assembly'

---

16. A corrupted text; other versions have: 'for example the assembly (כנסת) of
Israel before Mount Sinai'; this correction came from copyists who saw in the 'Great
Assembly' a tribunal, which gave rise to a problem, since it no longer existed.
Finkelstein, 'The Men', p. 233 gets round the difficulty by supposing that the saying
went back to a contemporary of this tribunal, therefore to a time when it was still
existing, but this cannot be demonstrated, and is very doubtful.

17. There is mention at times of 'Ezra and his companions'; cf. *Lev. R.*, 2.11;
Ezra is identified with Malachi (מלאכי 'my messenger') in *S. 'Ol. R.*, 74a.

18. Cf. also *Gen. R.*, 6.5, p. 45; *y. Ber.*, 7.3, p. 11c: 'Why were they called
"Men of the Great Assembly"? Because they restored the Greatness', that is to say,
the invocation to God in the prayer as 'great', just as Moses had established it (cf.
Neh. 8.6). It follows from this in particular that 'great' did not necessarily mean
'numerous'.

were attributed acts of major importance,[19] that no later tribunal could undo:[20] redaction of certain biblical writings and fixing the canon of the Prophets,[21] establishing the main prayers of the Synagogue, definition of the World to Come and who will be excluded from it[22] (*b. Sanh.* 104b).

Because of a lack of decisive elements to add to the documents, the modern discussions on the exact composition and the functioning of this authority have wavered among various solutions, going from pure literary fiction to a formal permanent existence, in passing by various formulas for occasional conventions, until Bickerman completely changed the question[23] by pointing out that it was never a question of the 'Great Assembly' as such, but always of the 'Men of the Great Assembly'. The difference is basic: we do not have to look for a synodal institution, but, as the various uses of the phrase 'the men of' (אנשי) indicate, it was the concern of a whole generation. This explains why they could make this authority and the generation of the tower of Babel parallel.

Other Tannaitic traditions expressed the same idea: for example, a teacher declared (*Midr. Ps.* on 38.8) that two generations had pronounced (licitly) the sacred name of God, namely, the 'Men of the Great Assembly' and the generation persecuted under Hadrian. Another saying (*Gen. R.* 35.2) on the divine promise no longer to punish

---

19.   L. Finkelstein, 'The Maxims of the *Anshe Keneset Ha-Gedolah*', *JBL* 59 (1940), pp. 465-69.

20.   The classical case is given in *b. Meg.* 2a: the feast of Purim had been instituted by the 'Great Assembly', and no other tribunal, even the great Sanhedrin, could take back its decrees.

21.   *b. B. Bat.* 15a: 'the "Men of the great Assembly" compiled Ezekiel, the Twelve, Daniel and Esther', which suggests, according to Rashi, that we should include with them Haggai, Zechariah, Malachi, Zerubbabel, Mardochai; this amounts to giving to this entity a great extension in time (and space).

22.   Seven biblical personnages were excluded, for having led others into sin; among those was listed Manasseh, king of Judah, whereas according to 2 Chron. 33.12-20 he had repented. On the other hand neither Antiochus nor Jason were mentioned, and Finkelstein, 'The Men', pp. 241-43, would want to conclude that the list had been established earlier, at a time when Chronicles had not yet been completed. However, we must not lose sight of the fact on the one hand that the rabbinic tradition ignored Judas Maccabeus, and had therefore nothing to say against Antiochus, and on the other hand that it did not share at all the royal and levitical ideology of Chronicles, as we see too in the interpretation given to Deut. 17.8-13 by a *baraita* (*b. Sanh.* 87a and parallels), which limited the authority of the central tribunal, contradicting 2 Chron. 19.5-7, which extended its competence in all domains.

23.   E.J. Bickerman, 'Viri magnae congregationis', *RB* 55 (1948), pp. 397-402.

depraved generations by water, states that two generations would not have needed the sign of the Covenant (the rainbow): that of Hezekiah and that of the 'Men of the Great Assembly'. Still another passage, attributed to Jose ben Ḥanina (end of the first century) and commenting on the list in Ezra 2.1 of those repatriated, referred to them, according to two parallel recensions, either on the one hand as 'exiles' (גולה בני) or 'those returned from exile' (עולי הגולה), or on the other as 'Men of the Great Assembly' (*Gen. R.* 71.3). Now, according to the figures provided (Ezra 2), they were several thousands.

This identification opens the way to understanding a paradox: on the one hand, there was an authority issuing legitimate decrees, and, on the other, the same entity was identified with a whole generation, which could seem to be a considerable crowd. By bringing the two together, we obtain a whole generation of *the repatriates* gathered together in a founding assembly, in short a small number from among the exiles, a fortiori from among the Israelites in general. A tradition (*y. Meg.* 1.5) describing this assembly explained that it was composed of 85 Elders, plus[24] over 30 prophets. According to another version, (*b. Meg.* 17b), it was a matter of 'one hundred and twenty, of whom some were prophets'. The 85 corresponds to the list of those signing the agreement of Neh. 10.1-28, and the total of 120 corresponds to the minimum adult male population so that a locality could be considered a city (an organized one) and not a simple village (collection of dwellings).[25]

The 'Great Assembly' thus acquires a configuration already identified from another angle: it is something like the 'city of Nehemiah', that is to say, in this particular case, a restored Jerusalem (or the quarter), which he had some trouble to repopulate. In such circumstances, the maxims attributed to these people by the prologue of *Pirke Abot* take on a new depth, not without a historical echo: 'to make many disciples' corresponds to the concern of Nehemiah to build up his little community; 'to build a fence around the Torah'[26] corresponds to the principle of separation (from the 'peoples of the land'), with the rampart, the control of

24.   By correcting ומהם 'of which' to ועמהם 'and with them'; cf. J. Dérenbourg, *Essai sur l'histoire et la géographie de la Palestine* (2 vols.; Paris: Impr. Impériale, 1867), I.35, n. 1.

25.   *m. Meg.* 1.6; the reason given is that in 120 there will be found ten men available (בטלנים 'idle') to form the *minyan* for the synagogue. This number 120 was characteristic of the founding community of Acts 1.15 as well.

26.   Understood in this way in the rabbinic tradition: establish rules (*halacha*) which ward off transgressions, and thus protect the Torah; cf. *m. Ber.* 1.1, and elsewhere and Moore, *Judaism*, I, p. 33.

the gates and the repudiation of foreign women. Of course, the assembly is only 'great' because of its importance in the tradition, since even the Sanhedrin could not undo its work.

If these 'Men of the Great Assembly' simply formed a constituent community, there remain certain questions to be more specific about, in regard to time and place. we look first at the social context of the time of Antiochus III: the Jews, numerous in Babylon, are scattered elsewhere, in particular in Judaea, and the king wanted to give (or restore) a privilege to the community of Jerusalem, in connection with the Temple, where the Pentateuch had not yet arrived (but some of the Prophets and Judaean chronicles were perhaps available). The library of Nehemiah was therefore already existing at the time when Simon the Just carried out his task within the framework of the charter. Incidentally, in regard to chronology, the rabbinic tradition makes some suggestive short cuts: only 52 years were allocated between Cyrus and Alexander by the *Seder Olam*, and what is more it was Simon the Just who had received Alexander. In other words, after Zerubbabel, there was no difficulty in understanding Nehemiah and his 'Great Assembly' as comprising only one generation before Simon the Just. According to a *baraita* intended to set the legal dates, the duration of the various reigns that followed one another during the period of the Second Temple are specified (*b. 'Abod. Zar.* 9a): 'The kingdom of Persia in front of the Temple 34 years, the kingdom of Greece [...] 180 years, the kingdom of the Hasmonaeans [...] 103 years, the kingdom of the House of Herod 103 years; then we should count the years after the ruin of the Temple.' We thus obtain a total of 420 years for the Second Temple period. Of course, none of these numbers exactly agrees with the durations provided by the historians, but they provide the order of comparative length, with the exception of the first: according to these numbers, the coming of the Greek kingdom would have been in 316 BCE, and the whole Persian period 'in front of the Temple' would have begun in 350, which drastically compressed the whole period from Cyrus to Darius III. In both these cases, the time is in some way reduced to a length useful for providing a space for the information available. We see moreover in contrast with this that Josephus, who was not really better informed on the Judaism that existed before Antiochus III, but who tried hard to adhere to a more objective chronology, had some difficulties in stretching over three centuries the salient events. All things considered, the prologue of *Pirke Abot* constitutes, even in its staidness, a perfectly usable historical source.

The conclusion is self-evident: the 'Men of the Great Assembly' constituted the founding generation, which can without any difficulty be connected to Nehemiah, as founder of the sacred library. Chronologically, this whole development would have to have taken place, not in the Persian period, but in the second half of the third century; this presents a problem, since at that time Judaea was under Lagide domination. I examine in Chapter 8, §4, whether it is possible to interpret the adversaries of Nehemiah and the Jews, though provided with a 'Persian' firman, as owing allegiance to Egypt.

Several related questions still remain to be resolved: first, what was the relationship of this founding group to Scripture, since it professed opinions distinct from what we read in the Pentateuch? Then, what connections did it have with other groups, Israelite or Judaean, since the 'model of Nehemiah' was based on separation and since especially its relations with the Temple were obviously ambiguous. In particular, finally, if these 'Men of the Great Assembly' represented at least in the beginning a group so small and so intense, therefore a tiny minority of the Jews in general, it is hard not to attempt a comparison with the other small and very intense group, the Hasidaeans, who already before the Maccabaean crisis had great moral weight.

3. *The Oral Tradition*

In rabbinic culture, as among the Pharisees of Josephus, the oral tradition, as distinct from, and not reducible to, the Bible, played a major role. Josephus, who was not a Pharisee, at first had a vague perception of them: in the account in *War* 2.162, he merely said that they were 'considered exact interpreters [δοκοῦντες ἐξηγεῖσθαι] of the laws'. According to this definition, their traditions therefore were a sort of jurisprudence surrounding the Scriptures. Later, his knowledge became more precise and, in *Ant.* 13.297, he identified the Pharisees as 'having introduced among the people many customs [νομιμά] which they had received from the Elders [ἐκ πατέρων διαδοχῆς], but which were not inscribed in the laws of Moses, and which for this reason the Sadducees rejected'. These customs were not a supplementary jurisprudence,[27] as was for example the decision of Mattathias to fight on the Sabbath (*Ant.* 12.275-77; cf. Chapter 2), but of legislative elements independent of what was written, and even at times contrary to it.[28] Moreover, it has long been recognized that the Sadducees were not narrow fundamentalists, but that they had interpretations to fill the gaps in the

27.   Although that element counted, since the teachers of one generation could legislate, even against a 'voice from heaven' (בת קול), and since the decisions are reversible; cf. *b. B. Meṣ.* 59b and H. Maccoby, *Early Rabbinic Writings* (Cambridge Commentaries on Writings, 3; Garden City, NY: Doubleday, 1988), pp. 4-7.

28.   Cf. the texts gathered together by P. Lenhardt and M. Collin, *La Torah orale des pharisiens* (Cahiers Evangile, 73; Paris: Cerf, 1990).

writings,[29] and we can understand in this sense Josephus's observation according to which 'to dispute with the teachers of the wisdom which they follow is reckoned in their eyes as a virtue' (*Ant.* 18.16). In other words, the tradition was only valid for them when compared with Scripture.

How then could a tradition *independent* of Scripture have arisen? The example of Christianity does not enlighten us on this point, since the whole literary effort of the New Testament, and then of patristic exegesis, consisted of showing that Scripture had spoken of Jesus from the beginnings. The Pharisees, at least before the great attempt at a synthesis of Aqiba (and his predecessors), do not mention any comparable event.[30] The sources provide some evidence that the oral was prior to the written, not only logically and pedagogically (since the written cannot designate itself[31]), but chronologically as well. A passage cited above attributed to the 'Men of the Great Assembly' the redaction of some of the biblical books. According to a text studied in Chapter 5, §4, the Pentateuch had been given to Israel in Hebrew script, and it was Ezra who had rewritten it in Aramaic characters. This hints at a reappropriation of a pre-existent text, still in the time of the same assembly. We can even bring up again the ceremony of Nehemiah 8, in which the solemn reading of the Law seemed to be something very new, facing a group already clearly identified. All this authority *over* the written text implies in fact a minimum of cohesion apart from the text. This is precisely what was implied by the 'tradition of the Elders'.

An interesting passage of the Mishnah gives a definition of the extension of the Torah (*m. Ḥag.* 1.8):

---

29. Since Geiger, *Urschrift*, pp. 133-36 (cf. *Meg. Ta'an.*, scholion for 4th Tammuz, in which the abolition of a 'book of the decrees' of the Sadducees is celebrated).

30. In a polemical passage with very technical vocabulary (Mt. 15.1-11), Jesus contrasted the commandments of God (written) with the ancestral tradition of the Pharisees (παράδοσις τῶν πρεσβυτέρων), which he called purely human. He is however close to the Pharisees (resurrection, synagogue).

31. A celebrated anecdote (*b. Šab.* 31a) tells of a pagan who came looking for Hillel to ask him to convert him, but by teaching him only the written Torah; Hillel did not argue with him, but taught him the alphabet in the usual order. The next day, he again taught him the alphabet, but in the inverse order. When the pagan protested, Hillel replied: 'You believed me then! Rely on me likewise in regard to the oral Torah.'

The *halakhot* [practical rules] for prayer[32] float [פורחים] in the air and have nothing to which they can attach themselves; the *halakhot* on the Sabbath, the pilgrimage sacrifices, and the sacrileges are like mountains hanging by a hair, since there is little Scripture and much *halakhot*; as for civil suits, the service in the Temple, things clean and unclean, and pro-hibited marriages, they have something on which to depend. All these categories[33] are the great domains of the Torah [גופי תורה].

This list is remarkable for more than one reason: first of all, it placed the matters most foreign to the Bible first, which expresses clearly the fact that the *halakha* alone mattered, whether it had a scriptural foun-dation or not. Next, the organization of the list of items is significant: whatever concerned daily life far from the sanctuary came first, and the *non-scriptural* singularity of the Sabbath was accentuated, as observed in Chapter 2, §4. These elements integrated perfectly into the 'model of Nehemiah', a protected community, separated from the Temple, about which it dreamed.

The Tosefta on this passage ignores the first category[34] (which 'floats in the air') and presents the other two a little differently: the domains for which there is little of the written and much of the *halakha* 'have *nobody on whom* to lean', whereas those which have much *halakha* and a good scriptural base are a product of exegesis (מדרש) and have for this reason '*something on whom* to lean'. Consequently, the precepts deduced from Scripture proceed from human acts of interpretation, and not from Scripture itself. On the contrary, whatever is not deduced is not attributable to anyone, and a maxim is cited: 'A pincer is made with another pincer. Who made the

---

32.   In the synagogue; the text has התר נדרים, 'absolution of vows', which presents a difficulty, since vows are dealt with in Num. 6.21, etc., as *b. Ḥag.* ob-serves, which makes it necessary to restrict the question to the limited problem of the competence of teachers to release from vows. On the contrary, by putting εὐχή 'vow, prayer' (perhaps under the form אבכי) under התר נדרים, we can see the nu-merous prayers and blessings, a considerable area, which really had no scriptural base (but which *Ant.* 4.212 was not afraid to attribute to Moses).

33.   In understanding הן והן (literally 'the ones and the others') with *b. Ḥag.* 11b; the manuscripts of the Mishnah and *y. Ḥag.* 2.7, have הן הן (literally: 'these', that is the last category), which may imply (but not necessarily) that the real *halakha* is that which has a scriptural foundation, which causes difficulty; cf. Lieberman, *Tosefta kifshuṭah*, III, p. 470.

34.   The list then begins with the Sabbath, and for that reason the passage appears also at the end of *t. 'Erub.*, which deals, without any scriptural support, with the extension of the private domain of the Sabbath to a public courtyard, or even to a completely closed quarter, which too can fit into the 'model of Nehemiah'; cf. Chapter 2, §1.

first? Was it not created?' This indirect allusion to the Creation, at the moment when one would have expected a commentary declaring that the Torah which was purely oral had been given too by Moses,[35] is an indication again of the chronological priority, in matters of usages and customs, of the oral over the written.

It is clear that the preceding considerations were not an attempt to demonstrate that the whole collection of rabbinic traditions went back as such to the pre-Maccabaean period, but only to show that they preserved a very lively remembrance of the priority of the oral. This contributes towards clarifying the contours of the 'Great Assembly': this entity had at its disposition earlier traditions. As for the origin of the latter, it is certainly necessary to look for them in Babylon: 1. The massive testimony of the books of Ezra–Nehemiah, even if their dating is doubtful, situates there the origin of all the tendencies contributing to the creation of Judaism. 2. The books edited by the 'Great Assembly' are, apart from the Minor Prophets (because of its last three), Ezekiel, Daniel, Esther, that is to say, those which embody explicitly Babylonian elements (*b. B. Bat.* 15a). 3. The Aramaic alphabet utilized is an intruder in Judaea; 4. the Babylonian story of Asineus and Anileus (*Ant.* 18.310-79), studied in Chapter 2, §2, shows the permanence, long after the Maccabaean crisis, of non-Scriptural customs relative to the Sabbath.

Furthermore, if the written and the oral are found together, the question necessarily comes up of knowing in practice how to deal in an authorized way with new situations, that is to say, in what way to interpret them, whether this would be for passing events or for creating a jurisprudence. To begin with, it must be observed that the first clear distinction between written Torah and oral Torah was connected to Hillel and Shammai in the time of Herod (*b. Šab.* 31a). Although late, this was the epoch in which the rabbinic tradition got the internal controversies started, and we may ask whether in the prologue of *Pirke Abot*, the term Torah ('teaching') did not principally refer to the oral, a place par excellence for teaching. The controversy did not necessarily imply blocks of opposing traditions, but rather a certain creativity: new things were said and taught, and the problem was to verify which ones were not arbitrary. Tradition was acquainted with all kinds of principles and several systems of rules of interpretation, of which the oldest (and the most brief) was attributed precisely to this same Hillel the Elder.

35.   This is the common opinion; cf. W. Bacher, *Die exegetische Terminologie der jüdischen Traditionsliteratur* (2 vols.; Leipzig: Hinrichs, 1899), I.89, and Urbach, *The Sages*, pp. 298-300.

Now, the latter, who had a pivotal role, was Babylonian. For lack of older definite elements on the oral traditions in contact with Mesopotamia, we will now consider some of the evidence in regard to him.

4. *Hillel the Elder and the Passover*

The accounts of the accession of Hillel to the rank of patriarch (נשיא) are composite, and are found under several forms. I begin with the most synthetic[36] (*t. Pasha* 4.13-14).

> A. One time the 14th Nisan, the eve of the Passover, fell on the Sabbath. They asked Hillel the Elder: 'Does the paschal sacrifice [פסח] prevail over the Sabbath?'

[The question came up since the immolation involved preparations and activities prohibited on the Sabbath. In his reply Hillel did his best to prove that the Passover prevailed, by means of various arguments using the rules of interpretation, and then he concluded]:

> 'Furthermore, I received from my teachers the tradition that the paschal sacrifice prevails over the Sabbath, and not only in the case of the first Passover, but also of the second, and not only the sacrifice of the community, but also the individual sacrifice.'
> B. They said to him: 'What will the rule be for those who would not have brought their knife and the paschal lamb to the sanctuary?'
> He said to them: 'Leave them alone. The Holy Spirit is over them. If they are not prophets, they are sons of prophets [בני נביאים].'
> What did Israel do at that moment? Those whose sacrifice was a lamb concealed [the knife] in the wool. If it was a kid, they attached it between the horns. In this way they brought the knives and the victims to the sanctuary and they immolated the sacrifices.
> C. That same day they named Hillel patriarch, and he taught them the precepts of the Passover.

This passage presents complex problems. To begin with, it is astonishing that they seemed to be ignorant of what happened when 14th Nisan fell on a Saturday, since that concurrence should have happened on average one year in seven in a lunar calendar, and since in the end the people knew what to do, just like the teachers of Hillel. Furthermore, the corresponding passage of the Mishnah (*m. Pes.* 6.1) expressly specified, in the case of the whole sacrificial activity of the Passover, the

---

36.   We follow the literary divisions (but not the conclusions) proposed by J. Neusner, *Le Judaïsme à l'aube du christianisme* (Paris: Cerf, 1986), pp. 113-15; cf. *idem*, *The Tosefta: Second Division, Moed* (New York: Ktav, 1981), pp. 136-37.

actions that could be done in spite of the Sabbath and those that the Sabbath prohibited. This presents a problem then at least in regard to the nature of the Mishnah in the time of Hillel, and in a related way a problem about the calendar, as well as a question about the identity (with respect to 'Israel') of the assembly who questioned Hillel and then appointed him as a patriarch. Next, an important divergence should be noted between the initial question about the Passover, which was a very general one (A), and the new formulation given in (B), which touched on a very specific point. Under the first form, it ignored the Mishnah, whereas under the second form it presented a more subtle question, on a point which is not treated in it but which in fact presupposes it. There is thus a certain plausability about a split in the narrative: the first part is more theoretical and in a scholarly style, and leads to the decisive superiority of tradition over subtle arguments; the second practical part shows that the people, under the influence of the Holy Spirit, had a tradition too which rendered learned debates useless. It is clear in these circumstances that the conclusion about the promotion of Hillel (C), directly connected to the established fact that he complied with tradition, applied equally well to the first part as to the second.

Another recension of this account provides supplementary details (*y. Pes.* 6:1):

> That law was unknown to the Elders of Bathyra.
>
> [The topic is the breaches of the Sabbath permitted for the preparation of the paschal lamb: *m. Pes.* 6.1]
>
> 1. It happened one time that the 14th Nisan coincided with the Sabbath and they did not know if the paschal sacrifice [פסח] prevailed over the Sabbath or not. They said: 'There is here a certain Babylonian whose name is Hillel, who has studied with [שמעי] Shemaiah and Abtalion. He knows whether the paschal sacrifice prevails or not over the Sabbath'— 'Can he be of some help?'[37] They sent for him. They said to him: 'Have you ever heard it said whether, when the 14th Nisan coincided with a Sabbath, it prevailed over it or not?...'
>
> [Hillel tried to prove the point with various biblical arguments, but the others rejected his reasons or refuted them, and concluded]:
>
> 'There is nothing to get from this Babylonian!'
>
> Although he stayed giving them explanations all day, they did not agree with him until he said to them: 'Curses on me [יבוא עלי]! This is what I received from Shemaiah and Abtalion.' When they heard him say that, they stood up and appointed him patriarch [נשיא].

---

37. Or, less probably: 'Perhaps he is of some help' (without irony).

2. When they had proclaimed him patriarch, he began to criticize them, saying: 'What was it that prompted you to have need of this Babylonian? Is it that you do not serve the two great ones of this world, Shemaiah and Abtalion, who are seated among you?' In criticizing them, he forgot the *halacha* on it.

3. They said to him: 'What will we do for the people who have forgotten their knife?' He answered them: 'I have heard the answer, but I have forgotten. But do not worry about Israel. If they are not prophets, they are disciples of the prophets.' Immediately, those whose passover was a lamb hid [the knife] in the wool; those who had a goat fastened it between the horns. Thus their victims happened to bring their knives with them. When he saw what they did, he remembered the *halakha*. He said to them: 'Curses on me if this was not what I had heard[38] from Shemaia and Abtalion!'

Each of the three numbered parts of the account ends with the mention of Shemaiah and Abtalion, the immediate predecessors of Hillel (and Shammai) according to the passage cited from *Pirke Abot*, but they are not present. The middle part serves as a bridge between the other two, which are parallel to those of the Tosefta: the first part is a general question, which explicitly ignores the Mishnah; the last is a very specific question, which presupposes it, and which more or less clearly sets the scene at the Temple, in conformity with tradition which wanted the immolation of the paschal victim to take place in the sanctuary, and its consumption in the precincts, or at least in Jerusalem (*t. Pasha* 8.16-17). I show below that this mishnaic opinion conceals other older usages: at least in certain circles, the paschal lamb was sacrificed and consumed outside the Temple, before as well as after the destruction. The account just studied is therefore a composite collection, which integrates other customs into a mishnaic perspective. Let us consider here only these other customs, which underlie the first part, namely, the actual enthronement of Hillel.

It could be asked which of the two recensions[39] is older, indeed the more original. Chronologically, the final edition of the *Yerushalmi* (about 400) is some two centuries later than that of the Tosefta, and its version of the account includes additions and digressions that are obviously late

---

38.   Reading of the Geniza (Schechter: יבוא עליי אם לא שמעתי, in S.Z. Schechter, *Aboth de rabbi Nathan* [Vienna: Lippe, 1887]); cf. S. Lieberman, *Hayerushalmi kiphshuto* (Jerusalem: Magnes, 1934), p. 466; the manuscripts have יבוא עליי כך שמעתי, 'Woe betide me! Thus have I heard...' (correction).

39.   A third exists, in *b. Pes.* 66a, which is intermediate between the two cited.

(some being omitted above): technical developments in scholarly style; irony about the Babylonians; criticism, through Hillel, of the patriarchs, who were not above their teachers. Certain details, however, appear more original in the *Yerushalmi*, in particular the proper names. Shemaiah and Abtalion formed the fourth pair of transmitters of the *Pirke Abot*; Bathyra was a Jewish colony in Batanea, far away from Jerusalem. In the first version, furthermore, the enthronement of Hillel as patriarch in proximity to the sanctuary, in the total absence of his teachers as well as of priests, is rather unlikely; at most, he could in such circumstances have been appointed head of a more or less dissident school, which is not suggested in any way, since there is an allusion to 'all the people'.

In regard to Shemaiah and Abtalion we know very little. There is a saying which mentions that they were both proselytes and descendants of Sennacherib (*b. Git.* 57b), which suggests some Babylonian connection; another, that two tanners (a foul-smelling craft, at the bottom of the social scale) were listened to when they testified about their teaching before the doctors (*m. 'Ed.* 1.3), which implies a discontinuity; still another, that the people, on a day of Pardon, stopped escorting the high priest and started following them, when they saw them passing (*b. Yom.* 71b), in other words, when they were not with the people at the Temple. This again looks like dissidence, or at least distrust in regard to the high priesthood. According to *b. Pes.* 66a, one of them was patriarch, and the other president of the Sanhedrin, which was not possible, unless 'sanhedrin' is understood as a limited school, but then that excludes the idea of 'patriarch'.

Josephus provides some not very coherent information, which helps however to put things in perspective: according to *Ant.* 15.3, 'the Pharisee Pollion and his disciple Sameas' were in favour with Herod, since they had advised the inhabitants of Jerusalem to open their gates to him. If Pollion is really a (Latin) equivalent of Abtalion,[40] the transcription 'Sameas' could come from Shemaiah, his colleague, or from Shammai, his disciple, with this latter being the more probable here. However, *Ant.* 14.172 reports that a certain Sameas, a member of the Sanhedrin, 'a just man and as a result beyond all fear', reproached the court and King Hyrcanus[41] for their cowardice when faced with the

---

40. Cf. Feldman, 'Pollion', pp. 53-62.

41. In *b. Sanh.* 19a-b, a similar account tells of a direct intervention by Simon ben Shetah before Alexander Janneus.

crimes of Herod (in 47 BCE) at the time of a trial in the Sanhedrin in which the latter, still young, had to answer for the murder of Ezekias, ancestor of the Galilean movement. Later, the same Josephus attributes the intervention to Pollion (15.4), who would have dared to recommend to the Sanhedrin to get rid of Herod. He is confusing them therefore, which induces us rather to presume them to be of the same generation, so that Sameas would be Shemaiah, the contemporary of Hillel. In reality, the question is to a great extent artificial, since Shemaiah and Shammai are two forms of the same name, and both can be transcribed 'Sameas'.[42] Furthermore, we surmise that Josephus was uncomfortable with his sources, since on the one hand Herod repressed the Pharisees, who were not afraid to stand up to the king (17.41-45), and on the other, when he had the whole Sanhedrin put to death, the one he spared was precisely Sameas, the only one who had dared to criticize him. Josephus tried afterwards to come up with an explanation (14.176), which really only dealt with Pollion (15.370), and not Sameas. He had some inklings therefore of these individuals, but he totally ignored Hillel the Elder.

In other words, Josephus, who was favourable to Herod and who at the same time was anxious in the *Antiquities* to appear to be Pharisaic, did not really know Pollion, Sameas 'and their school' except from secondary (Pharisaic) sources, which he worked hard to reintegrate into the official chronicles (Nicolaus of Damascus), since the latter referred only to politically important individuals. Finally, he did not really explain how this school could at the same time have been important and have escaped the condemnation of Herod. It was indeed a rather marginal movement: to reinterpret Pollion and Sameas as ethnarch and president of the Sanhedrin amounted then to putting them back into a normative and therefore central vision of the tradition.

In these circumstances, it must be concluded that the account of the enthronement of Hillel according to the *Yerushalmi*, which is characterized by a very tenuous link between the court (Sanhedrin, in fact the school of Bathyra) and the pair Shemaiah and Abtalion, fits in with the

---

42.   שמאי being a hypocoristic for שמעיה, as Janneus (ינאי) is of John (יחנן), etc.; cf. Dérenbourg's discussions and examples, *Histoire*, p. 95 n. 1. We cannot exclude the possibility that Shammai would be a doubling of Shemaiah-Sameas, deliberately put after the enthronement of Hillel; cf. J. Neusner, *The Rabbinic Traditions about the Pharisees before 70* (3 vols.; Leiden: Brill, 1971), I, pp. 158-59, who challenges any connection between Josephus and the rabbinic tradition.

other pieces of information, and that the presentation of the Tosefta, which leaves unexplained the absence of connections between the teachers of Hillel and the court, is tendentious, since it hides these facts. The theme of the quasi-discontinuity of the oral tradition is met again, moreover, in *b. Qid.* 66a, in an account already mentioned which relates that this tradition disappeared when Alexander Janneus (יָאַ) had all the teachers massacred, until Simon ben Sheṭaḥ 'restored the Torah in its primitive state'. It is necessary moreover to retain from these accounts that the rabbinic tradition admitted that under the Hasmonaeans just as under Herod the functioning of the Temple was not regulated by Pharisaic customs, which could explain why Hillel, in our account, left it up to the people on the matter of the knives (at the Temple).

Another explanation is possible however, acknowledging that the information provided by Josephus is true, although difficult to sort out: the announced succession of Hillel (and Shammai) to Shemaiah and Abtalion could be just a simple literary device. In the second part of the account, in fact, Hillel became angry and maintained that the whole assembly had heard the teaching of Shemaiah and Abtalion at Jerusalem. In the first part, on the contrary, no one had heard them, and furthermore no one said that they were dead. In that case, the elevation of Hillel with an anachronistic title would be a simple literary composition, resulting from the combining of the Babylonian origin, represented by the colony of Bathyra and Hillel, and the Pharisaic teaching of Jerusalem. This two-fold source would correspond then, as will be shown below (§5), to the duality of founders of the school of Yavneh: Yohanan ben Zakkai, a Galilean disciple of Hillel, and Gamaliel, an eminent Pharisee from Jerusalem.

Following the view of Josephus, who wanted to be known as a Pharisee but was only acquainted with its social aspects, leads to the conclusion that Shemaiah and Abtalion, who had been somewhat marginal at Jerusalem, had become important because of a posterity which he had to take into account, whereas Hillel, completely absent from his perspective, represented for him (in his time) an even more marginal entity, of whom he had perhaps never heard.[43]

---

43. In a similar way, Josephus only discovered Christianity belatedly at Rome, when he could no longer deny it a certain social importance. Furthermore, what he knew of Jesus came to him from Christians; cf. Nodet, 'Jésus et Jean-Baptiste', pp. 321-26.

Furthermore, the 'Elders of Bathyra',[44] who questioned Hillel and who had oddly the competence to promote him to patriarch, were not widely known in the rabbinic tradition, but Josephus provided some details (*Ant.* 17.23-27): Herod, wanting to shield Galilee from plundering by Trachonitis, created a buffer zone by establishing in Batanea (the present Golan) a Babylonian Jewish colony, and gave them tax exemptions, since the region lay fallow. The head of the colony, Zamaris, built a town which he named Bathyra and established forts. He brought in from everywhere people very faithful to Jewish customs, and the country became densely populated since the people 'felt secure'. This out-of-the-way location can explain the precariousness of the connection with Shemaiah and Abtalion, after a persecution of the Sanhedrin in Jerusalem: there was an attempt at a 'restoration' within this Babylonian colony, which tried, at least afterwards, to claim for itself a traditional legitimacy. In this way can be explained the importance in the account of the *vox populi*, heir of the prophets, and of the superiority of oral tradition over creative arguments, under either of its forms.

The nature of the link in the tradition which joined Simon the Just to Hillel begins to become apparent. It was very remote from the history of the reigning dynasties, as Josephus conceived them, and perhaps even too from the main Pharisaic movements, which had a considerable social extension at that time, in Judaea and elsewhere. The problem of the rabbinic tradition was rather that of the affirmation of the permanence of a central authority, a guarantee of the 'customs of the fathers', and therefore, for reasons that are still obscure, independent of the bodies set up in Jerusalem since Simon the Just (and Judas Maccabeus).

Now it is appropriate to consider the question posed to Hillel, since the choice of the sacrifice of the lamb to examine a problem linked to the Passover was not an innocent one.

The biblical information is extensive, but not very coherent. According to 2 Chron. 35.1-18, the Passover of Josiah was organized around the Temple: the small livestock for the sacrifices (goats and sheep) were offered by the king; the Levites immolated the victims and the priests sprinkled the blood which they received from their hands; then the Levites prepared the sacred dishes which they then brought to the people; finally, they prepared the Passover for themselves and the priests, the latter being occupied until dark with the daily service of the burnt offerings. It is

---

44.   The parallel version of *b. Pes.* 66a has בני בתירא 'those of Bathyra'. A Yehuda ben Bathyra is known, at the end of the first century, as head of the academy of Nisibis in Babylon; cf. *b. Pes.* 3b.

remarkable that the very brief parallel in 2 Kgs 23.21-23 mentions only the order given by Josiah to all the people to carry out the Passover at Jerusalem, without any allusion either to the Temple, or to priests or to Levites, but in insisting on the observance of the commandments of the 'book of the Covenant' discovered by Hilkiyahu. The contrast between the two presentations can be considerably reduced if the reference to the Book is speaking of Deut. 16.5-8: 'You are not permitted to offer the Passover sacrifice within any of the towns that YHWH your God is giving you; it is only in the place chosen by YHWH your God as a dwelling for his name that you will offer the Passover sacrifice, in the evening at sunset, the time of day when you departed from Egypt.' The exclusiveness of the 'chosen place', which can be interpreted either as Jerusalem or the Temple, corresponds then to a novelty, underlined by the fact that the Passover of Josiah was the first of this kind since the time of the Judges (or of the prophet Samuel, according to 2 Chron. 35.18).

The difference between the two accounts of this Passover can be reduced to a limited controversy: should the Passover be immolated and eaten in Jerusalem, or specifically in the sanctuary? The rabbinic tradition is not explicit in regard to this, but it reveals some oddities. In principle, according to Num. 9.9-12, anyone prevented from celebrating the Passover on 14th Nisan, because he was too far away or unclean because of a death, had to do so on fourteenth of the second month (Iyyar). In practice, the postponement to the second month for those who were impure only took place if a part of the people was in a state of purity, but it was not held if the people and all the priests were impure. The Passover was immolated for all 14th Nisan and furthermore, since the precept was to eat, and not just to immolate, it was granted that all could participate in it (*m. Pes.* 7.6). The result of this, even if the case seems rather theoretical, was that the day of Passover, the Temple was susceptible to impurity. A related controversy (9.4) can be interpreted as a disagreement about whether the Passover must be eaten in the Temple, or simply in Jerusalem,[45] and we meet again the difference between the two parallel accounts under Josiah. Moreover, one of the protagonists in this discussion was Eliezer ben Hyrcanus who had lived in Jerusalem before the destruction and had studied with Yohanan ben Zakkai (*Gen. R.* 41.1), and who could then be considered a witness. It was he in fact who declared that the Passover should be eaten in the sanctuary, and who maintained on the other hand (9.2) that it is necessary to consider as 'distant', therefore subject to the second Passover, whoever was outside the precincts (עזרה) at the time of the immolation of the victims. This last opinion agreed with the known customs relating to pilgrimages.[46] On the contrary, a later opinion (Aqiba) defined as distant those who were more distant than Modein (in all directions, about 25 miles), that is to say, those who are outside Judaea. This is an extreme opinion, not without allusion to the Maccabees, and made pilgrimages impossible for the Diaspora, and in fact made

45. Finkelstein, 'The Men', p. 239 n. 1.

46. Cf. S. Safrai, *Pilgrimage at the Time of the Second Temple* (Tel Aviv: Am ha-Sefer, 1965), pp. 123-25: the sources show that the custom was to arrive at least six days before the feast, that is, the time needed for a purification, especially for pilgrims from the Diaspora.

allowance only for those who could reach Jerusalem within 14th Nisan (*b. Pes.* 93b).

These debates could appear to be trivial, but they show in the backgound two quite different visions: the first, of Eliezer, one of those who was concerned with the problem of a judicious diffusion of the Bible in Greek, enhanced the importance of the Temple to the maximum, as a centre of the Jews wherever they might have been; the second was more attentive to Jerusalem and Judaea. The first was connected on the whole to the spirit of the charter of Antiochus III, and the second rather to the 'model of Nehemiah', all this taking place at a time when the Temple had disappeared, which allowed for a scholarly debate on contradictory doctrines relative to an ideal Temple, clearly distinct from the Herodian edifice and its customs. The rabbinic tradition, in fact, as heir of the academy at Jamnia-Yavneh and of those in other places (Bene Berak, Lod), had inherited varied echoes and doctrines. There are good reasons to think[47] that the four 'philosophies' described by Josephus were represented among them, and that the primacy of the Pharisees, in his time, involved the Diaspora more than Judaea. In this variety, the prologue of *Pirke Abot* selected one tradition as normative, which in no way implied that all the material in the Tannaitic collections were connected to it: the many controversies prove this, as well as incidents such as the excommunication of Eliezer, who had known the Temple and was renowned for his fidelity to his teachers.

In regard to the immolation of the Passover, two debates show a redactional dialectic at work, independent of any testimony about what really happened in Herod's temple. The first concerned the time of the immolation: according to all the texts (Exod. 12.6; Lev. 23.5; Num. 9.3, 5, 11) the Passover must be 'kept' in the evening (בין הערבים 'between the two evenings'[48]), with the same phrase as for Aaron's perpetual offering (Exod. 30.8; LXX ὀψέ). This expression contrasts with the morning in Exod. 16.12 (manna), 29, 39 and Num. 28.4 (daily burnt offerings). This is how the Samaritans and the Karaites naturally interpreted it. And yet, the unanimous rabbinic tradition understood it as 'beginning at noon', not without some lexical difficulties,[49] but emphasizing that in Josiah's Passover the priests were busy sacrificing till nightfall (2 Chron. 35.14), and therefore that they had begun soon after midday. That unanimity proceeded then from a tradition foreign to the Pentateuch.

As for the Passover sacrifice itself, a distinction was made between the 'Passover of Egypt', at the end of the ten plagues, and the 'Passover of the generations' that came later (*m. Pes.* 9.5), that is to say, after the gift of the Torah at Sinai. The distinction is obvious, since in the first case the Passover was in the home, while in the second it was linked up with the sacrifices in the sanctuary. It is so evident in fact that all that is needed to convince oneself is to compare the corresponding texts of the Pentateuch (as *b. Pes.* 96a does). It seems then that the Mishnah only expressed a truism on the matter, namely, that the oral tradition has nothing to say of significance.

---

47.   Cf. Nodet *et al.*, *Flavius Josèphe*, p. xxxvi.

48.   The LXX transposed ἀνὰ μέσον τῶν ἑσπερινῶν, or translated πρὸς ἑσπέραν.

49.   Between בין הערבים, בין השמש כבוא צאתך מועד; cf. *y. Pes.* 5.1; *MekhRI*, bo' 5; cf. Lieberman, *Hayerushalmi*, p. 450.

Such a conclusion is however improbable, since it is too contrary to the constant style of the Mishnah which is concise and dependable.

Contrary to the official doctrine, there are indications of the survival of the domestic Passover sacrifice. In particular, there is an account (*b. Pes.* 53a, on the preservation of local customs) of a Jewish notable in Rome, Theodosius,[50] who had restored in the community the custom of preparing all the lambs for the Passover, from which, after a debate, there followed a prohibition of such practices (*m. Beṣ.* 2.7), to make sure that no one thought that it was permitted to eat sacred foods outside of Jerusalem.[51] Josephus himself (*Ant.* 2.313) declared, after the account of the Passover in Egypt: 'Hence it happens that we still today [ὅθεν νῦν ἔτι] keep this sacrifice in the same customary manner.'[52] Now, he certainly would not have advanced a custom that he knew to be contrary to Pharisaic customs. In the same way, *m. Pes.* 7.2 reports that Gamaliel II, successor to Yohanan ben Zakkai at Yavneh, ordered his servant Tabi to roast 'for them' the Passover on a grill (and not directly in the fire), which suggests the persistence of the sacrifice of the paschal lamb after the destruction of the Temple.

Elsewhere however there is some criticism of the 'relaxations', that is to say, 'the lax tendencies', of Gamaliel (cf. *m. 'Ed.* 4.11). Yehoshua (same epoch) testifies on the other hand (*m. 'Ed.* 8.6) to having heard it said that sacrifices can be offered even without the Temple, and that very sacred things (קדשי קדשים) can be eaten even outside the enclosure of the precinct, since the sanctity of the place is permanent (cf. *m. Meg.* 1.11). But this testimony only refers to a theoretical possibility, and not to a fact.[53] Nevertheless, while it is well attested that the daily sacrifices had ceased after the destruction (*m. Ta'an.* 4.6[54]), it is advisable not to include the Passover

50.   Literally תודס, תוודוס; cf. Lieberman, *Hayerushalmi*, p. 480.

51.   גדי מקולס: cf. *t. Beṣ.* 2:15 and Lieberman, *Tosefta kifshuṭah*, V, pp. 957-58.

52.   Philo, *Spec. Leg.* 2.146, declares that, before the destruction of the Temple, for the Passover all the people were priests, *as in the time of Moses*. We can even add that the Synoptics, certainly edited after the destruction, implicitly assume a well-known custom in regard to this: 'Where do you want *us to prepare to eat* the Passover?' (Mt. 26.17 par.). But the problem at the beginnings of Christianity is complex, since Jn 19.30-31, which had ignored the paschal meal, situated the death of Jesus at the exact moment of the immolation of the paschal lamb in the temple, as attested by Josephus (*War* 4.317) and in accordance with the Passover of Josiah (2 Chron. 35.7-18).

53.   The same thing is true of the precepts relative to the temple of Onias (*m. Men.* 13.10; cf. Isa. 19.21): it is not stated whether they could be effectively carried out.

54.   The 17th Tammuz; cf. too Schürer, *History*, I, p. 522.

automatically, since it is of a different kind, as much because of its lesser frequency as because of the fact that the essential precept is to consume it, and not to sacrifice it. I mentioned above the oddities that could have come up in the Temple on matters of purity, according to rabbinic law.

These pieces of evidence lead to some clear conclusions: 1. There existed a Pharisaic custom to immolate and eat the paschal lamb in a domestic ritual, just like the Passover of the exodus from Egypt, therefore independently of the Temple. 2. This custom is well attested, in particular by the patriarch Gamaliel, who belonged to a strictly Pharisaic dynasty. 3. For reasons which go beyond the present exposition and deal with the development of the rabbinic ritual[55] of the paschal *Seder* in the second century, the decision which finally prevailed was the cessation of the family ritual of the lamb, so a rabbinic distinction was coined between 'Passover of Egypt', a bygone event, and 'Passover of the generations', an immolation necessitating a sanctuary; the latter could no longer be carried out since the sanctuary had disappeared. This necessity was derived from the Passover of Josiah according to Chronicles, in which the ritual of the paschal lamb was linked with sacrifices in gen eral, as again at Jerusalem in the time of Josephus. On the contrary, the Samaritans had maintained a paschal custom in accordance with Deuteronomy: there was no longer a temple, but the 'chosen place' was irremovable, which was enough, since the ritual of the paschal lamb was not intrinsically linked to the shrine. The book of Chronicles introduced a decisive difference.

This somewhat long preliminary review allows for an interpretation of the double form of the question posed to Hillel on the occasion of a 14th Nisan falling on the Sabbath, a concrete and urgent question, and not a school exercise: the Mishnah combined several doctrines, among which was the obligation of the paschal sacrifice in the Temple, which ended up as the dominant one. The fragments of traditions which resisted this unification are therefore significant. In the case of Hillel, the context of the Elders of Bathyra and the Babylonian atmosphere indicate therefore that the overall question had been submitted to him outside of Jerusalem, and even outside Judaea. The specific question about the knives, which presupposed the Mishnah and the Temple, and more

---

55. For some preliminary indications, cf. E. Nodet, 'Miettes messianiques', in I. Gruenwald, S. Shaked and G.G. Strumsa (eds.), *Messiah and Christos: Studies in the Jewish Origins of Christianity* (Festschrift D. Flusser; Texte und Studien zum Antiken Judentum, 32; Tübingen: Mohr [Paul Siebeck], 1992), pp. 119-41.

generally the final redaction of the episode given in the Tosefta conceals this fact, in the context of the 'standardization' indicated. All this resulted then from a reformulation. In other words, only the question of the Passover's superiority over the Sabbath is appropriately connected to Hillel, that is to say, the first part of the passage. We must examine and be more specific about a few points.

1. The body which questioned Hillel had the power to name him patriarch: nevertheless, it is not stated that it was a sanhedrin, but only the 'Elders of Bathyra', who are rarely mentioned elsewhere, but who had Babylonian connections, as we have seen. This raises too a question on the origin and nature of that patriarchal institution.

2. The teachers mentioned, Shemaiah and Abtalion, are known or at least recognized by all, but they were absent and had not been replaced. The statements of Josephus show that they must have been accorded a notable rank, at least in certain Pharisaic spheres (of Judaea or elsewhere). In any case, other passages indicate a discontinuity between them and their successors (cf. *m. 'Ed.* 1.3). Here, their authority is intact, but they are inaccessible: it is necessary then to consider them dead or killed, in either case without having been able to establish an acknowledged succession.

3. The profile of the candidate sought and promoted was unusual: a Babylonian who would have studied with the Pharisaic teachers of Judaea. Some challenge the Babylonian part as such. There is therefore a problem of unifying different tendencies.

4. The context of the proposed question was not an academic one, but indicated a specific urgency, for which an oral tradition and a teacher were needed; there was lacking therefore an authority on two levels, a traditional one and an immediate one. The Mishnah as edited two centuries later was not known, which is understandable, but above all there was then no guiding authority, no teacher invested with the desired decision-making authority.

5. The question itself was peculiar, since according to the usual lunar calendar Passover fell on the Sabbath one year in seven on average. If it had been a matter of a very specific point as in the third part, we could understand how the collective memory would have been hazy and how it would have been necessary to cut short a discussion; but even such was not the case, since in the third part all the people were 'sons of prophets', and recalled the necessary item. Here, the question was general, so in his argument Hillel sought a global solution, and the final

response was not even given clearly. There is then a certain strangeness in the fact that the whole assembly entitled to promote Hillel, or at least recognized as such after the event, would have forgotten such a general and simple customary point. This deservedly was the object of Hillel's anger in the connecting paragraph (second part).

6.   In his responses, Hillel called upon no Babylonian custom, personal or not, relative to the Passover. It is true that they did not directly ask him about this, but it is no less true that he knew how to miss the point of the question, in developing his scriptural arguments.

The redaction of the episode presents in a very compact form a bundle of problems. The discontinuity which preceded the appearance of Hillel has been considered above. As for the problem of the calendar, it is strange, and leaves room for a suspicion of an institutional novelty.

According to the primitive acceptance of the Sabbath as a full moon, the question proposed does not make much sense, since the Passover *was* a Sabbath. With regard to the weekly Sabbath, I have shown above (cf. Chapter 3, §1) that the rabbinic tradition, which preserved many non-scriptural elements, placed at Pentecost the ritual completion (עצרת) of the Passover, at the close of a cycle of seven weeks, which consecrated the supremacy of the weekly rhythm. There would be a paradox then in having the Passover, connected with the full moon, supplanting the Sabbath, which asserted itself as independent of the moon, and whose fixing did not depend on any authority. The problem however was in no way extraneous to the evolution of the Decalogue, as suggested in Chapter 3, §2, in which only the weekly Sabbath is perceptible in the present form of the Decalogue, with at most some traces of the Passover. The Decalogue would constitute then an exemplary case in which 'the Sabbath supplanted the Passover'. In this way, the inverse question posed to Hillel took on a fundamental meaning, all the more so since there was competition between two major symbolisms, related to the beginning of history and its centre: the Creation (general), with the Sabbath; and Redemption (particular), with the Passover.[56] But this still does not explain why the problem would have come up suddenly, since the accounts of the Maccabees already attested the extreme (non-scriptural) importance of the Sabbath, not without some Babylonian aroma.

---

56.   This is a very different perspective from that of the Palestinian targum on Exod. 12.42, which associated the paschal night with the Creation, in a sacrificial perspective, with the Sabbath remaining secondary; cf. R. Le Déaut, *La nuit pascale* (AnBib, 22; Rome: Pontifical Biblical Institute, 1963), pp. 213-15.

In the 364-day calendar of Jubilees, the year began on a Wednesday, and the Passover, on the fourteenth of the first month, was always a Tuesday. In such a system then, the feast cannot fall on a Sabbath. Although we do not know how the periodical corrections were carried out to make up for the time-lag in relation to the solar year, it is certain that this calendar was in use in certain groups with more priestly tendencies; some of the sectarians at Qumran and the Samaritans used this computation too.[57] So we can interpret the question posed to Hillel as the indication of some kind of transformation: at the time of the dispersal of the Sanhedrin by Herod, the community of Bathyra, filled with many members faithful to the Law who had arrived from all directions, had customs remote from those of Jerusalem: domestic immolation of the paschal lamb, an autonomous calendar. It was just a small group, and had perhaps some sectarian traits.[58] At the time of the persecution of the Pharisees, who, although a widely dispersed movement, had the lunar calendar in common, the problem came up of restoring in a safe place a religious authority to regulate matters (cf. Chapter 3, §1). This did take place at Bathyra, with some compromises: the surviving Pharisees, that is to say from the school of Shemaiah and Abtalion, agreed to go along with this on condition that the group abandon the sectarian calendar, so as to remain in contact with the many Jews scattered in Judaea and elsewhere. The result of this, some time later, was the famous problem of the Passover on the Sabbath, and the urgent necessity of connecting its solution to the aforementioned school, which explains the question to Hillel the Babylonian, to verify his fidelity to the Pharisees. This was a decisive test, carefully chosen for the selection of a patriarch, or at least, in these circumstances, for a head of a school. It is

57.   Abel and Starcky, *Maccabées*, p. 58, even considered that the acceptance of the Seleucid lunar calendar by the Hasmonaeans must have some connection with the Essene schism; but, if the latter are descended from the Hasidaeans, it is not a matter of a late schism, and it is on the contrary the Hasmonaeans who adopted the Seleucid custom.

58.   According to *Ant.* 18.19, the Essenes sent votive offerings (ἀναθήματα) to the Temple, but they performed their sacrifices elsewhere, with other rituals for purification; cf. Loeb, *ad loc.*, and the discussion of J. Strugnell, 'Flavius Josephus and the Essenes: *Antiquities* XVIII. 18-22', *JBL* 87 (1958), pp. 106-115, and that of J. Nolland, 'A Misleading Statement of the Essene Attitude to the Temple (Josephus, *Antiquities* XVIII, I, 5, 19)', *RevQ*, 9 (1978), pp. 555-62. As there is no mention of an altar, which is indispensable if the precept is to sacrifice, it could relate to the Passover, or else the precept is only about consumption.

even possible that the initiative had been entirely from the side of the Elders of Bathyra, without any request from the Pharisees, but done in order to regain control over them.

As for the celebration of the Passover, curiously so poorly known, another dimension should be mentioned here, since there are precisely some traces of an eminently biblical Babylonian tradition unaware of this feast.

1.   The book of Esther is the account of the foundation of the feast of Purim commemorating the liberation of Jews *locally* at the time of a persecution in 'Babylon'.[59] This account contrasts with the Exodus story, in which the liberation of the Israelites, commemorated by the Passover, is linked with the migration from Egypt towards a promised land. The feast of Purim is usually considered a much later local episode. But Esther, at the time of the oppression, had a fast of three days proclaimed on a 13th Nisan (3.12 and 4.1-16), which is remarkably incompatible with the precept to eat the Passover on the 14th, to which there is no allusion.[60] There is no longer any question of a possible migration to Judaea, although in biblical terms the episode (under Xerxes) was well after the restoration under Cyrus-Darius.

2.   The treatise of the Mishnah on the proclamation of Scripture (*Megillah*) is attached first to the Esther scroll (which must have been written in Hebrew, but with Aramaic script), and secondarily to the Pentateuch; it is the vestige of a great importance, at a certain point, of the feast of Purim (or 'Day of Mordecai', according to 2 Macc. 15.36), due to Pharisaic or Babylonian influence.

3.   A Talmudic discussion (on *m. Meg.* 1.1) took pains to explain the mishnaic pre-eminence of the Sabbath over Purim, that is to say, the circumstances of a downgrading of this feast, while the question to Hillel presupposed a context of promotion of the Passover (as more important than the Sabbath); it is remarkable moreover that it would have been the

---

59.   Which in itself certainly has a complex history; cf. *Epic of Gilgamesh* X, VI, p. 19 and W. Hallo, 'The First Purim', *BA* 6/1 (1983), pp. 20-23.

60.   N.L. Collins, 'Did Esther Fast on the 15th Nisan?', *RB* 100 (1993), pp. 533-61, tries to show that the calendar of feasts controlling the Passover was moved forward slightly in comparison to the civil calendar, in use at the court, and that in this way the three days of fasting beginning 13th Nisan could have concluded just before the Passover. This solution highlights the problem, rather than resolving it, since the day of the commemoration of the fast has been maintained by the Jewish calendar of feasts, but, to avoid the coincidence, the fast has been advanced a month (13th Adar), just before the feast itself.

Sabbath which served as a reference point in the two cases.

4. There are reasons to think, in taking into consideration the LXX and particularly the 'Lucianic recension', which is close to the Hebrew, but contains the additions, that the brief and secularized MT of Esther corresponds to the rabbinic downgrading. Likewise, Josephus was a witness to a long *Hebrew* text[61] (with prayers), but dissociated himself from this feast that was not very Judaean: he said that it was celebrated by 'the Jews' (*Ant.* 11.295), and not by 'us', as was his way of speaking of other solemnities.

In the background of the technical debate on the preferment of Passover over Purim, there was evidently the essential problem of the importance or not of immigration to the land of Israel which became a priority issue due to the importance given to the Passover:[62] it would seem surprising, but is in no way improbable, that the Babylonians preferred Purim *at home* up to a fairly late date, and that they would have had little to say about Passover, all the more so since the oral tradition was not derived from the Pentateuch. Conversely, it is remarkable, but ultimately very natural, that Esther would be the only book of the Hebrew Bible of which there is no trace in the manuscripts of the desert of Judaea.[63]

Too many facts are missing to be more specific about any detail, but such a merging of various groups as is presupposed by the events at

61.   A few examples will show that Josephus, for Esther as for the rest of the Bible, translated from the Hebrew, without making use of the LXX: in *Ant.* 11.187, 'feasts during seven days' corresponds to Est. 1.5 MT and Luc. rec.; §207, Bagathoos and Theodestes are unknown to Est. 2.21 LXX, but the MT has בגתן and תרש (read as תרדש and Hellenized); §209, 'Haman, the son of Amadathos, who was of Amalekite descent', which is ignored by Est. 3.1 LXX Αμαν Αμαδάθου Βουγαῖον ('braggart'), whereas MT specifies המן בן המדתא האגגי, in which 'Agagite' refers to Agag the Amalekite (cf. 1 Sam. 15); §245, the wife of Haman was Zarasa, transcribed from זרש (Est. 5.10-14) and not from Σωσαρα LXX, etc.

62.   Later, about 110–120, a controversy developed in Judaea over whether the feast was simply a commemoration to be observed in minute detail (*t. Pasḥa* 10.12), or whether it lived on in a current political dimension (five sages of the Passover *Haggada*); cf. Nodet, 'Miettes messianiaques', pp. 127-29.

63.   The texts studied by J.-T. Milik, 'Les modèles araméens du livre d'*Esther* dans la grotte 4 de Qumrân', *RevQ* 15 (1992), pp. 321-99, accentuates the eastern origin of the book, and the author concludes, with a completely different argument based on the versions, that the MT was a late *translation*. This result is interesting, but it seems odd to have it connected to an idea of a *promotion* of the feast of Purim after 70.

Bathyra makes it possible to understand why, according to the rabbinic tradition, it was only from Hillel onwards that the *internal* controversies over the oral tradition began. These are indications of divergent customs or sensibilities, and we can consider schematically that opposite Hillel the Babylonian was regularly found Shammai the Judaean, about whom we know nothing very precise, and who perhaps is nothing more than a double for Shemaiah, introduced in this way into the assembly as heir of the Sanhedrin of Jerusalem.

We thus see that if the Babylonian outflow was permanent, if the popular diffusion of the Pharisaic movement was unquestionable, especially in the Diaspora, as Josephus emphasized, the establishment of a Pharisaic continuity in *Judaea* was always very tenuous, and came up against civil and priestly power. Certain conclusions follow from this: first, this Pharisaic precariousness in Judaea seemed to contrast with a more distinct, although more discrete, presence in Galilee, which I shall elaborate upon below; then, the affair of the Passover shows that Babylonians and Pharisees were not identical; moreover, various indications, especially the apolitical marginality and questions about calendar, suggest a certain parallel between the people of Bathyra and the Essenes,[64] which provides an entrance into Hasidaean circles prior to the Maccabaean crisis; finally, the rabbinic tradition, which toned down the marginal and precarious status of Hillel, clearly concealed these facts, as we are going to see, so as to emphasize that it was the heir of all the legitimate Jewish institutions before the destruction of the Temple. The next step consists now of an examination of Jewish Galilee.

---

64. Indications coming at least in part from Judaea, perhaps from Qumran, but the fragments found in the caves represent a complex sociology (unknown to Josephus). For example *4QMMT* and the Temple Scroll contain elements of *halacha* derived from Scripture, which provides an element of comparison with the Sadducees, indeed even with the Samaritans; cf. L.H. Schiffman, 'Miqsat Ma'aseh ha-Torah and the Temple Scroll', *RevQ* 15 (1990), pp. 435-57. In the same way, the Damascus Document shows a *halacha*, deduced from what is written, by means of techniques found later among the Karaites, which was close to the thinking of the Sadducees; cf. L.H. Schiffman, *The Halakhah at Qumran* (SJLA, 16; Leiden: Brill, 1975), pp. 134-36, and *idem, Sectarian Law in the Dead Sea Scrolls: Courts, Testimony and the Penal Code* (BJS, 33; Chico, CA: Scholars Press, 1983), p. 212. While omitting mention of the Sadducees, Schiffman makes a comparison with the Pharisees because of some similarity with Tannaitic opinions; this conclusion is arbitrary, since the rabbinic sources mingled elements of oral tradition with others which were deductions from what was written (cf. §5 below).

5. *Jewish Galilee*[65]

The colony of Bathyra was in the Golan, east of the Sea of Tiberias, that is to say, in Galilee, at least in the broad sense which Josephus gave it (*War* 3.35-40). Later, the Mishnah, a foundation document of rabbinic Judaism, came from Galilee as well: it was edited shortly after 200 and, alongside numerous recollections of Jerusalem and the Temple, its general atmosphere is rural. Furthermore, at a time when the Roman dynasty of the Severi showed itself more favourable to the Jews, going so far as to grant them Roman citizenship (in all the towns and cities of the Empire), this Mishnah could be transferred to Babylon and adopted there, but nowhere is there any mention of it spreading throughout the Mediterranean basin. On the contrary, generations of later commentators on the Mishnah produced two collections, known as the *Jerusalem Talmud* (really issued at Tiberias) and the *Babylonian Talmud*, which are culturally twins; this indicates an obvious kinship between the schools of Galilee and those of Babylon. Nevertheless, the Mishnah is presented as the work not of Babylonians, but of schools founded by survivors from Judaea, after the defeat of Bar Kochba, in which case this isolated region of Bathyra would have been a simple fallback position. From this there arises a question about the nature and origin of this subsequent Galilean Judaism, and about what seems to be a Babylonian connection.

Going back in time, we see that Galilee, which practically corresponded to the four northern tribes of Asher, Zebulun, Naphtali and Issachar, did not play any appreciable role in the Hebrew Bible. Meanwhile, in the New Testament, the Galilean milieu in which Jesus grew up was rural, since there was no question of a Sephoris or a Tiberias in it, and nevertheless it is remarkable that it was religiously very much in ferment: expectations, discussions, conflicts between groups and varying tendencies. Since the subsequent development of Christianity was decidedly urban (Caesarea, Antioch, Rome), this rural dimension of the beginnings should be accepted as a fact. Once again then, the issue is to know the nature and origin of this Jewish milieu away from the great cities, and, what is more, separated from Jerusalem by a hostile Samaria.

65.   This section resumes and clarifies the details assembled in E. Nodet, 'Galilée juive, de Jésus à la *Mishna*', in F. Blanchetière and M.D. Herr (eds.), *Au sources juives du christianisme* (Louvain: Peeters, 1993), pp. 13-61.

Between these two epochs, we find the testimony of Josephus on the Galilean war in 66, in which he took an active part. The two accounts he gave of it (*Life* and *War* 2.430-32), some 20 years apart, are so lacking in consistency between them that no overall view clearly emerges. For our purpose, we simply keep in mind, as S. Cohen has shown,[66] that one of the keys to understanding the new presentation in *Life* is Josephus's concern to appear to be an observant Pharisee, and therefore to disparage systematically the religious fidelity of the Galileans, or at least their leaders. If we take the opposite of that tendentious view, we find a very strong Jewish Galilee, with a notable Zealot fringe, already considered above in regard to the Sabbath (Chapter 2, §2).

A certain continuity therefore begins to emerge. First, Herod had had some problems with Galilee. In 47 BCE, after the death of Pompey, Caesar rewarded Hyrcanus II and confirmed him as ethnarch for his fidelity (*Ant.* 14.137-44). It was at this time that the young Herod 'was put in charge' of Galilee, in circumstances that are not clear. He crushed Ezekias and his band, who had been acting ruthlessly on the frontier of Syria (14.159-60), with the resulting accusation by the Pharisees and proceedings before the Sanhedrin in Jerusalem. This trial, already mentioned above in regard to Sameas, is surprising: if it was just a matter of a police operation intended to neutralize pillagers, there would be no basis for legal proceedings. However, this Ezekias is not any bandit, since he was regarded as the forefather of the movement of Galileans and in particular the inspirer of the famous Judas. There is therefore a political[67] and religious stake involved. Politically, Herod's victims cannot be linked with the adversaries of Hyrcanus, since the tearful mothers come to implore Hyrcanus himself at the time of the proceedings. It could be argued that Herod had sought to carve out a fief against Hyrcanus, from which there arose court jealousies, but his actions earned him the good graces of Sextus Caesar, who could not be opposed to Hyrcanus, a protégé of Julius Caesar, and could not be any more favourable to a revolt. Herod, as a consequence of these vigorous initiatives,

---

66.   Cohen, *Josephus in Galilee and Rome*, p. 242.

67.   Cf. S. Freyne, 'Bandits in Galilee: A Contribution to the Study of Social Conditions in First-Century Palestine', in J. Neusner, *et al.* (eds.), *The Social World of Formative Christianity and Judaism* (Philadelphia: Fortress Press, 1988), pp. 50-68, who insists on the politico-social circumstances. H. Schwier, *Tempel und Tempelzerstörung* (Novum Testamentum et Orbis Antiquus, 11; Göttingen: Vandenhoeck & Ruprecht, 1989), pp. 145-48, discusses various opinions on these bandits.

was even named governor of Coele-Syria and Samaria by Sextus, and it is necesary to credit him with an exceptional political sense, as is shown afterwards thoughout his career.

The conclusion is crucial: these 'brigands' are anti-Roman Jews, but not necessarily adversaries of Hyrcanus; the proceedings instituted against Herod came from Jews who were defending the Law. There was therefore definitely a Galilean Judaism to which the Pharisees were favourable. It had perhaps shown some signs of irredentism, but there is no doubt that it could only be opposed to Herod the Idumaean, who was even referred to as a 'half-Jew' (*Ant.* 14.403). The converse is true as well: one of Herod's first steps on coming to power was to annihilate the Sanhedrin at Jerusalem, and he was always in conflict with the Pharisees, whose influence he feared.

In 40 BCE, Herod had himself named king of Judaea by the Roman senate (*Ant.* 14.381-85), while Antigonus, the last Hasmonaean king, had just obtained the same throne thanks to the Parthians, who had driven the Romans from Syria and taken Hyrcanus prisoner. In 39, Herod, helped by the Romans in a campaign against the Parthians, landed at Ptolemais to reconquer Judaea. Josephus states that all Galilee rapidly went over to him 'except for a few' (§395), and that he was able to head towards Jerusalem with increasing forces. The situation was thrown into confusion due to the venality of the Roman general Silo, who tried to derive profit from the two camps, and Herod had to consolidate his conquests. He set off again for Galilee, where Antigonus still held some fortified towns. He entered Sepphoris without encountering any opposition, but he soon had to commit considerable forces in a difficult struggle with 'bandits dwelling in caves'. In other words, the resistance of the supporters of Antigonus was negligible, but we meet again a problem with brigands, who obviously constituted a distinct party, strong enough to disturb Herod. Josephus describes, after the defeat of most of this enemy, the assault on the last caves where the refugees had gathered. These were situated on the cliffs of Arbela, which overlooked Magdala on the shores of the Lake (§§421-24). There is one remarkable incident: on the point of being captured, an elder preferred to kill his wife and seven children before throwing himself down the precipice. Herod was present at this scene and holding out his hand offered him mercy, but the man had time to shout abuse at him, reproaching him about his family origins. For the 'bandits', the stake was hardly an economic one, and it is hard not to imagine that these indomitable resisters were similar to Ezekias, defeated by the same Herod ten years earlier. Herod's extended hand gave an indication of the hope he had not only of conquering, but especially of being recognized as a Jewish king, which had considerable political implications. Shortly afterwards, Herod left Galilee, leaving behind him a governor, but revolts broke out continually.

Later, at a time not precisely known, but probably shortly after the beginning of his reign,[68] Herod wanted to guard against pillaging from Trachonitis by creating a buffer zone in Batanea with the establishment of rural colonies, as a way to protect the region as well as the route of pilgrimages. He installed there, exempt from taxation, a group of Babylonian Jews whose leader, Zamaris, founded in particular the town of Bathyra. Such was the origin of the colony of Bathyra, where Hillel was promoted. Herod's choice of Babylonian Jews without political ambitions was certainly clever, taking into account the neighbouring Galileans who had been resisting him on the other shore of the Lake, but who were long before of Babylonian origin, therefore of the same culture.[69] In the time of Jesus the two shores of the Lake, with strongly motivated groups, were at the same time related and discordant, which gave a context for his activity.

Josephus, who hated the Galileans, wanted to give the impression that they were Jews of recent date. He mentioned first the expansionist policy of John Hyrcanus (*Ant.* 13.254-58) with the conquest of Shechem and forced judaizing of Idumaea, then the capture of Samaria and Scythopolis, which did not include Galilee itself. Then, Josephus went on to say, citing Strabo, that Aristobulus, who succeeded John Hyrcanus briefly, conquered and circumcised by force some of the Itureans, a

---

68.   Josephus situated the call of Zamaris (*Ant.* 17.23-31) at Daphne near Antioch where he had been settled by Saturninus, who was governor of Syria at the end of Herod's reign (9–6 BCE), therefore after the time when the latter was already engulfed in domestic difficulties; cf. Schürer, *History*, I, p. 257. This is not plausible. It is necessary to look instead to the period in which he was consolidating his authority (37–25 BCE). Now, there had been a governor Calpurnius in 34–33: the date is better, and the names can be confused. Josephus's error, which tends to obscure the issue, is not necessarily accidental.

69.   Eusebius, *Historica ecclesiastica*, 1.7.14 cites a letter of Julius Africanus (a native of Emmaus-Nicopolis), according to which the 'family of Jesus' (δεσπόσυνοι) originated from the Jewish villages of Nazara and Kokhaba, the latter being in Batanea. Despite the legendary elements in this testimony, it is remarkable that this doubling of the locality was superimposed on the doubling (east and west of the Lake) organized by Herod.

tribe who are believed to have originated in the mountains of Lebanon. In following this progression towards the north, we are tempted to conclude that Galilee was included in these conquests and this judaizing.[70] But Josephus, who did not know too well where Iturea was, did not really say this, and had to depend on another author to help him understand. In addition, according to Luke 3.1, Iturea, which formed part of the tetrarchy of Philip, was clearly distinguished from the Galilee of Herod Antipas.

Jewish Galilee therefore had a respectable antiquity and continuity, in which we still find certain traces going back as far as the charter of Antiochus III. On the other hand, S. Safrai, in a thoroughly documented study,[71] shows that the rabbinic tradition fully recognized the Jewish character (in the sense of the rabbinic tradition) of first-century Galilee, before and after the destruction of Jerusalem, and even concludes that Judaism, in the sense of the aforementioned tradition, was perhaps better established there than in Judaea.[72] This result could be extended.

Rabbinic tradition claimed to be the heir of the academy at Yavneh, in Judaea, which became a flourishing centre after the destruction of the Temple, under the aegis of two key figures: the founder Johanan ben Zakkai, and his successor Gamaliel II. I examine first the external sources. The town of Yavneh-Jamnia, located between Jaffa and Ascalon, six miles from the sea, but endowed with a port and some territory, had

70.   Cf. Schürer, *History*, I, pp. 141, 562; II, pp. 8-10, who considers without real proof that the conquered 'part of Iturea' referred to Galilee; this opinion, which follows the suggestion of Josephus, implies (or presupposes) that the Judaism of Galilee was marginal.

71.   S. Safrai, 'The Jewish Cultural Nature of Galilee in the First Century', *Immanuel* 24/25 (1990), pp. 147-86.

72.   He completes in fact the study of A. Oppenheimer, *Galilee in the Mishnaic Period* (Jerusalem: Zalman Shazar Center, 1991), who points out, with all the necessary references, that the works on Jewish Galilee, as it was before the destruction of the Temple and in particular in the time of Jesus, are often marred by apologetic prejudices. For some (cf. Schürer, *History*, quoted above), Galilee was, in comparison to Judaea, a marginal region, where the Judaism was more 'liberal'; for others (in particular Büchler), the two regions were culturally homogeneous, although distinct in development. Oppenheimer himself belongs in this second camp; cf. a review and discussion in *RB* 100 (1993), pp. 436-46. Earlier, W.D. Davies, *The Setting of the Sermon on the Mount* (Cambridge: Cambridge University Press, 1964), pp. 450-51, had glimpsed in a brief appendix some slight differences between Jewish Galilee and Jewish Judaea, but in underestimating traditional *legal* observance in Galilee.

been given by Herod to his sister Salome (*War* 2.98). At her death it passed to the Empress Livia and afterwards it seems to have been a personal property of Tiberias, therefore administratively outside Judaea. Philo mentioned however that the population was in majority Jewish[73] (*Leg. Gai.* 200-203). Later, in 68, at the time of the extension into Judaea of the Galilee war, Vespasian had brought with him 'many citizens who had surrendered in return for some privileges', and had installed garrisons at Yavneh and Ashdod (*War* 4.130). Next, in circumstances about which Josephus gives no details, Vespasian put down among others the insurrections at Lod and Yavneh, and 'installed there as inhabitants a sufficient number of Jews who had come over to him' (*War* 4.444). The sequence of events is confused, but we detect in the background a precise policy, at a time in which unrest threatened the last years of the reign of Nero: like Herod at the time of the colony at Bathyra, he installed in some well-chosen places Jews who were loyal to him, or rather who were little involved in political affairs. Later, it was Titus, son of Vespasian, who led the Roman army in the war in Judaea in 70. He tried a similar policy. When the high priests and other notables came to surrender to the Roman command during the siege, they were transferred and put under house arrest at Gophna in Judaea; but when a little later the rumour went round in Jerusalem that they would not be seen again because they had been killed, Titus had them shown to the besieged to convince them to surrender—but without great success[74] (*War* 6.114).

It is in this context that we are able to interpret the rabbinic information on the foundation of Johanan ben Zakkai, since by itself this information is very confused. On the one hand, it was stated that he surrendered to Vespasian, predicted to him that he would become emperor, and managed to be installed at Yavneh with a few teachers. On the other hand, it was reported that having tried in vain, in a Jerusalem

73.   The non-Jews were foreigners, which suggests that the Jews had status (as in an imperial city), but the town was administered by a procurator. Philo explained that the affair of the statue of Caligula in the Temple began with a provocation at Yavneh, where the foreigners erected a brick altar and sacrificed on it. According to Strabo, *Geography* 16.2.28, the region of Jamnia (which he described in the time of Herod as a village, and not as a *polis*) could arm 40,000 men, which is a considerable number.

74.   This submission of priests raises the problem of a possible restoration of cult after the war; cf. K.W. Clark, 'Worship in the Jerusalem Temple after 70', *NTS* 6 (1960), pp. 269-80.

unrelentingly besieged, to persuade his fellow citizens to bring a futile war to an end, he had fled the city hidden in a coffin in order to surrender to Vespasian and obtain concessions from him (*ARN* A, 4).[75]

These accounts have been analyzed for a long time, since they are difficult to reconcile. The matter of the flight during the siege of Jerusalem fits under Titus but not under Vespasian, while the prediction can only fit Vespasian and not Titus. The discussions of modern historians are most often solely directed towards the point of knowing under which of the two generals the episode took place, even if that means interpreting it as a possible treason, but always supposing that Joḥanan ben Zakkai came from Jerusalem, Now, this fundamental point is doubtful.[76] In the first place, Josephus, who omitted nothing which was socially important, did not know him, whereas he knew Simon ben Gamaliel, a Pharisaic personality from Jerusalem and father of Gamaliel II. Then, the working life of Joḥanan before Yavneh, known only from rabbinic sources, consisted of having run a school at Arab, near Sephoris, therefore in Galilee, but with very moderate success (*y. Šab.* 16.8). Furthermore, a curious Christian legend recounts, always in Galilee, that his father (Zakkai/Zacchaeus) had to bow before the knowledge of the child Jesus.[77] Some rumour was therefore preserved about the Galilean connections of Joḥanan ben Zakkai, perhaps in Judaeo-Christian circles in Galilee.[78] Finally, he is made out to be the last disciple of Hillel the Elder (*b. Meg.* 13a). Now, the latter, a Babylonian, had been promoted precisely by the 'Elders of Bathyra', therefore again in (eastern) Galilee.

75.   These accounts have been transmitted in several versions, which have been presented and commented on by J. Neusner, *A Life of Yohanan ben Zakkai, Ca. 1–80 CE* (SPB, 6; Leiden: Brill, 1970), pp. 152-54. We adopt quite different conclusions here, except for the date of the arrival of Johanan at Yavneh.

76.   Despite some accounts presenting him as a witness to the burning of the Temple (*ARN* B, §7); to console a colleague, he declared that there was a form of expiation which was as efficacious as the cult, namely, charity (*ARN*, A, §4), which was a way *of denying* the Temple, since this precept had existed long before; cf. *m. Ab.* 1.2, which attributes it to Simon the Just. In the same spirit, the famous declaration of Hillel to a proselyte ('Do not do to others what you do not wish that they do to you. This is the essential point of the Law; the rest is just commentary. Go and study it', *b. Šab.* 31a) denies the cult as well, or instrumentalizes it.

77.   *Gos. Thom.* 6-8. The legend had circulated, since it was known to Irenaeus, *Adversus Haereses* 1.20.1. There were besides some relationships between some of the parables (on the kingdom) of Jesus and Joḥanan ben Zakkai; cf. *Mt.* 22.1-14 par. and *b. Šab.* 153a.

78.   Neusner's discussion, *Yohanan ben Zakkai*, pp 53-56.

There is nothing to indicate that Hillel or Joḥanan ben Zakkai had ever settled on a long-term basis in Jerusalem, which does not of course exclude the possibility that they had come as pilgrims or even had taught and had disciples there.[79] The Galilean connections, with Babylonian Judaism in the background, are on the contrary very clear, as well as a certain political innocence, which cannot help but remind us of the Hasidaeans of 1 Macc. 7.13-18, whom the high priest feared (since he killed them). Under these conditions, the foundation of the school at Yavneh is accounted for by a very simple hypothesis, in the proposed setting of Vespasian's campaign in 68: Johanan, unknown in Jerusalem, would have been one of the submissive Galileans installed at Yavneh, a Judaean town detached from Jerusalem.[80] His prediction to Vespasian would then have come from Galilee, just like that of Josephus to Jotapata (*War* 3.401), but with another meaning. Priority should be given then to the first of the versions cited. As for the escape of Joḥanan from a starving Jerusalem *under Vespasian*, as the second version indicated, it would be the result then of the fusion of two motifs: an escape of Joḥanan under Vespasian from some unknown place under siege, as in the first version, and an escape out of Jerusalem under Titus of unknown or unspecified persons. This second motif could have been a very deliberate reinterpretation of the deportation of priests to Gophna by Titus, in such a way as to show that the school of Yavneh, although unaffected by actual priestly influence, was nevertheless heir to the traditions of Jerusalem relative to the Temple. Various accounts show besides some tensions between certain priests and Joḥanan ben Zakkai, who was always opposed to the Sadducees[81] (cf. *m. ʿEd.* 8.3, *m. Šeq.* 1.4, etc.).

This conclusion, establishing a modest and Galilean beginning for the school at Yavneh before the destruction of Jerusalem, explains very well

79.   According to *b. Pes.* 26a, they taught just about everywhere in the squares; in *t. Hag.* 2.11, he teaches on the occasion of a pilgrimage.

80.   According to *b. Roš. Haš.* 29.2, people from Bathyra (בני בתירא) were also found at Yavneh right from the beginning and with notable rank; later, a Juda ben Bathyra was a contemporary of Akiba (*m. Kel.* 2.4), but left to found (or to go back to) a school at Nisibis in Mesopotamia (*Sifre Deut.* 80).

81.   A. Guttman, 'The End of the Jewish Sacrificial Cult', *HUCA* 38 (1967), pp. 137-48, who, although maintaining the traditional views on the patriarchal authority at Jerusalem of the Hillelites (Gamaliel, Simon) insists with good references on the opposition of Joḥanan to the war against the Romans as well as to the Sadducees, the priests and the Temple cult.

why Josephus would ignore it. Among the known attitudes of Joḥanan ben Zakkai, we note that he feared the growing authority of scriptural references, which risked altering the primacy of the oral tradition.[82] From Judaea, he therefore had to fear, apart from politico-social upheavals, the priesthood and the importance given to Scripture. That could be enough to explain why he would have accepted a situation closer to the Romans.

His successor Gamaliel II was a person of a different calibre, but especially of a different origin. His grandfather Gamaliel, St Paul's teacher, and his father Simon, whom Josephus knew, were Pharisaic notables known in Jerusalem. However, the tradition claimed that Gamaliel I was the son or perhaps the grandson of Hillel, himself a descendant of David, but this assertion should be considered doubtful, since it amounted at most to the subsequent legitimation of the patriarchal dynasty, and especially of the patriarch Judas, at the end of the second century: in fact *m. Ab.* 1.16 introduced Gamaliel I, in the chain of transmitters, immediately after Hillel (and Shammai), but without any indication of any privileged family ties[83] or academic connections, and mentioned besides that one of his aphorisms was that it is necessary 'to choose a teacher', which could be an echo of his own situation, or less probably the indication of a certain liberalism. In literary terms, the discontinuity was even greater than between Hillel and his predecessors, and what is more it is Joḥanan ben Zakkai and not Gamaliel who in the same passage is presented as the heir of Hillel and Shammai (2.8). Only traces of this discontinuity however survived: the two of them were clearly considered heirs of Hillel's authority, and this synthesis was really the pivot of the rabbinic tradition. Hillel himself, we have seen, combined an origin (or a culture) that was Babylonian with the education of the Pharisees of Judaea, which is really a way of saying that he is the common ancestor of Joḥanan and Gamaliel, but the matter is so much in conformity with that tradition that it can be presupposed to be a bit contrived.

---

82.   According to *Soṭ.* 5.2, he feared that in the future the status of impurity of the third degree would be forgotten, for lack of a scriptural support. However, Akiba ended up finding one, based on a detail of the Hebrew letter; the laws on impurity are traditional, and he held them to be fundamental, but the problem of their being forgotten is *new*.

83.   According to *y. Ket.* 12.3, p. 35a, Judas the Patriarch expressly introduced himself as a descendant of Hillel, while expressing his admiration for the Elders of Bathyra. Real consanguinity cannot therefore be entirely ruled out.

Gamaliel II increased the prestige of the school of Yavneh, brought teachers and disciples of considerable merit there, maintained good contact with the Roman authorities, and visited Jewish communities, in particular in Galilee and at Rome. These authorities permitted the development of other schools, among them Lod, and attracted to Yavneh a spectrum of people with various opinions. Gamaliel was a Pharisee, which represented a less strict tendency than that of many Galileans.[84] Several anecdotes[85] show that Gamaliel or his sons submitted without protest to more restrictive local customs, on the occasion of journeys in Galilee. He had therefore a particular respect for the Galilean tradition, but at the same time, at Yavneh, he maintained a greater open-mindedness. This was however out of concern for unity more than out of liberalism, for he was set on controlling the accreditations for teaching (*b. Nid.* 24b) and practical decisions, not without harshness at times; he was insistent on having the last word on the fixing of the calendar, without for all that pretending to be the most learned (*m. Roš. Haš.* 2.8-9). Johanan ben Zakkai, who ended his days at Beror Hayil, really seems to have been dismissed; Eliezer ben Hyrcanus his disciple, known for his fidelity to accepted teachings, was banished (*b. B. Meṣ.* 59a-b), since he would not submit to the majority. It was a question again, at least in the last two cases, of Galilean traditions, perhaps defended in sectarian ways.

The coexistence of complex sensitivities was not easy to maintain, as several indications clearly suggest: in the first place, there was the famous affair of the blessing against the 'sectarians' (or 'heretics', *minim*) which had trouble in being adopted (*y. Ber.* 28b). Whether or not it had been directed against Christians, which is unlikely,[86] its difficulty in getting through attests to a struggle between several tendencies. In fact, numerous rabbinic sayings, which it would take too long to analyze here, could be connected to the parties described by Josephus, or could presuppose them. As a matter of fact, if Gamaliel was a Pharisee, Johanan was more readily connected with the Hasidaeans, therefore with the Essenes; subsequently, Aqiba, and hence also his predecessors, took

---

84. The case of war on the Sabbath illustrated one difference between Jerusalemites and Galileans; cf. Chapter 2, §2.

85. Translation and commentary by Safrai, 'Jewish Cultural Nature', pp. 178-80.

86. D. Flusser, 'Some of the Precepts of the Torah from Qumran (4QMMT) and the Benediction against the Heretics', *Tarbiz* 61 (1992), pp. 333-74, shows in particular that the existence of such a benediction was really earlier than Christianity.

after the Zealots in their support of political activism and at the same time after the Sadducees in their imperious concern in wanting to connect the oral tradition to the Scriptures. In this connection, it is remarkable to see Josephus, who had at first written in *War* 2.119-66 of three traditional parties (*haireseis*) which were the Pharisees, the Sadducees and the Essenes, introduce some twenty years later a fourth, the heirs of Judas the Galilean (*Ant.* 18.23-25), and therefore the Zealots. Their ideas, he explained, were close to those of the Pharisees, but it amounted to madness, responsible for the ruin. An exterior factor had therefore led him to consider as a party in its own right this tendency which he judged to be disastrous, back when he had fought and hated it. As he defined all these parties, however, uniquely on the basis of certain doctrines, without any direct link either with the Temple or the priesthood or any official institution like the Sanhedrin, it must be concluded that his reference to them is after the war, and that it was a matter of scholarly tendencies, and not of a description of all the people. It is very possible that he would have heard about the growing moral authority of the school of Yavneh under Gamaliel, indeed even about a beginning of a special status granted by the Romans (cf. *m. 'Ed.* 7.7). In fact, right after the war, the Jews of Judaea had been deprived of their own jurisdiction (a so-called situation of *dediticii*),[87] and many like Josephus had chosen integration into a Roman status. Nevertheless, it could not stand to reason that the school of Yavneh, even with a Gamaliel conciliating the Romans and receptive of Greek culture, would be recognized by all as the unique heir of the complex of Jerusalem institutions, in particular because of the complete absence of priestly authority; we can imagine that Josephus would have respected it, but in a convoluted way.

In a general way, however, the authority of Gamaliel as ethnarch remained unstable: he was once momentarily deposed (*b. Ber.* 27b), and none of his sons directly succeeded him at his death, perhaps in part because of the Roman authorities, since he died around the time of the revolts under Trajan. Other elements make it possible to outline a little more his profile and his teaching: it was recounted that after this revolt, it was decided to prohibit the study of Greek (or study in Greek; *t. Soṭ.* 15.8-9), but that the house of Gamaliel was permitted to continue it, because it was close to the Roman government; there was therefore potentially a rupture at a critical time. On the subject of Greek, it was

87.   But religious liberty was maintained for them (except for the *fiscus iudaicus*); cf. Schürer, *History*, III, pp. 122-24.

reported in *b. Soṭ.* 49b that a thousand boys had been studying in his school, five hundred the Torah, five hundred Greek wisdom,[88] but that there remained only Simon his son and a cousin on the run. That school had not had the expected outcome, but not just for political reasons, since there are reasons to think that the problem of Greek was not irrelevant to the propagation of the New Testament in Judaea.[89]

This same Simon II, son of Gamaliel, proud of the school of his father, reappeared later in Galilee, after the war of Bar Kochba (132–135), in circumstances which throw light on the Pharisaic characteristics of Gamaliel, and therefore are worth examining. The immediate causes of that war are disputed[90] but in any case it was very bitter and lasted three and a half years. Jerusalem was then rebuilt under the imperial name of Aelia, and Jews were banned. Circumcision remained illegal through-out the Empire. After the death of Hadrian in 138, Antonin the Pious re-stored circumcision for the Jews. It was in this context that the survivors from Judaea emigrated to Galilee, especially the disciples of Aqiba, this teacher who had believed in Bar Kochba and had been tortured to death by the Romans. There had no longer been a Sanhedrin or a patriarchate from long before the war, at least according to the rabbinic tradition, since the finds in the desert of Judaea show that Bar Kochba had had the title of patriarch (נשׂיא),[91] and a certain Batnia ben Mesah, unknown

88.   That is to say, the language and the literature; cf. S. Lieberman, *Hellenism in Jewish Palestine* (New York: Jewish Theological Seminary of America, 1950), p. 102 n. 18.

89.   Cf. Nodet, 'Miettes messianiques', pp. 128-30.

90.   Cf. Saul Lieberman, 'Persecution of the Jewish religion', in *Festschrift S.W. Baron* (3 vols.; Jerusalem: Magnes, 1979), III, p. 214; M.D. Herr, 'Causes of the Bar Kokhba Revolt', *Zion* 43 (1978), p. 6, with bibliography. Ever since Graetz (cf. Schürer, *History*, I, p. 535), it has been assumed that it was because Hadrian, after having promised to restore the sanctuary, had changed his mind under Samar-itan pressure; this has been challenged by G. Alon, *The Jews in their Land in the Talmudic Age (70–640 CE)* (2 vols.; Jerusalem: Magnes, 1984), II, pp. 435-37. We may however wonder, in the opposite direction, whether it was the town-planning projects of Hadrian (on top of the prohibition of circumcision) which, by threatening the final cultic possibilities at Jerusalem, would have triggered a Maccabaean-type revolt. This question is tied up with the existence or not of some cult in Jerusalem after 70.

91.   From the coins dated according to the era of the 'liberation of Israel'; cf. references in Schürer, *History*, I, p. 544 n. 133. The rabbinic tradition, which had banished the memory of Bar Kochba, left a gap just about corresponding to the reign of Hadrian between the patriarchates of Gamaliel II and Simon II his son, but

from the classical sources, was referred to in several documents by a name normally reserved for the patriarch[92] (רבנו), which indicates that the school of Aqiba, enhanced in status subsequently, was not at that time the central authority.

The inaugural assembly of the survivors took place at an unspecified date at Usha,[93] not far from Haifa, with in particular Yehuda bar Ilai, who was born there and had studied there with his father (*b. Men.* 18a). He had also been a disciple of Aqiba at Bené-Berak, and was like him a master of *midrash halakha*, that is to say, of the joining of oral traditions to Scripture (*b. Sanh.* 86a).

That assembly at Usha without a patriarch, but led by Yehuda,[94] invited the Elders of Galilee to join them for study (*Cant. R.* 2.16, on Cant. 2.5); these came from the East, travelling 10-40 miles, which corresponds to a region going from Sepphoris to the east bank of the Lake. In other words, Yehuda bar Ilai, the heir of Aqiba, returned home to Galilee, and his authority was accepted by the local sages. Simon ben Gamaliel returned later, but had some difficulties in having himself accepted as patriarch. A colourful account (*b. Hor.* 13b-14a) depicts how, on the occasion of a conflict over precedence, Natan, president of the academy (or of the tribunal), and Meir an expert, thinking one day that they had been humiliated, planned to ridicule him the next day by forcing him to display in public his ignorance of a whole treatise. It amounted to a dismissal of his pretension of taking over the institution, by showing that he had nothing to contribute. The plot was thwarted

---

suggests that the family was settled at Betar, the place of the final defeat (*b. Soṭ.* 48b, *y. Ta'an.* 4), and had been harshly dealt with there. The information, which would put Betar around *Beth Jimal* is geographically doubtful (but not in literary terms; cf. A. Neubauer, *La géographie du Talmud* [Paris: M. Lévy, 1868], pp. 103-104), but it emphasizes the solidarity of the patriarchal family with the victims.

92.   In the letters from Nahal Hever; cf. N. Avigad, 'The Expedition to the Judaean Desert, 1960', *IEJ* 2 (1961), pp. 3-72, and P. Benoit, J.-T. Milik and R. de Vaux, *Les grottes de Murabba'at* (DJD, 2; Oxford: Clarendon Press, 1961), pp. 124-26.

93.   Identified with *Husha*, at the foot of Carmel; it was two Sabbath distances from Shefar'am according to *b. 'Abod. Zar.* 8b.

94.   Another version situated the event in the 'vineyard of Yavneh' (*b. Ber.* 63b-64a), but the context presupposes that Yehuda was in fact at home, in Usha, and he is presented as the 'leader of the participants'. The transfer of the name of Yavneh symbolized a displacement of the centre of authority, indeed of associated institutions.

however.[95] Other passages show that he often quoted other sages,[96] but always his contemporaries and never his teachers or the Elders; he only rendered decisions that conformed to the proceedings of his court.[97] Compared to Simon ben Yohai, another important disciple of Aqiba, he was 'like a fox facing a lion', which was a sign of ignorance.[98] Nevertheless, he always respectfully emphasized the importance of the school which his father Gamaliel II had established (*b. Soṭ.* 49b).

In actual fact, the weaknesses of Simon ben Gamaliel were solely in regard to the *oral tradition*: the plot referred to above was aimed at showing his ignorance of the treatise *Uqṣin*, which was concerned with the impurity of the inedible parts of foods, a subtle subject without any scriptural foundation and apparently unknown too to his father's school in Judaea. Elsewhere, he declared in regard to a controversy over the use of Samaritan unleavened bread that 'with regard to every precept (*miṣva*) that the Samaritans observe, they are stricter than Israel' (*t. Pasha* 1.15); to put it plainly, he appreciated their *biblical* exactness. In another context (*t. Ter.* 4.12), he said from the same perspective that the Samaritans are 'like Israel', whereas Judah the Prince, who had as a criterion only the oral tradition, said later on that they were 'like the pagans'. Simon had pedagogical responsibilities too, and in particular he allowed the students to light a lamp on the Sabbath so that they could prepare their biblical readings (*t. Šab.* 1.12), whereas the oral tradition prohibited this, in order to avoid any temptation to rekindle the flame (*m. Šab.* 1.3); such a custom, which he must have received from his father's school, where they studied Scripture, shows again the great importance given to what was written.[99]

95.   But things were awkward, since there was mention, in an important list of 'decrees of Usha', the prohibition to excommunicate an Elder (*y. M. Qat.* 3.1, p. 81d); *y. Bik.* 3.3, p. 65c, gives a different account, but one which shows too a resistance to the installation of Simon ben Gamaliel.

96.   *m. Ber.* 6.9; *m. B. Meṣ.* 8.8; the evidence of the Tosefta is significant because of its frequency: *t. Ber.* 5.2; *t. Ma'as. Š.* 3.18; *t. Suk.* 2.2; *t. Yeb.* 10.16; *t. Kel.-BQ* 4.2, 5.4.

97.   *y. B. Bat.* 10.2. It has been deduced from this that he possessed an unaccustomed humility, which his son Judah the Prince stated as well (*b. B. Meš.* 84b).

98.   *m. Ab.* 4.15 and *y. Šab.*, 10.7.

99.   The later justifications for this discordant tradition, trying to prove that it was rational, simply sought to 'normalize' Simon, since they made it incomprehensible that this usage would have later disappeared; cf. *b. Šab.* 13a and Lieberman, *Tosefta kifshuṭah*, III, p. 10.

By gathering together these small pieces of information relative to Gamaliel II and his son Simon, we see that these Pharisees who had come from Jerusalem had a tendency that was decidedly more biblical than the strictly Galilean milieux, which gave rise to some problems. This conclusion clarifies in passing a paradox about Josephus: he called himself a Pharisee, but when he paraphrased the Bible, in the *Antiquities*, he stated very clearly in the prologue that it was the only source of wisdom and law, which is an opinion rather Sadducean in appearance; then, when he presented these laws in detail, he gave numerous practical interpretations, sometimes remote from the literal sense, which we meet again in the rabbinic sources. In other words, he definitely had, as regards Scripture, a Judaean and not a Galilean way of being faithful to the oral tradition.

The other protagonists on the scene at Usha came from different backgrounds: Meir was supposed to have been the most faithful disciple of Aqiba (*b. Sanh.* 86a), and the first of the five 'teachers from the South' (*b. Yeb.* 62b); it is therefore significant that he should have been the academic authority referred to in the assembly. Nathan, the president of the court, was the son of the Babylonian exilarch, which is worth noting. The assembly of Usha represented then a confluent of tendencies, at the close of the dark period of Hadrian, with some competition there for power: the heirs of Aqiba, towards whom the available sources (Mishnah, etc.) were favourably disposed, linked up first with the Galileans, then with a branch of the Babylonian patriarchate, with the integration of the Judaean patriarchate being the most difficult. The last remained in abeyance for decades.

On the other hand, it is clear that the Judaean tendency, or more exactly the Jerusalemite tendency, was secondary in comparison to Galilean (Babylonian) Judaism, and not the other way around, since it had been subjected to the influence of other parties. As for the term 'Pharisee', which meant 'separated', it was a name stemming from opposing groups (cf. *m. Yad.* 4.6-71), therefore in Jerusalem rather than in Galilee. Scholars agree then, for the sake of clarity, that it should be reserved for the party identified at Jerusalem, and so to follow practically the definitions of the Jerusalemite Josephus. The term 'Galilean' remains however ambiguous, since Josephus already said in his account (*Ant.* 18.11-25) that the Pharisees and the Galileans (the fourth party) had the same ideas, particularly concerning the primacy of ancestral traditions. As these Galileans were none other than the Zealots, therefore an active minority coming from that region, this means that the Pharisees were also widespread in Galilee, as the New Testament clearly confirms. As for the Galilean branch represented by Hillel, Johanan ben Zakkai or Yehuda bar Ilai, among whom questions of purity were of major importance, they have been linked with that reduced minority made up of the Hasidaeans-Essenes. By taking some schematic indicators in the New Testament, to clarify ideas, if Paul is connected more with the Pharisees, John the Baptist should be compared to the Essenes, and Jesus is situated between the two of them.

As for the development from the Hasidaeans to the Pharisees, it is represented to perfection by the book of Nehemiah. It put in place what has been called the 'model of Nehemiah', according to Babylonian norms which have been connected to the Hasidaeans. Then, between the two missions of Nehemiah the law of Moses was proclaimed to a group which obviously already had its own cohesion and customs. Scripture was valued, but customs which were expressly not scriptural were maintained, as we saw in Neh. 13.1-3, with the manipulation of a verse of Deuteronomy to support a practice that was contrary to it.

6. *The 'People of the Land'*

The extreme precariousness of the group who were the bearers of the Torah and ancestral traditions, as appears from the ups and downs of the 'model of Nehemiah', the history of the Hasidaeans, the epics of Mattathias and Judas, the erring ways of the Pharisees in the time of Hillel or the formation of the rabbinic tradition in Galilee, practically gives the impression of a quasi-nomadic group, in the strict as well as in the broad sense, which struggled to settle down on a long-term basis among the settled population, at least in Judaea. These difficulties form a contrast with what we glimpse of a structural permanence in Babylonian Judaism, and of its wide diffusion in the Seleucid and then the Roman empires, except perhaps in Alexandria. We note meanwhile, at certain salient moments, that the founding groups or reorganizing groups, which subsequent traditions presented as central and well-received, were in reality marginal and very restricted in size, which did not rule out the presence of strong personalities, but just the contrary. Nehemiah had trouble in filling up his city: the 'Men of the Great Assembly', described as a whole generation, had the dimensions of a village; Mattathias and Judas Maccabeus only represented small groups at the beginning, subsequent increases notwithstanding; the promotion of Hillel came from a small distant colony; the schools of Yavneh and Usha had very modest beginnings. We obviously could say the same thing about the beginnings of Christianity. The general outline was of the 'small remnant' type: after a crisis a small more or less marginal group, very well-motivated and firmly rooted in a tradition, created in precarious conditions a new synthesis and then, when a posterity developed in an appreciable manner, the latter reinterpreted the outcome in terms of a continuity, not without bringing about selections and choices in the tradition: the marginal offspring became the principal heir; the Davidic sonship constituted a remarkable example of this process. It is advisable therefore to distinguish clearly such a small group, a school, from the population as a whole, necessarily more amorphous, or more unstable in case of a crisis. This distinction, which I am going to develop for the Tannaitic period, had some biblical antecedents.

Already, in Gen. 34.30, Jacob criticized Simeon and Levi, after the massacre of the Shechemites, because in this way he had been rendered odious among 'the inhabitants of the country' (יושב הארץ). This would be a remark of a nomad who did not have a covenant with a powerful sedentary community. Exod. 34.11-12 contains restrictive instructions: 'I am going to drive out ahead of you the Amorites, the Canaanites, the Hittites [...] Take care not to make a covenant with the inhabitants of the land you are about to enter [...].' We encounter the reality of being members of a minority again in Judges, which reduces to their proper proportions the stereotypes of Joshua. Before the conquest, the Reubenites and the Gadites declared: 'Our young children will stay in the fortified towns, safe from the inhabitants of the country' (Num. 32.17). The Pentateuch therefore deferred the conquest to the future, announcing complicated relations with the inhabitants of the country.

In the period in focus, the Hasmonaeans, and then Herod, tried to unify the population, and it is clear that the group that chose Hillel as patriarch was socially dissident, and, what is more, distant from the Temple.

The Talmudic literature was familiar with a concept of 'people of the country' (עם הארץ, literally: 'people of the land'), which it clearly distinguished from the pagans; this was frequently used in the *halakha*. It came up again especially over questions about the tithe (in relation to the Temple) and about purity (in relation to the neighbourhood). The expression is interesting for its own sake, since it presupposes that the group using it did not consider themselves by right and/or in fact as the ordinary population of the place, but on the contrary as separate from it.

The phrase is well attested in the Bible,[100] where it sometimes has a simple meaning, similar to 'inhabitant of the land': in Gen. 23.7, 12-13, Abraham bowed before the 'people of the land', who were just sons of Heth at Hebron (cf. 34.30 on Jacob). In Gen. 42.6, Joseph distributed grain to all the 'people of the land', therefore to the Egyptians; but in Exod. 5.5, Pharaoh refused to interrupt the forced labour of the 'people of the land' (LXX ὁ λαός) who had become numerous, so the Israelites were meant.[101] Elsewhere it referred to the Canaanites, 'the people of the land' (Num. 14.14, after the return of the scouts). In the time of the monarchy, the meaning became clearer, since it concerned the Israelite or Judaean people, as subjects of the king (2 Kgs 11.14-20; 15.5; 16.15; 21.24; 24.30, 35; Isa. 24.4; Jer. 1.18; 34.19; 37.2; 44.21; Ezek. 7.27, etc.; Job 12.24; Dan. 9.6), sometimes with a cultic nuance (Ezek. 46.9). According to 2 Kgs 24.14, under Nebuchadnezzar, only the poorest part of the people of the land escaped the exile (דלת עם הארץ; LXX οἱ πτωχοὶ τῆς γῆς), with a rural shade of meaning (25.3 and 19). On the return from exile, Hag. 2.4 encouraged the high priest Jeshua and the people of the land, and Zech. 7.5 laid stress on the local people who had forgotten the Temple, and not on the repatriated, who are rather intrusive. On the contrary, according to Ezra 4.4 the 'people of the land' were opposed to the restoration. In this sense, the expression occurs several times in the plural, designating the adversaries (Ezra 3.3; 9.1,11; Neh. 9.30), and in general those from whom they should keep away (Ezra 10.2, 11; Neh. 10.29 LXX; 10.31-32; 1 Chron. 5.25; 2 Chron. 13.9[102]); in these passages, the idea (which we meet in Deut. 28.10, Josh. 4.24; 1 Kgs 8.43-61; Ezek. 31.12; Zeph. 3.20; Est. 8.17; 2 Chron. 32.13) that the 'peoples of the land', or 'peoples of the earth' would have to recognize YHWH is entirely absent.

This rapid study of the 'people of the land' in the Bible points to two clearly distinct senses: when there happened to be a cult and a king, it was simply the people of the territory, that is to say, those who had no particular role; when there was no central authority, the 'people of the land' referred to the adversaries of the Israelites. The distinction is particularly suggestive for the texts relative to the restoration. The prophets, who spoke of the cult in the Temple, encouraged all the people. For Ezra–Nehemiah, which said little about it, it was a matter of local

100.   Cf. de Vaux, *Ancient Israel*, pp. 70-72, with references.

101.   Instead of רבים עם הארץ 'the people of the land had become numerous'; SP has, more logically, רבים מעם הארץ 'they have become more numerous than the people of the land', that is to say, the Egyptians.

102.   '[…] to make you priests *like the peoples of the lands* [כעמי הארצות]'; the LXX has ἐκ τοῦ λαοῦ τῆς γῆς (from מעם הארץ) 'descended from the people of the land', which is a quite different meaning.

adversaries (in particular in the plural), which comes close to the nomadizing accounts of the Pentateuch. There is therefore a comparison to be made between this last concept and the use of the turn of phrase in rabbinic literature.

In juridical material, only two texts involve the 'people of the land'. The first, Lev. 20.2-5. made it obligatory for the 'people of the land' to stone anyone, whether a son of Israel or a stranger resident (מן הגר הגר, LXX ἀπὸ τῶν προσγεγενημένων προσηλύτων) in Israel, who gave of his posterity (זרע, σπέρμα) to Molech.[103] It is a matter of a people dealing with an individual, as the Targum understood it.[104] The second concerned faults through inadvertence: Lev. 4.27 stipulated that if anyone of the 'people of the land' sins through inadvertence and becomes culpable, that person will bring a she-goat to be sacrificed. But, in a parallel manner, Lev. 5.17 says that if someone sins without knowing it and makes themselves culpable, they will bring in reparation a ram. The second occurrence is isolated, while the first occurs in a list of faults by inadvertence, in which 'anyone of the people of the land' is listed after the high priest, the entire people and the leader, and we find the distinctions envisaged above. In a characteristic way, the rabbinic tradition (*b. Ker.* 22b) discerns a nuance in the doublet: the culprit is the same, but when he is found among the 'people of the land', there is a connotation of pure ignorance, while in the second case the fault follows from a doubt, that is to say, from incomplete knowledge.

For the Talmudic sources, the expression 'people of the land' had become a sort of term denoting a deficiency.[105] One text shows that the definition had evolved: according to *m. Ber.* 7.1, the invitation to prayer after the meal (ברכת המזון) was obligatory as long as there were three eating together, even if one of them was a Cuthaean (Samaritan). In regard to this case, the *Talmud* developed a debate (*b. Ber.* 47b):

> 'Why are they not simply considered as "people of the land"? since it is taught [*baraita*]: An invitation is not extended to one who belongs to the "people of the land". Abbayé says: It is about a Cuthaean who is also an "associate".[106] Raba said: You can also certainly say that it is about a

103. Or: '...will have lain with an idolatrous woman' (through incitement), according to Ibn Ezra.

104. *Targ. Onqelos*; Rashi adds that the people could only inherit the land by extirpating idolatry from it; *Targ. Jonathan* introduced the procedure of formal condemnation, in order to avoid lynching.

105. For a presentation of various opinions on the meaning of the expression, in relation or not to the origins of Christianity, cf. A. Oppenheimer, *The 'Am ha-aretz* (ALGHJ, 8; Leiden: Brill, 1977), pp. 2-4.

106. חבר, a member of a brotherhood concerned about Levitical purity, similar to the Essenes (therefore also to the Hasidaeans; cf. 2 Macc. 5.27) or to the community following the Rule of Qumran; for references and discussion, cf. Urbach, *The*

Cuthaean who belongs to the "people of the land", for here [in the *baraita* above], it is about the "people of the land" as defined by the teachers [רבנן], for it has been taught [*baraita*]: Who belongs to a "people of the land"? Anyone who does not eat secular food in a state of levitical purity; this is the opinion of R. Meir. But the sages [חכמים] said: Anyone who does not tithe his produce properly. However the Cuthaeans tithe their produce properly, and carefully observe what is written in the Torah, for a teacher[107] has said: For in all the precepts which they observe, the Cuthaeans are more meticulous than Israel.'

'The teachers pointed out [*baraita*]: Who belongs to the "people of the land"? Anyone who does not recite the *Shema Israel* morning and evening; this is the opinion of R. Eliezer. R. Joshua said: Anyone who does not wear the phylacteries. Ben Azzai said: Anyone who does not have fringes on his garment. R. Nathan says: Anyone who does not have a *Mezuzah* at his door. R. Jonathan ben Joseph said: Anyone who has sons and does not train them to study the Torah. Others said: Anyone who has studied Scripture and the Mishnah, but has not been in the company of the teachers, is considered to be one of the "people of the land".'

Several small variants[108] of this last *baraita* show that it is not the result of an open discussion, but is a compilation of opinions expressed in various contexts. The suggestion that the Samaritans are 'people of the land', perhaps through allusion to Ezra 4.4, is ruled out, since they are observant, whereas the 'people of the land', in all the definitions then listed, are characterized by a failing in observance. These definitions divide up into two categories: 'people of the land relative to the commandments' (עם הארץ למצוות), in which it is a matter of non-observance of *biblical* precepts relating to the life of an individual, and 'people of the land relative to the Torah' (עם הארץ לתורה), in which it is a matter of the non-frequentation of the teachers, therefore of the *oral tradition*. In this latter sense, the Samaritans can be considered 'people of the land'. For our purpose, we should observe that all the definitions bring up perceptible marks of social differentiation, whether it was about purity or various visible signs. The case of the tithe is in the same category and is worth a brief examination.

Among the taxes on produce provided for in the Pentateuch, a distinction must be made between: the first fruits, intended for the priests (Num. 18.11-13), which were set by *m. Ter.* 4.3 at between the fortieth and the sixtieth of the value produced

---

Sages, pp. 583-84 and notes. The comparison between Samaritans and such confraternities is interesting.

107.   Simon ben Gamaliel, according to *b. Qid.* 76a.

108.   Cf. Urbach, *The Sages*, p. 633 nn. 55-57.

(תרומה גדולה); and the tithes, which followed more complex dispositions. According to Num. 18.26-32, a tenth of the produce was to be received by the Levites because of their service in the sanctuary, but they had in their turn to give a tenth to YHWH. According to Lev. 27.30-33, the tithe, vegetable and animal, belonged to God. According to Deut. 14.22-29, the tithe, in produce or in money after redemption, was intended to be consumed in the presence of YHWH in the place chosen, but every three years it was to be kept at home for the Levite, the poor and the orphan, and that legal relinquishment had to be solemnly declared in the place chosen (Deut. 26.12-15). It has been assumed that these precepts, contradictory in appearance, are traces of varying local customs, therefore of varying codes.[109] In any case, the known *halakha*, which we can call theoretical, since it was decided after the destruction of Jerusalem, combined them into a single system: after the offering of the first fruits, the tithe of the Levites was separated, and the latter, who could receive it any place, gave a tenth of it to the priests (תרומת מעשר). Then a second tithe was set aside to be eaten afterwards in Jerusalem (מעשר שני), but in the third and sixth years of the sabbatical cycle it was left for the poor[110] (מעשר עני).

The practice before the ruin of the Temple, as we discover in several sources, corresponded neither to the biblical data as a whole, nor to the structures of the *halakha*. According to Neh. 13.5-14, Jdt. 11.13, Tob. 1.6-7, the (one and only) tithe was brought to Jerusalem,[111] which corresponds to Lev. 27.30-33 alone. According to 1 Macc. 3.49-50, the Hellenization of the Temple made it impossible to fulfil[112] the precepts of the first fruits and the tithe. Josephus (*Ant.* 14.203) cites a decree of Julius Caesar confirming for Hyrcanus II, ethnarch and high priest, the privilege of receiving the tithe at Jerusalem, like his forefathers. According to *y. Ma'as Š.* 5.9, p. 56d, the tithe was, before John Hyrcanus, brought to Jerusalem and distributed in three parts: a third for the friends (מברים)[113] of the priests and Levites, a third for the treasury and a third for the poor and the 'associates' of Jerusalem.[114] John Hyrcanus

---

109. Cf. J. Wellhausen, *Prolegomena zur Geschichte Israels* (Berlin: Reimer, 3rd edn, 1905), pp. 150-52.

110. This is approximately the synthesis given by Josephus (*Ant.* 4.68, pp. 205, 240), which seems to say that the tithe of the poor was a *third* tithe (like *Jub.* 32.11, *Temple Scroll* col XLIII, and Tob. 1.8 [rec. AB]: his source was Pharisaic, and probably largely theoretical, without practical application).

111. According to the addition of 1 Sam. 1.21 LXX and Vulg. (repeated in *Ant.* 5.346), Elkanah brought to the temple at Shiloh the 'tithes of his land'.

112. In understanding τί ποιήσωμεν τούτοις (v. 50) as 'what shall we do with these things', and not 'with these people'; cf. Oppenheimer, *The 'Am ha-aretz*, p. 31. Likewise Philo, *Spec. Leg.* 1.132-52 indicated that the tithes and offerings had to be brought to Jerusalem.

113. Very likely the Temple 'guards' (משמרות); cf. S. Lieberman, 'Emendations on the Jerusalmi', *Tarbiz* 3 (1932).

114. Oppenheimer, *The 'Am ha-aretz*, p. 34, thinks that it must refer to 'associated' priests, or poor 'associates', so as to guarantee that the consumer was pure; this interpretation is however uselessly harmonizing, since the whole key to the

imposed then the collection of the tithe, and suppressed the solemn declaration of Deut. 26.12-15, since everything was confiscated and there was no longer any personal responsibility.

Later, Josephus described too (*Ant.* 20.181) the rapacity of the high priest Ismael ben Phiabi, his contemporary, who sent slaves to collect by force the tithes on the threshing floors, to the point of starving the ordinary priests, who were deprived of their due. At the time of the Galilean war (*Life* 181), he boasted about turning down the tithes to which he could lay claim. The declarations of Josephus are always under suspicion of being distorted, since he wanted to appear to be a Pharisee, or at least to be accepted by that school, but, precisely for this reason, he clearly showed that the Pharisees were at odds with the Temple over the basic problem of the tithe. In fact, the rabbinic tradition made no allusion whatsoever to the duty of bringing the tithe to the Temple. What is more, Josephus spoke of his own conduct in Galilee, and, if we suppose his statements to be coherent, it must be concluded that the high priestly tax collectors did not operate there, since the tithes were offered to him. This remark is related to two other facts about Galilee. First, the district of Batyra (east of the Lake), created by Herod and populated with pious Jews, was dispensed from the Judaean tax, in particular from the poll tax of a half-shekel, expressly intended for the cult.[115]. In addition, the movement of Judas the Galilean (or the 'Gaulanite', from Gamala[116]) the ancestor of the Zealots, had according to Josephus (*Ant.* 18:23), the same doctrines as the Pharisees, and the rebellion began with a refusal to obey the high priest Joazar, who had demanded the tax submission in the setting of the census by Augustus. Certain ties, at the end of the Hasmonaean period, of the Pharisaic movement with Galilee, far from the Temple, converged with what has been indicated in the nomination of Hillel the Babylonian.

In order to be more specific about the nature of the customs of this group, it is necessary to enquire about what became of the tithes, if they did not go to the sanctuary. According to Neh. 12.44-47, the whole of Israel, in the days of

---

distribution described as an ancient custom is neither biblical nor rabbinic. The phrase used, לעניים ולחבירים, seems to have been altered: the *waw* of liaison is explanatory (or restrictive) and not supplementary, since there is no reason why the 'associates', if they are neither priests nor poor, would have access to public charity.

115.   According to Exod. 30.11-15, the tax of a half-shekel was connected to a census, and therefore did not seem to be permanent; according to 2 Kgs 12.5 and 2 Chron. 24.6-10 (Judaean historiography), we can understand that it was an annual tax, as Josephus did (*Ant.* 3.194). This tax was collected even in Babylon (*Ant.* 18.312), and was confiscated by the Romans after the destruction (*War* 7.218, *fiscus iudaicus*). At the time of Bar Kochba, didrachmas were issued, with the representation of the Temple (of Solomon and not of Herod), in view of the restoration of the half-shekel, but the rabbinic tradition was content afterwards to collect (non-pharisaic) memories connected to the Temple (*m. Šeq.*, especially ch. 5).

116.   According to the expression, perhaps justified, of *Ant.* 18.4; he is probably to be identified with Judas son of Ezekias of Sepphoris, who revolted during the regency of Archelaus (*War* 2.56); cf. Hengel's discussion, *Die Zeloten*, p. 337 n. 1.

Zerubbabel and in the days of Nehemiah, deducted the parts that the Law had allocated to the priests and Levites; the legal benefits were paid and the functions of the Temple were assured. This ideal description is suspected of being highly embellished, and especially harmonized with the precepts of the Pentateuch. In fact, Nehemiah saw at the time of his second mission (13.10-14) that the portions of the Levites were no longer being delivered, and that the latter had abandoned their duties to work in their fields. Moreover, the rabbinic tradition (*b. Yeb.* 86b) acknowledged that since the time of Ezra the tithe was principally given to the priests, since they were ten times more numerous than the Levites (Ezra 2). Another passage (*b. Soṭ.* 47b) explained that if John Hyrcanus had abolished the solemn declaration of Deut. 26.13, it was because it could no longer be recited, since it presupposed that the tithe was given to the Levites, whereas it was the priests who received it.

A later controversy (c. 100) is informative (*b. Yeb.* 86b, *baraita*). According to Aqiba, the advocate of the unity of the oral tradition and Scripture, the first tithe belonged to the Levites, but according to Eleazar ben Azariah, known for his fidelity to his teachers, it belonged to the priests. It is recounted in this connection that the same Aqiba through trickery prevented the priest Eleazar from receiving a first tithe.[117] In other words, there is a conflict between the biblical precept, restored from the texts, and the older *halakha* to which Josephus and Philo bear witness. This debate in interesting in that it shows that there was not a general deep-rooted custom, but that the time had come for a 'restoration'. In fact, in a discussion connected to Joḥanan ben Zakkai, a *baraita* states (*y. Šeq.* 8.6, p. 51b) that there was no longer any consecration or first fruits or tithes[118] after the destruction of the Temple, and in particular that if a tithe had been separated, it should be burned. On the other hand, the documents from the desert of Judaea signed by Bar Kochba,[119] in whom Aqiba had believed he saw the Messiah, prove that the tithe was observed. Likewise, after the revolt, the separation of the tithe and the first fruits was prohibited by the Romans (*m. Maʿas. Š.* 4.11). Later however, among the successors of Aqiba in Galilee, that is to say, in the current that led to the Mishnah, the tendency progressively developed (*y. Maʿas. Š.* 5.5, p. 56c, etc.) to allocate the tithes to the 'associates', in particular to the teachers, since they observed ritual purity and bore more and more the burden of the community.

In brief, these indications show that the allocation of the (first) tithe to the priests away from the Temple, which instituted a non-biblical practice, existed before the destruction of the Temple among the Pharisees, particularly in Galilee. The dissenting opinions amount to two: 1. a tradition, which perhaps had come from Jerusalem, stating that there was

---

117. We even find some arguments to establish that the tithe was for priests; cf. *t. Peʾah* 4.5 and Lieberman, *Tosefta kifshuṭah*, I, pp. 180-81.

118. This *baraita* appears also in *b. Yom.* 66a (and par.), but with the first fruits and the tithe omitted, through harmonization with the later (Pharisaic) *halakha*.

119. Cf. Benoit, Milik and de Vaux, *Les grottes*, p. 124 n. 24.

no longer a separation of the tithe after the destruction; 2. an attempt at reform according to the letter of the Bible, wanting to reintroduce the right of the Levites; its protagonist was Aqiba. At no time do we detect any demand from the Levites.

As for the collection itself, it never became an object of any coercion, and they deplored at times extensive tax evasion: 'in the past the people submitted their products for the tithe, but now [...]' (*b. Ber.* 35b). Without going into the question here of the collection of tithes in the Diaspora,[120] it is now possible to be more specific about the term 'people of the land' given to those who did not deduct the tithe *properly*, even in the time of the Temple. The issue concerns those who remained outside Pharisaic circles, in that they abstained from the offering, *or sent it to the sanctuary*. They could therefore be Judaeans, Samaritans, or anyone irreligious. The Pharisees, or at least their purest representatives, were therefore like the Essenes, a distinct movement, separated from the 'people of the land', in the most usual sense of the term.

These observations are thrown into relief when we recall that the great difference in practice between the Pharisees and Sadducees, according to Josephus, was that the first observed the traditions of the Elders, whereas the second, who were more aristocratic, rejected them, because they were not scriptural. We have seen several important examples indicating that these traditions were not supplements to the Pentateuch, but were independent, or even conflicting, arrangements (Sabbath, Passover, prayer, tithes), which presupposed venerable customs, earlier than the adoption of the written work. The Tannaitic tradition, especially Aqiba, tried hard to produce a synthesis, which was sometimes difficult in the case of certain precepts still in vigour.

Before the destruction, these Pharisees indicated a great distrust (or a great claim) in regard to the Temple such as it was, whether Hasmonaean or Herodian, and perhaps this was the origin of their name (פרישין 'those separated'). Now the Temple, at least since the time of Jonathan and the affair of the Spartans, had at its disposal sacred texts, and preserved them. Moreover, the very name Sadducee, which was connected to the Zadokite descendants of Mattathias, clearly indicated that they were advocates of the Temple, which fitted in with the primacy accorded to what was written. More than a century before Herod, Judas Maccabeus and the resistance fighters had carried on a campaign against the Hellenization of Judaea and the Temple: according to 1 Maccabees,

120. Oppenheimer, *The 'Am ha-aretz*, pp. 49-51.

the result of this was an Aaronite dynasty, but according to 2 Maccabees (which called to mind the resurrection, in regard to the martyrs), there emerged from this not a high priesthood, but a sort of ideal image of the Temple. This difference corresponds to a fairly great extent to the difference between the Sadducees and the Pharisees, which does not imply however that either one or the other would have been in favour of armed resistance.

7. *Conclusions*

The list given in the prologue of *Pirke Abot* of the transmitters of the tradition, from the 'Men of the Great Assembly' and Simon the Just to Hillel, conceals then some rather complicated facts. This is so, on the one hand, because of historical disputes insufficiently well-known, between tendencies claiming to be the true Israel, indeed even to know what was the correct use of the Temple; and, on the other hand, the fact that the Tannaitic traditions, developed in Galilee (Sepphoris, Tiberias, Beth Shearim) at the end of the second century, had accumulated all sorts of elements, whether of Pharisaic origin or not, by extensively reworking them in the light of the thesis of the unity of the Torah, that is to say, of the oral and the written. Josephus, between the publication of the *Jewish War* and that of the *Jewish Antiquities*, had tried to take on the look at the same time of a Pharisee and of a good Roman citizen, and provides in this way a useful reference point: he wrote in Greek, then, on matters of concern to his Jewish readers, for use in the Diaspora. The influence of the Pharisees was therefore very substantial, perhaps even dominant in the Diaspora. The example of Saul of Tarsus suggests this, as well as the privileges granted by Caesar to various Jewish communities situated on the perimeters of the Mediterranean. There is no reason to doubt that the Pharisees bore the stamp of Jerusalem, but they did not originate there. In fact, Nehemiah as a prototype, then for various reasons Simon the Just, Judas Maccabeus, Hillel the Elder and all the Galilean developments attest to repeated Babylonian influences, relative to the 'ancestral tradition' and to the customs contrary to Scripture. These collided more or less head-on with the practices in Judaea, from which there arose all sorts of divisions, reconciliations and transformations, with the last episodes being the debates around Aqiba and then the return and the reorganization of his successors in Galilee, through which is reread the restoration attributed to Hillel.

The relationship of the Pharisees and then the Tannaim to Scripture is illustrated by the question of the copies deposited in the Temple.[121] According to *y. Ta'an.* 4.2, p. 68a, three scrolls (of the Pentateuch) were found in the court of the Temple; they were characterized by certain textual differences, and a new edition was prepared, retaining the variants that were in the majority, apart from the deliberate corrections of the scribes and teachers,[122] and apart too from the question of the *qere-ketib*. This declaration amounts to saying that the rabbinic text is reconstructed on an eclectic base, with an effort besides to lose nothing, which corresponds to the general intention of the Tannaim in regard to oral tradition. One of the forms rejected, and through it a type of text rejected (זעטוטי for נערי or אצילי, Exod. 24.5, 11), characterized, according to *b. Meg.* 9a, 'what had been written' in the copy sent for the translation commissioned by Ptolemy (cf. Chapter 5, §5); this is a discreet way of saying that the source of the LXX was a regrettably different text. Many discussions preserved in the rabbinic sources only make sense if we take into consideration the LXX, which implies that a Hebrew *vorlage* was still accessible, at least partly.[123] We can recall in this connection that the Hebrew Pentateuch used by Josephus had a close relationship with the LXX (B). Furthermore, that the high priest would have had at his disposal sacred writings since the time of Jonathan clearly emerges from an examination of the affair of Spartan kinship (cf. Chapter 6, §5). The presence of these divergent and still authoritative scrolls in the Temple marks a further very interesting supplementary stage, since it presupposed a certain cohabitation of diverse tendencies. What is more, if none of these texts, for the rabbinic tradition, has *a priori* a superior authority to the others, it is reasonable to conclude from this that none of them was specifically Pharisaic.

The Pharisaic movement was not priestly, whereas the guardians of Scripture were the priests, as it itself states. Josephus confirms this on several occasions. In *War* 3.352, in speaking of his aptitude for

121. S. Talmon, 'The Three Scrolls of the Law That Were Found in the Temple Court', *Textus* 2 (1962), pp. 14-27, with a detailed discussion of the parallel recensions.

122. Lieberman, *Hellenism*, pp. 22-24.

123. For example, in *t. Ber.* 1.10, a debate on the return (or not) of the coming out of Egypt in Messianic times, to which Jer. 23.7-8 refers, corresponds exactly to the difference between the MT and the LXX; cf. Nodet, *'Miettes messianiques'*, pp. 122-24.

divination, he explained that being a priest he was versed in the interpretation of the prophecies of the sacred books; in *Apion* 1.54, he declared that he was able to translate the Scriptures, since being a priest he was trained to interpret them. More generally, in *Apion* 2.187, he attributed to the priestly body as a whole the responsibility for the application of the Law.[124] In his notes on the Pharisees, he attributed to these latter great legal authority, but his information is difficult to fit into the historical developments on the Hasmonaeans or in the time of Herod,[125] and we can suspect that he has projected into the past rambling details to give more consistency to the party which he had had to choose after the destruction. We can thus perceive a considerable gap between his spontaneous convictions and the assumed doctrines. Contrary to this importance given to priests, the rabbinic tradition is hard on John Hyrcanus and Alexander Janneus, and it implied that the high priest was so ignorant (*m. Yom.* 1.1-3) that he had to comply with what the teachers told him.

In the Pentateuch, the appearance of the Law given to Moses at Sinai was a very late episode, compared to the Creation and the patriarchs. Philo, *Dec.* 1 interpreted this arrangement by saying that the great personnages prior to Moses were in themselves 'living Laws', or 'non-written Laws'. This presentation forms a contrast with the book of *Jubilees*, which had Samaritan connections and presented, in a strict chronological framework, all the history from the Creation up to the coming out of Egypt as if revealed at Sinai (in the week of Exod. 24.16-18): therefore only what is written counts. Moreover, in the Exodus, the precepts relative to the Passover (a family sacrifice) and the Sabbath (staying at home) were earlier than the revelation at Sinai, and I have shown, with regard to the 'model of Nehemiah' and the enthronement of Hillel, that the Jews (in contrast with the Judaeans) and the Pharisees (as opposed to the Temple rulers) preserved traces of non-scriptural or at least 'pre-Sinaitic' customs with regard to the Passover and the Sabbath. These customs are hardly detectable in Judaea before Mattathias and Judas, and at best can be seen before Simon the Just.

To conclude, the results of this chapter, combined with those from the

124. Cf. S.N. Mason, 'Priesthood in Josephus and the "Pharisaic Revolution"', *JBL* 107 (1988), pp. 657-61.

125. Cf. S.N. Mason, 'Was Josephus a Pharisee?: A Re-Examination of Life 10–12', *JJS* 40 (1989), pp. 31-45, with a discussion of numerous opinions.

preceding chapters, may be summed up in the form of a list of characteristic points going back over time.

1. The rabbinic tradition represented by the Mishnah, and firmly
fixed in Galilee, was a combination of two branches with different des-
tinies, whose common beginning was made up of Jews of a Hasidaean
type, who had immigrated to Palestine and were bearers of oral traditions that were Babylonian and non-biblical. The first branch, not Zealot
in any way, had remained or was reassembled in Galilee, while keeping
themselves at a distance from the Herodian sanctuary; it had scarcely
been affected by the disturbances in Judaea in 70 and 135. A second
branch had made a detour through Judaea. It stemmed from the foundation of Joḥanan ben Zakkai at Yavneh, which had been unpretentious
in the beginning, then sometime after 70 was strongly influenced by the
Pharisees of Jerusalem, who also preserved the oral traditions, but as
well paid very strong attention to the Bible. It had absorbed numerous
traditions and customs relating to the Temple and all the parties that had
existed in Jerusalem, but remained aloof from priestly circles. It had been
involved in fairly sharp debates over Zealot activism and finally, after
135, it returned as a school to Galilee, with the memory of all this, and
linked up with those who had never left or who had continued to arrive
from Babylon, with which traffic back and forth had never broken off.
In the successive redactions of the Mishnah, the Pentateuch, duly edited,
was not commented on as such, but was nevertheless placed as much as
possible up-stream from it, most of the time implicitly.

2. This synthesis was already quite well represented by Hillel the
Elder in the time of Herod. This pivotal person in fact united two
currents: the groups of the faithful in Bathyra, connected at least partially with the priestly calendar of *Jubilees*, and the Pharisees persecuted
in Judaea, using the usual Seleucid calendar. The mediation was carried
out by a Babylonian, that is to say, by someone native to the place from
which all the non-scriptural traditions came. As for the colony of Bathyra
itself, it was of Babylonian (not Zealot) origin, and according to Josephus
it had attracted as colonists very observant and very exclusive groups,
which must be connected to the Nehemiah of the second mission and to
his model, to the Hasidaeans and Essenes (who had to be Jews by race,
Josephus clearly specifies in *War* 119); proselytism was therefore missing from these circles.

3. The Pharisees constituted the branch of the Babylonians who had
reached Judaea, had more or less settled there and had experienced a

very strong biblical influence, without losing for all that their oral traditions. The composition of the book of Nehemiah illustrates very well what took place, at least in regard to Deuteronomy. They were more biblical (and less given to activism) than Judas Maccabeus himself, but were very similar to the book of 2 Maccabees, with a vision of the Temple as a divine dwelling and with an efficacious desire to influence the Diaspora, as the festal letters show. We must then situate their appearance between Jonathan and John Hyrcanus. Staying independent of the high priests and kings, they had become influential over the people, especially in the diaspora.

4.   The Sadducees had a completely different origin. We have noted their original relationship with the Samaritans, but they were the heirs of the ruling circles surrounding the dynasty stemming from Mattathias, and therefore fixed firmly in Jerusalem. However, they are not mentioned in 1 Maccabees, which should constitute their foundation narrative, guaranteeing their authority over Jews in general (through their connection with the Hasidaeans, and their absorption of Judas Maccabeus). For this reason, their emergence, as a party having a specific claim on the Zadokite high priesthood, has been situated after the direct dynasty had come to an end, that is to say under Alexander Janneus, therefore after the definitive split between Jerusalem and Gerizim. Josephus attributed to them a significance from the time of Simon, father of John Hyrcanus. We can accept this, if he wished to speak of ruling circles, but the denomination must be considered something later.

5.   Before the Maccabaean crisis, the person who dominated at Jerusalem was Simon the Just, in the time of the charter of Antiochus III. He apparently succeeded in coordinating in Jerusalem the Bible (but not necessarily the Pentateuch under the form in which we know it, which was missing from the library of Nehemiah), the Babylonian oral tradition and the requirements of the high priesthood, with Simon himself being of Egyptian origin. The equilibrium was precarious, and his successors were less fortunate, facing dissidents, sects and conflicts, then finally persecutions under Antiochus IV, Jason and Menelaus, with the fiscal element being the crucial factor.

6.   The 'Men of the Great Assembly' constituted schematically the preceding generation. They did editorial work on the Bible, which brought them closer again to Nehemiah, as founder of the library. They should be considered repatriates from Babylon, with venerable non-biblical customs, in particular the weekly Sabbath. These were Jews of a

Hasidaean-type, clearly distinct from the Judaeans of Jerusalem and their Temple. It was at that moment that there began, perhaps imposed by the supervisory political authority, some exchanges with the Samaritans, that is to say, between groups of limited size, from which there came compilations which led to the Pentateuch, with Deuteronomy emerging belatedly.

7.   This simplified sketch in no way rules out a restoration by Cyrus and Darius of a Judaean sanctuary in Jerusalem, provided with priests and prophets, but it postpones until much later the appearance in Judaea of Judaism itself, whose relationship to the Temple remained very complicated. The legend of the reception of Alexander tries to simplify that relationship, and to give it an honourable antiquity.

This sketch must now be collated with the book of Ezra–Nehemiah, left aside since the inventory of historical difficulties presented in Chapter 1.

Chapter 8

EZRA AND NEHEMIAH

A brief examination of the difficulties found in the accounts of the restoration under Cyrus and Darius, then in the accounts of the reforms under Ezra and Nehemiah, showed (Chapter 1) that all the events were enveloped in such uncertainty that the simplest historical synthesis was the paraphrase of Josephus, which merely replaced Xerxes with Cambyses, which unified the work of Zerubbabel, then systematized the Samaritan opposition, and finally emphasized that Ezra and Nehemiah were contemporaries. There remains the fact that the books of Ezra and Nehemiah are composite and uneven, which cannot escape notice in the most superficial reading. The conclusion of the analysis was that the impossibility of clarifying the facts, few as they were, due to certain systematic doublings, led to the supposition that the final composition of the books, far from being a simple collection of differing sources, conformed to a deliberate and highly organized purpose, or perhaps under the influence of a series of such revisions, to a succession of such intentions. What is more, the results of the preceding chapters only fairly remotely agree with the obvious content of these books, and definitely disagree with the synthesis of Josephus.

The purpose of this chapter then is to sketch a literary analysis of these books, in order to attempt a general comparison. The expected results are of two kinds: to discover through the redactional effects the trace of facts and institutions and, more importantly, to attempt to understand for what purpose the facts have been reinterpreted. In other words, the aim is to grasp the mechanisms at work in the formation of collective memories, namely, traditions. Certain transformations have long been recognized, as for example the flagrant anachronism of texts which put Daniel or Ezra in the time of Nebuchadnezzar. To work out the analysis, I will try to utilize several distinctions or contrasts established in other contexts: between Israel (or Samaritans) and Jews, between Jews and Judaeans, between the Temple with its cult and the immigrants from Babylon, and so on.

However, the preceding considerations (Chapter 7) have led to the establishment of a link on the one hand between Ezra–Nehemiah and the Pharisees and on the other hand between Chronicles and the Sadducees; they would have come then from opposing milieus. Nevertheless, these books are often attributed to the same author, the Chronicler. So we have to begin then with some comprehensive questions, relative to the books being taken together.

1. *The Chronicler and the 'Compiler'*

Since the work of Leopold Zunz, it has often been held that Ezra–Nehemiah as a unit, which to begin with here will be considered a joint work, makes up a segment which had been detached from the book of Chronicles.[1]

His argumentation is made up of two parts. First he makes some observations on some external connections: the prologue (Ezra 1.1-3) repeats the closing verses of 2 Chron. 36.22-23; Ezra 3, with the joyful celebration of the feasts, is in the style of Chronicles, just like Ezra 6.16-22. Then there follow some internal observations, showing that neither Ezra nor Nehemiah could have written certain passages. Ezra 7.1-11 and 10.1-14 speak of Ezra in the third person, and cannot be from his hand. Nehemiah 8–9 repeats events already mentioned in Ezra, while they are from another time, and tend to make Ezra and Nehemiah contemporaries. Nehemiah 11–12 repeats the same error (12.26 and 36), and the passage is swollen with lists and notices which are later than Nehemiah. Nehemiah 13 contradicts itself (vv. 3, 23), and the whole episode of the foreign women is superfluous after Ezra 9 and Neh. 9.2. Likewise, certain passages contemporaneous with Ezra cannot be attributed to him: the list of repatriates (Ezra 2) stands on its own, since Nehemiah 7 repeats it in another context. The documents in Aramaic cited in Ezra 4–7 precede Ezra, and furthermore the account continues in Aramaic with an interpolated clause (5.4 'we said to them', indicating the Persian authorities), which suggests that it is no longer about Ezra. Finally, only an eighth of the book of Ezra at most can be attributed to Ezra, with the rest being made up of earlier or later pieces, and among these latter some passages are due to Nehemiah. In other words, it is no longer possible to see in the book a work of Ezra amplified by additions, but on the contrary a subsequent work comprising among other things fragments of Ezra.

---

1.   L. Zunz, *Die gottesdienstlichen Vorträge der Juden, historisch entwickelt* (Frankfurt am Main: Kaufman, 2nd edn, 1892), pp. 13-36; Hebrew translation edited and provided with a commentary by H. Albeck (Jerusalem: Bialik, 3rd edn, 1974), pp. 7-20.

So an obvious hypothesis emerges, based on the first of the observations just presented: Ezra and Chronicles, which have in common the liking for lists and numbers, the mentioning of the Levites, the cantors and sacrificial details, which deal with history in a casual way, could well make up two separate parts of a same work. At the end of a careful lexical and stylistic analysis, Zunz considers his hypothesis well-founded, and attributes the following passages to the Chronicler: Ezra 1; 3; 6.18b–7.11; 10.1-17; Neh. 7.72b–9.37; 10.29; 11.11, 17, 22-24; 12.10-26, 27b, 30, 35, 36, 43, 44b-47; 13.1-3. This view is confirmed by the example of 1 Esdras, Josephus's source, which joins together in a continuous account 2 Chronicles and Ezra.

In regard to dating, Zunz puts the Chronicler well after the time of Ezra and Nehemiah, a little before Simon the Just, about the middle of the third century. It can be objected that all the ancient lists of the Hebrew canon[2] separate Chronicles from Ezra–Nehemiah, so that they amount to two distinct works, but he tried to account for this fact by conjecturing that Ezra–Nehemiah, placed most often first and containing facts without parallel in the other historical books, constituted the part introduced first into the canon.[3]

With the unity of the final redaction established in this way, there followed a search in this unified work for a single theological vision, or more exactly for an absorption of Ezra–Nehemiah into the obvious concepts of Chronicles, with the assembling of all Israel under the law of Moses around Jerusalem, with its levitical cult and its Davidic king.[4] By way of a preliminary remark, it should be noted that this generalization does not fit in with what has been defined and verified as the 'model of Nehemiah', which was only moderately interested in the Temple, but emphasized the importance of the Sabbath and of separation, especially by the walls, by the language and by the sending away of foreigners. At a more technical level, Sara Japhet has begun, after more than a century of consensus, to call into question the stylistic and linguistic unity of the two books. Without contesting the fact that there are similarities, which are connected to a late stage of biblical Hebrew, she concentrates on

---

2. Collected by Leiman, *Canonization of Hebrew Scripture*, pp. 37-40; in general, Ezra–Nehemiah form just one book in that canon, and the MT only separates them with a minor division (*setuma*), with the nearest major divisions (*petuḥa*) being in Ezra 10.9 and Neh. 3.1.

3. Cf. O. Eissfeldt, *Einleitung in das alte Testament unter Einschluss der Apokryphen und Pseudepigraphen* (Tübingen: Mohr [Paul Siebeck], 3rd edn, 1964), pp. 19f.

4. Especially since S.R. Driver, *An Introduction to the Literature of the Old Testament* (Edinburgh: T. & T. Clark, 1913), pp. 535-39.

noting the differences in language proper to the final redaction, that is to say, abstracting from earlier sources inserted into each of the two books.

In addition to systematic orthographic differences, she notes more substantial differences in language, of which two call for special mention. First, Chronicles insisted on the 'sanctification' (התקדש) of priests and Levites before every ceremony, even adding it where the parallels in Samuel and Kings ignored it. On the contrary, Ezra–Nehemiah was unaware of the term, or spoke of 'purification' (הטהר) of the officiants, whereas in Chronicles this term is only used for the purification of the Temple or of the country. Although the notions of 'sanctification' and 'purification' are connected, and almost interchangeable (2 Sam. 11.4), the first implies the addition of a quality, while the second is rather the removal of some corruption, and this slight divergence fits in with the theological differences between the two books. The second example concerns the organization of the people and the cult personnel: Chronicles frequently refers to the division of the people and the officiants into small units, with a set terminology (מחלקת), whereas Ezra–Nehemiah pays no attention to the organization of the people, and only gives fairly vague indications as to that of the cult personnel. These minor details underline the limited interest of Ezra–Nehemiah in 'all Israel' and in the Levitical functioning of the Temple. As for the argument drawn from 1 Esdras, which ignored the separation between the two books, it can be neutralized by the fact that it was a kind of compilation, which presupposes earlier works, and we cannot conclude from this whether they were separate or joined together.[5] Finally, the argument stemming from the identity of the concluding verses of 2 Chronicles and the beginning of Ezra is not decisive, since it can be taken in the opposite sense, especially if it is observed that the concluding verses surprisingly break off in the middle of a sentence. It could be held that it was to assert a unity that was in no way evident between the two books that the beginning of the second copied the end of the first.[6]

5.   Cf. H.G.M. Williamson, *Israel in the Books of Chronicles* (Cambridge: Cambridge University Press, 1977), pp. 12-16, with Bibliography.

6.   Cf. Williamson, *Israel*, p. 9. In a review of this work, H. Cazelles, *VT* 29 (1979), pp. 379-83 brings up the hypothesis of a very late canonization of Chronicles, due to the opposition of the Sadducees. In fact, it should be noted that the rabbinic tradition retained a vestige of opinions and customs to the letter contrary to Chronicles (cf. Chapter 7), that the New Testament never cites passages peculiar to Chronicles, and that there are reasons for presupposing that Josephus in his paraphrase was acquainted with longer forms of Samuel–Kings and did not have to use Chronicles to fill them out; cf. E.C. Ulrich, *The Qumran Text of Samuel and Josephus* (HSM, 19; Missoula, MT: Scholars Press, 1978), but the complete analysis of this remains to be done. The late canonization is therefore plausible and fits in with the considerations proposed above relative to a late publication. However, it is very doubtful that the Sadducees would have delayed it, since the ideology of Chronicles is close to theirs; it is therefore necessary to go so far as to presuppose a late *redaction*.

To close the debate here is out of the question, so I confine myself to two series of remarks on the connections between Chronicles and Ezra and on the links between Ezra and Nehemiah, in order to justify considering from here on Ezra–Nehemiah together as a unit, even if it were a part of a more extensive whole.

First of all, Ezra 1.1 asserts that there was a connection between the prophecy of Jeremiah and the proclamation of Cyrus relative to the restoration of the Temple. Now, the only passages of Jeremiah announcing a return from captivity are of little help. Jer. 25.11-12 had announced that after an exile of seventy years YHWH would deal severely with the king of Babylon, but it is only from external sources that we learn that Cyrus absorbed Babylon into the Persian Empire in 539. Jer. 29.10-14 stated still more briefly that after 70 years YHWH would fulfill his promises in regard to a return. Jer. 31.38 referred to the definitive restoration of Jerusalem, but made no direct allusion to the Temple. Josephus, who saw clearly that the connection was very tenuous, strengthened it by stating that Cyrus read in Isaiah the prophecies concerning himself and wanted to fulfill them[7] (*Ant.* 11.5, quoting Isa. 44.28): 'It is my will that Cyrus, whom I will have picked out to reign over many and powerful peoples, shall send back my people to their homeland and build my Temple.' On the contrary, the final verses of 2 Chronicles are more coherent, since the *mise en scène* of Cyrus fulfilling the prophecy is preceded on the one hand (36.20b) by the clear indication that the Persian Empire would supplant the successors of Nebuchadnezzar, and on the other hand by calling to mind the prophecy of Jeremiah: 'Until this land has enjoyed its Sabbath rest, it will keep the Sabbath throughout the days of its desolation, until 70 years have gone by.' However, only the duration of 70 years can be clearly connected to Jeremiah, whereas the allusion to the Sabbaths comes from Lev. 26.34-35. In addition, the conclusion in 2 Chron. 36.20-23, considered as a whole, involves exactly the section in which 2 Chronicles 36 stops following its source (2 Kgs 25.14), and we can consider v. 20a a redactional seam, summing up the deportation, as a way to introduce the edict of Cyrus. Finally, the abbreviated form of the proclamation of Cyrus has not the same meaning as the long form: Cyrus, commanded to build a temple at Jerusalem, invited all those who formed part of 'all his people' to go up. In other words, Cyrus did the financing, and launched a very

---

7.   Josephus had the same fabrication in regard to Alexander, to whom they showed what concerned him in Daniel (*Ant.* 11.337); cf. Chapter 4, §3.

broad invitation, at least to 'all Israel'. On the contrary, according to Ezra 1.4-6, it was a matter of Judah and Benjamin alone, and Cyrus restricted himself to restoring the cultic apparatus, while the exiles were bound to make a contribution to the undertaking. We encounter again the difference in points of view between the two books as already indicated: on the one hand, openness to a departure from the centre, on the other a restriction within a certain perimeter.

These observations show then that the conclusion of 2 Chronicles complied with a compositional plan, meant to assimilate two literary facts, namely, the allusion to Jeremiah and the putting of the Persian king in the picture. This remark does not imply of itself any conclusion on the primitive unity or not of the two books, nor even, if they were actually two distinct works, in regard to the original place of the proclamation of Cyrus. However, if we include the observations of Japhet and Williamson referred to above, which are of another kind, and Bickerman's arguments showing the authenticity of the proclamation of Cyrus, the probabilities favour a secondary composition of 2 Chronicles, derived from Ezra as well as from other sources. For the present study, we retain only the idea that it is legitimate to take seriously the traditional separation between 2 Chronicles and Ezra; there is at least a change in overall vision, which in no way excludes a relationship in epoch, language and ideas, as has been shown ever since Zunz.[8]

With that separation posited, the next question is deciding whether Ezra and Nehemiah are two distinct works, or a single final composition, as the canonical tradition would have it. Handled correctly, this problem does not depend on the historical reconstruction of facts. The composition is nevertheless marked by a rigorous chronological framework, which stretches certain facts: from the decree of the first year of Cyrus (Ezra 1.1) to the resumption of the work in the second year of Darius (4.24) and to the inaugural Passover of the sixth year (6.15), the continuity is indicated by the permanent presence of Zerubbabel and Joshua, but this setting does some violence to the resumption of the cult according to the law of Moses, mentioned under Cyrus (3.2-6), and to an important series of episodes under Xerxes and Artaxerxes. Next, the mission of Ezra and the missions of Nehemiah are carefully situated, one at the beginning (Ezra 7–10), the others toward the end (Neh. 1.1; 13.6) of the reign of Artaxerxes, but the proclamation of the Law by Ezra

8. Cf. the synthesis of B.S. Childs, *Introduction to the Old Testament as Scripture* (London: SCM Press, 1979), pp. 628-32.

(Neh. 8–9), and some summarizing verses (12.26) make them contemporaries, whereas they seem to be unaware of each other. Genetically, we could just as well consider, on the contrary, that the chronological frameworks are only derived from the sources, and that the elements that disrupt them would be due to the intention directing the final composition. The result is the same: a unified Ezra–Nehemiah is in a sort of violent state, which is not resolved by any simple manipulation, as we have shown, since even if we gather together everything involving Ezra, by connecting Nehemiah 8–9 (and perhaps 10) to some point in the narrative of Ezra 7–10, the whole account about Nehemiah becomes quite incoherent, because of his second mission, and especially because the sequence from Cyrus to Darius remains confused.

On the fringe of this difficult chronological framework, however, one can detect a progression in the present narrative in five phases, clearly separated by the successive appearances of the characters Ezra and Nehemiah.

1. Ezra 1–6 relates the outcome, long awaited, of the decree of Cyrus, with the restoration of cult and the Temple, whereas the walls were not rebuilt, because of local opposition and the official prohibition of Artaxerxes.

2. Ezra 7–10 speaks of the mission of the scribe Ezra, sent to introduce 'the law of his God, which is the law of the king' just about everywhere in Transeuphrates (7.25-26). Having arrived at Jerusalem, he organized the cult with the repatriated priests, then he set to work to purify the people, since the exiles had taken foreign wives, and the account ends with a long list of priests who had sent away their wives. This second phase, therefore, led to the strengthening of the bond between the Law, the cult and the establishment of an appropriate priestly body.

3. Nehemiah 1–7 recounts the mission of Nehemiah, sent to restore Jerusalem, without any definite link either with the Law or with the Temple. He overcomes various kinds of opposition, and the account ends with the difficulty of populating the rebuilt city, notwithstanding an important list of repatriates from exile.

4. Nehemiah 8–12 combines several pieces in a great inaugural feast uniting Ezra and Nehemiah: proclamation of the Law, festivities in the setting of a feast of Booths 'as there had not been since Joshua, son of Nun', a ceremony of penitence and praise, commitment of the community to observe the Law and finally a clear indication that 'the leaders of

the people had settled in Jerusalem' and that Judaea was repopulated. This inauguration, in which there was no question of the cult in the Temple, forms a striking counterpoint to another feast of Booths, on which occasion the cult was resumed under Cyrus (Ezra 3.4). There is therefore competition between two systems.[9]

5.	The last phase in Nehemiah 13 corresponds to the second mission of Nehemiah, in which he reformed the Temple and the priestly corps, dealt sternly with the family of the high priest, energetically defended the observance of the Sabbath, and once again expelled the foreign wives. This passage is very much superimposed on the mission of Ezra, but the newness is that the accent is no longer put on the cult itself, but on the reform, according to the Law, of the Jews in general and of the cult personnel in particular.

This last aspect corroborates the observation made on the double feast of Booths: the observance of the Law, from which there followed in particular the separation from foreigners, had become like a thread running through these five phases and something more important than the formal reality of the Temple, even according to the law of Moses. Relative to the Temple, a struggle for power should be noted: Nehemiah, who was not a priest, legislated still more than Ezra, who was a priest, and claimed to be taking control in the name of the Law. As for the law of Moses itself, it was mentioned in connection with the cult (Ezra 3), and thereafter was especially connected with Ezra. Nehemiah was placed in its wake, but it should be noted that neither his activity, nor the commitment of the community (Neh. 10.1, 29-40) exactly agrees with the letter of the Pentateuch.

Of course, all these observations are based only on the general arrangement of the two books, and leave intact the difficulties and inconsistencies of their constituent material, especially their historical sources. In other words, the progression pointed out in the five phases is an interpretation forcing the facts, and not the history itself. As a result—this point will be examined further—this history, if we manage to reconstruct it, should be notably different, and probably spontaneously lends itself quite poorly to the meaning that is attributed to it.

Other structural facts indirectly confirm the preceding analysis. It has

9.	The analysis of vocabulary by H.G.M. Williamson, *Ezra, Nehemiah* (WBC, 16; Waco, TX: Word Books, 1985), pp. 29-32, shows that these two feasts of Booths are connected to the two long and almost identical lists of repatriates of Ezra 2 and Nehemiah 7; see below.

long been observed that almost a quarter of Ezra–Nehemiah is made up of lists, which are never (except for Neh. 12.10-11) descending genealogies, unlike 1 Chronicles 1–9.[10] It has been claimed that the repetition of the same list of the repatriates in Ezra 2.1-70 and Neh. 7.6-72a, with slight modifications, was an indication that the two books, at first separated, independently used one and the same source, and that the preservation of the useless doubling, at the time of their later union, was due to the meticulous respect for the sacred text. The book of Chronicles as a whole and the anthologies from Qumran however do not indicate such scruples at those times.

Other points of view are in fact possible. After a review of various opinions on the origin of these archives, Tamara Eskenazi,[11] influenced by studies on biblical narration and the importance of repetitions, detects a literary strategy in the doubling of this list which is interminable (and tedious, according to Josephus, *Ant.* 11.68). The repetition forms an *inclusio* (of the A–B–A form), namely, the simplification of a chiasm (A–B–B–A), a structure which has as its role to unify everything contained within it. Here, the procedure focuses on the unit going from Ezra 2 to Nehemiah 7, or approximately the first three phases of the progression described above. That observation opens the way to drawing out some supplementary points: first of all, Ezra 1, with the decree of Cyrus and the restitution of the cultic objects to Sheshbazzar, prince of Judah, stands out as a prologue. Next, the long section just mentioned represents as a unit a realization of this decree, with a sort of contraction of time into a single moment. Finally, the new feast of Booths celebrates this successful outcome. The lists deliberately break the narrative sequence (Josephus omits them) and impose a schematizing of time, while insisting on an identification of the people as the sum total of repatriates, and not as 'all Israel' of Chronicles.

Some supplementary remarks can be advanced as well: the lists in question comprise Zerubbabel, Jeshua and their companions, and the long section specified is therefore centred on these persons. In the beginning, they effectively presided at the inauguration of the cult and the restoration of the Temple; then in the end, when Nehemiah tried to

10. Cf. M.D. Johnson, *The Purpose of Biblical Genealogies with Special Reference to the Setting of the Genealogies of Jesus* (SNTSMS, 8; Cambridge: Cambridge University Press, 1969), pp. 69-73.

11. T.T. Eskenazi, 'The Structure of Ezra–Nehemiah and the Integrity of the Book', *JBL* 107 (1988), pp. 641-56.

repopulate the city, which was rebuilt but empty, they constituted the most notable absentees (cf. Neh. 7.5), and their presence is nothing more than something textual. One detail is therefore significant: wherever in the first list it is a question merely of 'heads of families' (Ezra 2.69), the second introduces 'the rest of the people' (Neh. 7.71). The great event presided over by Zerubbabel is over and (obsolete), but there is a small residue. In the same way, the law of Moses was in force under Zerubbabel and Ezra, but that is no longer the case at the time of Nehemiah's activities (cf. Neh. 5). We discern then, under the formal setting dominated by Zerubbabel, perceptible traces of a negative evolution: like the rebuilt city, the cult and its law had become empty envelopes. In fact, the whole section, which extended over numerous reigns, represents a long period of time, with royal interventions and expansive projects, but all that was, in short, past history. In contrast, the new feast of Booths in the following phase, under Ezra and Nehemiah, in which the celebration of the Law replaced the cult, ended up with the formation of a new community, defined by a contractual agreement, and no longer by a genealogical dignity.

Furthermore, there is an incontestable continuity between the block framed by the two lists and the following section. This is indicated by the fact that the break between the end of the second list (Neh. 7.72a) and the setting up of the feast of the Law with Ezra (Neh. 7.72b) is deliberately vague. There is no terminology to indicate a change of scene, and in the MT the end of the first sequence and the beginning of the second are included in a single verse, which is however divided in two by a *setuma*. An ambiguity still remains then, and the question comes up of determining whether the block between the lists is isolated in the overall structure, as if a parenthesis, or is integrated, that is to say, its value weighed, positively or negatively. The response is provided in what follows by other lists. The fourth phase, or feast of the Torah with Ezra and Nehemiah, concludes with a list of the 'priests and Levites who came back with Zerubbabel, son of Shealtiel and Jeshua' (Neh. 12.1-9), followed by an enumeration of priestly families, then by the mention of the high priest who was the contemporary of Ezra and Nehemiah (v. 26). There followed next a reminiscence of the festive dedication of the rebuilt wall (v. 27), and a conclusion showing schematically an ideal epoch (vv. 44-47). There is therefore the trace of a crisis, with a new system replacing the old, but the unity of a long history is nevertheless affirmed. The method for reaching this is principally the juxtaposition of various documents, incidentally facilitated by minute redactional effects.

These observations on the intelligibility of the general structure of Ezra–Nehemiah lead us to attribute it to a certain 'compiler' who thoughtfully rearranged the documents or earlier compilations into a unique whole. The clues for identifying him as the Chronicler are not decisive, but just the contrary, since their methods and concepts differ widely, and especially because it is not proved that Chronicles would be an earlier work. I shall then retain as useful the canonical division into two books: Ezra–Nehemiah and Chronicles. Whatever the ultimate justification of this choice, the striking result is the contrast between the relative clarity, according to the point of view adopted, of the general plan of Ezra–Nehemiah and the inextricable web of historical difficulties outlined in Chapter 1. There is therefore an advantage in supposing that the work is not the disappointing result of an exceptional number of scribal errors, but results, at least to a great extent, from a well-motivated editorial activity. Some closer analyses should now fill out this analysis or reject it as useless.

2. Zerubbabel and the Proclamation of Cyrus

The prologue to the whole book of Ezra–Nehemiah—the first phase of the progression described above—presents some difficulties. It opens with the famous decree of Cyrus, by which, in the first year of his reign, he prescribed the construction of a temple to YHWH at Jerusalem. This document in fact appears in two forms already mentioned, then serves as a reference.

The first form is in a circular proclaimed and displayed in his whole kingdom (Ezra 1.2-4; 2 Chron. 36.23):

> 'Thus speaks Cyrus, king of Persia: "YHWH [Esdras B of the LXX omits], the God of heaven, has given me all the kingdoms of the earth, and it is he who has ordered me to build him a temple at Jerusalem in Judah. Any among you forming part of all his people, may [2 Chron. adds YHWH] his God be with him! Let him go up [end of 2 Chron.] to Jerusalem [end of LXX (B), which jumps from "Jerusalem" to "Jerusalem"] in Judah, and build the temple of YHWH [LXX (A, etc.) omits], the God of Israel—this is the God who is in Jerusalem [...]".'

The case of the LXX (Esdras B) is interesting: it is a very literal translation (in 1.1 וגם is rendered by καίγε) and is independent of the text of

2 Chronicles, as may be verified immediately. Besides, the Vaticanus (B) is brief, since, on the one hand, it systematically omits κύριος (יהוה) and, on the other hand, makes a jump which results in a final clause almost identical (ויעל לירושלים) to the truncated verse of 2 Chronicles (ויעל). It could be thought that the absence of the divine name from the proclamation of Cyrus is a correction, in order to make more probable the authenticity of this act of a pagan king. Furthermore, the jump could be nothing more than an accidental homeoteleuton, but it must be noted that in this latter case the meaning of the decree is greatly changed: the long text invites the repatriates to rebuild the sanctuary, and the collections that follow are therefore intended to finance the project. On the contrary, the short text leaves the work to Cyrus, as was mentioned above for 2 Chronicles, and asks the exiles to come to the rebuilt sanctuary, bringing offerings. To choose between the short text and the long one, the simplest thing is to compare their content with the memorandum found at Ecbatana, on a presumption that two texts literarily independent but stemming from the same act, as Bickerman proposes, should have a related content. Now, this memorandum speaks only of God or of the temple of God, but never of YHWH, and says that 'the expense will be met by the king's household' (Ezra 6.4). So this is not to be the work of the community of exiles, and it is surprising that the royal proclamation, as it appeared in the MT, dissolved the official aid of a generous monarch.

Furthermore, the structural study has shown that the inaugural act of Cyrus was the prologue of a collection of dissimilar pieces which were artificially united. Now, among these documents, we find several examples in which work was undertaken against the advice of the authorities: in Ezra 4.11-16, under Artaxerxes, the repatriated Jews who were rebuilding the city were denounced. In Ezra 5.3-17 the governor of Transeuphrates was surprised that the Temple was being rebuilt without permission. Again under Artaxerxes, the works of Nehemiah, with the long list of collaborators (Neh. 3.1-32) and the obstacles from some neighbouring potentates, were clearly the result of the Jewish initiative (2.18), and do not appear to have been drawn from the treasury, despite the kind words attributed to the king (2.8). All these episodes have in common their insistence on the initiative and commitment of the exiles and the repatriates. In these conditions, it is more natural for the prologue, which could not omit the inaugural act of Cyrus, to have insisted at least as much on Jewish solidarity: the restoration was the work of the community, aided by their God, and not by the king. The form in Esdras B seems then in the end less in harmony with the overall arrangement of the book, and therefore more primitive.

Other facts confirm this conclusion. First of all, Josephus, in his paraphrase (*Ant.* 11.3-7), insisted on the construction at Cyrus's initiative and at his expense, through the agency of neighbouring satrapies and with the contributions of the 'friends of the king'. He had read then a short form of the proclamation,[12] but we cannot tell whether it contained the tetragrammaton or not, since he always renders it by 'God' or 'the divinity'. Then, the actual form of 2 Chronicles contains, in comparison with the parallel passage of Ezra, one instance more of YHWH, which corrects the very pagan formula 'May his god be with him'.[13] It must be presumed then that the additions of the name are the work of the Chronicler, who was not afraid to create a prophecy of Jeremiah to clarify his account. These additions are partially passed on, as a result of the harmonization of the Hebrew, in the parallel passage of Ezra 1. Bickerman himself, who brilliantly defended the authenticity of the proclamation, concedes that if the designation 'the god who is at Jerusalem' suits a pagan king, the presence of the proper name of the god, which is unparalleled in the Achaemenid texts, constitutes an anomaly.[14] Incidentally, this leads to another argument in favour of the borrowing (and the revising) by the Chronicler of the proclamation of Ezra 1, rather than the reverse.

The content of the notice that was circulated presents other problems: the dispute under the same Cyrus between the exiles who rebuilt under the direction of Zerubbabel and Jeshua and 'the enemies of Judah and Benjamin' (Ezra 4.1-5, readily understood as Samaritans), revolved around the point of knowing who was entitled to build a temple to YHWH, the God of Israel: there were already the local populations, who claimed a right. In fact, the Aramaic memorandum, more prudently,

12. Josephus utilized a compilation of the 1 Esdras type; but, according to the known manuscripts, the proclamation had the long form in this collection; so he knew a compilation that was a little different, probably in Hebrew; cf. below, §6.

13. This was clearly seen by the rabbinic tradition (*Esther R.*, prologue §8) which interprets the proclamation in a very polemical way, illustrating it through use of Qoh. 10.12-13: 'The words of the wise bring them favour [corresponding to: "It is he who has asked me to build him a temple..."], the lips of the fool ruin him [corresponding to: "This is the god who is at Jerusalem"]: the beginning of his words is foolishness [corresponding to: 'May his god be with him"].'

14. Bickerman, 'Edict of Cyrus', pp. 82-84.

spoke of the construction of the temple of God at Jerusalem, and made
no allusion to a return of exiles. Furthermore, the order to restore the
cultic furnishings taken by Nebuchadnezzar, which appeared in the
memorandum (6.5), was in fact carried out, according to the document
mentioned in Ezra 1.7-11; everything was handed over to the treasurer
Mithredath, and the latter prepared a detailed account of them for
Sheshbazzar, prince of Judah. According to the text, there is no reason
to presuppose that this prince did not reside in Judah, and even in
Jerusalem. The final verse however makes a connection with the return
of the exiles: 'All this Sheshbazzar brought up when the exiles were
brought up [עם העלות, *niphal*; LXX ἀπὸ τῆς ἀποικίας] from Babylon
to Jerusalem.' It is not stated that Sheshbazzar was the head of the
convoy, but the wording induces us to think so.[15]

In fact, the carrying out of Cyrus's decree comprised two parts: in the second, just
cited, the utensils were returned by Cyrus to the prince of Judah, but in the first (vv.
5-6), the heads of families of Judah and Benjamin, priests and Levites, 'all whose
spirit had been roused by God', left to build the temple of YHWH at Jerusalem, with
all kinds of help from their neighbours. In this first notice, not only is there no
allusion to the order of Cyrus, but there is a sort of literary substitution through the
repetition of an identical formula: God had roused the spirit of Cyrus (v. 1), he then
roused that of the exiles, and we find again the conspicuous theme of the autonomy
of the Jewish initiative. What is more, the information about the assistance from
neighbours (v. 6) repeats, in a briefer way, the corresponding passage of the edict
(v. 4) and clarifies it retroactively, since the ambiguous formulation can suggest that
Cyrus's subjects aided the Jews,[16] as Josephus understood it. There is therefore a

15.	Rudolf Kittel (*Biblia Hebraica*) suggests in this case a *hiphil* vocalization;
this is reflected in the translation of J.M. Myers, *Ezra. Nehemia* (AB, 14; Garden
City, NY: Doubleday, 1965): 'Sheshbazzar brought all those along when he brought
up the exiles [...]'; the same is true of the initial summary of de Vaux, 'Décrets de
Cyrus', pp. 29-57.

16.	The text is obscure: וכל הנשאר (LXX καὶ πᾶς ὁ καταλειπόμενος) can be
understood, out of context, as the remnant of the exile spared by God (as in the usual
translations), but it is then historically difficult (despite Josephus) to understand why
Cyrus would have ordered his pagan subjects to subsidize directly the survivors.
According to others (1 Esd., Vulgate, Ibn Ezra, Rashi), it amounted to those who
had not been able to carry out the order to go up. Nevertheless, as Bickerman, 'Edict
of Cyrus', p. 85, has shown, if we take the context into account, that is to say, the
report of the implementation, the meaning changes (understanding כל הנשאר as a
collective, replaced by אנשי מקומו): it was a matter then solely—and more probably—
of a small number of repatriates, inspired by God and helped by those who
remained. However, it will be shown below that the redactional ambiguity was
warranted.

chiastic structure, which encompasses a central element: it is the second part of the edict (v. 4) which corresponds to the first part of its implementation. Now, it is this central element (doubled), with the repatriation and assistance for the exiles, which is precisely missing from the memorandum. As a result of this then, that part is secondary in literary terms, which is the same as saying that the function of the chiasm is to force its integration into the decree of Cyrus: the conclusion (v. 4) is in fact only a more fulsome and less idiomatic development of the aid by neighbours of v. 6. What is more, the ambiguity of that conclusion, mentioned already, has some meaning within the decree, since it suggests that the Persians helped the survivors. The proclamation of Cyrus is therefore limited to vv. 2-3, and, if we consider its short version (B), it is remarkably like the conclusion of 2 Chronicles.[17]

The note about the repatriates of Judah and Benjamin has therefore a different origin and should be disjoined. It spontaneously refers back to the episode mentioning the difficulties caused by Judah and Benjamin under Zerubbabel, and therefore as well, in this way, to the long and significant list (Ezra 2) of those who had returned with Zerubbabel. This list is composite,[18] since among the various categories of repatriates, it mixes those of Judah and 'the people of Israel', and adds the intrusive indication (וישובו [...] אשר, v. 1) that it was a matter of the return of 'those that Nebuchadnezzar had deported to Babylon', which puts the deportees parallel to the cultic objects taken by the same Nebuchadnezzar, with the whole thing cancelling the exile. In the same way, the genealogy given for Ezra in Ezra 7.1-5 cancelled the exile (cf. Chapter 1, §2).

By removing the redactional seams and grouping together the notice of 1.5-6, the list of the repatriated, and the difficulties of 4.1-5, a literary sub-set is obtained which clearly stands out from the proclamation of Cyrus, which is itself limited to 1.2-3. The connecting sentences, 4.4-5, which bring the work to a standstill from Cyrus to Darius, but not from any direct action, is therefore just a redactional effect used to introduce the continuation of the work under Darius (4.24), beyond a series of episodes under Xerxes and Artaxerxes.[19] This sub-set is therefore the story of a group of repatriates who had come with Zerubbabel and Jeshua to build a temple at Jerusalem, with a conflict arising over the question of who was the guardian of the cult to the God of Israel. In

17. Likewise, the stirring up of the spirit of Cyrus, in the introductory verse, is an addition derived from v. 5 (replacing אלהים by יהוה), which is added to the addition on the prophecy of Jeremiah: we recover the primitive verse in jumping from מלך פרס to מלך פרס.

18. Cf. the review of various opinions in Eskenazi, 'The Structure', p. 644 n. 14.

19. Talmon, 'Ezra and Nehemiah', pp. 317-28, includes Ezra 4.4-5 among the redactional summaries which recapitulate the sections by delimiting them; here, the function of this summary would be to group together the restoration of the altar and a beginning of construction under Darius.

literary terms (and therefore also in historical terms), this question is completely distinct from the Persian initiative to rebuild a temple for God at Jerusalem. Incidentally, this is therefore a confirmation of the fact that in the proclamation of Cyrus, the mention of the temple of YHWH, the God of Israel, is intrusive, which is confirmed by the testimony of manuscript (B).

3. *Zerubbabel and Darius*

The document of the chancellery discovered in the archives of Ecbatana in the time of Darius and dated to the first year of Cyrus, prescribed the reconstruction of the temple of God at Jerusalem at the expense of the king, as well as the restoration of the cult objects carried off by Nebuchadnezzar (Ezra 6.3-5). This piece contained neither the name of YHWH nor any allusion to Israel, and ignored any return of captives. It belongs to the Aramaic section, Ezra 4.6–6.18, which can be presumed to be earlier than the comprehensive edition in Hebrew, but had beforehand its own history.

According to the context of the rediscovery of the edict of Cyrus, the governor of Transeuphrates, who had come to discover for himself the reason for the work undertaken at Jerusalem, sent a letter to Darius which presents several oddities. First of all, the prologue of this scene is split in two. In 5.1-2, the prophets Haggai and Zechariah started to prophesy, without any further details being given: then Zerubbabel and Jeshua began to build the temple of God (בית אלהא); and finally it is recalled that the prophets are definitely with them. This apparently not very useful repetition forms an *inclusio* which gives reason to believe that the juxtaposition of the prophets and builders is artificial. Next, in 5.3, the inspection by Tattenai, governor of Transeuphrates, is loosely connected to the preceding persons: the chronological link is vague (בה זמנא), and the MT has a major division (*petuḥa*); finally, the builders are no longer mentioned subsequently except by the term 'Elders', until the reception by Tattenai of the royal response. At this point, a summarizing verse (6.14), inserted before the mention of the completion of the work, reunites 'the Elders of the Jews' and the prophets. What is more, according to the report sent to Darius, these 'Elders' defended their undertaking by explaining that it originated from the order given by Cyrus, which had led to the return of the cultic objects by Sheshbazzar (5.12-16), governor of Judah (cf. 6.7). The renewed mention of the latter allows for a comparison with the two literary sources isolated in Ezra 1: the whole Tattenai episode is connected to the proclamation by Cyrus, but it is surrounded by connected pieces, in which the activity of Zerubbabel and Jeshua is merged with the intervention of the prophets and a dedication of the temple. These complex episodes will be examined later. The useful result here is that Zerubbabel and Jeshua, and with them the account of the Jewish initiative, stand out from the matter of the report of Darius, just as they came loose from the proclamation of Cyrus.

Another difficulty comes up in regard to the response of Darius: it is stated that it was at Ecbatana that a scroll was found, which is cited (6.2-5: 'Memorandum. In the first year of Cyrus the king, King Cyrus has decreed: temple of God at Jerusalem [...]'); then there immediately follows the response of Darius to Tattenai (v. 6: 'And now [כען, LXX νῦν], Tattenai, governor [...]'), without any transition or formal way of address to indicate the author of the letter. Certain critics [20] have seen in the oddity of the abrupt passage from the edict of Cyrus to that of Darius a presumption of authenticity, since a forger would not have failed to restore the missing phrases, as Josephus did (*Ant.* 11.104: 'King Darius to Tattenai, governor, to Shethar-bozenai and to their associates, greetings. I am sending you a copy of the letter that I found in the archives of Cyrus [...]'). This same Josephus, or a collaborator, made however a valuable error: by putting the document of Cyrus in its primitive context, he reshaped it and added an address: 'King Cyrus to Tattenai and Shethar-bozenai [...]' (*Ant.* 11.12). The context makes it difficult to understand how Tattenai and Shethar-bozenai could be contemporaries of Cyrus, but this is nevertheless the most immediate sense, if we consider only the beginning of Cyrus's order in Ezra 6.2, without going farther to vv. 12-13, which recall that these are the instructions of Darius. Cyrus's order in fact had a title ('temple of God at Jerusalem', Ezra 6.2), a first part giving (or recalling) the general order to build, and a second part giving the specific order to Tattenai to remove every obstacle and to organize the assistance (Ezra 6.6-12).

It is necessary however to delimit clearly the memorandum found at Ecbatana. If it contained only the edict of Cyrus, it would lack anywhere an address of Darius, which recalls the document cited, and if the edict of Cyrus is prolonged by the order to Tattenai, we end up with the error of Josephus, since that order is unambiguously attributed to Darius; in

20. Cf. de Vaux, 'Décrets de Cyrus', p. 55.

both these cases, the result is difficult. There is however a problem in interpreting vv. 2-3. The usual translations follow the LXX: 'We found at Ecbatana [...] a scroll which ran thus: "Memorandum. The first year of Cyrus [...]".' The end of v. 2 וכן כתיב בגוה דכרונה can also be understood,[21] in respecting more the division of verses of the MT: '[...] (a scroll) on which was written [or "whose main point was"] a memorandum: "The first year of Cyrus [...]".' In this way, the term 'memorandum', describing the nature of the document, ceases to form part of it, which presents several advantages: first, the indication that the archival document was a memorandum no longer appears in the document itself, which is more logical; next, the absence of formal phrases at the beginning (address) and at the end (date) becomes understandable, since it is a partial copy; finally, the content of the memorandum is composed very naturally of the repetition of the decree of Cyrus, followed by the order of Darius to Tattenai. The document no longer presents difficulty in regard to structure, since two clear cases can then be considered: either, if the memorandum is the copy of a written dispatch, the missing address is to be restored at the beginning (v. 3) and not in the middle (v. 6), which created an odd effect; or it was a matter of a draft of an oral decision, destined for internal administration, as Bickerman proposes.

It could then be objected that it is unusual that the searches prescribed by Darius should end up with the discovery of a document signed by the same Darius. The difficulty could be overcome by supposing that it was another Darius, since there were three of them, but it is premature to give up on literary analysis. We then observe that the introduction to the document is abrupt: Darius had a search done in the archives of Babylon (v. 1), and the find took place at Ecbatana (v. 2). To resolve the double difficulty of the two places and the two Dariuses, it suffices to separate in time the two actions: Darius had the search done in Babylon, and there the account about Darius ends. Later, they found at Ecbatana the memorandum about the edict of Darius, making reference to an order of Cyrus, and this piece proves that the request addressed to Darius had been successful. In other words, the edict of Cyrus was at Babylon, and that of Darius was in the archives at Ecbatana. Such a process of composition, consisting of pure juxtaposition, is not rare in Ezra–Nehemiah. Here, the insertion of the rediscovered document into a

---

21. According to Ruben Yaron, *Introduction to the Law of the Aramaic Papyri* (Oxford: Clarendon Press, 1961), pp. 16-17, the term בגוה designates the important part of a document, and not its totality.

narrative framework which precedes the find is controlled by the addition of v. 13, which declared, repeating the wording of the edict, that the latter had been punctually carried out.

In regard to the 'Elders' questioned by Tattenai, they seemed to have known the decree of Cyrus, since he referred to their testimony in his letter (Ezra 5.13). This testimony is remarkable since it repeated, with the same vocabulary, elements of the decree as found in the memorandum, therefore different from the proclamation of Ezra 1: an order to rebuild the temple of God, restitution of the cult objects, absence of any allusion to a repatriation. What is more, they attribute to Sheshbazzar an essential mission: appointed governor, he brought the objects and laid the foundations of the Temple, and the work was continued without interruption, which contradicts several passages on their interruption (under Cyrus, Xerxes, Artaxerxes), not to mention what is known of the policy of Cambyses, successor of Cyrus and predecessor of the first Darius. Finally, it is a little strange, if the work had been ordered by the king at his own expense, that the departments of a governor of Transeuphrates knew nothing about it, and that they would not have been involved in any identifiable expenses, whereas they constituted the authority of ordinary supervision of Judaea.

These difficulties are cleared up if we take into account the fact that the whole narrative about Tattenai, Shethar-bozenai and their associates, all high officials of Transeuphrates, contains no information not in the memorandum, as restored above, or in the short notice on the governor Sheshbazzar (Ezra 1.7-11a): in fact, the memorandum contains the trace of a crisis in the time of Darius, which was settled by recalling an edict of Cyrus, followed by a series of measures in regard to the financing of the rebuilding and the support of the cult. It suffices then to assume that the narrative is only used to present this crisis, making a point of not providing any new content. The illogicality of Tattenai's move then disappears, and it is no longer difficult to understand the rupture between the order given by the Darius of the account to search in the archives and then the discovery at Ecbatana of a memorandum relative to an act of the same Darius (of history). It is clear finally that the redactor of the account had a literary concern only, and was as unaware of all the Achaemenids as of the rest of the book, which explains why he tried to find a continuity between Cyrus and Darius.

This composition from the hands of an editor extends from 5.3 to 6.13, and to it must be added v. 15, which indicates the date of the completion of the Temple, under Darius. This verse could have come from the memorandum or from an appended document. On the other hand, v. 14 serves to bind together the story of Tattenai with the introduction on Zerubbabel and the prophets; and the conclusion of the passage in Aramaic (vv. 16-18), which speaks of the Israelites inaugurating the temple of God, with sacrifices and a reference to the twelve tribes and to the law of Moses, confirms this binding: the temple of Cyrus and Darius was really dedicated by all the people, without specific allusion to the altar of sacrifices.

The simplest thing therefore is to attribute these passages to the editor of the introduction to the whole episode (5.1-2), who had associated Zerubbabel with the prophets: in fact, we have seen that this association was artificial, since the final inauguration was aware of just the prophets and various classes of Israelites.[22] Zerubbabel and Jeshua therefore did not form an integral part of the redaction, which associated the work of Darius and the Israelites. They were artificially integrated into the work of construction as well as into the dedication by all Israel. More exactly, their work as repatriated restorers, developed previously (Ezra 3), is united by this process with the affair of the edict of Darius, which is itself connected to the restoration by Israel. It would appear then that the material peculiar to this editor is to be clearly distinguished as well from the sources relative to Zerubbabel and Jeshua. As for the prophets Haggai and Zechariah, they play a quite specific role in the redactional parts: they prophesied in the beginning for the Jews of Judah and Jerusalem in the name of the God of Israel (5.1), then inspired the Elders of the Jews who were building (6.14), and the outcome of this was a dedication by all Israel, in which they are no longer mentioned. Their (literary) role over the Jews was therefore to extend as well the meaning of their action to all Israel. This literary role is evidently of prime importance, since the worship of the God of Israel by Jews alone did not make sense, and turned out to be a source of conflict.

Zerubbabel and Jeshua are again linked to the edict of Cyrus in another way, in connection with the foundation of the Temple. According to Ezra 3.7, the preparations for the construction of the Temple, and

---

22. Williamson, *Ezra*, pp. 73-75, isolates 5.1-6; 6.1-2 and 6.13-22 as editorial additions. This includes the bringing of Tattenai into the narrative, but he maintains the authenticity of his letter (5.7-17). However, the first two passages (5.1-6 and 6.1-2) are themselves composite, and the letter not only gives no information, but creates useless historical complications, because of Sheshbazzar.

in particular the forwarding of the materials, were carried out in conformity with the authorization (רִשְׁיוֹן, LXX ἐπιχώρησις) of Cyrus. This
authorization seemed to be limited here to a marketing franchise, allowing Phoenician artisans to import cedars from Lebanon. There is no
question of total financing by the king, since the money and resources
came from those who offered sacrifices (3.6-7). The connection with the
edict of Cyrus, under the one or the other form, is therefore very
tenuous.

Moreover, the whole of this passage calls for observations on
structures, since it is strange that the altar and the sacrifices should be
entirely restored according to the law of Moses (3.1-5) before there
would have been the slightest groundwork for the sanctuary of YHWH,
and it seems that there was uncertainty about the exact cultic role of the
Temple. As has already been noted, each of the long parallel lists of Ezra
2 and Nehemiah 7 is followed by a feast of Booths, and in both cases,
the Israelites were in their cities, then all the people assembled together
in Jerusalem. In Ezra 3.1-5, the feast of Booths took place in the
sanctuary, with the sacrifices prescribed by the Law, offered on the altar
rebuilt by Zerubbabel and Jeshua. In Nehemiah 8–10, it was a feast of
Booths, in the strict sense of huts (of boughs), done without sacrifices
and of a new type, since nothing like it had been seen since Joshua. It is
framed by the proclamation of the law of Moses and a commitment by
the community to observe it. On the one hand, the Law culminated in
the cult, and there resulted from this the laying of the foundations of the
Temple, celebrated by the people. On the other, the Law culminated in
penance and praise, and there resulted from this a contractual engage-
ment founding the community. Moreover, the allusion to Joshua, son of
Nun, is very interesting, since he was the first to have legislated (and
secondarily to have introduced the law of Moses), and if he fostered no
link with Jerusalem or with the Temple, he contended for 'all Israel',
while remaining centred on Shechem.

The formal parallelism between the two feasts of the Law is so strong
that the typological meaning prevails over the exactness of the narrative,
since it was a matter of bringing together different models. The second,
which will be studied below, led to a peaceful Jewish installation in
Judaea and Jerusalem. The first, on the contrary, opened up a long series
of difficulties through several reigns but especially referred to something
different: 1. it has been noted for a long time that the formulation of the
preparations (3.7-9) recalled strongly—and therefore deliberately—those

for the temple of Solomon (1 Kgs 5.5-18); 2. The builders began their work 'the second year of their arrival at the temple of God' (v. 8), which indicates that the important thing was the place of the ancient Temple, and not the construction to come (v. 10). 3. The celebration of the foundations was carried out according to the ordinances of David, king of Israel (v. 10). 4. Finally, it is mentioned, at the time of the inauguration of the foundations (v. 12), that some aged notables had seen the ancient Temple (Haggai 2.3 and Zech. 4.10). It very simply follows from this that the importance of the Temple came from its antiquity (David and Solomon), therefore its foundation. The account in that case takes on a typological meaning: it is the restoration of the law of Moses, under a cultic form, which should permit the recovery of the ancient Temple, and through it an Israelite legitimacy.

To clarify this result, we can wonder what might be the meaning of the account if the order of the two parts were reversed, that is to say, if the laying of the foundations had preceded the inauguration of the altar: it would be a matter then of a simple more or less slow and intermittent mechanical restoration of a prior state, simply connected to the edict of Cyrus which prescribed it. On the contrary, the fact that the cultic restoration of the Law was placed *before* the foundations of the Temple indicates that the restoration, consequently the reconstitution of the heritage of Solomon, remained a problem. Now, it is certain on the other hand that the accounts of the construction by Solomon made no allusion to the law of Moses, and were in no way in accordance with the dispositions laid down by the Pentateuch. The problem can be expressed in this way: How did the fulfilment of that Law allow for the recovery of Solomon's heritage? That Law was a novelty, connected with the repatriates (Ezra 3.8).

On the contrary, at the time of the second feast of Booths, the novelty was admitted, through the reference to Joshua, and the only connection with the past that was sought was with the patriarchs and Moses, that is to say, with the persons of the Pentateuch, therefore, with the history of ancient Israel, through a repudiation of the kings (canticles of Neh. 9.5b-37). The stake in the connection with the monarchy is announced by a parenthesis indicating the fear of the 'people of the land', at the moment of the restoration of the altar, then clarified by the crisis that immediately followed the foundation (Ezra 4.1-3): the 'enemies of Judah and Benjamin' wished to take part in the building of the temple of YHWH, the God of Israel. In literary terms, then, the episode of the laying of the foundations (3.10-13) becomes detached, as do the feast of Booths which serves as a prologue (vv. 1-6) and the mobilization of the Phoenicians artisans (v. 7). Since these elements make sense in the overall composition of the work, there is no objection to attributing them to the 'compiler'. There remains then a note, with a chronology and proper names, on the work undertaken by Zerubbabel and his companions on the site of the temple of God (vv. 8-10), which is extended by an adverse intervention (4.1-3), and which is connected to a part at least of the list of Ezra 2. This notice contains an allusion to the order of Cyrus intended to guarantee the exclusive right of the exiles to rebuild the Temple, but the edict contains no such thing, in fact just the contrary: the argument is therefore purely literary.

These brief analyses show the very clear consistencies in composition, which bring closely together scattered sources. The historical record, since it is necessary to return to it, happens to be considerably simplified in this process.

1. The edict of Cyrus-Darius, supplemented by a notice about Sheshbazzar, constitutes a source about which there is no reason to be suspicious. We meet again the conclusions of de Vaux and of Bickerman, being mindful that this restoration of the temple of Jerusalem has a direct connection neither with a repatriation of exiles, nor with the law of Moses.

2. As for the identification of Darius, his position in the Aramaic document, after Xerxes and Artaxerxes, leads us to think of Darius II (425–405) here, but it is not certain that the order of reigns is exact, and the usual choice of Darius I (521–486) is simpler, since we know incidentally of a Tattenai, governor of Transeuphrates and a contemporary of the latter.[23] The crisis indicated by the correspondence between Darius and Tattenai is otherwise unknown, but ultimately there is no difficulty in seeing it as resulting from a change in policy under Cambyses, as Josephus proposes (from another perspective).

3. Likewise, there is no reason to disregard the indication that the Temple had been completed the sixth year of Darius (6.15), but the celebration of the Passover, which follows (6.19-22), is a discordant independent piece: the text becomes Hebrew again, following a Masoretic

---

23. A Babylonian document from 502 BCE refers to a Tattenai (*Ta'at[tan'ni]*), governor (*pahat*) of Transeuphrates (*Ebirnari*), with the same vocabulary as in Ezra 5.3, and elsewhere; cf. A.T. Olmstead, 'Tattenai, Governor of Across the River', *JNES* 3 (1944), p. 46.

division (*setuma*). Furthermore, it was without any doubt an account of a feast of restoration of the Israelites, with those repatriated and with those who had broken off relations with the neighbouring nations, but the feast did not take place in the Temple, the victims were immolated by the Levites, and there was no allusion to the law of Moses. A final verse (6.22) ensures the liaison with the preceding episode, by connecting the festivities to the work on the Temple, but with several discrepancies (or inaccuracies): in it the Passover became seven days of Unleavened Bread, and the benevolent monarch is described as 'king of Assyria' and not as 'king of Persia' (cf. Ezra 4.3). This carelessness implies a devout but poorly documented redactional effort. This account, or more exactly the insertion of this account here, reminds us of the Passovers of Hezekiah and Josiah, after restorations of cult (2 Chron. 30 and 35). As for the inauguration of the altar according to the Law, independently of the Temple, it is difficult to see in it a single event, but it strongly resembles the dedication by Judas Maccabeus (according to 1 Macc. 4.52-59), with the persistence in the background of the question of the relative importance of the Dwelling and the altar.

4.   The name of Zerubbabel brings together several pieces, which point to a group returned from exile, with the priest Jeshua, to restore the ancient sanctuary. This group, independent of Cyrus-Darius as well as of Zechariah-Haggai, was Jewish and did not take itself to be all Israel. There are few details to help situate it in time. The usual joining of Zerubbabel to Darius is due to the setting with the Tattenai affair (5.2), but this is artificial. However, if we consider the succession of kings between Cyrus and Darius, the absence of Cambyses, and the presence of an Artaxerxes tend to suggest that it is a matter of a later Darius. It has been observed[24] that this succession is artificial: all of 4.6-23 (Xerxes and Artaxerxes) is framed by connecting verses which to a great extent repeat themselves, and which insist on the interruption of the work on the temple of God, whereas the complaints under these two kings did not speak of this. Just as the repetition of the list of companions of Zerubbabel made this same Zerubbabel survive up to Ezra, in the same way the stretching out of the chronology between Cyrus and Darius made this same Zerubbabel survive during all these reigns. Another possible reason is that the historical Zerubbabel would have been a contemporary of Darius II or Darius III, and that the chronological displacement of the Darius of the decree would be by the hand which

24. Cf. Williamson's discussion, *Ezra*, pp. 57-59.

connected the enterprise of Zerubbabel with him. Whatever is thought of these suppositions, the only definite point is that Zerubbabel was prior to the redaction of the Memoirs of Nehemiah (Neh. 7.5), but his attachment to the law of Moses leads us to presume that he was quite late.

5. Finally, the discussions about the genuine Israel and about the heritage of David and Solomon, as well as the opposition between the two forms of the feast of Booths are very real questions, which the redaction tends to extend back to Cyrus and Darius I. At the present stage of the examination of Ezra 1–6, the emergence of these problems cannot be dated however, no more than the intervention of the prophets can be. It is emphasized however that the promulgation of the law of Moses was done in two phases: a restoration of the cult which failed to re-establish a continuity with ancient times, then a community institution, which persisted in the 'model of Nehemiah'.

4. *Nehemiah*

In the accounts which we have at our disposal, the two persons Ezra and Nehemiah were unaware of each other, and according to the chronological indicators provided, they were not even contemporaries. Still, it is with their twinning that the book of Ezra–Nehemiah reaches its highest point, with the feast of the Law, whose continuation formed a peaceful era (phase 4, p. 343 above). The literary arrangement is certain, and we therefore continue the observations on structures.

We begin with the examination of this phase 4, which is extremely complex. The account of the reconstruction of the ramparts by Nehemiah (1.1–7.4) continued, in the general opinion of commentators, with the installation at Jerusalem of leaders of the people and volunteers (11.1-3), that is to say a tenth 'of the people'. The interruption comes from a series of related pieces, among which were the elements constituting the feast of the Law.

1. The long list (7.6-72), parallel to Ezra 2, replaces the missing volunteers with a list of those repatriated who, with Zerubbabel and many cult officials, were settled in Jerusalem and 'in their own towns'. This list is introduced by a connecting verse which shows that it is an archival document; it identifies those absent therefore. The settlement of the city by Nehemiah, from this perspective, was or should have been the high point of Zerubbabel's undertaking, after the restoration of the altar and then the Dwelling. That however was not the way it was, and

this emphasizes by way of contrast that the first account in the Memoirs of Nehemiah was not concerned with those repatriated from exile, but those 'who had escaped the captivity'[25] (Neh. 1.2-3). Nehemiah alone had made the trip, from the court of Babylon.

2. The solemn reading of the Law by Ezra (8.1-18) was connected to the preceding list by 7.72b: 'Now, when the seventh month came— the Israelites being in their towns [ובני ישראל בעריהם]—all the people gathered as one [...].' The interpolated phrase on the Israelites in their towns interrupts the sentence, by repeating the end of the list (7.72a: 'gate-keepers, cantors and "some of the people" in their own towns, and all the other Israelites in their own towns'). There is therefore a seam between two fragments which had different origins, and the issue of knowing whether this operation was prior to the insertion of the whole thing into the Memoirs of Nehemiah, or whether it was the result of the same project, is secondary here.[26] According to 8.17, the assembly is formed of repatriates, and according to 8.7-8, the law had to be explained and translated.[27] Next, the 'discovery' by the leaders and the priests of the feast of Booths (or Huts) in the written Law posed a problem, since the stipulations mentioned do not agree with what we read in Lev. 29.39-43,[28] without even speaking about the absence of the prescribed sacrifices (Num. 29.18-38). The important thing here however is the allusion to the written Law of Moses, as well as the identification of the assembly of repatriates with the Israelites, with everything taking place in a climate of entire newness, in which the people were

25. The wording of this verse is ambiguous, הפליטה אשר נשארו מן השבי 'the remainder, those who had been left of the captivity', which can be understood either as 'who had remained in captivity', so after the departure of the repatriates (Zerubbabel), or 'who had remained [in Judaea] at the time of the captivity', so who had not left ruined Judaea. H.C.M. Vogt, Studien zur nachexilischen Gemeinde in Esra–Nehemia (Werl: D. Goelde, 1966), pp. 45-51 shows that the first meaning is a harmonizing one, and that only the second is a natural one; cf. the discussion in Williamson, Ezra, p. 171.

26. Cf. C.C. Torrey, The Composition and Historical Value of Ezra–Nehemiah (BZAW, 2; Giessen: Riecker, 1896), pp. 29-34.

27. The term used, מפורש, is interpreted in various ways, and here I follow R. Le Déaut, Introduction à la littérature Targumique (Rome: Pontifical Biblical Institute, 1966), pp. 23-32, who makes use of the meaning 'translate' in Ezra 4.18.

28. Cf. the review of the problem and the discussion of C. Houtman, 'Ezra and the Law: Observations on the Supposed Relation between Ezra and the Pentateuch', OTS 21 (1981), pp. 91-115.

determined to listen to and learn the Law. The newcomers having originated from Babylon, the translation must have been to Aramaic, and therefore the original was in Hebrew. Despite the difficulties, it is hard not to look for a parallel between the Law read in this way and a certain phase of the Pentateuch. As for dates, this piece is connected to a seventh month, which fits in with the feast of Booths (Neh. 8.1; cf. Ezra 3.1), but there is no chronological connection to any reign.

3. The atonement ceremony that follows (Neh. 9) is somewhat incongruous, since the fast follows upon jubilation, and the principal sin announced is mixing with foreigners, which cannot be claimed immediately about voluntary repatriates. On the contrary, as has long been seen, the date (twenty-fourth day of the month) and the allusion to race fit the context of the 'Memoirs of Ezra', in which the assembly took place on the twentieth day (Ezra 10.9). The best place for the reinsertion of the episode (with or without the 'psalm' of Neh. 9.5-37) is between Ezra 10.15 and 10.16,[29] but it could have undergone some modifications at the time of the transfer. Apart from the indication of the day of the month, this piece does not entail an absolute date either.

4. The last piece (Neh. 10) is the statement of a written commitment made by the community to observe the law of God, 'given by Moses'. There is inserted into it (vv. 2-28) a series of signatories, the first of whom was Nehemiah, son of Hacaliah. This list interrupts the syntax of a sentence formed by vv. 1 and 29, and therefore is not in its natural place. The question of knowing whether it was originally the real list of the signatories to the commitment, or an *ad hoc* composition, gathering together a maximum of names to strengthen its impact, is still debated,[30] but the solution does not directly affect the purpose here. Once again, no date appears, and there is no allusion to Ezra. As for the content of the commitment, it was made up of a complete adherence to the Law of Moses, followed by specific measures. We may wonder whether these latter were added to the law of Moses as a kind of case law,[31] or

29. Cf. the discussion and conclusions of Williamson, *Ezra*, pp. 309-11, who follows W. Rudolf, *Esra und Nehemia, samt 3. Esra* (HAT, 1/20; Tübingen: Mohr [Paul Siebeck], 1949), pp. 154-56.

30. A. Jepsen, 'Nehemia 10', *ZAW* 66 (1954), pp. 87-106, and Williamson's discussion of this point, *Ezra*, pp. 326-29.

31. D.J.A. Clines, 'Nehemiah 10 as an Example of Early Jewish Biblical Exegesis', *JSOT* 21 (1981), pp. 111-17, who sees here a beginning of the 'tradition of the Elders', understood as jurisprudence and therefore after Scripture.

whether they merely emphasize certain points in which the trans-gressions are more clear-cut. However, the points on which Nehemiah insisted at the time of his second journey (Neh. 13), namely, the straightening out of the cult, the observance of the Sabbath and the breaking up of marriages with foreigners correspond quite exactly to the specific stipulations of the commitment, so that many commentators have considered that the latter merely clarified some sensitive precepts.

Consequently the most common opinion among the commentators is that this commitment was later than the second mission of Nehemiah, and therefore originally constituted an annex to Nehemiah 13. This solution however is not satisfactory, since it presupposes what is in question, namely that what was added to the law of Moses only served to emphasize it. The Pentateuch did not prohibit foreign marriages (Abraham and Hagar, Gen. 16.3; Joseph and Asenath, Gen. 41.45; Moses and Zipporah, Exod. 2.21; etc.), but pointed out the dangers of idolatry from the introduction of foreign women (Exod. 34.11-16, etc.). The prohibition of buying from foreigners on the Sabbath (Neh. 10.32), which was not lucrative work unlike the activities that Nehemiah prohibited in 13.15, was not biblical either. The stipulations relative to cult contain non-biblical precepts: an annual assessment of a third of a shekel, offerings of wood, the first fruits of fruit trees, and so on. These arrangements seem therefore to have completed the written work, like a jurisprudence. An instructive example of this literary mechanism is provided besides in 13.1-3: from a passage (Deut. 23.4-6) which pro-hibits admittance of Ammonites and Moabites to the assembly, they decided to exclude foreigners, and the account that follows ended up, after the expulsion of Tobiah the Ammonite, with the elimination of for-eign wives. The extension in the meaning was considerable, and contrary besides to the spirit of the cited passage (cf. Deut. 23.8-9). If we must speak of a jurisprudence, it follows the dictates of new principles.

Furthermore, in the commitment, one case at least represents a retreat from the precepts of the Pentateuch, namely, the giving up of the harvest and of debts every seven years (cf. Chapter 3, §3). The term jurisprudence therefore becomes inappropriate, all the more so since the exact content of the Pentateuch at that moment cannot be ascertained, especially on the subject of the Sabbath. All that has been said on the autonomy of the 'tradition of the Elders', with its Babylonian connec-tions in relation to Scripture, can therefore be applied here. Further-more, the account of the first mission of Nehemiah ignored the Temple, as well as the precept about the year of remission of debts (5.10-12). The signed commitment adds to the law of Moses rules about personal life and regulations on the upkeep of the Temple. We therefore arrive at the juxtaposition of three components whose somewhat unstable merging has been attributed to Simon the Just (Chapter 7, §2): written law (Pentateuch), oral law ('model of Nehemiah') and cult. A rabbinic tradition compared the inserted list of signatories to the 'Great Assembly', of which Simon was one of the last members, which agrees with the interpretation of that entity proposed above.

The second mission of Nehemiah is composed of two parts: one on the reform of the cult (13.4-14), and the other on the straightening out of Jewish practices (foreign wives and the Sabbath, 13.15-27), which culminated in the expulsion of the high priest Eliashib. It all ended with a conclusion which summarizes the two parts. The second part, which is strictly and explicitly Jewish, reveals no particular harshness, but the first, as regards the reform of cult, is centred on a unique problem, the proper usage of the storerooms of the Temple. We observe first the affair of Tobiah, installed by the high priest Eliashib in the room where they normally stored the offerings, incense, the utensils and the portions of the Levites and priests, and vigorously evicted by Nehemiah. Next, Nehemiah realized that the tithes were no longer coming in, and correlatively that the Levites were neglecting their duties. He restored the various duties by reorganizing the storerooms and their provisioning. Moreover, the preceding passage (12.44-47), which concludes the dedication of the ramparts by depicting an ideal epoch, was centred too on the proper administration of the storerooms, on which depended the quality of all the services of the priests and Levites. It is therefore definitely the same theme, which serves as a sort of summary of what follows,[32] since a chiastic structure is connected with it. This summary is due to an editor, since it calls to mind the time of Zerubbabel and the time of Nehemiah, not without recalling the precepts of David and Solomon on the offerings. Clearly, all this construction shows that Nehemiah, acting as a royal official, redressed the fiscal organization. He

---

32. Cf. Williamson's excellent analysis, *Ezra*, pp. 380-82. The story of Eliashib begins (13.4) with לפני מזה 'previously', an expression which produces a connection either with the expulsion of foreigners (13.3), or with the summary on the success of Zerubbabel and Nehemiah (12.44-47); if A designates the re-establishment of the warehouses and B the expulsion of foreigners, there is a chiastic structure: A (12.44-47), B (13.1-3), B (13.4-9), A (13.10-14).

was not interested in the cult itself or in the feasts, but in the proper functioning of the administration. Whatever the religious motivations, the important thing was that the taxes came in, even if the high priest was unworthy, we may add.

This apparent clarity hides some difficulties. According to 13.6, Nehemiah was not on an official mission, but on a private holiday (נשאלתי). His authority, which is nevertheless great in this passage, owes nothing therefore to the Persian government. Furthermore, the chronological information, which recalls precisely the dates of the first mission, is at the same time redundant, since we already know this (5.14), and incomplete, since the date of this new expedition is missing. Finally, Artaxerxes is referred to as king of Babylon, when the Persian designations are more important. As Sigmund Mowinckel shows, it would be a gloss.[33] The proposed comparison with Ezra 8.1, in which the words 'in the reign of king Artaxerxes' disrupt a sentence '[...]went up with me from Babylon' and are obviously a gloss, really has no foundation however, since here we find no disruption in syntax. It is necessary then to go even further, and consider either that the whole verse, explaining the wrongly dated absence of Nehemiah, is a gloss, or that the whole passage is an addition, composed in the style of the Memoirs of Nehemiah. The choice between these two options brings up the topic of an evaluation of the meaning of these Memoirs, outside the purview here. It suffices here to keep in mind that there is some literary manipulation whose purpose was to derive from the civil power, and not from the priesthood, the authority of the reformer, who is to bring about important changes.

But if the artifice fails, Nehemiah becomes again a purely Jewish reformer, and the story of his success, based on persuasion alone without authority or coercion, becomes a sort of epic, and not a simple exposition of facts. Moreover, if the administrative connection of the second mission to a Persian (or Seleucid) authority vanishes, there is no longer any difficulty in situating it at a time of Lagide domination or influence, that is to say in the third century or at the beginning of the second. In these circumstances, it is significant on the contrary that Nehemiah would have a *moral* connection not with Persia, but with Babylon.

---

33. S. Mowinckel, *Studien zu dem Buche Ezra–Nehemia*. II. *Die Nehemia-Denkschrift* (Oslo: Univesitets Forlager, 1964), p. 37.

The narrative in Nehemiah 8–13 has no longer therefore any necessary link with the Persian period, if we exclude the various lists of persons. This collection exactly corresponds to phases 4 and 5 of the general progression of the book of Ezra–Nehemiah, or again to all that follows the block enclosed by the doubled list of Ezra 2 and Nehemiah 7. The structuring separates it in particular from the actual mission of Nehemiah, from the twentieth to the thirty-third year of Artaxerxes. At the time of that mission, Nehemiah was governor (Neh. 5.14), and his main project, supported by the king, was the restoration of the ramparts. It is clear that he strove according to neither the law of Moses[34] (cf. 5.9-13), nor any stipulation about subsequent community commitment (10.31-40). The account of this mission was edited; it contains the classical difficulty of the opposition of Artaxerxes to any restoration of Jerusalem (Ezra 4.17-23), but there is no need to remove it from the Persian period, and this does not affect the purpose here. According to Sir. 49.13, 'His memory is great', which adequately explains that later episodes would have been lodged under his name. In particular, it is suggested below (§7), based on considerations about the Dedication, that the second mission (Neh. 13) should be attributed to Judas Maccabeus.

As for Nehemiah looked upon as founder of a library, this means that it resulted from a Babylonian impetus. The composition of this library is instructive: 'It collected together the books dealing with the kings, the writings of the prophets and of David, the letters of the kings on the subject of offerings' (2 Macc. 2.13). The reference to royalty is dominant, and the law of Moses is missing, then eventually included, as I have said. Babylonian Judaism always considered itself as exiled from a fallen kingdom. It must be noted in fact that what had been called 'city of Nehemiah', with the wall, the Sabbath, and the expulsion of foreigners, is connected likewise to his literary personality, such as it appears from the book, but not to his actual work as Persian governor.

5. *Ezra*

Unlike Nehemiah, Ezra was closely connected to the law of Moses: he was introduced as a zealous scribe (סופר מהיר, Ezra 7.6 γραμματεὺς ταχύς, 1 Esd. 8.3 γραμματεὺς εὐφυής) of the law of Moses, and it was he who eventually proclaimed it in Jerusalem.

The account does show tensions. The introduction (7.1-10) has a very

---

34. The prayer of Nehemiah (1.5-11a) is an insertion in Deuteronomic style.

laboured and repetitive style. At the beginning (vv. 1-5), the sequence without any chronology 'after these events, in the reign of Artaxerxes'[35] as well as the genealogy concluded with a repetition 'this Ezra [...]' (v. 6) are artificial, all the more so since this genealogy, identical to the posterity of Aaron given in 1 Chron. 5.29-41, would make Ezra a brother of the high priest exiled by Nabuchadnezzar.

Next, in v. 7, it is said, without any connection with Ezra, that the Israelites arrived at Jerusalem in the seventh year of Artaxerxes, then, in v. 8, that Ezra arrived at Jerusalem in the fifth month, without any mention of a connection to the repatriates, but nevertheless 'the seventh year of the king'. But this repetition has the effect of fusing together Ezra and the repatriates, in accordance with the mechanism observed to bring together Zerubbabel and the prophets in Ezra 5.1-2. Next, in v. 9, the indication of the duration of the voyage of Ezra, from the first to the fifth month, is concluded with the repetition of a formula ('The kindly favour of his God was with him') already used in v. 6. Various textual corrections have been proposed to improve the genealogy of Ezra and his cohesion with the repatriates,[36] but they do not take into account the signs of a revision,[37] and Ezra, the zealous scribe come up from Babylon, at an unspecified date, must be separated from the Israelites who arrived in Jerusalem in the seventh year. The apparent reason for this fusion was that subsequently there were two accounts: a convoy of repatriates came up with Ezra to Jerusalem (Ezra 8), then he expelled the foreign wives among the residents of Judah and Jerusalem, therefore independently of any repatriation event.

This doubling is met again in the rescript of Artaxerxes (7.12-26), which first of all sent Ezra and his volunteers to restore the cult at Jerusalem, at the expense of the treasury, then assigned to Ezra alone the mission to establish scribes in Transeuphrates, with the power to deal ruthlessly with any deviants. A double title for Ezra corresponded to this double undertaking: as priest, he arrived at the Temple at the head of a convoy of repatriates; as scribe, he examined, disseminated and applied the Law. The combination of these two titles is precisely the proper object of the introduction just studied, not without literary rough spots.

The rescript of Artaxerxes is given in Aramaic, with a short prologue

---

35. This vague indication is a gloss which is found also in Ezra 8.1.
36. Williamson, *Ezra*, pp. 89-92.
37. Cf. M. Noth, *Überlieferungsgeschichtliche Studien* (Halle: Nemeyer, 1943), p. 125.

(v. 11). Ezra is presented there as a priest–scribe: the double title is given without any trace of manipulation. The document is made up of four parts, and to the first three correspond the developments in the accounts that follow: 1. Permission to anyone who formed part of the people of Israel to go to Jerusalem (v. 13), which corresponds to the caravan of Ezra 8. 2. A mission entrusted to Ezra to go inspect Judah and Jerusalem according to the law of his God (v. 14), which corresponds to the matter of mixed marriages in Ezra 9–10. 3. Arrangements for the transfer of royal money and offerings (vv. 15-20), which corresponds to the goods taken along by the caravan (8.30-34), with the annexed citation of an order to the treasurers of Transeuphrates ensuring provisions and exemptions from duties (vv. 21-24), an order which only corresponds to the brief redactional note[38] of 8.36. 4. Instructions to Ezra to appoint scribes in all Transeuphrates (vv. 25-26), but it has no corresponding development.

The first three parts with their subsequent development present the great anomaly of speaking of the people of Israel and the God of Israel at Jerusalem and in Judah, which was certainly not likely on the part of a Persian king, even if he were repeating the phraseology of a Jewish request. These three parts (without the annexed citation) are therefore additions to the document, intended to lay the foundations for Ezra's authority in the narratives that follow, in which there is no longer any reference to Artaxerxes. There remains then the order to the treasurers, who prescribed subsidies of foodstuffs and silver, with express reference to orders from the God of heaven, and there remains too the mission throughout Transeuphrates. The order is strange, since there is nothing about support for the cult, except perhaps implicitly through the subsidy of 100 talents of silver, which is an enormous sum.[39]

As for the task of establishing scribes to teach the Law to anyone who was ignorant of it, this meant the promulgation of the written Law, become the Law of the king, without specific reference to Jerusalem. It was then a new phenomenon, in connection with the Jewish communities dispersed in Transeuphrates. Ezra being a scribe, and closely bound to the law of Moses, it must be concluded that his mission, since

38. Cf. the anomalies picked out by Williamson, *Ezra*, p. 122; moreover, the letter to Ezra implies that the order to the treasurers was transmitted independently of him.

39. According to Herodotus, *History* 3.91, the total amount of the annual taxes in Transeuphrates did not exceed 350 talents.

he left from Babylon (7.6), consisted of implanting it in an authoritarian way. It is in this way moreover that we can understand the proclamation of this Law at Jerusalem (Neh. 8), to a community which at the outset had other affinities.

To sum up, to subsidize Jerusalem and reform a widely extended Judaism through the written Law, without any idea of repatriation or of restoration of the Temple, such were the missions which remained. For lack of more precise information, it is hard to see how to connect these missions to Artaxerxes, but they match perfectly the policy of Antiochus III in regard to the Jews, at the time of the granting of the Charter (cf. Chapter 5, §6).

6. *Conclusions*

Josephus provides no new information on the Persian period, outside of some brief notes just before the arrival of Alexander. His principal source was the compilation of 1 Esdras[40] and the book of Esther, to

40. Josephus followed this collection and not Ezra–Nehemiah directly. Numerous details, but especially the overall composition, prove this. The story of the selection of Zerubbabel from the bodyguards of Darius (*Ant.* 11.31-74; cf. 1 Esd. 3–4); the work under Darius and its interruption by the 'enemies of Judah and Benjamin' (11.75-87; cf. 1 Esd. 5.47–7.15); the story of Nehemiah began after the death of Ezra (11.159), and the proclamation of the Law by Ezra is taken out of the context of the mission of Nehemiah, as in 1 Esd. 9.37-55; after the end of the present 1 Esdras, Josephus (11.156) fairly freely summarizes Nehemiah, and we may suppose that he would have known a now-lost continuation of that compilation. Cf. as far back as H. Bloch, *Die Quellen des Flavius Josephus in seiner Archäologie* (Leipzig: Teubner, 1876), p. 76, and Williamson, *Israel*, pp. 12-36. As for the form of 1 Esdras which he knew, there is a number of indications to show that he translated from the Hebrew: *Ant.* 11.12, Σισίνης (Tattenai) corresponds to Σισίννης in 1 Esd. 6.3, and to תתני in Ezra 5.3, and this alternating ת/שׁ indicates a Hebrew original: *Ant.* 11.26, in response to the complaint of Rehum, a governor, and Shimshai, a secretary, the king Cambyses (Artaxerxes according to Ezra) addressed 'Rathymos, secretary, Beelzemos and Semelios', committing the same error as 1 Esd. 2.19, of taking טעם בעל as a proper noun; but the writing of proper names ('Ραούμος, Βεελτεέμος, Σαμσαῖος) is so different that there could not be direct dependence: the two of them came therefore from the same Hebrew text; in particular, a characteristic error, 'Ραούμος came from reading רתום for רחום. *Ant.* 11.50-51: 'thanks to [the women], care and vigilance rule within us, and we are not able to detach ourselves from them' corresponds to 1 Esd. 4.17: οὐ δύνανται οἱ ἄνθρωποι εἶναι χωρὶς τῶν γυναικῶν, or something like לא יוכלו בני האדם להיות בלא נשׁים, and through Josephus we find the same expression, but with לחיות ('live without them') for להיות. These minor

which he added the remembrance of a letter of Xerxes recommending Nehemiah to Addaios, prefect of Syria, Phoenicia and Samaria (11.167). He made some deviations with regard to these sources, but these are only redactional effects, as can be easily seen.

We have seen that in order to put the dedication of the new Temple under Darius I, he had to omit the allusion to Xerxes in Ezra 4.6, then replace Artaxerxes of Ezra 4.7-23 by Cambyses. He then had to find a place for two independent units, the events relative to Ezra and Nehemiah (under Artaxerxes according to Ezra–Nehemiah), and the story of Esther (under Xerxes according to MT, under Artaxerxes according to the LXX). In order to have continuity with the restoration of the Temple under Darius I, he placed Ezra and Nehemiah right after him, under Xerxes (11.120), by suggesting that these episodes filled the whole reign (§183). Next, he filled the whole reign of Artaxerxes with the story of Esther[41] (he concludes in §296: 'Such were the events that took place in the reign of Artaxerxes'). Then he gives (§297) brief episodes under 'another Artaxerxes' (τοῦ ἄλλου[42]), and finally cites Darius, conquered by Alexander. It can be seen, by comparing this outline with the Achaemenid chronologies, that Josephus *omitted* an Artaxerxes and a Darius, since, due to the fact that he used Herodotus, he clearly did not have enough material to fill that many reigns. Since it was Darius III whom Alexander defeated, Josephus has therefore omitted Darius II.

As for that 'other Artaxerxes', he could have been the second (Mnemon) or the third (Ochos). To determine which of them is meant, we note first of all that the principal person in these events under this Artaxerxes was Bagoses, a general administering Judaea, who can be identified with a Bigvai known from the Elephantine papyri,[43] the Persian governor of Judaea in 408, therefore under Darius II, but a little before Artaxerxes II. However, Diodorus of Sicily (16, 47) mentioned a general of Artaxerxes III named Bagoses. According to Josephus, Bagoses was a contemporary of the high priest Johanan, whose sons Jaddua and Manasseh were

---

observations show that the text of Josephus is useful for determining the origin of 1 Esdras. According to the information assembled by J.M. Myers, *I & II Esdras* (AB, 42; Garden City, NY: Doubleday, 1974), pp. 5-7, there would be serious objections to the existence of an original compilation in Hebrew, in particular because of the story of the election of Zerubbabel (3.1–5.3), but the evidence from Josephus, curiously missing from this dossier, is of a kind that would overcome these objections.

41. We read in *Ant.* 11.184: 'After the death of Xerxes, the kingdom passed to his son Cyrus [Κῦρον], whom the Greeks called Artaxerxes.' The editors opportunely corrected Κῦρον to Ασύηρον 'Assuerus' (אחשורוש) or Xerxes, which corresponds to Est. 1.1 MT and the Lucianic recension. The equivalence presented by Josephus is false, but it is found too in Est. 1.1 LXX.

42. The summary (11.7) has τοῦ νεωτέρου, 'the second' or 'subsequent'.

43. Cowley, *Papyri*, pp. 108-22 nn. 30-31.

contemporaries of Alexander. The probability therefore favours Artaxerxes III,[44] all the more so since the author knew Diodorus.

Since the classical authors do not provide any new details, the useful results from this chapter can simply be gathered together.

1.   The book of Ezra–Nehemiah, clearly distinct from Chronicles, forms a unit, in which quite diverse material is organized according to deliberate procedures. The work of one or more compilers, which is noticeable in the Aramaic sections as well as in the Hebrew parts, originated from an apologetic purpose which profoundly transformed the initial meaning of its sources.

2.   The traces of a temple in Jerusalem in the Persian period are certain: the edict of Cyrus-Darius, sufficiently foreseeable from the general policy of these kings, stands up to criticism. Then, there remain recollections of a governor Nehemiah under Artaxerxes. The Elephantine documents assume a Judaean cult, without any connection with the law of Moses. In these periods, however, the quantity and nature of local customs and of Babylonian importations remain difficult to estimate, but different lists of high priests and notables must be connected with them.

3.   The literary activity of the persons Ezra and Nehemiah culminated in a founding ceremony, in which the proclamation of the law of Moses, followed by a feast of Booths outside the Temple ('feast of Huts'), replaced the inauguration of the altar, which had been followed by a feast of Booths in the sanctuary. The commitment of the community, which came next, focused on the law of Moses, on ancestral customs and the contributions to be made to the Temple. It agrees quite well with the situation created by the charter of Antiochus III and the work of Simon the Just. The second mission of Nehemiah was fictional, or rather a fictitious attribution to Nehemiah and corresponded to the eventual way of life of the Jewish community in Jerusalem, centred on customs of Babylonian origin, in interesting discordance with Deuteronomy. This very discrepancy permitted a comparison with the Pharisees.

4.   As for Ezra, he was the one who introduced the law of Moses, something very distinct from the 'model of Nehemiah', as is shown especially by the preceding discord. On the margins of the fictions indicated, this difference explains well the reciprocal ignorance of Ezra and Nehemiah, as well as their literary twinship. The narrative insists on the arrival of Ezra at Jerusalem, but his mission was directed towards all

44. Cf. H.G.M. Williamson, 'The Historical Value of Josephus' *Jewish Antiquities* XI. 297-301', *JTS* NS 28 (1977), pp. 49-66.

the Jewish communities of Transeuphrates. Such an authoritative action, in which we can detect the emergence and forced diffusion of a Pentateuch of mainly Samaritan origin is again to be situated around the 'Great Assembly' and Simon the Just, in the setting of the Jewish policy of Antiochus III.

5. The doubling of the feast of Booths, each built up against one and the same list of the repatriates, is open to interpretation too. The first (Ezra 3.5), celebrating the inauguration of the restored altar was connected to Zerubbabel and stands out because of its conformity with a law of Moses supposedly well known; the second (Neh. 8.14), which was a feast of Huts properly so called, without any ritual at an altar, is expressly connected to the proclamation of the law of Moses by Ezra; its novelty is emphasized, but not without an allusion to Joshua, which calmly jumped over the whole period of the monarchy. The first feast, going back in time all the way to Cyrus, is followed by a maze of complications, in which history gets lost; the second, from a later time, ends up with the commitment by the community and with the second mission of Nehemiah, which succeeded. This presentation contains a thesis: the restoration and control of the temple of Solomon, even in conformity with the law of Moses, did not succeed, whereas the institution of the 'model of Nehemiah' worked. That thesis was the exact opposite of the one supported by 1 Maccabees, but it came very close to the ideal of Judas according to 2 Maccabees, especially if we omit the account of the purification of the sanctuary,[45] acknowledged to be intrusive (2 Macc. 10.1-8). Moreover, it must be noted, in regard to Nehemiah, that the proclamation of the Law by Ezra shook up the community, but the event was easily absorbed: not only did it lead to new celebrations, but on top of that the commitment of the community and then the action of Nehemiah which followed were not in conformity with the letter of that Law. The 'model of Nehemiah' is capable of absorbing *at Jerusalem* the written Law, but it proceeded from another culture, of Babylonian origin. The overall redaction is not polemical, but it brings up the question of knowing where the authority of Ezra came from. If we follow Ezra 7, it came from the royal mandate, but it could just as well be a matter of the emergence of a new document, which it is not difficult to situate very late, towards the time of the Maccabaean

---

45. For the analysis of the difference between 1 Maccabees and 2 Maccabees as well as of two possible meanings of σκηνή, which correspond to these two forms of the feast of Booths, cf. Chapter 6, §5.

crisis, since the so-called library of Nehemiah did not contain it.

Certainly many problems remain relative to Ezra and Nehemiah, as well as relative to the introduction of the authority of the law of Moses, and in particular of Deuteronomy. All that was needed here was to show that the conclusions of the preceding chapters are not weakened by these books, despite their outward content. On the contrary, these conclusions have facilitated the analysis of their compositional difficulties, and in return have been enriched by them.

7. *Excursus 2: Nehemiah, Judas and the Dedication*

The story of the expulsion of Tobiah (Neh. 13.4-9) by Nehemiah and the recovery of the places where the offerings and the cult utensils were stored provided a very good context for the rabbinic explanation of the feast of the Dedication (*Ḥanukka*) and of the symbol of lights. That explanation, which was very brief, ignored the Judas epic and called into question the purification of the Dwelling, but not of the altar (*b. Šab.* 21b):[46]

> When the Greeks penetrated into the Dwelling [היכל] they made all the oils found there impure. When the power of the Hasmonaeans was strengthened and they were able to defeat them, they looked for and found only one vial, with the seal of the high priest, which had not been defiled. There was enough to light [the candlestick] for just one day, but there was a miracle [נס] and they were able to light it for eight days [...].

Of course, this account does not correspond to a dedication properly so called, but only to a restoration, since it emphasizes the re-establish-ment of a continuity. However, when it is separated from its legendary amplifications, the finding of the vial resulted first of all from a return to the storerooms, which completes very well the expulsion by Nehemiah of Tobiah and his entourage, with it being understood that the problem of the oil and its purity was fundamental, at least according to the Babylonian tradition.[47]

---

46. This text is found as well at the beginning of the scholion of *Meg. Ta'an.* (25th Kislev), with other passages clearly inspired by 1 Macc. 4.29, but the incon-sistency of an inauguration of the altar in *eight* days (and not in *seven* as in Lev. 8.33; Num. 7.12, 28; and 2 Chron. 7.9) is emphasized there, and Judas is never men-tioned.

47. As seen in *War* 2.591-93 and *Life* 74, in which the exclusive usage of an oil of Jewish manufacture was a custom proper to the 'Jews of Syria'. S. Zeitlin,

Doubtless, this brief account could be completely fictitious,[48] but on the one hand it was never connected to the book of Nehemiah, which could have served as an excuse for it; on the other hand, and especially, it explains the predicament of Josephus, who failed to explain clearly that the dedication of the altar by Judas, which he had recounted according to 1 Maccabees, ended in a 'feast of Lights' (*Ant.* 12.325). That feast is well attested, and as this name only makes sense with an account culminating with light, it must be concluded that the legend was an ancient one, and reaffirmed that the whole underlying episode could go back to the Persian period, under Artaxerxes. The mention of the Hasmonaeans should be interpreted in the light of the rabbinic tradition, which knew and then rejected 1 Maccabees in Hebrew, for whom Judas was the first of the dynasty. For lack of anything else to lean on, the simplest thing is to admit that the rabbinic explanation and the expulsion of Tobiah constitute two versions of one mighty deed, which must be attributed not to Nehemiah, but to Judas Maccabeus, or if need be to another rival person. As a result Tobiah represents 'the Greeks', that is to say the Hellenized Judaean circles, more or less conniving with the Hellenistic powers.

As supplementary indications we can note: 1. According to 2 Macc. 2.13, the Memoirs of Nehemiah and Judas Maccabeus were contemporary, or at least close. 2. According to 2 Macc. 3.4-12, the whole process of persecution had as a beginning a conflict relative to revenues and storehouses of the Temple, which constituted variants of the same problem. 3. Josephus ignored the whole second mission of Nehemiah (Neh. 13), not only because he did not speak of it, but also because his statements on the expulsion of the son-in-law of Sanballat (*Ant.* 11.302) contradict Neh. 13.28. He utilized and revised 1 Esdras and Nehemiah 1–12, which indicates that the last chapter of Nehemiah did not have a very firm connection to the rest of the book. 4. The affair of Tobiah expelled from the sanctuary fits without difficulty into what is known in other ways (cf. *War* 1.30-32 and Chapter 6, §3) on the relationship

'Hanukkah: Its Origin and its Significance', *JQR* 29 (1938), pp. 1-36, has collected the documentation that can be used, but his conclusions, based on the absolute primacy of the mighty deed of Judas Maccabeus, are peculiar.

48. This is the opinion of later rabbinic tradition, since, according to the recognized ways of propagating legal impurity, the Greeks could not have defiled the interior of *closed* vials; cf. *b. Šab.* 21b, *Tosafot* שהיה and Lichtenstein, 'Fastenrolle', pp. 275-79.

between the Tobiads and Jerusalem at the beginning of the second century.

These considerations clarify the results explained above (§5): the analysis has shown that chs. 8–13 of Nehemiah could be detached from the Persian period, but they are a collection of diverse pieces. In this collection, the first part, which combined the law of Moses with some elements, written or not, which were foreign to that Law, can be connected to the time of the 'Great Assembly' or of Simon the Just. The last part (Neh. 13), linked to the time of Judas, has as frontispiece a citation from the 'book of Moses' (Deut. 23.4-6), which seemed new at the time of the redaction, and even subsequent to the events reported. This citation is in fact connected to the second part of the mission (13.15-27), on the observance of the Sabbath and the expulsion of foreigners. The episode is introduced by a vague indication 'in those days', which does not necessitate that it would have taken place after the first part. This intertwining unified the second mission, while showing that it remained complex. On the one hand, the episode of Tobiah and the storerooms of the Temple is an extension of the commitments made in the preceding period (cf. 10.33-40); on the other, the matter of the Sabbath and of foreigners, without any connection to the Temple, falls in the strict sense under the 'model of Nehemiah'.

This interpretation gives a general picture of Jerusalem after the charter of Antiochus III, but it indicates that under the Dedication or the feast of Lights are met quite diverse commemorations of the origin of the cult, representing as many divergent traditions. Moreover, that solemnity remained largely in competition with the feast of Booths, which can be separated from the inauguration of the sanctuary.

Chapter 9

CONCLUSION AND PERSPECTIVES

At the end of this study, it is advisable to retrace the route, since the succession of surveys put forward could have given the impression of being disunited. In fact, none of the areas covered was studied for its own sake, but was always examined from the angle of a search for 'residual' details, those details which would lead one to think that the available documents can be read on two levels: as an ancient stage of laws or narratives, existing as traces or as semantic constraints; and as one or several subsequent stages, reshaped in view of new preoccupations. Now, Judaism under all its forms, examined from the time of the return from the exile up to the founders of the rabbinic tradition, is moderately well documented, but it constantly leaves itself open to that kind of double reading, since it has this characteristic that after each troubled epoch the heritage of the preceding epochs is reformulated, under the form of successive writings and multiform accounts or legends, by circles whose authority was never established in the first place. This can be seen particularly well in the case of the name of Israel, which epitomized the heritage; it was always a sign of legitimacy and therefore a stake of greatest importance, since different groups or tendencies sought to claim it for themselves, not without conflicts, with the most characteristic being the struggle between Jews and Samaritans. In other words, a written work, despite its authority, was not at once something stable, a permanent archive: it circulated, reinterpreted the story and became diversified. The literary process which led to the edition of the New Testament as an authoritative text was going on for several centuries. On the contrary, non-written customs have been able to endure through many changing circumstances, as they were being put into practice.

Besides the Bible in all its forms, the principal sources utilized have been the works of Josephus and rabbinic literature. The general outcome is that these complement one another very well, as long as we manage to distinguish the information that they convey from the point of view or the theological ideas with which this information is presented. In particular, each renewal took its start from a small group that called itself traditional, but was always marginal, and its posterity then presented it very naturally as central.

1. *Summary of the Search*

The different stages in the process can be condensed, for each of the eight chapters, under the form of brief statements:

1. An introductory overview gives a list of classical difficulties in the history of Judaea, from the decree of Cyrus up to the establishment of the difference between the Pharisees and Sadducees, difficulties that Josephus tries hard to smooth away, but is not able to resolve. First of all, the interpretation and dating of the principal episodes of the Persian period are made uncertain, in Ezra–Nehemiah, due to the phenomenon of systematic doubling (Cyrus-Darius, Ezra-Nehemiah) which prevents the precise zeroing in on facts and institutions and so prevents any firm dating. However, this effect did not result from negligence by compilers or copyists, but from editorial objectives.

Next, Josephus's account of the coming of Alexander the Great to Jerusalem (332 BCE) is intended to prove the antiquity and prestige of the temple at Jerusalem, and especially its precedence over that of the Samaritans at Gerizim, but the story is so legendary and so isolated that it suggests opposite conclusions, and in no way consolidates the uncertain facts of the preceding period. A question then comes up about the origin of the Samaritans.

Then, before the Maccabaean crisis, information is again sparse, at least up until the establishment of Seleucid control over Coele-Syria, about 200, but it does allow for establishing a distinction, even a tension, between Judaeans around the Temple, and Jews observing the Law and especially the Sabbath according to Nehemiah. At the time of the Hellenization crisis under Antiochus IV, which is difficult to sort out because of an excess of contradictory documents, the Samaritans, who were not yet really enemies of the Jews, admitted having received the Sabbath from them, which brings up a problem about their Pentateuch. The crisis itself seems to have been gradually sorted out with the installation of the Hasmonaean dynasty, following the resistance by Mattathias, who brought together the pious Jews, and of his son Judas Maccabeus, who restored the Temple and the Law. But shortly after, Josephus draws attention to different parties like the Pharisees, the Sadducees, then the Essenes, with deep-seated antagonisms, especially in connection with Scripture. The abrupt emergence of these divisions, without a definite cause, is not very understandable after the Hasmonaean normalization.

As for the rabbinic tradition, which claimed that it was the main heir at the same time of the Pharisees and of the customs of the Jerusalem temple, it only put down roots toward the end of the second century CE, in Galilee. It presented very new features, it fitted in clearly with none of the other ancient sources known, and it hardly spoke of its origins prior to 70, which seems to contradict its pretension of proceeding from an immemorial oral tradition, and not from a renewal derived from Scripture. There is however room to look for older traces of this tradition since it presents remarkable relationships with the Judaism of the book of Nehemiah, in particular a common Babylonian origin. Throughout all these obscurities, which extended over more than four centuries, one particular institution of first importance emerged, the Sabbath as well as its literary complement the Sabbatical year, since they were often at stake, and gave rise to facts visible to an external observer. The ups and downs of the Sabbath will serve as a thread guiding us through the maze.

2. The problem of tolerating war on the Sabbath seems at first elementary, since it involved conquests (Joshua) or the security of the state (period of the monarchy). However, the decision of the priest Mattathias to permit counterattacks on the Sabbath at the time of the Seleucid persecutions, was strangely late (167 BCE), and made no reference to any precedent. The strict Sabbath, thus weakened by this decision, is a *non-biblical* novelty, since it was a concern of only a small group of Jews, heirs of Nehemiah, who had insisted on the ramparts for the city and the closing of the gates on the Sabbath, what we have called the 'model of Nehemiah'; this model was characterized by a closure, counterbalanced by a tension towards an external point, Jerusalem in general, or the Temple in particular. This institution of the Sabbath, with very clear Babylonian connections, is well attested by various accounts of massacres on the Sabbath of Jews refusing to defend themselves, but it was not very ancient under this form, and came up against political necessities for the first time with Mattathias. It is remarkable however that Judas Maccabeus, presented as a son of Mattathias by 1 Maccabees,

knew nothing of the decision of his father, and that he would appear as scrupulously observant, but never as a priest.

3. If the Sabbath under this form was a Jewish novelty, the Pentateuch's legislation must be examined. The Sabbath in its old form, attested in the prophets and in some narratives, referred to the full moon and the associated ceremonies. The Passover, the fourteenth of a lunar month, was therefore a Sabbath in this sense. The Mesopotamian sources were likewise acquainted with a *šabattum*, corresponding to the full moon. They were acquainted too with 'dangerous days', the seventh, fourteenth, twenty-first and twenty-eighth. Practically, the rhythm of the quarters of the moon was close to the weekly Sabbath, but with the computation beginning over again each month, therefore in dependence on the moon. The weekly Sabbath had at the outset the same rhythm, but was freed from that lunar servitude, which implied a change in cult of major significance, since the moon, governing human fertility, was easy to divinize. The evolution from the ancient form to the new form of the Sabbath, while conserving the same name, can be interpreted in this way, and even ritualized: in the Jewish tradition, the feast of Passover (a lunar Sabbath) was extended up to Pentecost (49 days), which is a kind of 'feast of 7', with an encroachment on two new moons. Incidentally, in the first form of the Decalogue (Deut. 5.12-15), in the precept on the Sabbath, which is the longest of all the precepts, the weekly reference can easily be severed, and there remains then the observance of the Sabbath in remembrance of the coming out of Egypt, that is to say, a commandment on the Passover (monthly or annually). The other passages mentioning the weekly Sabbath, in particular the developments on the account of the manna, can also be removed, and there remains in this way a Pentateuch lacking this institution, whose most obvious traces are then found in the book of Nehemiah. Such a 'Pentateuch', under a form difficult to determine exactly (including or not Deuteronomy) could have suited the Samaritans, especially since the narrative part gives great importance to Shechem, and since in the genealogies Israel was father of Juda.

4. Josephus by turns deals with the Samaritans as Assyrian colonists or dissident Jews. This lack of logic becomes understandable, if we observe that the term 'Samaritan' is ambiguous, since it can designate the inhabitants of a region, the citizens of a town, or the faithful of Gerizim. It was the latter, dwelling around Shechem, who could have been the dissidents, degraded by foreign marriages and lax observances. In fact,

they constituted a limited group, and had undergone some Jewish influence (Sabbath, Sabbatical year). Yet, before these influences, they had been the heirs of the Israelites (Jacob, Joseph). Their cult at Gerizim and their priesthood existed and were perhaps not very much later than the time of Alexander (after 300 BCE), which constituted a very respectable antiquity, in comparison with what we note about Judaism.

5. The biblical account of the origin of the Samaritans does not hide the fact that, although they were described as Assyrian colonists, they connected themselves to Jacob-Israel and the commandments it had received, all of this in relation to a cult at Bethel. Furthermore, Aaron and his golden calf has a literary link with Bethel, which must be identified with Shechem, or rather a neighbouring sanctuary, despite a certain separation imposed by Genesis. The Aaronite cult of Gerizim had therefore a noteworthy local 'pedigree', even if its origins had been lost. In addition the Samaritan Pentateuch has interesting contacts with the Qumran fragments and with the least revised forms of the LXX (Philo, New Testament). The *Letter of Aristeas* which presents a Jerusalem high priest ruling over the twelve tribes, conferred authority on a revision, in a more Judaean or more balanced sense, of a translation of the Pentateuch that had been judged to be too 'Samaritan'. Since Antiochus III, the importance of Judaea had only kept on growing, but the Samaritan text, despite later corruptions, should be regarded as the first heir of the primitive edition. The Samaritan book of Joshua, despite a very poor transmission of the text, has remarkable similarities to the Joshua used by Josephus; it represents therefore a tradition worthy of attention. In particular, it tells of an assembly at Shechem (Josh. 24) in which Joshua made a briefer discourse, without any allusion either to the Patriarchs come from Mesopotamia, or to the coming out of Egypt. There existed therefore an Israelite tradition that was deliberately local and independent of Moses, and a fortiori of his Law, which clearly encourages a search for the Yahwism with local origins, Canaanite or Phoenician; from Joshua to 2 Kings, the Bible provides furthermore a substantial documentation for this.

6. If the Samaritans constituted a very local reality, it was not the same for the Jews, scattered as far as the Tigris. In the prehistory of the Maccabaean crisis, the Jerusalem charter granted by Antiochus III (about 200) is of prime importance, since it attempted, in order to ensure their fidelity, to federate a Jewish population of Babylonian culture scattered throughout his whole kingdom, by reorienting it on the city and its

temple. The high priest at that time was Simon the Just, son of Onias, who was of Egyptian origin. The situation was unstable, however, since the high priest installed on this occasion was a royal official who would have had a tendency to adapt to Hellenization (out of self-interest), whereas the observant Jews retained traditions that were quite independent of the sanctuary. To pinpoint the crisis itself, we must first of all interpret the major differences between 1 Maccabees and 2 Maccabees. The conclusion from this is that Judas Maccabeus was artificially introduced into the genealogy of Mattathias, as a way to 'judaize' him. In fact, he was neither a son of Mattathias nor even a priest, but he went into the wilderness as a defender of the Law according to Nehemiah, springing to the aid of all the persecuted communities of the region. Mattathias, on the contrary, was a priest with Samaritan connections; he had withdrawn from Jerusalem because of its decadence, but dreamed of seeing the Temple again. It is important to note that both took new initiatives, but perhaps these were of modest proportions, since the Hasidaeans were a literary guarantee for each of them, in 1 Maccabees for Mattathias, in 2 Maccabees for Judas.

In a parallel way, the analysis shows that the city of Jerusalem was comprised of two very distinct zones, each with its own protective system: the citadel controlling the Temple, which is obviously a characteristic peculiar to Jerusalem, and a properly Jewish quarter conforming to the 'model of Nehemiah', like many others in other places. We see that as a result the crisis was a double one: on the one hand, under the priest Onias, son of Simon, there was a slow Hellenization of cult, therefore something leading astray from the stipulations of the Charter, which was perhaps inevitable, since the king was the real patron of the Temple. On the other hand, there was a bitter phase under Antiochus IV, who was short of money. To increase his revenues, he wanted to control the possessions of the Temple, and therefore also the substantial contributions which were sent to it by Jews from the whole kingdom. When therefore the high priest wanted to formalize that evolution by obtaining for Jerusalem the status of a *polis*, with a clear-cut connection to Antioch, this endeavour not only led to incompatibilities with Jewish observance, which would have been a local problem, but especially was an attempt to cut off relations between Jews and Jerusalem, specifically the fiscal links.

The result of this was revolts on two fronts: at Jerusalem on the part of the priests (Mattathias) and *in the whole kingdom* for Jews in general.

It was then that Judas went underground and began to wage war, so that finally the Hellenized high priest Menelaus, seeing that this policy was ineffective, obtained from the same king the abolition of measures intolerable for the Jews. In view of these facts, we must follow the rabbinic tradition on *Ḥanukka* (Dedication or feast of Lights), and not attribute to Judas a valiant feat of the real restoration of the altar and cult on 25th Kislev 164. A ceremony of royal cult took place the twenty-fifth of each month, and the episode was at most a raid carried out at the time of the cult of the twenty-fifth of that month, shortly after the announcement of the death of Antiochus IV. A link with the winter solstice is not excluded, which confronts us in passing with a calendar problem. As for the other crisis, namely, the struggle among priests for control of the Temple, it was only resolved much later, when in 152 Jonathan was named high priest, on the occasion of a weakening of Seleucid power due to internal rivalries. In the meantime, the high priestly office had been held by others, evidently acceptable to the Seleucids. It was only much later, apparently under John Hyrcanus, that the 25th Kislev episode was considerably magnified, to the point of becoming a foundation event, but with varying interpretations. It was under this same king that the schism with the Samaritans was sealed with the destruction of Gerizim by John Hyrcanus in 107, but for political reasons; previously, hardly any serious conflicts with the Jews had come up, but on the contrary reciprocal influences were at work.

7. The rabbinic traditions provide useful supplementary information. First of all, the only high priest that they venerated since Moses was Simon the Just, who reigned at the time of the charter of Antiochus III. However, he was neither a Zadokite nor an Aaronide, but was apparently of Egyptian origin. It must be understood however that he had been the only one to effect the synthesis of the Judaism of Nehemiah, the law of Moses (under a form earlier than the one we know) and the Temple. Just before him, our attention is drawn to a generation of 'Men of the Great Assembly', an imprecisely defined entity, but one which corresponded well, at some time in the second half of the third century, to the exchanges between Samaritans and Jews which led to a Pentateuch close to the present one, integrating in particular the weekly Sabbath. This in no way implied however the disappearance of the oral traditions, which evolved in a parallel way. The Pharisees continued their attachment to non-scriptural traditions, and we see, from various examples, that these remained *contrary* to Scripture. It was not a matter then

of a jurisprudence developing the writing, but of customs of Babylonian origin, *earlier* than the adoption of the Pentateuch by the 'Great Assembly'. The book of Nehemiah is enlightening on this point: the proclamation of the law of Moses by Ezra created something new *at Jerusalem*, but the community to which he spoke already had its own cohesion and customs, since the commitment they then made was not identical with what we read in the Law, and since the action of Nehemiah himself at the time of his second mission, which excluded all proselytism, was contrary to a verse of Deuteronomy expressly cited at the beginning by the book. This arrangement portrayed at Jerusalem represented very well the attitude of the Pharisees, who honoured Scripture but normally preferred to it their ancestral customs; this could allow for flexibility, even for conflicting tendencies. Josephus himself, to appear Pharisaic, developed the same system, since under the guise of presenting Scripture as a unique legal source, he added many non-scriptural traditions. As for Nehemiah and the traditions peculiar to him, if we omit the scriptural disruption of Ezra and the redactional arrangement, he is not specifically the ancestor of the Pharisees, but should be compared to the Hasidaeans or the Essenes, and also to the activist fringe led by Judas Maccabeus.

This opposition between tradition and Scripture is met again on the occasion of the enthronement of the father of the rabbinic tradition, Hillel the Elder, at Bathyra in Batanea (east of the Sea of Galilee), in the time of Herod the Great. In this region, observant Jews and/or sectarians, using the calendar of *Jubilees* (or of Qumran), had gathered together; there too Pharisees who had survived the persecutions of Herod took refuge. With Hillel the Babylonian as an arbitrator, a first synthesis developed, let us say between the Essenes and Pharisees, according to the lunar calendar in use in Judaea and the Diaspora; the occasion for this was furnished by an urgent debate over the relative importance of the Sabbath and the Passover, since this feast was still strangely unknown at this time in Babylon, where they preferred to it Purim, which was a feast of liberation *without* a migration. Later, the foundation and the development of the school of Yavneh in Judaea provided more clarification. It was established in 68, under the aegis of Vespasian, by Johanan ben Zakkai, an apolitical teacher come from Galilee and a last disciple of Hillel; after the war, it was developed by Gamaliel II, a Pharisee who had come from Jerusalem, and as such was much more versed in Scripture. This school and its annexes remained distant from the priesthood, but they developed diverse doctrinal and political tendencies, including many memories of Jerusalem and the Temples, not without a Zealot fringe. After the defeat of Bar Kochba, the disciples of Aqiba emigrated to Galilee, and, as we saw, this was a return to the fold. Establishing the profile of Jewish Galilee necessitates a correction of the systematic bias introduced by Josephus, since as a good Jerusalemite he saw only sedition and irresponsibility there; in reality, it was the region where at least since the charter of Antiochus III numerous Babylonian pilgrims and colonists had not ceased passing through or settling there. Nehemiah was their model, while the Hasidaeans-Essenes, in urban communities or on collective farms, were their spearhead, in towns as well as in the country. Since before Herod, there had been a Zealot nationalist fringe, and this was the main reason why he had created the colony of Bathyra, while exempting it from taxes to keep them apolitical: it was a matter of putting close at hand people of a same culture but with contrasting attitudes. The Pharisees constituted the branch which had reached Jerusalem and had undergone the influence of Scripture, close to the Temple, but in the end they were scattered everywhere, including Galilee, as we saw in the synthesis on Hillel. This greater Jewish Galilee, that is to say, including the two shores of the Lake, was rural, traditional, very intense, not without conflicting tendencies, and quite closed to the outside world. The appearance of the movement of Judas the Galilean, then of Jesus and his disciples in such a rural milieu, with Pharisees, Zealots and Baptists, took place then in an intelligible environment.

As for the Sadducees, they must be assigned a completely different origin. On the one hand, they were close to the Temple and Scripture, just like the Samaritans, and on the other hand, they constituted a strictly Jerusalem-based legitimist party, which dreamt of a Zadokite dynasty as prescribed by Ezekiel. Now Mattathias, while officiating as a priest at Jerusalem, came in fact from Samaria, but his sons Jonathan and Simon, likewise attached to Scripture, had indeed taken power at Jerusalem, and therefore were settled there. Afterwards, there was a dynastic break between John Hyrcanus and Alexander Janneus, with the latter having been considered unfit to be high priest because of questionable origins. The dynasty of Mattathias up to John Hyrcanus, descending from the class of Joarib, was Zadokite as well according to the suggestion of the book of Chronicles. The Sadducees, starting from Alexander Janneus, the first of the Hasmonaeans in the strict sense, would then be the legitimist party supporting the extinct dynasty. If we go back to

Josephus's classification of parties, we see that the extremes, Essenes (Hasidaeans) and Sadducees, had very stable definitions, whereas the Pharisees, in the middle, nourishing themselves from two sources, written and oral, could give rise to an unsteady equilibrium, in doctrine as well as in politics. In this sense, even if it is a little inexact, there is no objection to qualifying as Pharisaic primitive Christianity, Josephus and the whole primitive rabbinic tradition since Hillel.

8. All these statements on the Hellenistic and Roman periods overwhelmingly contradict the obvious content of the book of Ezra–Nehemiah, which situates the restoration of Judaism and its definite association with the law of Moses and the Temple well before the time of Alexander. As a matter of fact, the decree of Cyrus, in 539, and its confirmation by Darius I stand up to criticism. What was really prescribed at the expense of the Great King was the restoration of the temple of God at Jerusalem, without any allusion either to the law of Moses or to the formal repatriation of the exiles. The column led by Zerubbabel formed a clearly distinct episode, at a date difficult to determine, and set off local opposition, since it was the people of Judah and Benjamin who declared, in the name of all Israel, that they had the monopoly on the cult of YHWH. Nehemiah was a Persian governor who restored the city, without any link with the Law, in the time of an Artaxerxes. His stature grew and it was under his redactional patronage that a synthesis was proposed between the law of Moses, proclaimed by Ezra, and the commitment of the community to honour that Law, but this was in fact reinterpreted through Babylonian customs. The transformation based on the law of Moses came from the priest Ezra, who had been sent by Artaxerxes into all Transeuphrates to impose this Law on all the Jews, which implied some recognition of the authority of the priesthood and the Temple. There was therefore an authoritarian act of tutelary power, which asserted itself especially at Jerusalem. Artaxerxes was certainly a loan name, since the episode is difficult to situate in the Persian period, whereas it fits in very well with the reforms of Antiochus III, attempting to upgrade Jerusalem in order to stabilize the Jews. In this way an insight is provided into the problems of community life at Jerusalem subsequently, but before the Maccabaean crisis. In brief, the book of Ezra–Nehemiah, which contains ancient information, not only offers no serious obstacle to the proposed conclusions, but even makes it possible to clarify the functions of these two persons: to Ezra was precisely connected the written Law (all or part of the Pentateuch), with

views about all Israel and a dominant high priesthood governing the Law and the cult; whereas under the name of Nehemiah and his library were gathered together the traditions of the Elders, various writings and a Jewish nostalgia for a monarchy having control over the cult.

2. *Perspectives*

The preceding sketch should not be considered a collection of established facts, but a sort of 'model' grouping together in a single plan some scattered and very diverse pieces of information. As such, it must therefore always be verified and extended. In conclusion then, I propose a series of supplementary questions or problems.

1. If the final composition of the Pentateuch was as late as I have suggested, it took place in a period in which the presence in Palestine of Attic ceramics and of traces of the importation of wine indicates a clear Greek presence. We can then look into eventual literary, and even institutional influences. The strange affair of the Spartan kinship in the time of Jonathan calls for this, as do the odd contacts between the cult at Delphi and Leviticus, or even under Antiochus IV the dedication, accepted by the Samaritans, of the temple at Gerizim to Zeus 'Patron of Strangers' or 'Hellenic'. The name of Moses, poorly explained in the MT, has in the LXX a form which is very clear in Demotic. Likewise, in Genesis, the account of beginnings brings to mind the Metamorphoses of Ovid, and 'the Spirit of God brooding over the waters' cannot help but recall the Orphic myth.

2. The difficulties relative to the Hellenization of the Jerusalem temple certainly did not disappear with the arrival of the sons of Mattathias. In the margin of the distrust of that dynasty and its activities by the Pharisees and the rabbinic tradition, it should be noted that in the booty from the Temple at the time of the war in 70, the chandelier (*Menorah*) represented on the Arch of Titus has some elements of a Greek symbolic system. We may wonder moreover what was the meaning, in the *Letter of Aristeas*, of the sending by Ptolemy II, a pagan monarch of Alexandria, of a complete set of cultic furnishings in meticulous conformity to the Law, and obviously intended for the Dwelling. This stands in contrast with the importance attributed to the altar, particularly at the time of the dedication by Zerubbabel, when the Temple (Dwelling) did not yet have its foundations. There seem to have been some difficulties in coordinating these two elements, in which one, very much closed, is

of an Egyptian type, and the other, very accessible, is of a Syro-Phoenician type.

3. As opposed to Jerusalem, characterized by external influences (Babylonian, Egyptian, Hellenistic), the Samaritans of Shechem represented the permanence of local traditions connected to the Navel of the Earth (Judg. 9.37), absorbing external influences more sparingly. After strong reciprocal influences, their definitive separation from Judaism was late, but their beginnings, before the emergence of the Gerizim temple, are lost in Israelite pre-history, and we have to hope for something new from the present excavations on the summit of Gerizim. There were several tendencies or sects, whose origin is vague, since we know very little about the relations between the city of Samaria and Shechem. On the other hand, on the margin of the schism and of the formation of the Pentateuch, the particular problem of the emergence of Deuteronomy comes up. It is certainly excessive to connect it to the time of Joshua: although it mentions Ebal and Gerizim, it does not name the 'place chosen by YHWH', but insists vehemently that it was to be unique, which implies that there were conflicts. It tends to supplant or at least influence the other books in the second century, since we see the Samaritan texts and the fragments from Qumran dotted with excerpts from it. For the Nehemiah of the second mission, the 'book of Moses' suddenly appears, but it is not natural to the writer of memoirs.

4. The tendencies, parties or sects were numerous within Judaism, at least from the time of the tensions induced by the charter of Antiochus III. Mattathias and Judas had not been long-lasting unifiers, and all elements coexisted under the Hasmonaeans. It is strange then that the 'gerousia', namely, a simple council of elders or notables, a banal institution, was replaced by order of the Romans in 57 BCE, by regional 'sanhedrins', an odd term which brings to mind rather a confederation of diverse parties. There is therefore some trace of a desire for some grouping together or at least some coordination, which furthermore confirms the coexistence in the storerooms of the Temple of different biblical copies, all of them valid. These facts draw attention to marginal groups, who resisted integration, in particular to the sectarians of the documents from the desert of Judaea, whether Essenes or not, who in any case had Babylonian connections. Galilee, where all tendencies were mixed together, should be connected to these marginal and sectarian groups, who were convinced that they were at the centre.

5. The feasts and celebrations (Passover, Booths, Sabbath) have two forms, one without a Temple and one with a Temple and a pilgrimage. Even if there are remains of agrarian cult, these dualities are in no way superimposed on the difference between the wandering in the desert of the Exodus and the taking up of sedentary life, since they are both still found after Herod, and even in this period there were serious doubts about the practice of the Passover among those in Babylon. Likewise, the feast of the Dedication, theoretically stemming from the Maccabees, was superimposed on a feast of Lights, apparently with a different origin. The history and sociology of these festivities in the Hellenistic and Roman periods still have to be worked out. These dualities in the feasts must in particular be collated with the two sources of Judaism, represented schematically by Ezra and Nehemiah. This duality of sources left some traces, at times strange, in the ancient historians, whom it is advisable to consult, especially if they do not agree with the biblical presentation: for example, Strabo, *Geography* 16.2.35, contrasted Moses, creator of a monotheism without images at Jerusalem, with the superstitious high priests, who later introduced strange customs.

6. The history of the sacred library (including the apocrypha) remains complex in any hypothesis, as much for the history of its redaction as for the ancient history of the texts. The so-called Deuteronomistic literature, from Judges to Kings, recounts the history from a Judaean point of view, but Deuteronomy itself and Joshua have ties with the North. The Prophets were linked to the cult and had hardly any connections with the traditions imported by the Jews from Babylon, but they appear in the library of Nehemiah and then in that of Judas, and their absence from the Samaritan Bible calls for an explanation. Furthermore, the universalist views of a Zechariah, for example, form such a contrast with the sectarian tendencies of a Nehemiah that it is hard to see how they originated in the same culture, short of trying to compare this difference with the tensions between the Jews and those associated with the Temple before the period of Maccabees, all the more so since the two books culminate in a feast of Booths; we can imagine these opposite reactions to the opening up instituted by the Charter of Antiochus III.

The book of Chronicles, which stands downstream from the law of Moses and especially from Judaean historiography, has cultic views and advocates the gathering of all Israel around Jerusalem; it affirms too that humans are authors of their own destiny, which amounts to a denial of Providence. This book constructs then an image difficult to situate at a particular time, but one which was certainly late and had some similarities to the ideology of the Sadducees. On the contrary, Ezra–Nehemiah should certainly be separated from Chronicles, since, besides the technical arguments, the final image which it presents exactly corresponds to the Pharisees of Jerusalem. As for the biblical text itself, the MT must be considered a careful rabbinic edition, more or less contemporaneous with the Mishnah, which among other things downgraded the feast of Purim, eliminated 1 Maccabees (Heb.) and tended to make Christian interpretation more difficult. However, an inventory needs to be done of all the ancient rabbinic discussions whose stake only comes to light if we take into consideration other versions, in particular the LXX (or its Hebrew source). In other words, these discussions were of use in establishing and memorizing the MT.

7. All the issues elaborated have consequences for the sociology of primitive Christianity, which was something marginal, but certainly did not stem from 'liberal' milieus. I have sketched a specific portrait of Jewish Galilee in the first century CE, on both sides of the Lake, in which the Essenes were not absent. But there is more to it than that, since I have also turned up connections between the Essenes and the Samaritans, in particular the so-called calendar of *Jubilees*, traces of which survive in the Gospels. Now, according to the Gospel of John, contrary to what is in the Synoptics, Jesus and John the Baptist were both baptizers, and had close connections with Samaria. Later, it was the same in the case of Philip, who baptized in Samaria. As it is faulty method to prejudge the non-sectarian character of the Baptizers, the connection between them and the Essenes should be reappraised, especially by considering the testimony of Epiphaneus (*Panarion* 19.5.6), who gives a list of primitive Christian 'sects' remarkably similar to the surrounding Jewish 'sects'. It is in fact possible that Jesus' sentence 'You will worship neither on this mountain [Gerizim] nor at Jerusalem' could be a trace of milieus of diverse origins brought together by a common mistrust in regard to the two priesthoods.

BIBLIOGRAPHY

Abel, F.-M., 'Alexandre le Grand en Syrie et en Palestine', *RB* 43 (1934), pp. 528-45; 44 (1935), pp. 42-61.

—'Tombeaux récemment découverts à Marissa', *RB* 35 (1925), pp. 267-82.

—*Les livres des Maccabées* (EBib, 38; 2 vols.; Paris: Gabalda, 1949).

Abel, F.-M., and J. Starcky, *Les livres des Maccabées* (Paris: Cerf, 3rd edn, 1961).

Aberbach, M., and L. Smolar, 'Aaron, Jeroboam, and the Golden Calf', *JBL* 86 (1967), pp. 129-40.

Ackroyd, P.R., *Israel under Babylon and Persia* (The New Clarendon Bible, OT, 4; Oxford: Oxford University Press, 1970).

—'The Jewish Community in Palestine in the Persian Period', in Davies and Finkelstein (eds.), *The Cambridge History of Judaism*, I, pp. 130-61.

Adler, A., *Suidae Lexicon* (5 vols.; Lexicographi Graeci; Stuttgart: Teubner, 1928–38).

Adler, E.N., 'Une nouvelle chronique samaritaine', *REJ* 44 (1901), pp. 188-22; 45 (1902), pp. 71-98.

Albeck, H., *Introduction to the Mishnah* (Tel Aviv: Devir, 1959).

Albright, W.F., 'New Light on Early Recensions of the Hebrew Bible', *BASOR* 140 (1955), pp. 27-33.

—'The Elimination of the King "So"', *BASOR* 171 (1963), p. 66.

Allegro, J.M., with the collaboration of A.A. Anderson, *Qumran Cave 4, I (4Q158–4Q186)* (DJD, 5; Oxford: Clarendon Press, 1968), to be completed by the lengthy recension of J. Strugnell, 'Notes en marge du volume V des "Discoveries in the Judaean Desert of Jordan"', *RevQ* 26 (1970), pp. 163-276.

Alon, G., *Jews, Judaism and the Classical World: Studies in Jewish History in the Times of the Second Temple and the Talmud* (Jerusalem: Magnes, 1977).

—*The Jews in their Land in the Talmudic Age (70–64 CE)* (2 vols.; Jerusalem: Magnes, 1984).

—'The Origin of the Samaritans in Halachic Tradition', *Tarbiz* 18 (1947), pp. 146-56.

Alt, A., *Kleine Schriften zur Geschichte des Volkes Israel* (3 vols.; Munich: Beck, 1953–59).

Aptowitzer, V., 'Die rabbinischen Berichte über die Entstehung der Septuaginta', *Haqedem* 2 (1909), pp. 11-27 and 102-22.

Audet, J.-P., 'Jésus et le "calendrier sacerdotal ancien": Autour d'une variante de Luc 6, 1', *Sciences Ecclésiastiques* 10 (1958), pp. 361-83.

Auerbach, E., 'Die Herkunft der Sadokiden', *ZAW* 49 (1931), pp. 327-28.

—'Der Wechsel des Jahres-Anfang in Juda im Lichte der neugefundenen babylonischen Chronik', *VT* 9 (1959), pp. 113-21.

—'Das Zehngebot–Allgemeine Gesetzes-Form in der Bibel', *VT* 16 (1966), pp. 255-76.

Auld, A.G., *Joshua, Moses and the Land: Tetrateuch–Pentateuch–Hexateuch in a Generation since 1938* (Edinburgh: T. & T. Clark, 1980).

Avi-Yonah, M., 'The Caesarean Inscription of the 24 Priestly Courses', *Eretz Israel* 7 (1964), pp. 24-28.

Avigad, N., 'The Expedition to the Judaean Desert, 1960', *IEJ* 11 (1961), pp. 3-72.

Bacher, W., *Die Agada der Tannaiten* (2 vols.; Strasbourg: Trübner, 1890).

—*Die exegetische Terminologie der jüdischen Traditionsliteratur* (2 vols.; Leipzig: Hinrichs, 1899–1905).

Baillet, M., 'Le texte samaritain de l'Exode dans les manuscrits de Qumrân', in A. Caquot and M. Philonenko (eds.), *Hommages à A. Dupont-Sommer* (Paris: A. Maisonneuve, 1971), pp. 363-81.

Barc, B., 'Siméon le Juste, rédacteur de la Torah?', in M. Tardieu (ed.), *La formation des canons scripturaires* (Patrimoines: Religions du Livre; Paris: Cerf, 1993), pp. 123-54.

Barthélemy, D., *Les devanciers d'Aquila* (VTSup, 10; Leiden: Brill, 1963).

—'Notes en marge de publications récentes sur les manuscrits de Qumrân', *RB* 59 (1952), pp. 199-203.

Barthélemy, D., and J.-T. Milik, *Qumran Cave I* (DJD, 1; Oxford: Clarendon Press, 1955).

Bartlett, J.R., 'Zadok and his Successors at Jerusalem', *JTS* NS 19 (1968), pp. 1-18.

Baumgarten, A.I., 'The Rabbinical Accounts of the Translation of the Torah into Greek' (a paper to be published).

Beauchamp, P., *Création et séparation: Etude exégétique du premier chapître de la Genèse* (Bibliothèque de Sciences Religieuses; Paris: Aubier-Montaigne, 1969).

Ben-Zevi, I., 'The Samaritan Script in the Gaonic Literature', *BJPES* 7 (1939), pp. 30-33.

Benoit, P., J.-T. Milik and R. de Vaux, *Les grottes de Murabba'at* (DJD, 2; Oxford: Clarendon Press, 1961).

Berger, P.R., 'Zu den Namen ששבצר und שנצר', *ZAW* 83 (1971), pp. 98-100.

Bettenzoli, G., 'Lessemi ebraici di radice "SBT"', *Henoch* 4 (1982), pp. 129-62.

Beyerlin, W., *Herkunft und Geschichte der ältesten Sinaitraditionen* (Tübingen: Mohr [Paul Siebeck], 1961).

Bickerman, E.J., 'Un document relatif à la persécution d'Antiochus IV Epiphane', *RHR* 115 (1937), pp. 188-223; republished in *Studies in Jewish and Christian History*, II, pp. 105-135.

—*From Ezra to the Last of the Maccabees: The Historical Foundations of Post-Biblical Judaism* (New York: Schocken Books, 1962).

—*Der Gott der Makkabäer: Untersuchung über Sinn und Ursprung der makkabäischen Erhebung* (Berlin: Schocken Books, 1937). ET: *The God of the Maccabees: Studies on the Meaning and Origin of the Maccabaean Revolt* (SJLA, 32; Leiden: Brill, 1979).

—*Institutions des séleucides* (Bibliothèque Archéologique et Historique, 26; Paris: Geuthner, 1938).

—*The Jews in the Greek Age* (Oxford: Basil Blackwell, 1988).

—'Origines Gentium', *Classical Philology* 47 (1952), pp. 66-74.

—*Studies in Jewish and Christian History* (AGJU, 9; 3 vols.; Leiden: Brill, 1974–86).

—'Viri magnae congregationis', *RB* 55 (1948), pp. 397-402.

Bloch, H., *Die Quellen des Flavius Josephus in seiner Archäologie* (repr.; Leipzig: Teubner, 1968 [1876]).

Boismard, M.-E., and A. Lamouille, *Les Actes des deux Apôtres* (EBib NS 13; 3 vols.; Paris: Gabalda, 1990).

—*L'évangile de Jean* (Synopse des quatre Evangiles, 3; Paris: Cerf, 1977).

—*Le texte occidental des Actes, réconstruction et réhabilitation* (Synthèse, 17; Paris: Etudes et Rech. sur les Civilisations, 1984).

Bowling, R.G., and G.E. Wright, *Joshua* (AB, 6; Garden City, NY: Doubleday, 1982).

Bowman, J., *Samaritanische Probleme: Studien zum Verhältnis von Samaritanertum, Judentum und Urchristentum* (F. Delitzsch Vorlesungen, 1959; Stuttgart: Kohlhammer, 1967). ET: *The Samaritan Problem: Studies in the Relationships of Samaritanism, Judaism and Early Christianity* (trans. A.M. Johnson; Pittsburg: Pickwick Press, 1975).

Braude, W.G., *The Midrash on Psalms* (2 vols.; New Haven: Yale University Press, 1976).

Briend, J., 'Sabbat', *DBSup* 10 (1985), cols. 1132-70.

Bringmann, K., *Hellenistische Reform und Religionsverfolgung in Judäa: Eine Untersuchung zur jüdisch-hellenistischen Geschichte (175–163 v. Chr.)* (Abhandlungen der Akademie der Wissenschaften zu Göttingen, 3/132; Göttingen: Vandenhoeck & Ruprecht, 1983).

Büchler, A., *Die Oniaden und die Tobiaden* (Vienna: Hölder, 1899).

—'La relation de Josèphe concernant Alexandre le Grand', *REJ* 36 (1898), pp. 1-26.

Bunge, J.G., 'Untersuchungen zum zweiten Makkabäerbuch' (unpublished dissertation, Bonn, 1971; cited in P. Schäfer, 'The Hellenistic and Maccabaean Periods', in J.H. Hayes and J.M. Miller, *Israelite and Judaean History* [London: SCM Press, 1977]), p. 562.

Burkitt, F.C., 'The Hebrew Papyrus of the Ten Commandments', *JQR* 15 (1903), pp. 392-408.

Caldwell, T.A., 'Dositheos Samaritanus', *Kairos* 4 (1962), pp. 105-107.

Caquot, A., 'Jubilés', in A. Dupont-Sommer and M. Philonenko (eds.), *La Bible: Ecrits intertestamentaires* (Paris: Gallimard, 1987), pp. 635-810.

Cazelles, H., 'Ex XXXIV, 21 traite-t-il du sabbat?', *CBQ* 23 (1961), pp. 223-26.

—'Les origines du Décalogue', in A. Malamat (ed.), *W.F. Albright Volume, Eretz-Israel* 9 (1969), pp. 14-19, included in *Autour de l'Exode: Etudes* (Sources Bibliques; Paris: Gabalda, 1987), pp. 113-23.

Charles, R.H., *Apocrypha and Pseudepigrapha of the Old Testament* (2 vols.; Oxford: Clarendon Press, 1913).

Childs, B.S., *Introduction to the Old Testament as Scripture* (Philadelphia: Fortress Press, 1979).

Clark, K.W., 'Worship in the Jerusalem Temple after 70', *NTS* 6 (1960), pp. 269-80.

Clines, D.J.A., 'Nehemiah 10 as an Example of Early Jewish Biblical Exegesis', *JSOT* 21 (1981), pp. 111-17.

Cody, A., *A History of Old Testament Priesthood* (AnBib, 35; Rome: Pontifical Biblical Institute, 1969).

Cogan, M., 'Israel in Exile—The View of a Josianian Historian', *JBL* 97 (1978), pp. 40-44.

Cogan, M., and H. Tadmor, *II Kings* (AB, 11; Garden City, NY: Doubleday, 1988).

Coggins, R.J., *Samaritans and Jews: The Origin of Samaritanism Reconsidered* (Oxford: Basil Blackwell, 1975).

Cohen, S.J.D., *From the Maccabees to the Mishnah* (Library of Early Christianity, 7; Philadelphia: Westminster Press, 1987).

—*Josephus in Galilee and Rome: His Vita and Development as a Historian* (Columbia Studies in the Classical Tradition, 8; Leiden: Brill, 1979).

Collins, N.L., 'Did Esther Fast on the 15th Nisan?', *RB* 100 (1993), pp. 533-61.

Conder, C.R., *Tent Work in Palestine* (2 vols.; London: Bentley, 1878).

Conder, C.R., and H.H. Kitchener, *The Survey of Western Palestine* (4 vols.; London: Palestine Exploration Fund, 1881–89).

Cook, S.A., 'A Pre-Massoretic Biblical Papyrus', *Proceedings of the Society of Biblical Archaeology* 25 (1903), pp. 34-56.

Cowley, A.E., *Aramaic Papyri of the Fifth Century BC* (Oxford: Clarendon Press, 1913).

—*The Samaritan Liturgy* (2 vols.; Oxford: Clarendon Press, 1909).

Cross, F.M., *The Ancient Library of Qumran and Modern Biblical Studies* (Garden City, NY: Doubleday, 1958).

—'Aspects of Samaritan and Jewish History in Late Persian and Hellenistic Times', *HTR* 59 (1966), pp. 201-11.

—'The Development of the Jewish Scripts', in G.E. Wright (ed.), *The Bible and the Ancient Near East: Essays in Honor of W.F. Albright* (New York: McGraw–Hill, 1965), pp. 215-42.

—'The History of the Biblical Text in the Light of Discoveries in the Judean Desert', *HTR* 57 (1964), pp. 281-99.

—'Papyri of the Fourth Century BC from Daliyeh', in D.N. Freedman and J. Greenfield (eds.), *New Directions in Biblical Archaeology* (Garden City, NY: Doubleday, 1971), pp. 54-69.

—'A Reconstruction of the Judean Restoration', *JBL* 94 (1975), pp. 4-18.

Cuq, E., 'La condition juridique de la Coelé-Syrie au temps de Ptolémée V Epiphane', *Syria* 8 (1927), pp. 143-62.

Dagut, M.B., 'II Maccabees and the Death of Antiochus IV Epiphanes', *JBL* 72 (1953), pp. 149-57.

Daniélou, J., *Théologie du judéo-christianisme: Histoire des doctrines chrétiennes avant Nicée* (Tournai: Desclée, 1958).

Danthine, H., 'L'imagerie des trônes vides et des trônes porteurs de symboles dans le Proche-Orient ancien', in *Mélanges syriens offerts à R. Dussaud* (Bibliothèque Archéologique et Historique, 30; 2 vols.; Paris: Geuthner, 1939).

Davies, W.D., *The Setting of the Sermon on the Mount* (Cambridge: Cambridge University Press, 1964).

Davies, W.D., and L. Finkelstein (eds.), *The Cambridge History of Judaism.* I. *Introduction: The Persian Period*; II. *The Hellenistic Age* (2 vols.; Cambridge: Cambridge University Press, 1984–89).

Delcor, M., 'La correspondance des savants européens, en quête de manuscrits, avec les Samaritains du XVIe au XIXe siècles', in J.P. Rothschild and G.D. Sixdenier (eds.), *Etudes samaritaines, Pentateuque et Targum, exégèse et philologie, chroniques* (Collection de la Revue des Etudes Juives, 6; Louvain: Peeters, 1988), pp. 27-43.

—*The Early History of Israel* (Philadelphia, 1978).

—'Hinweise auf das samaritanische Schisma im Alten Testament', *ZAW* 74 (1962), pp. 281-91.

—'Qumrân. Livre de la Guerre', *DBSup* 9 (1983), cols. 919-31.

—'Vom Sichem der hellenistischen Epoche zum Sychar des Neuen Testaments', *ZDPV* 78 (1962), pp. 34-48.

Delorme, J., *Gymnasium* (Bibliothèque de l'Ecole Française d'Athènes, 196; Paris: de Boccard, 1960).

Dérenbourg, J., *Essai sur l'histoire et la géographie de la Palestine* (2 vols.; Paris: Impr. Impériale, 1867).

Díez Macho, A., *Neofiti I, Targum palestinense, ms. de la biblioteca vaticana* (6 vols.; Textos y Estudios, 7–11 & 20; Madrid: Consejo Superior de Investigaciones Científicas, 1968–79).

Dillmann, A., 'Beiträgen aus dem Buche der Jubiläen zur Kritik des Pentateuch-textes', *Sitzungsberichte der deutschen Akademie der Wissenschaften zu Berlin* 11 (1883), pp. 320-40.

Donner, H., and W. Röllig, *Kanaanäische und aramäische Inschriften* (3 vols.; Wiesbaden: Otto Harrassowitz, 1966–69).

Doran, R., *Temple Propaganda: The Purpose and Character of 2 Maccabees* (CBQMS, 12; Washington: Catholic Biblical Association, 1981).

Driver, S.R., *An Introduction to the Literature of the Old Testament* (Edinburgh: T. & T. Clark, 9th edn, 1913).

Droge, A.J., *Homer or Moses?* (Hermeneutische Untersuchungen zur Theologie, 26; Tübingen: Mohr [Paul Siebeck], 1989).

Duhaime, J., 'The War Scroll from Qumran and the Greco–Roman Tactical Treatises', *RevQ* 13 (1988), pp. 133-51.

Edgar, C.C., *Zenon Papyri* (5 vols.; Paris: Institut Français d'Archéologie Orientale, 1925–31).

Egger, R., *Josephus Flavius und die Samaritaner: Eine terminologische Untersuchung zur Identitätsklärung der Samaritaner* (Novum Testamentum et Orbis Antiquus, 4; Fribourg: Vandenhoeck & Ruprecht, 1986).

Eichrodt, W., 'Der Sabbat bei Hezekiel: Ein Beitrag zur Nachgeschichte des Propheten-textes', in H. Gross and F. Mussner (eds.), *Festschrift H. Junker* (Trier: Paulinus Verlag, 1961), pp. 65-74.

Eissfeldt, O., *Einleitung in das Alte Testament unter Einschluss der Apokryphen und Pseudepigraphen* (Tübingen: Mohr [Paul Siebeck], 3rd edn, 1964). ET: *Introduction to the Old Testament* (trans. P.R. Ackroyd; Oxford: Basil Blackwell, 1965).

—*Hexateuch-Synopse* (Leipzig: Hinrichs, 1922).

—*Kleine Schriften* (6 vols.; Tübingen: Mohr [Paul Siebeck], 1962–79).

Ellis, R.S., *Foundation Deposits in Ancient Mesopotamia* (Yale Near Eastern Research, 2; New Haven: Yale University Press, 1968).

Epstein, J.N., *Mavo lenusah hamishna* (Jerusalem: Magnes, 1964).

Epstein, J.N., and E.Z. Melamed, *Introductions to the Tannaitic Literature* (Jerusalem: Magnes, 1957).

—*Mekhilta d'Rabbi Sim'on b. Jochai* (Jerusalem: Mekize Nirdamim, 1955).

Eshel, H., 'The Prayer of Joseph: A Papyrus from Masada and the Samaritan Temple on ΑΡΓΑΡΙΖΙΜ', *Zion* 56 (1991), pp. 125-36.

Eskenazi, T.T., 'The Structure of Ezra–Nehemiah and the Integrity of the Book', *JBL* 107 (1988), pp. 641-56.

Feldman, L.H., 'The Identity of Pollion, the Pharisee, in Josephus', *JQR* 49 (1958), pp. 53-62.

—*Josephus and Modern Scholarship (1937–1980)* (Berlin: de Gruyter, 1984).

Ferguson, W.S., 'The Attic *Orgeones*', *HTR* 37 (1944), pp. 91-107.

Field, F., *Origenis hexaplorum quae supersunt, sive veterum interpretum graecorum in totum vetus testamentum fragmenta* (2 vols.; Oxford: Clarendon Press, 1875).

Finkelstein, L., 'The Maxims of the *Anshe Keneset Ha-Gedolah*', *JBL* 59 (1940), pp. 465-69.

—'The Men of the Great Synagogue (circa 400–170 BCE)', in Davies and Finkelstein (eds.), *The Cambridge History of Judaism*, II, pp. 229-44.

—*Siphre ad Deuteronomium H.S. Horovitzii schedis usis cum variis lectionibus* (Berlin: Jüdischer Kulturbund, 1939).

Flusser, D., 'Some of the Precepts of the Torah from Qumran (4QMMT) and the Benediction against the Heretics', *Tarbiz* 61 (1992), pp. 333-74.

Freyne, S., 'Bandits in Galilee: A Contribution to the Study of Social Conditions in First-Century Palestine', in J. Neusner, *et al.* (eds.), *The Social World of Formative Christianity and Judaism* (Philadelphia: Fortress Press, 1988), pp. 50-68.

Gabba, E., 'Sul libro siriaco di Appiano', *Atti dell' Accademia nazionale dei Lincei* 9 (1957), pp. 339-51.

Gall, A.F. von, *Der hebräischer Pentateuch der Samaritaner* (Giessen: Töpelmann, 1914–18), with the supplements of M. Baillet, 'Corrections à l'édition de von Gall du Pentateuch samaritain', in W.C. Delsman *et al.* (eds.), *Von Kanaan bis Kerala* (Festschrift J.P.M. van der Ploeg; AOAT, 211; Neukirchen–Vluyn: Neukirchener Verlag, 1972), pp. 23-35.

Garbini, G., *History and Ideology in Ancient Israel* (London: SCM Press, 1988).

Gaster, M., 'Das Buch Josua in hebräisch-samaritanischer Rezension', *ZDMG* 62 (1908), pp. 209-79, 494-549.

—*The Samaritans: Their History, Doctrine and Literature* (London: British Academy, 1925).

Geiger, A., *Nachgelassene Schriften* (Leipzig: Kauffmann, 1876), IV.

—*Urschrift und Übersetzungen der Bibel in ihrer Abhängigkeit von der innern Entwicklung des Judenthums* (Breslau: Heinauer, 1857).

Gelston, A., 'The Foundations of the Second Temple', *VT* 16 (1966), pp. 232-35.

Ginsburg, M.S., 'Sparta and Judaea', *Classical Philology* 29 (1934), pp. 117-22.

Glaue, P., and A. Rahlfs, 'Fragmente einer griechischen Übersetzung des samaritanischen Pentateuchs', in *Mitteilungen des Septuaginta-Unternehmens* (Berlin: Weidenmann, 1914), II, pp. 71-72; republished by E. Tov, 'Pap. Giessen 13, 19, 22, 26: A Revision of the LXX?', *RB* 78 (1971), pp. 355-83.

Goedicke, H., 'The End of "So, King of Egypt"', *BASOR* 171 (1963), pp. 64-66.

Goldstein, J.A., 'The Dating of the Book of Jubilees', *PAAJR* 50 (1983), pp. 64-65.

—'The Tales of the Tobiads', in J. Neusner (ed.), *Christianity, Judaism and Other Greco–Roman Cults* (SJLA, 12/3; Leiden: Brill, 1975), pp. 85-123.

Goldstein, J.A., *I Maccabees: A New Translation with Introduction and Commentary* (AB, 41; Garden City, NY: Doubleday, 1976).

—*II Maccabees: A New Translation with Introduction and Commentary* (AB, 41A; Garden City, NY: Doubleday, 1983).

Goodman, M., 'Proselytism in Rabbinic Judaism', *JJS* 40 (1982), pp. 174-85.

Grabbe, L.L., 'Josephus and the Reconstruction of the Judean Restoration', *JBL* 106 (1987), pp. 231-46.

Graf, G., 'Zum Alter des samaritanischen "Buches Josue"', *Bib* 23 (1942), pp. 62-67.

Greenberg, M., 'Another Look at Rachel's Theft of the Teraphim', *JBL* 81 (1962), pp. 239-48.

—'The Stabilization of the Text of the Hebrew Bible in the Light of the Biblical Materials from Qumran', *JAOS* 76 (1956), pp. 157-67.

Gunneweg, A.H.J., *Leviten und Priester* (FRLANT, 89; Göttingen: Vandenhoeck & Ruprecht, 1965).

Guttman, A., 'The End of the Jewish Sacrificial Cult', *HUCA* 38 (1967), pp. 137-48.

Habicht, C., 'Royal Documents in Maccabees II', *Harvard Studies in Classical Philology* 80 (1976), pp. 1-18.

Halbe, J., *Des Privilegrecht Jahwes Ex 34,10-26* (FRLANT, 114; Göttingen: Vandenhoeck & Ruprecht, 1975).

Halévy, J., *Mélanges de critique et d'histoire relatifs aux peuples sémitiques* (Paris: A. Maisonneuve, 1883).

Hallo, W., 'The First Purim', *BA* 46/1 (1983), pp. 19-29.

Hammer, H., *Traktat von Samaritanermessias: Studien zur Frage der Existenz Jesu* (Bonn: Carl Georg, 1913).

Hanson, R.S., 'Jewish Palaeography and its Bearing on Text Critical Studies', in F.M. Cross *et al.* (eds.), *Magnalia Dei, The Mighty Acts of God: Essays in Memory of G.E. Wright* (Garden City, NY: Doubleday, 1976), pp. 561-76.

Harl, M., *et al.*, *La Bible d'Alexandrie, LXX.* I. *La Genèse* (Paris: Cerf, 1986); II. *L'Exode* (1989); III. *Le Lévitique* (1988); IV. *Les Nombres* (1994); V. *Le Deutéronome* (1992).

Harrington, D.J., *The Maccabaean Revolt: Anatomy of a Biblical Revolution* (Old Testament Studies, 1; Wilmington, DE: Michael Glazier, 1988).

Hartman, L.F., and A.A. di Lella, 'Daniel', in R.E. Brown, J.A. Fitzmeyer and R.E. Murphy (eds.), *The New Jerome Biblical Commentary* (London: Geoffrey Chapman, 1990), pp. 406-409.

Heinemann, I., 'Die Lehre vom ungeschriebenen Gesetz in jüdischen Schrifttum', *HUCA* 4 (1927), 149-71.

Hengel, M., *Judaism and Hellenism* (trans. J. Bowden; 2 vols.; Philadelphia: Fortress Press, 1974).

—'The Political and Social History of Palestine from Alexander to Antiochus III (333–187 BCE)', in Davies and Finkelstein (eds.), *The Cambridge History of Judaism*, II, pp. 35-78.

—*Die Zeloten: Untersuchungen zur jüdischen Freiheitsbewegung in der Zeit von Herodes I bis 70 n, Chr.* (AGSU, 1; Leiden: Brill, 1961).

Hermann, J., *Ezechiel* (Sellin Kommentar zum Alten Testament, 11; Leipzig: Hinrichs, 1924).

Herr, M.D., 'Causes of the Bar Kokhba Revolt', *Zion* 43 (1978), pp. 6-25.

—'Hanukkah', *EncJud*, VII, cols. 1280-86.

—'The Problem of War on the Sabbath in the Second Temple and the Talmudic Period', *Tarbiz* 30 (1961), pp. 242-56 and 341-56.

Hoffmann, D., 'Sarbane El', *MGWJ* 15 (1933), pp. 179-80.

Hoffmann, G., 'Lexikalisches', ZAW 1 (1881), p. 334.

Holleaux, M., *Etudes d'épigraphie et d'histoire grecque* (6 vols.; Paris: A. Maison-neuve, 1938–57).

Hölscher, G., *Die Hohenpriesterliste bei Josephus und die evangelische Chronologie* (Sitzungsberichte der Heidelberger Akademie der Wissenschaften, 30/3; Heidelberg: Carl Winter, 1940).

Horn, S.H., and L.H. Wood, 'The Fifth-Century Jewish Calendar at Elephantine', *JNES* 13 (1954), pp. 1-20.

Horovitz, H.S., *Siphre D'be Rab. Fasciiulus primus: Siphre ad Numeros adjecto Siphre zutta* (Leipzig : G. Fock, 1917).

Horovitz, H.S., and I.A. Rabin, *Mechilta d'Rabbi Ismael* (Frankfurt: Kauffmann, 1930; repr.; Jerusalem, 1970).

Hossfeld, F.-L., *Der Dekalog: Seine späten Fassungen, die originale Komposition und seine Vorstufen* (OBO, 45; Fribourg: Vandenhoeck & Ruprecht, 1982).

Houtman, C., 'Ezra and the Law: Observations on the Supposed Relation between Ezra and the Pentateuch', *OTS* 21 (1981), pp. 91-115.

Isser, S.J., *The Dositheans: A Samaritan Sect in Late Antiquity* (SJLA, 17; Leiden: Brill, 1976).

Janssen, E., *Juda in der Exilszeit: Ein Beitrag zur Frage der Entstehung des Judentums* (Göttingen: Vandenhoeck & Ruprecht, 1956).

Jastrow, M., *Hebrew and Babylonian Traditions* (London: Fisher–Unwin, 1914).

Jaubert, A., *La date de la Cène: Calendrier biblique et liturgie chrétienne* (EBib; Paris: Gabalda, 1957).

Jepsen, A., 'Nehemia 10', *ZAW* 66 (1954), pp. 87-106.

Jeremias, J., *Jerusalem in the Time of Jesus* (London: SCM Press, 1969).

Johnson, M.D., *The Purpose of Biblical Genealogies with Special Reference to the Setting of the Genealogies of Jesus* (SNTSMS, 8; Cambridge: Cambridge University Press, 1969).

Johnstone, W., 'The Decalogue and the Redaction of the Sinai Pericope in Exodus', *ZAW* 100 (1988), pp. 361-65.

Juynboll, T.W.I., *Chronicon samaritanum arabice conscriptum, cui titulus est Liber Josuae* (Leiden: Brill, 1848).

Kahle, P., *The Cairo Geniza* (Schweich Lectures, 1941; London: Milford, 1947).

—'Untersuchungen zur Geschichte des Pentateuchtextes', in *Opera minora* (Leiden: Brill, 1956), pp. 3-37.

Kampen, J., *The Hasideans and the Origin of Pharisaism: A Study in 1 and 2 Maccabees* (SBLSCS, 24; Atlanta: Scholars Press, 1988).

Kasher, M.M., *Hagadah Shelemah: The Complete Passover Hagadah* (Jerusalem: Tora Shelema Institute, 1967).

Katz, P., *Philo's Bible: The Aberrant Text of Bible Quotations in Some Philonic Writings* (Cambridge: Cambridge University Press, 1950).

Kaufman, S.A., 'A Reconstruction of the Social Welfare Systems of Ancient Israel', in W.B. Barrick and J.R. Spencer (eds.), *In the Shelter of Elyon: Essays on Ancient Palestinian Life and Literature in Honour of G.W. Ahlström* (JSOTSup, 31; Sheffield: JSOT Press, 1984).

Kellermann, U., *Nehemia: Quellen, Überlieferung und Geschichte* (BZAW, 102; Berlin: Töpelmann, 1967).

Kelso, J.L., *et al.*, *The Excavations at Bethel (1934–60)* (AASOR, 39; Cambridge, MA: American Schools of Oriental Research, 1968).

Kennedy, J., *The Note-Line in the Hebrew Scriptures, Commonly Called* paseq *or* pᵉsîq (Edinburgh: T. & T. Clark, 1903).

Kennett, R.H., 'The Origin of the Aaronite Priesthood', *JTS* 6 (1905), pp. 161-86.

Kippenberg, H.G., *Garizim und Synagogue: Traditionsgeschichtliche Untersuchungen zur samaritanischen Religion der aramäischen Periode* (Berlin: de Gruyter, 1971).

Klausner, J., *The History of the Second Temple* (2 vols.; Jerusalem: Massada, 1952).

Klostermann, E., *Eusebius Werke. I. Das Onomastikon der biblischen Ortsnamen* (3 vols.; Leipzig: Hinrichs, 1904).

Knohl, I., 'The Sabbath and the Festivals in the Priestly Code and in the Laws of the Holiness School', *Shnaton* 7-8 (1983–84), pp. 109-46.

Koch, K., 'Esdras and the Origins of Judaism', *JSS* 19 (1974), pp. 173-97.

Kohut, A., *Aruch completum sive lexicon* (9 vols.; repr.; Jerusalem: Makor, 1969–70).

Kosmala, H., 'The So-Called Ritual Decalogue', *ASTI* 1 (1962), pp. 31-61.

Kuhrt, A., 'The Cyrus Cylinder and Achaemenid Imperial Policy', *JSOT* 25 (1983), pp. 83-97.

Lagarde, P. de, *Anmerkungen zur griechischen Übersetzung der Proverbien* (Leipzig: Hinrichs, 1863).

Landau, Y.H., 'A Greek Inscription Found near Hefzibah', *IEJ* 16 (1966), pp. 55-70.

Landsberger, B., *Der kultische Kalender der Babylonier und Assyrer* (Leipziger Semitische Studien, 6; Leipzig: Hinrichs, 1915).

Lauterbach, J.Z., *Mekilta de-Rabbi Ishmael* (3 vols; Philadelphia: Jewish Publication Society of America, 2nd edn, 1976).

Le Déaut, R., *Introduction à la littérature Targumique* (Rome: Pontifical Biblical Institute, 1966).

—*La nuit pascale* (AnBib, 22: Rome: Pontifical Biblical Institute, 1963).

—*Targum du Pentateuque* (SC, 245, 246, 261, 271; Paris: Cerf, 1978–80).

Leaney, A.R.C., 'Greek Manuscripts from the Judaean Desert', in J.K. Eliott (ed.), *Studies in New Testament Language and Texts* (Festschrift G.D. Kilpatrick; NovTSup, 44; Leiden: Brill, 1976).

Leiman, S.Z., *The Canonization of Hebrew Scripture* (Transactions of the Connecticut Academy of Arts, 47; Hamden, CT: Archon Books, 1976).

Lemaire, A., 'Le Décalogue: Essai d'histoire de la rédaction', in A. Caquot and M. Delcor (eds.), *Mélanges bibliques et Orientaux en l'honneur de H. Cazelles* (AOAT, 212; Neukirchen–Vluyn: Neukirchener Verlag, 1981), pp. 259-85.

—*Histoire du peuple hébreu* (coll. "Que sais-je?", n. 1898; Paris: Presses Universitaires de France, 1981).

—'Le sabbat à l'époque royale israélite', *RB* 80 (1973), pp. 161-85.

Lemche, N.P., 'The Manumission of Slaves—the Fallow Year—the Sabbatical Year—the Vobel Year', *VT* 26 (1976), pp. 38-59.

Lenhardt, P., and M. Collin, *La torah orale des pharisiens* (Cahiers Evangiles, 73; Paris: Cerf, 1990).

Lestienne, M., 'Les "dix paroles" et le Décalogue', *RB* 79 (1972), pp. 484-510.

Lewy, J., and H. Lewy, 'The Origin of the Week and the Oldest West Semitic Calendar', *HUCA* 17 (1943), pp. 1-152.

Lichtenstein, H., 'Die Fastenrolle: Eine Untersuchung zur jüdisch-hellenistischen Geschichte', *HUCA* 8-9 (1931–32), pp. 257-351.

Lieberman, S., 'Emendations on the Jerusalmi', *Tarbiz* 3 (1932), pp. 62-97.

—*Greek in Jewish Palestine* (New York: Jewish Theological Seminary of America, 1942).

—'The Halakhic Inscription from the Beth-Shean Valley', *Tarbiz* 45 (1975), pp. 54-63.

—*Hayerushalmi kiphshuto* (Jerusalem: Magnes, 1934).

—*Hellenism in Jewish Palestine* (New York: Jewish Theological Seminary of America, 1950).

—'Persecution of the Jewish Religion', in J. Schatzmiller (ed.), *Festschrift S.W. Baron*, (3 vols.; Jerusalem: Magnes Press, 1979), III, pp. 214-31.

—*Tosefta kifshuṭah: A Comprehensive Commentary on the Tosefta* (8 vols.; New York: Jewish Theological Seminary of America, 1955-73).

Livingstone, D., 'Location of Biblical Bethel and Ai Reconsidered', *WTJ* 34 (1970–71), pp. 20-44.

Loza, J., 'Exode XXXII et la rédaction JE', *VT* 23 (1973), pp. 31-55.

—*Las palabras de Yahve; estudio del decálogo* (Biblioteca Mexicana, 4; Mexico City: Universidad Pontificia, 1989).

—'La tradición antigua de Exodo XXXII y su prehistoria' (in press).

Maccoby, H., *Early Rabbinic Writings* (Cambridge Commentaries on Writings, 3; Garden City, NY: Doubleday, 1988).

Macdonald, J., *Memar Marqa* (2 vols.; BZAW, 84; Berlin: Töpelmann, 1962).

—*The Samaritan Chronicle No. II (or: Sepher ha-Yamim) From Joshua to Nebuchadnezzar* (BZAW, 107; Berlin, Töpelmann, 1969).

—*The Theology of the Samaritans* (London: SCM Press, 1964).

Magen, Y., 'A Fortified Town of the Hellenistic Period on Mount Gerizim', *Qadmoniot* 19 (1986), pp. 91-101.

—'Mount Gerizim—A Temple City', *Qadmoniot* 23 (1991), pp. 26-38, and 24 (1991), pp. 70-96.

Main, E., 'Les sadducéens vus par Flavius Josèphe', *RB* 97 (1990), pp. 161-206.

Martin, C.H.R., 'Alexander and the High Priest', *Transactions of the Glasgow University Oriental Society* 23 (1969), pp. 102-114.

Mason, S.N., 'Priesthood in Josephus and the "Pharisaic Revolution"', *JBL* 107 (1988), pp. 657-61.

—'Was Josephus a Pharisee? A Re-Examination of *Life* 10–12', *JJS* 40 (1989), pp. 31-45.

Mathews, K.A., 'The Background of Paleo-Hebrew at Qumran', in C.L. Meyers and M. O'Connor (eds.), *The Word Shall Go Forth: Essays in Honor of D.N. Freedman* (ASOR, Special Volume Series, 1; Philadelphia: American Schools of Oriental Research, 1984).

McKenzie, J.L., *Second Isaiah* (AB, 20; Garden City, NY: Doubleday, 1968).

Meinhold, J., 'Die Entstehung des Sabbats', *ZAW* 29 (1909), pp. 81-112.

Mercati, G., *Psalteri Hexapli reliquiae*, I (Rome: Vatican Library, 1958).

Meyer, E., *Die Entstehung des Judentums* (Halle: Niemeyer, 1896).

Michaeli, F., *Le livre de l'Exode* (CAT, 2; Neuchâtel: Delachaux & Niestlé, 1974).

Mildenberg, L., *The Coinage of the Bar Kokhba War* (Typos, 6; Frankfurt: Sauerländer, 1984).

Milik, J.-T., 'Les modèles araméens du livre d'*Esther* dans la grotte 4 de Qumrân', *RQ* 15 (1992), pp. 321-99.

Momigliano, A., *Prime linee di storia della tradizione maccabaica* (Rome: Foro Italiano, 1930).

Montgomery, J.A., *The Samaritans, the Earliest Jewish Sect* (Bohlen Lectures, 1906; Philadelphia: J.C. Winston, 1907; repr.; New York: Ktav, 1968).

Moore, G.F., *Judaism in the First Centuries of the Christian Era: The Age of Tannaim* (2 vols.; Cambridge, MA: Harvard University Press, 1927; repr.; New York: Schocken Books, 1971).

—'Simeon the Righteous', in G.A. Kohut (ed.), *Jewish Studies in Memory of Israel Abrahams* (New York: Jewish Institute of Religion, 1927), pp. 348-64.

Mørkholm, O., *Antiochus IV of Syria* (Classica et Mediaevalia, Diss. 8; Copenhagen: Gyldendal, 1966).

Motzki, H., 'Ein Beitrag zum Problem des Stierkultes in der Religionsgeschichte Israels', *VT* 25 (1975), pp. 470-85.

Mowinckel, S., *Studien zu dem Buche Ezra-Nehemia. II. Die Nehemia-Denkschrift* (Oslo: Universitets Forlaget, 1964).

Mras, K., *Eusebius Werke. VIII. Die Praeparation Euangelica* (2 vols.; Berlin: Akademie Verlag, 1954–56).

Murphy-O'Connor, J., 'The Judean Desert', in R.A. Kraft and G.W.E. Nickelsburg (eds), *Early Judaism and its Modern Interpreters* (Philadelphia: Fortress Press, 1986), pp. 119-56.

Myers, J.M., *I & II Esdras* (AB, 42; Garden City, NY: Doubleday, 1974).

—*Ezra. Nehemia* (AB, 14; Garden City, NY: Doubleday, 1965).

Myre, A., 'Les caractéristiques de la loi mosaïque selon Philon d'Alexandrie', *Science et Esprit* 27 (1975), pp. 35-69.

Na'aman, N., 'Shechem and Jerusalem in the Exilic and Restoration Period', *Zion* 8/1 (1993), pp. 7-32.

Negretti, N., *Il settimo giorno* (AnBib, 55; Rome: Pontifical Biblical Institute, 1973).

Neubauer, A., *La géographie du Talmud* (Paris: M. Lévy, 1868).

Neusner, J., *Comparative Midrash: The Plan and Program of Genesis and Leviticus Rabbah* (BJS, 111; Atlanta: Scholars Press, 1986).

—*A History of the Jews in Babylonia. I. The Parthian Period* (SPB, 9; Leiden: Brill, 1965).

—*Le judaïsme à l'aube du christianisme* (Paris: Cerf, 1986).

—*A Life of Yohanan ben Zakkai, Ca. 1–80 CE* (SPB, 6; Leiden: Brill, 2nd edn, 1970).

—*The Rabbinic Traditions about the Pharisees before 70* (3 vols.; Leiden: Brill, 1971).

—*The Tosefta: Second Division, Moed* (New York: Ktav, 1981).

Niese, B., *Flavii Iosephi opera* (7 vols.; Berlin: Weidmann, 1885–95).

—*Kritik der beiden Makkabäerbücher: Nebst Beitragen zur Geschichte der makkabäischen Erhebung* (Berlin: Weidmann, 1900).

Nodet, E, 'La Dédicace, les Maccabées et le Messie', *RB* 93 (1986), pp. 321-75.

—'Flavius Josèphe: Création et histoire', *RB* 100 (1993), pp. 5-40.

—'Galilée juive, de Jésus à la *Mishna*', in F. Blanchetière and M.D. Herr (eds.), *Au sources juives du christianisme* (Louvain: Peeters, 1993), pp. 13-61.

—'Jésus et Jean Baptiste selon Josèphe', *RB* 92 (1985), pp. 321-48.

—'Mattathias, Samaritains et Asmonéens', *Transeuphratène* 7 (1994), pp. 94-106.

—'Miettes messianiques', in I. Gruenwald, S. Shaked and G.G. Strumsa (eds.), *Messiah and Christos: Studies in the Jewish Origins of Christianity* (Festschrift D. Flusser;

Texte und Studien zum Antiken Judentum, 32; Tübingen: Mohr [Paul Siebeck], 1992), pp. 119-41.

Nodet, E., *et al.* (eds.), *Flavius Josèphe: Les antiquités juives, livres I à III* (Paris: Cerf, 2nd edn, 1992).

Nolland, J., 'A Misleading Statement of the Essene Attitude to the Temple (Josephus, Antiquities, XVIII, I, 5, 19)', *RQ* 9 (1978), pp. 555-62.

Noth, M., *Das Buch Josua* (HAT, 1/7; Tübingen: Mohr [Paul Sieback], 1953).

—*Exodus: A Commentary* (OTL, 2; Philadelphia: Westminster Press, 1962).

—*Überlieferungsgeschichtliche Studien* (Halle: Niemeyer, 1943).

Olmstead, A.T., 'Tattenai, Governor of Across the River', *JNES* 3 (1944), p. 46.

Oort, H., 'Die Aaroniden', *TT* 18 (1884), pp. 289-335.

Oppenheimer, A., *The 'Am ha-aretz* (ALGHJ, 8; Leiden: Brill, 1977).

—*Galilee in the Mishnaic Period* (Jerusalem: Zalman Shazar Center, 1991).

Paul, A., *Le judaïsme ancien et la Bible* (Paris: Desclée, 1987).

—*Leçons paradoxales sur les juifs et les chrétiens* (Paris: Desclée, 1992).

Pelletier, A., *La lettre d'Aristée à Philocrate* (SC, 89; Paris: Cerf, 1962).

Perlitt, L., *Bundestheologie im Alten Testament* (WMANT, 36; Neukirchen–Vluyn: Neukirchener Verlag, 1969).

Petersen, D.L., 'Zerubbabel and Jerusalem Temple Reconstruction', *CBQ* 36 (1974), pp. 366-72.

Porten, B., 'The Diaspora. D—The Jews in Egypt', in Davies and Finkelstein (eds.), *The Cambridge History of Judaism*, I, pp. 372-400.

Powels, S., *Der Kalendar der Samaritaner: Anhang des Kitab Ḥisab al-Sinn und anderer Handschriften* (Studia Samaritana, 3; Berlin: de Gruyter, 1977).

Préaux, C., 'Esquisse d'une histoire des révolutions égyptiennes sous les Lagides', *Chroniques d'Egypte* 11 (1936), pp. 522-52.

Prigent, P., *Justin et l'Ancien Testament* (EBib; Paris, Gabalda, 1964).

Puech, E., *La croyance des esséniens en la résurrection des morts: Immortalité, résurrection, vie éternelle* (EBib, NS 21; 2 vols.; Paris: Gabalda, 1993).

Pummer, R., 'ΑΡΓΑΡΙΖΙΜ: A Criterion for Samaritan Provenance', *JSJ* 18 (1987), pp. 18-25.

Purvis, J. D., 'Exile and Return', in H. Shanks (ed.), *Ancient Israel* (Washington, DC: Biblical Archeological Society, 1988).

—'Samaritan Pentateuch', *IDBSup*, pp. 772-75.

—*The Samaritan Pentateuch and the Origin of the Samaritan Sect* (HSM, 2; Cambridge, MA: Harvard University Press, 1968).

—'The Samaritans', in Davies and Finkelstein (ed.), *The Cambridge History of Judaism*, II, pp. 591-613.

—'The Samaritans and Judaism', in R.A. Kraft and G.W.E. Nickelsburg, *Early Judaism and its Modern Interpreters* (Philadelphia: Fortress Press, 1986), pp. 81-98.

Rainey, A.F., 'Bethel is still Beitin', *WTJ* 34 (1970–71), pp. 175-88.

Ratner, B., *Seder Olam Rabba: Die grosse Weltchronik* (Vilna: Rehm, 1897).

Reinach, T., *Contre Apion* (Coll. Budé; Paris: Les Belles Lettres, 1930).

Reinach, T., and S. Reinach (eds.), *Œuvres complètes de Flavius Josèphe: Antiquités judaïques; Guerre des Juifs* (6 vols.; Paris: Leroux, 1900–32).

Reventlow, H.G., *Gebot und Predigt im Dekalog* (Gütersloh: Gerd Mohn, 1962).

Richter, W., *Recht und Ethos: Versuch einer Ortung des weisheitlichen Mahnspruches* (SANT, 15; Munich: Kösel, 1966).

Robert, L., and J. Robert, 'Bulletin épigraphique', *Revue des Etudes Grecques* 83 (1970), pp. 469-73.

Robert, P. de, 'La naissance des études samaritaines', in Rothschild and Sixdenier (eds.), *Etudes samaritaines*, pp. 15-26.

Robinson, E., and E. Smith, *Biblical Researches in Palestine* (3 vols.; Boston: Crocker & Brewster, 1841).

Robinson, G., 'The Idea of Rest in the Old Testament and the Search of the Basic Character of Sabbath', *ZAW* 92 (1980), pp. 32-42.

Ross, W., 'Is Beitin the Bethel of Jeroboam?', *PEQ* 73 (1941), pp. 22-27.

Rostovtzeff, M., *Social and Economic History of the Hellenistic World* (Oxford: Clarendon Press, 1941).

Rothschild, J.-P., and G.D. Sixdenier (eds.), *Etudes samaritaines, Pentateuque et Targum, exégèse et philologie, chroniques* (Collection de la Revue des Etudes Juives, 6; Paris: Peeters, 1988).

Rowley, H.H., *Men of God: Studies in Old Testament History and Prophecy* (London: Nelson, 1963).

—'The Samaritan *Schism* in Legend and History', in B.W. Anderson and W. Harrelson (eds.), *Israel's Prophetic Heritage* (Festschrift J. Muilenburg; New York: Harper, 1962).

—'Zadok and the Nehustan', *JBL* 58 (1939), pp. 113-41.

Rudolf, W., *Esra und Nehemia, samt 3. Esra* (HAT, 1/20; Tübingen: Mohr: [Paul Siebeck], 1949).

Ruprecht, E., 'Stellung und Bedeutung der Erzählung vom Mannawunder (Ex 16) im Aufbau der Priesterschrift', *ZAW* 86 (1974), pp. 269-307.

Sachs, A.J., and D.J. Wiseman, 'A Babylonian King List of the Hellenistic Period', *Iraq* 16 (1954), pp. 202-212.

Safrai, S., 'The Jewish Cultural Nature of Galilee in the First Century', *Immanuel* 24/25 (1990), pp. 147-86.

—*Pilgrimage at the Time of the Second Temple* (Tel Aviv: Am ha-Sefer, 1965).

Sandmel, S., *Philo's Place in Judaism: A Study of Conceptions of Abraham in Jewish Literature* (New York: Ktav, 1971).

Saulnier, C., *Histoire d'Israël. III. de la conquête d'Alexandre à la destruction du Temple (331 AC–135 AD)* (Paris: Cerf, 1985).

Schäfer, P., 'The Hellenistic and Maccabaean Period', in Hayes and Miller, *Israelite and Judaean History*.

Schalit, A., 'Die Denkschrift der Samaritaner an König Antiochos Epiphanes', *ASTI* 8 (1972), pp. 131-83.

Schechter, S.Z., *Aboth de Rabbi Nathan* (Vienna: Lippe, 1887; repr.; New York: Feldheim, 1967).

Schiffman, L.H., *From Text to Tradition: A History of Second Temple and Rabbinic Judaism* (Hoboken: Ktav, 1991).

—*The Halakhah at Qumran* (SJLA, 16; Leiden: Brill, 1975).

—'Miqsat Ma'aseh ha-Torah and the *Temple Scroll*', *RevQ* 15 (1990), pp. 435-57.

—*Sectarian Law in the Dead Sea Scrolls: Courts, Testimony and the Penal Code* (BJS, 33; Chico, CA: Scholars Press, 1983).

Schürer, E., *The History of the Jewish People in the Age of Jesus Christ* (trans. and ed. G. Vermes *et al.*; 3 vols.; Edinburgh: T. & T. Clark, 1973–87).

—'Zu II Macc 6,7 (monatliche Geburtstagsfeier)', *ZNW* 2 (1901), pp. 48-52.

Schwartz, D.J., 'Josephus and Nicolaus on the Pharisees', *JSJ* 14 (1983), pp. 157-71.

Schwartz, D.R., 'On Some Papyri and Josephus' Sources and Chronology for the Persian Period', *JSJ* 21 (1990), pp. 175-99.

Schwartz, J., 'The "Temple of Jacob" and the Cult in Bethel during the Second Temple Period', in *Proceedings of the Ninth World Congress of Jewish Studies 1985* (6 vols.; Jerusalem: World Union of Jewish Studies, 1986), 1, pp. 7-12.

Schwartz, J., and J. Spanier, 'On Mattathias and the Desert of Samaria', *RB* 98 (1991), pp. 252-71.

Schwartz, S., 'A Note on the Social Type and Political Ideology of the Hasmonean Family', *JBL* 112 (1993), pp. 305-309.

Schwier, H., *Tempel und Tempelzerstörung: Untersuchungen zum ersten jüdisch-römischen Krieg* (Novum Testamentum et Orbis Antiquus, 11; Göttingen: Vandenhoeck & Ruprecht, 1989).

Sievers, J., *The Hasmonaeans and their Supporters: From Mattathias to the Death of John Hyrcanus I* (University of South Florida Studies in the History of Judaism, 6; Atlanta: Scholars Press, 1990).

Simon, M., 'Les sadducéens', *DBSup* 10 (1985), cols. 1545-56.

Skehan, P.W., 'The Biblical Scrolls from Qumrân and the Text of the Old Testament', *BA* 28 (1965), pp. 87-100.

Smith, M., *Palestinian Parties and Politics that Shaped the Old Testament* (Lectures on the History of Religion NS 9; New York: Columbia University Press, 1971).

Sperber, A., *The Bible in Aramaic* (4 vols.; Leiden: Brill, 1959–73).

Starcky, J., and F.-M. Abel, *Les livres des Maccabées* (La Sainte Bible; Cerf: Paris, 1961).

Stern, E., *Material Culture of the Bible in the Persian Period 538–322 BC* (Warminster: Aris & Phillips, 1982).

—'The Persian Empire and the Political and Social History of Palestine in the Persian Period', in Davies and Finkelstein (eds.), *The Cambridge History of Judaism*, I, pp. 70-87.

Stern, M., *Greek and Latin Authors on Jews and Judaism* (3 vols.; Jerusalem: Magnes, 1974–84).

—'Review of M. Hengel's "Judentum und Hellenismus"', *Kiryat Sefer* 46 (1970), pp. 94-99.

Strack, H.L., and G. Stemberger, *Einleitung in Talmud und Midrasch* (Munich: Beck, 7th edn, 1982). ET: *Introduction to the Talmud and Midrash* (trans. M. Bockmuehl; Edinburgh: T. & T. Clark, 1991).

Strugnell, J., 'Flavius Josephus and the Essenes: *Antiquities* XVIII. 18-22', *JBL* 87 (1958), pp. 106-115.

Talmon, S., 'Ezra and Nehemiah', in *IDBSup*, pp. 317-28.

—*King, Cult and Calendar in Ancient Israel* (Jerusalem: Magnes, 1986).

—'The Three Scrolls of the Law that Were Found in the Temple Court', *Textus* 2 (1962), pp. 14-27.

Tcherikover, V.A., 'The Documents of II Macc.', *Tarbiz* 1 (1930), pp. 39-43.

—*Hellenistic Civilisation and the Jews* (Philadelphia: Jewish Publication Society of America, 1959).

—'Was Jerusalem a Greek Polis under the Procurators?', *Eretz Israel* 1 (1951), pp. 94-101.

Tcherikover, V.A., and A. Fuks, *Corpus papyrorum iudaicarum* (Cambridge, MA: Harvard University Press, 1957).

Thackeray, H. St. J., 'The Letter of Aristeas', *JQR* 15 (1903), pp. 337-91.

Torrey, C.C., *The Composition and Historical Value of Ezra–Nehemiah* (BZAW, 2; Giessen: Ricker, 1896).

Tov, E., 'Hebrew Biblical Manuscripts from the Judaean Desert: Their Contribution to Textual Criticism', *JJS* 39/1 (1988), pp. 5-37.

—'A Modern Textual Outlook Based on the Qumran Scrolls', *HUCA* 52 (1982), pp. 11-27.

—'The Rabbinic Traditions Concerning the "Alterations" Inserted into the Greek Pentateuch and their Relation to the Original text of the LXX', *JSJ* 15 (1984), pp. 66-89.

Tuland, C.G., '"*Ussaya*" and "*Ussarna*": A Clarification of Terms, Date and Text', *JNES* 17 (1958), pp. 269-75.

Ulrich, E.C., 'Horizons of Old Testament Textual Research at the Thirtieth Anniversary of Qumran Cave 4', *CBQ* 46 (1984), pp. 613-36.

—*The Qumran Text of Samuel and Josephus* (HSM, 19; Missoula, MT: Scholars Press, 1978).

Urbach, E.E., 'Class-Status and Leadership in the World of the Palestinian Sages', in *Proceedings of the Israel Academy of Science and Humanity* 2 (1968), pp. 38-74.

—*The Sages: Their Concepts and Beliefs* (Jerusalem: Magnes, 1973).

Valentin, H., *Aaron* (OBO, 18; Göttingen: Vandenhoeck & Ruprecht, 1978).

Van Hoonacker, A., 'Néhémie et Esdras, une nouvelle hypothèse sur la chronologie et la restauration juive', *Le Muséon* 9 (1890), pp. 19-36.

Van Seters, J., *Abraham in History and Tradition* (New Haven: Yale University Press, 1975).

—'Joshua 24 and the Problem of Tradition', in Barrick and Spencer (eds.), *In the Shelter of Elyon*.

VanderKam, J.C., 'Hanukkah: Its Timing and Significance according to 1 and 2 Maccabees', *JSP* 1 (1987), pp. 23-40.

Vaux, R. de, *Ancient Israel* (New York: McGraw–Hill, 1961).

—'Les décrets de Cyrus et de Darius sur la reconstruction du Temple', *RB* 46 (1937), pp. 29-57.

—'Israël', *DBSup* 4 (1949), cols. 729-77.

—'Le lieu que Yahwé a choisi pour y établir son nom', in F. Maass (ed.), *Das ferne und nahe Wort* (Festschrift L. Rost; BZAW, 105; Berlin: Töpelman, 1967).

Vogt, H.C.M., *Studien zur nachexilischen Gemeinde in Esra–Nehemia* (Werl: D. Goelde, 1966).

Walter, N., *Der Thoraausleger Aristobulos* (TU, 86; Berlin: Akademie Verlag, 1964).

Weber, M., *Ancient Judaism* (Glencoe: Free Press, 1952).

Weinfeld, M., *Deuteronomy and the Deuteronomic School* (Oxford: Clarendon Press, 1972).

Weisman, Z., 'Reflexions on Lawgiving at Sinai and its Interpretations', *Shnaton* 5–6 (1978–82), pp. 55-68.

Weiss, I.H., *Dor dor udorshav* (2 vols.; Berlin: Platt & Minkus, 1871).

—*Sifra debé Rab, hu' sefer Torat Kohanim* (Vienna: Schlossberg, 1862).

Wellhausen, J., *Prolegomena zur Geschichte Israels* (Berlin: Reimer, 3rd edn, 1905).

Wendland, P., *Aristeae ad Philocratem epistula* (Leipzig: Teubner, 1900).

Widengren, G., 'Israelite–Jewish Religion', in C.J. Bleeker and G. Widengren (eds.), *Historia religionum* (Leiden: Brill, 1969), pp. 225-317.

—'The King and the Tree of Life in Ancient Near Eastern Religion', *UUÅ* 4 (1951), pp. 64-67.

—'The Persian Period', in Hayes and Miller (eds.), *Israelite and Judaean History*, pp. 489-538.

Will, E., *Histoire politique du monde hellénistique. I. D'Alexandre à Antiochos III* (Annales de l'Est, 30; Nancy: Publications de l'Université, 1979).

Will, E., and C. Orrieux, *Ioudaïsmos, Hellènismos: Essai sur le judaïsme judéen à l'époque hellénistique* (Nancy: Presses Universitaires de Nancy, 1986).

Williamson, H.G.M., *Ezra, Nehemiah* (WBC, 16; Waco, TX: Word Books, 1985).

—'The Historical Value of Josephus' *Jewish Antiquities* XI. 297-301', *JTS* NS 28 (1977), pp. 49-66.

—*Israel in the Books of Chronicles* (Cambridge: Cambridge University Press, 1977).

Wilms, F.-E., *Das jahwistische Bundesbuch in Exodus 34* (SANT, 32; Munich: Kösel, 1973).

Wintermute, O.S., *Jubilees* (a new translation and introduction), in J.H. Charlesworth (ed.), *The Old Testament Pseudepigrapha* (2 vols.; Garden City, NY: Doubleday, 1985), II, pp. 35-142.

Wright, G.E., *Shechem: The Biography of a Biblical City* (New York: McGraw–Hill, 1965).

Würthwein, E., *Die Bücher der Könige (1 Kön. 17–2 Kön. 25)* (ATD, 11/2; Göttingen: Vandenhoeck & Ruprecht, 1984).

Xella, P., *I testi rituali di Ugarit*, I (Studi Semitici, 54; Rome: Consiglio Nazionale di Ricerca, 1981).

Yadin, Y., *The Temple Scroll* (3 vols.; Jerusalem: Magnes, 1977–83).

Yahuda, A.S., 'Über die Unechtheit des samaritanischen Josuabuches', *SPAW* 39 (1908), pp. 887-913.

Yarden, L., 'Aaron, Bethel and the Menorah', *JJS* 26 (1975), pp. 39-47.

—*The Tree of Light: A Study of the Menorah* (Uppsala: Scriv Service, 1972).

Yaron, R., *Introduction to the Law of the Aramaic Papyri* (Oxford: Clarendon Press, 1961).

Yeivin, I., *Introduction to the Tiberian Masorah* (trans. and ed. E.J. Revell; Masoretic Studies, 5; Missoula, MT: Scholars Press, 1980).

Zeitlin, S., 'Hanukkah: Its Origin and its Significance', *JQR* 29 (1938), pp. 1-36.

—*Ner Ma'arabi* (1925).

Zuntz, G., 'Aristeas Studies. II. Aristeas on the Transmission of the Torah', *JSS* 4 (1959), pp. 109-126.

Zunz, L., *Die gottesdienstlichen Vorträge der Juden, historisch entwickelt* (Frankfurt: Kauffmann, 2nd edn, 1892 [1832]). Hebrew translation provided with a commentary by H. Albeck (Jerusalem: Bialik, 3rd edn, 1974).

INDEXES

INDEX OF REFERENCES

OLD TESTAMENT

NEW TESTAMENT

PSEUDEPIGRAPHA

INDEX OF AUTHORS